Bible Records

of

Caroline County

Virginia

Families

Herbert Ridgeway Collins

HERITAGE BOOKS
2008

HERITAGE BOOKS
AN IMPRINT OF HERITAGE BOOKS, INC.

Books, CDs, and more—Worldwide

For our listing of thousands of titles see our website
at
www.HeritageBooks.com

Published 2008 by
HERITAGE BOOKS, INC.
Publishing Division
100 Railroad Ave. #104
Westminster, Maryland 21157

Copyright © 2008 Herbert Ridgeway Collins

Other books by the author:

Caroline County, Virginia Bureau of Vital Statistics: Death Records, 1853-1896

*Caroline County, Virginia Death Records (1919-1994) from
The Caroline Progress, a Weekly Newspaper Published in Bowling Green, Virginia*

Cemeteries of Caroline County, Virginia, Volumes 1–3: Public Cemeteries

All rights reserved. No part of this book may be reproduced or transmitted in any form or by any means, electronic or mechanical, including photocopying, recording or by any information storage and retrieval system without written permission from the author, except for the inclusion of brief quotations in a review.

International Standard Book Numbers
Paperbound: 978-0-7884-4758-7
Clothbound: 978-0-7884-7508-5

LIST OF ACKNOWLEDGMENTS:

The late James Patton
Kim C. Campbell
King and Queen Historical Society
Virginia State Library
Virginia Historical Society
Pearl Phillips Mills
The late Mrs. Nettie Leitch Major
The late Judge Leon Bazile
Mrs. L.W. Ledgerwood, Jr.
Helen Cross Covington
Bernie and Patty Driver
The late George H.S. King
Shirley Ball Plesur
Barbara Farmer Bird
The Late Virginia L.H. Davis
The late Alma Green
Ethel Broaddus Andrews Barlow
The late Ropon Bowers
John Pratt
The late Kathleen Sizer
Ray Smith Campbell
Gloria Gatewood
R. Arnold Ricks
The late Elizabeth Woolfolk Furr
Jean Broaddus
Walton Mahon
John Frederick Dorman
Kathy Coleman McVay
Daniel T. Hansen
Robin S. McAfee
Maxie Rozell
June Upshaw Giles
The late Ralph E. Fall
Chip Steele
Jason Bradshaw
William Roy Southworth
Mary Robertson Boulware Campbell
Joyce Pitts Carter
Tommy Upshaw
Lloyd Coleman Huckstep
Rachael Puller Harris
Helen Kay Yates
Vivian Jackson

TABLE OF CONTENTS

ACREE BIBLE	1
ALLEN / HOOMES / TUNSTALL BIBLE	1
ANDERSON BIBLE NO. 1	2
ANDERSON BIBLE NO. 2	3
ANDREWS BIBLE NO. 1	5
ANDREWS BIBLE NO. 2	6
ARNALL BIBLE	7
ATKINSON BIBLE	8
AYLETT BIBLE	9
BAGBY BIBLE	10
BARLOW BIBLE NO. 1	13
BARLOW BIBLE NO. 2	13
BAYLOR BIBLE NO. 1	14
BAYLOR BIBLE NO. 2	16
BAYLOR BIBLE NO. 3	17
BAYLOR BIBLE NO. 4	18
BAYLOR BIBLE NO. 5	19
BAYLOR BIBLE NO. 6	21
BEASLEY / BEAZLEY BIBLE	23
BEAZLEY / SAMUEL BIBLE	24
BERNARD BIBLE NO. 1	26
BERNARD BIBLE NO. 2	28
BLANTON / ALLEN BIBLE	29
BLAYDES BIBLE	30
BONDURANT BIBLE	31
BOULWARE BIBLE NO. 1	32
BOULWARE BIBLE NO. 2	33
BOULWARE BIBLE NO. 3	34
BRIDGES BIBLE	37
BROADDUS BIBLE NO. 1	39
BROADDUS BIBLE NO. 2	43
BROADDUS BIBLE NO. 3	45
BROADDUS BIBLE NO. 4	46
BROCKENBROUGH BIBLE	47
BROOKS BIBLE NO. 1	48
BROOKS BIBLE NO. 2	49
BROWN / SHEPPARD BIBLE	50
BRUCE BIBLE NO. 1	51
BRUCE BIBLE NO. 2	52
BRUCE / EDWARDS BIBLE	53
BUCKNER BIBLE NO. 1	55

BUCKNER BIBLE NO. 2	56
BUCKNER BIBLE. NO. 3	58
BUCKNER / HAWES FAMILY RECORD	59
BURRUSS BIBLE	61
BURTON BIBLE	62
BURTON / QUARLES BIBLE	62
BUTLER BIBLE	63
BUTLER / WRIGHT BIBLE	64
CALLAWAY BIBLE	66
CALLIS BIBLE	67
CAMPBELL BIBLE NO. 1	68
CAMPBELL BIBLE NO. 2	69
CAMPBELL / HENDERSON BIBLE	70
CARTER BIBLE NO. 1	71
CARTER BIBLE NO. 2	73
CASEY BIBLE	74
CASH BIBLE	75
CHEWNING BIBLE	76
CHILES BIBLE	77
COLE BIBLE	78
COLEMAN BIBLE	80
COLLINS BIBLE NO. 1	81
COLLINS BIBLE NO. 2	82
COLLINS / JOHNSON / RAWLINGS BIBLE	84
CONWAY BIBLE	86
CORBIN BIBLE NO. 1	88
CORBIN BIBLE NO. 2	89
DeJARNETTE BIBLE	90
DICKINSON BIBLE NO. 1	93
DICKINSON BIBLE NO. 2	94
DICKINSON BIBLE NO. 3	96
DICKINSON BIBLE NO. 4	97
DICKINSON / COLLINS BIBLE	99
DODD BIBLE	99
DONAHOE BIBLE	100
DORSEY BIBLE	102
DOWNING FAMILY RECORD	103
DUDLEY PRAYER BOOK	104
DUDLEY / EATON BIBLE	105
DURRETT BIBLE	105
DUVAL BIBLE	107
ENGLAND / BRAMHAM BIBLE	109
ENGLAND / SUTTON BIBLE	110

ENNIS BIBLE	111
FARINHOLT BIBLE	113
FARMER BIBLE NO. 1	113
FARMER BIBLE NO. 2	114
FARMER / HARDY BIBLE	115
FARISH BIBLE NO. 1	116
FARISH BIBLE NO. 2	117
FARISH BIBLE NO. 3	118
FAUNTLEROY BIBLE	119
FITZHUGH BIBLE NO. 1	120
FITZHUGH BIBLE NO. 2	122
FITZHUGH BIBLE NO. 3	123
FLIPPO BIBLE	123
FREEMAN BIBLE	125
GARRETT BIBLE NO. 1	126
GARRETT BIBLE NO. 2	127
GARRETT BIBLE NO. 3	128
GARRETT BIBLE NO. 4	129
GAYLE BIBLE	130
GEORGE BIBLE	131
GLASCOCK BIBLE	132
GOODWIN BIBLE	134
GORDON BIBLE	138
GOULDIN BIBLE NO. 1	140
GOULDIN BIBLE NO. 2	141
GOULDIN BIBLE NO. 3	142
GOULDMAN BIBLE	142
GRAHAM BIBLE	143
GREEN BIBLE NO. 1	144
GREEN BIBLE NO. 2	145
GUEST BIBLE	146
HARGRAVE BIBLE	147
HARRIS BIBLE	149
HAWES BIBLE	151
HAWES / BUCKNER / WALKER FAMILY RECORD	152
HAWES / TAYLOR BIBLE	153
HEWLETT / LUCK / WIGGLESWORTH BIBLE	156
HOGE / REYNOLDS BIBLE	156
HOOMES BIBLE NO. 1	158
HOOMES BIBLE NO. 2	160
HUDGIN BIBLE	163
HUDGIN FAMILY RECORD	167
HUTCHESON BIBLE NO. 1	168

HUTCHESON BIBLE NO. 2	169
JESSE / COLLINS BIBLE	171
JOHNSTON BIBLE	173
JONES BIBLE	174
KAY BIBLE NO. 1	175
KAY BIBLE NO. 2	176
KIDD BIBLE	176
KNOX BIBLE	177
LEAVELL BIBLE	179
LIGHTFOOT BIBLE NO. 1	179
LIGHTFOOT BIBLE NO. 2	181
LIGHTFOOT BIBLE NO. 3	182
LINDSAY BIBLE	183
LINDSAY / LOMAX DIARY	184
LIPSCOMB / WILSON BIBLE	185
LUCK BIBLE	187
MADISON BIBLE	188
MAHON BIBLE	190
MARSHALL BIBLE	191
McGRUDER (MAGRUDER) BIBLE NO. 1	192
McGRUDER BIBLE NO. 2	192
McGRUDER BIBLE NO. 3	193
McGRUDER BIBLE NO. 4	194
MICOU BIBLE	195
MILLER BIBLE NO. 1	195
MILLER BIBLE NO. 2	195
MINOR BIBLE NO. 1	196
MINOR BIBLE NO. 2	199
MINOR BIBLE NO. 3	201
MORRIS BIBLE	202
MORSON BIBLE NO. 1	202
MORSON BIBLE NO. 2	203
MOTLEY BIBLE	204
NOEL BIBLE	204
OVERTON BIBLE	205
PARKER BIBLE	206
PARSONS FAMILY RECORD	206
PARTLOW BIBLE	207
PENDLETON BIBLE	209
PENN BIBLE	214
PENNEY BIBLE	214
PITTS BIBLE NO. 1	216
PITTS BIBLE NO. 2	216

POLLARD BIBLE	217
PRATT RECORD BOOK NO. 1	218
PRATT RECORD BOOK NO. 2	218
PULLER BIBLE	219
REDD / ANDERSON BIBLE	220
RICHARDS BIBLE NO. 1	224
RICHARDS BIBLE NO. 2	225
RICHERSON BIBLE	226
ROSE BIBLE NO. 1	226
ROSE BIBLE NO. 2	227
ROW / ROWE BIBLE	228
ROY BIBLE NO. 1	233
ROY BIBLE NO. 2	233
ROYSTON BIBLE	236
ROZELL BIBLE	238
SALE BIBLE	237
SAMUEL(L) BIBLE	239
SATTERWHITE / REID BIBLE	241
SCHOOLS BIBLE	242
SCOTT BIBLE	242
SEAL BIBLE	243
SHEPHERD BIBLE	245
SIZER BIBLE NO. 1	246
SIZER BIBLE NO. 2	248
SMITH BIBLE	247
SMITH REGISTER	248
SOUTHWORTH BIBLE	251
SPILLMAN BIBLE	253
SPINDLE BIBLE	253
STARKE BIBLE	255
STERN / STERNE BIBLE	256
STHRESHLEY BIBLE	257
SUTTON BIBLE	258
SWEENEY / HUTCHESON BIBLE	260
TALIAFERRO BIBLE NO. 1	261
TALIAFERRO BIBLE NO. 2	262
TALIAFERRO REGISTER	264
TAYLOR BIBLE NO. 1	267
TAYLOR BIBLE NO. 2	270
TAYLOR BIBLE NO. 3	271
TAYLOR / BARLOW BIBLE	273
TAYLOR / BORKEY BIBLE	274
TAYLOR / PITTS BIBLE	274

TERRELL BIBLE NO. 1	275
TERRELL BIBLE NO. 2	276
TERRELL BIBLE NO. 3	276
TERRELL BIBLE NO. 4	277
TERRELL BIBLE NO. 5	278
TERRELL BIBLE NO. 6	280
TERRELL BIBLE NO. 7	281
TERRELL / COBB BIBLE	282
TERRELL / RICKS BIBLE	282
THOMAS BIBLE NO. 1	284
THOMAS BIBLE NO. 2	288
THOMAS BIBLE NO. 3	289
THOMSON BIBLE	290
THORNLEY BIBLE NO. 1	290
THORNLEY BIBLE NO. 2	291
THORNLEY BIBLE NO. 3	293
THORNLEY BIBLE NO. 4	294
THORNTON BIBLE NO. 1	296
THORNTON BIBLE NO. 2	297
THORNTON BIBLE NO. 3	298
THORNTON BIBLE NO. 4	299
THORNTON BIBLE NO. 5	300
TOD(D) BIBLE	300
TOMPKIINS BIBLE	301
TRIBBLE BIBLE	302
TUNSTALL BIBLE NO. 1	303
TUNSTALL BIBLE NO. 2	303
TURNER / THORNTON BIBLE	304
TURNER / WRIGHT BIBLE	307
TYLER BIBLE	308
UPSHAW BIBLE NO. 1	309
UPSHAW BIBLE NO. 2	310
UPSHAW BIBLE NO. 3	311
VAUGHAN BIBLE NO. 1	312
VAUGHAN BIBLE NO. 2	313
VAULX BIBLE	313
WALDEN BIBLE	316
WALLER BIBLE	317
WARE BIBLE NO. 1	320
WARE BIBLE NO. 2	321

WASHINGTON BIBLE 322
WASHINGTON / BURKE BIBLE 324
WHITE BIBLE NO. 1 326
WHITE BIBLE NO. 2 327
WHITE BIBLE NO. 3 331
WILLIS BIBLE NO. 1 332
WILLIS BIBLE NO. 2 333
WILTSHIRE / DUGGINS BIBLE 334
WOODFORD BIBLE 335
WOODFORD FAMILY RECORD 335
WOOLFOLK BIBLE 339
WORMELEY BIBLE 343
WORTHAM BIBLE NO 1 344
WORTHAM BIBLE NO. 2 347
WRIGHT (EUGENE) BIBLE 350
WRIGHT (LOUIS) BIBLE 351
WRIGHT (ROBERT) BIBLE 351
WRIGHT (WESLEY) BIBLE 353
WYATT BIBLE 354
YATES BIBLE 359
YOUNG BIBLE 361

INTRODUCTION

The family registers in the Bibles of Caroline County families are one of the few remaining sources which record the vital statistics and family relationships of Caroline families. Most influential families purchased these Bibles at the beginning of the 19th century. Although a few date to the 18th century, many of the 19th century Bibles record family members who lived in the 18th century. Many of the 19th century Bibles were published by Matthew Carey of Philadelphia. The Reverend Mason Locke Weems, known as "Parson Weems", the author of the famous Washington biography with the cherry tree legend, was a traveling salesman for Matthew Carey. He traveled extensively through Caroline County and the surrounding areas, frequenting the taverns in Caroline. During that time he peddled these Bibles, many of which have survived today.

During the mid-19th century, many of the Caroline family Bibles went with the settlers to points west as they moved in covered wagons. The two most important things they carried with them were the Bible and a clock. Unfortunately, many of the Bibles have been lost through fires and carelessness.

Since Colonial times, Virginia families have recorded their births, marriages, deaths as well as stories and tragedies in these Bibles. In a number of cases, the slaves are also recorded with the white families in the family register. Since the state taxed by age, the slave owners often kept their own vital statistics. These are extemely important, since the Pre-Civil War census did not record slaves by name, only number. In other cases, information on the weather and family pets are also recorded in the Bibles. The Boulware Bible recorded: "A Mule Colt foaled the 28th day of May 1801. The property of Mark Boulware and his Name is called Jack 1809". One Bible dating to the early 1800's noted: "November 12th 1833 The Stares (sic) was a falling from heaven all night. My arm got broake (sic) March 18th 1835". A lengthy recording of a bad storm in portions of King and Queen, Essex and Caroline County which killed wild animals, destroying crops, and having hail 2 and 3 inches deep is recorded in the Gouldin Bible on 5 August 1869. On the fly sheet of the Thomas Chandler's Family Bible is the following reference: "The first steamboat in the Pamunkey River was on Saturday, the 27th of November 1791". The Woodford Bible has two references to unusual weather: "June 11th, 1773, A smart Frost that bit the vines, some snow fell mixed with hail and rain. May 4th 1774, a violent frost that bit the corn, wheat, and destroyed the fruit entirely. January 14, 1831 the great snow commenced falling and continued until the 17th of the month." Physical descriptions also are given such as birth of a child: "fair skin, blue eyes and chesnut (sic) hair". In another Bible, the time of birth is recorded as thus: "Jno Roy Baylor born at early candle light on\ Tennessee on Monday the 14th 1840". Another was quick to point out the hardships their relatives could endure: "Thomas Pollard at age 73 rode on horseback from Kentucky to Caroline County a year or two ago and means to return shortly". In many cases newspaper notices of marriages and deaths have been clipped from papers and placed in Bibles. Entries from family Bibles have been considered legal records for matters such as proving birth or marriage dates, especially since Social Security was inaugurated.

The Library of Virginia started collecting copies of family entries in Bibles as early as 1928, when the state began seeking unofficial documents to make up for the lack of official vital statistics. In the 82 years that the library has been collecting these records, more that 5,000 family Bible records are now in their archives. The Virginia Historical Society, the Alderman Library at the University of Virginia, and many other repositories throughout the country also have Bible records from Caroline County, Virginia. The Maryland Hall of Records began collecting the Bibles when that institution was established. The Bibles grew rapidly and much valuable space was required. Sometime prior to 1960, they had to resort to removing the family registers and destroying the Bibles after the records were removed.

ACREE FAMILY BIBLE

This family Bible register was submitted for a Revolutionary War pension and appears in *Virginia Revolutionary War Pension Applications* by Frederick Dorman, Volume I, p. 10. The information in brackets comes from *Abstracts of Revolutionary War Pension Applications* by Virgil White, Volume 4. John Acree declares "he was born in Caroline Co. Va. on 2 March 1760, married 21 November 1794 in King & Queen Co., to Lucy Schools and that the family now lives in Sullivan Co., Tenn." This name could be a variation of the present name Acors or another different family entirely, neither of which the author has attempted to prove.

John Acree the son of [Abraham] Adam Acree and Anne his wife was born March 2nd day 1760.
Lucy Schools the daughter of John Schools and Salley his wife was born June 30th 1774, also was married to her beloved husband November 21, 1794.
Elizabeth Acree the daughter of John and Lucy Acree was born February the 24th day in the year 1795.
Matthew [Y.] Acree the son of John and Lucy Acree was born [June] July 21st day in the year 1796.
Salley Acree the daughter of John and Lucy Acree was born July 21st day the year 1798.
Uriah Acree was born Decr. 2nd day the year 1800.
Susanna Acree was born April 19th in the year 1803.
Fanney Acree was born February 2222228th day in the year 1806.
Polley Acree was born August 4th day in the year 1808.
John Acree was born Decr. 13th day in the year 1810.
[Lucy Acree was born Decr. 5th day in the year 1812.]
[William Acree was born June 7th day in the year 1815.]

ALLEN / HOOMES / TUNSTALL FAMILY BIBLE

This Bible record was reproduced in *The First Tunstalls in Virginia and Some of Their Descendants* by Whit Morris, Press of The Clegg Company, San Antonio, Texas 1950 at page 228. The original owner of this Bible was probably Richard Allen of New Kent County. Colonel John Hoomes, son of George and Frances Hoomes of "Old Mansion", Bowling Green, Caroline County, married into this Allen family, as evidenced in the records. The Tunstall family also appears in Caroline County records.

Richard Allen [son of Robert Tunstall Allen & Frances "Fanny" Byrd] of New Kent County Va. married Elizabeth Ferrell. Children:
Betty Allen Born 26 Nov. 1734.
Mary Allen Born 11 Apr. 1736.
Richmond Allen, born 7 Nov. 1737, died 17 Apr. 1794.
Martha Allen, born 13 May 1740.
Richard Allen, born 10 Dec. 1741.

Rebecca Allen, born 18 Aug. 1743.
Dorcas Allen, born 22 June 1745.
Priscilla Allen, born 7 June 1747.
Judith Churchill Allen, born 1 July 1749, died 10 Aug. 1822, married 20 Oct. 1768 John Hoomes.
William Allen, born 8 Oct. 1751.
Mildred Allen, born 7 Feb. 1753.
Richard Allen, above, married Elizabeth Wilson, born 6 Mar. 1745, died 8 Feb. 1805. Children: Richard, Margaret, Susan, Betsy, Wilson.
Wilson Allen, born 15 Feb. 1774, died 21 July 1844, married Sophia Hoomes.
Richmond Allen, born 2 Feb. 1778, died 12 Mar. 1858.Colonel John Hoomes son of George and Frances Hoomes [of "Old Mansion"], born 20 Oct. 1749, married Judith Churchill Allen, above.
Sophia Hoomes, daughter of John Hoomes & Judith Churchill Allen (born Dec. 14, 1788).
Adaline Margaret Allen, daughter of Wilson Allen & Sophia Hoomes, born 27 Aug. 1811, died 1853, married Robert Byrd Tunstall 8 Oct. 1840.
Children of Robert Byrd and Adaline Margaret Tunstall:
Fanny Byrd Tunstall b. 18 Mar., 1842, d. 8 Dec. 1843.
Allen Hoomes Tunstall, b. 15 July 1843 (went to Hot Springs, Ark.)
Richard Cuthbert Tunstall, b. 20 July 1845, d. 28 June 1911 (went to Nevado, Mo.)
Lelia Sophia Tunstall, b. 6 Apr. 1847, d. 22 Sept. 1900 m. Col. Thomas R. Thornton (went to St. Louis).
Robert Byrd Tunstall, b. 25 Sept. 1848, d. unmarried 1921 (went to St. Louis).
Fanny Byrd Tunstall, b. 31 Aug. 1850 in Bowling Green, Va., d. 16 Jan. 1936 at "Wilton" Hanover, Va.
Anne Carter Tunstall, b. 21 Feb. 1852, d. 30 June 1852.
Mary Adaline Armistead Tunstall, b. 8 Jan. 1853, d. 12 Nov. 1920 (went to Hot Springs, Ark.)

ANDERSON FAMILY BIBLE NO. 1

This Bible record was submitted as proof for a Revolutionary War pension and is from *Virginia Revolutionary War Pension Applications* by John Frederick Dorman, Volume 2, p. 36. It is part of leaf cut from the reverse title page of a Bible printed in London by Thomas Baskett in 1769. On 13 August 1850 Herbert Anderson of Caroline Co., age 50, declared that he was the oldest son of William Anderson and Sally Anderson and that the births of the children were cut out of the family Bible 12 August 1850 by Robert R. Chapman and Reuben J. Chapman.

William Anderson was born the 4th of August 1773 and departed this life the 14th of June 1836.
Sarah J.[Jones] Anderson was born the 19th of July 1790 and died the 21st of July 1839.
Richard Anderson of Cumberland Co., Va., once Caroline Co., Va., married Martha Meadows in Cumberland Co. 2 December 1784 by Rev. Charles McRae.

Family Register on back of title page published at Edinburgh, 1782.
James Anderson son of Richard Anderson and Patty his wife was born October 11th 1785.

Salley Anderson was born 1st day December 1787.
Bettey Anderson was born 20th November 1789.
John Anderson was born 2nd November 1791.
_____ Anderson was born ___ January 1794.
Fran[c]is Anderson was born 15th March 1796.
Rebekah Anderson was born _____.
R. Laurence Anderson was born May 22nd ____.
Sally Anderson, relict of William Anderson, departed this life on Friday (sic) morning, the 28th of August 1840.

NOTE: In the same pension record is a document dated 16 August 1850, Mickelborough Young, age 75, [who operated the tavern at "White Chimneys", Caroline County] states "he knew Nathaniel Anderson who married Sally Jones and died in 1798 or 1799. She afterward married William Anderson who died in June 1836, and she died in Aug. 1840. She left only four children surviving her: Herbert Anderson, Armistead Anderson, Mary wife of John Richardson, and Catharine wife of William E. Green." [According to Hopkins' *Abstracts of Caroline County, Virginia* at page 65, When Nathaniel Anderson Jr. died soon after March 1797, and before June 1803, he left a widow, Sally Anderson and three infant children: Sally Jones Anderson, William Skelton Anderson and Catherine Terrell Anderson.]

ANDERSON FAMILY BIBLE NO. 2

This Bible belonged to the family of Robert Semple Anderson of Hanover and Caroline Counties and the City of Richmond and dates from 1859 to 1936. It was published by Jasper Harding and Sons, Philadelphia, 1859. Also included is a copy from an earlier Bible of Garland Anderson and his wife Maria Burbidge Anderson 1747-1793. A copy of both of the records is in the Library of Virginia. Garland Anderson owned land in New Kent, Caroline, Hanover, and adjoining counties. Garland Anderson's son, John Burbidge Anderson, married Martha Tompkins of Caroline County and had six sons and three daughters. Their sixth son, Henry Tompkins Anderson was a Disciples of Christ minister and another son, Benjamin Anderson was a prominent physician in Caroline County. For further information concerning this family, see *A History of Caroline County Virginia* by Marshall Wingfield, Richmond, Virginia, 1924. Littleton Goodwin Anderson was probably named for another Caroline family, that of Littleton Goodwin.

Inscribed "Presented to Robt Semple Anderson By His Affectionate Mother, Maria D. Anderson October 8, 1859."
Robt. S. Anderson, son of Genet and Maria D. Anderson of Hanover Co. was married in Richmond by Rev. Jos. B. Taylor to Miss Bettie A. Wheat, daughter of Francis and Edna E. Wheat on Thursday evening Jany 29th, 1852.
Married in Staunton, Va Nov 15th 1881 by Rev Wm Hough, Ro. Cabell, son of R.S. & Bettie A. Anderson to Miss Katie E. Cushing, daughter of E.M. Cushing.
Imogen J. V. Anderson, daughter of Robert S. Anderson and Bettie Anderson was married Wednesday night October 28th, 1885 to Samuel M. Buchanan of Richmond, Va.
Bettie Frank Anderson was married to Robert H. Hall June 1, 1892.

Wythe Davis Anderson of Richmond, VA was married to Miss Mary Lee Hunt in Winchester, KY, April 26 (27) 1904.

Cabell J. Buchanan, son of Imo. J. and Samuel M. Buchanan was married in Richmond, Va to Clara Otey April 17, 1911.

William Judson Anderson married to Margaret Johnson June 15, 1920.

Edwin R. Anderson and May Stratton married July 1913.

Robert Anderson Buchanan married to Maud Whitehorn Feb. 1917.

Genet Buchanan married to Marie Ford December 17, 1916.

Samuel Buchanan married to Addie Williby May 10, 1926.

Frances E. Anderson daughter Wythe D. and Mary Lee Anderson married Beecher Ernest Stallard, July 13, 1935.

Mildred E. Anderson daughter of Wythe D. and Mary Lee Anderson married Alton Whiteside Williams, June 10, 1936.

Genet Anderson was born August 4th 1793.

Maria D.(Drummond) Harris his wife was born Sept. 16th 1803.

Mary Elizabeth Anderson, daughter of Genet and Maria D. Anderson was born Sept 4th 1822.

John Garland Anderson their son was born July 24, 1824.

Littleton Goodwin Anderson, their son, was born Mar 7th 1827.

Genet Anderson, their son was born Janu 23, 1827.

Addison Lewis Anderson, their son was born Aug 26th 1830.

Robert Semple Anderson, their son was born Mar 8th 1832.

Marcia Thomas Anderson, their daughter was born Sept. 28th 1834.

Robt Semple Anderson, son of Genet and Maria D. Anderson was born in Hanover County, March 8th, 1832.

Bettie A. Wheat, daughter of Francis and Edna E. Wheat was born in Caroline Co., Aug 29th 1832.

Robert S., infant daughter of Robt. S. and Bettie A. Anderson was born and died in Hanover County April 1853.

Robert Cabell Anderson, son of Rob. S. and Bettie A. Anderson was born in Richmond cty., July 1st 1854.

Marcia Edmonia Anderson, daughter of Rbt. S. Anderson and Bettie A. Anderson was born at Lagrange in Hanover Co., July 7, 1857.

Imogene Joanna Vivian Ariadna daughter of Robt. S. and Bettie A. Anderson born at Cedar Fork, Caroline Co Oct 31st 1858.

Bettie Frances Anderson, daughter of Robt. S. and Bettie A. Anderson was born at Cedar Fork, Caroline Co., Va. Aug. 6, 1865.

Genetta Wheat Anderson, daughter of Robt. S. and Bettie A. Anderson was born in Richmond cty Va Saturday Jany 11, 1873. Wythe James Davis Anderson born February 9th 1877 in the city of Richmond, VA son of Robert S. and Bettie A. Anderson.

Mildred Elizabeth Anderson, daughter of Wythe D. and Mary Lee Hunt Anderson was born in Winchester, Ky. March 8th, 1906.

Frances Edmonia daughter of Wythe Davis and Mary Lee Anderson was born in Richmond, Va September 17, 1907.

George Hunt Anderson, son of Wythe D. and Mary Lee Anderson was born March 2, 1911.

Robert Semple Anderson, son of Genet and Maria D. Anderson died in the city of Richmond, January 28, 1889. Aged 56 years, 10 months and 20 days. Double pneumonia.

Bettie A. Anderson, daughter of Edna E. and Francis Wheat and wife of Robert Anderson died Sunday November 5, 1905 in her 74th year. Brights disease.

Marcia E. Anderson, daughter of Bettie A. and Robert S. Anderson died in Richmond, Va Feb 22, 1915, 58 years, 1 month and 15 days Pneumonia.

Bettie Frank Anderson Ball daughter of Bettie A. and Robert S. Anderson died Nov. 3, 1920. Pellagra.

Robert Cabell Anderson son of Robt. S. and Bettie Anderson died in Staunton, Va Oct. 24, 1924, age 70 years, 3 months and 23 days. Chronic kidney trouble, hardening of the arteries and heart trouble.

Katie Cushing Anderson, wife of Cabel Anderson died April 22, 1930.

Genetta Wheat Anderson died May 1948.

Wythe Davis Anderson died June 29, 1960, Richmond, VA pneumonia.

Mary Lee Anderson, wife of Wythe Davis Anderson died Oct. 30, 1966.

COPIED FROM THE PAGE OF AN OLDER BIBLE, FOR WHICH A PHOTOSTAT IS ENCLOSED. GARLAND ANDERSON, BORN HANOVER COUNTY, VIRGINIA 1742: DIED HANOVER COUNTY MARCH 8, 1811, WAS GRANDFATHER OF ROBERT SEMPLE ANDERSON. THIS WAS INCLUDED IN THE BIBLE USED.

Garland Anderson, born 1742.

Marcia Elizabeth Burbidge his wife, born April 19, 1747.

John Burbidge, their son, born June 2, 1765, Sunday.

Martha Garland, their daughter, born August 1, 1767 between 10 and 11 o'clock at night, depart August 25, 1783.

Garland, their son, born August 6, 1769 in the morning between 5 and 6 o'clock.

Burbidge, their son, born March 13, 1772, Fryday [sic] between 10 and 11 o'clock at night.

William, their son, born August 4, 1773, Wednesday between three and four o'clock in the afternoon.

Elizabeth Burbidge, their daughter, born November 17, 1774.

Armstead, their son, born Monday, November 10, 1777.

Mary, their daughter, born June 4, 1779 between six and severn [sic] o'clock in the morning.

Ann, their daughter, born November 19, 1783.

Marcia, their daughter, born October 24, 1785.

Dorothy Peay, their daughter, born December 5, 1788.

Lucy, their daughter, born January 13, 1791. Departed Aug. 1798.

Genet, their son, born August 4, 1993.

ANDREWS FAMILY BIBLE NO. 1

Two pages of this Bible were copied by Ethel Broaddus Andrews Barlow of Caroline County, however, the marriage page and death page were not. The present owner of the Bible is unknown. James William and Mary E. R. Green Andrews lived at "Riverview Farm", located on Reedy Mill Road, Caroline County, Virginia.

This Certifies that the Rite of Holy Matrimony was celebrated between James William Andrews of Caroline and Mary Ellen Richard Green of Caroline on 25 th of March 1884 at Mt. Hermon [Baptist Church at Shumansville, Va.] by Rev. Andrew Broaddus.

James William Andrews son of John J. and Emma Andrews born Jan 28th 1859.

Mary ["Mollie"] Ellen R.[Richard] Green daughter of Richard W. and Mary Ellen Conduit Green born Aug. 29th 1862. [Died Sept. 22, 1947].

Thelma Elaine Andrews, born June 26, 1906. Fifth daughter. [Died March 4, 1925].

Mary Emma daughter of James W. and Mary R. Andrews was born August 17th 1886.

Everett Walden Andrews son of James W. and Mary R. Andrews was born Dec. 26th 1888. [Died March 5, 1960].

Nellie Clyde second daughter of James W. and Mary R. Andrews was born June 29th 1891. Died February 2, 1975.

James Carl Andrews 2nd son of James W. and Mary R. Andrews was born Oct. 7th 1893. [Died April 11, 1960].

Iva Dale Andrews was born May 9th 1896.

Eugene ["Eugie"] Fletcher [Andrews] 3rd son was born June 25th 1899.

Eula Vern Andrews 4th daughter born October 21, 1902. [Died April 14, 1998].

ANDREWS FAMILY BIBLE NO. 2

This Bible was copied by Ethel Broaddus Andrews Barlow July 28, 1994. The location of the Bible is now unknown. Mrs. Barlow owns the Bible of Harriette Lilian Broaddus who married Melville Walker Andrews September 25, 1895 at Upper King and Queen Baptist Church. This Bible was given to Harriet Lilian Andrews by her brother June 18, 1879 and published by the American Bible Society, New York, 1876. No family records seem to appear in that Bible. She also owns the Bible of Melville Walter Andrews, published by Oxford University Press, New York and London, 1898, but again it does not include a family register.

On the 25th day of Sept. 1895 Melville Walker Andrews, the son of Lawrence Battaile Andrews and Mary Susan Hutchinson Andrews and Harriett Lillian Broaddus the daughter of James Mordecai Broaddus and Millicent Coleman Jones Broaddus were married at Upper King and Queen Church by Rev. Frank Beale.

From this union five children were born:

1. Mordecai Walker Andrews the 1st son of Melville W. & Lilian B. Andrews was born July 7, 1896.
2. Millicent Randolph Andrews the 1st daughter of Melville W. & Lilian B. Andrews was born Nov. 4, 1897.
3. Mary Battile Andrews the 2nd daughter of Melville W. & Lilian B. Andrews was born Sept. 7, 1899.
4. Jonathan Evans Andrews the 2nd son of Melville W. & Lilian B. Andrews was born Feb. 22, 1903. Jonathan died Feb. 22, 1903. "Of Such is the Kingdom of Heaven".
5. Charles Albert Andrews the 3 son of Melville W. & Lilian B. Andrews was born Feb. 26th 1905. Charles died Apr. 8, 1905. "Thy will O Lord not ours be done".

ARNALL FAMILY BIBLE

This Bible was published by J. A. Wilmore & Company, New York. A copy of the family register is in the Library of Virginia.

Geo. W. Arnall born 1833 Caroline Co. died Oct 5th 1903 Richmond, Va.
Matilda F. Arnall born May 1833 Caroline Co. died Oct 19, 1895 Caroline Co.
Alpheus S. Childrey born Henrico Co. died Apr 9, 1897 Henrico Co.
Harriett A. Childrey born Henrico Co. died 1868 Henrico Co.
Pascal Arnall born 1862 Caroline Co. died July 5th 1928 Henrico Co.
M.S. Arnall born 1865 Henrico Co. died May 2, 1944 Richmond Va.
   Pascal Arnall & M.S. Arnall were married July 4th 1894 at Denny St. Church by W. A. Laughon.
Mary F. Arnall was born April 25, 1896 Richmond Va. married Linwood T. Butler Dec 23, 1915, died July 27, 1977.
William J. Arnall born Feb 11, 1899 Henrico Co. married Mary K Shobe Dec 21, 1921.
Edner V. Arnall born Feb 7, 1901 Henrico Co. married John H. Eache Oct 30, 1929.
Mabben A. Arnall born Sept 7, 1906, married Hunter B. Bailey Oct 24, 1942.
Pascal Arnall Jr. born Aug 26, 1908 Henrico Co. Va. married Ruth A. Whitehead March 28, 1937, died April 22, 1969.
Linwood Taylor Butler Born May 5, 1892 married Dec 23rd 1915.
Mary F. Arnall Butler Born April 22, 1896.
Matilda Frances Butler Born Oct 9th 1916. Died Oct. 1st 1919.
Bernice Virginia Butler Born Feb 9th 1919.
Mary Catherine Butler Born May 12th 1921.
Bernice Virginia Butler married Robert Milton Edwards.
Mary Catherine Butler married May 3rd 1945 Kenneth Lawerence [sic] Gotthelf Key West Fla.
Mary Lynn Gotthelf Born Feb. 20, 1946.
Bernice Elizabeth Gotthelf Born Sept. 4, 1947.
Catherine Sue Gotthelf Born Sept. 22, 1950.
Kenneth Joseph Gottrelf Born Feb. 23, 1956. Died Dec. 8th 1974.
Lawrence Milton Edwards Born Feb 15, 1948.
Joan Frances Edwards Born Oct. 7, 1949.
Lois Virginia Edwards Born Aug. 7, 1952.
Mallew Alice Edwards Born Aug. 26, 1954.
Edna May Edwards Born January 17, 1957.
Pascal Arnall Sr. Born Aug. 23rd 1862 Caroline Co. died July 5th 1944 Henrico Co.
Mary Susan Childrey Arnoll Born June 3rd Henrico died May 2nd 1944 Richmond Va.
Henry David Shobe [no further info]
Elizabeth C. Shobe [no further info]
William Jennings Arnall Born Feb. 11th 1898 Richmond, Va. Died Sept. 11 1984.
Mary Catherine Shobe Arnoll Born July 2nd 1897 died April 29, 1980. Died April 29, 1980.
Married Dec. 21st 1921 Preacher's Parlor, Carson, E.V.
Mary E. Arnall Born Sept. 19th 1922 Henrico Co., married Ernest Bendle April 18, 1942.

Ruth M. Arnall Born Dec. 16th 1923 Henrico Co.
Gearldine [sic] N. Arnall Born Mar. 14th 1926 Henrico married Wilbur Bendle.
Kathryn J. Arnall Born Mar. 11th 1928 Henrico Co. married Joseph Austin.
William Ernest Bendle Born Dec. 6, 1942.
Dwight Bendle Born July 9, 1948.
Lewis Jennings Bendle Born Dec. 13, 1956.
Judy Ann Bindle Born 1958.
Edna Virginia Arnall Born Feb. 7th 1901 married John Herbert Eacho, Born Aug. 23rd 1903, Washington, D.C. Oct. 30th 1929

ATKINSON FAMILY BIBLE

This Bible, originally owned by Lucy W. Atkinson, contains records of King William and Caroline Counties, 1800-1879. A copy is in the Library of Virginia and has also been published in *Tidewater Virginia Families*, Volume 2, pp. 42-43, 1992.

Iverson L. Atkinson was married to Lucy W. Thomas by Rev. Wm. Starr on 24th April 1832.
Iverson Lewis Atkinson son of Charles & Winefred Atkinson was born 23rd June 1807.
Lucy Walker Thomas daughter of Allen & Elizabeth Thomas was born 27th January 1800.
Lucy Jane Atkinson Daughter of Iverson L. & Lucy W. Atkinson was born in march the 14 1833.
IRA Lewis Atkinson Son of Iverson L. & Lucy W. Atkinson was born in July the 17 1835.
Laura Ann Atkinson was born in May the 2 1837.
Ritty Walker Atkinson was born in September the 22 1838.
Willie Columbus Atkinson son of Ervin and Cornelia Atkinson was born August 2[?] 1882.
Benjamin Oliver Atkinson was born June 29, 1880.
James Bradley Atkinson was born June 30, 1884.
Douglas Atkinson was born August 16, 1886.
Benjamin Oliver [Oliver marked through] Overton Atkinson was born July 2, 1915.
Virginia [illeg] Atkinson daughter of Benjamin and [illeg] Atkinson born February 5th 1921.
Iber Atkinson was born in September the 25 1852 Daughter of I..L. Atkinson & L. Atkinson.
Ervin Atkinson was born in April the 17 1854.
John W. Atkinson was born December the 5th 1856.
Calladonia C. Atkinson was born May the 23 1860.
William C. Floyd was born July 26th 1840.
Americus Floyd was born June the 28 1844.
Died Nancy Thomas departed this life in 1837..19 September
Ira Lewis Atkinson Departed this life in 1840..September the 22.
Laura Ann Atkinson Departed this life in April the 28 1853.
Ider Atkinson departed this life in February the 5 1883.
Bettie Floyd Departed this life April the 23 1887.

AYLETT FAMILY BIBLE

This Bible belonged to Philip Aylett, who was born in King William County and whose descendants married into Caroline County families and later lived in Caroline County. The Bible was published by Matthew Carey, Market Street, Philadelphia, Pennsylvania. It was owned by Mrs. Patrick Henry Fontaine, Woodsdale, North Carolina in 1931. A copy of the family register is in the Library of Virginia. Reverend Fontaine was rector in St. Margaret's Parish, Caroline County.

Philip Aylett
  Born 12 Mar. 1767 in King Wm. Co., Va.
  Died Sept. 1831 at Montville, King Wm. Co., Va.
July 13, 1815 Mary Macon Aylett daughter of Philip & Elizabeth Aylett to Philip Fitzhugh of Caroline.
Feb. 20, 1823 Philip Aylett son of P. & E. Aylett to Judith Page Waller.
May 29, 1831 (21?) Anna Henry Aylett daughter of P. & E. Aylett to Thomas Moore of Chelsea King Wm. Co. Va.
Feb. 3, 1831 Martha Dandridge, daughter of P. & E. Aylett to Silas Duncan Captain in the U.S. Navy.
July 9, 1832 Sarah Shelton Daughter of Philip & Elizabeth Aylett
  to Wm. Spotswood Fontaine of Henry Co. Va.
                    (Myra Hazard's record)
Elizabeth Taylor Moore daughter of Th. & Anna Moore was born at Montville Va. 9th February 1821.
Anna Henry Moore daughter of Thomas & Anna Moore was born at Roselea 12 December 1827.
Wm. Spotswood Fontaine was born 7 Nov. 1810 at the Sellow House
  Hanover Co. Va. His father was William Winston Fontaine -- His Mother was Martha Hale Dandridge.
Wm. Winston, son of Wm. S. & Sarah Fontaine was born at Montville King Wm. Co. Va. Nov. 27th 1834.
Alexander Spotswood son of W.S. & Sarah Fontaine born [no date] Fontainebleau King Wm. Co. Va.
Nov. 14 1818 Elizabeth Henry Aylett, daughter of Philip & E. Aylett aged 20 years 9 months.
Aug 19 1822 Louisa Fontaine daughter Philip & E. Aylett aged 17 years 4 months.
Jan 2nd 1828 Anna H. Moore daughter of P. & E. Aylett aged 24 years.
Jan 28 1829 Patrick H. Aylett son of P. & E. Aylett aged 20 years 9 months Died at the University of Va.
Feb. 9 1829 William Aylett son of P. & E. Aylett Aged 22 years at Montville.
Sept. 1831 Philip Aylett Senior at Montville King William Co. Va aged 64 years.
1833 Martha D. Duncan, at Aylett's warehouse Daughter P. & E. Aylett.
Sept. 24 1842 At Fontainebleau King Wm. Co. Va. Mrs. Elizabeth Aylett daughter of Patrick Henry & Sarah Shelton Henry, and wife of Philip Aylett of Montville King Wm. Co. Va.
Mar 5 1875 Sarah Shelton Fontaine, at Reidsville N.C., wife of Wm. S. Fontaine, and daughter of Philip & Elizabeth his wife and daughter of Patrick Henry, 64 yr. & 9 mo.

BAGBY FAMILY BIBLE

This Bible was published by Matthew Carey, Philadelphia, 1834. A copy is in the Virginia Historical Society. This family lived at "Cedar Grove", which was located 1 mile south of Lauraville on Route 654 (Lauraville Lane), thence 2 miles on private road to the site where the house and cemetery stood. The cemetery is still there in a grove of flowers and shrubs. There are three marked graves here, those of Travis Bagby, his wife and one-year-old son. The tombstones have been pulled up and placed against a tree in the cemetery. Other family members are buried in Lakewood Cemetery, Bowling Green, Virginia.

The original house was incorporated into the present bungelow built near the original site. The place was originally known as the Old Kidd Place. Travis Bagby married John & Ann Kidd's daughter, Mary Ann Kidd, and it then was called the Bagby place. Robert Harrison Upshaw was overseer of the Bagby estate at the time of Travis Bagby's death in 1849. A family member not mentioned in the Bible, but found in the Caroline Death Register is Mary A. Spindle, daughter of James and Mary Bagby, who died August 1861 at the age of 57. Nearby was located Bagby Post Office in Caroline County, named for this family.

The death notice of Travis Bagby appeared in the *Religious Herald* of 14 March 1850 and states that he died at his residence in Caroline County 31st December last, in the 43rd year of his age and was a native of King and King County. The same paper, bearing the date 29 October 1874 carried the death notice of his widow, Mrs. Mary A. Kidd Bagby, who died October 17, 1874. It states that she was baptized into the Upper King and Queen Church by Rev. Andrew Broaddus in September 1833.

The list of Travis Bagby's servants was found in the Travis Bagby's Journal, Seventh Account. This book was found in the settlement of Travis Bagby's estate and the original book has been placed in the Library of Virginia as of 2004.

Richard Bagby, son of John & Mary Bagby was Born March the 7 1749   (changed to 1750) Was married to Susannah Jeffries August the 29 1783.
Susannah Jeffries Born November the 9 1765.
Mary Bagby their Daughter was Born September 9 - 1784. Departed this life August the 29 1785.
George Bagby their Son was Born the 23 of October 1786. Departed this life April 20, 1810. 23 years 8 mo.
Rachel Bagby Born May 1st 1789. Died March 6th 1852.
John Bagby Born May 1st 1792.
Richard Bagby their son was Born April 15 1796.
Martha Bagby Born 15th Aprl 1795.
Robert [B.]Bagby Born 18th Jany 1801.
Mary Bagby Born 28 Septr. 1805.
Travis Bagby Born the 8th August 1807.
Susannah Elizabeth born May 15th 1810.
William Cornelius Haynes Son of John Haynes & S. E. Haynes was born the 25th October 1827.

Mary Ann Kidd was born Nov. 3rd 1809. Departed this life Oct 17th 1874.

John Bagby was married to Elizabeth Courtney (who was born Augt 28 1794) on the 15th day of March 1814.

Richard Bagby was married to Dorothy Ann Fleet on the 14th Feby 1821.

John Haynes was married to Susan E. Bagby on the 30th day Nov. 1826.

Robert B. Bagby was married to Elizabeth Bagby daughter of Capt. John Bagby 21st December 1825.

William C. Wyatt was married to F. G.W. Bagby on the 31st day of May 1827.

Travis Bagby was married to Mary Ann Kidd daughter of John & Ann Kidd on the 28th day of Jany 1834.

Ann E. Bagby daughter of Travis & Mary A. Bagby was married to Col J .O. Butler January 1850.

Emmaline Courtney Bagby daughter of John & Elizabeth born October 9th 1815.

[Name scratched through] born March the 26th 1829.

Ann Elizabeth Bagby their daughter was born 24th August 1836.

Travis Bagby their son was born 29th day of March 1838.

Thos. Gresham Bagby was born 19th August 1840.

Mary Louisa Bagby was born May 15th 1847.

Sallie Maria Bagby was born december[sic] 6th 1848

Juliet Bagby daughter of R.B. & Elizabeth Bagby was born 8th Jany 1827.

Mariah Elizabeth Bagby was born 30 Octo 1828.

Mattie V. Butler daughter of J.O. & Nannie E. Butler was born on Nov 2nd 1853.

Edward E. [Everett] Butler son of J.O. & A.[Ann] E. Butler was born August 28th 1856. [Dentist in Bowling Green, died in 1949 and buried in Lakewood Cemetery, as is his mother Ann E. Butler (1836-1919)].

Leonidas C. Butler son of J. C. & A. E. Butler was born Nov 8th 1859.

Departed this life Lizzie Butler Mahon Oct 9 1904.

Departed this life Travis Bagby Feb 14th 1907 Age 68. [buried in Lakewood Cemetery]

Richard Bagby departed this life April 23rd 1818 aged 69.

James D. Haynes departed This life Oct 1st 1828.

Susannah Bagby departed this life March 28th 1832 aged 67.

John Richd. Bagby son of Travis & Mary Ann Bagby died 14th March 1846.

Rachel Kidd wife of John Kidd & daughter of Rd. & Susannah Bagby departed this life March 6th 1852. Aged 62 years 10 Mos & 6 days.

J.O. Butler departed this life April 10th 1857. Aged 56 years 3 months.

Thos. G. [Gresham] Bagby son of Travis and Mary A. Bagby died upon the field of Sharpsburg Sept 17, 1862 Aged 22 years.

Ann Kidd widow of Thos. Kidd and daughter of Ann Lumpkin died July 26th 1838. Aged 37 years and 7 mo.

John Kidd Father of Mary Ann Bagby wife of Travis Bagby died 23rd May 1839 aged 70.

Ann Kidd wife of John Kidd and Mother of Mary Ann Bagby died Apl 14th 1847 Aged 80 years.

Travis Bagby departed this life December 31 1849 aged 42 years and five months.

Sallie Maria Bagby daughter of Travis & Mary A. Bagby departed this life April 15th 1855 aged 6 years 5 months 9 days. [Caroline Death Register list her as "Sally" M. Bagby, dying Apr. 15,

1856, age 4y 4m]

Mattie V. Butler daughter of J. O. & Annie E. Butler died March 29th 1860 aged 6 years & 5 months.

[Register of Travis Bagby's Servants as found in his journal]:

Juliet was born Feby. 5th 1811
Eliza was born Jany. 20th 1813
Richard was born Jany. 18th 1817 (three above all children of Crissy)
Lucindy was born Septr. 19th 1818
Caroline her child was born 27th Dec. 1838
Sarah her child was born 5th Jany. 1841
Mahaley daughter of Silvy born June 7th 1820
George son of Andrew Born July 1809
Harry son of Eliza born Feby. 1832
Washington son of Eliza born Septr. 1834
Richard son of Eliza born Mar. 1836
Godfrey son of Eliza born 4th July 1839
Nancy daughter of Juliet born 1831
Isaac son of Juliet born Mar. 1834
Crissy daughter of Juliet born 1836
Alexander son of Juliet born Octr. 8th 1838
John Alfred son of Winny born June 1835
James son of Eliza born 24th Feby. 1842
Ben. Son of Mahaley born 30th Octr. 1842
Priscila daughter of Juliet born Septr. 18th 1843
Matilda daughter of Juliet born Septr 18th 1843
Jane daughter of Lucinda Octr. 8th 1843
Andison son of Mahaley born 25th Augt.. 1845 dead
Mariah daughter of Eliza born 1st day Feby. 1844
Susannah daughter Eliza born Augt. 8th 1846
John Henry son of Lucinda born Septr. 26th 1846 dead
Lucy Ann daughter of Mahaley born Octr. 21st 1846 dead
Catharine daughter of Juliet born Jany. 10th 1847
Lavina daughter of Eliza born July 6th 1848
Charles son of Lucinda born June 6th 1849
Robert son of Mahall born Aug. 17th 1849
Sarah Ellen of Mahall born June 21st 1852
Alfred son of Lucinda born Nov. 24th 1851
Silva daughter of Mahala born Sept. 5th 1855
Winney daughter of Emmerline born Nov. 7th 1855
William son of Mahala born Sept. 7th 1861
Lucy daughter of Caroline born Dec. 17th 1861
Maria daughter of Caroline born Sept. 13th 1862

Agnes daughter of Jane born June 11th 1868 dead
Albert son of Jane born Sept. 9th 1864

BARLOW FAMILY BIBLE NO. 1

This Bible belonged to John Walter Barlow who lived on Frog Level Road, Caroline County, Virginia. The Bible is now owned by Ethel Broaddus Andrews Barlow of Caroline County. John Walter Barlow was the son of William & Joanna Seal Barlow. Henrietta Morris was the daughter of Thomas Morris and Elizabeth C. N. Barlow. They were married in Caroline County February 11, 1878.

John Walter Barlow born November 11, 1840. Died February 12, 1926.
Married February 13, 1878 to Nettie [Henrietta] Elizabeth Morris born February 15, 1855. Died July 21, 1919.
Children are:
Thomas Franklin Barlow born November 29, 1878. Died May 17, 1968.
Clarence Welford Barlow born March 1, 1880. Died January 24, 1940.
John Samuel Barlow born December 9, 1881. Died October 28, 1947.
Cora Lillian Barlow born April 26, 1883. Died February 28, 1884.
Bertha Lillian Barlow born December 18, 1884. Died August 1, 1954.
Lewis Walter Barlow born March 13, 1886. Died January 30, 1956.
Melvin Lloyd Barlow born December 20, 1887. Died May 5, 1972.
Josie Elizabeth Barlow born May 1, 1889. Died June 7, 1890.
Harry Alexander Barlow born December 25, 1891. Died June 2,1956.
Peter Maurice Barlow born June 14, 1892. Died April 7, 1895.
Willard Bradford Barlow born September 23, 1893. Died September 24, 1964.
Eddie Shephard Barlow born December 10, 1895. Died November 19, 1970.
Nettie Elizabeth Morris Barlow Died July 21, 1919.
John Walter Barlow Died February 12, 1926.

BARLOW FAMILY BIBLE NO. 2

This Bible was published by The Southwestern Co., Nashville, Tennessee. It is now owned by Ethel Broaddus Andrews Barlow, Caroline County, Virginia. It originally was owned by Lewis Walter Barlow, (son of John Walter Barlow and Nettie Elizabeth Morris), and his wife Pearl Catherine Edwards, daughter of Henry Clay Edwards and Louisa Frances Reynolds. This family lived on Frog Level Road in Caroline County.

This is to Certify that Lewis Walter Barlow and Pearl Catherine Edwards were united in Holy Matrimony at Richmond on the 17 day of January in the year of our Lord 1916 by Rev. John J. Parsons. Signed Lloyd Barlow and Mrs. J. J. Parsons.
Marriages:
Leona Barlow to Robert Carter March 1, 1941.
Dorothy Barlow to Charles [F.] Street Jr. March 29, 1942.

Ethel [Broaddus] Andrews to Francis Barlow Oct. 17, 1942.
Verna Mitchell to Lewis W. Barlow Jr. 7-10-43.
Nancy Peatross to Henry Clay Barlow June 18, 1949.
Betty [Anne] Peatross to C. [Clarence] Ray Barlow Mar. 24, 1951.
Demple Chenault to Anthony Earl Barlow June 12, 1954.
Iola Barlow to Kenneth Utz December 31, 1955.
Shirley Barlow to James L. Minter March 19, 1960.

Births:
Lewis Walter Barlow March 13, 1886.
Pearl Cathleen Barlow Sept. 5, 1897.
Francis Monroe Barlow June 2 - 1917.
Leona Elizabeth Barlow Sept. 21 - 1919.
Dorothy Kathleen Barlow Dec. 18 - 1921.
Lewis Walter Barlow Jr. March 26 - 1924.
Henry Clay Barlow Jan. 30, 1927.
Clarence Ray Barlow June 23, 1929.
Anthony Earl Barlow August 30, 1931.
Iola Virginia Barlow August 24, 1934.
Shirley Ann Barlow July 17, 1940.

Deaths:
Lewis Walter Barlow January 29, 1956.
Pearl Catherine Edwards Barlow August 19, 1991.
Glenn Charles Street March 31, 1967.
Majorie Laverne Barlow September 8, 1947.
Ivan Walter Barlow December 3, 1948.
Gail Frances Barlow August 8, 1950.

BAYLOR FAMILY BIBLE NO. 1

This Bible was printed by Matthew Carey, Philadelphia, 1812. The records date from 1750 to 1869. A copy of these records were deposited in the Library of Virginia by Mr. E.M. Baylor. They have also been reproduced in the *Virginia Genealogical Society Quarterly*, Volume 19, 1981, pp.22-24. The Baylor family lived at "New Market" plantation, Caroline County, Va. It has all been printed in *Virginiq Bible Records* by Jeannette Holland Austin, Willow Bend Books, Westminster, Maryland 2000.

In the margin of the Bible, B. H. Baylor supplied the following information: "This record is from the Bible of his grandfather Dr. George Daniel Baylor of Lockleys [near Bowling Green] Caroline County, Virginia. One of Dr. Baylor's daughters, Julia Ann Baylor, married Joseph Bray whose only surviving great grandchild was Miss Georella B. Jefferis. Dr. Warner Lewis Baylor, Asst. Surgeon, C.S.A., married, first Miss Chappell -- no living descendants; secondly, Miss Lizzie Hoskins Wright, Tappahannock, Essex County, Virginia. By the marriage of Dr. Warner Lewis Baylor & Lizzie Hoskins Wright, there were the following living children, Elizabeth Lewis, Bernard Hoskins, Thomas Booth, Frances Warner and George Daniel, all of whom were married with descendants."

George Daniel Baylor son of John & Frances Baylor of New Market & County of Caroline was married September the 24th 1814 to Eliza Lewis Fox daughter of John & Eleanor Fox of Greenwich & county of Gloucester.

John Baylor & Frances Norton were married at the Parish Church of St Olave Hart Street London by the Revd Mr Pett on the 18th day of November 1778 Recorded by their grandson W.L. Baylor.

W.L. Baylor third son of George D. & Eliza L. Baylor Caroline County, Va. was married 27th of January 1864 to Mary A. E. Chappell daughter of R.W. Chappell city of Petersburg. We were married by the Rev C.J. Gibson pastor of Grace Church at the residence of her mother on Halifax Street in the same city three o'clock P M Wednesday.

John Norton Baylor son of George Daniel & [Eliz Lewis] Baylor was born the 19th day of August 1816.

Ellen Augusta Baylor daughter of George Daniel and [Eliz Lewis] Baylor was born the 15th day of May 1818.

George Robert Baylor son of George Daniel and [Eliz Lewis] Baylor was born the 24 day of May 1820.

Frances Courtenay Baylor daughter of George Daniel and [Eliza Lewis] Baylor was born the 15th day of December 1822.

Warner Lewis Baylor son of George Daniel & [Eliz Lewis] Baylor was born 22d of June 1825.

Julia Ann Baylor daughter of George Daniel and [Eliza Lewis] Baylor was born the 3d day of February 1828.

Louisa Henrietta Baylor daughter of George Daniel and [Eliza Lewis] Baylor was born the 13th day of October [1830?].

Thomas Wiltshire Baylor son of George Daniel and [Ellen Lewis] Baylor was born the 28th day of May 1833.

Alexander Galt Baylor son of George Daniel Baylor and Eliza Lewis Baylor was born the 5th day of October 1835.

George Daniel Baylor son of John & Frances Baylor was born at New Market, Caroline County, January 29th 1789.

Eliza Lewis Fox daughter of John & Eleanor Fox was born at Greenwich Gloucester County, December 8th 1794.

Frances Courtenay Baylor daughter of John & Frances Baylor was born October 10th 1779 & died April 3rd 1780 aged 5 months.

Courtenay Orange Baylor daughter of John & Frances Baylor was born May 31st 1781.

Susanna Frances Baylor daughter of John & Frances Baylor was born March 2nd 1783 & died February the 19th 1837.

Warner Lewis Baylor son of Dr. Warner Lewis & Mary A. E. Baylor was born on Thursday October 27th 1864 in the city of Petersburg, Va.

Departed this life Febry 6 1808 John Baylor of New Market county of Caroline Virginia Son of John & Frances Baylor of same place aged 58 years and upwards. He was born September 4, 1750.

Departed this life Feby 18, 1816 Frances Baylor born at York Town Virga and daughter of John

& Courtenay Norton of Gould Square Crutchet Friars London aged 55 years and upwards. She was born December the 5th 1759.

Departed this life April 3rd 1837 Mrs Eliza Lewis Baylor daughter of John and Eleanor Fox of Greenwich county of Gloucester aged 41 years and upwards. This is recorded by her bereaved husband George D. Baylor To whom she was the fond devoted and faithful wife.

Departed this life April the 17 Monday night at a quarter before 3 o'clock [1848] Doctor George Daniel Baylor, son of John and Frances Baylor of New Market Caroline aged 59 years and upwards. This is recorded by an affectionate son to whom he set the best example.

Departed this life in the city of Petersburg, Va. April 25, 1857 Saturday evening Ellen Augusta Garnett in the thirty ninth year of her age. She was buried in the Blanford churchyard.

Departed this life 10 PM Sunday night April 26th 1868 at her mother's, Halifax Street Petersburg, Va. Mary A. E. Chappell, wife of Dr. W.L. Baylor of Caroline Co. Va. and daughter of R.W. & Harriett Chappell of Petersburg born at the same house on Sunday 10 AM April the 22d 1828. She possessed a lovely character; was a devoted wife & Mother; & won the respect of all who knew her. W L B.

Departed this life Wednesday evening September 8th 1869 Warner Lewis Taylor, son of Dr. W.L. Baylor and the late Mary A. E. Baylor aged four years, ten months and 8 days. Buried in Blanford Churchyard September 10th 1869.

Departed this life Wednesday evening, September 15th 1869, George Marie Baylor son of Dr. W.L. Baylor and the late Mary A. E. Baylor aged one year six months and seven days. Buried in Blanford churchyard September 15th 1869.

Died Mrs Frances C. Pollard wife of Charles W. Pollard on Thursday July 23d 2 1/2 PM 1868 in the city of Petersburg.

BAYLOR FAMILY BIBLE NO. 2

Known as the George Wythe Baylor Bible, the records of which were copied by Mrs. J.M. Cunningham-Dale in 1925, appeared in the *Virginia Magazine of History and Biography*, Volume 35, 1925, pp.404-405. This Bible was in the possession of Susan Thornton Henning (Merriwether), a grand-daughter of George W. Baylor, of Allendale Farm, Shelby County, Kentucky in 1925. The present whereabouts of this Bible is unknown. The seat of the Baylor family in Caroline County was known as "New Market".

George W. Baylor, born January 5th. 1785 and married to Betsy D. Timberlake on the 3d day of December 1807.

He was the son of Major Walker Baylor, who was the son of Col. John Baylor of Caroline County, Virginia, who intermarried with Frances Walker. She [Betsy Timberlake] was a Friend-Quaker. They were descendants from England.

George W. Baylor's mother was the daughter of Joseph Bledsoe.

Betsy Davis Timberlake born October 19, 1789 and married George W. Baylor on the 3d day of December, 1807.

Mary Jane Baylor married to Joseph Henry Bledsoe November 18th, 1729.

John P. Allen born March 3d 1810 and was married to George Ann Baylor on the 25th day of September, 1824, who was born August 25, 1818.

Richard Walker Baylor born 13th day of December, 1808, first son of George W. and Betsy Davis Baylor.

Mary Jane Baylor born 20th July, 1810, first daughter of George W. and Betsy Davis Baylor.

Courtenay Baylor born 20th May, 1813, second daughter of George W. and Betsy Davis Baylor.

George Ann Baylor born 25th August, 1818, the third daughter of George W. and Betsy Davis Baylor.

Walker Baylor Allen was born 31 of July 1835.

Died on the 9th day of March, 1812 Philpot Curran Baylor an infant son of George W. & Betsy Davis Baylor.

Died on the 16th day of April, 1822 Courtenay Baylor, second daughter of George W. & Betsy Davis Baylor.

Died on the 5th day of March, 1838 Betsy Davis Chinn, consort of Aquilla Chinn. She was Betsy D. Timberlake and consort of George W. Baylor.

Died on the 14th of Sept. in the morn 1822 Major Walter Baylor, father of George W. Baylor.

Mistress Mary Timberlake, 2d wife of Richard Timberlake & formerly the wife of Samuel Smith, dec'd. born in the month of May 19, 1747, the daughter of Thomas Munden & Rachel Munden, who was the daughter of John Payne and Nancy Page, who was the daughter of Carter, all of whom were originally from Great Britain except Thomas Munden, whose father was from France and married in England, and Mrs. Mary Timberlake is the mother of Betsy D. Timberlake, now the wife of George W. Baylor, her youngest child.

BAYLOR FAMILY BIBLE NO. 3

This Bible is a record of the Baylor family of Caroline County and covers the period 1743-1811. The family seat was known as "New Market". Some of the records duplicate those in early Baylor Bibles listed above. A copy of these records are in the Library of Virginia and they have been printed in the *Virginia Genealogical Society Quarterly*, Volume 18, 1980, p.120. This Bible record has also been printed in *Virginia Bible Records* by Jeannette Holland Austin, Willow Bend Books, Westminster, Maryland, 2000.

John & Frances [Norton] Baylor were Married at the Parish Church of St.Olave, Hart Street, London by the Revd Mr. Pett on the 18 day November 1778. [the bride and groom were cousins. The bride was 19 years of age].

John Horace Upshaw Esquire of Essex County was married the 25th November 180_ at New Market to Lucy Elizabeth Todd Baylor of Caroline County by the Revd Mr. ____.

Frances Courtenay Baylor Daughter of John & Frances Baylor Born Octor. ye 10th 1779 Died April ye 3d 1780.

Susanna Frances Baylor Daughter of John & Frances Baylor Born March ye 2d 1783: Sponsors Miss Fanny Armistead, Mrs. Shield, Miss Pitt, Miss Betsey Baylor, Mr. Thomas, Mr. George Norton.

I went to Alexandria in April 1797 when C.O. B. and E. B. had the small pox. Frances Baylor Mary [illeg] Daughter of John & Lucy born at New Market [illeg] 1811.

John and Courtenay Norton [parents of Frances Norton who married John Baylor] were Married in York Town Virginia December ye 10th 1743. They went over to England in Novembr 1764, said John Norton of London Mercht died Octr ye 25th 1777 aged 58 years and was buried in St Olave Heart Street, Crutchet Fryers Parish Church in the Doctr's Vault Middle Isle. Doctr Owen Rector of said Parish buried him -- his wife Courtney Norton died in Barbadoes ye 8th of August 1780 -- also his son Henry Norton died in Barbadoes in November 1780. Their loving daughter Frances Baylor left Gould Square Crutchet Fryers London where her Father and Mother had resided for some years -- on the 21st of November 1778 for America by way of Holland and St Eustatia and Arrivd at New Market in June 1779. John [illeg] on 4 April [illeg]. [The John Norton & Sons' papers 1750-1795 are in the possession of Colonial Williamsburg. An account of this business has been published entitled *John Norton & Sons Merchants of London and Virginia* by Frances Norton Mason, Dietz Press, Richmond, Va. 1937. Also *The Virginia Genealogist*, Volume 12, Number 2, p.76 gives further information concerning this family business].

BAYLOR FAMILY BIBLE NO. 4

This Bible is of the Baylor family of "New Market", Caroline County, Virginia and starts with the oldest son of John and Maria Baylor. Copies of this Bible are found in both the Alderman Library at the University of Virginia and at the Library of Virginia. The rest of this Bible, not reproduced here, is too faded to read but refers to the Bland family of King and Queen County.

Was born on the evening of Thursday at early candlelight John Baylor first Son of John and Maria Baylor May the Twenty Ninth One thousand Eight hundred and Twenty One at Locust Hill, the residence of his Grandmother Roy.

Departed this life at Locust Hill on Sunday evening February the 19th 1837 at five o'clock Mrs Susanna Frances Sutton, daughter of the late Jno & Frances Baylor of New Market Aged Fifty four a pious member of the Baptist Church.

Our ever blessed Mother Frances Baylor, died at New Market on the night of 18 February 1815 in the 56th year of her age, and on the night beginning the 17th her old servant Peatross each asking after the other. Written at Locust Hill Monday Morning February 20, 1837. Buried at New Market Tuesday Morning 21st [February 1815].

Departed this life Mrs. Jean Jones, the consort of Thomas Jones late of the County of Gloucester Feb, the 12th 1823 much lamented by her friend.

At his seat Locust Hill Departed this life Mrs. Catherine Roy May the 11th 1727 much lamented by her children, and Friends.

Married on the Evening of Thursday the 6th of May 1819 by the Reverend Mr. Wilson Fredg. Presterian [sic] Church, Jno Baylor of New Market to Maria, Youngest daughter of Mungo & Catherine Roy all of Caroline County.

BAYLOR FAMILY BIBLE NO. 5

This Bible was published by the American Bible Society, New York, 1850. A copy is in the Virginia Historical Society. This family lived at "New Market" plantation, Caroline County. The Blackford family, descendants of the Baylor family were the last to own New Market.

Jno. Baylor of Tiverton England died at Norfolk the 11th Sep.1721.
Jno. Son of Jno. & Lucy Todd died at New Market Caroline 3d Apl 1772.
Fanny Walker Wife of Jno. Baylor Died at New Market 9th July 1783.
Lucy Armistead 3rd Daughter of Jno. & Fanny Walker Baylor Died at Alexandria 9th July 1783.
Jno. Baylor 2nd Son of Jno. & Fanny Walker died at Bowling Green the 5th Feb. 1808 and was buried at New Market.
Fanny Norton Baylor wife of Jno. Baylor died at New Market 18th Feb. 1815.
George 3rd Son of Jno. & Fanny W. Baylor A Colonel of Horse in the Revolutionary & aide to Genl. Washington, died at Bridgetown Barbados of wounds received at Tappan in New Jersey in Sep 1778, on the 9th of Nov 1784.
Robt. 4th Son of Jno. & Fanny W. Baylor died at Pearl River Miss. in the year 1826 leaving a family.
Fanny Baylor, then Nicholson, died at New Market 10th Oct 1815.
Courtenay 5th daughter of Jno. & F.W. Baylor, then Clayton, died in Gloucester Co in 1795.
Walker 6th Son of Jno. & Fanny W. Baylor died in Kentucky in the year 1826 leaving a family.
Elizabeth 6th daughter of Jno. & Fanny W. died at Richmond on the 5th Decr. 1831.
Maria Wife of Jno. Baylor Daughter of Mungo & Catharine Roy died at Locust Hill the 23d day of March 1850.
Jno. Baylor son of Jno. and Fanny Norton Baylor died at New Market Caroline Co on Saturday the 4th of November 1865 in the 80th year of his age.

Dr. John Roy Baylor died at the St. Claire Hotel, Richmond, Va. July 26, 1897.
Ann Bowen Baylor, wife of Dr. John Roy Baylor died at 404 Vine St., Chattanooga, Tenn at the home of her son John Roy Baylor Nov. 21, 1901.
Ellen Bona Baylor wife of Jas. Bowen Baylor died on Madison (Church) St., Washington D.C. on Oct. 27th 1899.
Jno. Baylor son of Jno. & Lucy Todd Baylor was Born 12 May 1705. Moved to New Market Caroline in the year 1726.
Betty only Daughter of Jno. & Lucy Todd Baylor was born in 1718 and died unmarried.
Jno. eldest Son of Jno. & Fanny Walker Baylor was born 14th Aug 1744 & Died an infant.
Fanny & Elizabeth Daughters of Jno. & Fanny W. Baylor were Born 20th Oct 1745. Died Infants.
Lucy 3rd Daughter of Jno. & Fanny W. Baylor was Born Oct. 12th 1746.
Jno: 2d Son of Jno. & Fanny Walker Baylor was Born at New Market the 4th Sep 1750.
Fanny Norton Only Daughter of Jno. Norton Esqr of London was Born at York town Virginia while her Father resided there her mother being Courtenay Walker before marriage.[no date given]
Geo. 3d Son of Jno & Fanny W. Baylor Born 17th Jan 1752.

Robt. 4th Son of Jno. & Fanny W. Baylor Born 19th Jan 1754.

Fanny 4th Daughter of Jno. & Fanny W. Baylor Born 27th July 1756.

Courtenay 5th Daughter of Jno. & Fanny W. Baylor Born 13th Apl 1758.

Bernard 5th Son of Jno. & Fanny W. Baylor Born 23 June 1759 and died an infant.

Walker 6th Son of Jno. & Fanny W. Baylor was Born 13th Oct. 1762.

Elizabeth 6th Daughter of Jno. & Fanny W. Baylor was Born 5th Decr. 1766.

Jno: Son of Jno. & Fanny Norton Baylor was Born 18th May 1786 there being 2 Sons and 6 Daughters of the same parentage.

Maria Wife of Jno. Baylor & youngest Daughter of Mungo and Catharine Roy was born at Locust Hill on the 27th day of Sept.1790.

Jno. Roy Son of Jno & Maria Baylor was born at Locust Hill on the 29th day of May 1821 he being the only child of this marriage.

Sarah Evelyn Bayloe [sic] daughter of Jas. Bowen Baylor and Ellen Bruce Baylor was born at Staunton Hill, Charlotte Co., Va. Oct. 5th 1883.

James Eldest Son of Jno. Roy & Annie Baylor was born at Mirador Albemarle the residence of his Grandfather Bowen on the 30th day of May 1848. [Mirador later became the home of the Longhorne family where Lady Aster was raised.]

Jno. Roy 2d Son of Jno. Roy and Annie Baylor was born at Mirador on the 10th day of April 1851.

Maria Roy Daughter of Jno. Roy & Annie Baylor was born at New Market Caroline County Va on the night of the 6th Jan 1855.

Ann Courtenay Baylor daughter of James Bowen Baylor and Ellen Bruce Baylor was born in the Exchange Hotel, Richmond, Va. Mar.20d 1887.

John Baylor, son of James Bowen Baylor and Ellen Bruce Baylor was born in Richmond, Va. at the N. W. Corner of Grove Ave. & Reed St. on Nov. 5th 1889.

Eloise Barfoot Baylor daughter of Jno. Roy Baylor and Julia Howard Baylor was born at The Willer School Albemarle Co. Va. Sep. 14, 1884.

Pelham Blackford Jr. son of Pelham Blackford and Evelyn Baylor Blackford born at Richmond, Va. April 27 1905.

Jas. Baylor Blackford son of Pelham and Evelyn Baylor Blackford was born in Richmond, Va. July 5th 1907.

Ellen C. Bruce daughter Charles Bruce and Sarah Seddon Bruce was born at Staunton Hill Charlotte Co. Va. Jan: 29, 1858.

Ellen Bruce Fisher daughter of Dr. Wm A. and Ann Baylor Fisher was born at 715 Park Ave. Baltimore, Md. April 4th 1908.

Ellizabeth Gault Fisher daughter of William A. and Ann Baylor Fisher was born at 715 Park Ave Baltimore Md. April 29th 1909.

Anne, oldest daughter of James M.(Marshall) and Frances (Skark) Bowen was born at "Green Wood", Albemarle Co. Va. Novr 21 - 1821.

John Baylor Son of Jno. & Frances Baylor was Born at Tiverton Devonshire England 1750. Moved to Virginia settled in Gloucester & was married to Lucy Todd O'Brien of New Kent in 1698.

Jno. Son of Jno & Lucy Todd was Married to Fanny Walker at York Town 2d Jan 1744.

Lucy 3d Daughter of Jno & Fanny Walker was Married to Jno. Armistead 17th Mch 1764.

Jno. Baylor the Son of Jno. & Fanny Walker was Married in London at Crutchet-Friars Church by the Rev. Mr. Pett to Fanny Norton only Daughter of Jno. & Courtenay Norton of Goulds Square.

Geo. 3rd Son of Jno: & F.W. Baylor was married at Mansfield to Lucy Page Daughter of Mann Page Esqr on the 17th Feb. 1776.

Robt. 4th Son of Jno. & F.W. Baylor was Married at Gwinn Island to Fanny Gwinn Decr 1778.

Walker 6th Son of Jno. & F.W. Baylor was Married to Jane Bledsoe in 1782.

Jno. Son of Jno. & Fanny Norton Baylor was Married at Locust Hill by the Rev. Nicholson to Maria youngest Daughter of Mungo & Catherine Roy, on the 6th May 1819.

Jno. Roy Son of Jno. & Maria Baylor was Married to Annie oldest Daughter of James M. & Frances Bowen at Mirador Albemarle County by the Rev. Dr. Waller on the 6th Day of Jan. 1844.

James Bowen Baylor, son of Dr. John Roy Baylor and Ann Bowen Baylor was Married at Staunton Hill, Va. Jan. 5th 1881 to Ellen C. Bruce, daughter of Charles Bruce and Sarah Seddon Bruce by Rev. Dr. Drew of Presbyterian Church.

John Roy Baylor, brother of Jas. Bowen Baylor was Married at Randolph, Charlotte Co., Va. Nov. 28th 1883 to Julia F. Howard, daughter of Philip Howard and Ella Barfoot Howard by Dr. Drew of the Presbyterian Church.

Sarah Evelyn Baylor daughter of Jas. B. Baylor was married to Pelham Blackford at Staunton Hill Charlotte Co. Va. June 13th 1904 by Rev. Arthur Selden Lloyd & Rev. A.B. Kinslong.

Ann Courtenay Baylor daughter of Jas. Bowen and Ellen Bruce Baylor was married at Staunton Hill Charlotte Co, Va. to Dr. Wm. Alexander Fisher Jr of Belview Md. Oct 17th 1906 by Rev. A.B. Kinslong.

Also included in this record is a newspaper clipping of the wedding of Mr. Arthur H. Clayton of Glo'ster to Miss Jane Baylor, youngest daughter of late John Baylor Esq. of Caroline County (1823) by the Rev. Mr. Woolfolk. From *Richmond News Leader*.

BAYLOR FAMILY BIBLE NO.6

This Bible originated with Richard Baylor and covers the period 1808-1943. A copy was in the possession of Mrs. Wythe Davis Bowe, Chance, Virginia in 1982. A copy of the record is also in the Virginia Historical Society. Richard Baylor's wife was born at Port Tobago, just outside of Port Royal, Caroline-Essex County line, on Route 17. Some members of this family are buried at nearby Vaulter's Church in Essex County. "Edenetta", mentioned is this Bible record is in Essex County and is still standing in restored condition.

Richard Baylor Son of Robert Baylor & Ann Brooke was born at Pearl Bank 1808.
Lucy Waring, Wife of Richard Baylor, was born at Port Tobago Sepr 2nd 1814.
Virginia Williamson Tunstall (wife of Robert Baylor) was born at Norfolk Dec 7th 1844.
Isabella Thorburn McIntosh (wife of Richd Baylor Jr. was born in Norfolk Dec 8th 1857.
Mary Blake Baird (wife of Richd Baylor (3)) was born at Epping Forest Essex Co, Va. Apr 26, 1879.
Lucy Waring Baylor (daughter of V.W. & I.T. Baylor) was born in Norfolk Feb 25th 1869.
Isabella McIntosh Baylor (daughter of R. & I. T. Baylor) was born in Norfolk at 20 Minutes past

eleven o'clock P.M. Oct 12th 1880 Tuesday.

Lucy Latane' Baylor (daughter of Richd & I. T. Baylor) was born in Norfolk at 1 1/2 o'clock P.M. Tuesday Feb 28 1882.

Richard Baylor (son of Richd & I.T. Baylor) was born in Norfolk Thursday Sept 27th 1883 - 2:45 P.M.

Mary McIntosh Baylor (daughter of Richd & I. T. Baylor) was born in Norfolk February 18th 1885 Thursday 12 A.M.

Charles McIntosh Baylor (son of Richd & I. T. Baylor) was born in Norfolk Va. March 11th 1888 Sunday 5:10 A.M.

Elizabeth Waring Baylor daughter of Richd & I. T. Baylor was born in Norfolk Va. January 25th 1890 Saturday 6:30 A.M.

Rosalie Brooke Baylor (daughter of Richd & I. T. Baylor) was born in Norfolk Va. Thursday Jan 28, 1892 7 o'clock A.M.

Robert Payne Waring Baylor (son of Richd & I. T. Baylor) was born in Norfolk, Va. Thursday Aug 30th 1894 2:20 P.M.

Fannie Baylor daughter of Richard & I. T. Baylor was born in Norfolk Va. Sat Oct 17th 1896 at 2:30 A.M.

Katherine Latane' Baylor daughter of Richard & I. T. Baylor was born in Norfolk Va. [no date listed].

Lucy Waring and Richard Bayler were married May 19th 1834 at Edenetta. [Essex Co., Va.]

Virginia W. Tunstall & Robert Payne Baylor were married April 30th 1868 at Norfolk, Va.

Isabella Thorburn McIntosh & Richard Baylor Jr. were married Dec 4th 1879 in Norfolk Va.

Virginia Barron Baird & Henry Latane' Baylor were married Nov 7th 1901 at Vauters Church Essex Co Va.

Lucy Waring Baylor & Wilson Elliott Durce were married at St. Paul's Church Norfolk Va. 1896.

Mary Blake Baird & Richard Baylor Jr.(3) were married June 9th 1914 at Fredericksburg Va.

Isabella McIntosh Baylor & Wythe Davis Bavas Jr. were married at Vauters Church June 6th 1943.

Ann Waring Baylor daughter of Richd & Lucy Baylor born Sept 4th 1835.

Lucy Latane' Baylor daughter of Richd & Lucy Baylor was born July 7th 1837.

Robert Payne Baylor son of Richd & Lucy Baylor was born June 14th 1840.

Mary Baylor, daughter of Richd & Lucy Baylor was born June 13 1842.

Elizabeth Payne Baylor daughter of Richd & Lucy Baylor was born May 30 1844.

Harriet Rouzee Baylor daughter of Richd & Lucy Baylor born Feb 25th 1846.

Helen Stanley Baylor daughter of Richd & Lucy Baylor Sept 20 1847.

Richd Baylor Son of Richd & Lucy Baylor was born May 1st 1849.

Katherine Brooke Baylor daughter of Richd & Lucy Baylor was born Nov 24th 1851.

Henry Latane' Baylor son of Richd & Lucy Baylor was born July 29th 1853.

Isabella McIntosh Baylor (daughter of Richd & Mary B. Baylor) was born in Richmond Wednesday July 17th 1918 at 6:10 A.M.

Died at Kinlock, at half past twelve o'clock A.M. Wednesday the 5th of March 1862, Lucy Baylor, Wife of Richard Baylor in the 48th year of Her Age.

Died at Kinlock at 10 minutes past eleven o'clock P.M. on Tuesday the 25th of November 1862 Richard Baylor in the 60th year of his age.

Died in Norfolk on the 2nd June 1872 Robert P. Baylor in the 32 year of her age.

Died at Kinlock Aug 3rd 1882 Thursday evening Isabella McIntosh Baylor, daughter of R. & I. T. Baylor aged 21 months.

Died at Kinlock Sept. 26th 1901 Thursday Ann Waring Baylor, daughter of Richard & Lucy Baylor aged 66 years.

Died at Kinlock Nov 25, 1863 Elizabeth Payne Baylor daughter of Richard & Lucy Baylor aged 19 years.

Died in Norfolk Va. at eleven minutes past ten o'clock A.M. on Friday the 6th of November 1914 Richard Baylor in the 66th year of his age.

Died in Norfolk Va. at half past two o'clock P.M. on Saturday April 20th 1918 Isabella Thorburn McIntosh Baylor in the 61st year of her age.

Died at Edenetta on the 9th of December 1930, Henry Latane' Baylor age 77 (son of Richard & Lucy Baylor).

BEASLEY/BEAZLEY FAMILY BIBLE

This Bible originally belonged to Thomas H. Beasley 1817 or 1821 and contains records from 1801-1894. It was photocopied through the courtesy of Mrs. Harry Cabel Dunlop, Richmond, Virginia in 1983 and given to the Virginia Historical Society by Mrs. Roland Schools, Milford, Virginia. This record exists of several sheet of paper, in different handwriting, which probably accounts for the discrepancies in the recording dates. Part of this family lived at Picardee's Fork, now at the intersection of Mattaponi Trail and Sparta Road in Caroline County.

Married on the 29th of Nov. 1891 Mr. Thomas H. Beasley to Miss Eiser F. Beasley by the Reverend Mr. Richards.

Susan P.[Parker] Beasley Was born the 8th day of Sept. 1842.

Charles H.[Hay] Beasley Was born the 18th day of Sept. 1844.

Robert T. Beasley Was born the 29th day of Feb. 1848.

Heneny C. Beasley Was born the 19 day of August 1850.

Alexander M. Beasley Was born Oct. the 8th 1853.

Patsy Beazley was Born October the 29th 1801.

Thos. Beazley was Born Febury the 17 1821.

Adeline Beazley was Born the 5th of April in the year 1827.

Charles H. Beasley Departed this life Aug the 25th 1853 aged 6 years.

Eliza F. Beasley Departed this life Nov 25th 1873. Age 55 years.

Elen V. Beasley Died July 26 1894. Aged 64 years.

Married on the 25 day of Nov 1843 Thomas H. Beasley to Miss Eliser F. Beasley by the Revent. Mr. Richards.[second entry]

Thomas H. Beasley was born June the 19th 1817.

Eliser F. Beasley was born Jan the 31st 1818.

Susan P. Beasley was born the 8 day of Sept. 1844.[second entry, different year of birth]

Charles H. Beasley was Born the 18th day of Sept. 1847.[second entry, different year of birth]

Robert T. Beasley was born the 25th day of Feb. 1850.[second entry, different day and year of birth]

Charles H. Beasley Departed this life August the 29th 1857 Age 6 years.[second entry, different year of death]
Luther Silas Beasley was born the 28th of September 1855.
Alice H. Beasley Was born 11th day of July 1856.
Thomas W. Beasley Was born 28th day of Jan. 1862.
Thomas H. Beazley Born Feb 17 1821.
Henry C. Beasley was born the 19 day of Aug. 1852.[second entry, different year of birth]
Alexander M. Beasley was Born Oct. the 8 1853.
Luther S. Beasley was born the 28th day of July 1857.[second entry, different year of birth]
Alice H. Beasley was [born] the 11th day of July 1860.[second entry, different year of birth]
Thom H. Beasley was born the 25 day of Jan. 1863.

BEAZLEY / SAMUEL FAMILY BIBLE

This Bible was printed by A.J. Holman & Co, Philadelphia. There is no date of publication. No owner's name is recorded. The records exist in two sections. The first are handwritten pages inserted into the Bible. The actual Bible record pages begin with the records of Philip Samuel and Lucie Beazley, his wife. The Samuel family lived at a place known as "Bath", no longer standing, nine miles from Bowling Green near Woodford, Virginia. The place was on the South River and for some years was also owned by the Coghill family. For more information concerning the Samuel, consult *The Samuell/Samuel Families of Tidewater Virginia* by Dorothy S. Samuel and Colonel Taliaferro L. Samuel III, Montgomery, Alabama, 1997. The Beazley family lived at a place known as "Mount View" which was located at 17806 Rogers Clark Boulevard (Route 207). The cemetery is located back of the house spot and here is buried Philip Arthur Beazley and Mildred Penn Collins, his wife. For more information concerning this Collins family, consult *The History and Genealogy of the Collins Families and related families* by Herbert Ridgeway Collins, The Dietz Press, Richmond, Va., 1954.

The Jackson family lived at "Oak Hill" on Route 30 at the Caroline-King William line just beyond Bethel Methodist Church were there is a memorial window to Thomas Price Jackson Jr. Many of the Jackson/Samuel family are buried at " Oak Hill". See *Cemeteries of Caroline County, Virginia*, Vol. 2 by Herbert R. Collins, Willow Bend Publications, Westminster, Md., 1995.

M.A. Beazley & R. L. Jackson married May 27th 1891.
Lucy A. Beazley & Philip Samuel were married June 2, 1903.
Births:
Archibald S. Beazley was born May 26th 1824.
M.C. Beazley was born May 2, 1859.
M.A. Beazley was born Feb. 13th 1861.
A. L. Beazley was born Nov. 2nd 1862.
J. W. Beazley was born June 15th 1866.
G. L. Beazley was born Nov. 23, 1868.
L.A. Beazley was born April 10th 1870.

Wm. A. Beazley was born June 18th 1871.
F.M. Beazley was born Feb. 8th 1873.
R. C. Beazley was born December 14th 1874.
O. B. Beazley was born Feb. 9th 1878.
Gertrude L. Beazley & J.P. Jennings were married April 17, 1895.
Deaths:
Oliver Beazley died Dec 28th 1869.
Martha Samuel Beazley his wife, died July 11th 1873.
Maria E. Wilson Beazley wife of A.J. Beazley died Feb. 20th 1892.
Archibald S. Beazley died Dec. 24th 1895.
Annie Beazley Jackson wife of R.L. Jackson died Jan. 21st 1896.
Gertrude Beazley Jennings died June 21st 1907 - wife of J.P. Jennings.
Capitola Stone wife of Lee Stone Died Aug 1907.
R.H. Thompson husband of Maude Beazley Thompson died June 20th 1923.
Mother [of Oliver Beazley] was Major Corbin's daughter.
Oliver Beazley & Martha Samuel were married Sept. 4th 1823.
Archibald S. Beazley & Maria E. Wilson were married Dec. 23rd 1856.
Thomas B. Coghill & Bettie A. Beazley were married Aug. 27 1854.
Philip Arthur Beazley & Millie [Mildred Penn] Collins were married Dec. 18th 1856.
William L. Beazley & Amelia E. Henderson were married Dec. 25 1859.
Emeline Beazley married Waller Allen in 1880.
M.C. Beazley & Leeonidas [sic] Stone Married Mch. 7th 1888.

Philip's Grand Mother on Mother's side Jane Catherine Johnson. Great Grand Mother Kate Price White. Grandfather Thos. Price Jackson. Great Grand father Major John Jackson. His Grand Mother's father was Wm Daniel Johnson. On his father's side his Grand Mother was Sarah Woodford [Woodford marked through and changed to Woolfolk} Hill daughter of Henry Hill of Mt. Gideon. His Grandfather was Philip Samuel.

Died Nov. 30, 1932 William Alpin Beazley. Aged 61.
Died Feb. 24, 1933 John Wilson Beazley aged 67.
Died June 28, 1945 Archibald Llewellyn Beazley in his 83 year.

Family Register
Parents Names
Husband Philip Samuel
Born Dec. 23rd 1870
Wife Lucie Beazley Samuel
Born April 10th 1870
Married June 2nd 1903

Marriages:
Boyd Latane Samuel & Lucie Margaret Frances July 10, 1937.
Children's names:

Lois Samuel daughter of Philip & Lucie Beazley Samuel Feb. 28th 1904.
Philip Samuel Jr., son of Philip & Lucie Beazley Samuel was born Mch. 23rd 1905.
Boyd Latane Samuel son of Philip & Lucie Beazley Samuel was born Oct. 30th 1906.

Marjorie Frances Samuel daughter of Boyd and Lucie Samuel was born Dec. 18, 1940.
John Boyd Samuel son of Boyd and Lucie Samuel was born Oct. 18, 1945.
Lois Samuel daughter of Philip & Lucie B. Samuel died Mch. 1904.
Philip Samuel Jr. son of Philip and Lucie B. Samuel died Mch. 23rd 1905.
Lillie Almetar Beazley Samuel died July 5, 1948.
Philip Samuel died Aug. 30, 1949.

BERNARD FAMILY BIBLE NO. 1

This Bible was printed in London for R. Ware in 1765 at the Bible and Sun in Amen-Corner, near Pater Noster-Row. The Bible was owned by John James Bernard, attorney-at-law in Arlington, Virginia in 1954 when it was copied by George H.S. King of Fredericksburg, Virginia. It is now owned by his son. The Bible is very large and leather bound, measuring 18 1/2" x 11 1/4". A typewritten copy was in the possession of the late James Patton, Port Royal, Virginia. The information included in brackets was added by Mr. Patton. This Bible record has been published in the *Magazine of Virginia Genealogy*, Volume 37, Number 3, August 1999. "Mansfield", which is mentioned in this Bible was south of Fredericksburg on U.S. Route 2 and was destroyed during the Civil War. It is now the site of the Fredericksburg Country Club.

William Bernard the son of Richard Bernard and Elizabeth his wife Hart was born the 6th of September O.S.1730 and on the 25th Nov. 1750 was married to Winnifred Thornton the only Daughter
  Anthony & Winnd. Thornton of the County of Stafford: the Children of that marriage are as follows:
Richard born 10 April 1753 (Tuesday); Died 22d Jany: 1785.
Elizabeth born 11 Sept. 1755 (Thursday); Died 20 Oct. 1756.
William born 21 Feby. 1758 (Tuesday); Died 1759.
John born 20 Oct. 1761 (Tuesday); Died 1782.
William Thornton born 24 Feby. 1764 (Friday); Died Sept. 8, 1769.
Francis Peter born 22 Sept. 1765 (Sunday); Died Oct. 1768.
Winnifred the wife of William Bernard was born on the 23 day of
  Septr. 1729 and departed this life on the 29 day of Sept. 1765.
William Bernard was married to Sarah Savin July 25, 1767. Children of second marriage:
Elizabeth Richardson born 10 Sept. 1768 (Friday night).
William born 3 September 1770 (Monday morning).
Sarah born 2 Feby. 1779 (Tuesday morning).
Sarah Savin wife to William Bernard departed this life on the 27th day January 1790.
William Bernard the son of William Bernard and Sarah his wife formerly Sarah Savin was born
  3d of September 1770 and on the Ninth day of April 1789 was married to Fanny Hipkins the
  only Daughter of John & Elizabeth Hipkins of the County of Caroline & Town of Port Royal:

the Children of that Marriage are as follows:

Sarah Savin born 7th March 1790 (Sunday Morning).

John Hipkins born 10th Jany. 1792 (Tuesday morning).

Eliza Pratt born 21st April 1794 (Monday night); Died 6 July 1803.

William Born 15 May 1796 (Sunday morning).

Fanny wife of William Bernard was born on the 14th May 1775 and departed this life on the 30th day of April 1801.

Eliza Pratt departed this life on the 7th of July 1803 between 11 & 12 O'clock at night.

Sarah Savin was married to Philip Lightfoot 31st August 1804.

William Bernard was married to Elizabeth Fauntleroy (formerly Elizabeth Hooe) daughter of William Hooe Senr of King George on the 29th day of December 1804 - the Children of that Marriage are as follows:

Fanny Margaret born 17th October 1805 (Thursday Evening); Died June 24, 1891.

Arthur Howson Hooe born 16 Octr 1808, Sunday Morning 3 o'clock [died Aug 1891, buried at Mansfield].

Alfred born 5 November 1810, Monday morning 4 O'clock; died 15th July 1811.

Virginia Ann born 31st July 1812, Friday Evening.

Elizbeth Thacker born 9th March 1814, Wednesday morning; Died Mch. 25, 1866.

Anna Rosetta Byron born 1 Nov. 1815, Ditto, Noon 1/2 past 12; Died Dec. 13, 1831 [at Mansfield, bur at Mansfield].

Nathaniel Alfred born 14 Oct. 1819, Thursday evening; Died Nov. 25, 1892.

Virginia Ann was married to Richard H. Carmichael on the 9th Apr.[Apr. marked out, Sept inserted] 1830.

William Bernard departed this life at Mansfield on the 25 November 1841 aged 71 years 2 months and 22 days. 9A.H.H.Bd scrips it - taken from obituary in Va. Herald of Fredericksburg of 1st December 1841).

Virginia A. Carmichael died in Fredericksburg on Friday morning at 4 o'clock A.M. January 22, 1886 and was buried the next day in the Fredericksburg Cemetery (AHHB.)

Richard H. Carmichael [Jr.] died in Fredericksburg on [4th] day of February 188[2] and was buried the next day in the Fredericksburg Cemetery. [born Oct. 12, 1838].

Elizabeth Bernard consort of Wm. Bernard died in Fredericksburg on 20 day of Nov. 1870 and was buried in the cemetery at Mansfield. She was born Oct. 9, 1774. (See her monument for dates).

Nathaniel Alfred Bernard, son of Wm Bernard and Elizabeth Fauntleroy Bernard was married to Isabella Butler Roberts, daughter of John H. Roberts & Ellen Badger on the 21 day of November 1867. The children of that marriage are as follows:

[infant son d. at 4 weeks, bur Sept 28, 186?, bur at Mansfield]

William Bernard born 1 Jan. 1869; Died Sept. 21, 1944 [Bur. City Cem.]

Ellen Bernard born; Died Sept. 27, 1870.

Elizabeth Hooe Bernard born 11 Dec. 1873; Died May 17, 1948 (Mrs. Pollock) [bur City Cem]

John Roberts Bernard born 3 July 1877; died March 7, 1946. [bur City Cem]

William Bernard, son of Nathaniel Alfred Bernard and Isabella R., his wife, was married to Loulie Minor Young, daughter of Edgar M. Young & Mary Constance Calwell on the 25th day of October, 1899. The children of this marriage are as follows:

William Bernard Jr. born 3 August 1900, Friday morning, 2 o'clock.

Constance Calwell born 24 December 1902; Friday night at 9 o'clock.[d. Dec. 3, 1983, bur in City Cem]

Isabella Roberts born 21 June 1904, Tuesday morning 7 o'clock.

Edgar Young born 17 Feby. 1906, Saturday morning 2 o'clock. [died Sept 1988]

Alfred Nathaniel born 18 Jany 1909, Monday morning 5 o'clock; died Nov. 19, 1909.

John James born 8 March 1914, Sunday 11:20 A.M. [died Mar. 30, 1971, bur in City Cem]

Isabella Butler Roberts wife of Nathaniel Alfred Bernard departed this life on Dec. 20, 1913. She was born Jan. 9th 1837. [bur in City Cem]

Isabella Roberts, daughter of William Bernard and Loulie M. Young Bernard, his wife, was married to William John Scheyer, Liuet U.S.M.C. on July 25, 1925.

Constance Caldwell Bernard, daughter of William Bernard and Loulie M. Young Bernard his wife, was married to Augustus William Cockrell 3rd Lieut. U.S.M.C. on May 6, 1926.

Augustus William Cockrell IV, first child of this marriage was born Feb. 24, 1927.

Edgar Y. Bernard married Katherine W. Micks May 22, 1930. [He died Sept 23, 1988, bur in Confederate Cemetery at Spotsylvania Courthouse]

William Bernard Cockrell second son of Constance Bernard Cockrell & Lieut: A.W. Cockrell died in Shanghai, China, July 13, 1932. He was born March 6, 1931.

Bernard Young Cockrell 3rd son Constance Bernard Cockrell and Lieut. A.W. Cockrell born Nov. 22, 1933.

Wiliam Bernard Jr, son of William Bernard and Loulie Young Bernard, was married on March 18, 1932 in San Francisco to Anna Louisa Evans. (no issue).

John James Bernard son of William Bernard and Loulie Young Bernard, was married to Aglae Louise Van Valzah December 25, 1940. [He died 1971, she June 26, 1981, both bur in City Cem]

Issue of the union of John James Bernard and Aglae Louise Van Valzah are:

William Robert Bernard born June 2, 1942 at Washington, D.C.

John Van Valzah Bernard born February 23, 1945 at Washington, D.C.Nov. 20, 1948 -

Loulie Young Bernard [Born Mar 15, 1874] was buried this day at the City Cemetery, Fredericksburg, Virginia. She died at the family home, 407 Hanover St., Fredericksburg on Nov. 18, 1948. She is survived by all of her children except Alfred Nathaniel who died in infancy. (signed) John James Bernard.

BERNARD FAMILY BIBLE NO. 2

This Bible originally belonged to John H. Bernard and his wife, Jane J. Gay Robertson, who resided at "Gay Mont" near Port Royal, Caroline County, Virginia. This Bible was published in New York in 1813. It resided for many years in the book press along with some sixty other books at Gay Mont until 1958, when the house was sold. A member of the family purchased the press and books and they were stored off the premises in a wet basement and eventually hauled off to the dump. Fortunately the late James Patton made extracts from the Bible records which today are preserved. These records have been published in the *Magazine of Virginia Genealogy,*

Gay Robertson Bernard, born Feb. 25, 1817.
Anne Skipwith Bernard, born Feb. 9, 1819, died May 1, 1821.
John Hipkins Bernard, born Jan. 12, 1821, died Aug. 7, 1822.
Sally Savine Bernard, born Feb. 5, 1823, died Apr. 26, 1831.
William Bernard, [twin to above], born Feb. 5, 1823, died Mar. 22, 1823.
Mary Eliza Bernard, born July 1, 1824.
William Robertson Bernard, born Dec. 17, 1825.
Lelia Bolling Bernard, born July 18, 1827.
Caroline Pocahontas Bernard, born Feb. 17, 1831.
Powhatan Bolling Bernard, born Sept. 22, 1833, died Mar. 24, 1835.
Helen Straun Bernard, born Jan. 11, 1836. The first little girl baptized in St. Peter's Church, Port Royal, Va. on the day of its consecration by Bishop Moore, with Mrs. General Scott as sponsor, May 15, 1836.

BLANTON / ALLEN FAMILY BIBLE

The earliest entry in this Bible is Richard Blanton, son of Charles and Charlotte, born 1786 in Essex County. They lived in the area of Caroline County called "Blantons" near Balty and attended Emmaus Christian Church at Penola. The second entry, Sarah "Sallie" Holladay Goodloe, daughter of Aquilla & Elizabeth Goodloe, married George William Blanton. For a complete history of this family see *Todds of Virginia* by Rubey, Stacy and Collins, Artcraft Press, Columbia, Missouri, 1960.

The records enumerated below are from loose pages from a family Bible, the pages now in the possession of Dollie Allen Prohaska.
They appear to have come from a nineteenth century Bible. This record has been published in the *Virginia Genealogical Society Quarterly,* Volume 18, p. 127. It has also been reproduced in *Virginia Bible Records* by Jeannette Holland Austin, Willow Bend Books, Westminster, Maryland 2000.

Richard Blanton died July 5th 1870 in the 84th year of his age.
Sallie H. Blanton Wife of George W. Blanton died May 22nd 1877 in the 44th year of her age.
Laura O. Blanton Wife of Julian A. [Allen] Blanton died May 26 in 1878 age 20 years & 27 days.
George W. [William] Blanton died Aug. 13th 1908 age 80.
Aquilla J. [James] Goodloe died Mar. 29, 1912 age 85 years.
John T. [Thomas] Allen died Oct. 4, 1912 age 58 years & 17 days.
Bettie L. Allen died Oct. 29, 1937 age 82.
Sons of the above couple:
John Shelby Allen died Oct. 17, 1949, age 64 [married Virginia Fowler]
Emmett Lewis Allen died July 1, 1950 age 63. [married Virginia Laurence]
Lawrence Berkley Allen died Mar. 27, 1956 age 62.

George W. Blanton to Sarah H. Goodloe Nov. 17th 1853.

Laura O. Blanton Daughter of George W. & Sarah Blanton to Julian A. Blanton December 12, 1876.

George W. Blanton of Caroline Co. Va. [married secondly] to Mrs C. [Caroline "Callie"] H. [Harrison Arnold] Mountjoy, [widow of William Mountjoy] of Washington, D.C. Sept. 16th 1880.

Bettie L. Blanton of Caroline Co. Va. to John T. Allen of the same Dec. 16th 1880.

Richard Blanton, Essex Va. [was born] Oct. 30, 1786.

Mary Blanton Prince William [county] [was born] Apl. 27, 1790.

Nettie S. Blanton Daughter to C.H. and George W. Blanton born September the 3, 1881.

George W. Blanton son of Richard and Mary Blanton born September the 15, 1828.

Sarah H. Blanton daughter of Aquilla and Elizabeth Goodloe born April the 29, 1834.

Betty I. Blanton daughter of George W. and Sarah H. Blanton born September the 20, 1855.

Laura O. Blanton daughter of the same born April the 29 1858.

George Goodloe Blanton [married twice Blanche Sutton and Ann Eliza Martin] son of George W. and Sarah H. Blanton born June 28th 1861.

James R. [Rawlings] Blanton son of the same born February the 15 1864.

Sallie H. Blanton daughter of the same born May the 28th 1867.

Isla G. Blanton daughter of the same born April the 6 1870.

Mary J. Blanton Daughter of the same born September the 26, 1872.

George O. Allen son to Bettie I. and John T. Allen born February 6th 1883.

John Shelby Allen Son to same born March 24th 1885.

Emmett I. Allen Son to same [born] March 13th 1887.

Mary G. Allen daughter to same born November the 29 1890.

Berkley Allen to same born July 26 1893.

Sallie W. Allen to same born March 8 1895.

Earl Allen the son of the same born in the month of July 14 year of 1900.

BLAYDES FAMILY BIBLE

This Bible record is in the Alderman Library, Charlottesville, Virginia and a copy is also in the Library of Virginia. The Blaydes family lived in both Spotsylvania and Caroline Counties. Stephen Blaydes was in Caroline County as early as 1854 and Hugh F. Blaydes as early as 1857. William M. Blaydes, son of Hugh & Mary E. Blaydes died September 24, 1860 in Caroline County and Charles E. Blaydes, infant son of Jo. and Augy Blaydes, drowned at Guinea, Caroline County September 1873. Robert Hughes Blaydes, born September 9, 1881 in Spotsylvania, son of Samuel Chiles Blaydes married Evie Sanford of Caroline County and operated a large store at Guinea. He died November 11, 1930, his wife March 2, 1953, both buried in the family cemetery at Guinea. Samuel Chiles Blaydes was born in 1858 in Caroline County and married Ida M. Blackley, daughter of John & Sarah Jane (Timberlake) Blackley and ran a store with his son Hugh. For more information concerning this family, see *More Than Skin Deep* by Mary Douglas Blaydes.

William B. Blaydes and Frances B. McGehee were married December 8th 1829 by R.G.C.
Simeon G. Duerson & Ellen V. Blaydes were married July 27th 1853 by R.L. Coleman.
William G. Duke & Mary E. Blaydes were married July 18th 1853 by R.L. Coleman.
Frederick Lindsey and Mary ____ Bennett November 10th 1886 by Rev. P.T. Warren.
Willie B. Duerson and Ann Eliza Pleasants were Married Nov. 30th 1898 by Rev. C.J. Haley.
William Bibbs Blaydes was born March 18th 1797.
Frances Barbara McGhee was born February 5th 1800.
Frances Ann Blaydes was born October 5th 1830.
Mary Elizabeth Blaydes was born December 12th 1831.
Ellen Virginia Blaydes was born November 2nd 1833.
Isabella Matilda Blaydes was born July 23rd 1837.
John Coleman Blaydes was born January 6, 1839.
William Hawes Blaydes was born February 15th 1842.
Frederick Lindsay Duerson was born April 21st 1850.
Willmonia Frances Duerson was born October 5th 1857.
Willie Blaydes Duerson was born August 15th, 1861.
Virgil O. Duerson was born December 18th 1808.
Wilmonia Frances Duerson departed this life June 7th 1858.
Virgil O. Duerson departed this life Aug. 4th 1890.
Simeon Goodloe Duerson departed this life July 2nd 1898.
John Coleman Blaydes departed this life May 31st 1839.
William Bibb Blaydes departed this life October 15th 1857.
Frances _____ Blaydes departed this life February 7, 1865.
Mary Elizabeth Duke departed this life August 1899.
Frances Ann Blaydes departed this life June 23rd 1805.
William Hawes Blaydes departed this life June 26th 1904.
Ellen Virginia Duerson departed this life April 12th 1917 10 P.M.
Frederick L. Duerson departed this life Jan. 18 1924.
Mary Bennett Duerson departed this life [blank] 1937.
Willie Blaydes Duerson departed this life June 25th 1939.

BONDURANT FAMILY BIBLE

This Bible was printed and published by M'Carty & Davis, Philadelphia, 1882. The Bondurant family intermarried with the Smith and Campbell families of Caroline County. A copy of this Bible record is in the Library of Virginia. It has also been reproduced in *Virginia Bible Records* by Jeannette Holland Austin, Willow Bend Books, Westminster, Maryland 2000.

Robert M. Bondurant was born 9th of April 1801.
Pamelia A. Bondurant was born 13th of April 1801.
Mary A. J. Bondurant daughter of Robert and Pamelia A. Bondurant was born the 3rd of November 1825.
Edward Bondurant son of Robert and Pamelia A. Bondurant was born the 10th Oct 1826.
Peter M. Bondurant son of Robert and Pamelia A. Bondurant was born the 29th of May 1829.

Robt. M. Bondurant departed this life 16th of April 1865.
Pamelia A. Bondurant Departed this life the 26th of February 1845
  in her 44 year.
Mary A. J. Murrell Departed this life the 26th of January 1855 in her 30th year.
Edward Bondurant departed this life the 16th of July 1827.
Ida May daughter of Rebecca B & John W. Bondurant was born 14th of December 1858.
Bessie Bondurant Smith daughter of Ida May and A.G. Smith was born March 27, 1881.
Lilburne Mason daughter of A.G. and Ida May Smith was born August 28, 1882.
Mary Ella daughter of A.G. and Ida May Smith was born June 26, 1884.
Thomas Dillard son of A.G. and Ida May Smith was born July 26, 1887.
John W. son of A.G. and Ida May Smith was born August 14, 1889.
Ida George daughter of A.G. and Ida M. Smith was born August 23, 1891.
Robert M. Bondurant married Pamelia Moseley daughter of Peter Moseley 11th of November
  1824.
Mary A. J. Bondurant was married to B. F. Murrell the 8th June 1840.
P.M. Bondurant was married to L. B. Hilliard the 5 of April 1854.
John M. Bondurant & Rebecca R. Owen were married 30th of August 1857.
Ida May Bondurant and H.G. Smith were married April 1, 1880.
Bessie Bondurant Smith was married to T. E. Campbell April 26, 1904.
Robert M. Bondurant son of Robert and Pamelia A. Bondurant was born January the 10th 1831.
John W. Bondurant son of Robert and Pamelia A. Bondurant was born 18 of Oct. 1833.
Sarah Adaline daughter of Robert and Pamelia A. Bondurant was born the 19th of December
  1837.
Joseph W.W. Bondurant Son of Robert and Margaret W. Bondurant was born the 23rd of June
  1848.
Infant son of A.G. and Ida May Smith born July 30, 1893. Died August 10, 1893.
Vernon Owen son of A.G. and Ida M. Smith was born November 15, 1894.
Adrian George, son of A.G. and Ida M. Smith was born April 2, 1897.
Cornelius son of A.G. and Ida Smith was born March 2, 1899.
Robert M. Bondurant departed this life the 17th of July 1832.
Sarah Adaline departed this life the 26 of November 1845.
Cornelius son of A.G. and Ida May Smith died October 26, 1966.

BOULWARE FAMILY BIBLE NO. 1

This Bible was owned by Miss Maude Motley, who moved from the Upper Zion area of Caroline to the Milford area in 1941. Her mother's maiden name was Boulware. It is now owned by James Presgraves, Wytheville, Virginia. The records run from 1780-1802. A copy of the family register is in the Library of Virginia.

Turner Boulware, son of Mark Boulware, moved to Wood County, Virginia, now West Virginia, in 1810. He helped build the court house and old Bell Tavern there. He enlisted in the American

Army in 1812 and helped defend Fort Meigs and later died in Parkersburg, West Virginia.

Franky Boulware daughter of Mark Boulware & Milley his wife was born July the 5, 1780.
Molley Boulware born Decm. 23rd 1781.
Richd. Boulware born Novemr. 15th 1783.
Dolley Boulware born Novemr. 25th 1785.
Eliza Boulware born June 15th 1788.
Turner Boulware son of Mark Boulware & Agatha his wife Born Octo 4th 1792.
Lucy Boulware the daughter of Marke Boulware and Agatha his wife was born November 6th 1793.
Elliott Boulware born 12th September 1795.
Judah Boulware born January 5th 1797.
James Boulware born April 13 1799.
Ofelia E. Boulware born January 18th 1801.
Battle Boulware born July the 20th 1802.

A Mule Colt foaled the 28th day of May 1801. The property of Mark Boulware and his Name is called Jack 1809.
A Mule Colt foaled the 17th day of April 1811.

Obit enclosed from Newspaper:
"Died in Caroline county on the 26th of January 1872 of inflamation of brain, Gennie, son of James and Caroline Boulware, aged about five years. The remarkable sprightness of the little boy and his amirable disposition had greatly endeared him to his parents which was heightened by increasing watchfullness by the bedside of their little sufferer. Weep not parents, at this dispensation of Devine Providence, not rejoice that your little boy is a shining angel among the redeemed."

BOULWARE FAMILY BIBLE NO. 2

This Bible was owned until recently by Miss Maude Motley who moved from the Upper Zion area of Caroline to the Milford area. Her mother's maiden name was Boulware. The records run from 1792-1836. The Bible is now owned by James Presgraves, Wytheville, Virginia. A copy of the family register is in the Library of Virginia.

Turner Boulware Son of Mark Boulware and Agatha his wife both of Caroline County Virginia was born in Said County October the 4th 1792 who emigrated to Wood County Virginia 18th - 1810 was Married on the 28th day of May 1829 to Mary Anne Creel of Wood County, Va. Daughter of George Creel Jr. and Clara his wife who was daughter of Anthony Buckner of Prince William County Va. who was born August 5th 1807.
Mark Boulware departed this life March 15th 1811.
Agatha Boulware wife of Mark Boulware departed this life February 22nd 1836.

BOULWARE FAMILY BIBLE NO. 3

This Bible was published by C. Ewer and T. Bedlington, Boston, 1825. The Bible is now owned by Mrs. Mary Robertson Boulware (John A.) Campbell, of Redmond, Washington, who furnished the copy transcribed here and, who also has placed a copy in The Library of Virginia. The earliest record in the Bible is that of Harriet Terrell in 1787, and that of her husband Gray Boulware in 1793. According to family tradition, Harriet Terrell's mother was a Tyler.

The Boulware family originated in Essex County before coming to Caroline County. The family which owned this Bible lived at "Arcadia", a 745-acre estate, now within the confines of Fort A.P. Hill in Caroline County. The estate joined the Royston family and also that of the Kay family. It was originally the home of the Thomas Slaughter family before it was acquired by Gray Boulware. Andrew Lee Boulware married Ann Trippe Slaughter. Arcadia appears in the Mutual Assurance Society records of 1803, when it was owned by Thomas Slaughter. The Boulware house at Arcadia was built around 1830 and taken down in 1913 and replaced by a new one. Arcadia was last owned by Luther Kay.

The graveyard, enclosed with an iron fence and arched gate with the name "Gray Boulware" on its gate, was moved to Greenlawn Cemetery, Bowling Green, Virginia, when the government created the military reservation there in 1941. Four graves were moved, including one marked grave of Sally Hudgins Boulware and the three unmarked graves, which included those of Gray Boulware and his first wife, Virginia Louisa Wright, and another child. The iron fence was not moved and its whereabouts is unknown today.

Andrew Lee Boulware died the 8th of August 1827.
Bettie Tyler died 9 Sept 1825.
Virginia Louisa Boulware died the 15th of April 1849.
Geo. L. Boulware died April 27-1852.
Judith T. [Terrell] Boulware died December 7, 1850.
Gray Boulware Sr died February 2d 1855 [1855 marked out and changed to 1857].
Sally Hudgin Boulware died October Thursday 15, 1857.
Gray Boulware Jr. son of G. Boulware and Milly G. Boulware died the 12th of November [1895]. [buried in Lawrence Co, Kansas].
Gray Boulware son of Gray Boulware Jr. died Oct 26, 1895.
[Louise] Loulie Judith Boulware Murphy June 30th 1894 in Lawrence Kans.
Gray Boulware husband of Millie Boulware on February 13th 1895 in Topeka, Kans. Buried in Lawrence Co., Kans. 2/15/95.
Thomas G. son of G. and M.S. Boulware died in Cripple Creek Colo June 26, 1896.
Millie Hudgin Boulware wife of Gray Boulware Died in Silver City June 23, 1906.
Margaret Boulware Hoover dau. Of G. and Millie S. Boulware died Sierra Madre, Calif. Jan 4, 1918.
Frank, son of H.E. and Harriet B. Ray died Topeka, Kans., July 2, 1896.
Mary Scott, wife of Frank Boulware died Feby 12, 1920 Silver City, N.M.

Robt. H. Jr., son of R.H. and Blanche died May 1st 1920, Silver City, N.M.

Robert Hudgin Boulware Sr., son of Gray Boulware and Millie Hudgin Boulware, died December 20, 1929 Silver City, New Mexico.

Gray Estes Murphy son of Wm. E. Murphy & Loulie Boulware Born Feb. 16th 1889 Topeka, Kans.

Born to Horace E. Ray & Harriet Boulware twins February 10th 1896. Named Thomas Franklin & Margaret Elizabeth Ray the boy died July 2, 1896 at Topeka, Kansas.

Born to A.J. Boulware and Lizzie Porter Boulware, a daughter, Florence Millie Sept. 5th 1897, at Topeka, Kans.

Born to Thomas G. and Lillie Adams Boulware, a son Francis Rogers, March 4, 1891 Hillsboro, N. Mex.

A son Walter Wesley Boulware, Nov. 24, 1893 Hillsboro, N. Mex.

A daughter, Bessie Lillie Boulware, Mar. 15, 1895 Blanco, Castillo Co, Colo.

Hodge Casey Boulware died July 1, 1983 Charlottesville, Virginia.

Mary Boulware married John Allen Campbell July 5, 1969 in Charlottesville, Virginia.

Born to Mary Boulware Campbell and John Allen Campbell a son Matthew Allen Campbell, April 20, 1971 Huntington Beach California.

Born to Mary Boulware Campbell & John Allen Campbell a son Robert Hodge Campbell September 15, __, in Middletown, Pennsylvania.

Born to Horace Edgar Ray and Harriet B. Ray, a daughter Katherine Lou Feby. 6, 1905 at Topeka, Kans.

Born to Charles Edwin Hoover and Margaret B. Hoover, a son Ned Hoover, July 10 - 1905. Died August 10 - 1905 at Topeka, Kans.

Born to Charles Edwin and Margaret Boulware Hoover, a daughter Margaret Jane Oct. 3rd 1906 Jackson, Miss.

Born to Robert H. and Blanche Casey Boulware, a son Hodge Casey Boulware, December 15, 1906 Silver City, N. Mex.

Born to Robt. H. and Blanche Casey Boulware, a daughter Mary Blanche March 17, 1909 Silver City, N. Mex.

Born to Robt. H. and Blanche Casey Boulware, a son Robt. Hudgin Boulware Jr. in July 22nd 1914. Silver City, N. Mex.

Hodge Casey Boulware, son of Robert Hudgin Boulware, married Helen Agee Turner March 23, 1946 Haverford, Pennsylvania.

Mary Robertson Boulware born to Hodge C. and Helen A. Boulware June 20, 1947 Long Branch, New Jersey.

Mary Blanche Boulware died December [22nd] 1969 in Manassas, Virginia.

Gray Boulware and Harriet Terrell were married 4th January 1821.

Gray Boulware & Virginia Louisa Wright were married the 21st of April 1846.

Richard H.[Henry] W.[Washington] Buckner & Judith T. [Terrell] Boulware were married the 29th of Feb., 1848.

Gray Boulware and Milly S.[Stone] G. [Gray] Hudgin were married the 18 of August 1852.

A. [Alfred] J. [Jackson] Boulware and A. [Ann] T. [Trippe] Slaughter Nov. 15th 1853 by Eld. G. George.

Loulie Judith Boulware to William E. Murphy March 4th 1886.

Harriet Gray Boulware to Horace Edgar Ray June 20th 1894 in Lawrence Kans. By Rev Ayres.

Thomas Gray Boulware and Lillie Gertrude Adams married in Chloride Sierra Co., N.M. by Justice of the Peace H.E. Rickert Dec. 12, 1889.

Millie Noland Boulware and James Warren Hairston, Married in Silver City, N. Mex. By Rev. J.R. Goss, June 5, 1900.

Alfred Jackson Boulware and Elizabeth Mary Porter Married in Chicago, Ill. On 21st day of Oct. 1895 by Rev. F.W.E. Werner.

Robert Hudgin Boulware and Blanche [Eleanor] Casey June 14, 1905 in Silver City, N. Mex.

Margaret Hudgin Boulware and Charles Edwin Hoover, in Silver City, N. Mex. By Rev. Goss, Pres. June 14, 1904.

Millie Boulware Hairston and Andrew Jackson Adams Sept. 2, 1905 Silver City, N. Mex. By Rev. John Armstrong.

Gray Boulware was born the 15th of May 1792.

Harriet Terrell was born 17th February 1787.

Judith Terrell Boulware was born the 7th Dec. 1821.

Gray Boulware Jr. was born the 22 of April 1823.

Bettie Tyler was born the 9th Sept. 1824.

George Lee Boulware was born 27th of Oct. 1825.

Andrew Lee Boulware was born 27th of Feb. 1827.

Alfred Jackson Boulware was born the 3rd of Nov. 1829.

Virginia Louisa Wright was born the 28 of Jan. 1830.

Milly Stone Gray Hudgin was born the 27 of June 1830.

Judith Louisa Boulware August 27 1853 Daughter of M.G. Boulware.

Bessie Luckett Boulware born March 22nd 1855.

Sally Hudgin Boulware born October 1st 1856.

Gray Boulware Jr., son of G.B. and Milly G. Boulware born the 5 of April 1858.

Thomas Boulware, son of Gray & M.G. Boulware born 19 December 1860.

Robert Hudgin, son of Gray & M.G. Boulware born December 5th 1862.

Alfred Jackson Son of Gray & M.G. Boulware born January 16th 1865.

Harriet Gray Boulware born May 1st 1868.

Milly Noland Daughter of Gray & M.G. Boulware born August 6th 1870.

Margaret Hudgin Boulware, daughter of M.G. & G. Boulware born September 28th 1872.

Walter Hudgin Boulware August? 28th 1874.

Frances Rogers Boulware born Chloride, Sierra Co. New Mex. March 4th 1891.

Walter Wesley Boulware Born in Hillsborough Sierra Co. New Mex. Nov. 24th 1893.

Bessie L. Boulware born Blanco, Castillo Co. Colo. Mch 15th 1895.

David Houston & Florence Mildred Boulware married Sept 10, 1915.

Kathryn Ellen born Jan. 27, 1917.

David Houston Jr. & Bryon Jackson born Oct 3, 1918 [twins].

Gray Boulware Jr. & Virginia Louisa Boulware & Judith T. Buckner were baptized by Col. L.W. Allen [Littleberry Woodson Allen was Colonel and chaplain in the Confederate Army] the 28 of April 1848 & united with Liberty Church. Milly G. Boulware united with Liberty May 27th 1856.

The following newspaper printed death notices lay in the Bible:

Died, at the Grove, his farm in Spotsylvania County, on Monday the 2nd day of February, 1857, Mr. Gray Boulware, of Caroline county, in the 65th year of his age, leaving a widow, two sons and numerous other relations to mourn their loss.

  Brother Boulware embraced religion in the prime of life; was baptized by Elder Laurence Battaile in 1831, and united with Liberty church, where he continued as efficient member for more than 20 years. He was constitutionally, particulary systematic in his management and by industry and frugality acquired an independent fortune by farming alone. As a Christian he was liberal. Nobly did he aid in the erection of houses for the worship of God; and in his contribution to the various benevolent objects, his love of righteousness might be clearly perceived. Thou an economist from principle, he had nothing of the niggard; only convince him that a cause was right, and he would engage in it with all his heart, nor think much of any expense. For some years back he was rather infirm, 2 months, and preceding his death, closely confined to his room, with much difficulty of breathing. His sufferings he bore with characteristic patience and resignation, often conversing on the subject of death, and gave particular directions in reference to his burial, and he died without a murmur.

                              T____

  At a meeting of Liberty Baptist church, Caroline county, held on Saturday the 21st of Feb., 1857, the following preamble and resolutions, were unanimously adopted:

  Whereas, God, in his inscrutable wisdom, has removed by death, from our midst our beloved brother, Gray Boulware, who for more than 25 years, was a member of this church---

  Resolved 1st: That in him this church has lost one of its most efficient members, who spent his best efforts to promote its interest; and while we bow with resignation in the decree which summoned him to another world; we deeply sympathize with the afflicted family of our deceased brother.

  Resolved 2d: That as a token of respect by his church, to our departed brother that the pastor be, and is hereby requested to preach funeral discourse at Liberty meeting house on the 4th Sunday in March next.

  Resolved, 3d: That the clerk of our church be requested to record this preamble and these resolutions on our church book, and to send a copy to the afflicted family of the deceased, and one also to the Religious Herald, with request to be published. By order of the church.

        G.[George]W.[Washington] TRICE, Mod.
C.[Charles] T. Jesse, Cl'k.

The slaves of Acadia were listed on a separate document dated 22 December 1857 as Lynah, Jim, Soloman, Abraham, Joe, Billy, Jeff, Mac, Jacob, Ned, Frank, Lee, John, Ella, Sally, Griffin, Harriett, Kitty, Evelina, Susan Fleata & Children, Robert, Sarah, Edm, Milly, Walter, Julia, Alice, Eliza, Dick, Lizzie, Milly, Lucinda, Edward, Emma, Bob, Lucy, Kisiah, Miltilda, Martha, Nelson, and Hatty.

BRIDGES FAMILY BIBLE

This Bible record was submitted for a pension for services in the American Revolution and was printed in *Virginia Revolutionary Pension Applications* by John Frederick Dorman, Volume 10, p. 9. The Bible originally belonged to Joseph Bridges of Caroline County, and who was a private, lieutenant and sergeant during the Revolution in the regiment of Colonel William Woodford of Caroline County. After his discharge, he moved to Granville County, N.C. and later to Chatham County, N.C., where he died March 22, 1837. The Bridges family lived at "Broad Plains" in the Reedy Mill area of Caroline County and married into the Pollard, Norment, Young, and other families. Joseph Bridge's son Horace Bridges went to reside in Tennessee.

Joseph Bridges and Francess [sic] Davis were married On the 24th of December A.D. 1788.
Horace D. Bridges and Martha Gee were married on 22nd of October A.D. 1812.
William H. Bridges & Sally Justice were married on 1st of October A.D. 1816.
Horace D. Bridges and Louisa G. Johnson were married on the 26th day of May 1825.
Nicholas R. Bridges and Emma P. Johnson were married on 20th of December 1827.
Joseph Bridges born February 1st 1750.51.
Francess Bridges wife of Joseph Bridges Born January 30th A.D. 1755.
Horace D. Bridges son of Joseph & Francess Bridges born July 20th A.D. 1790.
William H. Bridges son of Joseph & Francess born July 1st 1793.
George Rodney Bridges son of Joseph and Francess born January 18th 1795.
Nicholas Richard Bridges son of Joseph and Francess Bridges born December 15th A.D. 1796.
Cornelia Adaline daughter of William H. Bridges and Sally his wife born 25th November A.D. 1818.
Joseph Morgan son of Wm. H. Bridges & Sally his wife born 21st October 1820.
Delhi Cochran Bridges daughter of Wm. H. Bridges & Sally his wife born 10th December A.D. 1822 at 10 Oclock A.M.
Martha Emila Bridges daughter of Wm. H. Bridges & Sally his wife born 30th day of September 1825.
Seniora Susannah Bridges daughter of Wm. H. Bridges & Sally his wife was born October 25th A.D. 1827.
Mary Sibbella Daughter of Nicholas R. Bridges and Emma P. his wife Born September 29th 1837.
Elizabeth Wilson was Born the 29th July A.D. 1840.
Frances Ann daughter of Nicholas R. Bridges and Emma P. his wife was born 13th January 1829.
Horace Hampton son of Nicholas R. Bridges and Emma P. his wife Born 15th of July A.D. 1830.
Eving Livingston son of Nicholas R. Bridges and Emma P. his wife, was born 24th of March A.D. 1832.
Preston Johnston Son of Nicholas R. Bridges and Emma P. his wife Born 3rd of January A.D. 1834.
Pauline Agness [sic] Daughter of Nicholas R. Bridges & Emma P. his wife Born 30th November 1835.
Lieutenant George Rodney Bridges of the army of the United States died February 21st A.D.

1816 in the 22nd year of his age: he was shot dead near Fort Montgomery (Mississippi Territory) by a deserter whom he attempted to apprehend.

Mrs. Martha Bridges Consort of Horace D. Bridges died on 28th of September 1823.

Horace Hampton Bridges son of Nicholas R. and Emma P. Bridges died October 3d A.D. 1831.

Preston Johnston Bridges Son of Nicholas R. and Emma P. Bridges died September 30th A.D. 1835.

Mr. Joseph Bridges, Esqr. died March 22nd 1837.

Mrs. Frances Bridges Consort of Joseph Bridges Esqre. Died May 3rd 1841.

BROADDUS BIBLE NO. 1

This Bible consist of only the Old Testament. It was published by Matthew Carey, Philadelphia, Pennsylvania October 3, 1805. Behind the title page is a list of the "Subscriber's Names", which includes 84 names and addresses of those who pledged to purchase this edition of the Bible. Those names include John Broaddus of Caroline, the owner of the Bible in question, as well as names of persons in Essex, King and Queen and other counties in Virginia in addition to persons in other states. The Broaddus Bible originated with John Broaddus. This family lived in the Sparta area of Caroline County and were affiliated with the Salem Baptist Church. The Bible was owned by Mr. H.G. Motley, Upper Zion Post Office, Caroline County in 1937 and a reference to it appears in the WPA Survey of Caroline historic sites. Mr. Motley also owned a second Bible, that containing the records of Mark Boulware, who moved to Wood County, West Virginia in 1810.

The Broaddus Bible contains records of John Broaddus, his three wives and their children. John Broaddus was the fifth son of Thomas Broaddus, who was a Lieutenant in the Continental Army of 1779. A copy of the family register from the Bible is in the Library of Virginia. For more information concerning this family, one should consult *The History of the Broaddus Family* by Rev. Andrew Broaddus, St. Louis, 1888.

John Broaddus, son of Thos. & Ann Broaddus, was born May 7th in the year of our Lord 1764.

America Broaddus wife of John Broaddus was born November the 28th 1778.

Nancy R. Broaddus and Sarah Broaddus, daughters of John & America his wife were born November 12th 1794.

James H. Broaddus was born January 3d 1797.

Mordecai W. Broaddus was born January 26th 1799.

Theresa Broaddus was born August 9th 1801.

John Broaddus was born August 8th 1803.

Thomas Broaddus was born May 5th 1805.

Amanda Broaddus was born April 5th 1807.

[Mary] Polley A. Broaddus was born April 28th 1809.

Warner Broaddus was born June 26 - 1811.

Caroline Broaddus was born March 20th 1813.

Jane Broaddus daughter of John & Martha his wife was born October 12th 1814.

William H.[Hyter] Broaddus [son of John & Martha] was born January 21st 1816.

Robt Sample [also spelled Semple] Broaddus was born October 6th 1817.
Joseph Andrew Broaddus son of John Broaddus & Catherine his wife was born Sept 6 '21.
Adaline Atway [Attaway] Broaddus daughter of John Broaddus & Catharine his wife was born April 10th 1826.
Catherine Gatewood [3rd] wife of John Broaddus was born March 20 1782.
John Broaddus [Jr., son of John & America] and Harriet E. Puller were married together October 3rd 1833.
Wm H.[Hyter] Broaddus & Elizabeth C. Puller were married 22 Feby 1838.
Ro S.[Sample] Broaddus [son of John & Martha] & Letitia E. Miller were married Decr 18 - 1838.
Jos. A. Broaddus [son of John & Martha] & Mary C. Gatewood were married December 1839.
Sarah Broaddus daughter of John & America Broaddus his wife departed this life January 12th 1795.[age 2 months]
America Broaddus [lst] wife of John Broaddus departed this life May 24th 1813.
Caroline Broaddus departed this life July 1813.[age 4 months]
Martha Broaddus [3rd] wife of John Broaddus departed this life February 10th 1819.
Warner Broaddus son of John & America Broaddus his wife departed this life November 18th 1820.
Adaline Atway [Attaway] departed this life October 1829.
John Broaddus and America his [2nd] wife were Married together February 13th 1794.
Nancey [sic] Broaddus daughter of John Broaddus & America his wife was married to John G. Cole October 7th 1812.
John Broaddus & Martha [Richeson] his [2nd] wife was Married together December 1813.
John Broaddus & Catherine [Gatewood] his [3rd] wife was married together November 2d 1820.
James H. Broaddus, son of John & America his wife, was married to Lucy Gatewood March 1821.
Mordecai W. Broaddus son of John & America his wife was married to Elizabeth Dejarnett Daughter of Joseph Dejarnett & Pheby his wife May 20th 1820.
Theresa Broaddus [dau. of John & America] was married to George Marshall December 1824.
Amanda Broaddus [dau. of John & America] was married to John C. Gravatt 28 April 1825.
Mahalia Broaddus [dau. of John & America] was married to Willis Pitts Decr 1825.
Mary A. Broaddus [dau. of John & America] was married to James Puller February 7, 1827. [Car. Mar. Reg. shows 1828]
James H. Broaddus was married to Ophelia Boulware, Daughter of Marke & Agness [sic] Boulware August 18, 1832.
Jane R. Broaddus was Married to James P. Broaddus October 31st 1832.
John Broaddus Son of Thomas Broaddus & Ann Broaddus Departed this Life September 2 1836.[age 73]
Mor [Mordecai] W. Broaddus Minister of the Gospel Departed this life November 26th in the year of our Lord 1840 Aged 4 yrs 10m.
William H.[Hyter] Broaddus, Son of John Broaddus and Martha his wife departed this life Novr 4th 1844 in the 28th year of his age.
Jane Broaddus departed this life in the [blank] year of her age.
Nancy Cole departed the (Apr 1?) 1862.

James H. Broaddus Departed this life June 1868.
Catherine Broaddus wife of John Broaddus Departed this life July 1852. Age 70 years born in 1782.
John Broaddus Departed this life April 1884 Age 80.
[Mary] Polley A. Puller Departed this life March 1890 born 1809.
R. S. [Robert Sample] Broaddus Departed this life March 8 1893 age 75.

In the front of this Bible is a listing of the subscribers who advanced their orders for this edition of the Family Bible.

SUBSCRIBERS' NAMES

Joseph Alexander, New Lisbon, Ohio.
Ellis Armstrong, Essex.
John T. Burton, Madison, New-York.
Silas Betton, Salem, New Hampshire.
Beasin Beale, New Lisbon, Ohio.
Samuel Bransford, Bent-Creek.
Josiah Bagbey, Buckingham.
Luke W. Barber. Chaptico.
Peter Bumigarner, Hawksbill Mills.
John Broaddus, Caroline.
Ephraim Beezly, Essex.
Jesse Coc, Brunswick, Virginia.
Rev. John Cook, Washington Co. Maryland.
Bethuel Covalt, Bedford County.
Dudley Curin, Salem, New-Hampshire.
Robert Coleman, Buckingham.
John Coleman, Buckingham.
George Christian, Buckingham.
Robert Campbell, Salem, New-Hampshire.
Isaac Carpenter, Marshalton.
Isaac Clayton, Marshalton.
Lewis Day, Deerfield, Ohio.
Benjamin Davison, Newton, Ohio.
John Donovan, Washington, Co. Maryland.
Philip Duval, Buckingham.
Samuel Duval, Buckingham.
Lewis Ely, Deerfield, Ohio.
James C. Fennel, Greensville, Vermont.
Samuel Forrer, Mundellsville.
Phineas Gordon, Salem, New-Hampshire.
David Graham, New Lisbon, Ohio.
Joseph Graves, Bedford County.

Nathaniel Gorrill, Salem, New-Hampshire.
Samuel Gresham, King & Queen.
Samuel Grove, Mundellsville.
Robert Harris, Buckingham.
Samuel Hoffmire, Bedford County.
John Hindman, Ball-Creek, Ohio.
John Henderson, Buckingham.
Jacob Hart, Bedford County.
Nathaniel Hart, Bedford County.
William Holloway, Mundellsville.
John Johnson, Washington County.
James Kinney, New Lisbon, Ohio.
Lesis Kinney, New Lisbon, Ohio.
John Kelly, Buckingham.
Caleb Linn, Washington County.
John Lucas, Madison, New-York.
William McKiby, Palmyra, Ohio.
John Meason, New Lisbon, Ohio.
John P. Malone, Brunswick, Virginia.
William Meredith, Brunswick, Virginia.
Caleb Morse, Salem, New-Hampshire.
William Mills, Chaptico.
Robert March, Mundellsville.
William L. Marye, Mundellsville.
Edwin Motley, King & Queen.
Joshua Marshal, Marshalton.
Benjamin H. Munday, Essex.
Thomas Neal, Brunswick, Virginia.
Martha Nircus, Salem, New Hampshire.
Isaac Powers, Madison, New-York.
James Pendleton, King & Queen.
David Rollins, Salem, New-Hampshire.
Thomas Roane, King & Queen.
Asa B. Sizer, Madison, New-York.
Joseph Saunders, Brunswick, Virginia.
John Stiger, Bedford County.
Samuel Stephens, Bedford County.
John Seayres, Buckingham.
George Smith, Buckingham.
John Scruggs, Buckingham.
Thomas Scholfield, Chaptico.
James Sale, Essex.
Eleanor Thomas, Washington Co. Maryland.
William Thorn, Salem, New-Hampshire.

John Wyche, Brunswick, Virginia.
James Wyche, Brunswick, Virginia.
John & James Wyche, Westward Mill.
John Watt, Washington Co. Md. 2 copies.
Jesse Webster, Salem, New-Hampshire.
Edward Wright, King & Queen.
Isaac Wright, Mundellsville.

[Note: This subscriber's list for pre-publication sales of the October 3, 1805 edition of the Family Bible published by Mathew Carey, Philadelphia, a copy of which was purchased by John Broaddus of Caroline County, is included here in this compilation for several reasons. First, it identifies the location of a person at a given time. Second, it shows there was a Bible for a certain family at a given time and thirdly, it identifies the publisher and date for any one of these Bibles which may have lost it's title page over the years.]

BROADDUS FAMILY BIBLE NO. 2

This Bible is in bad condition. There are no center sheets.
Information has been inserted in space available. The last three sheets are just inserts in the Bible, probably information from Alexander Woodford Broaddus Sr.'s Bible of "Cherry Grove", Caroline County. The records pertain to members of the Broaddus family who lived at "Cherry Walk", Essex Co. and "Cherry Grove", Caroline Co. Va. The Bible was printed by Matthew Carey, Philadelphia, 1808 and is presently owned by Mr. and Mrs. Sterling P. Anderson, Jr. Placed in the bible are newspaper obituaries of Mrs. Attie M. Kidd, Rowland F. Broaddus, Mrs. Sarah Ann Broaddus, John P. Broaddus, and Thomas A.[A.T.] Broaddus. Attie M. Broaddus was the widow of William B. Kidd of "Hedge Hill", located at Kidds Fork in Caroline County. He was a soldier in the Confederate Army and died young, buried at Old Salem Church at Alps, Caroline County. A copy of this Bible record is in The Library of Virginia. It has also been printed in the *Virginia Genealogical Society Magazine*, Volume 17, No. 4, p.118, October 1979. A copy has also been reproduced in *Virginia Bible Records* by Jeannette Holland Austin, Willow Bend Books, Westminster, Maryland 2000.

Cherry Walk, also known as "Cherry Row", is located between Miller's Tavern and Dunbrooke and has been in the Broaddus for over 150 years. Alexander Woodford Broaddus of Caroline County came to live at Cherry Walk in 1854. His first wife was Fanny Ellen, daughter of Carter Croxton. In 1859, he married Sally Haile, daughter of Captain R. G. Haile. He was treasurer of Essex County for many years and died in office in 1883.

Born on the 27 Feb. 1834 Alexander Woodford Broaddus, son of M.[ordecai] R.[edd] and
S.[arah] A. Broaddus, Cherry Grove, Caroline Co., Va.
Born on the 29th Feb. 1836 at Cherry Grove, Caroline Co. Va. Attaway Miller Broaddus,
daughter of the same.
Born on the 23rd March 1838 John Prince Broaddus, son of the same, Cherry Grove, Caroline
Co. Va.

Born on the 21st August 1840 at Cherry Grove, Caroline Co. Va. Preston Broaddus, son of the same.

Born 16th Feb. 1843 at Cherry Grove, Caroline Co. Va. Arch[ibald] Thomas Broaddus, son of same.

Born 17th Feb. 1846 Susan S. Broaddus at Cherry Grove, Caroline Co. Va., daughter of the same.

Born 5th Feb. 1856 at Cherry Walk, Essex Co. Va. Roland F[alconer] Broaddus, son of A[lexander] W[oodford] & F[annie] E[llen] Broaddus.

Alexander Woodford Broaddus, son of Mordecai Red[d] & Sarah Ann Broaddus was born near Sparta Caroline Co. Va. on the 27th Feb.1834.

Sallie Matilda Haile, daughter of Capt. Robert G. & Elizabeth Haile, was born at Beaver's Hill, Essex Co. Va. on the 25th Feb. 1839.

Junius M. Broaddus, son of A.W. & S.M. Broaddus was born at Cherry Walk, Essex Co. Va. on the 26th Feb. 1860.

Nannie P. Broaddus, daughter of A.W. & S.M. Broaddus, was born at Cherry Walk, Essex Co. Va. on the 24th July 1861.

Alexander Woodford Broaddus, son of A.W. & S.M. Broaddus, was born at Cherry Walk, Essex Co. Va. on the 21st Aug. 1867.

Lena Madison Broaddus, daughter of A.W. & S.M. Broaddus was born at Cherry Walk, Essex Co. Va. on the 21st Dec. 1866.

[Matilda] Mattie Haile Broaddus, daughter of A.W. & S.M. Broaddus was born at Cherry Walk, Essex Va. Va. on the 7th March 1869.

Lucy Virginia Broaddus, daughter of A.W. & S.M. Broaddus was born at Cherry Walk, Essex Co. Va. on the 17th Feb. 1871.

Attie Miller Broaddus, daughter of A.W. & S.M. Broaddus was born at Cherry Walk, Essex Co. Va. on Feb. 4th 1873. [She is buried in Richmond, her husband at old Salem Church, Caroline]

Alexander Preston Broaddus, son of A.W. & S.M. Broaddus, was born at Cherry Walk, Essex Co. Va. on the 4th Feb. 1875.

Sarah Elizabeth Broaddus, daughter of A.W. & S.M. Broaddus, was born at Cherry Walk, Essex Co. Va. on the 26th March 1879.

John William Broaddus, son of A.W. & S.M. Broaddus was born at Cherry Walk, Essex Co. Va. Sept. 22nd 1880.

Alexina Woodford Broaddus, daughter of A.W. & S.M. Broaddus was born at Cherry Walk, Essex Co. Va. Sept. 12th 1883.

Roland F. Broaddus, son of A.W. & S.M. Broaddus was born at Cherry Walk, Essex Co. Va. on the 5th Feb. 1856.

Married by the Rev. A[ndrew] Broaddus, Nov. 18th, 1858 at Salem Church Caroline Co. Va. Mr. William B. Kidd to Miss A[ttaway] M[iller] Broaddus.

Married on the 19th April 1859 at Beaver's Hill, Essex Co. Va. by Elder H.W. Montague, Mr. A[lexander] W[oodford] Broaddus to Miss Sallie M[atilda] Haile, both of Essex Co. Va.

Alexander Woodford Broaddus & Fanny Ellen Croxton were married at Laurel Grove, Essex Co. Va. on the 15th March 1855.

Alexander Woodford Broaddus & Sallie M. Haile were married at Beaver's Hill, Essex Co. Va. by the Rev. Howard W. Montague on the 19th April 1859.

Died on the 6th Jan. 1837 Mordecai Broaddus long afflicted with asthmetic affection. It was apprehended by himself that he would died from suffocation, but it pleased God to favor him with a gentle demise sooner.

Died on the 21st Jan. 1838 John P[rince] Miller after a short but very severe illness of bilious pleuracy.

Died in Caroline Co. May 29, 1859 Mordecai R[edd] Broaddus, in the 52nd year of his age.

Died in Caroline Co. Sept. 24th 1887, Mrs. Sarah Ann [Miller] Broaddus in the 76th year of her age.

Died Aug. 24th 1886 in Caroline Co Miss Susie S. Broaddus in the 40th year of her age.

Died Oct. 7th 1883 in Caroline Co. Va. Alexander Woodford Broaddus in the 49th year of his age.

Died in Caroline Co. Dec. 27th 1875 William B. Kidd [son of Capt.William Kidd and Harriett M. Wright and husband of Attie M. Broaddus and is buried at old Salem Baptist Church site, Alps].

Alexander Woodford Broaddus, Jr., son of A.W. & S.M. Broaddus, departed this life on the 15th July 1869. Funeral by the Rev. H.W. Montague.

Alexander W. Broaddus, son of M.R. & S.A. Broaddus departed this life on the 7th Oct. 1883. Funeral by the Rev. Dr. Garlick.

Mattie H. Broaddus, daughter of A.W. & S.M. Broaddus, departed this life on the 8th May 1890. Funeral by the Rev. W.R.D. Moncure.

S.M. Broaddus, daughter of Capt. R.G. & E. Haile, departed this life Dec. 29th, 1901.

Died on the 20th April 1915 A.T. Broaddus in the 73rd year of his age.

Entered into eternal rest Dec. 4th 1914 at Memorial Hospital, Roland F. Broaddus in the 59th year of his age.

Died at his home 708 Wickham Street, Barton Heights, Va. Jan. 25th 1911, John P. Broaddus, aged 73 years. Raised at Sparta Caroline Co. Va.

Died at her home 708 Wickham Street, B[arton] H[eights] Aug. 6 1916 at 4-10 P.M. Mrs. Attie M. Kidd in the 81st year of her age.

BROADDUS FAMILY BIBLE NO. 3

This Bible belonged to Hervey E. Broaddus and Cordelia B. Glenn of Illinois who were married December 22nd 1881 at Magnolia, Illinois and which appears on the certificate of matrimony page in the front of the family section. The Bible is now owned by Betty Frances Elizabeth Broaddus, Uarna, Illinois. The earliest recordings in the Bible are those of Hervey E. Broaddus, born 1858 and his wife, Cordie B. Broaddus, born 1859. This Broaddus family are descendants of the Andrew Broaddus family of Sparta, Caroline County, Virginia.

Grace I. Broaddus to Chas. F. Rogers Dec. 21, 1904.
Young Glenn Broaddus to Nina Lee Scarborough Jan. 25, 1911.
Leland H. Broaddus to Gertrude Florence Justice Dec. 30, 1912.
Hervey E. Broaddus [born] March 27, 1858.
Cordie B. Broaddus [born] Dec. 25, 1859.
Grace Idell Broaddus [born] Sep. 14, 1882.

Young Glenn Broaddus [born] Dec. 28, 1887.
Leland Hervey Broaddus [born] Sept. 14, 1890.
Mary Elizabeth Rogers [born] Jan. 21, 1908.
Edwin Russell Broaddus [born] Jan. 22, 1912.
William Hervey Rogers [born] April 11, 1913.
Virginia Lee Broaddus [born] August 4, 1913.
Alan Richard Broaddus [born] August 1, 1914.
Cordelia Pearl Rogers [born] May 5, 1916.
William Elliott Broaddus [born] July 3, 1916.
Infant to Nina Glenn, still born [born] July 22, 1917.
Frances Elizabeth Broaddus [born] August 28, 1918.
Warren Elliott Broaddus [born] October 1, 1920.
Grace Idell Rogers [died] Feb. 17, 1919, 36 yrs. 5 mo. 3 days.
Cordelia B. Broaddus [died] May 8, 1934, 74 yrs. 4 mo. 13 days.
Hervey E. Broaddus [died] Oct. 6, 1935, 77 yrs. 67 mo. 9 days.
Young Glenn Broaddus [died] July 26, 1961, 73 yrs. 6 mo. 28 days.
Nina Lee Broaddus [died] no date listed.
Leland H. Broaddus [died] April 24, 1967.
Alan R. Broaddus [died] March 8, 1973.

BROADDUS FAMILY BIBLE NO. 4

This Bible was published by the American Bible Society, New York, 1872. It was originally owned by Eugene Broaddus, son of J. Wilbur Broaddus and is now in the possession of Bernard Walton Mahon, Bowling Green, Virginia.

Eugene Broaddus born Jany 4th 1872.
Wilbur Russell Broaddus was born May 16th 1872 [1873].
Charles Aubrey Broaddus was born Nov. 14th 1876.
Alice Maud Broaddus born 26th July, 1878.
Blanche Dulaney Broaddus daughter of Eugene and Blanche Broaddus born July 26, 1899.
Emma Louise Broaddus Born Aug. 1881. Died February 1887.
Eugene Broaddus Born Jany 4th 1872. Baptised by Rev. J.H. Davis May 1872.
W. Russell Broaddus Born May 16th 1873. Baptised by Rev. E.P. Wilson December 1873.
Chas. Aubrey Broaddus born Nov. 14th 1876. Baptised by Rev. E.P. Wilson August 1877.
Alice Maud Broaddus Born 26th July 1878. Baptised by Rev. Wm E. Evans March 20th 1880.
Carrie Mastin Broaddus was born Jan. 10th 1883. Baptised Dec.18th by Rev. E.G. Mastin.
2nd Marriage
Grace Whitney Broaddus Born June 17th 1888.
Florence Webb Broaddus Born July 21, 1889. Baptised 29th Dec 1889 by Rev. S.S. Ware of St. Peters Pt Royal. Godmother Mrs. Mary Webb.
Helen Hope Broaddus Born 28th Nov. 1890. Baptised May 31st 1891 by Rev. S.S. Ware. Godmother Mrs. Grace Bull.
Births of Grandchildren:

Blanche Dulaney daughter of Eugene & Blanche Broaddus. Born July 26 1899.
Eugenia "Jean" Walton Broaddus daughter of Eugene & Blanche Broaddus born May 2, 1906.
Linda Wirt daughter of Russell and Pauline Broaddus born Nov. 2, 1906.
Emily Elizabeth daughter of Eugene and Maud Travis born Aug. 10,1907.
Wilbur James son of Eugene and Blanche Broaddus born Dec. 22, 1908.
Helen Satterlee Travis daughter of Maud and Eugene Travis born Oct. 22, 1911.
Russell Garman Broaddus son of Russell and Pauline Broaddus Aug.10, 1912.
Emma Louise Broaddus died February 1881.
Carrie Mastin Broaddus died April 13th 1894.
Charles Newbill son of Charles and Ethel Broaddus born Feb. 22, 1913.
William Ennis son of Eugene and Blanche Broaddus Born Mar. 31, 1915.
Emily Harrison daughter of Poindexter and Florence Irby born Apr 1, 1921.

BROCKENBROUGH FAMILY BIBLE

These family records were kept in an English Prayer Book and a typewritten copy was placed in the Virginia Historical Society. The Brockenbrough family, whose record was recorded in this book, lived in the town of Port Royal, Caroline County. Their house still stands in Port Royal, awaiting restoration. They married into the Peyton, Bowie, Quarles, Thornton, Taliaferro, Pratt and Turner families, all Caroline County connections. Some of the Brockenbrough family lie buried in a cemetery surrounded by a brick wall in Tappahannock, Essex County.

Austin Brockenbrough son of William, born 1685, Married Mary Metcalfe.
William Brockenbrough son of Austin and Mary born 15th day of June 1715, and married Elizabeth Fauntleroy.
Austin Brockenbrough son of William and Elizabeth born the 3rd of November 1738 and married Lucy Champe, the 22nd of October 1761 he died the 19th of March 1810, she died 5th of May 1775, leaving six children.
William Brockenbrough son of Austin and Lucy Champe born the 25th of August 1762 and baptized the 12th of September by the Rev Mr. Dawson. Col William Brockenbrough his Grandfather. Mr. John Champe jr his uncle (God Father). Mrs. Jane Champe his GrandMother. Miss Maria Carter of Cleve (God Mother). died 22nd of August 1777.
Lucy Brockenbrough born 26th of July 1765 and baptized the 18th of August by the Rev William Gibberne. Col William Brockenbrough (God Father). Mr. Moore Brockenbrough (God Father). Mrs. Bettie Champe (God Mother).
Jane Brockenbrough born 7th of February 1767 baptised 17th of May by the Rev William Gibberne. Mr. John Brockenbrough and Mr.Moore Brockenbrough (God Fathers). Mrs. Mary Gibberne, Mrs .Sarah Brockenbrough (God Mothers). Miss Jennie Fauntleroy (God Mother).
Champe Brockenbrough born 8th of April 1768, baptised 9th of July by Rev Wm Gibberne. Mr. Newman Brockenbrough and Mr. Moore Fauntleroy of Crondall (God Fathers). Miss Mary Fauntleroy (God Mother).
Elizabeth Brockenbrough born 17th of December, 1772, baptised on Tuesday 30th of March by the Rev William Davies rector of Hanover parish. Mr. John Brockenbrough of Tappahannock (God Father). Lucy Brockenbrough (God Mother).

John Champe Brockenbrough, born the 13th day of February 1775, baptised 2nd day of May by Rev Wm Davies. The Rev John Champe Brockenbrough died in the city of Richmond Va. 22nd of November 1808, leaving one son called Austin (U.S. Army).

Lucy Married Philip T. Alexander in 1784, and in 87, married William Quarles, died 27th June 1788.

Elizabeth married the Rev James Elliot Champe married Sarah Skinker Bowie, 1795.

Rev John Champe married Lucy Hipkins, was educated in England, and was an Episcopal Clergyman, his only son Austin graduated at West Point served a while in the U.S. Army, resigned his commission, married a daughter of General Jacob Brown of Washington City, moved to Indiana, 1831, and died in 1843, the Western Brockenbroughs are his descendants, you can now have the relationship between the Western branch and the Port Royal branch. My Mothers Father who was Dr. Champe Brockenbrough and the Rev John Champe Brockenbrough were the only surviving sons of Austin Brockenbrough who married Lucy Champe the daughter of old Col Champe who built old Lambs Creek Church. My Mothers Father left five daughters, eldest Miss Sally Champe Brockenbrough, never married.

Mrs. Lucy Austin Thornton.
Mrs. Elizabeth Fauntleroy Peyton.
Mrs. Mary Metcalfe Fitzhugh.
Mrs. Cathrine Augusta Turner.

Mr. Champe Brockenbrough had two sisters Jane and Elizabeth Brockenbrough, Jane married

Mr. Thomas Pratt in 1785. He died leaving her a widow with four daughters, one married Dr. Dangerfield Lewis of "Marmion" King George, another married Mr. Ben Grymes, another Dr. Wm Grymes and another Mr. Ashton, all of King George from these marriages are Lewis family, the Grymes, Washingtons, Ashtons and Snowdens of Alexandria.

Elizabeth Brockenbrough married the Rev Mr Elliot and settled in Kentucky.

Can give you no information of this branch as years have elapsed since heard from Mr Thomas Pratt's widow married Mr. Frank Taliaferro of Epson near Fredericksburg. (This is where the record ends in the prayer book).

BROOKS FAMILY BIBLE NO. 1

This Bible was copied by George K. Cleek October 18, 1988. At that time, the Bible was owned by Mrs. Dorothy Edna Morton Taylor, General Delivery, Sparta, Caroline County, Virginia.

Marriages
Alpheus Brooks of Caroline and Hauzie Haynes of Caroline on Mch. 19, 1893 at home Rev. Andrew D. Broaddus.
Hilda Haynes Brooks to Curtis T. Moore June 18, 1921.
Alma Letitia Brooks to Robert G. Fisher June 18, 1923.
Archibald Brooks to Dorothy Morton Feb. 15, 1946.
Births
Alpheus Brooks was born Mch. 5, 1868.
Hauzie E. Haynes was born Oct. 10, 1873.
Maude Brooks was born June 11, 1894.

Alma L. Brooks was born Aug. 6, 1895.
Overton Brooks was born Aug. 8, 1898.
Hilda H. Brooks was born June 6, 1901.
Linda P. Brooks was born June 1, 1904.
Claude Brooks was born May 1, 1907.
Archibald Brooks was born Sept. 5, 1916.
Joyce Moore was born Jan. 13, 1923.
Marguerite Brooks Fisher was born Mar. 18, 1924.
Curtis T. Moore, Jr. was born Oct. 6, 1927.
Archibald Brooks, Jr. was born Dec. 10, 1946.
James Morton Brooks was born Feb. 29, 1948.
Lewis Haynes Brooks was born Oct. 18, 1951.
Nancy Carol Brooks was born Jan. 10, 1957.
Deaths
Maude Brooks died Aug. 4, 1894.
Letitia E. Haynes died July 1924.
Joyce Moore Baker died Mar. 7, 1942.
Hauzie Haynes Brooks died May 30, 1948.
Alpheus Brooks died Sept. 14, 1948.
Archibald Brooks, Sr. died Aug. 13, 1969.

BROOKS FAMILY BIBLE NO. 2

This Bible was copied by Cathrine Cleek Mann October 18, 1988. At that time it was in the possession of Dorothy Edna Morton Taylor, General Delivery, Sparta, Caroline County, Virginia.

Marriages
Lewis Haynes of Caroline Co., Va. and Letecia E. Beazley of Caroline County on 18th of
 August 1870 at home by Rev. A. Broaddus.
Irene R. Haynes was married December 23rd 1891 to J. J. Kay both of Caroline Co., Va. by Rev.
 O. Ellyson.
Hauzie E. Haynes was married March 19th 1893 to A. Brooks both of Caroline Co., Va. by Rev.
 A. Broaddus.
Births
Lewis Haynes born 31st Aug 1804 Caroline Co., Va.
Letecia E. Haynes born 20th Aug 1845 Caroline Co., Va.
Irene R. Haynes born 23rd Nov 1871 Caroline Co., Va.
Hauzie E. Haynes born 10th Oct 1873 Caroline Co., Va.
Susie J. Haynes born 12th June 1875 Caroline Co., Va.
Hannah L. Haynes born 14th July 1879 Caroline Co., Va.
Charlie T. Haynes born 8th Nov 1882 Caroline Co., Va.
Deaths
Lewis Haynes Died May 24, 1885.
Irene Kay Died May 24, 1911.

Letitia Haynes Brooks Died May 30, 1948.
Susie Haynes Taylor Died Jan 16, 1935.
Charles T. Haynes Died _____.
Hannah Haynes Beasley Died Nov 3, 1957.

BROWN / SHEPPARD FAMILY BIBLE

This Bible belonged to a family which lived in both Caroline and Hanover counties. John Dudley Brown was a graduate of the University of Virginia and was a member of the General Assembly in 1845 from Hanover County. The Bible was last owned by the Campbell family in Hanover County. It was copied by Judge Leon M. Bazile in 1962 and published in *The Virginia Genealogist,* Volume 6 at page 111. "Glen Cairn", once a part of Scotchtown, was sold by Edmund Pendleton of Caroline County in December 1799 to help settle the debts incurred by Speaker of the House of Burgesses John Robinson.

John Brown and Martha George were married in Caroline County on the 20th day of August in the year 1782.
John M. Sheppard and Sarah Pulliam were married in 1789, on the 19th day of December.
Births
John George was born 18th August 1704.
Ursula Dudley was born 26 September 1720.
John Brown, the elder born [no date listed].
Mary Rapier was born [no date listed].
John Brown senior was born 26 March 1754.
Martha George was born 19 September 1761.
John M. Sheppard was born 14 February 1763.
Sarah Pulliam was b orn 23 March 1769.
Joseph M. Sheppard was born 23 September 1790.
Anne M. Sheppard was born 14 July 1792.
Samuel Sheppard was born 19 March 1794.
Lucy Sheppard was born 19 July 1795.
Mary Sheppard was born 20 September 1797.
Harriet Sheppard was born 3 August 1799.
Samuel M. Sheppard was born 9 March 1801.
Lavinia Sheppard was born 10 November 1802.
Elizabeth Sheppard was born 14 June 1804.
John M. Sheppard was born 2 July 1807.
Nathaniel Sheppard was born 4 January 1810.
[space]
Booth Brown was born 9 May 1785.
Fleming Brown was born 18 July 1787.
John D.G. Brown was born 25 June 1789.
Mildred W. Brown was born 9 January 1792.
Mary D. Brown was born 2 October 1797.

[space]

Mrs. Wm. Hugh Campbell died 1908.

[space]

Deaths

John M. Sheppard died at Scotchtown April 1817.

Sarah Sheppard died at Scotchtown December 1823.

John Brown Senior died at his residence in Caroline County 6 June 1816.

Martha Brown died 14 December 1823.

Fleming Brown died April 1844.

Sarah Brown died 19 September 1864.

Booth Brown died June 1850.

Mary D. Hutchinson died 23 June 1862.

John D.G. Brown died 20 January 9 o'clock A.M. at Hickory Bottom.

Mrs. Sallie Elizabeth Campbell wife of William Hugh Campbell died at his home Glen Cairn 3 April 1908. She left two sons John and Hugh and 5 daughters Hattie, Sallie, Fannie, Maud and Mrs. Carter Redd.

William Hugh Campbell died at Glen Cairn 16 December 1910 at 2 o'clock P.M. He was born at Glen Mount, King & Queen County 22 March 1827 son of Hugh Campbell & Mary Hill Fleet.

Additional notes

William Hugh Campbell married Sarah Elizabeth Brown, daughter of John Dudley George Brown and Harriet Sheppard, his wife.

Lucy Sheppard, born 19 July 1795, married Landon Berkeley.

Harriet Sheppard, born 3 April 1799, married John D.G. Brown.

Lavinia Sheppard, born 10 November 1802, married John J. Taylor.

Nathaniel Sheppard, born 4 June 1810, died unmarried.

BRUCE FAMILY BIBLE NO. 1

The Bruce family first settled in Rappahannock County, then Richmond County, King George County, Caroline County and Stafford County before moving into Tennessee, Kentucky and Missouri. This is an early Bible of that family, a photostat which is found in the Bruce folder, George H.S. King Papers, the Virginia Historical Society. The whereabouts of the original was not revealed.

Robert Yound and Elizabeth daughter of Wm & Sarah Bruce were married [illeg].

Joseph Carr and Sarah, daughter of Wm & Sarah Bruce were married Oct the 10th A.D. 1820.

John Bruce, son of Wm and Sarah Bruce, married to Harriett Owen [illeg].

William H. Bruce, son of Wm and Sarah Bruce was married to Margaret Middleton January 27th 1824.

Thomas V. Bruce son of Wm and Sarah Bruce was Married to Elizabeth [illeg].

John F. Strother and Lavinia, daughter of Wm and Sarah Bruce were married January the 21 A.D. 1830.

Lovell M. Bruce, son of Wm and Sarah Bruce, was married to Mary Williams [illeg] 1830.

Aaron [F or H] Bruce, son of Wm and Sarah Bruce was married to Jane Robison November 10, 1831.

William Bruce Son of Elijah Bruce and Sallis his wife was Born January the first day in the year of our Lord 1771.

Sarah Bruce wife to William Bruce was born January the third day in the year of our Lord January 3 1777.

Elizabeth Bruce daughter of Wm Bruce and Sarah his wife was born October 3rd in the year of our Lord 1794.

John Bruce Son of Wm Bruce and Sarah his wife was born April 24th in the year of our Lord 1797.

William H. Bruce, Son of Wm Bruce and Sarah his wife was born March 15th in the year of our Lord 1800.

Thomas V. Bruce Son of Wm Bruce and Sarah his wife was born July 30th in the year of Lord 1802.

Sarah Bruce daughter of Wm Bruce and Sarah his wife was Born February 14 in the year of our Lord 1805.

Aaron Bruce Son of Wm Bruce and Sarah his wife was Born July 12 in the year of our Lord 1807.

Lovel M. Bruce Son of Wm Bruce and Sarah his wife was born January the 6th in the year of our Lord 1810.

Lavinah Bruce daughter of Wm Bruce and Sarah his wife was Born August 21st day in the year of our Lord 1812.

Emily Bruce daughter of Wm Bruce and Sarah his wife was born July 5th day in the year of our Lord 1815.

George William Strother, son of John Whetcher Strother and Lavinia his wife was born in the year of our Lord August the 11th A.D. 1832.

Sarah Jane, daugh of Gilbert and Jane his wife was born in the year of Lord January 24 1832.

SLAVES

Harriet was born January 1820.

Soloman was born December 1821.

Benjamin was born In October 1823.

Mary Ann was born in June 1825.

Hyrum was born April 1827.

Wesley was born February 1829.

[end of listing of slaves]

William H. Bruce departed this life the 9th of August in the year of our Lord 1825.

Emily Bruce departed this life the 25 of November 1827.

Aaron Bruce departed this life the 25 of November 1866.

Wm Bruce Sr. died in Henry County Ky July 4, 1862.

Sarah Bruce wife of Wm Bruce departed this life Dec. 26, 1862.

BRUCE FAMILY BIBLE NO. 2

This Bible belonged to William N. Bruce, who was born in Chesterfield District, South Carolina. He was the son of Charles and Catherine Bruce. He married twice, his first wife was Sarah Ann Williams. His second wife was Mary S. Bates, daughter of William D. Bates and Susan A. Boulware of Caroline County, Virginia. They were married at "Cleveland", Caroline County, Virginia on July 24, 1854, his occupation being that of a physician. The Bible is presently owned by Mrs. Sallie Gaines, Bainbridge, Georgia. The Bible records have been published in *Virginia Bible Records* by Jeannette Holland Austin, Willow Bend Books, Westminster, Maryland, 2000.

William N. Bruce married Sarah Ann Williams March 23, 1850.
Sarah Ann Williams Bruce died June 18, 1853, aged 20 yrs, 8 mos, 24 days, second dau. of W. Williams. She was buried beside her mother at Fowlstown Church.
William N. Bruce married in Cleveland, Caroline Co., Va. by Rev. G.[George] W.[Washington] Trice to Mary Susan Bates, dau. of William D. Bates July 24, 1857.
William N. Bruce born October 13, 1811 6 miles north of Cheraw, S.C.
Mary Susan Bates born December 4, 1831 in Caroline Co., Va.
Louisa Powell __.
Lucy Estelle Bruce born May 4, 1858.
Mary Susan Bruce, born April 23, 1853.
George William Bruce, born August 3, 1867.
Robert Lee Bruce, born April 24, 1864.
John Potter Bruce, June 9, 1866.
Charles Potter Bruce, born February 5, 1869. Named for his grandfather living at Darlington, S.C. and his great-grandfather of Guilford, N.C.
Sarah Bruce born October 26, 1872.
Mary Susan Bruce married O. B. Floyd March 14, 1881.
Lucy Estelle Bruce married Benjamin Griffin February 12, 1885.
Sallie, 8th child of William N. Bruce, married William A. Gaines November 13, 1902.
John Potter Bruce died July 10, 1884.
William A. Gaines died January 8, 1926, aged 83 yrs.
Mary Susan Bruce died December 29, 1816, aged 85 yrs, 24 days.

BRUCE / EDWARDS FAMILY BIBLE

This is the Bible of Maria S. Bruce Edwards, who was the daughter of William Sale Bruce and Mary Hampton Andrews and granddaughter of William H. Bruce & Maria Campbell, all of Caroline County. She married Augustine "Guss" Edwards and the children listed are of that couple. The original Bible is now owned by Lewis Garrett of Hanover Court House and a copy is in the archives of the King and Queen County Historical Society, as well as the Library of Virginia. A family data sheet is enclosed with the Library of Virginia copy and that information is enclosed in brackets by the author. This family lived at the Edwards home place, "Spring Cottage", Route 639 & Mattaponi River, Owenton, King and Queen County, Virginia. They are buried at St. Stephen's Baptist Church, King and Queen County. Augustine Edwards married first Lucy Trimmer of King William County. He married secondly Maria Sale Bruce. After his death, she married secondly Claiborne L. Wilson, who died July 7, 1898. There were four children by Augustine Edwards' first marriage and were raised by he and his second wife.

Arlena [Lena] V. Edwards was born Jan. 24th 1862.
Charley [Charles] B. Edwards was born Aug. 15th 1863.
Maria L.E.[Eulalie] Edwards was born Nov 4th 1866.
William S.[Sylvanus] Edwards was born April 5th 1869.
Zotilla [Zoe] C. Edwards was born 8th of March 1875.
Mary C.[Cincinnata] Edwards was born 25 of Dec 1877.
Waverley C. Edwards was born Feb 15 1880.
Nancie M. Edwards was born the 13th of Dec. 1882.
Reacie [Theresa] Fleet Edwards was born 4th day of May 1866.
Maria S. Edwards was born Aug 10th 1844.
Conelious [Cornelious] A. Edwards born 16 Sept 1849.
Brittania [Travis] L.A. Edwards born 28th Apr 1855.
Adolphus C. Edwards born 16th of May 1858.
Mary Cincinatta Edwards born Dec. 25th 1877; Died Nov. 30th 1957.
[There were 4 children of Augustine and Lucy Edwards. They included Cornelious A.(born in King William County), Zotilla L. (died young), Brittania L.A., and Adolphus C. Augustine and
Maria Edwards had 10 children, who included Arlena V., Charles, Maria L., William Sylvanus (married Ora Bruce), Covossa Elwood, Zotilla Zoe C., Mary Cininnata, Waverly C., Nannie M., and Theresa F. Edwards]
Augustine [Guss] Edwards was born May 16th 1821.
Charlie B. Edwards was born the 15 of Aug 1863 and departed from this life Dec 8 1889 age 26 years three months & 22 days.[never married]
Waverley C. Edwards was born 15 of Feb 1880 & departed from this life Aug 24 1881.
Eulalie Wilson was born Nov 4th 1866 and departed from this life Sept 29 1891 age 25 years.
Arlena V. Kay departed from this life May 24 1924.
Maria S. Wilson departed from this life June 2nd 1928.
Maria S. Bruce & Augustine Edwards was married Jan 9 1861.
Brittania L.A. Edwards was married to W.L. Goddin Feb 21 1884.
M.L. Eulalie Edwards was married to F.[Fred] C. Wilson Feb 22 1885.
Arlena V. Edwards was married to J.[John]T. Kay.
Claborne L. Wilson departed from this life July 7th 1898.
Reacie Fleet Edwards was married to E.L. Garrett Jan 3 1906.
Mabel N. Edwards was married to G. Norman Dec 23 1903.
[Covossa Elwood "Guss" Edwards married Marian Lee Selph December 28, 1898 and died January 21, 1959]
[Zotilla C. "Zoe" Edwards married Clarence "Clary" Franklin Elliotte and died November 17, 1965]
[Mary Cincinnata Edwards never married and died November 30, 1975]
[Nannie Mable Edwards married George Washington Norman December 23, 1903 and died May 9, 1973]
[Theresa "Reacie" Fleet Edwards married Edward L. Garrett January 3, 1906 and died September

BUCKNER FAMILY BIBLE NO. 1

This family lived at the "Neck Plantation", earlier known as "The Grange", Caroline County, now a part of Fort A.P. Hill reservation. The family record was copied by Miss Mary Buckner in 1907 and sent to Mr. Crozier to be published in *The Buckners of Virginia* by William Armstrong Crozier, published by The Genealogical Association, New York, 1907 and appears at page 129. This Bible was owned by Miss Margaret Ann Buckner, Fredericksburg, Virginia in 1960. They were reproduced in her book *Early Virginians*, published near that time.

Washington Buckner, son of Richard and Charlotte Buckner, his wife, was born July 31, 1783; died July 22, 1801.

Caty, daughter of the above, was born Jan. 25, 1785.

Charlotte, daughter of the above, was born Feb. 13, 1787.

Elizabeth, daughter of the above, was born Jan. 25, 1789.

Bailey, son of the above, was born Oct. 11, 1789, and departed this life Jan. 15, 1832.

Ann Hawes, daughter of the above, was born Sept. 1, 1792.

Mary Hawes, daughter of the above, was born Aug. 3, 1794.

Caty and Richard were married by the Rev. A. Waugh, Dec. 23, 1801. Richard Buckner was born Dec. 7, 1775.

Richard Henry Washington Buckner son of Caty and Richard Buckner, was born Dec. 9, 1810.

Charlotte Hawes, daughter of Samuel Hawes and Ann, his wife, was born Oct. 1, 1766, and departed this life Dec. 17, 1831.

Wm Aylett Buckner was born Feb. 13, 1766, and departed this life Jan. 2, 1830.

Wm Aylett Buckner and Charlotte Buckner were married Friday, June 23, 1797, by Rev. Abner Waugh.

Wm. Smith Buckner, son of Wm. Aylett Buckner and Charlotte, his wife, born April 16, 1798; departed this life Monday, March 21, 1836.

Unnamed daughter of Wm. Aylett Buckner and Charlotte, his wife, born Aug. 23, 1799; departed this life Sept. 8, 1799.

Lucy Ann Buckner, daughter of Wm. Aylett Buckner and Charlotte, his wife, born Nov 13, 1800; died July 7, 1801.

Washington Buckner, son of Wm. Aylett Buckner and Charlotte, his wife, born Feb. 19, 1803; died July 24, 1803.

Emily Buckner, daughter of Wm. Aylett Buckner and Charlotte, his wife, Oct. 27, 1804.

Ellen Buckner, daughter of Wm. Aylett Buckner and Charlotte, his wife, born March 17, 1807; died Sept. 15, 1807.

Ellen Buckner, second daughter of that name, born July 27, 1808. Name changed to Jane and christened by Rev. Saml. Low, May 3, 1810. Married to Thomas Hawes, and secondly, Henry Anderson.

William S.B. Buckner and Mildred Hawes were married Oct. 7, 1817.

Mildred Charlotte Buckner, daughter of William S.B. and Mildred Buckner, was born Friday,

Aug. 25, 1818, and died Oct. 20, 1836.

Ann Hawes Buckner, daughter of William S.B. Buckner and Mildred, his wife, was born March 17, 1820, in King William County.

William Aylette Buckner and Ann Hawes Buckner were married Tuesday, Oct. 17, 1837, at "The Neck," Caroline County by Rev. Lawrence Battaile of the Baptist Church.

BUCKNER FAMILY BIBLE NO. 2

This Bible was published by William Darling, Edinburgh, 1776. It originally belonged to John Buckner of "The Neck Plantation", Caroline County, Virginia. This place is now in the Fort A.P. Hill area. See Robert Wright Bible elsewere in this study.

Richard Buckner [born] 7th Dec. 1775.
Catherine E. Buckner [born] 25th Jany. 1785.
Colin Buckner Son of Richard & Catherine Buckner Born Decemb. 20th 1802.
Charlotte, daught. of above Born 7th April 1803.
Richard Henry Washington Buckner Born December 9th 1810.
William Aylette Buckner son of above Born the 14th May 1814.
Mary Dorothy Buckner Born 1st March 1821.
Ann Eliza Buckner Born 10th March 1823.
Wm Smith Bickley Buckner Son of Wm A. and C.H. Buckner was born 11 of April 1839.
Ella Wright daughter of Robert & Mary D.[Dorothea Buckner] Wright Born 3 October 1842.
  [1843 in Wright Bible and tombstone].
Mary Smith Buckner daughter of Wm. A. and Ann H. Buckner Born 2 February 1840.
Richd. Wright, Son of Robert and Mary D. Wright born 10 July 1844.
William Lewis Son of Robert M.[Moseley] Wright & Mary D. Wright Born the 11th August 1846.
Richard Henry Washington Buckner Son of W.A. & A.H. Buckner was born 24 October 1845.
William Aylett Buckner Jr. son of last named Born 11 November 1847.
Mildred Charlotte daughter of last named Born 19 October 1849.
Walker Hawes Buckner son of William A. and Ann H. Buckner Sept.1851.
Richard and Catherine Buckner were married by the Rev. A. Wingo December 23rd 1801.
William A. and Ann H. Buckner were married by Rev. Lawrence Battaile October 17th 1837.
Mary D.[Dorothea] Buckner [daughter of Richard Buckner] and Robert M.[Moseley] Wright [son of Robert Wright] 17th August 1841.
Wm. A. Buckner & Charlotte Buckner was Married Friday June 23rd.1797 by Rev. Abner Wingo.
William Smith Bickley Buckner Son of William a. Buckner & Charlotte his wife Born the 10th April [1839] and departed this life on the 21 March 1841.
[blank] Daughter of William A. Buckner and Charlotte his wife was Born 23rd day of August 1799 and departed this Life September 8th 1799.
Lucy Ann Buckner Daughter of Wm. A. Buckner & Charlotte his wife Born Novembr. 12th 1800.
Lucy Ann Buckner departed this life July 7th 1801.

Washington Buckner son of Wm & Charlotte Born February 19th and departed this life July 24th 1803.

Emily Buckner Daughter of the above born October 27th 1804.

Ellen Buckner daughter of the above born March 17th 1807 and departed this life September 12th 1807.

Ellen Buckner the second, Daughter of the above, born July 27th 1808 since changed to Jane and christened by the Rev'd. Saml. Low on May 3rd 1810.

William S.B. Buckner & Mildred Hawes were married the 7th Oct. 1817 Tuesday.

Mildred Charlotte Buckner was born Tuesday 25 August 1818 and died _____ on the 20th Octr. 1830 (Thursday) daughter of Bickley & Mildred Buckner.

Mildred Hawes Buckner died Nov. 18th 1867.

Jane Walker, daughter of Wm. S.B. Buckner & Mildred H. Buckner died March 4 ___.

Ann H. Buckner daughter of above died Nov. 19th 1880.

Bettie Pollard [Buckner] died [unmarried] May 16th 1895 [age 80].

Catharine M.[Margaret Katherine] Wright daughter of Robert M. Wright and Mary D. Born the 7th November 1848. [1850 in Wright Bible and tombstone].

Judith A. Wright daughter of Robert M. Wright and Mary D. was born the 11th of January 1850. [1851 in Wright Bible and tombstone]

Mary Moseley Wright was born Novr. 25th 1857.

Fannie Kate Fitzhugh daughter of S. & A.E.B. Fitzhugh was born December 9th 1858 in the County of Orange.

Colin, Son of Richd. & Catherine Buckner departed this life the 22 July 1803.

Charlotte daughter of as above departed this life August 1805.

Wm. Smith Bickley Buckner Son of Wm. A. and Ann H. Buckner Departed this life 15th Decr. 1841.

Catherine E. Buckner Departed this life 16th September 1850.

Richard Buckner Departed this life 8th May 1864.

Richard Henry Washington Buckner died Feb. 25, 1895 [Caroline County Baptist minister].

Wm. Aylett Buckner died Aug 2nd 1865.

Washington Buckner Son of Richd. H. Buckner & Charlotte his wife was born July 31st 1783 and departed this life July 22nd 1801.

Cathy Daughter of the above was born Jany. 25 1785.

Charlotte Daughter of the above was born Feb 13th 1787.

Infant Daughter [daughter marked out] Son of Wm & Charlotte Born February 19th 1803 and departed this life July 24th 1803.

Charlotte Hawes, daughter of Samuel Hawes & Ann his Wife was born October 2nd 1766 and departed this life December the 17th 1831.

Wm. A. Buckner was born February 13th 1766 and Departed this life January 2nd 1830.

Kate Bickley Buckner died Jan. 1886.

Mary Susan Buckner Thornton daughter of Wm. Smith Bickley Buckner & wife of Majr. Wm. M. Thornton died in Prince Wm. Co. Aug 17th 1893.

Mary Smith Buckner, daughter of William Aylett Buckner and Anne Hawes Buckner, born Feb 2nd 1844 at Rappahannock Academy and died at Locust Grove near Mica Dec. 14, 1927. Buried at old family burying ground Rappahannock Academy, later moved to Green Lawn cemetery, Bowling Green, Va.

J.B. Buckner Sr. and Allie Blackstone White were married in Mexico, Texas Nov. 8, 1885.

J.B. Buckner Jr. was born in Mexico, Texas Oct 30, 1886.

Richard Campbell Buckner was born in Mexico, Texas Oct 24, 1889.

Mary Virginia Buckner was born in Mexico, Texas March 15, 1892.

Mildred Hawes Buckner was born in Mexico, Texas Dec. 19, 1895.

Sabra Allie Buckner was born in Caroline County, Va. Feb 11, 1900 at Locust Grove near Mica.

Annie Aylette Buckner was born in Caroline County, Va. Feb 11, 1900 Died March 24, 1900. Buried at Liberty Baptist Ch.

Henry Aylette Buckner was born in Caroline Co. Va. June 6, 1902.

William A. Buckner was born near Rappahannock Academy, Caroline County on 14th day of May 1814.

Ann H. Buckner was born on the 17th day of March 1820 in the County of King Wm.

Wm. Smith Brickley son of above was born on the 11th day of April 1839 at the Neck.

Mary Smith Daughter of above was born Friday the 2nd February 1894 at the Neck.

Richard Henry Washington, son of above was born on Friday the 24th of Octr. 1845 at Privilege [estate] near the Rappahannock Academy Caroline Co.

Wm Aylette son of above was born on Tuesday the 11th Novr. 1847 at Brainfield [estate] near Rappahannock Academy.

Mildred Charlotte Daughter of above was born on 19th October 1849.

Walker Hawes, Son of above was born Sept. 24, 1851.

Catherine Elizabeth daughter of above was born on Thursday the 4th of Augt. 1853.

[no name] Daughter of above was born on tuesday July 10th 1855.

John Breckenridge Son of above was born on Tuesday June 18th 1856.

[no name] Daughter of above was born on the [no date] 1858.

Wm. A. Buckner died Augst. 2nd 1865.

Wm. S.B. Buckner Son on Wm A. & Ann H. Buckner died on Tuesday the 15th day of Decemr. 1841 at Caroline Co.

Catherine E. Buckner daughter of Wm A. & Ann H. Buckner died on Thursday the 1st day of June 1854.

[no name] daughter of Wm A. & Ann H. Buckner died on Saturday Augst 4th 1856.

[no name] daughter of above died on Sunday the ___ day of ___ 1858.

Richard Henry Buckner son of Ann H. & Wm A. Buckner died (killed in Battle) June 9th 1863.

John B. Buckner Sr. died Sept 23, 1921.

Allie W. Buckner wife of John B. Buckner Sr. died May 4, 1930. Both buried at Liberty Baptist Church in Caroline Co., Va.

John B. Buckner Jr., oldest son of John B. and Allie W. Buckner died on April 8, 1935. Buried at Forest Lawn Cemetery, Richmond, Va. on Wed. April 10, 1935.

Ruth Dillard Buckner Jr. died on February 23, 1958. (Ruth Dillard Buckner married Wilbert Otis Atkins on June 23, 1948.)

BUCKNER FAMILY BIBLE NO. 3

This Bible was published by C. Alexander & Co., Philadelphia, 1834. The record of this Bible is in the Library of Virginia and covers the period 1810-1949. This family started in Caroline County and went into Tennessee.

F. W. Buckner was born 1st July 1811.
Sarah A. E. Buckner was born 2d December 1819.
Samuel Buckner Son of Francis & Sarah Buckner was born 23rd February 1836.
Sarah Buckner was born 23rd February 1836.
Ann Jackson Buckner was born 12th Nov. 1837.
George Buckner was born 30th September 1839.
William Francis Buckner was born 15th June 1843.
George Buckner Jr. Son of F. W. Buckner & Sarah A. E. Buckner departed this life June the 7th 1848.
Infant son of Francis & Sarah Buckner died Oct 3rd 1856.
Upshaw Buckner son of Francis and Sarah A. E. Buckner died Aug 2, 1929.
Sarah A. E. Buckner wife of F. W. Buckner died ____.
Mary Carter Kelly Buckner wife of Upshaw Buckner died Aug 21st 1946.
Henry C. Buckner was born 16th May 1854.
Infant son of Francis & Sarah Buckner was born Sept 24th 1856 . Upshaw Buckner son of Francis W. & Sarah A. E. Buckner was born 7th of January 1858.
Ernest Wordwell Buckner son of Henry K. Buckner and Mary Elizabeth Slay Buckner was born Sept 5, 1936.
Sarah Buckner Dunlop daughter of Mary Buckner Britt and Porter Dunlop Jr. was born Nov 27th 1849.
F. W. Buckner was married to Sarah A.E. Gordon 9th April 1835.
Saml G. Buckner was married to Kate S. Woolbridge 2nd April 1857.
Joseph C. Woolbridge & Annie M. Buckner were married 6th April 1858.
Henry Clay Buckner was married to Elizabeth Monroe _____.
Upshaw Buckner was married to Mary Carter Kelly 4th April 1894.
William Francis Buckner was married to Hattie E. Elliott ____.
Annie Elizabeth Buckner was married to James Edward Britt Jan.10th 1822.
Henry Kelly Buckner was married to Mary Elizabeth Stay Dec 30th 1925.
Mary Buckner Britt was married to Porter Dunlop Jr. September 2nd 1947.

BUCKNER / HAWES FAMILY RECORD

This record of the Buckner and Hawes families of Caroline County, Virginia was filed with the Woodford family record in the Library of Virginia by Elizabeth Buckner Steele, Paris, Ky, who owned the record in 1945.

Thomas Buckner was born August 31st 1755 and died Apr. 5, 1805.
Elizabeth Hawes was born Nov 20, 1859.
Walker Buckner son of Thomas Buckner was born March 7, 1781 died March 14, 1855.
The above Walker Buckner married to Elizabeth Walker Buckner daughter of Robert and Mary Buckner.

Wm. Buckner son [of Walker & Elizabeth Buckner] was born Aug..10th 1810 in Henderson Co. Ky.

Samuel Hawes was born Feb 1st. 1727 and departed this life Apr 1st 1794.

Ann Walker was born Aug. 23, 1731.

Samuel Hawes, was married to Anne [sic] Walker June 20, 1751.

Samuel Hawes, son of Samuel and Ann born 7th January 1754.

Samuel Hawes died Feb. 25, 1774.

Ann Hawes (daughter of Samuel & Ann) born Feb. 7, 1758 died Dec.1st 1776.

Elizabeth daughter of Samuel and Ann his wife was born Nov 20, 1759 and married Thomas Buckner May 25, 1780 who was born Aug. 31st 1755 Died Apr. 5th 1805.

Benjamin the son of Samuel Hawes & Ann was born March 13, 1752 died Nov 2, 1782.

Mary the daughter of Samuel Hawes and Ann was born Feb 2, 1764 married Robert Buckner Mar 28th 1782.

Charlotte, daughter of Samuel and Ann Hawes was born Oct 1, 1765 & was married to Richard Buckner Sept. 21, 1782.

Aylett the son of Samuel and Ann Hawes was born Apr. 21st 1768.

Richard the son of Samuel and Ann Hawes was born Feb. 3, 1772.

Walker the son of Samuel and Ann Hawes was born July 1st 1776.

Walker, the son of Thomas and Elizabeth Buckner born March 7, 1781 and died March 14, 1855.

Benjamin Hawes, son of Thos. & Eliz. Buckner was born Nov 3, 1782.

Ann Walker, daughter of Thomas & Eliz. Buckner was born May 24, 1784.

Wm. Thos. Buckner son of Thos. & Eliz. was born Jan 29, 1786.

Samuel son of Thos. & Eliz. was born Nov 18, 1787.

Richard, son of Thos. & Eliz. was born Jan. 25, 1789.

Mary Aylett, dau. of Thos. & Eliz. was born Nov 29, 1790.

Elizabeth Walker dau. of Robt. & Mary Buckner was born 1790.

Charlott[e] Daughter of Thos. & Eliz Buckner was b Aug. 18, 1792.

Frances Thornton son of Thos. & Eliz Buckner was b Feb. 12, 1794 d 1795.

Aylett son of Thos. & Eliz Buckner was b July 4, 1797.

Eleanor daughter of Thos. & Eliz Buckner was b Nov 2, 1799 d June 29, 1840.

Samuel son of Thos. & Eliz Buckner was b Nov 18 1801.

[Also 3 newspaper clippings]

Miss Clay Wornall, daughter of James R. Nornall, married in Clark County, Kentucky, Wm. T. Buckner, Jr., of Clark County, wednesday evening, December 8, 1875, ceremony performed by Rev. Mr. Van Leer.

Miss Jane Clay Kenney, eldest daughter of Mr. and Mrs. Clarence Kenney married Mr. Harry Martin Blanton Jr., son of Mrs. H.M. Blanton, Richmond, the ceremony being performed at 4 o'clock Wednesday afternoon, December 28, 1932 by Rev. W.E. Ellis, pastor of the Paris Christian church.

Miss Lucy Woodford Buckner, only daughter of Mr. and Mrs. William T. Buckner, married Mr. John Clarence Kenney, son of Mr. and Mrs. M.A. Kenney at the Second Presbyterian Church,

Paris, Kentucky, at 8 o'clock p.m., October 23, 1907, the ceremony being performed by Rev. Dr. E.H. Rutherford.

BURRUSS FAMILY BIBLE

This Bible belonged to Henry Burruss of Caroline County, Virginia. It is now owned by Alexander Burruss, Hage, Virginia. A portion of this Bible was published in *Tidewater Virginia Families*.

Married Nov. 29th 1893 by the Rev. J. Y. Downman, at No. 24 S. Adams St. Richmond Va. Cotesworth Pinckney Burruss and Sophie Scott Hancock daughter of Mrs. __ Hancock (formerly of Washington}

Married Nov. 27th 1894 in the Presbyterian Church, Hagerstown Md. Grayson Burruss and Sarah Elizabeth Beall daughter of Mrs. Wm R. Beall.

Married Sept. 8th 1857 - by the Revd. C. H. Read - C. P. Burruss and Kate V. Daughter of Mr. Charles Gennet and Mrs. Elizabeth E. Gennet.

Charles Henry - son of C. P. and Kate Burruss died Wednesday evening, September 12th 1860 - at the residence of his Uncle E. W. Burruss in Caroline Co.

Robert Lee - recently drew his last breath, Wednesday morning, May 15th 1862, at the Richmond House.

Mabel - eldest daughter of C. P. and K. V. Burruss, fell asleep in Jesus Aug. 9th 1884. Saturday - Ruther Glen Va.

Eyrand, taken away from earthly scenes July 4th 1884, laid to rest in Hollywood Friday afternoon July 6th.

In hope of a blessed immortality, Charles Cotesworth Pinckney Burruss departed this life, Sunday morning April 19th 1884, Aged 72 yrs 7 mos 1 day.

[entries made by Henry Burruss II]
Henry Burruss & Elizabeth Johnson 9th Oct 1794.
Henry Burruss & Sally T. Wortham 14th Nov 1805.
Henry Burruss born 23d Dec 1769.
Sally T. Wortham born 28 Nov 1782.
Grand Father Charles Wortham born 13 July 1759.
Grandfather Jno Burruss born [blank] 1745.
Sally T. Burruss born 25th March 1797.
Nancy Burruss born 18th August 1798.
Ra[chel] Burruss born 27 July 1800.
Elizabeth G Burruss born 25th Sept 1802.
Margaret Burruss born 10th April 1804.
Jno Burruss born 21 Sept 1806.
Daughter born 11 March 1809.
Mary Jane [Burruss] born 4 April 1810.
C[harles] C[otesworth] P[inckney] Burruss born 18 Sept 1812.
E[lliott] W. Burruss born 13 Jan 1815.

Grand Father Burruss died 8th April 1778.
Grandfather Wortham died 7 1/2 o'clock PM 4th June 1818.
Henry Burruss, My Father died 1/2 12 night 6th Dec 1839.

BURTON FAMILY BIBLE

This Bible originally was owned by May Burton, Jr. His father May Burton, Sr. was the son of John Burton of Caroline County, Virginia, and died there in 1735. May Burton, Jr. moved to Orange County, Virginia. The Bible leaves were filed with the application for pension for Capt. May Burton, Jr.'s service in the American Revolution. May Burton Sr. married Hannah Medley; May Burton, Jr. married Martha Head, daughter of Benjamin Head September 29, 1776. Some of the Burtons of Caroline County, Virginia are included in *Tidewater to Texas: The Scurlocks and Their Wives, Norman-Turk-Hendrick-Rose and Allied Lines* by Rosemary Corley Neal, Hampton, Virginia, 1998. The records of this Bible were published in the *William and Mary Quarterly*, Series 2, Volume 8, 1928, p.211. The records have also been reproduced in *Virginia Bible Records* by Jeannette Holland Austin, Willow Bend Books, Westminster, Maryland 2000.

Lucy Burton was born 28 April, 1778, married James Collins. [This family moved to Missouri}
Fanny [Burton] was born 6 February, 1780, married Baldwin M. Buckner.
Elizabeth Burton was born 17 June, 1781.
Benjamin Burton was born 22 June, 1784.
Hannah Burton was born 30 June, 1786, married Alexander Bradford.
Jarth Burton was born 9 September, married (lst) Mr. Blakey, (2nd) John Webb.
Sarah Burton was born 9 May, 1790, married Melton November ll, 1811.
Peggy Burton was born 13 February, 1792, married Mr. Douglass.
Martha Burton was born 31 May, 1794. [Martha married lst Edward Shipp, probably of Caroline County, 2nd James Craig of Augusta County.]
Harriet Burton [was born] 27 February, 1797.
Mary Mariah Burton was born 8 October, 1798. [she married Smith Eddins]

BURTON / QUARLES FAMILY BIBLE

Copied March 18, 1932, from the original by Clara C. Coile, Johnson City, Tennessee. The Bible, referred to as the Charles Burton Bible, was in the possession of Clara C. Coile, Johnson City, Tennessee, when she copied the record March 18, 1932 for publication in *Tennessee Bible Records and Marriage Bonds* by Jeannette T. Acklen, Nashville, Tennessee, 1932. The original Bible was printed and published by Matthew Carey, Philadelphia, 1813. Wm. P. Quarles, born in Caroline County, Virginia, about 1752, one of ten children of Roger Quarles and Mary Goodloe of Caroline County, married Ann Hawes, daughter of William Hawes and Tabitha Thompkins. Around 1800, he moved his family to Bedford County, Virginia, and in 1809 to White Plains, Putnam County, Tennessee. Ten children were born to this couple, seven girls and three boys. One of his children, Elizabeth Jane Quarles, married Charles Burton. Wm. P. Quarles and other members of his family are buried in the family cemetery just off the old Walton Road, three miles east of Cookesville, Tennessee.

Charles Burton, son of William Frances Burton, born Nov. 4, 1782.

Elizabeth Jane Quarles, daughter of Wm. and Ann Quarles, born March 27, 1790.

Frances Ann Louesia [sic] Penn Burton, daughter of Charles and Jane, born May 2, 1811.

Stephen Decatur Burton, son of Charles and Jane, born Friday, Oct. 8, 1813.

Charles Burton and Eliza Jane Quarles, married Dec. 14, 1808.

Stephen D. Burton and Polly Goodbar, married July 19, 1835.

William Burton, Sr., father of Charles Burton, died Jan. 7, 1811.

William Quarles, father of Eliza Jane Quarles, murdered on the road near White Plains April 2, 1814.

Departed this life Oct. 21, 1814, Eliza Jane Burton, after a severe illness of seventeen days.

Departed this life March 30, 1831, Frances Ann Louisa Penn Burton, after a severe illness of seventeen days, in the 20th year of here age.

Frances Burton, mother of Charles Burton, died Oct. 8, 1835.

Departed this life Aug. 17, A.D. 1842, Charles Burton, father of Stephen D. Burton, after a severe illness of fifteen days.

BUTLER FAMILY BIBLE

The Butler family lived on what is now called Signboard Road near Wesley Wright's place and St. Paul's Methodist Church in Caroline County. A copy of this Bible is in the Library of Virginia. For further information concerning this family, see *Tidewater Virginia Families* by Virginia Lee Hutcheson Davis, 1989. A copy is also in the Virginia Historical Society. This family is related to Dr. John Dabney Butler's family of Gether, Caroline County. His will was posted in Caroline County 2 February 1905. He descended from Isaac Butler, whose mailing address was White Chimneys, Caroline County, and whose will was posted in Caroline in 1875. John Butler's will was posted in Caroline 9 June 1810. All three wills have survived. Papers of the Butler family are located at Duke University in North Carolina.

The Age of myself, my wife, and children are as follows:

John Butler Sr Son of John Butler and Ann his wife was born March 14th 1723. Died 17 April 1810.

June Anderson, Daughter of Edward Anderson and Jane his wife was born October 10th 1832. We were Married December 26th 1752 And my dear wife departed this Life December 16th 1770.

Anderson Butler Son of John Butler and Jane his wife was born Dec 14 1753.

John, Son of John Butler and Jane his wife was born June 22nd 1755.

Samuel, Son of John Butler and Jane his wife was born April 30th 1857.

Thomas, Son of John Butler and Jane his wife, was born May 9th 1759.

Ann, Daughter of John Butler and Jane his wife, was born June 2d 1761.

Sarah, Daughter of John Butler and Jane his wife, was born May 4th 1763.

Lucy, Daughter of John Butler and Jane his wife, was born June 2nd 1765.

William, Son of John Butler and Jane his wife, was born May 31st 1867.

Neddy [Edward] Gee, Son of John Butler and Jane his wife was born April 3rd 1769.

John Butler was married to Mary Boughan May the 12th 1772.

Joseph, Son of John Butler & Mary his wife was born November 9th 1773.
Ann departed this life on May the 3d day 1770.
Mary Butler wife of John Butler Died 20th Jan 1843.
Nancy Daughter of John Butler and Mary his wife was born Jany 10th 1776.
John Son of John & Mary Butler his wife was born Sept 6th 1777.
Mary Butler daughter of John & Mary Butler his wife was born Decr 9th 1779.
James New, Son of John & Mary Butler his wife was born April the 27th 1781.
Elizabeth, Daughter of John & Mary his wife was born May 7th 1783.
Polly, Daughter of John Butler & Mary his wife, was born Nov 25th 1786.
Isaac Butler, son of John Butler & Mary his wife was born the 12th day of July 1790.
Lucy Butler, Daughter of John Butler and his wife was born 12th day of July 1793.

BUTLER / WRIGHT FAMILY BIBLE

This Bible was published by E. H. Butler & Co., Philadelphia, 1853. It was owned by Mary Butler Wright of Richmond, Virginia in 1962 and a copy placed in the Library of Virginia by Wesley Wright III, who was born in 1893. The original owners of this Bible were Wesley Wright and his wife, Lizzie Butler. They lived at "Locust Grove" farm which was next to St. Paul's Methodist Church in Caroline County.

Mayme also Mamie Wright Daughter of Wesley Wright & Lizzie B .Wright was born at Locust Grove Caroline Co Va 30th Decr. 1850.
Thos. Temple Wright Son of Wesley Wright & Lizzie B. [Butler] Wright was born at Locust Grove, Caroline County 21 of May 1883.
Aubin Boulware Wright Son of Wesley Wright & Lizzie B. Wright was born at Locust Grove, Caroline Co Va Octo 3rd 1885.
Wesley McCartley Wright Son of Wesley & Lizzie B. Wright was born at Locust Grove March 15th 1893.
James Raymond Wright Son of Wesley & Lizzie B. Wright was born at Locust Grove, Caroline Co Va Decr. 14th 1895 (Saturday A.M.).
Melville Garland Wright Son of B.[Burton] B.[Boutwell] Wright & Etta W.[Woodson Jesse] Wright was born May 6 1878 at "Elmwood", Caroline County].
Melville G. Wright Jr., Son of M. G. & M. B. Wright, was born Monday Aug 14th 1905 at Locust Grove Caroline Co. Va.
Janie Nance Wright, daughter of Wm M. & Gladys Joyner Wright was born Aug. 20, 1955.
Aubin Wesley Wright son of A.B. & Margaret F. Wright was born at Warsaw Va. June 4 1918.
Margaret Fisher Wright daughter of A.B. & Margaret F. Wright was born at Warsaw Va. March 28 1920.
Elizabeth Lee Wright daughter of Thomas T. and Fanny May Wright was born at Warsaw Va. July 25 1925.
William Morgan Wright son of Thomas Temple and Fanny May Morgan Wright was born at Warsaw Va. September 29 1927.
Wesley W. Wright son of Wesley & Anna Parker D. Wright was born in Richmond Va. Sept. 1929.

Thomas Parker Wright Son of Wesley & Anna P.D. Wright was born in Richmond Va. Feb. 29 1932.

Melville Garland Wright II, was born Sept. 6 1945 in Richmond Va., son of M.G. Jr. & Dorothy W. Wright.

Margaret Ida daughter of A. Wesley & Margaret Jean Wright, born June 17 1950.

Julia Jean daughter of A. Wesley & M. Jean Wright, was born July 1 1951.

Thos. Temple Wright II, Son of W.M. & G.J. Wright was born in Wilmington, Del. June 27, 1953.

Wesley Wright Sr. was born April 8th 1799 & died Septr 13 1879 Age 80 years 3 mos & 5 days.

Mary Ann Green nee White wife of Wesley Wright was born Aug 29 1816 & died 9th of July 1855.

Wesley Wright Jr. was born April 21 1844.

Lizzie Lee Butler daughter of James T. & Elizabeth Butler was Born in the city of Richmond, on the 14th of May 1856.

Thomas Herbert Butler only Son of James T. & Elizabeth Butler, was Born in the city of Richmond Virginia on the 20th of June 1859.

Danl Stephens McCartley was born [not filled in] 1806 [date marked through] & died in 1830.

Maria Humes was born Decr 1805 & died June 1879.

James T. Butler son of Thomas & Mary Eubank Butler, was Born in the County of Caroline Va. on the 1st Octo 1822.

Elizabeth McCartley Daughter of Dan'l & Maria McCartley was Born in the City of Richmond Virginia on the 18th Nov 1830.

Maria Daughter of James T. & Elizabeth Butler was Born in the City of Richmond Va on 5th Decemr 1851.

Mary Virginia Daughter of James T. & Elizabeth Butler was Born in the City of Richmond Va on the 14th of April 1883.

Thos. Butler, father of Jas T. Butler was born 2d Sept. 1799 & died March 1856.

Maria Butler died in the City of Richmond Virginia on the 6th of December 1861.

Mary Virginia Butler died in the County of Caroline Virginia on the 12th of May 1871.

Thomas Herbert Butler died in the City of Richmond on the 26th of June 1875.

Elizabeth Butler wife of James T. Butler died at Locust Grove Caroline Co Va on the 8th of Octo 1886.

James T. Butler was born 1 Octo 1822.

James T. Butler died at Locust Grove Caroline Co Va Jany 8 1895.

James T. Butler Sr died [smeared beyond reading] 1898.

Wesley Wright died at Locust Grove Caroline Co Va August 26 1911.

James Raymond Wright Son of Wesley & Lizzie B. Wright died Aug 17 1916 of typhoid fever at Spartansburg N.C. aged 21.

Lizzie B. Wright wife of Wesley Wright died in Phila. Oct 28 1916.

Melville Garland Wright died Oct. 16 1934 Phila Pa.

Aubin Boulware Wright died Feb. 12, 1956 in Phila. Pa.

[newspaper obituary:
WRIGHT - Feb. 12, 1956. AUBIN B., beloved husband of Margaret P. of 8805 W. 12th St.

Funeral Wed. 11 A.M. at Oak Lane Baptist Church, 12th & Oak Lane ave. Int. Thurs. 2 P.M. Hollywood Cem., Richmond, Va.]

James T. Butler and Elizabeth McCartley by the Rev. M.P. Hoge on the 28th of January 1849.
Melville G. Wright & Mamie D. Wright his wife were married Nov 3 1904..
Aubin Boulware Wright and Margaret P.____ were married Aug 19 1915.
Thos. Temple Wright and Fannie May Morgan were Married Nov. 27 1922 in Washington D.C.
Wesley Wright Jr (3rd) and Anna Parker Davidson were married in Boston Oct 4, 1924.
Melville Garland Wright Jr. & Dorothy Vernon Netzel Married Nov 21 1936 St. James Episcopal Church Richmond Va.
Wesley Wright and Lizzie Lee Butler by the Rev. A.B. Dunaway on the 26th of February 1880.
Margaret Fisher Wright and Herbert Wilmouth Starr married July 12 1947 Phila. Pa.
Aubin Wesley Wright and Margaret Jean Roberts of West Point Va. married March 17 - 1948.
William Morgan Wright and Gladys Joyner Wright Married Apr. 5 - 1952.

CALLAWAY FAMILY BIBLE

This family Bible is in the possession of Mr. Frank Hewitt, Ashville, North Carolina. A copy is in the Library of Virginia. Four other references have been used and combined with the data to prepare the biographical material preserved in the Library of Virginia copy.

Richard Callaway was born in Caroline County, Virginia, about the year 1724. When sixteen years of age, he removed to what later became Bedford County, east of the peaks of Otter. He was a sergeant, then a lieutenant, in the French and Indian War, from Bedford County, Virginia. He was trustee of the town of New London in 1761. He was a member of the first legislature of Kentucky, which met under a tree. He was a member of the Virginia Legislature in 1777, and also Justice of the Peace, and participated in the seize of Boonsborough.

In 1779, he was chosen trustee of the Town of Boonsborough, and was commissioned to open a ferry. In preparing the ferry boat, he was shot and instantly killed by the Indians Mar. 8, 1780.

Col. Richard Callaway married (1) about 1754, Frances Walton, daughter of George Walton, of Bedford County, Va. Their children were:
  1. Elizabeth, known as Betty, born in 1760. She, with her sister Frances and Jemima Boone, were captured by the Indians. She married Col. Samuel Henderson, just two weeks after she had been rescued, he being one of the rescue party.
  2. Frances, born 1762, married (1) Colonel John Holder, who was also of the rescue party. She married (2) John McGuire.
  3. Doshea, born Aug. 8, 1768, married William Callaway.
  4. Lydia, married (1) Christopher Irvine, born Sept. 11, 1755; died Sept. 11, 1786. Married (2) General Richard Hickman.
  5. Eliza, married John Patrick.
  6. Sarah, married Col. Gabriel Penn of Amherst County, Va., son of Robert Penn and Mary Taylor.

7. Molly (Mary), married Charles Gwatkin, who was born in 1741, and died in 1791. They lived in Bedford County, Va.

8. Nancy, of Amherst County, Va. as shown by deed of gift and power of attorney.

9. George.

10. Caleb.

Col. Richard Callaway married (2) Elizabeth (Jones) Hoy, widow of John Hoy. Their children were:

1. Richard Jr.

2. John.

3. Keziah, married Capt. James French, as shown by deed of gift from their mother, Elizabeth Callaway, widow of Richard Callaway, in Madison County, Kentucky, in 1796.

CALLIS FAMILY BIBLE

This Bible is inscribed "A present to Mrs. A.V. Callis 1873 by her husband W.S. Calliss on her wedding day." It was published by Charles H. Yost, Philadelphia. The Bible is now in the possession of Lillian Pearl Phillips Mills, who lives in the northern part of Caroline County. She is the daughter of Julia May Callis and James W. Phillips and granddaughter of the original owners. Most of the entries in the Bible contain only one "s" in Callis, although, the presentation entry contains two. There are approximately 6 pages in this Bible with photo insert spaces. All the photos have been removed. This family lived at the Callis homestead and the adjacent place called "Sunnyside" on route 301 near the old Delos Post office between Bowling Green and Port Royal. Both places are now in the Fort A.P. Hill Military Reservation. The Callis family originally were from Essex County. For more information on the Callis family, see *The Garretts of Essex and Caroline Counties Virginia* by Harry Lee Garrett, Miami, Florida, 1962.

Walter S. Calliss and Annie V. Powers was united in the holy ties of Matrimony Decr 20th in the year of our Lord 1866. By the Rev G.W. Trice of Caroline County.

James W. Phillips and Julia May Calliss was united in the holy ties of Matrimony Feb. 10th in the year of our Lord 1908. By the Rev McManaway of Bowling Green, Va.

Lillian E. Calliss was born July 4th 1868. Daughter of W.S. & A.V. Callis.

Fannie Birdie Erdine Callis was born June 7th 1871. Daughter of W.S. & A.V. Callis.

Richard Edward Callis was born Feb. 26th 1873. Son of W.S. & A.V. Calliss [this entry was recorded twice at the same place]

Walter Rowe Callis was born August 21st 1874 son of W.S. & A.V. Calliss.

Maggie Rosalie Callis was born October 14th 1877. Daughter of W.S. & A.V. Calliss.

Annie T. Calliss was born Sept. 14th 1880. Daughter of W.S. & A.V. Calliss.

Julia May Callis was born May 8th 1882.

Willy Scott Callis was born May 7th 1888. Son of W.S. Callis and Lucy D. Callis.

Mrs. Margarett J. Calliss mother of W.S. Calliss Departed This life Nov. 7th 1875.

Maggie Rosalie Calliss died Aug 1881.

Annie G. Calliss died Sept. 1881.

Ann V. Callis wife of W.S. Calliss departed This life March 23rd 1883.

Walter Rowe Callis died 25th of Aug 1889. Age 15 years & 4 days.

Walter Scott Callis husband of Annie V. Callis departed this life
June 13th 1895. Age 55 years 5 months & 10 days.
R.L. Garrett died March 25, 1922 age 76 [1846]
Julia F. Garrett died Nov. 3, 1912 age 8l [1831].
Richard Edward Callis died June 6, 1952 Age 79.
Julia Mae Callis died June 4, 1941 Age 59. Wife of J.W. Phillips Sr.
Lillian Callis Timberlake Died July 20, 1950 Age 82. Wife of J.D Timberlake.
Birdie Callis Greeman died March 12, 1965 Age 93 [he was from New York]
James W. Phillips Sr. died May 1, 1953. Husband of May C. Phillips.
Julia May Callis was married the 10 day of Feb. 1908 to James William Phillips.
Richard Henry Rowe Phillips was born Aug. 21, 1912. Son of James W. Phillips and May C. Phillips.
James William Phillips Jr. was born Dec. 9th 1908. Son of James W. Phillips and May C. Phillips.
Julia Birdie Phillips was born Oct. 22, 1910. Daughter of J.W. Phillips and May C. Phillips.
Wortley Margaret daughter of May C. & J.W. Phillips was born May 12, 1917 at Sunny Side, Va. [Caroline County].
Lillian Pearl Phillips daughter of May C. & J.W. Phillips was born Dec. 23, 1921. [the last two entries for Wortley and Lillian Phillips were written in the photo insert spaces].
Mr. Walter S. Calliss and Miss A.V. Powers were solemnly united by me in the Holy Bonds of Matrimony at the Residence of her Mother on the 20th day of December in the year of our Lord One Thousand Eight Hundred and 1866 conformably to the ordinance of God and the Laws of the State in Presence of Both families and neighbors. Signed G.W. Trice. [this is partly pre-printed and partly handwritten].

CAMPBELL FAMILY BIBLE NO. 1

This Bible was published by Thompson & Thomas, Chicago, 1900 and copyrighted by John E. Potter in 1898. It belonged to Susanna Dorothy Campbell Puller, Richmond, Virginia, who died July 15, 1959.

Married April 29th 1901 Thomas Valentine Campbell and Susanna Dorothy Campbell.
Married Oct. 15th 1913 Mordecai William Puller and Susanna Dorothy Campbell.
Married Sept. 25 - 1920 John Gordon Peatross and Sibyl Valentine Campbell.
Married Nov. 20th 1901 James Preston Campbell and Maria Louisa Terrell.
Married Aug 25 - 1926 Joseph Crawford Ginn and Vivian Ertelle Campbell.
Married Aug 25 - 1927 Durwood Carlino Campbell and Beatrice Eva Chenault.
Married Feb 4, 1933 Preston Terrell Campbell and Paulette Louise Shappard.
Married Mar. 16, 1935 Paul Ellis Serene and Vivian Ertelle Campbell Ginn.
Born Sept 29th 1902 Sibyl Valentine Campbell only child of Thomas V. and Susanna D. Campbell.
Born Aug 12, 1918, James Edward Puller, son of Mordecai W. and Susanna D. Puller.
Durwood Carlino Campbell, son of James Preston and Maria Louise Campbell born May 4, 1904.

Vivian Ertell Campbell, dau of James Preston & Maria Louise Campbell, born May 18, 1906.

Preston Terrell Campbell, 2nd son of James Preston & Maria Louise Campbell born Mar 4, 1911.

Leone Evelton Campbell, 2nd dau of James Preston & Maria Louise Campbell born May 10, 1917.

Henry Eugene Campbell, 3rd son of James Preston & Maria Louise Campbell born and died Oct 6, 1913.

Ralph Millard Campbell Born Oct 21, 1922 adopted son of James Preston & Maria Louise Campbell Feb. 25, 1923.

Vivian Crawford Ginn born July 18, 1928, dau of Joseph Crawford & Vivian Ertelle Ginn.

Died Oct 4, 1902 Thomas Valentine Campbell in the 28th year of his age.

Died June 26, 1911 Emmuella Campbell in the 68th year of her age. Mother of Minnie Peatross, Luola Sanford, Preston, Anna, Robert and Leslie Campbell.

Died Dec. 10, 1908 (Born Mar 3, 1855) Ella Anderson Terrell, wife of Jno T. Sr. & Mother of Eva A. Cobb, Louise Campbell, Connie Humphries, Aubin, John T. Jr. & Willie Terrell.

John T. Terrell Sr. died Aug 11, 1928 (Born Aug 20, 1850) father of Eva Cobb, Louise Campbell, Connie Humphries, Aubin, John T. Jr. & Willie Terrell, 78 yrs of his age.

Born Oct 24, 1874 Died April 21, 1953, James Preston Campbell 78 yrs 6 mos lacking 3 days - Father of Durwood C., Preston Terrell Campbell, Ertell C. Irby & Leone C. Brewer, Husband of Louise Terrell Campbell.

CAMPBELL FAMILY BIBLE NO. 2

This Bible belonged to William Hugh Campbell, who was born at "Poplar Grove", Caroline County, Virginia, July 6, 1813. He was the son of Elliott Peatross Campbell and Elizabeth Wilson of Caroline County. He settled in Washington County, Arkansas where he married Julia Rutherford [last name misspelled in the Bible], whose family is believed to have come originally from Essex County, Virginia. The Bible was destroyed by fire sometime after 1906 while it was in the home of James B. Campbell. Prior to that time, it had been copied in the fall of 1906 by Nama Carter Overshiner and was furnished in 1961 to Fanna Campbell Spicer for membership in the DAR. Another copy of the Bible record was sent to Mrs. L.W. Ledgerwood, Jr. in 1946, also made by Nama Carter Overshiner.

UNITED in holy wedlock on March 21, 1843, are Husband: William Hugh Campbell, born July 6, 1813 AND WIFE: Julia Rutiford [Rutherford], born January 19, 1823 AND OF this union there are the following children, born upon the following dates:

John E. Campbell born Jan. 5, 1844
James B. Campbell born April 18, 1845
William Campbell born Oct. 1st 1846
Joseph W. Campbell born March 21, 1848
Winnie Elizabeth Campbell born March 15, 1852
Julia Campbell born Oct. 28, 1853
Thomas Harrison Campbell born Feb. 23, 1855

Mary Campbell born Sept. 23, 1857
Noel G. Campbell born Aug. 23, 1859
Richard Dye Campbell born Jan. 9th 1862
William Hugh Campbell The father of the above recorded family departed this life Dec. 18-1861.
Julia Campbell The mother of the above recorded family died Dec. 30th 1885.
George Washington Carter b. Dec. 23-1800 d. May 7, 1875
Nancy Emmaline Arnold Carter born Sept. 4, 1815 died Feb. 22, 1892.
George Washington Carter [Jr] born May 7th, 1852 died April 2nd, 1928.
Winnie Elizabeth Campbell Carter born March 15th, 1852 died March 26, 1929.
Married Sept - 1880
Laud 1881 - Aug 28
Dilford 1883 - Dec 5
Nama 1885 - Oct 20
Witt 1887 - Oct 1st
Von 1889 - Sept 5th
Ral 1891 - Sept 6th
Millie E. 1896 - March 14th
Dad was the only child born to grandmother & grandfather. He'd been married before and had a big bunch. Uncle Charlie, Jerd, Louis etc. They were married in Tennessee about 1850 & came to Ark. where dad ___.

CAMPBELL / HENDERSON FAMILY BIBLE

This Bible, known as the Elliott Peatross Campbell bible, was printed and published by Matthew Carey, Philadelphia, 1812. It is now owned by the Corpew family of Richmond, Va. The Bible was published in *The Virginia Genealogist*, Volume 24, 1980, pp.117-118 with some minor differences from the original. The Bible was copied by Mrs. Nettie Leitch Major, Bethesda, Maryland.

John C. Henderson and Mary L. Campbell married Oct. 21st, 1828.
Edward W. Swann and Dorothy M. Campbell was married by the Revd Saint M. Faulkner
   October 26th in the year of our Lord 1841.
Edward W. Swann was born in the year of our Lord February 12th 1818.
Dorothy M. Campbell was born in the year of our Lord January 7th 1823.
Joseph W. Campbell, the son of Elliott & Elizabeth Campbell was born in the year of our Lord &
   Savior Jesus Christ the 23rd of March 1811.
William H.[Hugh] Campbell, the son of E.P. Campbell and E. Campbell was Born the 6th day of
   July 1813.
Elizabeth Frances Henderson Daughter of John C. Henderson and Mary L. Henderson Born
   22nd December 1829.
Lucy Ann Henderson Daughter of John C. Henderson & Mary L. Henderson born 25th February
   1831.
Mary Elizah Henderson Daughter of John C. Henderson & Mary L. Henderson Born February

the 5th 1833.

Jonathan W. Terrell was born the 25th of November 1845. [brother of Christopher Terrell, both of whom were son of David and Agatha Chiles Terrell].

Joseph Anderson, the son of Sarah Jane & Phillip S. Rennolds, was born the _ day of April 1851.

Dorothy Elizabeth Rennolds, the daughter of Sarah Jane & Phillip S. Rennolds, was born September [no further date]

Manasseh Campbell, the son Elliott and Elizabeth Campbell was born April the 22nd 1828.

Elizabeth Campbell was born April the 22nd 1828.

Mary Elijah Henderson died the 18th of February 1834 Age one year and thirteen days old.

Elizabeth P.[Wilson] Campbell died the 4th of February 1854 Age 66. Written by her Daughter Dorothy M. Swann.

Elliott P. Campbell died April the 9 1858 Age 74

Christopher Terrell died October 9th 1826 aged 79 years and 9 days. [family tradition says he was the father of Elizabeth Wilson Campbell's mother. The Terrell family book *Richmond, William and Timothy Terrell* by Barnhill, 1934, shows Christopher Terrell as having married Mary Wilson. We know that Elizabeth P. Wilson Campbell's Father was William Wilson and her mother was Lucinda Collins, so Christopher's connection is somewhat confused in family tradition].

Christopher Terrell died October Oct 1826 Aged 79 years and 9 days. Written by Joseph W. Campbell the 24th day of August 1828
[second entry of same person]

Mary Terrell the wife of Christopher Terrell died the 15th of Oct 1837.

Sarah Terrell died January 16, 18_8 [date smeared].

Atwell E. Campbell the Son of Elliott and Elizabeth was born 15 day of August 1819.

Margaret M. Wilson died July the 6th 1861.

Married by Andrew Broaddus the 23rd of December 1806 E.P. Campbell and Elizabeth Wilson Age 21 and 18 and she died 1854 February 4th In her sixty seventh year of age --- And in the bloom of maturity Surrounded by a Lovely group of children of whom any Mother might be proud. Blessed with comfort and care - Fascinating her Friends by winning attractions - Loving and beloved she was an ornament to her son and graced the Society in which she moved. Above all, she was Christian possessing that greatest of all Christian Virtues: Charity. Sweet spirit. A Friend who knew thy virtues in youth and in maturity bids ---
[page torn].

CARTER FAMILY BIBLE NO. 1

This Bible was published by C. Alexander & Co., Philadelphia, 1839. The records date from 1729-1924. It appears that most of the family lived in the Sparta area of Caroline County. Members of the Catlett family are buried at their home place, now in a cow pasture at 17269 Seals Road, Caroline County, where Phil and Florence Carter Catlett lived. A copy of this Bible record is in the Library of Virginia.

Jas. L. Carter Married to E.H. Garnett May 24th 1843.

Luther A. Carter Married L.[Lucy] A. Haynes July 4th 1867.

R.[Robert] S. Parr Married Sallie B. Carter Nov 23rd 1876.

P.R. Catlett Married to Florence A. Carter May 19 1887 By Andrew Broaddus Junior. Piece [sic] to thy soul.

Phillip B. Catlett Died Dec. the 8 1829.

Eugene P. Carter Married to Ida R. Carter June the 8 1883 by Rev. W.A. Baynard.

His daughter Mattie Carter died May the 3, 1924, 36 years old burried [sic] at Salem Church Sparta, Va.

Jas. L. Carter was Born January 20th 1812.

Emeline H. Garnett was born August 19th 1820.

[Following five children of Phil R. Catlett and Florence A. Carter]:

Maud[e] A. Catlett was born Oct. 13th 1888.

James Duey [Dewey] Catlett Born Sep. the 12, 1897.

Bernard Carter Catlett was born October the 24, 1901.

Julian B. Catlett was born October the 27, 1891.

Elmer B. Catlett was born July 15, 1894.

Luther A. Carter Departed this Life May 11th 1892.

Lucie Carter died [Mar. 24, 1918 moved to Greenlawn Cemetery].

James Samuell was Born Dec. 24th 1729. Ann Samuel his wife was born May the 17th 1744.

Ann B. Garnett Born Novm. 28, 1782.

P.[Phillip] R. Garnett son of Thomas & Susan Garnett Born November the 7th 1779.

[Following three children of Phillip R. Garnett and Ann B. Samuel and grandchildren of James and Ann Samuel]:

William G.S. Garnett Born March 11th 1823.

James T. Garnett Born May 21st 1825.

Sarah C. Garnett Born Feby. 18th 1827.

Sarah B. Andrews departed this life January 19th 1849 in her sixty eight year.

Maude J. Catlett died July 24, 1891 at 7 o'clock P.M. Not lost but gone before us ever thy most deeply feel.

James L. Carter was Born Jan 20th 1812.

James L. Carter died August 22, 1885.

Emeline H. Carter his wife died Feb the 4th 1891.[tombstone at Mt. Herman Baptist Church, Shumansville, Va. has Feb. 4, 1900].

Luther A. Carter died May 11th 1892.

Sallie B. Parr died March the 7th 1923. [Both she and her husband, Robert S. Parr are buried at Mt. Hermon Baptist Church, Shumansville, Caroline County, Va.]

Harriett Parr Departed this life Oct 10, 1841.

Elizabeth Carter Departed this life March 4th 1868.

Departed this Life on the 22 instant at 7-20 in the 73 year of his age after a Protracted affliction James L. Carter Aug. 22nd 1885 The Husband of E.H. Carter of Caroline Co. Va. Peace to thy Soul.

[Following five children of James L. Carter and Emeline Garnett]:

Luther A. Carter was Born June 11, 1844.

French H. Carter was Born July 6, 1847.

Eugene P. Carter was Born July 3, 1849. [died Mar. 15, 1928 and was buried at Salem Baptist Church, Caroline Co.]

Sarah C. Carter was born March 25, 1854.

Florrence [sic] G. Carter was born Oct 11th 1861. [died at Eastern State Hospital, where she is also buried. Others members of this family are buried at 17269 Seals Road, Caroline County, where Phil & Florence Carter Catlett lived. The cemetery, with unmarked graves is now in a cow pasture]

Harriett Parr Departed This Life Oct 10th 1811.

Elizabeth Carter Departed this Life Sept. 30th 1812.

James T. Garnett Departed This Life August 25th 1857.

Ann Samuell the Mother of Ann Garnett departed This life May 18th 1829.

Phillip R. Garnett Departed This Life February 14th 1866.

Ann B. Garnett his wife Departed this Life May 26th 1868.

Also included in this record is a newspaper article featuring Ruth Carter Vellines of Glen Allen, 93 years old with 3 children, 2 step children, 17 grandchildren & 27 great grandchildren.

CARTER FAMILY BIBLE NO. 2

This Bible was published by Cassell Publishing Company, New York, 1892. The Bible is now owned by Herbert Carter Covington, Ruther Glen, Caroline County, Virginia.

This is to certify that Miss Myrtle M. Donahoe and Mr. Rufus P. Carter were united by me in the bonds of Holy Matrimony at the bride's parents on the 19th Day of December in the year of our Lord 1888, in the presence of friends and relatives. Signed Robert E. Barrett "of the" Virginia Conference.

MARRIAGES

Ruby V. Carter & Lloyd E. Covington Mar 7th 1917

Myrtle Rea Carter & Zollie Peatross Oct 29 1919

Myrtle E. Covington & Timothy A. Fitzgerald Jun 1938

Herbert C. Covington & Adaline Lunesco Jun 22 1946

Lloyd P. Covington & Helen Anne Cross May 3 1947

Jeanne Fitzgerald & James Shelburne Jan 6 1962

Betty R. Fitzgerald & Carl Heath Jan 15 1963

David Fitzgerald & Grace Wade May 20 1965

BIRTHS

Rufus Page Carter born Mar 14 1862.

Myrtle M. Carter born Mar 18 1866.

Ruby V. Carter born Nov 29 1889.

Myrtle R. Carter born Mar 24 1892.

Myrtle E. Covington born Dec 17 1917.

Herbert C.[Carter] Covington born Mar 18 1922.

Lloyd P. Covington born Dec 3 1923.

Margaret J. Peatross born Apr 29 1924.

Zelma Peatross born Jan 21 1926.
Jeanne Page Fitzgerald born Sep 13 1939.
Ruby [Betty] Fitzgerald born Jan 13 1943.
David Fitzgerald born May 20 1944.
Barry Fitzgerald born Aug 23 1947.
Sylvia Gail Covington born Jan 1 1948.
Page Carter Covington born June 5 1949.
William Wade Covington born Jun 13 1950.
Lloyd P. Covington born Feb 9 1952.
Sandra Shelburne born Nov 29 1962.
Daniel Heath born Dec 7 1964.
Michael R. Heath born Feb 10 1966.
Deborah Fitzgerald born Apr 21 1966.

DEATHS

Myrtle M. Carter, wife of R.P. Carter departed this life on the twelth day of Nov. in the year of our Lord 1895.
Ellanora Hasteltine Flippo died April 29, 1927.
Rufus Page Carter died Sept. 8, 1928.
F.Z. Peatross died Mar 13, 1930.
Lloyd E. Covington died May 11, 1956.
Ruby V. Carter Covington died July 19, 1981.
Myrtle Rea Carter Peatross died July 7, 1984.
Timothy A. Fitzgerald died Apr. 29, 1993.
Lloyd P. Covington Sr. died Sept. 5, 1997.
Myrtle C. Fitzgerald died Sept. 4, 1998.
Page C. Covington died June 25, 2000.

CASEY FAMILY BIBLE

The name of Thomas Casey, the elder, appears on the Personal Property tax list of Caroline County for the first time in 1809. He married February 17, 1808 in Fauquier County, Virginia to Catherine Mitchell, daughter of Caleb Mitchell and his wife, Jane Campbell of Caroline County. He must have been living in Fauquier at the time of his marriage and must have moved soon thereafter to Caroline County. The Mitchells were originally from Caroline, but apparently were living in Fauquer at the time Catherine was married, as most marriages were performed in the home of the bride. Caleb Mitchell was the bondsman. Catherine's death certificate stated she was born in Fauquier ca. 1792. This Bible record was copied some years ago by Helen K. Yates and furnished the author. The whereabouts of the original Bible is unknown today.

Irene G. Casey was born Dec. 11th 1888.
Sadie Mabel Casey was born March 17th 1890.
Otho Lee Casey was born Jan. 30, 1892.
J. E. Casey and Phoebe Alice Gouldman were married March 3rd 1887.
Otho Lee Casey died Sept. 6th 1960.

Sadie Mabel Casey died Oct. 19, 1941.

CASH FAMILY BIBLE

The Cash family lived in that part of Caroline County which became Camp A.P. Hill and the graves were moved from the family cemetery to Greenlawn Cemetery, Bowling Green, Va. In 1941. The Bible was published by C. Alexander & Co., Philadelphia in 1839. Oscar F. Cash was born about 1809 in Virginia and married Mary Sterne, the daughter of David Sterne and Lucy Beazley on March 28, 1837. He built the house, which in 1941 was torn down by Camp A.P. Hill, around 1839-40. The house was next to the Garrett house where Booth was captured and killed. They had twelve children, all born at the Cash Homestead near Port Royal. Two, Adalaide and Baynham died in January 1863 died of typhoid fever. Oscar died at the early age of 54 on August 6, 1863 from injuries sustained from a runaway horse and sulky. A few days later, his wife, Mary, contracted typhoid fever and died December 10, 1863, leaving the youngest child, only nine months old at the time. The family slaves cared for the surviving children. Family tradition is that the Cash family originally came from England. The older son of Oscar and Mary Cash returned from the Civil War to the Cash Homestead in Caroline County, however, his children as they grew to adulthood left the homestead and moved from Caroline County. David and Mary Anne Cash had among their issue Walter Scott and Elmira Cash. David Cash died in Caroline County in 1911, having earlier participated in the dedication of the Confederate monument on the Caroline Courthouse lawn. Elmira Cash married Charles Lofurno late in her life and had only one child, Charles Lofurno, when she was 43 years of age. His family now lives in New Bern, N.C.

David Semple Cash, son of Oscar & Mary Cash born January 7th 1838.
Walter Scott Cash son of Oscar & Mary Cash born August 6th 1839.
Elizabeth Cash, daughter of Oscar & Mary Cash born January 7th 1841.
Lucy D. Cash daughter of Oscar & Mary Cash born November 8th 1842.
Died near Macon, Ills. (Mrs. John W Royston) in spring of 1970. The above was Lucy D. Cash.
  Adalade Cash daughter of Oscar & Mary Cash born 11th April 1844.
John [Taylor] Cash born February 13 1846. Died at Weston Missouri.
D.S. Cash died May 4th 1911 at the old home place.
W.S. Cash died on the battlefield April 4th 1865 and his body was never found by any of the family.
John G. Cash died at Weston, Mo. July 18 - 1925.
Henrietta Cash born March 20 1848.
Mary S.[Susan] Cash born July 14th 1850.
Betty [Betty marked through] Cash born February 12 1852.
Harriett S. Cash born February 12th 1852. Died Mrs. Harriett Attebery near Sutters, Oklahoma about Oct 1st 1938.
William Baynham Cash born March 20th 1852 [changed to 1853].
Arthur [Wise] Cash born June 8th 1859.
Oscar F.[or L?] Cash born March 25th 1863. Died at Patouse Washington about June 1st 1905.

Baynham Cash died Jun 9th 1863.
Adalade Cash died Jan 19th 1863.
Oscar F. Cash died Augst 6th 1863.
Mary Stern Cash died Dec 10th 1863 [changed from 1862].
Walter S. Cash died on the battlefield in Civil War April 4th 1865.
W.B. Cash died Jan 15 - 1943. Son of Arthur W. Cash.
Martha Cash* died April 12th 1894.
Oscar F. Cash died April 9th 1906.
Virginia Cash* died Jan 27 - 1910 Sister of Martha and Mary Ann Cash.
Oscar F. Cash & Mary Sterne was married March 28th 1837.
David S. Cash & Mary A. Cash married Nov. 26th 1866.
The Mary Stern (above) was the daughter of David Stern and Lucy Beazley Stern. David Stern
  was a Revolutionary War soldier wounded twice, 1st at Cowpens S.C. 2nd at Guilford Court
  House, N.C. He and his widow received a pension. Inscribed by W. S. Cash 1948.
Walter S. Cash Son of David S. & Mary A. Cash born October 6th 1867.
*Martha and Virginia Cash whose deaths are recorded on previous page were sisters of Mary A.
  Cash that married D.S. Cash.
David Semple Cash died May 4th 1911.
Mary Anne Cash mother of W. S. Cash died June 3rd, 1912.
Arthur Wise Cash Died May 19 - 19043 Decatur Illinois.
Harriet Attebery Sept 30 - 1938 - Died Luther, Oklahoma.
Mary Susan Cash Died June 4 - 1947 - Age 97 yrs. Marshalltown Iowa.

CHEWNING FAMILY BIBLE

This Bible was published in Philadelphia in 1884. Inscribed in the front of the Bible is "In 1885 Given to Lee J. Smith by Robt P. Smith". The Bible is now owned by Evelyn Hamilton, Evergreen, Virginia. Members of this family lived in the north western part of Caroline County.

Clarence C. Chewning son of Thos L. & Mattie Chewning was born the 6th of Jan. 1868.
Lynn P. Chewning son of Thos L. & Mattie L. Chewning was born on the 30th of April 1869.
Thomas H. Chewning son of T.L. & M.L. Chewning was born on the 26th of July 1872.
Ernest W. Chewning son of T.L. & M.L. Chewning was born on 4th of Nov 1874.
Rosa Evelin [also Evelyn and Elvie] Chewning daughter of T.L. & M.L. Chewning was born on
  the 30th of April 1877.
Mattie Maud Chewning daughter of T.L. & M.L. Chewning was born on the 21st of September
  1879.
_____[no name] died Mar 1, 1903. Age 27.
Married on the 23rd of January 1866 Thos L. Chewning & Mattie L. Partlow.
Lynn P. Chewning & Kate C. Waller were married Nov. 25th 1891. Married by the Rev C.T.
  Taylor at Bethany Church Caroline Co. Va.
Clarence C. Chewning & Irene Burruss were married Oct. 12, 1909 in Washington, D.C.
Thos Henry Chewning & Inez ____ were united in the Holy Bonds of Matrimony June 9th 1877
  in the City of Washington, D.C.

Ernest W. Chewning & Julia M. Davis were married Dec 22, 1911 at Waller's Church.
R. Evelyn Chewning & Lee J.[Johnson] Smith were married Nov 2, 1898 at Wallers Church.
Maud Chewning & William H. Murdox were married Dec 2nd 1903.
Madeline Smith and A. Bernard Driver were Married in Franklin County on the 2nd of July 1931.
Robert Thomas Smith son of Lee J. and Evelyn Chewning Smith was born July 15, 1900.
Mary Madeline Smith daughter of Lee J. and Evelyn Chewning Smith was born July 18, 1902.
Fannie Lee Driver daughter of A. Bernard and Madeline S. Driver was born Feb. 10, 1934.
Augustus Bernard Driver Jr. son of A. Bernard & Madeline S. Driver was born August 25, 1938.
Lee J. Smith died on 21st Jan 1933.
Evelyn C. Smith died on 23d Jan 1953.
The following newspaper death notices are in the Bible: Mrs. Denia Gatewood, whose funeral was preached at the residence of her son Mr. W.G. Dillard on Wednesday, February 6 at 1 o'clock and was laid to rest by the side of her husband of her youth. Also the death notice of Lee J. Smith of Chilesburg who died Jan. 23, 1933 at age 71 and who was buried at County Line Baptist Church, Caroline County.

CHILES FAMILY BIBLE

This record is of the family of Samuel Chiles, 1785, Caroline County, Virginia. It was copied by Mary Belle Ingram of Bay City, Texas. She is the great-granddaughter of Jesse Richeson and Selina Chiles and the great-great-granddaughter of Samuel Chiles of Caroline County. This record was published in *Tidewater Virginia Families, A Magazine of History and Genealogy*, Volume 12, Number 3, November/December 2003, pp.184-185.

Zmanda F.G. Chiles Born Feb. 18th 1808 Va. Died Feb. [illeg].
William I. Chiles Born May 12th 1801 Died [blank].
Robert R. Chiles Born Decem 19th 1811 Died Oct. 29th 186 [torn].
Sarah F. Chiles Born Mch. 28th 1814 Died [blank] 1862.
Selina G. Chiles Born Feb. 9th 1816
Caroline S.J. Chiles Born Nov. 22nd 1817.
Nary E. Chiles Born Aug 1st 1819.
John S.H. Chiles Born Nov 13th 1821 Died Decem 10th 18 [torn].
Thomas H. Chiles Born Aug 22nd 1823 Died August 23rd 1823.
Susan M.C. Chiles Born July 21st 1825.
Thomas B. Chiles Born Feb 14th 1827 Died June 6th 1869.
Elliott W. Chiles Born Feb 9th 1829.
Pamela A. Chiles Born May 10th 1831 Died June 27th [torn].
Clementina D.A. Chiles Born March 29th 1832 Died Sep 1st 1856.
Lucy C. Chiles Born Aug. 12th 1834 Died Aug [blank] 1865.
Samuel Chiles Father of the above Children Died Sep 15th 18[18].
Frances L. B. H[ewlett] Chiles Mother of the above Children Died June 1718 [torn].
Amanda F.G. Chiles married James McCluskey in Virginia.
William I. Chiles married Mrs. Jane Barnes in Maryland.

Robert R. Chiles married Lucy Cleer (died) married Molly Ann Fry in Alabama.
Sarah F. Chiles married Gregory Rozannia of Richmond, Virginia.
Salena G. Chiles married Jessie Richeson in Caroline Co. Virginia.
Mary F. Chiles married James Wallace {died} married James Hooker in Alabama.
John S.H. Chiles married Catherine Hurst in Alabama.
Susan M.C. Chiles married William M. Kent in Alabama.
Thomas B. Chiles married Mary E. Counts in Alabama.
Elliott W. Chiles married Catherine Kirkland (died) married Matilta Holliman in Alabama.
Clementina D.A. Chiles married William C. Ba[-]idfoot in Alabama.
Lucy C. Chiles married James M. Corsby in Alabama.
William M. Kent Born in Laurence Co. Alabama Sep [blank] 1828.
Susan M.C. Chiles Born July 21st 1825.
William M. Kent & Susan his wife were married September 13th 1849.
The Children of this marriage are as follows
Sarah Frances Elizabeth Ann Born July 10 1851 Died Aug 10th 1852.
Lucy Ellen Born Feb 27th 1853.
James Henry Born Jan 3rd 1855.
John Calvin Buchanan Born Sep 25th 1855.
Mary Josephine Born Sep 25th 1858.
Ida Catherine Born Decem 20th 1862.
Willie Bird Born Oct 15th 1865.

Also lying loose in the Bible is the printed obituary of Samuel Chiles, source not given.

At his residence in Franklin County, Alabama, Samuel Chiles died on 15th September after a short but severe illness of eight hours. He was formerly a deacon of Buris [Burruss] Church, Caroline County, Virginia. After removing to Alabama he became a member and deacon of the Bethel Baptist Church, Franklin County. He "used the office of deacon well, purchasing himself a good degree and a great boldness in the faith which is in Jesus Christ. He died as he lived, a happy Christian."

COLE FAMILY BIBLE

This Bible belonged to the James S. Cole family of Caroline, who lived in the Sparta area of Caroline County. The Bible dates from 1815-1926. James Singleton Cole was the son of John G. Cole and Nancy Broaddus. His brother Robert Walker Cole, who married Lucy F. Broaddus and died April 1868 at age 52 was a Baptist minister in Caroline County, being ordained in Salem Baptist Church. James S. Cole's sister Martha Semple Cole married a Mr. Wright and died February 10, 1885 at the age of 62 leaving among her heirs a son A.F. Wright. The Cole family lived at Sparta in a house that was located next to old Murray place, later Sam Pitts' place and next to Salem Baptist Church.

James S. Cole was Born Decr. 20th 1815.
Elizabeth A. Cole wife of the above Born March 25th 1818.
Martha Jane Thornley was born February 11th 1837.

Harriett George Thornley was born September the 29 1838.
Rosa D. Cole was Born September 24th 1843.
Bettie James Thomas Cole was Born May 25th 1850.
Henrietta G. Cole Born June 29th 1852 Died January 2nd 1855. [Caroline Death Register shows
   DOD as Jan. 2, 1856, age 6 years].
Maria Sandidge Cole was Born April 4th 1854.
Elsie G. Cole was Born June 17th 1856.
Helena A. Cole was Born May 14th 1858.
Julia Edward Cole was Born July 14th 1860.
Maria Sandidge Cole was Born April [illeg].
Maud Ethel Rhoads [died] December 29th 1895.
Clarence L. Rhoads [died] September 20th 1897.
Lena Elisabeth Rhoads [died] December 13th 1899.
Mary Jennette Rhoads [died] March 13, 1901.
[newspaper clipping:
"Ellsworth J. Baker and Miss Lena E. Rhoades, both of Fredericksburg, were married in Washington Wednesday by Rev. John E. Briggs"]
James S. Cole died October 26th 1870.
Rosa D. Cole Died October 11th 1871.
Elizabeth A. Cole died 1879.
[Newspaper clipping of Mrs. Silvio Tosi's death:
"Mrs. ___ddie J. Tosi, wife of Mr. Silvio Tosi, West Mulberry Street, died yesterday morning of Bright's disease. She was born about thirty-two years ago near Sparta, Caroline county, Va. and was a daughter of Mr. James S. Cole, a prominent citizen of that place. Both on the paternal and maternal sides Mrs. Tosi was descended from old English families which had settled in Virginia. On the paternal side she was a granddaughter of Nancy Broaddus and John G. Cole of Caroline county and on the maternal side her grandparents were Martha Sandidge [Sandridge?] and Anderson Trice of Louisa county, Va. She was a lady of refinement and possessed a charm of manner which made her many friends.

   Mrs. Tosi met her husband in Richmond, he having come to that city from Venice in 1880. The marriage took place fifteen years ago in Richmond, where for a year afterward Mr. Tosi continued to practice his profession as artist, architect and designer. About thirteen years ago they removed to Baltimore. Besides her husband Mrs. Tosi is survived by two young daughters, Misses Italia and Verona Tosi."]
Richard Kersey died June 16th 1900.
Emmett Mason Cole Born Aug 18 1894.
Married in Washington Feb. 26 - 1926 at Preacher's Parsonage by
   Rev. Tolson. [no name of bride and groom is listed].
James S. Cole was born Decr 20th 1815.
Eliz. A. Cole wife of the above was born March 25, 1818.
Martha Jane Thornly daughter of George and [torn page] Thornly was born July 11th 1839.
[torn page]ge Thornly _____ George and _____ was born _____.
Mary Ella Cole was Born March 2nd 1846.
Bettie J. Cole was born May 25, 1848.

Virginia T. Cole Born May 15th 1850.

Henrietta Cole Born [page torn].

James S. Cole and Elizabeth A. Thornly was married together August 25th 1842 by Bo. Wilkerson of Louisa.

Clarence L. Rhoads To Helena Dameron Cole January 3rd 1888.

Richard Kersey and Mary Ella Cole were Married March 15th 1894.

_____ Tosi [page torn].

COLEMAN FAMILY BIBLE

This Bible was published by J. H. Chambers & Co., Saint Louis, Missouri and copyrighted by A. J. Holman & Co. in 1882. It was presented to E.M. Coleman on April the 5th 1916 by his parents, H.F. Coleman and Jennie M. Coleman at "Fair View", Caroline County, Virginia. It was given to Julian Harwood Coleman, the oldest son of Emmett and Caddie Coleman, at the death of his mother. When Julian H. Coleman died in 1981, the Bible passed to his oldest son, Richard H. Coleman. In 1991, he passed the Bible to his brother, John Patrick Coleman of Seattle, Washington, the present owner. The Fair View farm, located in the north end of Caroline County was sold by its owner, H. F. Coleman on February 29th 1916 for the sum of $10,000. It has been carefully restored and is now owned by Dr. Joseph D. Paquette, a Fredericksburg pediatrician. Emmett Moffette Coleman was born at "West View", the Coleman home place at Penola, Virginia.

This Certifies that the rite of Holy Matrimony was celebrated between H.[Henry] F.[Frank] Coleman of Caroline Co. and Jennie M. Patrick of Albemarle on April 7th 1868 at Syloan Retreat by Rev. S.P. Huff at Hebron Church, Nelson Co. Va.

E.[Emmett] M.[Moffette] Coleman of Caroline County and Caddie D.[Dorsey] Campbell of Caroline County on June 21, 1899 at Emmaus Church, [Penola] Virginia.

Dr. H.[Hawes] Rees Coleman of Caroline County, Va. and Elizabeth Mae Hoffman of Rockbridge County, Va. on August 29, 1900 at Virginia, Cutler officiating.

Walter S. Hart of Chicago, Ill. and Evylyne [Evelyn] Gertrude Coleman of Caroline Co. Va. on May 20, 1908 by Rev. Martin in Cincinnati, Ohio.

Hawes Clyde Coleman of Caroline Co. Va. and Joceylin [Jocelyn] Coghill Jan 31, 1912 Va.

George Kemp Coleman of Caroline Co. Va. and Pearl Cobb Do. [no date].

Claude C. Coleman of Richmond, Va. and Julia Langhorne Cone on April 28, 1917.

Joseph Lee Potter and Hope Evangeline Coleman Mar. 12, 1912.

Dr. Julian Harwood Coleman and Margaret Julia Edmunds July 20, 1926.

Arthur Lee Beazley and Virginia Franklin Coleman June 15, 1936.

John Albin Vaughan Jr. and Clarice Louise Coleman Mar. 31, 1937.

Emmett Moffett Coleman Jr. and Christine Vaughan June 21, 1939.

Joseph Frank McVay and Ogenia Ellen Coleman Sept. 16, 1943.

Births:

Emmett Moffette Coleman Sept. 7th 1869 at 6 A.M.

Frank Selwyn Coleman Jan. 14th 1871. 8 P.M.

Hawes Rees Coleman Oct 21st 1872. 4 P.M.

Geo. Kemp Coleman Jan 18th 1876. 11 P.M.

Gertrude Coleman March 6th 1877. 11 P.M.

Claude Coleman July 21st 1879. 12 P.M.

Pearl V. Coleman Dec 8th 1880. 4 P.M.

Hope Evangeline [Coleman] March 15th 1882. 7 P.M.

Waverly Clyde Coleman Sept 2nd 1883 Sunday 3 o'clock A.M.

Custis Lee Coleman Oct 4th 1887. 5 o'clock A.M.

Lorene Moffette Potter August 6, 1916 Sunday 6:45 P.M. in Collinstown, Va.

Jane Coleman Hart April 22, 1912 Chicago, Ill.

Neely Snidder Hart June 23, 1910.

Caddie Dorsey (Campbell) Coleman Mar. 20, 1871.

Julian Harwood Coleman April 2, 1900.

Clarice Louise Coleman July 20, 1903.

Margaret Julia (Edmunds) Coleman Dec. 16, 1905.

Virginia Franklin Coleman May 11, 1906.

Emmett Moffett Coleman Jr. Oct. 11, 1908.

Henry Frank Coleman Jan. 20, 1911.

Ogenia Ellen Coleman Aug. 9, 1913.

Deaths:

J. W. Patrick died Aug 1840.

Mrs. Lucy Patrick died March 1863.

John M. Patrick died Dec. 1871.

Pearl Vernon Coleman died in Rd. Va. June 1st 1897 at 4 O'clock (age 16 years 5 months 7 days).

Curtis Lee Coleman died in Phila. Pa. June 28, 1913 Saturday 6:10 P.M.

Henry Frank Coleman died in Bowling Green, Va. January 13, 1919 Morning 11:30 A.M. Age 75 yrs.

Jennie M.[Moffette] Coleman died in Bowling Green, Virginia Friday Oct. 23, 1931 at 8:05 P.M. Age 86 yrs.

Emmett M.[Moffette] Coleman Died Jan. 9th 1936.

Frank S.[Selwyn] Coleman Died December 30th 1939.

Hawes Rees Coleman Died November 7, 1940.

Henry Frank Coleman Oct. 22, 1913.

Caddie Dorsey (Campbell) Coleman Feb. 5, 1951.

Emmett Moffett Coleman Sr. Jan. 9, 1936.

COLLINS FAMILY BIBLE NO. 1

The dedication page of this bible has the following: "This Bible is the Property of Clarissa Collins December 24, 1818. Written by James D. Wright. From To George T. Collins June 5th 1831 King George County." It passed from George T. Collins to his son Edgar B. Collins and from him to his grandchild William Webb. It is still in that family. A copy of the record is in the Library of Virginia. George T. Collins' family has lived at "Hickory Grove", Penola, Caroline County since before the Civil War and are buried there. For further information, see *The History and Genealogy of the Collins Family of Caroline County, Virginia* by Herbert Ridgeway Collins, Dietz Press, Richmond, Va. 1954.

James D. Wright and Lucinda Collins were married June 6th 1816 and to them was born a Daughter Clarissa Frances, July 5th 1817 also a Son William James, July 10th 1819.

George T. Collins and Ann J. Coleman were married May 15th 1834 and to them was born a Daughter (1) Clarissa Elizabeth March 30th 1835.

(2) James Clayton [Collins] was born July 20th 1836.
(3) Margaret Ann [Collins] was born February 10, 1838.
(4) Sarah Jenette Collins was born May 10th 1840.
(5) Catherine Virginia Collins was born November 10th 1841.
(6) George Robert M. Collins was born Oct 10th 1843.
(7) Emuella H.[Harris] Collins was born June 15, 1845.
(8) Ogenia Ellen Burke Collins was born April 8th 1847.
(9) John W.[Welford] Collins was born Jan. 25, 1849.
(10) William J. Collins was born July 5, 1850.
(11) Julian A.[Augustus] Collins was born July 15, 1852.
(12) Edgar Beauragaude Collins was born May 21, 1860.

Edgar B. Collins & Florence C. Baptist were married October 12, 1881 (Oct 25).

Florence C. Baptist was born March 6, 1860 and died January 6, 1941.

(13) Charlie L. [Lindsey] Collins was born March 25th 1854.

1. Edmund Collins was born November 25th 1776.
2. Frances [Fanny] Collins was born January 12th 1779.
3. Mary [Polly] Collins was born October 23rd 1785.
4. James Collins [Jr.] was born September 21st 1787 and deceased   August 5th 1815..
5. Jane Thompson Collins was born March 30th 1789.
6. Charles Collins was born January 28th 1793.
7. Lucinda [Lucy F.] Collins was born September 20th 1794.
8. Ann [Nancy] Collins was born September 16th 1796.
9. John Collins was born February 3rd 1798.
10. Joseph [Todd] Collins was born January 3rd 1800.
11. Phebe Collins was born March 28th 1802.
12. George T.[Todd] Collins was born March 3rd 1803.

COLLINS FAMILY BIBLE NO. 2

This Bible was published by the American Tract Society, New York City, 1861. It was a gift to C.L. and Bettie (Sutton) Collins of Woodford, Caroline County, Virginia. It passed to their daughter Annie Collins Jesse and to their daughter Ella Jesse Latham of Arlington County, Virginia. At her death the estate was settled and the Bible appeared for auction with a minimum bid of $100.00 on the internet ebay as item #233297389 January 8, 2000. The purchaser's name is not known. Charles Lindsay and his wife Bettie Sutton lived mostly in Bowling Green, Caroline County but owned and lived at other different places in the county. Some of the places were Clifton, Mt. Zephre, Holly Hill. They spent their last years in Arlington County. For more information concerning this family see *The History and Genealogy of the Collins Family of Caroline County, Virginia and related families* by Herbert Ridgeway Collins, Dietz Press, Richmond, Virginia, 1954.

C. [Charles] L. [Lindsay] and Bettie L. [Lula] Sutton 14th May 1874.
Mattye Pendleton Collins and Ferdinand Wiley Chandler 14th May 1902.
Charles Ridgely and Ruby Jean Smartt 14th February 1904.
Charles Thomas Jesse and Annie Graham Collins 5th Oct. 1904.
George Todd Collins and _____ 9th Mar. 1905.
Estel Lewis Collins and Willoughby Lindsey April 1912.
Lucille Burton Collins and George T. Frick 2 July 1915.
Mattye P. Collins Chandler and B. Bertram A. [Allen] Woolfolk 8th Dec. 1914.
Charles Lindsay Collins and Mary B. Rush 8 November 1918.
Lucille B. Collins Frick and Herbert O. McLean June 1920.
George Todd Collins and Ida F. [Frances] Camper 17th Sept. 1920.
Robert H. [Hugh] Collins and Florence Virginia Tonkin 17th March 1921.
Julia Thornton Collins and Frank Law Woolfolk 4th Sept. 1925.

Births
C.L. Collins 25 March 1854.
B.L. Sutton 18th Sept. 1855.
C. Ridgely Collins 1 May 1875.
Mattye P. Collins 9th Nov. 1879.
Geo. T. Collins 9th Mar. 1882.
Joseph P. Collins 9th July 1884.
Estelle Lewis Collins 9th Nov. 1887.
Julia Thornton Collins was born 21st Oct. 1889.
Robert Hugh Collins was born Oct. 29, 1891.
Lucille Burton Collins was born Mar. 28, 1893.
Charles Lindsay Collins Jr. was born May 28, 1895.
Willard Garnett Collins was Born Aug. 9th 1898.
[another child Annie Graham Collins, born July 6, 1877, birth not recorded in the Bible]

Deaths
Joseph P. Collins 15th _____ 1890.
Willard Garnett Collins 27th July 1899.
Edmund Pendleton Sutton 17th June 1900.
Charles Ridgely Collins 17 January 1907.
Elizabeth Lewis Chandler 3rd December 1902.
Charles Lindsay Collins 29th May 1921.
John Ridgely Chandler 11th June 1923.
Bettie Lewis Collins 26th June 1952.

George Todd Collins Oct. 4th 1956.

COLLINS/JOHNSON/RAWLINGS FAMILY BIBLE

This is a small New Testament published by the American Bible Society of New York in 1848. This Collins family lived at "Hickory Grove", Caroline County. The Rawlings family lived at "Ellan's Gowan" (or "Ellengowan"), a structure that stood in Spotsylvania County well over 200 years. Alfred Rawlings, father of Nannie Rawlings, was born in Spotsylvania County. Located 1 ½ miles south of Lewiston, the estate was once a part of the Bel Air tract. James Rawlings purchased this one thousand tract in 1731 and built the house shortly thereafter. In 1757, he willed the house and 792 acres to his son James Rawlings Jr. and was left from father to son until about 1937. The house was a solidly built brick structure with a three-bay facade. Photographs of the house are preserved in the Virginia Department of Historic Resources and a description is in the WPA Survey of Spotsylvania County. James Rawlings was the son of Judith Ann Johnson (daughter of John Lipscomb Johnson of Meadow Hill) and Alfred Rawlings. Judith Ann "Nannie" Johnson and Alfred Rawlings were married December 18, 1844. The house had been unoccupied for some time before its demise when flooded over at the time Lake Anna was made in the 1960's. A detailed description with pictures was featured in The Free Lance Star, July 29, 2006. For information on the Lipscomb family mentioned in the book, see the *Religious Herald*, the Baptist newspaper of the 19th century, May 26, 1910 issue. The New Testament book was presented to Judith Ann Rawlings by her father and by her to Nannie her daughter. A copy of the family register from the book is in the Library of Virginia. The records date from 1800-1941. See also "Autobiographical Notes by John Lipscomb Johnson", published in 1958.

Judith Ann Rawlings Presented by her Father August 27th 1848.
Presented to Nannie by her Mother March 30th 1879.
Alfred Rawlings Collins Son of Chastain F. & N.J. Collins was born September 1st 1882.
Chastain Frederick Collins was born May 3rd 1884.
Anne Judith Collins was born April 27th 1886.
James Clarence Collins was born Oct. 27th 1887.
Rebecca Jane Coleman Collins was born July 24th 1889.
Beatrice Collins was born Feb. 18th 1891.
Lewis Edgar Collins was born Aug 2nd 1892.
Clara Edmonia Collins was born July 18th 1894.
Mary Ridgley Collins was born Aug. 24th 1896.
Julian Augustus Collins was born March 8th 1898. Died August 24   1923.
Nannie Ashby Collins born July 15 1901.
Julian Augustus Collins Died August 24 1923. Buried at Hickory Grove.
Mary Ridgley Collins Noble died Aug 11 1924. Buried in Hollywood Cemetery Richmond Va.
Nannie Ashby Collins Kidd died Nov 5 1941. Buried at Hickory Grove Caroline Co Va.
Lewis Johnson was born September 24 1800 was married to Jane D. Lipscomb Dec 16th 1824.
  She was born March 24th 1800.
Judith Ann Johnson was born June 10 1826.

Elizabeth Mary Johnson was born Augst 27th 1828.
Fredonia Jane Johnson was born August 7th 1830.
Sarah Frances Camilla Johnson was born April 17th 1833.
John Lipscomb Johnson was born Augst 12th 1835.
Valentine Mason Johnson was born July 17th 1838.
Alfred Rawlings & Judith A. Johnson were married December 18 1844.
Alfred R. Collins was born at Bowling Green Sep 1st 1882.
 [above is duplicated entry]
GrandMother Rawling's Writing
James Lewis Rawlings was born 10 of July 1846.
Alfred Benjamin Rawlings was born May 26 1848.
Jane Dabney Rawlings was born 11th of July 1850.
Clara Lawrence Rawlings was born Augst 26th 1852.
Edmonia Frances Rawlings was born September 20th 1854.
Lewis Johnson Rawlings was born April 23rd 1856.
Julia Valentine Rawlings was born Augst 31st 1860.
Ashby Rawlings was born June 3rd 1862.
Louise Livingston Rawlings was born at Livingston Jan 24th 1872.
Elizabeth Margaretta Rawlings was born at Ellan gowan March 11th 1882.
Lewis Johnson was born September 24th 1800.
Jane D. Lipscomb was born March 24th 1800. [daughter of Hon. John Lipscomb].
  They were married at Meadow Hill Dec 16th 1824.
Alfred Rawlings was born December 28th 1822.
Judith Ann Johnson was born June 10th 1826.
  They were married at Forest Hill December 18th 1849.
Elizabeth Mary Johnson was born August 27th 1828.
Fredonia Jane Johnson was born August 7th 1830.
Sarah Frances Camilla Johnson was born April 17th 1833.
John Lipscomb Johnson was born August 12th 1835.
Valentine Mason Johnson was born July 17th 1838.
Chastain F. Collins son of George T. and Ann J. Collins was born October 6th 1858. Died 9 - 12 - 33.
Nannie J. Rawlings daughter of Alfred and Judith A. Rawlings was born February 5th 1858.
   Died 7 - 22 - 1901.
Married at Ellans Gowan Oct 14th 1880 Steve [Stephen] Branch and Clara L.M. Rawlings. [Stephen Branch and family lived near Farmington, Georgia.}
June 4th 1881 married at [illeg] Alfred R. Rawlings to M.L. Bailey.
Married at Waller's Church Spotsylvania Co Chastain F. Collins and Nannie J. Rawlings Oct 25, 1881.
Lewis Johnson was born September 29th 1800.
Jane Dabney Lipscomb was born March 24th 1800.
They were married at Meadow Hill December 26th 1824.
Alfred Rawlings was born Decr. 28 1822.
Judith Ann Johnson was born June 10 1826.

They were married at Forest Hill Decr. 18 1844.

Elder J.A. Billingsley and Elizabeth Mary Johnson were married September 28th 1851 at Forest Hills.

Jno L. Johnson and Julia Anna Taylor married July 12, 1860 in Norfolk Va.

Valentine M. Johnson & Eliza W. Bogus were married at Livingston May 1st [illeg].

Elizabeth Mary Johnson was born August 27th 1828 [looks like 1828].

Fredonia Jane Johnson was born Aug 7th 1830.

Sarah Frances Camilla Johnson was born April 17th 1833.

John Lipscomb Johnson was born August 12th 1835.

Valentine Mason Johnson was born July 11th 1838.

James Lewis Rawlings was born July 10, 1846.

Alfred Benjamin Rawlings was born May 26th 1848.

Jane Dabney Rawlings was born July 11th 1850.

Clara Lawrence Rawlings was born August 20, 1852.

Edmonia Frances Rawlings was born September 20th 1854.

Lewis Johnson Rawlings was born April 23rd 1856.

Julia Ann Rawlings was born Febry 5th 1858.

John Valentine Rawlings was born Augst 31st 1860.

Ashby Rawlings was born June 3rd 1862.

Louise Livingston Rawlings was born at Livingston on the 24th of January 1873.

Elizabeth Margarette Rawlings was born at Ellangown March 11, 1882.

Alfred Rawlings Collins was born at his father's in Bowling Green September 1st 1882. [duplicated entry]

Alfred Rawlings Branch was born in Ga. Feb 9th 1886.

Alfred B. Rawlings was born Oct 9th 1887. Departed this life at Forest Hill on Sunday evening 6th of Nov 1850?

Lewis Johnson aged 53 years 1 month and 12 days, bad heart.

Sarah Frances Camilla Johnson departed this life 23d day of February 1843 aged 9 years 4m 25d. Had St. Vitus dance.

Departed this life at the residence of his father John Valentine Rawlings aged 13 months 14 days on the 19th day of October 1861 of diptheria.

Departed this life at the residence of her son-in-law Alfred Rawlings Mrs. Jane D. Johnson relict of the late Lewis Johnson on the 30 of January 1863 aged 62 years 10m.

Departed this life at Ellengowan on the 22nd of March 63 Alfred Rawlings Aged 90 years 2 months & 25 days in the year of our Lord 1861 he had heart disease for two years and Apoplexy 4 days which took his life.

Frederick S.___Rawlings was born May 26th [no year listed].

Alfred Benjamin Rawlings [no further info given].

CONWAY FAMILY BIBLE

This Bible Record was copied by George H.S. King in 1948 from the Bible of Mrs. Gordon Conway, resident at the old Conway home-place, Mt. Sion, in Caroline County, Virginia. The Bible was published in Philadelphia in 1809. On the fly sheet is written: "The property of John

Conway made preasant (sic) to him by his mother, Elizabeth Taylor in 1810". A copy of this Bible record is in the Virginia Historical Society.

In a letter dated Sept. 5, 1883 from Mt. Sion, a relative states that Francis Conway lived at Port Conway, across the river from Port Royal, Caroline County, was born December 27, 1722, died May 17, 1761, married Sarah Taliaferro, who was born October 8, 1727 and died January 17, 1784 and that his son Francis Conway, Junior, was born March 7, 1748, died February 13, 1794, married Elizabeth Fitzhugh, who was born October 10, 1754, died February 25 1823, having married secondly to Col. Jas. Taylor.

Francis Conway, Senior, Born December 27th, 1722.
Sarah Conway, Born October 8th, 1727.
Francis Conway, Junior, Born March 7th 1749.
Elizabeth Conway, Born October 10th 1754.
Francis F. Conway, Junior, Born December 10th 1772.
Alice Conway, Born August 11, 1775.
John F. Conway, Born August 28th 1777.
Catlett Conway, Born February 7, 1780.
Sarah Tol. [Taliaferro?] Conway, Born October 7th, 1781.
Elizabeth Conway, Born July 11, 1783.
Edwin Conway, Born March 11th 1785.
John Conway, Born March 21st 1787.
George Conway, Born September 27th 1789.
Thomas Conway, Born November 29th 1791 [married Mary Hawes Buckner, 1811].
Harriet Conway, the wife of John Conway, Born August 1st 1798.
The [following four are]children of John Conway:
Francis H. Conway, Born February 15, 1816.
Ann R.F. Conway, Born March 16th 1818.
Catlett Conway, Born March 5th 1822.
Eleanor Conway, Born December 28th 1824.
Selina F. Conway, wife of Catlett Conway, Born January 4th 1831.
Edwin Conway, son of Catlett and Selina F. Conway was born Feby.16th 1851, Sunday, at Mt. Sion.
Fanny S. Conway was born March 6th 1850 at Mt. Sion.
Eugene Conway was born March 29th 1853 at Mt. Sion.
John Catlett Conway was born December 30th 1854.
Frank Henry Conway was born February 16th 1857.
Fulton Conway was born December 19, 1858.
Harriett Ann Conway was born in Mississippi August 20 1866.
Milton FitzHugh Conway was born in Mississippi August 20th, 1866.
Selina May Conway was born in Canton, Mississippi, March 31st 1869.
Catlett Conway was married to Selina F. Fitzhugh, daughter of John Fitzhugh of Prince William County, Va. on Dec. 19th 1848.
Eugene Conway was married to Lizzie E. Egliston [sic], daughter of _____ Egliston of

Viscburg [sic], Miss. Feb. 5th 1880.
Francis Conway Senior Died May 17th 1761.
Sarah Conway Died January 17th 1784.
Francis Conway Junior Died February 13th 1794.
Francis F. Conway Jr. Died December 27th 1803.
Alice Conway Died October 24th 1776.
John F. Conway Died April 4th 1784.
Catlett Conway Died June 17th 1781.
Elizabeth Conway (Alias Taylor) Died February 25th 1823.
Ann R.F. Conway, the child of John Conway, died October 10, 1825.
Thomas Conway Died in [Dallas Co.] Alabama July 11th 1826.
George Conway Died in Alabama Dec. 14th 1827.
Elizabeth Conway died June 29th 1832.
Edwin Conway died in Kentucky April 12th 1844.
Sarah T. Thornton died [no date listed].
John Conway died Mt. Sion March 22, 1865.
Harriett A. Conway died in Mississippi Oct. 13th 1868.
Frank H. Conway died in Sharon, Miss. June 22, 1872.
Frank H. Conway, Senr. Died Jany. 2nd 1873 at Mt. Sion.
Selina F. Conway died in Mississippi, Sept. 4th 1878.
Edwin Conway Died in Mississippi September 20th 1878.
Harriet E. Conway died at Mt. Sion November 17th 1879.
Ann R. Thornton Died June 20th 1808.
Henry F. Thornton Died February 27th 1829 (the father of Harriett E. Conway).
Henry F. Thornton, Jr., died September 20th 1819.
[Below is a separate sheet lying in the Bible, perhaps from an earlier Bible]
Francis Conway Was Born 27th [page torn] the Year 1727.
Sarah Conway Was Born 8th day of Octob [page torn] the Year 1727.
Betty Conway Was Born 8th day of D [page torn] about Ten a Clock [page torn] in the Morning in the Year 1745.
Mary Conway Was Born 28th day of October aBout [sic] Three a Clock in the Morning And in the year 1748.
Francis Conway Junior Was Born 7th day of March aBout Three a Clock in the Morning And in the Year 1748.
Catlett Conway Was Born 25th day of December Abouth [sic]15 Minets [sic] after One a Clock in the afterNoon [sic] Which was of a Wednesday in the Year 175_ [page torn].
One Daughter Dead Was Born October 1th [sic]1755.
Sarah Conway was Born the 27 Day of November about Half an Our [sic] after Twelve a Clock at Night Being of a Munday in the Year 1759.

CORBIN FAMILY BIBLE NO. 1

The following family Bible record was inserted in the suit of Dickinson vs. Poindexter, CR-LC-H, 1838, ID-56-Z in the Fredericksburg Circuit Court Clerk's Annex Office with the following note from the commissioner in 1838: "The foregoing is a correct copy of the entries made on one of the pages in a large Bible exhibited before the Commr as the family Bible of the Corbins of Laneville - The book is exhibited by the defendant's counsel at the suggestion of the counsel for the pltfs, the Commr has made a full copy of the entries, in addition to the extract forming a part of Mr. Wellford's deposition and his attention being called by the sd. counsel to the fact he states that it appears to him obvious that the first nine entries were made by the same person and with the same pen and ink, and he thinks it fair to presume at one and the same time - It does not appear in whose hand writing the entries are made. [signed] J.M. Herndon, Commr."

Henry Corbin, son of Thomas Corbin married Alice Eltonhead, daughter of Richard Eltonhead of Lancaster County, England, July 25, 1645. From this union descended the Corbins of Caroline County, who first lived at "Laneville" in King and Queen County. Laneville burned March 15, 1758. Four of this family settled in Caroline County, John Corbin at "Port Tobago", Gawin Corbin at "Yew Springs", Francis Corbin at "The Reeds", and Richard Corbin at "Moss Neck". Of these houses in Caroline County, only Moss Neck is presently standing. Gawin Corbin married as his second wife, Jane Lane, daughter of John Lane and Richard Corbin married Rebecca Parke Farley which accounts for the middle names recorded in the Bible. They also married into the Tayloe family of "Mount Airy" in an adjacent county. There are known family cemeteries at Moss Neck and also at The Reeds on Shuman Road, Caroline County.

John Tayloe Corbin was Married to Maria [born July 14, 1752 the daughter of Benjamin Waller] his wife the 16th Day of Feby 1771 from whom was descended as follows - viz
Richard Corbin born the 2nd Decr 1771
John Tayloe Corbin born 9th April 1775 obit 28th Augst 1775.
John Tayloe Corbin born 24th Nov - 1776.
Gawin Lane Corbin born 19th June 1778.
Betty Tayloe Corbin born 29th Augst 1780.
Martha Maria Corbin born 28 Feby 1786.
Anna Frances Maria Corbin born 21st Decr 1786.
Henrietta Matilda Corbin born 26 Apl 1792.
John Tayloe Corbin departed this life 16 Feby 1794.
Henry Elkinhead [Eltonhead] Corbin was born 22nd Sepr - 1794.
Maria Corbin departed this life 16 Sepr - 1796.

Richard Corbin eldest son of John Tayloe Corbin was married to Rebecca Parke [Farley] his wife 15th Nov. 1794 from whom are descended
John Tayloe Corbin born 26th Sepr 1795.
Elizabeth Farley Corbin born 13th March 1797.
Richard Corbin born 2nd Sepr 1798.
Gawin Lane Corbin born 12th April 1800 - died 1st Novr 1807.
Mary Byrd Corbin born 10 Jany 1802.
Richard Corbin departed this life in the 10th day of June 1809.
Rebecca Parke Corbin his wife departed this life on the 13th of April 1822 aged 43 years.

CORBIN FAMILY BIBLE NO. 2

This Bible was originally owned by Gawin Corbin and dates from 1739-1779. The records include the counties of Middlesex, King & Queen and Caroline as well as Norfolk and Williamsburg.

"The foregoing Gawin Corbin Bible Record is copied from an old yellow copy owned by Mrs. Ellelee Chapman Humes of Huntsville Ala. by Stella Pickett Hardy in August 1917."

Gawin Corbin & Joanna Tucker were married Nov. 17th 1762.
Gawin Corbin, son of Richard & Betty Corbin, born Dec. 15, 1739.
Joanna Tucker, daughter of Robert & Joanna Tucker, born April 12, 1744.
Betty Tayloe Corbin, born March 28, 1764 at 8 min. past 5 o'clock in the morning. Godfathers: Col. Robert Tucker and Capt Constantine John Phipps. Godmothers: Mrs. Bettie Corbin and Mrs. Joanna Tucker.
Ann Corbin, born Dec. 17, 1767 at 40 min. past 1 o'clock in the morning. Godfathers: Carter Braxton and Tayloe Corbin esqurs. Godmothers: Mrs. Bettie Corbin and Mrs. Eliza Corbin.
Felicia Corbin, born Feb. 1, 1770 at 25 min. past 8 o'clock in the morning. Godfathers: Richard Corbin, Esq and Dr. Robert Spratt. Godmothers: Miss Alice Corbin and Jane Tacker.
Jane Lane Corbin, born Oct. 3, 1773 at 1 o'clock in the morning. Godfathers: John Tayloe Corbin and Thomas Corbin, Esquires. Godmothers: Mrs. Maria Corbin and Miss Courtenay Tucker.
Richard Henry Corbin, born Aug. 4, 1775 at 4 o'clock in the morning. Godfathers: The Hon Ralph Wormley and John Page of North End, Esquires. Godmothers: Miss Sarah Tayloe and Miss Alice Corbin.
Jane Corbin, born Sept. 8, 1777, at night. Godgathers: George Bird and R. Corbin Tucker, Esquires. Godmothers: Mrs Ann Tucker, Bettie Braxton, Jane Wormley and Eliza Robinson.
Jane Lane Corbin died April 4, 1777 at 30 min. past 6 o'clock in the morning.
Gawin Corbin, died July 19, 1779 at 10 min. past 3 o'clock in the morning.

DeJARNETTE FAMILY BIBLE

This Bible was published by the American Bible Society, New York, 1851. It was originally owned by Daniel Coleman DeJarnette and his wife, Louisa Jane DeJarnette of "Spring Grove", Caroline County. Three DeJarnette brothers owned adjoining plantations in Caroline County. Robert DeJarnette owned "Clifton", no longer standing, Daniel Coleman DeJarnette owned "Spring Grove", and John Hampton DeJarnette owned "Hampton", the latter two still standing. This Bible is now owned by Daniel I. Hansen, great-great grandson of the original owners. For further information concerning this family, consult *William and Mary Quarterly*, Series I, Volume 25, pp.268-272; also the books *DeJarnette and Allied Families in America 1699-1954* by Earl C. & May (Miller) Frost, Pacific Coast Publishers, Redwood City, California, 1954 and *Listen to the Mockingbird - The Life and Times of a Pioneer Family* by Daniel Dunbar Howe.

On the front end-page are the following names:
Daniel C. DeJarnette 1844.

Daniel Coleman DeJarnette 1923.
Elliott C. Hoge.
Family record pages:
Daniel C. DeJarnette & Louisa Jane DeJarnette were Married the 7th of March 1843.
Daniel C. DeJarnette was born October 18th 1822 died Aug. 20th 1881.
Louisa J. DeJarnette was born March 9th 1824 Died Dec. 19 - 1892.
"Copied from old record"
Daniel DeJarnette and Jane T. Coleman were married the 25th Decmb 1808.
Daniel DeJarnette and Huldah H. Coleman were married 21st of Decmb 1817.
[new entries]
Joe Willis DeJarnette and Alice Purcell Richards were Married Oct 27th 1920 at the Methodist Church Bowling Green Va.
Nancy Richards DeJarnette and George W. Hansen were married November 8th 1947 at the Methodist Church in Bowling Green, Va.
Jo DeJarnette Hansen (Jo De) baby girl, daughter of Nancy Dej Hansen and George W. Hansen born July 23rd 1953 at Ft. Belvoir hospital.
[old handwriting]
Elliott DeJarnette was born the 24th of February 1846. Died Nov.14th 1898.
Sallie Lewis DeJarnette was born the 8th of July 1848.
Mary Louisa DeJarnette was born the 30th June 1850.
Lelia Hawes DeJarnette was born 9th Decr. 1852.
Bessie Garland DeJarnette was born the 22nd August 1855.
Daniel DeJarnette was born the 17th of October 1856.
Daniel Coleman DeJarnette was born the 14th May 1864. Died Feb- 21-1926 at Spring Grove.
Daniel Coleman DeJarnette and Nancy DeJarnette Willis were married Dec. 8th 1897.
Daniel DeJarnette Son of Mary Hampton & Joseph DeJarnette was born the 9th of Oct 1783.
My Father Joseph DeJarnette aged 77 years departed this life Saturday 31st day of July 1824.
Joe Willis DeJarnette was born Aug 29th 1898.
Alice Richards DeJarnette was born April 21 - 1899.
Nancy Richards DeJarnette was born July 2 - 1923.
Nancy Willis DeJarnette was born the 29th of May 1879.
George W. Hansen born Sept. 17th 1921 at Winside Nebraska.
Daniel Iler Hansen (Dan) Baby boy son of Nancy DeJ. Hansen and George W. Hansen born Aug. 9th 1956 at Stuart Circle Hospital Richmond, Va.
John DeJ. father of Joseph ---
Joseph DeJ. born 1716.
Joseph DeJarnette was born in the year 1847.
"Copied from the old family record"
Daniel DeJarnette was born the 9th Oct 1873.
Jane T. Coleman was born 16th May 1790 (1st wife).
Huldah H. Coleman was born 17th Sept. 1793 (2nd wife).
Elizabeth Mary Goodwin DeJarnette was born 27th April 1810.
Robert E. DeJarnette was born 20th Sept. 1812.
Joseph DeJarnette was born 30th Oct. 1814.

John Hampton DeJarnette was born 24th Sept. 1818 died Aug.10th 1897.
Jane T. Goodwin DeJarnette was born 26th Decmb. 1820.
Daniel Coleman DeJarnette was born 18th Oct. 1822 died Aug. 20th 1881.
Nicey Ann Hawes DeJarnette was born August 27th 1824.
Huldah Ann DeJarnette was born 13th Novmb. 1825.
Lucy L. DeJarnette was born 9th March 1827.
Virginia DeJarnette was born 16th Novmb. 1828.
Mary Virginia DeJarnette was born Sept. 12th 1830.
Caroline Harris DeJarnette was born 4th March 1833.
Johnny DeJarnette son of John Hampton & Caroline died Feb. 4th 1906.
James Daniel Coleman DeJarnette son of Alice & Elliott DeJ. Born Dec 2, 1871 died Jan. 17th 1914.
Dr. Elliott DeJarnette Jr. Born 9-25-1873 Married 11-25-1896 Died 10-21-1946.
Janie Thompkins Born 1874 d. 1941 - One son.
Alice Coleman DeJarnette born 1849 died April 22nd 1900.
Mary Lou DeJ. Cox daughter of Daniel & Louisa DeJ. died Nov. 17th 1923. Age 73.
Samuel Coleman DeJarnette son of Daniel & Louise DeJarnette died February 21st 1929 at Spring Grove age 61 years & nine months.
[begins old writing]
Daniel DeJarnette died ___ of July 1857.
Lelia Hawes DeJarnette died the 28th of May 1858. [tombstone has 1868]
Bessie Garland DeJarnette daughter of Daniel & Louisa DeJarnette died 6th day of July 1866 aged 11 years one month.
Daniel Coleman DeJarnette Son of Daniel DeJarnette & Huldah DeJarnette died at the Residence of his sister Mrs. Daniel Hoge in Montgomery Co. Va. He was born on the 18th of October 1822 died on Saturday August 20th 1881. Aged 59 yrs 10 m. & 2 days.
Louisa DeJarnette wife of Daniel C. DeJarnette died Dec. 19th 1892 at Spring Grove.
Caroline Harris Hoges died January 1st 1892.
Elizabeth Quisenberry died January 18th 1888.
Lucinda C. DeJarnette died Dec. 18, 1869.
John Hampton died August 10th 1897 aged 78 yrs.
Sallie DeJ. Baldwin daughter of Daniel and Louisa DeJarnette died Thanksgiving Day Nov. 28th 1907 at Spring Grove Age 59.
"Copied from the old family record"
Joseph DeJarnette son of Daniel & Hul died 31st day of July 1824.
Jane T. DeJarnette died 22nd of March 1815. The wife of Daniel DeJarnette.
Josheph [sic] infant son of D. and Jane DeJarnette died 20th August 1818.
Huldah Ann DeJarnette daughter of Daniel and Huldah DeJarnette died 13th of Jan. 1827.
Virginia daughter of Daniel and Huldah DeJarnette died 14th of Sept. 1829.
Mary Virginia daughter of Daniel and Huldah DeJarnette died 26 July 1832.
Jane Tullock G. DeJarnette daughter of Daniel and Huldah DeJarnette & wife of George Tyler died 1st of Jan. 1841.
Daniel DeJarnette died 22nd Sept. 1850.
Huldah Hawes DeJarnette wife of Daniel DeJarnette died July 1st 1861.

Elliott DeJarnette son of D.C. DeJarnette & Louisa Jane DeJarnette died Nov. 14, 1898.

Edmund Tompkins DeJarnette Born Aug.-22-1897 married 1st Emily Redd Carter born April 5th 1904 Died May 7th 1856. 2nd wife Rosamond Bering Born July 3rd 1897 Married Nov. 18th 1957.

Rosamond & Edmund were killed in an automobile Wednesday July 13th 1966. Edmund had 2 children by first wife Jane Elliott DeJ. Born Oct 10th 1936 & Edmund Tompkins DeJ. Jr. Born Jan. 15, 1938.

DICKINSON FAMILY BIBLE NO. 1

This Bible was published by Langdon Coffin, Boston, in 1830. A typewritten copy is in the Dickinson folder of the George H.S. King Papers, Virginia Historical Society, which is reproduced here. The seat of this family was "Chestnut Valley" in the upper end of Caroline County on U.S. Route 2 and had a summer home at "Moon's Mount", a 1,000 acre estate on Route 17 in Caroline County near Port Royal.

John & Jane H. Dickinson were married at Chestnut Valley in Caroline, the seat of her father, James Dickinson, by the Rev. Edward McGuire, Pastor of the P. Church in Fredericksburg on the 25th day of May 1820.

John was born 22nd of November 1790 at Planter's Farm in Caroline
 His parents were David and Ann Coleman. David the only son of
 Thomas and Elizabeth Page.

Jane is the only daughter of James Dickinson of Chestnut Valley
 in Caroline and Sarah Jones. James was the eldest son of Thomas Cooper Dickinson of Essex. Jane was born the 8th December 1803.

John Fayette Dickinson, first born of John & Jane H., was born the 29th of April 1821 at Bowling Green. Fair skin, blue eyes and chesnut hair.

James Edward Dickinson born 31st August 1822 at Chestnut Valley. Fair skin, hazel eyes and light hair. James Edward Dickinson and Ellen C. Middleton were married in Fredericksburg, Virginia the residence of her father, Henry O. Middleton, on the evening
 of the 30th of October 1844 by the Rev. Edward C. McGuire, pastor of the P. Episcopal Church of that place.

Addison Boliver Dickinson was born the 10th September 1824 at the Bowling Green. Brown complexion and black hair.

Addison Boliver, 3rd son of John & Jane H. Dickinson, departed this life at the Summer House at Moon's Mount on the 10th day of August 1825 after a protracted attack of Cholera infantum and was intered in the family graveyard at Chestnut Valley by the side of his Grandfather. He was a child of rare beauty.

Sarah Ann Dickinson was born at Moon's Mount the 21st of February 1826. Of brown complexion, black hair and eyes.

John Goodwin and Sarah Ann Dickinson were married at the Mount by the Rev. William Friend on the 3rd day of December 1844.

William Henry Dickinson was born in Fredericksburg the 16th of June 1828. Fair complexion, chesnut [sic] hair and black eyes.

Ellen Coleman Dickinson was born at Moon's Mount the 4th day of January 1830. Black hair and eyes.

Henry Byrd Lewis and Ellen C. Dickinson were married at Nottingham by the Rev. William Friend, October 18, 1849.

Edgar Dickinson was born at Moon's Mount the 30th of June 1832. Fair skin and black eyes; a large handsome child.

Edgar Dickinson departed this life at the Mount on the 25th day of March 1841 and was intered [sic] in the family graveyard by the side of his Father.

John Dickinson, the father of the aforementioned seven children, departed this life at the Mount on the 6th day of December 1835 and was interred in the family graveyard at Chestnut Valley.

Jane D. Goodwin, first born of John and Sarah Ann Goodwin, was born on the 26 of December 1845. Fair skin and blue eyes.

Hellen [sic] Goodwin was born on the 3rd of March 1847 at Woodland, Caroline County. Black eyes and hair.

Mildred Dickinson, first born of James and Ellen, was born the 13th of June 1847 with blue eyes and fair skin at Moon's Mount.

Ellen Byrd Lewis, first born of Henry B. and Ellen C. was born the 5th of August 1850. Black eyes and hair.

[There is a newspaper obituary pasted in the Bible]:

"Obituary

Died in Burleson County, Texas, December 23rd 1864, of congestive fever, Mrs. Sarah A., wife of John Goodwin, Esq., in the 30 year of her age. She was a daughter of John Dickinson, Esq., of Moon's Mount, Caroline County, Va. She professed religion about 16 years previously to her death, and united herself with the Baptist Church. In the year 1857 she removed to this State with her husband and family. Her husband and nine children, besides many relatives and friends in this and her native State mourn her untimely departure from mortal life. [Long eulogy follows] Triumphing through Christ, the great Conqueror, she fell asleep to await the mourn [sic] of the ressurection [sic].

January 14, 1865   W.C.C."

DICKINSON FAMILY BIBLE NO. 2

This Bible was published by the American Bible Society, New York, 1852. This is a second Bible of the Dickinson family of "Chestnut Valley", Caroline County. A photostat copy is found in the Dickinson folder of the George H.S. King Papers, Virginia Historical Society, from which this copy is reproduced.

John Fayette Dickinson was married to Virginia Saunders the 27th of June 1848 By the Rev. John P. McGuire. Virginia was the eldest child of Jno. Saunders & Sophia Bentley, of Loretta Essex Co.

Jno. F. Dickinson was born 29th April 1821 at Bowling Green county seat of Caroline Va. His parents were Jno. Dickinson and Jane Dickenson.

Minnie Walton Dickinson daughter of Jno. & Virginia was married to William W. Brown, at St. John's Church, King George Co. Va. by the Rev. Edward McGuire on the 5th July 1876.

Ada Virginia, third daughter of Jno. & Virginia, was married to Albert Turner Smith, second Son of Lieut. Wm Taylor Smith of Canning, by the Rev. Edward McGurie at Berry Plain the family seat, on 31st October 1877.

Jno. Saunders Dickinson was married to Allie Marie Lewis, second daughter of Fielding Lewis of Marmion, King George County, Va. on Tuesday 23 of November 1880.

Sophia B. Dickinson and Archille Murat Willis were married at Berry Plain on the 10th of March 1885.

Loula Estelle Dickinson and Forest Plater Tayloe were married at Berry Plain on the 1st day of March 1881.

Virginia G. Dickinson & Charles Tiernan Darling were married at Berry Plain Sat. Oct. 5th 1907. One daughter.

Virginia Klingle Darling & Webster Vincent Grymes were married in Washington Oct 5th 1930.

Loula Estel Dickinson and Forest Plater Taylor were married at Berry Plain the 1st day of March 1881.

Mary Ellen Dickinson born August 23rd 1850 at Berry Plain King George Cty Va.

Wm Cooper Dickinson born Aug 9th 1852 at Berry Plain King George Cty Va.

Minnie Walton Dickinson born December 23rd 1854 at Berry Plain King George Cty Va.

Jno Saunders Dickinson born December 23rd 1854 at Berry Plain King George Cty Va.

Sophia Bently Dickinson born June 6th 1859 at Berry Plain King George Cty Va.

Ada Virginia Dickinson born 31st May 1856 at Wheatland Essex Cty, Va.

Loula Estelle Dickinson born Aug 18th 1861 at Berry Plain King George Cty Va.

Robert Edward Dickinson born June 24th 1863 at Berry Plain King George Cty Va.

Mahlon Welby son of Minnie Walton & Wm. W. Brown, was born at Wavely, Jan 16th 1877 King George Cty Va.

Mary Imogen Lewis Dickinson Daughter of Jno & Attie Dickinson was born on Saturday 13th August 1881 at Marmion King George County Va. Died 1886.

Virginia Saunders[Saunders crossed through]Gertrude Dickinson 2nd daughter of John & Attie was born at Berry Plain Sept. 5th 1883.

Estelle Pollock 3rd daughter of John & Attie Dickinson born at Berry Plain Nov. 29 1885.

Zola 4 child of Attie & Jno Dickinson born Dec. 17. 1887 died March 13. 1890.

Ada Virginia Dickinson, daughter of Jno F. Dickinson & Virginia Saunders born at Wheatland Essex Co May 31st 1856 - Died at her home Adalbert [near Dogue in King George County].

Minnie Gertrude daughter of Ada Virginia & Albert Turner Smith, born at Berry Plain October 17th 1878.

Wm Taylor Smith born at Adalbert Apr 10th 1882 2nd child of Albert and Ada.

Helen Virginia Grymes daughter of Va. & Webster V. Grymes born Dec 5 1831 at Berry Plain.

Fielding Lewis Dickinson born at Marmion Feb. 5, 1894.

George Forest Dickinson born at Marmion July 3, 1895.

Imogen Lewis Dickinson born at Marmion October 9, 1898.

Nancy Louise Dickinson 1st dau of Louise & Fielding Dickinson born Wheatland Essex Aug. 31st 1918.

Elizabeth Randolf Dickinson born Sept 11th 1919 at Wheatland.

Mary Imogen [Lewis Dickinson born August 13th 1881] Died 1886 [written in pencil].

Mary Imogen born 22 May 1921 at Wheatland.

Fielding Lewis born June 27th 1928.

Mary Ellen Dickinson died the 23d twenty third of November eighteen hundred and fifty two 1852.

Virginia G. Dickinson wife of Jno F. Dickinson departed this life Jan 24th 1874.

Robert Edward youngest son os Jno & Virginia Dickinson was drowned on the 4th of August 1878 at Saunder's Wharf in Essex, where he was staying with his uncle Dr. Walton Saunders.

Wm C. Dickinson died at Wheatland Essex Co. Va. Jan. 21st 1932.

Zola Lewis Dickinson 2nd wife of Jno Dickinson died at Berry Plain May 28 1953 buried at Marmion 3rd May.

Attie Maria Lewis wife of Jno S. Dickinson died at Marmion 16 of March 1890 just four days after her little daughter Zola.

Virginia G. Dickinson wife of Chas Tiernan Darling died at Berry Plain Feb. 27 1913 buried at Marmion.

John S. Dickinson died in the Mary Washington Hos. August 3rd 1937 at 8:15 o'clock Age 82 & 8 months buried at Marmion.

Chas. Tiernan Darling husband of Virginia G. Dickinson died April 1919 buried at Marmion.

Ada Va. Dickinson wife of Albert Turner Smith died at her home Adalbert Dec. 9 1953.

Louise Broaddus & Fielding Lewis Dickinson married St Marys Rectory Sep 25, 1917 in Fredericksburg, Va.

4 children

Nancy

Betsy

Imogen married 1942

Fielding Lewis

Imogen married at Wheatland, Loretta, Essex Co Virginia Norman V. McElroy May 2, 1942.

lst. Norman V. McElroy Jr. Born June 1 1946.

2nd Nancy Elizabeth McElroy Born Jan 9, 1960.

Elizabeth Randolph Dickinson married Peter Bance June 16, 1950 St. Timothy Church, Tappahannock.

Children

Peter Charles Bance Nov 28, 1951

Edgar John Dickinson Bance Jan. 19, 1953.

Fielding the 4th child of Louise & Dielding D. married Laura Walton. 3 children.

DICKINSON FAMILY BIBLE NO. 3

This Bible originally belonged to David Dickinson (1756-1812) of Caroline County, Virginia and later passed into the possession of Mrs. Benjamin Early, nee Emma Dickinson of Caroline County, Virginia, great-granddaughter of David Dickinson through his second wife, Mary West, who resided in Pratt-on-Kanawa, West Virginia. The entries appear to be in the handwriting of David Dickinson and the entries deal largely with his first marriage to Ann Coleman and their children. A typewritten copy of the Bible made by George H.S. King in 1947 is in the Virginia Historical Society.

David Dickinson Born May 29, 1756.
Ann Dickinson Born October 29, 1756.
David and Ann his Wife were Married the 24th Day of November 1774, by the Reverend Archibald Dick.
The Ages of their Children--
Francis Coleman Dickinson born August 31, 1775 - Gossops Mr. Richard Johnson, Mrs. Hannah Coleman, Miss Aggatha Dickinson.
Betsey Wuiatt [Wyatt] Dickinson born June 10, 1777 - Gossops Mr. William Harrison, Mr. Thomas Jones, Mrs. Johnson, Miss Dorithy Bingir, Miss Fanny Coleman.
Lucy Dickinson born December 10, 1778. Mr. Phil Johnson, Mr. Charles Woolfolk, Mr. Dudley George, Mrs. Johnson, Mrs. Oliver.
Thomas Dickinson born August 9, 1780. Mr. Thomas Coleman, Mr. John Oliver, Mrs. Lucy George, Mrs. Ann Dickinson.
Ann Dickinson born October 26, 1782. Mr. Thos. Guy, Mr. George Guy, Miss Fanny Wortham, Miss Molly George.
Fanny Dickinson Born June 30, 1784. Mr. Vivion Minor, Mr. Sam Coleman, Miss Ann Woolfolk, Miss Jane Coleman.
David Dickinson Born Sept. 1, 1785. Mrs. Thos. Guy, Mr. John Sutton, Mr. William Dickinson, Mrs. Guy, Mrs. Watkins.
Samuel Dickinson Born October 6, 1787. Mr. Reuben George, Captain Mickleburough, Miss Lucy Chew Coleman.
John Dickinson Born October 22, 1789.
William Dickinson Born February 23, 1792. [went to Kentucky]
Lucy Dickinson Born Febry the 14 day 1794.
James O Kelly Dickinson Born March the 25 day 1796.
James O. Kelly Dickinson Departed this life February 3, 1799.
Ann Dickinson [his wife, nee Ann Coleman] Departed this life August 25, 1798.
[Two sons by his second wife, Mary West, as follows]
The ages of David and Mary Dickinson's sons Robert and George.
Robert Dickinson born June 28, 1805.
George W. Dickinson born October 2, 1802.

DICKINSON FAMILY BIBLE NO. 4

This Bible was published by The American Bible Society, New York, 1852. On the fly leaf: "Berry Plain Bible of the Dickinson Family", King George County, Virginia. A copy of this Bible record is located in the George H.S. King Papers, Virginia Historical Society. The Bible was in the possession of Miss Estelle Dickinson, King George, Virginia in 1973. For additional information concerning this family, see *Genealogies of the Families of the Presidents* by R.B. Henry.

John Fayette Dickinson was born 29th April 1821 at Bowling Green the county seat of Caroline County. His parents were John Dickinson and Jane Dickinson. He was married the 27th June 1848 at Loretto by the Rev. John P. McGuire to Virginia G. Saunders, oldest child of John Saunders and Sophia Bentley of Loretto, Essex County, Virginia.

Virginia G. Saunders Dickinson died January 24th, 1874.

Captain John F. Dickinson died October 1st 1902, aged 83 years.

The following children of Captain John F. and Virginia G. (Saunders) Dickinson were born at Berry Plain, King George County, Virginia, viz: (except #5)

Mary Ellen Dickinson born August 23rd 1850; died November 23, 1852.

William Cooper Dickinson born August 9th; died at Wheatland, Essex County, Va., January 21st 1932.

Minnie Walton Dickinson born December 23rd 1854; married July 5, 1876, William W. Brown.

John Saunders Dickinson born December 23, 1854 [twin to Minnie]. He m. 23rd November 1880, Attaway Maria Lewis, daughter of Fielding Lewis of "Marmion", King George County; she died at "Marmion", 16th of March 1890 four days after her little daughter, Zola. He m. [secondly] Helen Osceola [Zola] Lewis, sister of his first wife who died at "Berry Plain", 28th May 1953. John S. Dickinson died 3rd August 1937 at the Mary Washington Hospital, Fredericksburg, Va., aged 82 years and 8 months. He is buried at "Marmion" as are his two wives.

Ada Virginia Dickinson was born 31st May 1856 at "Wheatland", in Essex County, Va., the seat of her maternal grandparents. Ada Virginia Dickinson was married to Albert Turner Smith, second son of Lieut. William Taylor Smith at "Canning", by the Rev. Edward McGuire, at Berry Plain, the family seat, on 31st October 1877. She died at her home, "Adalbert", near Dogue in King George County, on 9th December 1953 and was buried at Emmanuel Church at Port Conway, King George County. Albert Turner Smith died 22nd May 1883 by a tractor accident and was buried at "Canning" and later removed to Emmuel Churchyard. This couple had a son and a daughter.

Sophia Bentley Dickinson was born 6 June 1859 at "Berry Plain" and was married there on the 10th of March 1885 to Achille Murat Willis.

Loula Estelle Dickinson was born 18th August 1861 at "Berry Plain", and was married there on the 1st day of March 1881 to Forrest Plater Tayloe. She died the 5th of March 1956 at "Ferry Farm", Stafford County, Va., the ancestral seat of her husband's ancestor, Captain Augustine Washington, father of General George Washington.

Robert Edward Dickinson was born at "Berry Plain", 24th June 1863, the youngest son of John and Virginia G. (Saunders) Dickinson. He was drowned on the 4th of August 1878 at Saunder's Wharf in Essex where he was staying with his uncle, Dr. Walton Saunders.

William Cooper Dickinson married Ann Daingerfield Lewis [issue]

Fielding Lewis Dickinson, born at "Marion" Feb. 5, 1894; married Sept. 25, 1917 at St. Mary's Rectory in Fredericksburg, Virginia, Louise Broaddus - four children: Nancy, Betsy, Imogen and Fielding Lewis Dickinson.

George Forrest Dickinson, born at "Marmion" July 3, 1895, married 23rd July 1940, Anna Paige Green.

Imogen Lewis Dickinson born at "Marmion October 9, 1898.

Mahlon Welby, only child of William W. and Minnie Walton (Dickinson) Brown, born 16th

January 1877 at "Waverley" in King George County, Va.

Children of John Saunders Dickinson and Attaway Maria Lewis:

Mary Imogene Lewis Dickinson, born 13th August 1881 at "Marmion". _____ Died 1886.

Virginia Gertrude Dickinson was born 5th of September 1883 at "Berry Plain", and married there 5th of October 1907, Charles Tierman Darling. She died 27 February 1913 at "Berry Plain", and he died April 1919; both are buried at "Marmion". Their only child, Virginia Klingle Darling.

Estelle Pollock Dickinson was born the 29th November 1885 at "Berry Plain".

Zola Dickinson, the fourth child of John and Attie Dickinson, was born 17th December 1887 and died 13th March 1890.

[children of Albert Turner and Ada Virginia (Dickinson) Smith}:

Minnie Gertrude was born 17th October 1878 at "Berry Plain".

William Taylor Smith was born 10 April 1882 at Adalbert", in King George County, Virginia.

There is a picture in the Bible of Robert S. Saunders, of Mississippi, brother to Mrs. John F. Dickinson.

DICKINSON/COLLINS FAMILY BIBLE

This Bible was published by the American Bible Society, New York, 1850. It was owned by the Dickinson family who lived at the old Dickinson family house on Main Street, Bowling Green, Virginia. This estate of some 900 acres was also known as "Robin's Roost" and later as the "Rains House". Members of the Dickinson family, including the graves of Festus Dickinson and his wife are buried in a cemetery just back of the house. This Dickinson family came to Caroline County from Pennsylvania and earlier members of this family founded Dickinson College in Carlysle, Pennsylvania. The Bible was originally owned by Julia M. and William F. Dickinson. In 1953, the Bible was owned by Elizabeth "Bess" Collins Liver, who was living in Gallion, Alabama, where her Collins ancestors went from Caroline in the late 1800's. They lived at "Landor" in Caroline County, where Joseph Todd Collins and Susan Wood Collins are buried. Elizabeth Collins Liver is now dead. For further information concerning this Collins family, see *The History and Genealogy of the Collins Family of Caroline County, Virginia and related families*, by Herbert Ridgeway. The Dietz Press, Richmond, Virginia, 1954. Laurel Grove and Hedge Hill mention here are names of family homes. A copy of this Bible was placed by Elizabeth Collins Liver in the Library of Virginia in 1953.

William Festus Dickinson Born July 7, 1823. Son of Samuel Coleman and Evalina Pendleton Dickinson.

Julia Magruder Dickinson Born 1831. Daughter of William Festus and Elizabeth Brashear Dickinson.

Married on the 11th of January, 1849 - William F. and Julia M. Dickinson at Laurel Grove, Virginia.

Died near Washington, D.C. at ten o'clock on the night of October 25, 1860 Julia M. Dickinson, wife of W.F. Dickinson, in the 29th year of her life.

Died at Gallion, Alabama, July 13, 1908 - William F. Dickinson. He was 85 years old.

Born on the 7th of June 1853 - Elizabeth B. daughter of Wm. F and Julia M. Dickinson.
Born on the 3rd of February, 1853 - John Walter Collins, son of Joseph Todd and Susan Wood Collins.
Married on the 5th of February, 1880, at Hedge Hill, Alabama - J. W. Collins and Lizzie B. Dickinson.
Died at Gallion, Alabama, June 4th, 1926 - John Walter Collins, age 73 yr.
Died at Gallion, Alabama, January 20, 1930 - Elizabeth D. Collins, wife of J.W. Collins, age 76.
Born on Saturday the 23rd of June, 1883 - John Walter, son of J. W. and Lizzie B. Collins.
Married on the 5th of February, 1880, at Hedge Hill, [Gallion]. Alabama - J. W. Collins and Lizzie B. Dickinson.
Died at Gallion, Alabama, June 4th, 1926 - John Walter Collins, age 73 yrs.
Died at Gallion, Alabama, January 20, 1930 - Elizabeth D. Collins, wife of J. W. Collins, age 76.
Born on Saturday the 23rd of June, 1883 - John Walter, son of J. W. and Lizzie B. Collins.
Born on the 16th of August, 1921 - John Walter Collins III, son of John Walter and Garnette Collins.
Married on the 27th of July, 1946, at Evanston, Ill, John W. Collins III and Virginia W. Mowry.

DODD FAMILY BIBLE

The family register from The New Testament, published in Edinburgh, was included in the pension application for services in the American Revolution and was published in the *American Revolutionary Pension Applications* by John Frederick Dorman, Volume 30, p.48. The New Testament belonged to Thomas Dodd and Anne Dillon, his wife, who were married 27 Oct 1768 in Caroline County Virginia by Parson Thomas Morton, an Episcopal minister at the Creek Church, Drysdale Parish (later St. Asaph's Parish) Caroline County. She was born in nearby Stafford County and was about 18 years old when she married. In about 1809, she and her husband, Thomas Dodd moved to Kentucky.

Thomas Dodd and Anne his wife was married the 27 of October in the year of our Lord 1768.
Henre [Henry] Dodd was Born September 12 1769.
Molle Dodd was Born Febuwary 18 1774.
Sallie Dodd was Born [Jan]uwary 15 1776.
_____ Dodd was born ____ 12 1781.
____an Dodd Son of [H]enre Dodd was [bo]rn May 15th 1788.
____is Abot Son of Joseph [Eales?] w[as] born June 22d 1793.
Mary abet Was Born October 11 1795.

Additional information not in Bible record, but found in Caroline County records:
In 1778 Mary Dodd had a husband in the Armed Forces and was awarded assistance money of 10 pounds.
Molly Dodd married Jessee Raines in Caroline County 1 Dec 1796 by Rev. Henry Goodloe.
John Dodd married Lucy Poe in Caroline County 2 Jan 1790 by Rev. John Shackleford.
Nancy Dodd married Thomas Harris in Caroline County 27 Jan 1803 by Rev. William Kenyon.
Mary Ann Dodd married Richard Jones in Caroline County 28 Oct 1822, bondsman Henry H.

Dodd.

DONAHOE FAMILY BIBLE

This Bible was published by B.F. Johnson & Co., Richmond, Va., 1885. It contains the "Temperance Pledge" page and signed by Emma F. Donahoe in Dec. 1902. The Bible originally belonged to Archibald Donahoe and his wife who lived where the Russell Stover Candy Outlet Store is presently located (2007). The walled-in cemetery is nearby where the family is buried. Archibald Donahoe served in the Confederate Army. Some of the other members of this family are buried in another cemetery across Rogers Clark Boulevard (route 207) from the present Russell Stover Candy Outlet Store. The Bible has recently been given by a member of the Donahoe family to Helen Cross Covington, Ruther Glen, Caroline County, Virginia.

This certifies that the rite of Holy Matrimony was celebrated between A. [Archibald] Donahoe of Caroline Co. and Martha J. Richardson of Caroline Co. on March 28, 1867 at St. Margaret's by Rev. L.W. Allen.

MARRIAGES
  Ada J. Donahoe & John B. Covington June 27, 1886
  Mattie E. Donahoe & Jos. T. Bryant Nov. 4, 1888
  Sallie E. Donahoe & Willie E. Baughan Nov. 14, 1894
  J.L. Donahoe & (1) Mamie L. Mitchell Aug. 11, 1897
  J.L. Donahoe & (2) Minnie LaLonde [no date]
  W.F. Donahoe & Lucy I. Baughan Sep. 28, 1905
  Mary A. Donahoe & Harry E. Mervin Sept. 3, 1907
  Inez L. Donahoe & William Madison Dec. 6, 1913
  Geo. D. Donahoe & Edith Coates Dec. 16, 1914

BIRTHS
  A. [Archibald] Donahoe born Jan 23, 1842
  Martha J. Donahoe born July 26, 1846.
  Ada J. Donahoe born July 1, 1868.
  Mattie E. Donahoe born Feb. 27, 1870.
  Julian L. Donahoe born June 11, 1872.
  Sallie E. Donahoe born Oct. 15, 1874.
  Julian L. Donahoe born Nov. 1, 1876.
  Willie F. Donahoe born Sept. 27, 1878.
  Mary A. Donahoe born May 20, 1881.
  Emma Floyd Donahoe born June 11, 1884.
  Inez Lynette Donahoe born Aug. 2, 1886.
  George D. Donahoe born Sept. 27, 1889.

DEATHS
  Julian L. Donahoe died July 11, 1874.
  Sallie E. Baughan died Feb. 28, 1916.
  Arch [Archibald] Donahoe died July 21, 1923.

Martha Donahoe died Mar. 12, 1923.
J.L. Donahoe died Mar. 27, 1943.
Emma Donahoe died May 30, 1943.
William F. Donahoe died Mar. 30, 1962.

DORSEY FAMILY BIBLE

This Bible was published by William W. Harding, Philadelphia in 1868. It was owned by Miss Margaret Dorsey, Bowling Green, Caroline County, Virginia until her death in 2002. It is now owned by her niece, Deborah Worthington Dorsey Trebilcock in New York City. The Bible was originally owned by Charles Ridgely Dorsey. This family is descended from the Dorsey and Ridgely families of Maryland. A complete genealogy of these two families appeared in *The Sun*, Baltimore, Maryland, January 12, 1908, written by Emily E. Lantz. Charles Ridgely Dorsey was born at Ellicott City, Howard County, Maryland. He served in the Confederate Army. After the War, he came to Caroline County and married Catherine Collins, daughter of George Todd Collins of "Hickory Grove", Penola, Caroline County. After her death, he married her sister, Margaret Ann Collins. He and his two wives are all buried in the cemetery at Hickory Grove.

Charles Ridgely Dorsey and Catharine Virginia Collins were married April 15th 1869.
Charles Ridgely Dorsey and Margaret Ann Collins were married December 28th 1871.
George Ridgely Dorsey and Estelle Shuman were married June 20, 1904.
Ridgely Corbin Dorsey and Leona Catherine Fehler married January 12, 1935.
Deborah Worthington Dorsey married William Anthony Trebilcock September 9, 1961.
Ridgely Corbin Dorsey and Frances E. Kirk married Jan 14, 1966.
Charles Ridgely Dorsey was born January 20th 1835.
Catharine Virginia Collins was born November 10th 1841.
Children of Chas R. & Catharine V. Dorsey.
Mary Ridgely Dorsey was born at half past three o'clock A.M. on the third day of December 1870.
Charles Samuel Worthington Dorsey was born at five minutes past five o'clock P.M. on the third day of December 1870.
Margaret A. Collins (Dorsey) was born Feb 10th 1838. Died Feb 21st 1919.
Child of Ridgely Corbin Dorsey and Leona Fehler Dorsey.
Deborah Worthington Dorsey, born Nov. 29, 1938.
Evelyn Dorsey Trebilcock born December 11, 1967.
Paul Ridgely Trebilcock born April 25, 1969.
Children of C.R. Dorsey & Margaret A. his wife.
George Collins [Collins lined through] Ridgely Dorsey was born November 18th 1872.
Children of Stella Shuman Dorsey and George Ridgely Dorsey:
Margaret Comfort Worthington Dorsey, born April 27, 1905.
Ridgely Corbin Dorsey, born January 15, 1907.
Catharine Virginia Dorsey beloved wife of C. Ridgely Dorsey died at 7 o'clock A.M. December

10th 1870.

C. Ridgely Dorsey the son of Charles S.W.D. and M.P. Dorsey died at half past 4 o'clock July 10th 1874.

Margaret Ann Dorsey, sister of Catharine Virginia and second wife of C. Ridgely Dorsey, died February 21, 1919.

Charles Samuel Worthington Dorsey, only son of C. Ridgely and Catharine V. Dorsey died November 15th 1871.

Mary Ridgely Dorsey only daughter of C. Ridgely Dorsey and Catharine V. Dorsey died July 1st 1872.

Stella Shuman Dorsey died Feb. 7, 1935 .

George Ridgely Dorsey died February 13, 1961.

Frances E. Dorsey died August 5, 1982.

Ridgely Corbin Dorsey died January 20, 1990.

DOWNING FAMILY RECORD

This is probably taken from a Downing Bible and probably owned at one time by Mrs. Ellen Downing of Bowling Green. The Downing family lived at the site of the first courthouse at Bowling Green which was located near the present New Yorker Restaurant on what was called the head of the courthouse creek branch. The name of the place was called "Rock Spring" after it was acquired by Mary Downing and her husband Thomas Cornet Rixey. This house burned about 1909. Buried here were Thomas Cornet Rixey Sr., husband of Mary E. Downing who died November 6, 1853 at age 39 years and Ellen Downing Rixey, daughter of Thomas C. and Mary E. Downing Rixey, born August 30, 1851 and died at the age of 3 years. Mary Ellen Downing Rixey and other members of the Rixey family are buried in Lakewood Cemetery, Bowling Green, Virginia. The whereabouts of the Rixey family Bible is not known. It was owned by Mrs. Andrew Taylor of Whites, Caroline County, in 1933. For more information concerning the Rixey family, see *The Rixey Family* by Randolph P. Rixey, 1933. This record was furnished by Mary Boulware Campbell of Redmond, Washington.

The original Downing property joined the Hoomes estate on the north east corner and encompassed a large area, which is now in the Fort A.P. Hill area. At the time the Fort took the place in 1941, it had dwindled to 140 acres and was owned by the Garrett family. Members of the Downing family were moved from their private cemetery to Greenlawn Cemetery, Bowling Green, Virginia. Those included Rufus Downing, who died in 1844 at age 61; William S. Downing, who died in 1848 at age 73, John P.[Pendleton] Downing, who died in 1856 at age 33 years, Fanny Downing, and four unmarked and unknown graves. Fanny Downing, the mother of John Pendleton Downing who was born in 1824, was still living in 1850 at the age of 60, which would make her born around 1790. The Death Register of Caroline County shows John P. Downing as having died in September of 1857 at age 30 of typhoid fever leaving a wife Frances Downing and father-in-law Robert Hudgin. This conflicts by one year from the Bible record.

John Pendleton Downing and his wife Lelia E. Morris, mentioned in the Bible record are both buried in Lakewood Cemetery, Bowling Green, Virginia.

Four miles north of Bowling Green on the west side of Route 2 was another home of the Downing family, called "River Hill". This house was built in the second half of the 19th century by members of the Downing family and was later owned by the Rixey family, This place probably fell on what is today Paige Road.

[Beginning of Bible record]
Eleanor Walker Hudgin, daughter of Robert Hudgin and Sarah Richards Graham Hudgin, was born July 12, 1832 and died in April 1906.
Eleanor Walker Hudgin married in 1853 to John Pendleton Downing who died in 1856 before the birth of his younger son.
Their children were:
Robert Hudgin Downing born 1854.
John Pendleton Downing, [Jr] born Dec. 19, 1856.
Robert Hudgin Downing married in Tyler, Texas, and had two children: James Loftin Downing and Ellen Walker Downing.
John Pendleton Downing [Jr] married Lelia E. Morris on Nov. 12, 1884. Their children were:
Ellen Hudgin Downing, born Oct. 22, 1888.
Annie Morris Downing, born Dec. 31, 1890.
John Pendleton Downing, [III], born June 5, 1893, Died June 30, 1895.
Charles Dabney Downing, born July 19, 1895.
Elizabeth Winston Downing, born Dec. 7, 1897.
Robert Graham Downing, born April 23, 1900.
Edmund Morris Downing, born July 28, 1902.
Alice Scott Downing, born Feb. 21, 1905.

Printed newspaper death notice:
Mrs. E.W. Downing. Mrs. Ellen W. Downing died Friday night in her home at Robert T. Glassell's after an illness since last Tuesday, the 73d year of her age. She was the daughter of the late Robert Hudgin, who for many years was clerk of Caroline county court, and was a sister of the late Captain John M. Hudgin. She leaves two sons-John P. Downing, of Kirkwood, Ga., and Robert H. Downing of Tyler, Tex. She is survived by a brother Judge Walter G. Hudgin at Hinton, W. Va. And a sister, Mrs. Willie Boulware, of Kansas City, Mo.

DUDLEY PRAYER BOOK

The family data here is taken from what is termed "Charles Dudley's Book", which is actually a Prayer Book and Psalms printed by Alexander Kinkaid, Edinburg, 1768. Charles Dudley lived in Caroline County, Virginia and in Surrey County, North Carolina. The family named "Poore" was connected with the Magruder family in Caroline County and then there was Ben Perley Poore's family in Washington, D.C. The author has not tried to make any connections with that family to this family.

Mary Dudley Daughter of Charles & Elizabeth Dudley was Born June the 23 1806.

Nancy Dudley Daughter of Charles & Elizabeth [illeg] was Born April the 10 1802.
Charles Poore was Born December 5, 1822.
Robert Poore son of Thos. & Nancy was born May 4 1830.
Charles Dudley Born Decr. 21st 1750.
Mary Dudley Born July 14th 1749.
Judith Dudley Born 5th Day of May 1770.
Robert Dudley Born 30th Day of Dec. 1772.
Daughter and Son of Charles and Mary Dudley [no further information listed]

DUDLEY/EATON FAMILY BIBLE

This Bible record is found in the Revolutionary War pension application papers and was reprinted in the *National Genealogical Society Quarterly*, Vol XXXII, No. 4, p.112, December, 1944. The record concerns the family of Guilford Dudley, son of Christoper and Elizabeth Dudley of Caroline County. Guilford Dudley was born in Caroline County, Va. April 17, 1756 and married Anna Bland Easton at Halifax, N.C. May 23, 1784. Anna Bland Eaton was born in Prince George County, Va. December 21, 1763, the daughter of Thomas and Anna Eaton of Bute, later Warren Co., N.C.

[Children of Guilford and Anna Bland (Eaton) Dudley]:
Frances Elizabeth, b. Woodberry, the seat of Col. Benjamin Williams in Johnson Co., N.C. 25 Feb. 1785.
Frances Bland, b. Tweedside, near Fayetteville, N.C., 30 June 1786; m. 26 Jan. 1815, Dr. Samuel Crockett of Franklin, Tenn.
Julia Ann Eaton, b. Fayetteville, N.C., 16 Oct. 1788; m. 11 Sept.1810, Dr. Elliott Hickman of Franklin, Tenn.
Theodorie Bland, b. at Mill seat, near Fayetteville, N.C., 5 May 1790.
Thomas Eaton, b. Fayetteville, N.C., 9 Aug. 1792.
Elizabeth Helen, b. Fayetteville, N.C., 18 Mar. 1794.
Sarah Bland*, b. on Appomottox River, Prince Edward Co., Va., 8 Sept. 1796. (*so christened by her own desire).
Guilford, b. Prince Edward Co., Va., 22 Jan. 1799.
Judith Randolph, b. Prince Edward Co., Va. 24 July 1800; m.Thurs, 23 May 1822, Nicholas L. Long of Maury Co., Tenn.
Caroline, b. Cumberland Co., Va., 28 Apr 1802.
Virginia, m. 9 A.M. Sun. 27 Aug 1830, Thomas Woodson Cash, Esq., Atty. at law of Franklin, Tenn.
Mary Matilda Pugh, m. Thurs. evening 6 Sept. 1830, James C. Hill, Esq., Merchant of Franklin, Tenn.

DURRETT FAMILY BIBLE

This Bible was published by Matthew Carey, Philadelphia, 1818.
It was originally the Bible of Jonathan Durrett and is now owned by Herman Baker of Woodford,

Caroline County, Virginia. The records were copied by Mrs. Bert Harter and published in *The Virginia Genealogist,* Volume 5, pp.28-30. A complete history of the Durrett family was published in the same reference in volumes 15, 16 and 17. Another Bible, that of Martin Durrett, brother to Johnathan, has been printed in *Mississippi Cemetery and Bible Records*, volume 2, at p.50 by the Mississippi Genealogical Society.

Jonathan Durrett was the son of William Durrett (28 July 1745-11 Aug. 1813) and Elizabeth Hines (2 Sept. 1746-11 Oct. 1821) of Caroline County. Jonathan Durrett was the son of Wm. and Elizabeth Hines Durrett of Caroline.

Jonathan Durrett was born April 4, 1771.
Polly H. Durrett, his wife, was born June 28, 1784.
Albert Durrett was born July 19, 1805.
William Hines Durrett was born Feb. 27, 1807.
Oscar Fitzallen Durrett was born Dec. 25, 1808.
Abigail Durrett was born Feb. 5, 1816.
Braxton Byrd Durrett was born Nov. 16, 1819.
Jonathan Jackson Durrett was born June 24, 1824.
Mary Elizabeth Durrett was born Sept. 3, 1829.
Nancy Hodges was born Aug. 7, 1797.
Mary Ann Johnson Durrett was born Dec. 4, 1828.
Martha Ellen Durrett was born Oct. 6, 1830.
Judith Terrell Durrett was born Feb. 24, 1833.
Elliott Vermanet Durrett was born Sept. 24, 1834.
Maria L. Hester was born June 15, 1837.
Mary Ann J. Carter was born Jan. 15, 1836.
William Porter Carter was born Nov. 28, 1837.
Wallis Marion Carter was born April 28, 1838.
Ellenorah Hassentine Carter was born Nov. 24, 1840.
Jonathan Melzar Carter was born March 13, 1849.
Kate Baker Durrett was born Oct. 16, 1856.
Cliveous Albert Baker was born Nov. 15, 1856.
Charles Lewis Durrett was born Apr. 14, 1859.
William Albert Durrett was born Mar. 30, 1868.
Judith T. Durrett was born May 13, 1870.
Everett Vermanet Durrett was born Apr. 18, 1872.
Robert Henry Durrett was born Mar. 18, 1874.
Mary Virginia Durrett was born Nov. 10, 1875.
Ann Lewis Durrett was born Oct. 9, 1877.
Laurence Blanton Durrett was born Mar. 25, 1880.
Harvey John Thomas Durrett was born Oct. 18, 1881.
Ann Elizabeth Blanton was born Oct. 9, 1878.
Joseph Hart Baker was born Jan. 24, 1879.
Emmet Todd Blanton was born Jun. 11, 1880.

Albert Riftin Baker was born May 22, 1881.
Richard Alfred Blanton was born May 26, 1882.
Herman Cliveous Baker was born Mar. 28, 1885.
Andrew Ellis Baker was born Mar. 6, 1888.
Jonathan Durrett and Polly H. Lively were married Oct. 23, 1804.
Albert Durrett and Nancy Hodges were married Feb. 22, 1827.
William H. Durrett and Mary I. Dunkum were married May 15, 1832.
Melzer Carter and Abigail Durrett were married Oct. 16, 1834.
Braxton Byrd Durrett and Ann E. Williams were married May 30, 1844.
Jonathan J. Durrett and Susan E. Jones were married Aug. 20, 1848.
Abner Hines and Mary Elizabeth Durrett were married Sept. 5, 1855.
Bushrod W. Baker and Judith T. Durrett were married July 26, 1855.
Elliott V. Durrett and Maria L. Hester were married Dec. 20, 1855.
Andrew Hart and Mary A.J. Durrett were married Jan. 16, 1867.
E.V. Durrett and Mary A. Blanton were married May 16, 1867.
Jonathan J. Durrett and Margaret J. Tompkins were married June 7, 1866.
Cliveous Albert Baker and Marie Lou Hart were married Dec. 19, 1877.
Oscar Pitzallen Durrett died Feb. 25, 1816.
Abigail Carter died Apr. 22, 1851.
Polly H. Durrett died May 2, 1851.
Jonathan Durrett died 9 o'clock AM Mar. 23, 1855.
Mary E. Hines died Apr. 26, 1856.
Judith T. Baker died Aug. 14, 1857.
Maria L. Durrett died Sept. 21, 1861.
Susan E. Durrett died Sept. 16, 1862.
Nancy Durrett died [illeg] 17, 1883.
Albert Durrett died Sept. 26, 1889.
Mary Ann Johnson Hart died Aug. 12, 1900.
Martha E. Durrett died Nov. 26, 1916.
Andrew Hart died Oct. 21, 1877.

DUVAL FAMILY BIBLE

This Bible was owned by Daniel DuVal and his wife Salley Carter of Caroline County. This Bible was published by Matthew Carey, Philadelphia, May 8, 1805. It was owned by Betty Douglas Hayes (Mrs. A.E. Hayes), in Fort Wayne Indiana in 1946. The notes in parentheses were made by her. The whereabouts of this Bible today is unknown. A copy of the family register is in the Library of Virginia and also at the Virginia Historical Society. The DuVal family lived in the lower end of Caroline County and the area today is locally known as "DuVal Town".
The Picardat family mentioned in the records operated a blacksmith shop at Picardati's Fork, later DeJarnette's at what is now the intersection of Mattaponi Trail and Sparta Road.

Daniel DuVal and Salley Carter married 2 December 1791.
John Bryant was married to Betsey DuVal, daughter of D. & S. DuVal, July, 1810 (day not

given).

Mary DuVal, daughter of Dan'l & Salley DuVal, was married the 3rd of January, 1812. (Groom's name not stated, but see Mary Proctor).

Lucy DuVal, daughter of Dan'l & Salley DuVal, was married to Nicholas Dillard the 11th of March, 1815.

Kitty DuVal, daughter of Dan'l & Salley DuVal, was married to William Allport the 27th of December, 1814.

John James and Ann DuVal married the 10th January, 1822. (Ann was dau. of Daniel and Salley).

Clinton Jones & Susan DuVal married 10th December in the year of our Lord, 1834. (Susan was dau. of Daniel & Salley).

George DuVal & Mary Ann Picardatt [daughter of Lewis C. Picardat] married August the 12th day 1830. (George was son of Daniel & Salley).

Richard Richards and Alice V. James married 12th January in the year of our Lord, 1838. (Alice was dau. of John James & Ann DuVal).

Daniel DuVal was born 21st February, 1770.

Salley Carter, Consort of Daniel DuVal, born 25th December, 1768.

Betsey DuVal, daughter of Dan'l & Salley DuVal, was born 9th December, 1792.

Mary DuVal, daughter of D. & S. DuVal, was born 26th December, 1793.

Lucy DuVal, daughter of aforesaid, was born September 21st, 1795.

Kitty DuVal was born May 18, 1797.

Susan DuVal was born April 5th, 1799.

Ann DuVal was born May 29th, 1801.

James DuVal was born 26th Octr 1803.

John & George DuVal, twins, born January 14th (?) 1807.

Thomas DuVal was born 3 June 1813. (Note: Kitty, Susan, Ann, James, John, George and Thomas were all children of Daniel & Salley Carter DuVal).

Thomas Bryant, son of John & Betsey Bryant, was born June 3d 1811.

Susannah Proctor, daughter of William & Mary Proctor, was born the 16th of November, 1812.

James Proctor, son of Wiliam & Mary Proctor, was born the 10th November, 1814.

Thomas Proctor, son of William & Mary Proctor, was born August the 7th 1817.

Ann Proctor, daughter of William & Mary Proctor, was born the 25th of October, 1819.

Richard Richards was born in the year of our Lord and Master, Sept 12th 1812.

Sarah DuVal, daughter of George & Mary Ann DuVal, was born May 29th day 1831.

Alice V. James was born the 1th November, 1822. ()Note: middle initial is blurred; might also be read "D" or "E").

Sarah Ann James was born 22th September, 1824.

Patsy James was born 29th December 1826.

John James was born 20th June 1829. (Note: Alice V (?), Sarah Ann, Patsy and John James were children of John James & Ann DuVal; John James, the son, was known to his family as John H. James, although the middle initial is not shown in this record).

Ann S. Miller Died August 30th, 1877, Aged 76 years, 3 months. (Note: This was Ann DuVal, dau. of Daniel & Salley Carter DuVal; she m. (1) John James; (2) a Mr. Miller).

Betsey Bryant died 24 August 1813.

John Bryant, consort of Betsey Bryant, died September 10th, 1814.

Thomas DuVal, son of D. & S. DuVal, died 2d January 1814.

John DuVal, Senior, Father of Daniel DuVal, departed this life the 7th of June in the year of our Lord 1820.

William Proctor died the 8th September in the year of our Lord 1821.

John James died the 1 July in the year of our Lord 1829. (lst husb. of Ann DuVal).

Sarah Ann James died 20th June 1826.

Alice V.(?) Richards died June 14 in the year of our Lord 1876, her fifty fourth year of life.

John DuVal died Sept 3d in the year of our Lord 1831.

Susan Jones, daughter of Dan'l & Salley DuVal, died 7th of September in the year of our Lord 1846.

Lucy Dillard died June 3rd in the year of our Lord 1849.

Sarah DuVal, consort of Daniel DuVal, died Nov. 12th in the year of our Lord 1849. (Salley).

Daniel DuVal died February 5th in the year of our Lord 1857.

James DuVal died June 19th in the year of our Lord 1860.

Kitty Allport died August 12, 1869.

Thomas Proctor died September 19th in the year of our Lord 1833.

Mary Elen [sic] Richards died August the 1. 1851.

Thomas J. Richards died Nov 7th in the year of our Lord 1865.

John W. Richards died March the 16th in the year of our Lord 1868.

Patsy Farmer died Dec. the 25th in the year of our Lord 1867.

Mary Proctor died May the 8 in the year of our Lord 1861.

ENGLAND/BRAHHAM FAMILY BIBLE

This Bible of the Bramham and England families covers the period 1796-1956 and was published by M. Carey, Philadelphia in 1815. It was owned by Dennis Jarrell Jefferies, Ruther Glen, Va. in 1990. A copy has been placed in the Virginia Historical Society.

This England family lived at "Aspen Hill" near Carmel Church in Caroline County. The house was built about 1830 by George England and was still standing in poor condition in 1937, but is now gone. There are five graves here, but only one is marked that of Ethelven Harrison England. The unmarked ones are George England, born 1792, his wife Martha H., born in 1810, John W. England, born 1841 and Clemintina T. England born 1839.

George W. England was born November 20th 1815 in the morning, son of George England & Matilda his wife.

Maria Forrest Daughter of Richard O. & Elenor Jeffries was born 24th October 1825.

John William England son of Geo. & Martha England Born December 14th 1838 in the morning at 3 o'clock.

Ethelven Harrison England Born March 20th 1814.

Maria Jackson Vass the Daughter of John & Adalaide his wife was Born July 31st 1856.

Etta James Born June 8th 1861.

Ann S. Bramham daughter of Benjamin & Jamima was born the 19th November 1828.

Benjamin Bramham Junr departed this life the day after Christmas 1811 he left a wife and three Small children to deploy his loss, to his family he was affectionate to his neighbors, he was Kind and all those who Knew him laments his death.

Benjamin Bramham Junr and Jemima Lanford Bramham, his wife was married after Great difficulty the 8th day June 1796.

Ann S. Bramham, the daughter of Benjamin and Jamima Bramham was born 39 minutes after three the 17th of May 1797 and Departed this life the 8th Day of March 1806.

Judith N. Bramham the daughter of Benjamin and Jamima was born the 4th July at night 1802 and Departed this life the 20th day of Sept. 1811.

Ellenor Ann Bramham daughter of Benjamin & Jamima was Born the 8th Day of June 1804 about 10 o'clock at night.

Pattie England died March 25, 1958.

Mary S. Bramham was born the 8th of January at 11 O'clock at night.

George W. England the Son of Geo. and Matilda England was born Novr. 20th 1815.

Mary Ann Daughter of Geo and Matilda England was born Decr 7th 1817.

Amanda Rebecker [sic, probably another spelling for Rebecca?] the Daughter of Geo and Matilda England was born March 24, 1821.

Adalaide Brent the Daughter of Geo and Matilda England was born June 2nd 1822.

Eliza June the Daughter of Geo and Matilda England was Born January 15 1825.

Quadrentus the Son of Geo and Matilda Born in Spotsylvania County Jany 25, 1822.

Maria Jackson England the daughter of G. & Martha Born the 20 of March 1830.

Martha Caroline Elenor Uginia Born Jany 3rd 1833.

Eliza Jane Born Jany. 26, 1835.

Clemmy Tina [Clementina "Clemmie" L.] Born Jany 24, 18__ [1839].

George England died Feb. 15, 1869.

Martha England, wife of George England died March 1887.

Ivord England died Dec. 22, 1903.

Maria J. England died March 6, 1893.

Martha E. England died August 18, 1917.

Eliza J. England died June 23, 1892.

Clemmie England died March 14, 1916.

John W. England died July 12, 1921.

Ethelvon Harrison England died [no date listed in Bible, but tombstone has October 6th, 1856].

ENGLAND/SUTTON FAMILY BIBLE

This Bible was published by H.M. Wharton, Baltimore, Maryland, 1881. A copy of the family register is in the Library of Virginia.

Wm. C. England of Westnd Co. Va and Emma C. Sutton of Westnd Co Va. on May 17, 1876 at Bushfield by Rev. John White of the M. E. Church. Witness C.H. Sanford.

John F. England and Emily Loving were united on the 27th day of December in the year of our Lord 1841 at Caroline County, Va. Witness Edwin B. Loving.

Kinsey Dawn England, born 27 October 1977.

Kori Rence' England born 28 September 1981 (Daughters of Wm B. Jr. and Cynthia England).
John David Slowinski born 24 June 1982.
James Craig Slowinski born 18 May 1985. (Sons of Marcia Lynn and Samuel Slowinski)
Jared Craig England born 30 April 1989 (Son of Earl Craig & Melanie England).
William Buchanan England Jr. and Cynthia Faye Glass were married 30 October 1972. Divorced 16 August 1991. (Son of Wm B. Sr. & Beatrice Jenkins England).
Earl Craig England and Melanie Paige Roadcap were Married 8 November 1985.
(Children of Ernest E. and Mabel Chatham England)
Ernest E. England and Daisy Mae Newton March 25, 1919.
William B. England and Beatrice Adeline Jenkins April 26, 1946.
Ernest E. England and Mabel Sophronia Chatham June 20, 1948. (Sons of Ernest E. & Daisy N. England)
Stuart Wilson England and Elizabeth Sanford January 13, 1944.
William Vernon England and Ernestine Nash (Kelmon, Knight) Apr 13, 1953 (Sons of Walter & Noria England) & to Lillian Bowen (2nd Marriage) June 18, 1971.
Wm C. England was born Sept. 6, 1845.
Emma C. England was born Oct. 9, 1855.
Walter H. England was born Feb. 20th 1877.
Willie C. England [twin] was born April 29, 1882.
Alfred L. England [twin] was born April 29, 1882.
Ernest E. England was born Aug. 25, 1883.
Lizzie Y. England Born May 20th 1892.
Emma K. England Born Sept. 22, 1896.
Wm B. England Born Aug. 17, 1920.
Ernest E. England Jr. Born Sept. 6, 1924.
William B. England Jr Son of William B. & Beatrice J. Boprn January 20, 1952.
Marcia Lynn England daughter of Ernest E. Jr & Mabel C. Born June 24, 1955.
Earl Craig England Son of Ernest E. Jr & Mabel C. Born January 13, 1959.
Randolph Wilson England Son of Stuart W. and Elizabeth England Born July 13, 1962.
Alfred L. England Died May 2nd, 1882.
Willie C. England Died March 17th 1885.
Lizzie Y. England Died Aug. 25, 1893.
Ernest E. England Died Nov. 30, 1943 of cancer.
Daisy N. England Died Dec. 23, 1961.
Waller H. England Died March 25, 1949.
Stuart Wilson England son of Walter & Nora England died 21 July 1967 (at age 50).
Vernon son of Walter & Nora England died Mar. 23, 1974 of a heart attack.
Ernest Earl England Jr. son of Ernest & Daisy England died March 18, 1975 at age 50 of a heart attack.
William C. England died November 24, 1926 John F. England (father of Wm C. England) died September 1, 1884 at age 70 of Typo Mil Fever (buried at Oakwood Cemetery, Richmond, Va.).

ENNIS FAMILY BIBLE

This Bible was published by William W. Harding, Philadelphia, Pennsylvania in 1869. The Ennis family has a street named for it in Bowling Green, Caroline County. This Bible originally belonged to Joseph J. Ennis, son of Samuel Ennis and Ann Moore. The Bible is now owned by Mrs. Woodford Broaddus, Gether, Caroline County, Virginia.

Joseph J. Ennis and Susan A. Bowen married September 14th 1854.
L.S. Read Sr. and Lizzie H. Ennis were married September 4th 1888.
Irving S. Ennis and Liza V. Reed were married March 31st 1891.
Joseph Ennis and Manie [sic] Doughty were married Dec 25th 1891.
Joseph Irving Ennis was borned April 11th 1822.
Susan Amanda Bowen was borned Feb 1st 1833.
Margaret Ellen daughter of Joseph Ennis and Susan his wife was borned August 4th 1855.
Mary Ann daughter of Joseph Ennis and Susan his wife was borned March 28th 1857.
Alice May daughter of Joseph Ennis and Susan his wife was borned January 12th 1859.
Irving Spence son of Joseph Ennis and Susan his wife was borned January 20th 1861.
William Moore son of Joseph Ennis and Susan his wife was borned December 8th 1862. Shot April 28th 1883 died April 30th 1883.
Joseph Ennis son of Joseph Ennis and Susan his wife was borned May 21st 1865.
Elizabeth Carcey daughter of Joseph Ennis & Susan his wife was borned April 21st 1867.
Elmer son of Joseph Ennis and Susan his wife was borned September 7th 1869.
Anna Mariah daughter of Joseph Ennis and Susan his wife was borned July the 19th 1871.
Samuel Ara son of Joseph Ennis & Susan his wife was borne June the 1st 1874.
Chas. Charlie Bowen son of Joseph Ennis and Susan his wife was born Feby 14. 1877. [this son was entered twice, first as Charlie Bowen and next as Chas. B.]
Margaret Ellen daughter of Joseph Ennis & Susan his wife died August 11th 1856 - Age 1 year and 13 days.
Mary Ann daughter of Joseph Ennis and Susan his wife, died September 28th 1859 - Age 6 months.
Alice May daughter of Joseph Ennis and Susan his wife died October 8th 1862 - Age 3 years, 8 months, 27 days.
Anna Mariah daughter of Joseph Ennis and Susan his wife died July the 29th 1872. Aged 1 year and 17 days.
Willie Moore Ennis son of Joseph J. Ennis & Susan his wife died April the 30th 1883. aged 20 years 4 months & 28 days.
Joseph J. Ennis Sr. died March 25th 1896. Aged 74 years 11 Months & 14 days - son of Samuel Ennis and Ann Moore his wife.

Also in this Bible is a newspaper death notice of Willie Ennis, son of Mr. Jos. J. Ennis, of Upshaw's neck while hunting on the Atlantic beach last Saturday. While out hunting a friend the gun of his companion accidently discharged in immediate proximity of his right leg, the whole charge entering the knee producing a frightful organization of the joint and fracture of the thigh bone. The leg was amputated on Sunday morning by Drs. Le Cato, E.B. Finnets and Mapp and every effort made to rally the young gentleman, but he died on Monday after from the shock of the injury. He was buried at Snow Hill, Md., his former home 1893. About 21 years old.

FARINHOLT FAMILY BIBLE

The Farinholt family lived at lot 19 in the town of Port Royal, Caroline County in the 18th and 19th centuries. This was the family Bible of William Farinholt, who died in 1846 and his wife Marie Kerle (or Keirle) Farinholt. This Bible has not been located, but was owned by William W. Farinholt in Atlanta, Georgia in 1973. See page 147 in Ralph Emmett Fall's *Hidden Village, Port Royal, Virginia 1744-1981*. A listing below of the information which probably appears in this Bible is reconstructed from the Census Record of 1850 and the Bureau of Vital Statistics Death Records for Caroline County. Two of the Farinholt children are buried in lot 19 on King Street in Port Royal. The family ran a hotel at Port Royal for several years.

Maria Kearle, daughter of Jno. W. Kearle, was born in Baltimore, 1810.
Maria Farinholt, daughter of Jno. W. Kearle of Baltimore, wife of William Farinholt and mother of Jno. K. Farinholt, died in Port Royal Dec. 12, 1875 at age 75.
Sarah H. Farinholt, daughter of William and Maria Kearle Farinholt, was born in 1832.
Robert Farinholt, son of William and Maria Kearle Farinholt, was born in 1833.
Emily Farinholt, daughter of William and Maria Kearle Farinholt, was born in 1834.
John Kearle Farinholt, son of William and Maria Kearle Farinholt, was born in 1835 (Postmaster at Port Royal)
Gertrude Farinholt, daughter of William and Maria Kearle Farinholt, was born in 1836.
Keirle Farinholt, son of William and Maria Kearle Farinholt, was born in 1839.
Eugene Farinholt, son of William and Maria Kearle Farinholt, was born in 1841.
Zoe Farinholt, daughter of William and Maria Earle Farinholt, was born in 1843.
Helen Emily Farinholt, daughter of William and Maria Farinholt, married Daniel Atwill and had seven children.
Robt. B. Farinholt, son of Maria Farinholt and brother of John R. Farinholt, died of hooping cough Dec. 25, 1857 at age 23. (managed and clerked in a general store in Port Royal)
Kerle Farinholt, son of William & Maria Farinholt, died of diptheria December 1862 at age 27.
Emma Farinholt, neice of John R. Farinholt, died in Port Royal of consumption Nov. 20, 1872 at age 16.
William H. Farinholt, Jr., son of Wm. Henry & Sarah Elizabeth Farinholt, was born in 1825.
Wm. Henry Farinholt, Jr., son of Wm. Henry & Sarah Elizabeth Farinholt, died Oct. 15, 1858
Ro. Farinholt, son of Wm. Henry & Sarah Elizabeth Farinholt, died Aug. 10, 1857 at age 5 months.
Louise Farinholt, daughter of Wm. Henry & Sarah Elizabeth Farinholt, died July 6, 1862.
Unnamed infant, still born daughter of E. & Emma G. Farinholt died at Port Royal Oct. 10, 1885.

FARMER FAMILY BIBLE NO. 1

This Bible, consisting of the Old and New Testament, was published by the American Bible Society, N.Y., 1837. It is in the possession of Mrs. Shirley Ball Plesur, Milford, Virginia.

Lewis Farmer son of Lewis Farmer and Susanna his wife was born

Nov. 4th 1816.

Ann Pitts was born 3rd of May 1816 and was married to Lewis Farmer 22 May 1839.

Meriallis Allis was born April 4the 1852.

[following three entries are 20th century entries]

Mariah Alice Farmer B. April 4, 1852.

Victory Farmer B. Sept. 14, 1852.

Mary Bety Farmer B. April 5, 1857.

[following entries appear to be 19th century]

William Rouse was born in 1825 the fifteenth day of September
and I hope that I shal--? W Rouse.

William Rouse and wife [no further info written. A subtraction is written beneath the Rouse entry, "1871-1823 = 48 and 1871- 1846 = 35", which should read 25].

FARMER FAMILY BIBLE NO. 2

This Bible, consisting of the Old and New Testament, was published by the American Bible Society, N.Y., 1883. It was originally owned by Pearl Farmer Morris, who lived in the Brandywine-Naulakla area of Caroline County, and now in the Fort A.P. Hill area. It passed from her to Gracie Farmer (Mrs. Ralph Chenault), daughter of Alma Farmer, granddaughter of Anderson Farmer, great-granddaughter of Samuel L. and Esther Rouse Farmer. Samuel L. Farmer was the brother of Pearl Farmer Morris. It is presently owned by Barbara Farmer Bird, Bowling Green, Virginia.

Samuel L. Farmer was born May 3, 1835.
Esther Rouse was born Sept. 21 - 1830.
John Hamilton Farmer was born Jan. 2 - 1858.
Henry Wilson Farmer was born Feb. 20, 1860.
Phemie Farmer was born Aug. 13th 1863.
Anderson H. Farmer was born Oct. 12 - 1866.
Ida Farmer was born Sept. 21 - 1868.
Baby Brother Born and died 1871.
Pearl Farmer was born April 13 - 1873.
Hauzie C. Bruce was born Oct. 12 - 1885.
Robt C. Bruce was born Oct. 6. 1889.
Sarah E. Morris. Born March 13th 1845.
Moses H. Morris. Born Jan. 18th. 1849.
Sarah E. Morris. Died Monday Dec. 19th 1904 at 10 A.M.
Moses H. Morris. Died Monday Dec. 24th 1917 at 1:48 A.M.
Samuel L. Farmer and Esther Rouse was Married July 18. 1856.
Pearl Farmer & Moses H. Morris were Married at the Parsonage of
  Union Station M.E. Church by the Rev. Mr. Potts July 30th 1908.
Frederick A[u]gusta Morris born February 10th 1888. Died November 18th 1920.
Lilliam Morris Nee Simms and Frederick A. Morris was Married March 4th 1914 by Reverand
  Engel Presbertain [sic] Minister In Elizet. City.

Virgie R. Farmer died Sept. 4th 1943.
James Leonard Farmer Died Nov. 11th 1945.
Anderson H. Farmer died May 5 - 1931.
Thomas Jackson Jordan died June 18 - 1943.
Peemie Jordan died January 27 - 1944.
Otis Arthur Farmer Died Dec. 13 - 1929.
Stephen Farmer Died June 1 - 1930.
Linda May Farmer Died Mar. 4 - 1937.
Edith May Farmer Died April 14 - 1940.
John Hamilton died Dec. 2 - 1858.
Ida Bruce died Dec. 8 - 1891.
French W. Bruce died Mar. 17 - 1904.
Robert C. Bruce died Aug. 14 - 1908.
Samuel L. Farmer died July 3 - 1913.
Esther Farmer died Feb. 27 - 1916.
Henry Wilson Farmer died September 4th 1918.

FARMER/HARDY FAMILY BIBLE

This Bible was published by John B. Perry, Philadelphia, 1853. It was given to Ann Farmer of Caroline County, Va. on the occasion
of her marriage to Thomas Lee Hardy on 16 May 1853. The Hardy family lived in Winchester, Virginia. The records were copied by Margaret Hickerson Emery and reproduced in the *Virginia Genealogical Quarterly*, Volume 19, 1881, pp.101-102.

James Young and Sarah Jane Farmer were married by the Rev. Lawrence Battaile in Caroline
  County Dec. 4th 1851.
Thomas Lee Hardy and Ann Farmer were married by the Revd Williams May 16th 1853 in the
  Town of Manchester, Chesterfield County, Va. By the Rev. Mr. Williams of Manchester.
Ann S. Farmer to Thomas L. Hardy, the former of Caroline, the latter of Winchester, Va. was
  married the 16th of May, 1853. [entered twice in two different handwritings]
Andrew B. Adams and Lucie L. Hardy were married at the Methodist Church by the Reverend
  Dr. Hough, November the 27th, 1875, Fredericksburg.
Lucy Lee Hardy, first child of Ann and Thomas Hardy, born April 14th, 1854.
Charles Churchwill Hardy, second child of Ann and Thomas Hardy,
  born Nov. 25, 1855.
William Henry Hardy was born Sept. 20th, 1857.
Thomas Wesley [Hardy] was born June 14th 1859.
Emma Jane Hardy born January 18, 1861.
Richard Lee Hardy was born April 13th 1863.
Nannie Martin Hardy born March 18th 1865.
Sarah Virginia Hardy born July 19th 1867.
Mary Lou Hardy, born October 12th 1869.
John Edward Young was born 30 Sept. 1855.

Charles Preston first child of Lucie and Andrew B. Adams,
  born Sept. the 27th, 1876.
Mary Lee Adams was born August 16, 1878.
Ernest Linwood Adams was born Sept. 21, 1880.
Bessie Adams was born Oct. 27, 1882.
Bessie Adams died June the 15th 1884.
Thomas L. Hardy died 4th of March 1885.
Thomas W. Hardy died 19th August 1894 at Colorado Springs, Colorado.
Willie H. Hardy killed 25th of July 1900.
Ann S. Hardy died 15th of March 1902.
Richard L. Hardy died 26th Aug. 1903 at Mary Washington Hospital.
Emma J. Hardy died Oct. 25th 1940.
Lucie Lee Adams died Dec. 4th 1941.
Nannie M. Hardy died May 8th 1946.

FARISH FAMILY BIBLE NO. 1

This Bible was owned in 1975 by Mrs. Roberta Farish Purvis Reed, Austin, Texas and was published in *The Virginia Genealogist*, Volume 19, pp.28-29. It was known as the Bible of Edward S. Farish, born 17 February 1791 in Caroline County, Virginia, married Sarah Goode of North Carolina, 23 April 1813 in Hopkinsville, Kentucky. Both are buried in Greenward Cemetery, Jackson, Miss.

Children of Edward S. & Sarah Goode Farish
Elizabeth B. Farish was born 8 March 1814.
Amerial Farish was born 1 June 1815.
Thomas S. Farish was born 1 April 1817.
Mary R. Farish was born 1 Dec. 1818.
Leven P. Farish was born 9 Mar. 1821.
Sarah C. Farish was born 27 March 1823.
Levinia Farish was born 10 Nov. 1825.
Robert Stevens Farish was born 26 Sept. 1827.
Edward Farish was born 29 July 1829.
George R.[or W] Farish was born 2 May 1831.
Joseph Zacharias Farish was born 21 July 1833.
Ann Eliza Farish was born 2 Oct. 1835.
Cornelia Smith Farish was born 10 July 1840.
Charles Henry Farish was born 16 June 1844.
Sarah [Goode] Farish died 23 Oct. 1851.
Edward S. Farish died 28 Sept. 1860.
Edward S. Farish was born 17 Feb. 1791 in Caroline Co.
Sarah Goode was born 4 Aug. 1797 in North Carolina.
Edward S. Farish and Sarah Goode were married 23 April 1813 in
  Hopkinsville, Christian Co., Ky.

FARISH FAMILY BIBLE NO. 2

This Bible was recorded with the Virginia Society of Colonial Dames in 1937 and a copy has been placed in The Library of Virginia. In 1937, the Bible was owned by Robert Farish Purvis in 1937. Since that time she married a Mr. Reed and lived in Austin, Texas. This was recorded in the *National Genealogical Society Quarterly*, Volume 61, p.78 and in *The Virginia Genealogist*, Volume 19, p.28. This family had its roots in Caroline County, Virginia. The title page has the following: "Present By Robt. S. Farish To his children Daniel C. Burford & Matilda D. Burford Christmas A.D. 1877". The name "Farish" is recorded in some places with two "r's". The names "Hazelwood" and "Stevens" were used by members of the family buried in Caroline County, Virginia. Stevens Farish lived at "North Point" on the Mattaponi River in Caroline County. A study of the Farish family was written by John Frederick Dorman and published in Richmond, Va. in 1967 entitled *The Farish Family of Virginia and its Forebears.* Two sons of Stevens Farish and Elizabeth Buckner, Robert S. and Edward S. Farish migrated from Virginia in their early lives. A brother George B. Farish remained in Caroline County, Virgina. Robert S. Farish was born ca. 1785 in Caroline County. His brother Edward S. Farish was born February 17, 1791 in Caroline County. For information on the Farish-Tilman connection, Elizabeth Farish, daughter of Robt & Sarah Farish, to Paul Tilman of Hanover County, Va. see *Virginia Genealogical Society Quarterly*, Volume 15, No. 4, p.126.

"This Certifies that the Marriage Contract between Robt S. Farish of Drew County State of Arkansas and Sarah J. Dowdy of Drew County State of Arkansas was duly solemnized by me at Drew County on this Eleventh day of June One Thousand Eight hundred and seventy four - Thos. P. Stone M.E.P."

Robt. Stevens Farrish was born September 26th 1827. Died Sept. 11, 1896.
S.D. Farrish his wife was born Febr 5th 1839.
Sarah J. Dowdy Farrish wife of Robt S. Farish was born Febr 5th 1839.
        Burford
Danl. Philemon Burford was born Sept. 27th 1878 died May 10, 1857, New York, N.Y.
Lucy Helen Burford was born April 3rd 1881.
Robert Farish Burford was born Nov 1st 1883 died Dec. 19, 1935 Pine Bluff, Ark.
Dudley Marshall Burford was born Jany 22d 1887.
Helen E.A. Farish first wife of Robt S. Farish was born March 22d 1832.
Jessie Lydia Farish daughter of R.S. & Helen Ann Farish was born February 11th 1853.
Helen Marshall Farish daughter of same was born July 20th 1854.
Matilda Durden Farish was born August 17th 1856. Died Mar 3 1930.
Edward Lafayette Farish was born Augst 24th 1859. Died Mar 1930.
Sarah Stevens Farish was born September 28th 1866.
Catharine Hazelwood Farish was born Oct. 6th 1868 died Oct. 18, 1957 Dellwood Cemetery Pine Bluff, Ark.
Robt S. Farish and Sarah J. Dowdy were married June 11th 1874.

Robt S. Farish and Helen A. Marshall his first wife were married Dec. 23d 1857.
D.C. Burford married Matilda D. Farish Feby 22d 1877.
        Children of D.C. Burford
Matilda Farish Burford _____ [not legible]
Jessie Lydia Farish died Decr 10th 1863.
Helen M. Farish died December 13th 1863.
Sarah Stevens Farish died Feby 18th 1868.
Helen Ann Farish wife of Robt S. Farish died Jany 7th 1874.
Catharine Elizabeth Burford was born March 24th 1893.
Catharine Elizabeth Burford died June 30th 1895.
Lydia Belton Marshall was born July 21st 1810.
Lydia B. Marshall died Feb. 5th 1895.
Martha Lydia Burford was born January 1st 1896. Died Dec. 23rd 1943.
Daniel Clark Burford died March 31st 1897 Aged 42 yrs.

Also included in the Bible are two newspaper death notices, one of Daniel C. Burford March 31, 1897 as a result of being kicked by a mule while looking at some merchandise in the street in Pine Bluff, Ark. leaving wife and 5 children, the other notice of Mrs. F.M. Moore who died in Pine Bluff Oct. 30, 1890 and whose first husband was a Burford.

FARISH FAMILY BIBLE NO. 3

This Bible was owned by Roberta Farish in 1937. "Hazelwood Plantation in Caroline County was owned by Hazelwood FarIsh before it was sold to John Taylor of Caroline.

Camelia Sarah Farish was born July 10, 1840.
Charles Henry Farish was born June 16, 1844.
initials R.S.F., perhaps the initials of the one recording the data.
Jessie Lydia Farish daughter of Robt S. & Helen Farish was born February 11th 1850.
Helen Marshall Farish was born July 20th 1856.
Matilda Durden Farish was born August 17th 1856.
Edward Lafayette Farish was born August 24th A.D. 1857.
Sarah Stevens Farish was born September 28th 1866.
Catharine Hazelwood Farrish [sic] was born Oct 6 1868.
Edward Stevens Farish was born February the 17 1791 and Sarah Goode his wife was born
  August the 4 1797.
        Marshall
Helen E.A. Marshall was born March 22 1832.
L.B.G. Marshall was born July 13th 1833.
W.B. Marshall was born May 23d 1837.
E.M. Marshall was born Mch 11th 1839.
Americal C. Farish Departed this life October the 9 1816.
Thomas S. Farish Departed this life October 1818.
Elizabeth B. Farish Departed this life August 1821.

Levin P. Farish Departed this life October 1822.
Lavenia Farish Departed this life July 19 1826.
Mary R. Farish Departed this life August the 3 1826.
Ann Eliza Farish died Oct 10th 1837.
Sarah C. Farish died July 11th 1841.
Sarah Farish died October 23d 1857.
Cornelia S. Farish died Nov 10th A.D. 1859.
Helen M. Farish Died December 13th 1863.
Edward S. Farish died Decr 10th 1863.
A.E.A. Farish died January 9th 1874.
Jessie L. Farish died December 6th 1854.
Sarah Farish died Feby 8th [or 18] 1868.
L. A. Marshall died Aug 21st 1857.
J.B.L. Marshall died November 7th 1858 [7th is scratched but looks right].
Eugene M. Marshall died Mch 8th or 18th [blurred] in hospital at Chattanooga Tenn.
Elizabeth B. Farish was born March 8th 1814.
Americal Farish was Born June the 1 1815.
Thomas S. Farish was Born April the 1 1817.
Mary R. Farish was Born December the 1 1818.
Leven P. Farish was Born March the 9 1821.
Sarah C. Farish was Born March the 27 1820.
Lavina Farish was Born November the 10th 1825.
Robert S. Farish was born September the 26 1827.
Edward Farish was born July the 29 1829.
George K.[Keeling] Farish was born May the 2 1831.
Joseph J.[?] Farish was born July the 21 1833.
Ann Eliza Farish was born October the 2 1835.
Edward S. Farish and his wife was married April the 23 1813.
Robt S. Farish and Helen Ann E. Marshall were married Decr 23d 1851.
Also included are two newspaper death notices, Dr. Robt S. Farish who died at his home in Drew county, Ark. Sept 11, 1896 in 69th year of age, a native of Mississippi and moved to Arkansas in 1856, cousin of Rev. Stephen Farish. The other notice is a tribute to Dr. Robt S. Farrish [sic].

FAUNTLEROY FAMILY BIBLE

While the Fauntleroy family lived at "The Mount" plantation in King and Queen, Virginia, near Banco Post Office, members of that family married into the Corbin family of Caroline County and the Waring family of Caroline and Essex Counties, as well as the Todd family of Caroline. Fourteen members of the family rests in the cemetery at "The Mount", while fourteen other members rests in the cemetery at "Holly Hill" in King and Queen County. Some members of this family also lived in Essex County. The Bible was owned by Miss Juliet Fauntleroy, Altavista, Virginia at the time it was copied in 1937.

Thomas Fauntleroy was born in Essex County. (1760-1765) and died in Middlesex Co., Va.

February 10, 1820.
Thomas Fauntleroy married Isabell Lorimer in Middlesex County in 1796.
Their children were:
Hannah Elizabeth, born June 26, 1797. Died Oct. 25, 1814.
Isabelle Lorimer, born Sept. 19, 1798. Married May 4, 1819, James C. Wiatt.
John, born Nov. 16, 1799, mar. Rebecca Parke Farley Corbin.
Thomas Waring, born Mar. 7, 1801. mar. Juliet Muse Healy.
Catherine Moore, born Aug. 7, 1802, mar. Richard Randolph Corbin.
William Lawson Epaphroditus Waring, born Aug. 7, 1804, mar. Kitty Carter Corbin.
Mary Lorimer, born April 3, 1806, mar. Charles C. Curtis.
Sarah Tomlin, born June 1, 1808, died October 10, 1813.
George Lorimer, born January 24, 1810, mar. his cousin, Apphia Bushrod Fauntleroy.
Apphia Bushrod, born June 19, 1811, mar. John I. Adams.
Martha Payne Waring, born January 11, 1813, mar. George Lewis Willis.
Judith Tomlin, born May 21, 1815, mar. Robert Cunningham Caldwell.

FITZHUGH FAMILY BIBLE NO. 1

This Bible record consists of two pages, written on each side and were found in the old Conway Bible at Mt. Sion, Caroline County, Virginia. They have been removed from the original Fitzhugh Bible and trimmed on both sides. They were copied by George H.S. King in 1948 on his visit to the Conway estate. A copy is in the Virginia Historical Society. Catlett Conway, formerly the owner of Mt. Sion married Selina Frances Fitzhugh, daughter of John FitzHugh whose Bible these pages were taken from.

Summerfield Fitzhugh, mentioned in this Bible record, was born in Prince William County January 29, 1830, served in the War Between the States, married Ann Eliza Buckner and died in Caroline County April 9, 1886. Their daughter Frances Katherine Fitzhugh married Aylett Hawes Conway and they became the parents of George Fitzhugh Conway, Judge of the Caroline County Courts from 1932 to 1958. This family lived in what is now Fort A.P. Hill and the graves have been moved to Greenlawn Cemetery, Caroline County.

Jno. Fitzhugh and Jane Champ Helm were married in Bath Steuben County Genesee N York on 14th Jany 1804.
Jno. Fitzhugh was married to Miss Frances Sharpe the 8th May 1823.
George Wm Fitzhugh was married Miss Sarah S.B. Henry on the 17 Apr 1828.
Elisa M.T. Fitzhugh was married to Dr. Edwd H. Henry on the 24th Augt. 1829.
Margaretta L. Fitzhugh was married to Thos Hughlett [Hewlett?] on 19th July 1832.
Jno. Fitzhugh and Ann Gallagher were married at Providence Prince William County on the 17th Jany. 1837.
John P.T. Fitzhugh & Sarah F. Aalxander [sic] were married 15th Augt 1837.
Jane Champ Fitzhugh was married to Mr. George Payne on the 8th Octr 1840.
Dr. Francis McKeldie FitzHugh and Mrs. Louisa J. Latham were married in Mississippi on the 21st of December 1843.

Catlett Conway and Selina F. Fitzhugh were married at Fairview on Tuesday the 19th Decr 1848.

Jno. P.T. Fitzhugh and Elizabeth Stephenson were married in Warrenton on the 15th June 1848.

Milton Fitzhugh and Mary Catlett Gibson were married on Tuesday the 17 Decr. 1850.

Eliza M.T. Fitzhugh was born in Bath N.Y. on Tuesday 16th of Octr 1804 Was baptized by the Revd. Mr. Phelps in Geneva had for Surities Mr. Alexander F. Rose and Miss Lucinda Phelps.

John Presley Thornton Fitzhugh was born in Bath on Friday 21st March 1806 Was baptized by the Revd. Mr. Phelps had for Surities [sic] Mr. Alexander F. Rose & Miss Lucinda Phelps.

George William Fitzhugh was born on Monday Evening 13th July 1807 Was baptized by the Revd. Mr. Phelps had for surities Mr. Alexander F. Rose and Miss Lucinda Phelps.

Margaretta Fitzhugh was born on Sunday the 18th Feby. 1810 was baptized by Mr. Davis. (was born at her Grandmother's home)

Wesley Fitzhugh was born at Elmwood on the 4th June 1812 was baptized by Mr. Davis.

Jane C. Fitzhugh was born on Thursday the 14th Decr. 1815.

Francis McKendree Fitzhugh was born Wednesday 20th August 1817 was baptized by Dr. [page torn] 1st day of Sept.

Jane C. Fitzhugh the second was born on Wednesday the 16th of August 1820 Baptized by the Revd. Christopher Fry.

Francis Fitzhugh's first child was born on the 21st March 1824 and died the same day.

Milton Fitzhugh was born on Tuesday the 3rd May 1825 and was baptized by the Revd. Jessee Chisney.

Summerfield A. Fitzhugh was born on Wednesday morning the 4th of Feby. 1829. Babtised on _____ by Revd. Francis McCarthy [buried in Greenlawn Cemetery, Caroline County].

Selina Frances Fitzhugh was born on Tuesday Evening the 4th of January 1831 baptized by the Rev. Stephen Smith.

Eugenia Fitzhugh was born on Wednesday the 23rd January 1833 Baptized by Revd. Charles Davis at the Campmeeting.

Mrs. Matilda Helm departed this life on Sunday evening the 10th June 1804.

John Thornton Fitzhugh, son of John Fitzhugh of Bellefield, Stafford County, departed this life on Thursday the ninth of February 1809 at twenty minutes after nine o'clock at night age fifty nine years four months.

Margaret Fitzhugh, wife of the above John Thornton Fitzhugh, departed this life on Sunday the thirteenth of February 1814 forty minutes after two o'clock in the day - age sixty two years and twenty two days.

Francis Fitzhugh was born on the 25th Decr 1814 and departed this life on 31 of same month.

Jane C. Fitzhugh departed this life on Wednesday the 18th Sept. 1816 aged 9 months & 4 days.

Fletcher Fitzhugh was born on the 18th April 1819 and departed this life on Sunday 25th of the same month.

Jane C. Fitzhugh wife of John Fitzhugh was born on the 4th May in the year 1785 and departed this life on Thursday the 8th of November 1821 12 o'clock in the day aged 36 years and six months.

Frances Fitzhugh wife of John Fitzhugh was born on the 18th Decr 1799 and departed this life on Sunday morning 1/2 after 3 o'clock on the 11th day of Jany 1835 Aged 35 years and twenty four days.

Wesley Fitzhugh died in the Texan Army on the 11 Sept 1836 Age 24y 3mo [page torn] days.

Dr. George William Fitzhugh died in Paris in Fauquier County on Friday the 21st July 1837. Age 30 y 0 mo 8 days.

Mrs. Sarah Frances Fitzhugh wife of Dr. J. P.T. Fitzhugh departed this life on Sunday morning 25th Nov. 1838.

Eliza M.T. Henry departed this life on 21st day of May 1840 at Mr. Thos Hughletts Northb. County.

Jane C. Payne wife of George Payne and Daughter of Jno. Fitzhugh departed this life on the 19th Sept. 1845 aged 25 years.

Margaretta L. Hughlett wife of Thos. Hughlett and Daughter of Jno. Fitzhugh died on the 29th Jany. 1849 aged 39 years.

FITZHUGH FAMILY BIBLE NO. 2

This Bible originally was owned by Philip Fitzhugh of Caroline County, Virginia. It was copied by Mrs. William Bullitt Fitzhugh, grandaughter of Philip Fitzhugh in 1932 and published in the *Virginia Magazine of History and Biography,* Volume 40, pp. 175-176 and in *Tyler's Quarterly,* Volume 13, pp. 273-274. The information in the brackets was added by Mrs. William Bullitt Fitzhugh, who was living in Machipongo, Virginia in 1932. A copy of the record has also been reproduced in *Virginia Bible Records* by Jeannette Holland Austin, Willow Bend Books, Westminster, Mary land 2000.

Mrs. Mary Macon Fitzhugh, Octo. 6th 1836.
Mr. Philip Fitzhugh was born 1760 d. Dec. 21st 1836.
Philip Fitzhugh and Mary Macon Aylett were Married July 13th
   Amno Domini 1813.
The ages of our dear children --
Elizabeth Henry, born May 12 1816.
Patrick Henry born Dec 2nd 1818--[was killed in Civil War June
   17th 1864 at Petersburg, Va.].
Lucy Redd, born Octo 8th 1819.
John Fitzhugh--born Dec 20th 1821 [died May 9th 1894].
Philip Aylett born June 14th 1824 [died June 7th 1908].
Child unnamed, born Jany 26th and died Feby 18th 1826.
La Fayette Henry, born May 9th, 1829 [died Aug. 1, 1905].
Edwin, born May 9th 1830.[died in 1852]
Thadeus born March 15th, 1855.
Sons and Daughters of John Fitzhugh of King George Co., Va. and
   his wife Lucy Fitzhugh [nee Reed] of Caroline Co., Va.:
Dennis eldest son, Married a Cousin, Miss Clark -- moved to
   Louisville, Ky. Was afterwards Judge.
Samuel Temple, married his Cousin, Miss Fitzhugh near Balto.
   Md. -- Daughter of Col. Fitzhugh -- moved to Ky.
Philip Fitzhugh Remained in Va. and married Mary Mason Aylett
   of King William Co., Va.

Lucy Married Dr. Hall and lived in St. Louis, Mo.
Alexander -- Went to Pike Co. Missouri -- Married a Miss Carson.
[The above was written by my father, the late Dr. Phillip Aylett
  Fitzhugh -- born June 14th, 1824, died June 7th, 1908].

FITZHUGH FAMILY BIBLE NO. 3

This Bible is believed to have originated with Battaile Fitzhugh (1771-1836) who lived at "Santee" a place off of Tidewater Trail in Caroline County, Virginia. This place joined "Prospect Hill" and "Claremont". Most of this family lie buried in the family cemetery at nearby "Flintshire". A copy was made by George S. H. King and is now in the Virginia Historical Society.

Married on the 14th of March 1809 Battaile Fitzhugh of Redford King George County to Elizabeth Taliaferro of Rose Hill Orange County.
Married on the 15th of December 1825 by the Rev. Edward C. McGuire - Samuel Gordon of Kenmore - Spotsylvania County Va. to Patsie Fitzhugh of Santee Caroline County Va.
Battaile Fitzhugh son of Henry and Sarah Fitzhugh. Born at Redford in King George County on the 15th day of March 1771. Died at Santee Caroline County Va. on the 22 of March 1836.
  Feb. 23 1883 - Santee - Mother died fifteen years ago this day.
Born - Elizabeth Taliaferro born at Rose Hill in Orange County Va. 2nd of September 1780 Daughter of Laurence Taliaferro and Sarah Dade and wife of Battaile Fitzhugh of Santee Caroline County Va. Died 29th of Oct 1853 at Santee.
Patsy Fitzhugh daughter of Battaile Fitzhugh and Elizabeth Taliaferro born at Albion in King George County on the fourth of September [marked to December] 1807 was married the 15 of December 1825 at Santee Caroline County - died Feb 23 1868 - in Fredericksburg at the home of her son in law Dr. J. G. Wallace.
Samuel Gordon - son of Samuel Gordon and Susan Knox - Born in Falmouth Stafford County Va. on the 29th of January - 1804 - now living April 28th 1887.
Katharine Gordon second daughter of Samuel Gordon and Patsie Fitzhugh - born at Santee Caroline County Va. October 27 1832. Unmarried April 28th 1882 still living at Santee.
Baptized by the Rev. Wm Friend first Rector of Grace Church Caroline County Va.
  Oct 27th 1887 - Today I am 55 hears old - in good health - and the full engagement of all the blessings of life Surely goodness and mercy have followed me all my days. Katharine Gordon - Santee.
[Envelope with following written on it]
  For Patsy Yerby Her Mother's hair/Died Feb 27th at 12 1/2 oclock/ at Dr. Jetts Port Conway/King George County Virginia/Buried at "Flintshire" Caroline Co Va./Feb 28th 1902.

FLIPPO FAMILY BIBLE

This Bible belonged to the Flippo family which lived at "Sycamore Hill", which is located one mile north of South River bridge on Bull Church Road in Caroline County. This place has been in the Flippo family since prior to 1800. The Bible was published by the American Bible Society, New York, 1848. This Bible is currently owned by Harry C. Duesberry, Jr., Mechanicsville, Va. Lying loose in the Bible is a four page obituary of Dr. J. A. Flippo of Caroline County, Va. by L.B. Anderson, M.D., Norfolk, Va. He was born October 18th, 1821. He died April 5, 1896 in Caroline County.

Marriages:

John W[oodson] Flippo & Mary Jane Flippo were married Jan. 19 1871 by Rev. L. W. Allen.

Addison Linwood Flippo, son of John W. and Mary Jane Flippo, married Jan. 21st 1903 to Elizabeth W. Waring.

Ethel Page Flippo, daughter of Addison and Elizabeth Waring Flippo married Nov. 18, 1925 to Henry C. Duesberry - married by Rev. John Ryland.

Elizabeth Waring Flippo, Daughter of Addison and Elizabeth Waring Flippo, married May 4, 1929 to Melville Graham Baseler married by Rev. W.D. Smith.

BIRTHS:

Addison L. Flippo was born 3rd Fbry eighteen hundred and Seventy-Two at Seven O'clock in the morning.

Gideon Flippo born Sept 23rd 1794.

Sarah Jane Woodson, daughter of Benjamin and Sarah Woodson was born June 22nd 1797.

Married to Gideon Flippo Dec. 22nd 1813. Their issue: 1)Evalina Susan Flippo born Feb 3rd 1816. 2)Joseph Bennett Flippo, born Nov 15, 1817. 3)Sarah Ann Flippo, born May 22nd, 1820. 4)John Wood Flippo, born Oct. 6th, 1822. 5)Louisa E. Flippo, born Oct. 11th, 1824. 6)Harriet T. Flippo, born June 6th, 1826.

Mary Jane Flippo, daughter of John Bennett and Mary T. Wood Flippo, born Feb. 2nd, 1830.

Ethel Page Flippo, daughter of Addison Linwood Flippo and Elizabeth Waring Flippo, born Dec. 29th, 1903.

Her sister Elizabeth W. Flippo, born Feb 17th 1905.

Henry Coleman Duesberry Jr., son of Henry C. Duesberry and Ethel Page Flippo Duesberry, born Sept. 27th, 1926 Henrico Cty, Va.

Elizabeth Westmore Waring Duesberry, daughter of Henry C. and Ethel Page Flippo Duesberry, born Dec. 18th, 1927, Henrico Cty, Va.

Lloyd Coleman Huckstep, son of Elizabeth H. W. Duesberry Huckstep and Julian B. Huckstep III, born March 1, 1952.

Elizabeth Page Huckstep, daughter of Elizabeth and Julian Huckstep, born April 19, 1955.

Julie Waring Huckstep, daughter of Elizabeth and Julian Huckstep, born Oct. 16, 1956.

Julian Brindleton Huckstep IV, son of Elizabeth and Julian Huckstep, born March 21, 1960.

DEATHS:

Sarah Jane Woodson Flippo, died Feb 21st, 1859 (included is her obituary by Rev. L. W. Allen)

John Woodson Flippo died April 29, 1901 at seven in the evening.

Harriet J. Flippo died Jan. 31st 1894.

Elizabeth Waring Flippo, died Sunday, March 12th, 1905. Formerly Miss Waring.

Mary Jane Flippo, wife of John Woodson Flippo, died Jan. 7th, 1908.

Addison Linwood Flippo died May 26, 1931, aged 59 yrs.

MORE MARRIAGES:
Hency C. Duesberry Jr. married Rose Feminella, Aug. 13, 1955.
Elizabeth Westmore Waring Fudsberry, married Julian B. Huckstep III, June 28th 1950.

FREEMAN FAMILY BIBLE

This Bible belonged to the descendants of Frances Foster of Caroline County, who married John Latham of Culpeper in 1754. The Bible was published and sold by Edmund Cushing, 1828. In 1944, the Bible was owned by Mr. G. L. Freeman of Culpeper County, Virginia, when Mary Lee Somerville made a copy for George H.S. King. The copy is found in the King Papers in the Virginia Historical Society.

John Latham of Culpeper was married to Frances Foster of Caroline County, 1754.
Thomas Freeman was married to Susanna Latham January 7, 1779 both of Culpeper.
John Hoomes Freeman was married to Ann Robertson daughter of Wm. & Elizabeth
  Robertson November 27th 1805 all of Culpeper. Her mother's maiden name was Elizabeth
  Collins a member of an opulent first class family of English people.
Thomas Freeman was born 23rd day of March 1752.
Susanna Latham wife of Thomas Freeman was born March 4-1785.
Now follows their children:
John Hoomes was born October 11th 1778.
Thomas was born Feby. 21st 1781.
Gabriel was born February 5th 1783.
Archibald was born October 19th 1785.
John Hoomes Freeman's children by his first wife.
Arthur Ryland born 28 day of September 1806.
Thomas Christopher born 21st February 1809.
William Hoomes born 11th Oct. 1810.
George Franklin born 26th Sept. 1812.
Edward Ann born Sept. 10, 1814.
Children by his second and last wife.
First an abortion.
Second _____ [illegible].
Daniel Grinnan born 19 Jan 1823.
Jane Susanna Frances born 12 April 1824.
Philip Latham born 13 June 1825.
Sarah Ann born 24 Nov 1828.
The twins Helen Mary and John Francis born 29 November 1828.
My Father Thomas Freeman was fifty nine years 11 months & 16 days old the day he died.
Mrs. Ann Freeman, John Hoomes Freeman's first wife, died 20 of August 1817 Aged 36 years
  and 27 days died about 2 o'clock in the evening.
John Hoomes Freeman died April the 30 1878. He was ninety 93 years old 7 months. Culpeper
  county, Va.

Philip Latham Freeman died at Point Lookout, Maryland, a prisoner to the Yankees he died in early part of March 1865 day not known.

Died at Gordonsville, Orange Co. Va., his residence, Arthur Ryland Freeman aged sixty one years 9 months & 13 days, he died Tuesday 9 day of June 10 o'clock 1868. He was twice married his first wife was Catherine Field daughter of Henry Field of Culpeper she lived to have 2 children ____[illegible] died & John the youngest one died soon after its mother. His second and last wife was Mary Kemper now a widow with a numerous family of children to mourn the loss of an affectionate Husband and Father. He was a member of the Presbyterian Church & a consistent and zealous member to the end of his life. He died of a carbuncle he was mentally deranged for days before he died.

John Latham died 1766.

Frances his wife died December 5 1789 of consumption.

Thomas Freeman died March 9th 1812 of a wound he received in the battle of Germantown in the revolution & made a prisoner to the British 9 months and 15 days. he died in his 60 year. Susanna his wife died March 9th 1830 in her seventy fifth year.

Their children

Thomas died September 1808 at fort Stodart, Louisiana.

Archibald died Nov.1832 of apoplexy.

Gabriel died April 27th 1852.

John Hoomes Freeman's children

Helen Mary Freeman died December 3rd 1860 aged 32 years and 5 days...[there follows a rather illegible eulogy].

Daniel Grinnan Freeman died at his residence near Culpeper Courthouse December 13th 1861 of palpitation of the heart in his 39th year.

George Franklin Freeman's death has been omitted in its proper place. He died at Madison Mills, Madison county, Mississippi State on the second day of October 1834 in the 23rd year of his age full of promise. A manuscript of his life will be found among his fathers papers.

John Frances was killed Saturday evening about sunset the 13th of Dec. 1862. He was a few paces ahead of his company landing on the charge of the enemy -.

John Hoomes Freeman was married to Sarah Grinnan September 4th 1821 and our first born was an abortion.

The 2nd is a son born 19 day of January 1823 and we call his name Daniel Grinnan.

The 3rd child born to us is - daughter and we call her name Jane Susanna Frances born 12 day of April 1824.

The 4th Child is a son and we call his name Philip Latham born 13 June 1825.

The 5 Child is a daughter and we call her name Sarah Ann born 24 November 1826.

The twins Helen Mary and John Francis born 29th day of November 1829.[listed earlier as 1828]

Sarah Freeman departed this life at 1 o'clock 12 day of May 1856. She died of Pulmonery consumption in the 64th year of her age. A zealous Christian she was the daughter of John and Frances Grinnan and the oldest of 9 brothers and sisters. S. born 29 July 1792.

GARRETT FAMILY BIBLE NO. 1

This Bible belonged to the family of Richard Henry Garrett (1806-1882). He was married twice, first to Elizabeth L. Boulware May 17, 1836, and secondly to Fannie B. Holloway November 29, 1859. The family lived near Port Royal on present day Route 301 on the farm where John Wilkes Booth was captured. The house was destroyed when Fort A.P. Hill was established in 1941. The graves in the family cemetery were moved to nearby Enon Baptist Church on the Caroline-Essex County line. A copy of this family register from this Bible is in the Library of Virginia.

Mary Elizabeth daughter of Richard H. & Elizabeth L. Garrett was born the 23 June 1837.
Cecilia Fleetwood second daughter of Richard H. & Elizabeth L. Garrett was born the 25th September 1838.
John Muscoe Son of R.H. & E. L. Garrett was born the 21st July 1840.
Catharine Adalaid the daughter of R.H. & E.L. Garrett was born the 30th September 1842.
William Henry Second Son of R.H. & E.L. Garrett was born the 18th April 1845.
Ann Judson fourth daughter of R.H. & E.L. Garrett was born the 28th February 1847.
Julia Frances fifth daughter of R.H. & E.L. Garrett was born the 3rd September 1850.
Richard Baynham, Son of [R.H. & E.L. Garrett, page torn].
Julia Frances daughter of R.H. & E.L. Garrett departed this life the 23d July 1851.
Richard H. Garrett was born the 14th December 1806.
Elizabeth L. Boulware was born the 16th October 1816.
Fannie B. Holloway was born the 7th day of January 1829.
Elizabeth L. Garrett wife of Richard H. Garrett departed this life the 8th October 1852.
Richard H. Garrett [died] about 7 o'clock A.M. on the 8th January 1878 aged 71 years and 25 days.
Fannie B. Garrett [died, page torn]
Richard H. Garrett & Elizabeth L. Boulware were married by Elder Henry G. Segar on Tuesday the 17th of May 1836.
Richard H. Garrett & Fannie B. Holloway were married by Elder William A. Baynham on tuesday the 29th of November 1853.
Robert C. Garrett & Maria L. Boulware were Married by Rev. W.A. Baynham on Sunday the 20th of June 1880.
Philip Taliaferro & Henrietta W. Garrett were married on Tuesday the 12th December 1882.

GARRETT FAMILY BIBLE NO. 2

This Bible belonged to the family of Theoderic Garrett (1798-1884) of Caroline and Essex Counties. He was brother to Richard Henry and Reuben Garrett of Caroline County. He lived near Spindles Shop. He married Catherine F. Callis. See the Callis family Bible elsewhere in this volume. A copy of the family register from this Bible is in the Library of Virginia.

Theod. Garrett to Catherine F. Calliss July the 13th 1820.
Silas S. Garrett To Rosa Ann Bates March the 10th 1836.
Henry S. Garrett & R.L. Davis was married March 1, 1883.
Richard H. Garrett To Elizabeth Boulware May 1836.
James M. Garrett To Catherine [Garrett, smeared through] December 24th 1840.
Julia C. Garrett to Ira Jeter December the 17 1857.

Sallie C. Garrett To Richard Ennis Dec 18 1860.
Hannah M. Garrett to Joseph Land[rum] Oct 4th 1853.
Dunaway B. Garrett born January 12 1884.
Henry L. Garrett born Jan 15 1886.
John L. Garrett born September 28 1889.
[Births]
Theod. Garrett June the 15th 1798.
Catharine F. Garrett May 30th 1802.
James M. Garrett Oct 4th 1821.
Richard L. Garrett Oct 20th 1823.
Isabellah A. Garrett Sept 11th 1825.
Annah M. Garrett Oct 9, 1828.
[page torn]lia C. Garrett [page torn] the 5th 1831.
[page torn]ton Garrett July the 4th 1836.
[page torn]?(M)ary S. Garrett [page torn] the 9th 1833.
[page torn]bert S. Garrett December the 14th 1838.
Sally Garrett July the 13th 1840.
Henry S. Garrett March the 4th 1843.
John C. Garrett March the 23 1845.
One without name Died making 12 Children all 8 of which is now living October the 5th 1867.[signed] Theod. Garrett.
Catharine F. Garrett departed this life March 8th 1884.
Sarah A. Calliss departed this life March 8th 1884.
Rosa L. Garrett was born September the 13th [no year given].
John Witton Ennis Son of Richard J. Ennis and Sally C. his Mother was Born the 19th of May 1862.
Richard F. Landrum [born] February 8th 1862.[complete entry marked through]
Isabella Addaline Garrett departed this life Augst 29th 1873.
Theoderic Garrett departed this life Feb. 9th 1875.
[entry illeg] Oct 1872.
[Births]
Louis R. Landrum Oct 26th 1854.
William P. Landrum April 17th 1857.
John B. Landrum July 11th 1859.
Richard F. Landrum Febury 8th 1862.
Joseph H. Landrum Nov 11 1865.
Mary K. Ennis born January 16, 1868.
Eddie R. Ennis born Oct 26, 18[blank].

GARRETT FAMILY BIBLE NO. 3

This Bible was printed by The Southwestern Co., Nashville Tennessee, no date. The original owner of this Bible was Aubrey Jones "Lock" Garrett and his wife Mary S. Blythe, who lived in Bowling Green, Virginia. The Blythe family ran the Blythe Millinery Company in Bowling

Green in the early 20th century. Benjamin Blythe's family lived near Rappahannock Academy in Caroline County, where he ran a store and was postmaster in 1880. The Bible came into the possession of Joe Willis DeJarnette and is now owned by his grandson, Daniel I. Hansen, Fredericksburg, Virginia.

This Certifies that Mary S. Blythe of Bowling Green Va. and Aubrey J. Garrett of Bowling Green were joined together by me in the Bonds of Holy Matrimony At Washington D.C. on the 26 day of Dec. in the year of our Lord 1908.
Winston Blythe Garrett [born] April 5th 1910 at 20 minutes to two A.M. Tuesday.
W.R.W. Garrett Died Nov. 9th 1916 at 6 O'clock in the Morning Thursday.

Additional information not in the Bible supplied from tombstone and death records. All of the following are buried in Lakewood Cemetery, Bowling Green, Virginia:
Mary Blythe Garrett 1889-January 20, 1962, wife of Lock Garrett.
Aubrey Garrett 1883-1962.
Winston B. Garrett, born 1910, only son of A.J. Garrett died at Bowling Green, August 1944 at age 34.
Clarence Wyatt Garrett, 85, born at Sheppard Hill Farm, son of W. R. W. & Margaret Jane Garrett, Deputy Commissioner of Revenue for Caroline County for 27 years, died May 7, 1914.
Aubrey Jones "Lock" Garrett, 78, died February 10, 1962.
William Thomas Garrett, only son of W.R.W. and Margaret Jones Garrett, died in Bowling Green October 1, 1946, age 79.
Margaret Jones Garrett 18 October 1843-8 October 1925.
Mrs. Maggie (W. R. W.) Garrett, died October 1925, age 83.
George Blythe died at age 25.
Benjamin G. Blythe died January 16, 1913, age 71 years.
Carrie Blythe Foster died April 1938.
Ida Blythe Sheppard 1883-1972.

GARRETT FAMILY BIBLE NO. 4

This Bible was given to Mrs. Charlotte Miller Garrett, wife of Robert Sample Garrett, on her wedding day, October 13, 1959 by her father and mother, Nathan Miller and Ann Loudenback Miller. The Miller family lived near Port Royal and were merchants in the town of Port Royal, Caroline County. Robert Sample Garrett was the son of Theodric Garrett of Caroline County. The records were copied by the great granddaughter of Nathan and Anna Miller and have been printed in *The Garretts of Essex and Caroline Couuties Virginia* by Harry Lee Garrett, Miami, Florida, 1962. It is ironical that this family would spend most of their life living in Lincoln country and one of the children would be buried in the same cemetery as Abraham Lincoln.

Robert Sample Garrett, born Caroline County, Virginia, December 14, 1836; D'd February 20, 1914 [in Jacksonville, Illinois].
Charlotte Jane Miller Garrett, born Loudoun, Ohio, December 25, 1940; D'd November 27, 1809 [in Dawson, Illinois].

Children
1. Lillie Belle (M. Scott Hunter), mother of Charlotte McCorkie B. Logan County, Illinois, November 17, 1860; M. March 4, 1885; D'd February 17, 1937 [stroke].
2. Essie G. (M. Ira Ridgeway) B. Logan County, Illinois, August 2, 1862; M. March 24, 1885; D'd December 23, 1887 [Typhoid fever].
3. James Henry (M. Mary Jane Hendricks) B. Sangamon County [Illinois] June 19, 1864; M. April 13, 1892; D'd February 8, 1932 [T.B. Sanatorium].
4. Lulie E. (M. John Rentschler) B. Sangamon County, October 14, 1865; M. January 19, 1888; D'd December 1933 [stroke].
5. Nettie Doris, single. B. Sangamon County, February 14, 1869, D'd July 9, 1897 [T.B. at home in Dawson].
6. George William, infant. B. Sangamon County, September 9, 1867; buried Oak Ridge, Springfield [Illinois].
7. Ruffus Roland (M. Grace Vaughn) B. Sangamon County, May 28, 1873; M. December 27___ ; D'd October 6, 1907 [injured foot infection].
8. William E.[Edward] (M. Mary Everett) B. Sangamon County, March 23, 1875; M. October 18, 1900.
9. Ada May (M. Robert Leslie Schultz) B. Sangamon County, April 22, 1878; M. October 7, 1903; D'd March 4, 1950 [stroke].
10. Charlie B.[Bertram], single. B. Sangamon County, July 8, 1880; D'd October 29, 1956 [in T.B. Sanatorium at Riverton, Illinois].

GAYLE FAMILY BIBLE

This Bible was published by A .J. Holman & Co, Philadelphia, 1873. This Gayle family lived on what was earlier the 18th century plantation of Mordecai Broaddus. The old brick house was built by the Broaddus family, whose daughter married into the Gayle family. It was located on the lands between the present day Reedy Mill Road and Burnetts Road off Mattaponi Trail. The house burned while the Gayle family lived here and they built another house in front of that one, which is also now gone. The newspaper death notice of Josiah P. Gayle is placed in the Bible at Psalm 150. Josiah P. Gayle, born in Caroline County in 1792, moved to near Spotsylvania Court House some thirty years before his death, died there 31 day of August 1875 in the 83rd year of his age, leaving seven children. His wife, Fannie Broaddus, preceded him in death two years before. He was buried in the family cemetery at "Rose Mount Farm", Spotsylvania County.

Josiah P. Gayle, the son of Mordecai J. and Virginia A. Gayle
   was born April the 3rd 1849.
Mordecai W. Gayle and Frances Elizabeth his twin sister were
   born the 19th October 1850.
Lillian H. Gayle was born December the 3d, 1852.
Annie E. Gayle was born September the 5th, 1854.
Virginia Gayle was born November the 30th 1856.
Seth Gayle was born March the 30th 1858.
Frederick Gayle was born October the 6th 1860.

John B. Gayle was born May the 30th 1863.

Josephine D. Gayle was born July the 18th 1866.

Ida Gayle was born February the 8th 1869.

Sands Gayle was born February the 13th 1870.

Frank Gayle was born February the 13th 1873.

Almeda Gayle and Mark, her twin brother were born April the 18th 1875.

At Edmondsbery Caroline county, Va., March the 9th 1848 by Rev. Andrew Broaddus, M. J. Gayle and Virginia Broaddus.

At Ridgeway Caroline County, Va., February the 12th 1873 by Rev. A.H. Sanus, F.T. Sutton and Lillian H. Gayle.

M. W. Gayle & Mattie S. Shepherd were married Feb 12th 1878.

Philip H. Coghill and Annie E. Gayle were married Nov. 26th 1878.

At Richmond Va. 30th January 1889 by Rev Dr. Dashiell, M. W. Gayle and Allice D. Willson.

At Ridgeway Caroline County Va. Sept 5th 1889 by Rev. Andrew Broaddus, John C. Fletcher and Josie D. Gayle.

At Oakwood Cemetery Henrico Co November 15th 1890 by Rev. S.C. Clopton, Jno B. Gayle and Ada B. Nuckols.

At Weldove N.C. Dec 22nd 1890 by Rev Fred [blank], Gayle and Willie Simmons.

Near Old Church Henrico Co January 14th 1892 by Rev Joel T. Tucker, Seth Gayle and Attie A. Broaddus.

At Gold Hill, Buckingham Co. Va. March 26th 1902 by Rev Boatwright, Sands Gayle and Sara Look Boatwright.

Frances Elizabeth Gayle Departed this life the 29th February, 1855.

Ida Gayle Departed this life, February 13th 1869.

Mark Gayle Departed this life, April the 25th 1875.

Virginia Gayle Departed this life March the 10th 1876.

Almeda Gayle Departed this life August 24th 1876.

Josiah P. Gayle Departed this life June 17th 1888 at Fredericksburg, Va.

Mordecai J. Gayle Born March 10th, 1823 Died Oct. 3rd, 1902.

GEORGE FAMILY BIBLE

This Bible record was submitted for Revolutionary War pension for services of William George, born in Caroline County and died in Goochland County, Virginia by his widow, Nancy George. It was reproduced in *Virginia Revolutionary Pension Applications* by John Frederick Dorman, Volume 43, p.6. His sister Anna (George) Gatewood was living in Caroline County at that time (31 Dec. 1847). Ann (George) Johnson, daughter of William and Nancy George, was living in Goochland County. The following record was taken from a family register kept by her father, William George. At the death of her mother on 21 June 1838, the register passed to Nancy "Ann" (George) Johnson and on 1 Nov. 1847, she gave it to her brother Edmund George. The register is believed to be in the handwriting of William George, their father. The marriage bond for William George and Nancy Garthright, daughter of Wm. Garthright of Henrico was secured in Henrico County 18 September 1786. Edmund George was living in Fluvanna County in 1848 and was 57 years old. The George family lived at several locations in Caroline County, most notably "Fairford" near Penola.

William George was married to Nancy Garthright the 21 of September 1786.
Samuel George was born 23 December 1787.
William George was born 17 March 1789.
Edmond George was born 9 of April 1791.
Reuben George was born 25 of September 1795.
Tabitha George was born 4 of November 1797.
Nancy [Ann] George was born 21 of August 1800.
John George was born 13 April 1802.
James George was born 21 of June 1804.
Eliza George born in February 25th 1808.
[end of register]

William George of Caroline County died in Goochland County 11 September 1827].
Nancy Garthright George, wife of William George and daughter of Wm. Garthright of Henrico Co., died 21 June 1838].
Children of William and Nancy Garthright George who died before their mother:
William George
Tabitha George

GLASCOCK FAMILY BIBLE

This Bible descended into the family of David Collins Glascock and Ione B. Collins, who lived at "Elson Green", Caroline County. The original was given to John K. Gott, Marshall, Va. and a copy is in the Library of Virginia. Also included but not copied here are the Bibles of Henry Glascock, Broad Run, Fauquier Co., and another, that of John Thomas Glascock. Also included is a Pension Declaration of Robert Combs of Fauquier County. A separate sheet included in the Bibles is a list of ten slaves, giving their names and dates of birth, all but one 18th century.

Burr Glascock and Emsey W. Lake were married the 30th of March 1845.
Sarah E. Glascock (daughter of the above) and Joseph E. Davis were married May 16th 1867.
Mahlon T. Glascock Son of the above and Isabel Gulick were married the 7th Feb. 1872.
Burr H. Glascock and Mildred Norman were married the 12th of Dec'm. 1878.
W.B. Glascock and Sallie E. Dewry were married Aug. 3rd 1887 [Wm. Beaureguard].
D.[David] C. Glascock (Grandson of Burr Glascock) and Ione B Collins [dau of Robert Emmett Collins] were married July 31, 1918.
Ida Glascock (Sheppard) Granddaughter of Burr Glascock and Raymond Cobb Moore were married Nov. 7, 1935.
Burr Glascock was born the 18th of Aug. 1812.
Emsey Winffred Lake wife of Burr Glascock was born the 14th Oct. 1816.
Sarah Edith Glascock their daughter was born the 22nd Jany. 1846 (Died April 12, 1921).

Susan Alice their Daughter was born the 7th of July 1817. Died Dec. 16, 1921.

Mahlon Isaac Glascock their son was Born the 7th of July 1849 - 12 o,clk. A.M. Died Oct. 23, 1928.

Mary Elen Glascock their Daughter was Born Feb. 20th 1851 - 12 o,clk. A.M. Died July 3, 1924.

Burr Hezekiah Glascock their son was born the 17th of July 1853 at 5 o clock (or sunrise). Died Dec. 12, 1921.

Louellen Lake Glascock Daughter of Burr & Emsey W. his wife was born April the 23rd 1855 between 1 & 2 oclock A.M. Died May 2, 1914.

Aquilla Asberry Glascock Son of Burr & Emsey W. his wife was born Mon. Sept. 7th 1857 between 2 and 3 oclock A.M. Died May 24, 1929.

William Beaureguard Glascock Son of Burr & Emsey W. his wife, was born July 6th 1861. Died Oct. 19, 1931.

Norman Lake Glascock son of Burr H. & Mildred Glascock was born Jan. 16th 1880.

West Glascock son of the same was Born May 8th 1884.

Maud Alice Davis Daughter of Joseph W. & Sallie E. Davis was born July 7th 1871.

Walter Cochran Davis Son of the above was born Nov. 22nd 1873.

Nora Lou Davis Daughter of J. M. & Sallie E. Davis was Born Oct. 25, 1876.

Isaac Eugene Davis daughter of J. M. & Sallie E. Davis was born Oct. 24th 1879.

Susan Emsey Davis daughter of J. M. & Sallie E. Davis was born Oct. 26th 1883.

Edith Alverta Davis daughter of J. M. and Sally E. Davis was Born Sept. 24, 1885.

David Clarence Glascock was born March 8, 1889 at Oak Hill, Prince William Co., Va. Son of Mahlon I. & Isabell Lee Glascock.

David Collins Glascock, son of David C. & Ione C. Glascock, was born Dec. 28, 1931, 11:00 A.M. at Doswell, Va.

James Henry Glascock Son of Mahlon I. & Belle L. Glascock was Born July 26th 18__ . Died March 9, 1893.

Burr Albert Glascock Son of Mahlon I. & Belle L. Glascock, was Born Apr.2nd at Fairfield, Prince Wm. Co. 1875, died 12-7-1954.

Ernest Lake Glascock Son of M.I. & Isabelle L. Glascock was Born January 28th 1877, at Oak Hill, Prince Wm. Co., Va. Died April 12, 1914.

Agnes Myrtle Glascock Daughter of M. I. & I. L. Glascock was Born Jany. 7th 1879.

Milton Ish Glascock was born Feb. 18th 1883 at Alto, King George Co ., Va. Died Dec. 15, 1918 at Oak Hill.

William Ashby Glascock was born March [May?] 2 [?] 1886.

Aubrey Gulick Glascock born May 3, 1891, died Nov. 6, 1956 in San Francisco, California.

Ida Lee Glascock born June 4, 1895. Died 16th June 1964 at Anne Arundel General Hospital, Annapolis, Md. Daughter of Mahlon I. and Isabelle Lee Glascock.

Hezekiah Glascock departed this life Oct. 18th, 1843 aged 70 yrs. 1 mo. & 22 days.

Edith Glascock departed this life Febr. 17th 1858 aged 74 years 6 mo. & 34 days.

Emsey W. Glascock wife of Burr Glascock Died Aug. 18th 1885 45 minutes after 1 oclock A.M. aged 68 years, 10 months and 4 days.

Burr Glascock died Apr. 3rd 1896 aged 84 years 7 months and 17 days.

John William Lake son of Isaac & Sallie Lake died March 21st 1903 in the 82nd year of his age.

Louellen Lake Glascock daughter of Burr & Emsey Glascock died May 2nd 1914 aged 59 years.

Isaac Lake died Mar. 26th 1851 in the 69th year of his age.

Sallie Lake Wife of the above Died May 18th 1821 in the 36th year of her age minus two days.

Susan Lake Daughter of the above Died Ap.4th 1852. Aged 68 years 6 days.

Agness Myrtle Glascock daughrer of M. I. & Isabell L. Glascock died Jan. 22nd 1883 aged 4 years 15 days.

James Henry Glascock son of M.T. & Isabelle L. Glascock died March 9th 1893 in the 20th year of his age.

Ernest Lake Glascock son of M. I. & Isabelle L. Glascock died April 1, 1914 in the 37th year of his age.

Milton Ish Glascock son of M. I. & Isabel [sic] L. Glascock died Dec. 15th, 1918 in the 35th year of his age.

David Clarence Glascock son of Mahlon I. & Isobel [sic] L. Glascock died 20 October 1963 at 8:10 A.M. aged 74.

GOODWIN FAMILY BIBLE

This Bible (1737-1882) belonged to Peter Goodwin, born February 17, 1737, married 1st Sarah Coleman, 2nd Sarah Coghill, and died October 5, 1793 at age 56. He was the son of James Goodwin, who died November 8, 1757, and his second wife Mrs. Elizabeth (Chapman) Chrisman. Peter Goodwin lived at "Oakley" farm near Paige in Caroline County. The Bible was published by The Bible Association of Friends in America, Philadelphia, 1831. The copy furnished here was provided by Irma Sacket, Long Beach, California. Another copy is in The Library of Virginia. This family was published as "The Goodwin Families in America" by John S. Goodwin in the *William and Mary Quarterly*, First Series, Vols VI (1897), VIII (1899) and Second Series, Vol XIV (1934). A copy is also in the Virginia Historical Society. Many members of this family are buried in the churchyard of St. George's Episcopal Church in Fredericksburg, Virginia.

Thomas Goodwin born Octo. 9th 1770 [in St. Margaret's Parish] was married to Ann Maria Smith who was born Feby. 18th 1775) on the 2nd. Octo. 1792 and had issue as follows

Wm P.[Peter] Goodwin born Nov. 20th 1793.

Sarah Goodwin born Sepr. 6th 1795.

Charles Goodwin born June 30th 1797.

Thomas Goodwin born March 16th 1800.

Arthur Goodwin born Feby. 3rd 1802.

Littleton Goodwin born Feby. 13th 1804.

John H. Goodwin born Decr. 29th 1806.

Mary Goodwin born Aug. 17th 1809.

Elizabeth Goodwin born March 7th 1812.

Ann Maria Smith Goodwin born Apl. 19, 1816.

Ann M.T. Goodwin married Edgar W.[Wilton] Harrison Sept. 18, 1851.

Wm M. B. Goodwin married Nannie T. Holloday Nov. 18th 1852.

Wm P.[Peter Goodwin] married [first] to Caroline Heiskell [daughter of Ferdinand Heiskell]

Septr. 26th 1816.
Wm P.[Goodwin] married to his second wife Mary B. Burke May 1st 1827.
Rev. E. H. C. [Edward Hackley Carmichael] Goodwin to Mary Van Bibber Oct. 26th 1858.
James H. Wilson to Eleanor Reat Goodwin Jan. 14th 1864 or 1865.
Charles [Goodwin] married to Janette G.[Gordon] Carmichael Decr. 21st 1819.
Littleton [Goodwin] married to Ann Maria Smock Octo. 2nd 1832.
Arthur [Goodwin] married to Anne Thom Octo. 16th 1834.
Ann Maria Smith married to John R. Hart Octo. 21st 1835.
John H.[Harrison Goodwin] married to Mary Ann Hart Octo. 31st 1837.
Ann Elizabeth married to John Thomas Goodwin son of Littleton & E.D. Goodwin of Caroline Decr. 19, 1838.
Evelina C.G.[Goodwin] married Arthur R.[Rose] Hart Oct. 26th 1843.
Thomas Goodwin married to Ellen Ayres Jany. 13th 1846.
Eleanor C. Goodwin married to George R.W. Allnutt March 2nd 1848.
Children of Wm & Caroline [Heiskell Goodwin]
Ann Elizabeth [Goodwin] born Apl. 27th 1818.
Maria Margaret [Goodwin] born March 15th 1822 died July 23rd 1822.
Evelina Caroline Sarah [Goodwin] born July 8th 1823.
Children of Wm P.[Peter] & Mary B.[Burke Goodwin]
Ann Maria Smith born July 5th 1828.
William Mary Byrd [Goodwin] born March 5th 1829.
Children of Charles & Janett G.[Gordon Carmichael Goodwin]
Thomas [Goodwin] born Sepr. 8th 1820.
James Carmichael [Goodwin] born Sepr. 17th 1823.
Eleanor Carmichael [Goodwin] born Augt. 28th 1825.
Edward [Hackley] Carmichael [Goodwin] born Novr. 22nd 1827.
Sarah Ann [Goodwin] & a still born twin born Augt. 23rd 1829.
Virginia still born Jany 9th 183_.
Children of Littleton & Ann Maria [Goodwin]
Thomas Esme [Goodwin] born June 27th 1834.
Casper Wislar [Goodwin] born 31st July 1837.
Littleton [Goodwin] born August 11th 1841.
Mary Byrd, Daughter of Wm M.B. & N.L. Goodwin [born] Nov. 18th 1854.
Frederic Van Bibber, the son of the Rev. E. H. C. Goodwin & Mary his wife was born August 4th 1859.
Wm Dallas [Goodwin] born [March 21] 1861.
Bettie Carter [Goodwin] born Dec. 2nd 1862.
Edward H. Goodwin born [blank].
Children of Arthur & Annie [Thom Goodwin]
Eleanor Reat [Goodwin] born 13 Sepr. 1835.
Mary Allen [Goodwin] born March 1st 1837.
Ann Smith [Goodwin] born Jan. 26th 1839.
Elizabeth Carmichael [Goodwin] born March 12th 1842.

Arthur [Goodwin] born Oct 17th 1843.
Janet Gordon [Goodwin] born Sept. 18th 1845.
Reuben T.[Thom Goodwin] born Jany. 2nd 1850.
Arthur Thomas [Goodwin] born Oct. 11th 1852.
Catharine Ware [Goodwin] born May 21st 1858.
Children of A.M.S. & John R. Hart
Catherine Rose [Hart] born Jany. 5th 1837.
Thomas Goodwin [Hart] born Jany. 10th 1839.
Robert Allason [Hart] born Decr. 8th 1840.
Ann Maria Smith [Hart] & a still born twins born April 7th 1843.
John G.[Goodwin Hart] born March 22nd 1845.
Arthur Maxwell [Hart] born February 14th 1847.
Charles Henry [Hart] [born] July 14th 1849.
Alexander Rose [Hart] [born] February 25th 1851.
Benjamin Allen [Hart] [born] May 30th 1853.
Laura Chapman [Hart] [born] Feby. 6th 1855.
Susan Jane [Hart] [born] Oct. 27th 1856.
Children of John Thomas & Ann Elizabeth Goodwin
Caroline Heiskell [Goodwin] born Apl. 12th 1841.
Clarence Littleton [Goodwin] born Sepr. 1st 1843.
William P. [Goodwin] born Nov. 19th 1845.
Elizabeth Glassell [Goodwin] [born] Feby. 12th 1848.
Sarah Byrd [Goodwin] Born Febr. 8th 1850.
Evelina Lewis [Goodwin] Born Sept. 11th 1852.
John T.[Thomas Goodwin] Born Sept. 30th 1859.
Children of Arthur & C.L. Hart
Ferdinand Heiskell [Hart] born Augt. 20th 1844.
William Goodwin [Hart] born Sept. 21st 1847.
Catharine W. daughter of W. M. B. & N.T. Goodwin born March 3rd 1866.
Children of Thomas & Ellen [Ayres Goodwin]
Charles [Goodwin] born Oct. 30th 1846.
J.S.Harden [Goodwin} born Mar. 21, 1848.
Jacob Ayres [Goodwin] [born] May 19, 1849.
Janet Gordon [Goodwin] [born] Sept. 13th 1850.
Charlotte Ayres [Goodwin] [born] July 14th 1853.
Sarah Ann [Goodwin] [born] July 15th 1855.
Ellen Thomas [Goodwin] [born] Feby. 21st 1858.
Thomas [Goodwin born May 12, 1864]
Children of G.R.W. & E.[Eleanor] Allnutt
Sallie Smith [Allnutt] born 14 Dec. 1848.
Janet Gordon [Allnutt] born Jany. 15, 1852.
Ellen [Allnutt] born April 23rd 1857.
Children of E.W. & A.M.T. Harrison
Mary Goodwin [Harrison] born July 28th 1852.

Edgar Wilton [Harrison] born March 14th 1854.
William [Harrison] born Dec. 24th 1855.
Ellen Byrd [Harrison] born Sept. 7 1858.
Maria Temple [Harrison] born Feby. 10 1861.
An Infant Son born June 12, 1864 lived not an hour.
Elizabeth Goodwin died Sepr. 3rd 1813.
Thomas Goodwin Jr. died Feby. 2nd 1823.
Maria Margaret Goodwin died July 23rd 1822.
Caroline, Wife of W.P.G.[Goodwin] [died] Decr. 29th 1824.
Mary Byrd, Wife of W.P.G. [died] Mar. 5th 1829.
Jas. Carmichael died July 25th 1830.
Thomas Goodwin Sen. [died] Jany. 14th 1836 aged 65 yrs 3 Mo & 5 days.
Catherine Rose Hart [died] Octr. 19th 1837 age 9 mo. 7 & 14 days.
John Harwood Goodwin [died] Jany. 1st 1842 aged 35 yrs 2 days.
J.G. Harris [died] 21 Mar. 1848.
Elizabeth Glassell [died] Sept. 8th 1849.
Casper W. Goodwin [died] Jany 1st 1851.
Arthur Thomas [died] Jany 22 1855 age 2yrs 3 mos 11 days.
Laura Chapman [Hart died] March 28, 1855.
E. Alnutt [died] July 14 1858 Aged 15 Mon.
C.W. Goodwin [died] June 29th 1859 Aged 13m 7 & 8 days.
Ann M.L. Hart [died] Feby. 1st 1860 Aged 6y 10m.
John T. Goodwin [died] August 5th 1860 Aged 6m 6d.
John G. Hart [died] 17 of May 1862 aged 17.
Clarence L. Goodwin [died] Nov. 4, 1862 aged 19.
Mary A. Goodwin [died] 19th Dec. 1862 25y 9m 19d.
Thomas Goodwin Hart died in Richmond of a wound received in a Battle near that place 1864.
Charles H. Hart died of Diptheria in Fauquier in 1864.
Alexander R. Hart killed 1864.
Ann Maria Goodwin [died] March 18th 1849 at 5 minutes before 5 P.M. aged 74 yrs 1m.
Wm P. Goodwin [died] Nov. 20 on his 66th Birthday on Sunday 1859.
Arthur Goodwin [died] Nov. 17th 1861, Aged 59 yrs 9m 12 days.
Sarah Goodwin [died] February 4th 1867.
Littleton Goodwin [died] May 31st 1871.
Charles Goodwin [died] August 1st 1874.
Ann E. Goodwin [no further info].
Evelina Hart [no further info].
Mary Goodwin died June 26, 1882. Buried by Dr. Edmond C. Murdaugh 1882 The bell was tolled [etc] Aged 67 years 9 months 19 days.
I, Peter Goodwin was married to Sarah Coleman April 2nd 1760. She departed this life 24th February 1766.
Leaving three children
James Coleman Goodwin born March 29th 1761.

Julius Coleman Goodwin born February 7th 1765.
Mary Goodwin born December 29th 1765.
Married to my second wife Sarah Coghill Nov 15th 1769.
Thomas Goodwin born Oct. 9th 1770.
Harwood Goodwin born Sept. 5th 1773.
Littleton Goodwin born July 7th 1776.
Elizabeth Hawes Goodwin born March 2nd 1779.
Peter Goodwin departed this life on Saturday 5th Oct. 1793. Aged 56 years, 7 months, 18 days, being born Feb. 17th 1737.
Sarah Goodwin, wife of Peter Goodwin, was born July 23rd 1746. She was the daughter of Thomas & Elizabeth Coghill. She departed this life on Saturday Aug 10th 1822 - 10 minutes aft. 3 o'clock P.M. Aged 76 years, 18 days.
Littleton Goodwin married to Elizabeth D.[Doswell] Goodwin on the 19th day January 1797. The former born 7th July 1776. The latter born 8 Sept 1781 daughter of John & Elizabeth Goodwin of Hanover.
Littleton Goodwin departed this life Sept. 5, 1822. Aged 46 yrs 1 month & 28 days.
Elizabeth L. Goodwin departed this life on Wednesday morning June 27th 1849 at 2 o'clock A.M. Aged 67 years 9 months 19 days.
Harwood Goodwin the second Son of Peter & Sarah Goodwin departed this life at the residence of his Son Dr. John M. Goodwin in Orange, July 15th 1859 Aged 85 years 10 Months & 10 days.
Miss Sally Goodwin Fredericksburg [no further info].
Mary Goodwin born August 17 - 1809 died June 26 - 1882. Was buried by Rev. Edmond C. Murdaugh Rect. of Trinity Church. The Church "bell" was Tolled while she was dying.

GORDON FAMILY BIBLE

This Bible was printed for Samuel Bagster in London and published by J.B. Lippincott & Co. in Philadelphia, 1848. It was in the possession of Miss Tallie Gordon, Fredericksburg, Va. in 1972. A copy is in the Virginia Historical Society. This family lived in upper Caroline County. Many are buried in Caroline County in existing cemeteries as indicated in the Bible records. They are related to the Gordon family buried next to the Kenmore house in Fredericksburg. A typewritten version of this Bible is included with the exact xerox copies, but is not reproduced in this compilation. One should consult it for variations of the original.

Carter Littlepage Stevenson Born Sep 21st 1817 [General, C.S.A. died August 15, 1888 and buried in Confederate Cemetery, Fredericksburg].
Martha Silvery Griswold Born Dec 27 - 1821 - [Died August 24, 1886 and buried in Confederate Cemetery, Fredericksburg].
Martha Silvery Griswold and Carter Littlepage Stevenson were married June 15th 1842.
Births
Virginia Stevenson Jan 29th 1844 Detroit Michigan.
William Herndon Stevenson May 8th 1845 Fort Wilkins Lake Superior.
Isabella Herndon Stevenson Aug 26th 1847 Detroit Michigan.

Clara [Talley] Guise Stevenson Aug 28th 1849 Fort Gibson Arkansas.
Edwin Whipple Stevenson Feb 7th 1854 Buffalo New York.
Carter Stevenson Taylor July 24th 1871 Fredericksburg Virginia.
Bernard Moore Taylor Sept 23 1880 Fredericksburg Virginia.
Tallie Carter Gordon December 28 1880.
Virginia Stevenson Born January 24 1844.
William Herndon Stevenson Born July 1845.
Isabella Herndon Stevenson Born Aug 26th 1847.
Clara Tallie Guise Stevenson Born Aug 28th 1849.
Edwin Whipple Stevenson Born February 7th 1854.
Isabella Herndon Stevenson & James Taylor Married April 25th 1867.
Carter Stevenson Taylor Born July 24th 1871.
Carter Stevenson Taylor Died Aug 11th 1872.
Born Jan 28th 1868 - Born Dec 1876 [these two dates listed but no names].
[Clara] Tallie Gussie Stevenson & Battaile F.[Fitzhugh] Gordon Married October 14th 1874.
Belle Stevenson Gordon Born Sept 29th 1875.
Patsie Fitzhugh Gordon Born May 2nd 1877.
Carter Littlepage Stevenson & Martha Silvery Griswold June 13th 1842 St. Paul Church Detroit Michigan.
James Taylor & Isabell Herndon Stevenson April 25th 1867 St. George's Church Fredericksburg Virginia.
Battaile Fitzhugh Gordon & Clara Gussie Stevenson October 14 1874 St. George's Church Fredericksburg Virginia.
Pattie Fitzhugh Gordon & Thomas P. Yerby Grace Church Caroline County Virginia Nov 30th 1898.
William I. Dickinson & Belle Stevenson Gordon Grace Church Caroline County Virginia Dec. 9th 1905.
Carter Littlepage Stevenson Wednesday August 15th 1848 2 1/4 o'clock P.M. 72 years of age.
Pattie Fitzhugh Gordon Yerby Port Conway King George Co. Va. Feb 27th 1902. Buried at Flintshire. [Caroline County]
Belle Stevenson Gordon Dickinson Clare Mont June 27th 1907. Buried at Flintshire.
Tallie Stevenson Gordon Clare Mont, November 11, 1912. Buried at Flintshire.
Deaths
Virginia Stevenson Detroit Michigan March 20th 1844.
William Herndon Stevenson Detroit Mich July 11th 1845.
Edwin Whipple Stevenson Buffalo N. York February 27th 1855.
Carter Stevenson Taylor Stellore Amherst Co Virginia August 11th 1872.
Bernard Moore Taylor Harrisburg Va. July 14th 1882.
Isabella Herndon Taylor Fredericksburg Virginia 39 years Sunday August 1st 1886 10 o'clock A.M.
Martha Griswold Stevenson Clare Mont Virginia 64 years. August 24th 1886 10 o'clock P.M.
Births
Belle Stevenson Gordon September 29th 1875 Claremont Virginia 4 o'clock.
Patsy Fitzhugh Gordon May 2nd 1877 ClareMont Virginia 5 o'clock.

Tallie Carter Gordon Dec 28 1880 10 o'clock Clare Mont Virginia.
Martha Griswold Gordon October 2nd [page torn] Clare Mont Virginia 5 o'clock.
Susan Knox Gordon Dec 15th 1889 Clare Mont Va. 5 7/8 o'clock.
Carter Stevenson Gordon Nov 15th 1887 Tuesday At 2 o'clock Clare Mont Va.
[The following three items are typewritten and added to the original handwritten Bible records]
Champe Carter Corbin & Carter Stevenson Gordon April 15, 1925.
Frances Elizabeth Wilkerson & Battaile Stevenson Dickenson, (son of Belle Stevenson Gordon & William I. Dickenson) January 8, 1829.
Champe Carter Gordon January 23, 1941, buried at Grace Episcopal Church, Caroline County, Virginia.
[The following is different handwriting}
Battaile F. Gordon December 15, 1920 Buried at Flintshire.
Martha G. Gordon Feb. 6, 1960 Buried at Fredericksburg Confederate Cemetery.
[Still another handwriting of an aged person with wavy writing]
Carter Stevenson Gordon Died March 27 1961.
[Printed newspaper death notices for John Griswold, Esq., son of Simeon Griswold of Nassau, Rensselaer county, N.Y., age 51 years. Miss Margaret G. Gordon, Feb. 1960, buried in City Cemetery [Fredericksburg].

GOULDIN FAMILY BIBLE NO. 1

This Bible was published by James A. Bill, Philadelphia, 1847. It belonged to the Gouldin family who lived at "Spring Hill", Central Point, Caroline County, Virginia. This Bible was buried during the Civil War. It is now in the possession of Thomas W. Upshaw, Milford, Virginia.

John William Gouldin Born the 9th Day of August In Caroline County Virginia The Year 1826.
John W. Gouldin & Rebecca M. Broaddus Married Feby 28 1847.
John W. Bouldin & Anna Broaddus Married Feby 19 1862.
This Do in Remembrance of Me. Jan 1874.
John Waller Gouldin Born Aug.. 9, 1826.
Rebecca M. Gouldin (his wife) Born Feby. 26, 1824.
Calvin Gouldin Son of Jno. W. Gouldin & Rebecca M. his wife Born Jany 25th 1878.
Chester Gouldin Second Son of W.G. & Rett? Gouldin his wife Born Nov 2nd 1850.
John Edgar Gouldin Born December 19th 1853 Son of J. Wm. Gouldin & Rebecca M. his wife.
Mary Morson Gouldin Daughter of Rebecca M. Gouldin and John W. Gouldin Born May 5th 1856.
Cleon J. Gouldin Second Son of John W. Gouldin & Rebecca M. his wife Born Nov 2nd 1850.
Calvin Gouldin first born of J.W. & Rebecca his wife Departed this life in the Month of November 1859 age one year three months and about 10 days.
Calvin Gouldin The first born of J. W. & R. M. Gouldin his wife Departed this life November 30th 1849 Age one year ten months and 6 days. [second entry]
C. Waller Gouldin Died Aug 2nd 1895. At rest with God.
On the 19th day of August 1859 Rebecca M. Gouldin without a murmur of complaint Died and as

her life had always Bore She passed from Earth, Sweet amble and forgiving her most Earnest Prayer was for her three little children. J. W. G.
Tis long since they Bore thee away from me
   and laid thee low in the grave
  But could I forget the my Soul would be
  Like the rock that replenishes waves
  And oh those departed Sainted ones
  In thy robes of glory clad
  Dust thou ever from thy bright abode look down on me deserved and Sad.
   Spring Hill August 21st 1860 Caroline County Virginia. J. W. G. John Wm. Gouldin 1847.

Lying loose in the Bible is a handwritten account of a storm in Caroline County
Chapter 1st of Joels read with Earnest Prayer as the 5th day of August 1869 will long Be Remembered as the great and Destructive Hail Storm Passing through Portions of both King & Queen and Essex County destroying whole crops of corn, tomato vines and most every thing else, killing forest hares, and other wild creatures, trees falling in immense quantities; covering the ground at least 2 & 3 inches deep and all heaped In large Banks, the tremendous winds that Blew all the time. It was up to 2 feet in depth and indeed it was of termination and prayer.
Spring Hill Caroline County Virginia
Near Central Point
August 20th 1869   J. W. G.

GOULDIN FAMILY BIBLE NO. 2

This Bible was published by B.F. Johnson & Co., Richmond, Virginia, 1886. It is now owned by Ann Upshaw Wright, Bowling Green, Virginia.

John W. Gouldin of Caroline Co. Va. and Anna Broaddus of Caroline Co. Va. On February 19th
   1862 at her Father's House by Revd. A. Broaddus D.D.
Children of J. W. Gouldin & Anna his Second Wife
Rhoderick Gouldin Born January 2nd 1863.
Reuben Gouldin Born March 26th 1865.
John Waller Gouldin Was Born March 10th 1868.
Philip B. Gouldin Born October 4th 1871.
Harriet Elizabeth Gouldin Born August 3d 1876.
John Waller Gouldin Was Born Aug. 9th 1826.
Anna Gouldin Second wife of J. W. Gouldin Born July 7th 1840.
Cleon J. Gouldin Son of J. W. Gouldin & Rebecca M. his wife Born November 2nd 1850.
John Edgar Gouldin Born December 19th 1863 (Son of J.W. Gouldin & Rebecca M. his wife).
Mary M. Gouldin Daughter of J. W. Gouldin & Rebecca M. his wife Born May 5th 1856.
Calvin Gouldin Son of J. W. Gouldin & Rebecca M. his Wife Died November 30th 1849. Age one
   year 10 Months & 6 days.
Reuben Gouldin Son of J. W. Gouldin & Anna Gouldin his wife Died May1865 Age 2 Months.

J. Waller Gouldin Died August 2nd 1895.
Cleon J. Gouldin Died at Flemingburg Kentucky August 11th 1896 Age 45 years 9 Months & 9 days.
Anna Gouldin Died April 29 1900 Age 59 years 9 Months & 20 days.
Emily Gouldin Departed this Life May 1 1947 Age 70 years & about 11 Months. The love of My youth is gone.

GOULDIN FAMILY BIBLE NO. 3

This Bible is missing the title page. It is now owned by Thomas S. Upshaw, Milford, Virginia. It was originally the Bible of Roderick B. Gouldin.

Bertha Anna Gouldin Born June 20, 1904.
[Bettie] Satie Gouldin Born Aug 15, 1906.
Roderick Butler Gouldin Born Oct 8, 1908.
Roderick B. Gouldin Sr. Died Dec 4th 1934.
Roderick Butler Gouldin Jr. Died Dec 3, 1964.

GOULDMAN FAMILY BIBLE

This Bible was copied some years ago by Helen Kay Yates and a copy furnished the author. The whereabouts of this Bible is now unknown. The Gouldman family lived in that part of Caroline County that is now in Fort A.P. Hill. See also Parker and Schools Bibles. There are two additional Gouldman Bibles in the King George Historical Society files, not included here.

Richard Gouldman was born January 19th 184_.
Sarah Gouldman the wife of Richard Gouldman was Born November 7th 1812.
Maria F. Gouldman was Born October 13th 1830.
Ann Catherine Gouldman was Born October 15th 1832.
Thomas Gouldman was Born July 30th 1835.
Richard Henry Gouldman was Born October 7th 1837.
Sarah Ann Gouldman was Born September 21st 1839.
J. E. Casey was born Oct. 17, 1856.
Mary Susan Gouldman was Born August 15th 1841.
John Musker Gouldman was Born December 30th 1845.
Robert Alpheius Gouldman was Born August 31st 1845.
William Banum Gouldman was Born May 15th 1848.
Louisa Etta Gouldman was Born May 19th 1850.
Phebe Alice was born June 29th of 1852.
Phebe Alice Gouldman was Born June 29th 1850. (listed twice)
Catherine A. Gouldman died March 26, 1913.
J. E. Casey died June 4th 1918.
Alice P. Casey died August 30th 1922 in the 70th year of her age.

Louise Etta Taylor died Jan 6, 1929 in the 78th year of her age.
W. H. Taylor died Aug. 11, 1914.
Charles B. Parker died Feb. 2, 1932.
Joseph Gouldman died April, 1929.
Sadie Mabel Casey died Oct. 19, 1941.
Richard Gouldman died January 24th 1874.
William Baynham Gouldman died Dec. 15, 1923.
Mary Susan Gouldman died 1825.
Sallie School Gouldman died 1893.
Sarah A. Gouldman died July 12, 1908.
Thos. L. Gouldman died Oct. 11, 1908.
John Musker Gouldman died Nov. 18, 1921.

GRAHAM FAMILY BIBLE

This Bible was originally owned by John Graham of Dumphries and a copy is in the possession of Mary Boulware Campbell of Redmond, Washington, who furnished this copy. The copy was made in 1896 by Miss Hartley Graham of Washington, D.C. and sent to her cousin in a letter of April 23, 1896, who stated that they were descendants of Dr. William Cocke, who married Elizabeth Catesby, and who was related to Mary Stuart, Queen of Scots. She states that his epitaph hangs in Bruton Parish Church in Williamsburg, Va. She also states that the family is related to Dr. William Bagby and Dr. Chamberlayne of Richmond, Virginia. In a letter dated April 28, 1896, from Miss Hartley Graham, sister to L.P. Graham, to Sara Graham Hudgin, she states that Graham family Bible was owned at that time by Mrs. Hartley Graham White in Prince William County, Virginia. According to Mary Boulware Campbell of Redmond, Washington, who furnished this information, the whereabouts of this Bible today is unknown to her.

Walter Graham, fourth son of John and Elizabeth Graham of Dumphries married Sally Richards, fourth daughter of John and Susannah Richards of Falmouth. Their daughter Sarah Richards Graham, born 1801, married Robert Hudgin of Caroline County and the surname of Graham descended into that family.

Following is the Bible record:
John Graham, born the 30th April, 1711, was the son of John Graham, Esq., of Mackenston in Perthshire, North Britain, who was nearly related to Graham of Garter of Orchill.
My mother was named Margaret, oldest daughter of John Graham, Esq., of Killiarn in the Shire of Stirling. He was heir-at-law to the estate of the Duke of Montross of Scotland, and the Duke left no issue. My father by my mother had nineteen children and there is none living only myself, my sister Catherine who married Mr. John Stuart of Balemuren near Belfast, Ireland (relative of hers), and my sister Jean, if married I know not to whom. I was married to Christian, the daughter of Dr. Gustavus Brown of Maryland the 18th day of August, 1742. She departed this life the 17th day of September following and lies interred under a marble at Dipple in Stafford County. On December 14th, 1746, I was the second time married to Elizabeth, daughter

of Catesby Cocke, Esq., by whom we had the following issue:

John, born the 14th day of Sept. 1747, died at the age of 3 months and lies interred at Belmont in Fairfax Co.

Duncan, born the 6th of Oct. 1748, Christened the same day and died that night. He lies interred with his brother John.

Margaret, born the 13th of October, 1749.

Robert, born the 3rd July 1751.

Mary, born 2nd May 1753.

John, born 4th May 1755.

William, born 1st April 1757 died Sept. 28, 1821.

Walter, born 18th March 1759 Wm. Bird, Esq., was his godfather.

Elizabeth, born 7th May 1751 died Aug. 21 1754, of the same disorder Catherine had which she got in the same way.

Catherine born 22nd Aug. 1763 died 6th of Aug., 1754, after being seized with a violent flux which she got from Allen, the son of Allen McCrae. Catherine was the comeliest child we ever had. She died the fourth day after being taken sick. Catherine and Elizabeth lie interred at Belmont near their brothers. When Catesby Cocke, Esq., their Grandfather sold Belmont he reserved a burying place which will appear by the deeds made by the second Catesby Cocke to Benj. Grayson recorded in Fairfax County.

Catesby, born Friday 13th Sept., 1765, privately baptized by the Rev. Mr. James Scott. He had Godfathers and Godmothers afterwards.

Jean, born Wednesday 23rd March 1768, and privately baptized by the Rev. Mr. James Scott. She had Godfathers and Godmothers afterwards as had all the children except Duncan.

GREEN FAMILY BIBLE NO. 1

This Bible is inscribed for Richard William Green and on the same page are the initials "GHG" [George H. Green] and the date "1857". It was printed by Hudson and Co, Hartford, Connecticut, 1818. It is now owned by Ethel Broaddus Andrews Barlow, Caroline County, Virginia. The Green family home was on the Sparta road from Pickadee's Fork and was a very large estate. You turn onto what is today "Cecil Road" and go to the old house spot and grave yard on the right. There are no markers there, but this was the home of George Green, who died in 1850. His son, Theophilus Green married Elizabeth "Patsy" Walden.

Elizabeth F. Green daughter of Theophilus F. Green and Patsy E. Green his wife born Nov. 26th 1817.

Nancy E. Green, born Jany. 26th 1820 and departed this life the 17th day of August 1822.

George W. Green born August the 12th 1822.

3rd Daughter born April 6th deceased 15th.

Juliet Ann 4th Daughter born 21st June 1825.

Miranda T. Green born 14 day of April 1831 deceased Nov. 7, 1900. Aged 72 yrs 7 m 18 days.

Richard Green born 14 day of April 1831 deceased 12th 1863 Aged 32 years.

John F. Green 4th son born 10 of June 1838. [He died Dec. 15, 1866 at age 25].
Thomas W. Green born June 12th 1842.
Theophilus R. Green son of W.G. & Martha E. Green was born July 31 1873.
Clara A. Green daughter of same was born Oct 6th 1879.
Written by Mary Ellen Green Andrews:
Married on the 22 of May 1856 by R.W. Cole at the residence of Mr. James Chapman Richard W. Green to Mary E. [Ellen] Conduit. Died in Caroline County Sept. 22nd 1863, Richard W. Green in the 33 year of his age. This young Christian brother was a member of the Sparta Greys, Company N, 30 Va. regiment in which company he had won for himself a name which will not soon be forgotten by his comrades who are left to mourn their loss, steady in his habits, uniform in his life he left behind him a name worthy of The Christian. On the eave of his departure for his rest beyond the grave, Taking leave of his brokenhearted wife he exclaimed, I am prepared. I have tried to live a pious and upright life. I hope I shall meet all my family in Heaven. He leaves a widow and three small children, who cherish The hope that he will rise again to a blessed immortality beyond the grave.
1. Julius E. [Everette] Green, son of Richard Wm and Mary E. Green was born 24th April 1857.
2. Eugenia Green, daughter of Richard W. and Mary E. Green was born 19th of November 1859.
3. Mary Ellen daughter of Richard W. and Mary E. Green was born on the 29th of August 1862.

GREEN FAMILY BIBLE NO. 2

This Bible was in the possession of Miss Alma Green, who lived at the Green homestead, built in 1898/9, located just north of Shumansville in Caroline County. It is now in the possession of Mrs. Verna Mitchell Barlow, whose mother was sister to Alma Green and who also lives in Caroline County.

Thos. W. Green and Martha Richards were married Jan. 24, 1872.
Eugenia Green, daughter of R.W. and Mary E. Green was married to Jno Adkinson the 23rd. of Dec. 1880.
Clara A. Green [daughter of T. W. & M.E. Green] & W. H. Kelley were married Jan. 5, 1892.
T. W. Green & Maggie G. Andrews were married March 3rd. 1892.
Theophilus R. Green, son of T. W. & Martha E. Green, was born July 31st 1873.
Clara A. Green, daughter of T. W. & Martha E. Green, was born Oct. 6, 1876.
Florence L. Green, daughter of T. W. & Martha E. Green, was born July 18, 1880.
Sallie J. Green, daughter of T. W. & Martha E. Green, was born Dec. 23, 1883.
Thos. Franklin Green, son of T. W. & Martha E. Green, was born April 3, 1886.
George Phillip Green, son of T. W. & Maggie G. Green, was born July 5, 1902.
Alma V. Green, daughter of T. W. & Maggie G. Green, was born September 28th 1904.
Edna E. Green, daughter of T. W. & Martha E. Green, was born Oct. 26th 1868.
Viola Myrtle Green, daughter of T. W. & Maggie G. Green, was born Nov. 3rd 1893.
John Walter Green, son of T. W. & Maggie G. Green, was born Oct. 11th, 1895.
Hilda V. Green, daughter of T. W. & Maggie G. Green, was born Dec. 26th 1897.
Floyd Green, son of T. W. Green, was born July 11, 1900.
Eldred Bradley Green, son of T. W. & Maggie G. Green, was born on Wednesday the 12 day of

June 1907 about 2 o'clock a.m.

Julia E. Green, daughter of T.W. & Maggie G. Green, was born on Wednesday 29 day of December 1909.

Maggie G. Green - born Oct. 11, 1868 Died April 23, 1929.

Thos. W. Green born June 12, 1842 Died Dec. 28, 1913.

Edna E. Green, daughter of T. W. & Martha E. Green died Feb. 1st 1889 Age 3 mo 6 days.

Martha E. Green, wife of T.W. Green, died June 17th 1891 age 41 years.

Floyd Green, son of T. W. & Maggie G. Green, died Sunday August 4th 1901.

Florence L. Green, daughter of T.W. & Martha E. Green, died Sunday June 8th 1902. Age 21 yrs. 10 mos 20 days.

John Walter Green died July 26, 1961.

George Phillip Green died May 2, 1968.

Myrtie Green Pitts died Aug. [5], 1968.

Hilda Green Mitchell died Oct. 18, 1972.

Julia Green Seal died November 10, 1972.

GUEST FAMILY BIBLE

This Bible was published by E. H. Butler & Co., 1857. The Guest family lived at "Beaumont", later named "Altona" in Fredericksburg, Virginia. The house is now destroyed. They married into several Port Royal families in Caroline County, particularly those at "Gay Mont". The Bible was owned by the late James Patton, Port Royal, Virginia.

George Guest son of John & Rebecca Guest (maiden name Hall) was born in London England on 22nd day of October 1806. Died on 2nd of July 1879 at 4:45 o'clock.

Married 1st in December 1842. Sallie daughter of Peter & Deborah Hoffman of Baltimore, Maryland who died without leaving issue in March 1845.

Nora, daughter of George and Mary E. Guest at "Beaumont" near Fredericksburg Va. May 16 1862.

Bernard Robertson, son of George and Mary E. Guest born in Halifax County, Va. Aug. 11, 1864. d. 4/10/48.

Frank Barksdale, son of George and Mary E. Guest born in Baltimore Md. Aug 11, 1867. d. 1/27/27.

Mary Bernard, daughter of Bernard R. and Eliza L. Guest was born at Savannah, Ga. March 20, 1898.

John Laurens, son of Bernard R. and Eliza L. Guest was Born at Birmingham Ala. August 13th 1899. d. 1/28/53.

Elizabeth Carter, daughter of Frank B. & Carol Wellford Guest was born at "Snowden" near Fredericksburg, Va. Aug 25, 1908.

John, son of Frank B. & Carol W. Guest, was born at Pasadena California May 27. 1919.

George Guest died in Baltimore Md. July 2nd 1879, and was buried in the Confederate Cemetery at Fredericksburg, Va. He was the son of John and Rebecca Hall Guest and was born in London, England October 22 1806 at No Great Ormord St.

Mary E. Guest died in Baltimore Md. Oct. 11, 1895 and was buried beside her husband at

Fredericksburg Va. She was the daughter of John Hipkins Bernard and Jane Gay Robertson, his wife, and was born in Richmond, Va. July 1, 1824. She was 8th in descent of John Rolfe and Pocahontas.

Nora Guest died at "Beaumont" near Fredericksburg Va. Feb. 12, 1863.

Frank Barksdale Guest died in Richmond Va. January 26, 1926 & was buried in Hollywood Cemetery (Wellford Section), Richmond Virginia.

Eliza (called Lula) Laurens Chisolm Guest died April 11th 1931 at Richmond, Va. and was buried in Confederate Cemetery, Fredericksburg Va. April 13, 1931. She was the daughter of Robert Chisolm & Margaret Horry Laurens his wife of Charleston S.C.

Caroline Wellford Guest died in Richmond Apr. 10 1972 buried in Hollywood Cemetery.

Bernard Robertson Guest son of George Guest and Mary Eliza Bernard Died in Richmond Va. on April 10, 1948. He was buried in the Confederate Cemetery in Fredericksburg Virginia, beside the graves of his father, his mother and his devoted wife.

John Laurens Guest son of Bernard R. Guest and Leila Laurens Chisolm, died in Richmond, Va. on Jan 28, 1953. He was buried in the Confederate Memorial Cemetery in Fredericksburg, Virginia with his father, mother & grandparents.

Mary Bernard Guest, dau of Bernard R. and Leila Guest died May 22, 1974. Buried in Confederate Cemetery, Fredericksburg on May 24th.

HARGRAVE FAMILY BIBLE

The Hargrave Bible was begun by John Terrell Hargrave of Caroline County and dates from 1793. He was the son of Garland Hargrave and the grandson of Joseph & Rachel Terrell Hargrave. The Bible has remained in the family since that time. A copy of the family record was sent for publication in *Tidewater Virginia Families*, Volume 3 by Fran Jones Surrett, Sun City, Arizona. Mrs. Surrett is a great granddaughter of John Terrell Hargrave. Material in brackets has been added by Herbert R. Collins from *Richmond, William and Timothy Terrell* by Celeste Jan T. Barnhill and from the *Quarles Family of Saint Margaret's Parish* by Garland Quarles.

Garland Hargrave was born January 30, 1793.
Lucy W. Bibb was born May 1, 1798.
Children of Garland and Lucy Hargrave:
Pleasant Hargrave was born August 15, 1815.
Mary Ann Hargrave was born August 19, 1816.
Clementina Hargrave was born August 7, 1818.
Elija P. Hargrave was born February 7, 1820.
Rachel T. Hargrave was born September 23, 1821.
Sophia J. Hargrave was born March 18, 1823.
Lucy Frances Ellen Hargrave was born July 31, 1825.
Nancy C. Hargrave was born July 15, 1827.
Catherine E. Hargrave was born March 10, 1829.
Joseph Hargrave was born March 17, 1831.
Sarah J. Hargrave was born June 8, 1833.
Hardenia B. Hargrave was born March 19, 1835.

Robert S. Hargrave was born September 22, 1837.
John T [Terrell] Hargrave was born January 11, 1839.
Mary Ellen Quarles was born March 17, 1849.
Children of John [Terrell] and Mary Ellen [Quarles] Hargrave:
George Samuel Hargrave was born May 11, 1867.
Maude Estell Hargrave was born February 27, 1869.
Hattie J. [Jessie] Hargrave was born October 28, 1870.
William Garland Hargrave was born December 16, 1872.
Mary Quarles Hargrave was born October 3, 1874.
John T. Hargrave Jr. was born January 3, 1877.
Effie Moreland Hargrave was born February 28, 1879.
Byrnal Clyde Hargrave was born February 5, 1883.
Julia Winston Hargrave was born September 13, 1884.
Lucie Ellen Hargrave was born May 5, 1886.
Robert Caleb [Redd] Hargrave was born June 7, 1888.
Mabelle Corrine Hargrave was born February 22, 1891.
Garland Hargrave died February 3, 1876
Lucy W. Hargrave died December 7, 1855.
Hattie J. Brock died August 11, 1900.
John T. Hargrave died March 11, 1913.
Lucy Ellen Haley died November 20, 1919.
Mary E. Hargrave died August 23, 1926.
Mary M. Hargrave died July 6, 1932.
William G.[Garland] Hargrave died January 1, 1936.
Charlie F. Brock died May 23, 1939.
Mary Quarles Axsell died August 5, 1939.
George Samuel Hargrave died January 12, 1940.
Maude E. Blanton died November 26, 1952.
Judson W. Smith died July 10, 1954.
Jessie C. Haley died December 26, 1954.
Robert L. Blanton died September 13, 1955.
Joseph R. Houston died February 15, 1959.
Emma C. Hargrave died May 14, 1957.
Robert C. Hargrave died December 29, 1968.
Mabelle C. Haley died March 24, 1970.
Effie M. Smith died October 14, 1967.
Alice M. Hargrave died January 7, 1970.
Byrnal C.[Clyde] Hargrave died August 18, 1972.
Julia H. Houston died August 30, 1972.
John T.[Terrell] Hargrave Jr. died October 1, 1974.
Ann Quarles, wife of William Quarles died April 22, 1854. [August 22, 1851 in Quarles Book].
Names of Martha Samuels children:
Frances E. Samuels died November 27, 1845.
Joseph Eli Pleasant Samuels died June 18, 1847.

Octavia Samuels died September 1, 1838

Cathsandra [or Casandra] Samuels died June 20, 1850.

Jane Elizabeth Samuels died April 11, 1852.

Lutrishia James Samuels died July 2, 1853.

Cornelius James Samuels died May 18, 1856.

Edmonia Agnes Samuels died October 24, 1858.

James V. & Catherine E. Lowry first son James G. Lowry born December 25, 1852.

James G. Lowry [son of the above] died April 23, 1853.

Samuel Terrell died August 14, 1844. [born January 8, 1770, married May 7, 1800 to Elizabeth Harris, dau of James Harris and was brother to Robert Terrell. Their sister Lucy Terrell married Samuel Hargrave January 10, 1779]

Robert Terrell died February 9, 1843, age 77. [brother to Samuel, born November 26, 1778 and son of Pleasant Terrell and Catherine Farish, who married in November 1762].

James D. Farish died February 10, 1845.

Ann Elizabeth Lowry died September 11, 1840, age 14 yr.

Pleasant Terrell died April 7, 1847.

Jessie G. Gilman died February 13, 1847, age 21.

William Hewlett died August 6, 1851.

Elizabeth Terrell, wife of Samuel Terrell died January 5, 1853.

George F. [Fox] Terrell died May 28, 1855.

Silas M. Luck & Hardenia B. Hargrave were married November 1, 1858.

John T.[Terrell] Hargrave & Mary Ellen Quarles were married June 6, 1866.

Children of John T. Hargrave & Mary Ellen Hargrave:

Robert L. Blanton & Maude E. Hargrave were married June 21, 1893.

Charles F. Brock & Hattie J. Hargrave were married November 23, 1893.

William G.[Garland] Hargrave & Mary Maude Mason were married November 22, 1899. [Quarles Book has 1894].

Judson W. Smith & Effie W. Hargrave were married April 29, 1903.

Joseph R. Houston & Julia W. Hargrave were married December 7, 1904.

John T. [Hargrave] Jr. & Alice Maude Lane were married June 20, 1906.

William Axsell & Mary Q. Hargrave were married July 23, 1906.

Jessie Cobb Haley & Lucy E.[Ellen] Hargrave were married October 31, 1906.

Robert C. Hargrave & Emma C. Pettway were married November 16, 1909.

Byrnal C.[Clyde] Hargrave & Cora Muse were married November 23, 1909.

Jesse Cobb Haley & Mabell C. Hargrave [Jessie Hall married second a sister of his first wife] were married April 6, 1921.

HARRIS FAMILY BIBLE

This Bible was published by Judd, Loomis & Co. in 1836. A copy of the family register from the Bible is in the Library of Virginia.

John Harris and Lucy Day were married June 8th 1785.

James Turner and Mary Richeson [daughter of John and Mary Richeson of Caroline County] were married [no date listed].
William L. Harris and Rebecca W. Turner were married January the 27th 1819.
Marcellus L. Goodman and Sarah E. Harris were married December 6th 1849.
James M. Harris & Zarilda Emmana Goodman was married the 18th of December 1851.
Robert E. Harris and Judith J. Davis were married June 4th 1856.
George A. Hudgins & Rebecca A. Harris were married 15th September 1857.
Oscar Gresham and Mary Ellen Harris were married Sept. 1st 1859.

[Births]
John Harris Aug 26th 1763.
Lucy Day June 20th 1768.
James Turner [no date listed].
Mary Richeson [no date listed].
Thomas T. Harris Feb 25 1788.
Milley Day Harris Jan 16 1790.
Sarah T. Harris March 31 1792.
John O. Harris April 4 1794.
Eliza Adams Harris was born Feb 14 1801
Rebecca W. Turner was born April 22 1799.
Marcellus L. Goodman was born June 17th 1828.
Zanilda E. Goodman was born Dec 3rd 1831.
Judith J. Davis was born Nov 27th 1837.
Children of William L. Harris and Rebecca W. Turner.
John Hortentius Turner Harris was born Mar 26th 1820.
William Watkins Harris was born Jany 20 1822.
James Madison Harris was born October 1st 1823.
Robert Franklin Harris was born October 23rd 1825.
Sarah Elizabeth Harris was born Sept 11th 1828.
Rebecca Ann Harris was born October 5th 1830.
Lucy Day Harris was born Dec 2nd 1833.
Thomas Henry Harris was born May 23rd 1836.
Mary Ellen Harris was born Jany 9th 1840.
George Albert Hudgins was born April 18th 1834.
Oscar Gresham was born February 12th 1836.
Child of Marcellus L. Goodman and Sarah E. Harris.
Sarah Elizabeth Goodman was born August 30th 1850.
Children of George A. Hudgins and Rebecca A. Harris.
Louisa Watkins Hudgins was born Sept 8th 1858.
Marion Preston Hudgins was born Feb 12 - 1861.
Rebeca [sic] Hudgins born Oct 14th 1863.
Henry Hudgins January 1866.
Children of Oscar & Mary E. Gresham.
Susan Gresham was born July 22nd 1860.
Oscar H. Gresham was born Sept 3rd 1861.

Sarah Ellen Gresham born Sept 5th 1863.
Children of Robert F. Harris and Judith J. Davis.
Mary Rebecca Harris was born Oct 18th 1857.
Sarah Willey Harris was born Oct 3rd 1860.
William Watkins Harris was born Sept 15th 1863.
Mary H. Davis departed this life Oct 28 1866.
Children of James M. Harris and Zarilda E. Goodman.
Lucy Ann Harris was born April 1859.
Lucy Ann Harris was born April 1859.
Lucy Harris December the 10 1845 aged 77 yrs 5 mo 11 days.
William L. Harris May the 17th 1847 aged 51 yrs 3 mo 22 days. Blessed are the dead that die in the Lord.
Mary L. Norment aged 48 yrs 7 mo 16 days died May 22nd 1847.
Mary Turner died the 10th of February 1849.
John R. Turner died Oct [11th] 1857.
Elizabeth Turner died 1861 [Car. Death Register gives Jan 13, 1862].
Judith Ann Thompson died Oct 6 - 1916.
Lucy Day Harris aged 1 year 8 mo 6 days Augt 8 1835.
Thomas Henry Harris aged 12 years 9 mo 25 days March 2d 1849.
Text 15th Cor 26 verse.
John H.T. Harris aged 30 years 3 mo 8 days July 4 1880.
Sarah E. Goodman aged 22 years 3 days September 14, 185[runs off the page].
Sarah E. Goodman Age 1 month 1 week Oct 6th 18[runs off the page].
Wm. W. Harris aged 31 years 4 mo 16 days June 5th 1853.
Susan Gresham age 2 mo 3 weeks Oct 14 1861.
Robert F. Harris departed the Sep 6 1864 age 39 years.
Man that is born of woman is of few days and full of trouble.
Mary Rebecca Harris died March 29 1879.
John D. Thompson died June [no year listed].

HAWES FAMILY BIBLE

This Bible was copied by Miss Mary Buckner in 1907 and furnished for the publication of *The Buckners of Virginia* by William Armstrong Crozier, The Genealogical Association, New York, 1907. It is also reproduced in the book, *Early Virginians*, privately published by Miss Margaret Ann Buckner of Fredericksburg, Virginia in the 1960's.

Samuel Hawes, born Feb. 1, 1727; married Ann Walker, June 20, 1751.
Ann Walker, born Aug. 23, 1731.
Elizabeth, daughter of Samuel and Ann Hawes, was born Nov. 20, 1759; married Thomas Buckner, May 25, 1780.
Mary, daughter of Samuel and Ann Hawes, was born Feb. 2, 1764; married Robert Buckner, March 23, 1782.
Charlotte, daughter of Samuel and Ann Hawes, was born Oct. 1, 1766; married Richard H.

Buckner, Sept. 26, 1782, and married secondly, to William Aylett Buckner Walker, son of Samuel and Ann Hawes, was born July 1, 1776; married to Polly Martin, Oct. 26, 1797; died May 18, 1828.

Polly Martin, daughter of Thomas and Mildred Martin, born Sept. 24, 1782.

Mildred, daughter of Walker and Polly Hawes, born Sept. 29, 1799; married Wm S.B. Buckner, Oct. 7, 1817.

Ann Hawes, daughter of Walker and Polly Hawes, born Sept. 2, 1803; married Col. John Washington, March 7, 1820.

HAWES/BUCKNER/WALKER FAMILY RECORD

This family record of the Hawes, Buckner and Walker Family was owned by Elizabeth Buckner Steele, Paris, Ky. in 1945. It was included in papers sent to Martha Woodroof Hiden, Registrar of First Families of Virginia, by Mrs. Harry M. (Jane Clay) Blanton, Paris, Kentucky in 1945 and was included with the Woodford Family Bible, see elsewhere in this book.

Samuel Hawes was born Feb 1st. 1727 and departed this life Apr 1st 1794.
Ann [sic] Walker was born Aug. 23, 1731.
Samuel Hawes was married to Anne [sic] Walker June 20, 1751.
Samuel Hawes, son of Samuel and Ann born 7th January 1754.
Samuel Hawes died Feb. 25, 1774 .
Ann Hawes (daughter of Samuel & Ann) born Feb. 7, 1758, d. Dec.1st 1776.
Elizabeth daughter of Samuel and Ann his wife was born Nov 20, 1759 and married Thomas Buckner May 25, 1780 who was born Aug 31st 1755 Died Apr. 8th 1805.
Benjamin the son of Samuel Hawes & Ann was born March 13th 1762 died Nov 2, 1782.
Mary the daughter of Samuel Hawes & Ann was born Feb. 2, 1764 married Robert Buckner Mar 28, 1782.
Charlotte, daughter of Samuel & Ann Hawes was born Oct 1st 1765 & was married to Richard Buckner Sept 21st 1782.
Aylett the son of Samuel and Ann Hawes was born Apr 21st 1768.
Richard the son of Samuel and Ann Hawes was born Feb 8, 1772.
Walker the son of Samuel and Ann Hawes was born July 1st 1776.
Walker, the son of Thomas and Elizabeth Buckner born March 7, 1781 and died March 14, 1855.
Benjamin Hawes, son of Thos. & Eliz. Buckner was born Nov 3, 1782.
Ann Walker, daughter of Thomas & Eliz. Buckner was born May 24, 1784.
Wm. Thos. Buckner son of Thos. & Eliz. Buckner was born Jan 29, 1786.
Samuel son of Thos. & Eliz. was born Nov 18, 1787.
Richard, son of Thos. & Eliz. was born Jan. 25, 1789.
Mary Aylett, dau. of Thos. & Eliz. was born Nov 29 , 1790.
Elizabeth Walker dau. of Robt. & Mary Buckner was born 1790.
Charlotte Daughter of Thos. & Eliz Buckenr was b Aug. 18, 1792.
Frances [Francis] Thornton son of Thos. & Eliz Buckner was born Feb. 12, 1794. d 1795.
Aylett son of Thos. & Eliza Buckner was b July 4, 1797.

Eleanor daughter of Thos. & Eliza Buckner was b Nov 2, 1799 d June 29, 1840.
Samuel son of Thos. & Eliza Buckner was b Nov 18, 1801.

HAWES/TAYLOR FAMILY BIBLE

This Bible was owned by Mallory Taylor of Maceo, Kentucky in 1954. It was transcribed by the late Miss H.M. Philibert of Arlington, Virginia and a copy placed in the Library of Virginia. It contains records of the Richard and Clary Walker Hawes family of Virginia and Kentucky and the Samuel Mitchell and Mildred Martin Taylor family of Virginia and Kentucky and their descendants. The Hawes and Aylett families were from King William and Essex Counties and were in Caroline County at the time of its formation. They intermarried into the Buckner family of Caroline. For further reading on these families consult *Hawes Family of Caroline County, Virginia* by Elizabeth Hawes Ryland, Richmond, Virginia, 1947, and *Buckners of Virginia and the Allied Families of Strother and Ashby* by William Armstrong Crozier, The Genealogical Association, New York, 1907.

Richd Hawes born 1770 Died Nov. 29th, 1829.
Clara Walker his wife was born Aug. 1st, 1776 Died Oct. 14, 1848.
Rich Hawes & Clara Walker were married Feb. 1792.
Children of the above named
Ann Hawes born Jan. 27th, 1793.
Saml Hawes born June 14, 1795.
Richd Hawes born Feb. 6, 1797.
Hugh Walker Hawes born Oct. 20th, 1798.
Kitty Walker Hawes born Oct. 17, 1800.
Aylette Hawes born Jan 12th, 1803.
Albert Galatin Hawes born April 1st, 1805 and Died March 14, 1849.
Edwin Hawes born Oct. 24, 1807.
Benj. Walker Hawes born Ap. 19, 1810.
Clara Mary Hawes born Oct. 28, 1811 and Died --- 1812.
Susan Elizabeth Hawes born Oct. 28th, 1816.
William Franklin Hawes born April 28, 1819.
Emma Nicholas born 1835, Died Friday April 14, 1854.
Her daughter Juliet Nicholas born Friday 7 Ap 1854.
The above named is the daughter of H.W. Hawes & Juliet Ryon.
Samuel M.(Mitchell) Taylor born Jan. 30, 1785.
Mildred E. Martin born June 9, 1793. They were married 1810.
Children of the two above named
Jonathan Gibson Taylor born March 15, 1811.
Mary Ann Taylor born July 3, 1813.
Sarah Elizabeth Taylor born Sept. 29, 1816.
John Martin Taylor born July 23, 1819.
Sam'l Francis Taylor born Oct. 8, 1821.
Robert William Taylor born Dec. 19, 1823.

Rachel Mildred Taylor born Augst 8, 1826.
Susan America Taylor born Sept. 27, 1828.
Hetty [sic] Hawes Taylor born Nov. 22, 1830.
George Edward Taylor, born Nov. 9th, 1833.
Benjamin Walker Hawes & Mary Ann Taylor were married March 28, 1832.
Children of the above named
Richard Walker Hawes born Ap. 14, 1833.
Saml Francis Hawes born May 4, 1835.
Mildred Ann Hawes born Oct. 21, 1836.
Clara May Hawes born August 28, 1839.
Kitty C. Hawes born Oct. 4, 1841.
Benjamin Walker Hawes born Oct. 9, 1845.
Infant daughter born Nov. 10, 1847 & died Nov. 22, 1847.
Sarah Elizabeth Hawes born July 22, 1849.
Susan Mitchell Hawes born April 22, 1851.
Hetty [sic] Gibson Hawes born March 29, 1854.
Albert Zachary Taylor son of Jonathan G. & Susan E. Taylor died Feb. 11, 1859 aged 11 years, 3 months & 16 days.
Benj. W. Taylor died Jan. 31, 1882.
Samuel M. Taylor died Sept. 30, 1837.
Robert Walker Taylor died Feb. 5, 1902 age 81 years.
George Edward Taylor died Nov. 29, 1915 aged 59 years.
Richard Hawes & Clara Walker were married Feb. 1792.
Jonathan G. Taylor & Susan Elizabeth Hawes were married the 1st day of June 1832.
Richard Hawes Taylor & Mary Feilder were married Dec. 23d, 1858.
George Trotter Hawes & Clara A. Taylor were married Feb. 20, 1857.
Mildred C. Taylor & Henry C. Herr were married on the 7th of May 1866 9 o'clock p.m.
Robert W. Taylor & Mary C. Martin married May 2, 1872.
George E. Taylor & Minnye F. Gibson were married Nov. 22, 1887.
Edwin Pendleton Taylor & Bettie Moreland were married Jan. 12, 1886.
Mallory Gibson Taylor & Lucy May Lyons were married June 8, 1916.
Jonathan G. Taylor was born March 15, 1811.
Susan E. Taylor was born Oct. 28, 1816.
Samuel Mitchell Taylor was born March 24, 1833.
Richard Hawes Taylor was born Jan. 29, 1835.
Clara Ann Taylor was born Dec. 14, 1836.
Gibson Taylor was born Jan. 14, 1839.
Robert Walker Taylor was born Dec. 8, 1840.
Mildred Catherine Taylor was born July 22, 1843.
John Aylett Taylor was born June 4, 1845.
Albert Zachary Taylor was born Oct. 25, 1847.
Edwin Pendleton Taylor was born Feb. 7, 1850.
Ben William Taylor was born Sept. 3, 1854.
George Edward Taylor was born Oct. 20, 1856.

Children of Richard & Mary Taylor
Mary Fielder was born Sunday, Sept. 25, 1859.
Susan Gibson Taylor born August 3, 1917.
William Mallory Taylor born May 15, 1921.
The above are children of Mallory Gibson Taylor and Lucy May Lyons Taylor.
Sue Gibson Taylor married Walter Harold Bigger June 15, 1940.
William Mallory Taylor married to Shirley Frances Cameron of Alberta, Canada on June 1947.

HEWLETT/LUCK/WIGGLESWORTH FAMILY BIBLE

These Bible records were found in an abandoned house on the edge of Caroline and Spotsylvania Counties in 1975 and published by Charles Austin Joy in the *Virginia Genealogical Society Quarterly*, Volume 13, p.77. The records appeared to be of the period of the events recorded. Hewlett, Virginia is named for this family.

John C. Hewlett and Sarah K. Hewlett was Married the 21st day of October 1828 by the Revd Robert G. Coleman.
John K. Luck and Sarah K. Hewlett was Married July the 31 1838 by the Revd William R. Powel.
Robert O. Wiglesworth and Mattie B. Dabney was married April 28 1878 by Rev. Mr. Roe.
Percy C. Wiglesworth and M. Ethel Davis was married Oct. 17, 1905 by Rev. Mr. Gill at Washington, D.C.
John C. Hewlett was born January 4th 1805.
Sarah K. Hewlett was born June 19th 1807.
Drusilla M. Hewlett was born September 27th 1829.
Robert O. Wiglesworth born Nov 7, 1898.
Ethel Lynn Wiglesworth born Jan 13, 1907.
Sarah E. Luck and Mary C. Luck was born February 5th 1841.
John K. Luck was born September 19, 1807.
George W. Luck was born the first day of September 1839.
Joseph C. Luck was born July 6th 1842.
John K. Luck Jr. was born October the 19th 1843.
Robert O. Wiglesworth born May 29, 1851.
Percy C. Wiglesworth born March 3, 1879.
Bessie D. Wiglesworth born Oct. 3, 1880.
Dursilla M. Wiglesworth born Aug. 23, 1889.
Robert G. Wiglesworth born Dec. 10, 1907.
H. S. Wiglesworth was born 28th June 1857.
D. M. Wiglesworth was Fifty Five years 3 months & 10 days old when she departed this life & lived a married life 40 years 9 months & 17 days.
John C. Hewlett died March 31st 1836.

George Boxley Jr. died the 17th day of October 1836.
Sarah E. Luck died July 16 th 1891 .
George Boxley died the 14th of April 1844.
Sarah K. Luck departed this life September 24th 1845.
Joseph C. Luck departed this life December 25th 1845.
John K. Luck departed this life Augus[t] the 16, 1860.
George William Luck died November 24th one thousand eight hundred & sixty one. 1861.
Mary E. Hancock died One thousand Eight hundred and Sixty five.

HOGE/REYNOLDS FAMILY BIBLE

This Bible was published by the National Publishing Company, Philadelphia in the 1870's. The records cover the two families who lived in Giles County, Patrick County and Stokes County, N.C. and Bristol, Tennessee 1783-1963. A copy is in the Library of Virginia. While the Reynolds family may have a tie to Caroline County, it could not be determined by the author and thus only the Hoge portion of the Bible, which definitely ties to Caroline County is reproduced here in this study. The Hoge family has ties to "Blenheim" and "Spring Grove" in Caroline County.

[Grant?] James Hoge [born] July 23rd 1783.
His wife
Elison Howe Hoge Dec. 1st 1792.
Married Jms Hoge & Elison Howe Jan 14th 1810.
Grant James Hoge [died] July 25th 1861.
Elison H. Hoge [died] Jan. 15, 1856.
Their children:
Born Daniel Howe Hoge Mch 11 1811.
Eliza Hoge Dec 11 1815.
James Foalton Hoge April 16th 1818.
Joseph Haven Hoge June 21st 1820.
William E. Hoge May 26 1822.
Married
Daniel H. Hoge & Ann H. Dejarnett [of Caroline Co.] Feby 14 1844.
James F. Hoge & Eliza Jane Johnson Oct 15 1840.
William E. Hoge & Jane Meek Aug 20th 1844.
Geo Tyler & Eliza Hoge Oct 2 1844. [parents of Gov. James Hoge Tyler, who was born at Blemheim, Caroline Co., August 11, 1846]
J.H. Hoge & Susan C. Sayers Sept 26 1843.
Deaths
Eliza Hoge Tyler Aug 10 1846. [mother of Gov. Tyler. Tombstone has Aug. 11]
Daniel H. Hoge Oct 2nd 1867.
His Wife Ann H. Hoge Dec 19 1876.
James F. Hoge Sept 4 1873.
Wm E. Hoge [no date given, James Hoge Tyler's book gives date of death as 3 Feb 1885].

Lizzie J. Hoge J.H. Hoge's 2nd wife born Mch 16th 1839.
Births Wyth County
Major Robt Sayers Born Aug 7th 1796.
His wife Sinah Ross Sayer Oct 12th 1804.
Married
Robt Sayers & Sinah Ross by Rev. Samuel Mc____ Aug 30th 1824.
Deaths
Major Robert Sayers [no date given, James Hoge Tyler's book gives 26 Nov 1876].
Sinah R. Sayers [no date given, James Hoge Tyler's book gives 11 October 1876].
Their children
Susan Crockett Sayers Born June 25 1825.
Robert Sayers Born Nov 16 1826.
Rachel H____ Sayers Born April 16 1828.
William Sayers Born Dec 18 1829.
John P. Sayers Born April 27 1831.
Samuel R. Sayers Born June 27 1833.
Ann C. Sayers Born Apl 16 1838.
Esther M. Sayers Born Feby 27 1837.
Deaths
Wm Ross Sayers Mch 7 1838.
Helen R. Sayers Mch 8 1841.
Births
Joseph Haven Hoge June 21 1820 Pulaski Co Virginia
Susan Crockett Sayers June 25 Wyth Co. Va.
Married
Joseph H. Hoge & Susan C. Sayers by Revd W.P.F. Pickman Sept 26 1843.
Their Children
Born Helen Mary Hoge September 12 1844.
James Robert Hoge Born June 3rd 1846.
Eliza Tyler Hoge Born March 22nd 1848.
Senah Ann Hoge July 20 1849.
Joseph C. Hoge Born May 5 1851.
Elianor James Hoge Born Jany 8 1853.
Osker Hoge Born June 11 [1855].
Samuel S. Hoge Born July 6 1856.
Willie S___ Hoge Born Nov 24 1858.
John T S Hoge Oct 9th 1861.
Marriages of Their Children
D W Mason & Helen M. Hoge By Revd Darnill June 10 1868.
A D Reynolds & Sinah A. Hoge by Revd W H Willhelm Oct 1st 1872.
J F Brewer & Willie S Hoge By Revd Ar____ Sept 13th 1881.
John Tompson Sayers Hoge & Florence Snyder By Rev _____.
Deaths
Susan C Hoge May 15 1883.

Joseph H Hoge Nov 17 1898 78 years.
Helen Mary Mason Died September 23d 1882.
Eliza Tyler Hoge June 11 1848.
James Robert Hoge Oct 6 1851.
Joseph C Hoge Feby 2d 1852.
Ellen James Hoge April 15 1852.[James Hoge Tyler's book list her death date as 15 Apr 1854].
Osker Hoge June 14 1855.

HOOMES FAMILY BIBLE NO. 1

This Bible was published in Edinburg and Printed by Alexander Kincaid His Majesty's Printer, 1762. The Bible belonged to the Hoomes family of the Bowling Green Farm, later called "Old Mansion". A copy is in the Virginia Historical Society. Sophia Hoomes Allen lived at "Oak Ridge", a few miles south of Old Mansion. That house is now destroyed by several burnings in the 20th century.

George Hoomes of the Bowling Green & Frances his wife died
leaving four children
1. Stephen F. Hoomes
2. Ann Hoomes
3. Frances Hoomes
4. John Hoomes, who was born 20th Oct. 1749 - died Dec. 16, 1805
    aged 56 yrs - Married to Judith Churchill Allen 20th Oct. 1768
    who was born July 1st 1749 - died 11th Augt 1822 aged 74 yrs.
Richard Allen of New Kent married Elizabeth Terrell
1. Betty Allen was born November 26 1734.
2. Mary Allen ------------- April 11 1736.
3. Richmond Allen -------- November 7 1737.
4. Martha Allen ---------- May 13 1740.
5. Richard Allen --------- December 10 1741.
6. Rebecca Allen ---------- August 15 1743.
7. Dorcas Allen ---------- June 22 1745.
8. Driscilla Allen ------- June 7 1747.
9. Judith Churchill Allen July 1 1749.
10. William Allen --------- October 5 1751.
11. Mildred Allen --------- February 7 1753.
John Hoomes and Judith his wife were married 20th Oct 1768.
1. Allen Hoomes was born Sept 2 1769.
2. George Hoomes --------- June 16 1771.
3. John Hoomes ----------- Mar 10 1773.
4. Edmund Hoomes --------- July 31 1774.
5. William Hoomes -------- Sept 18 1775.
6. John Hoomes ----------- Octr 27 1777 - died Mar 1824.

7. Geo. W. Hoomes -------- Novr 22 1779 - died in 1802.
8. Wm Allen Hoomes ------- Jany 28 1782 - died 26th Feby 1818.
9. Richard Hoomes -------- Mar 28 1784 - died in Decr 1823.
10. Not baptized.
11. Armistead Hoomes ------ July 3 1786 - died in Febry 1827.
12. Not baptized.
13. Not baptized.
14. Sophia Hoomes --------- Decr 14 1788 - died 9 April 1862 aged 74 yrs 3 mo 26 days.

Richmond Allen born Novr 7th 1737 - died April 17th 1794. Married Elizabeth Wilson, who was born Mar 6th 1745 died Febry 8, 1805.

1. Richard Allen
2. Margaret Allen
3. Susan Allen
4. Betsey Allen
5. Wilson Allen born Febry 15th 1774 - died July 21 1844 Aged 70 yrs 5 mos 6 days.
6. Richmond Allen born Febry 2nd 1778 - died Mar 12 1808 Aged 30 yrs.
7. Wilson Allen

Judith Allen Hoomes and Robert T. Pendleton Married Nov 1829.
Children
1. Robert Lewis Pendleton born 24 Jany 1830 - Died Dec 12, 1880. Aged 50 yrs 10 mos 19 days.
2. Hannah Battaile Pendleton [born] 8 June 1837.

Wilson Allen & Sophia Hoomes Married Jany 22 1807.
1. William Hoomes Allen born Oct 31st 1807 - died Mar 20th 1867 Aged 61 yrs 4 mos 20 days.
2. Robert Wilson Allen ------ April 7 1809 - died March 14th 1856.
3. [no name listed] --------- Augt 1810.
4. Adaline Margaret Allen --- Augt 22 1811 - died June 21 1853.
5. Ann Armistead Allen ------ June 11 1814 - died Mar 2nd 1873.
6. Mary Churchill Allen ----- May 29 1817 - died Dec 4 1846.
7. John Richmond Allen ------ Febry 23 1821 - died Apl 22nd 1873.
8. George Richard Allen ----- April 2 1823 - died Novr 5th 1823.
9. [no name listed] --------- Octo. 1824.
10. Betty Maupin Allen ------- Octo. 4 1825 - died April 15th 1826.
11. [no name listed] --------- Feby 1827.
12. Alfred Dandridge Allen --- March 20 1828.

George W. Hoomes and Martha Waller Married Octo 20 1799.
1. John Waller Hoomes born 9 Aug 1800 - died Aug [no year listed]
2. Caroline Virginia Hoomes ---- 2 April 1802 - died July 1802.

Richard Hoomes and Hannah Battaile Married 19 April 1803.
Children
1. Not Named born 1805.
2. John Allen Hoomes   "   10th May 1806.
3. Hay Hoomes   "   1808.

4. Richard Hay Hoomes " 22 April 1810 - died Jany 7 1884.
5. Judith Allen Hoomes " 9 Mar 1812 - died July 20 1856.
6. George Wilson Hoomes " 16 July 1814 - died 1862.
7. Hay Battaile Hoomes " 9 Mar 1816 - died Aug 27 1880.
8. Mary Willis Hoomes " 13 Dec 1821 - died Mar 16 1844.

Armistead Hoomes and Ann C. Willis Married Novr 12 1806.

Children

1st George Churchill Hoomes born 21st Mar 1808.
2nd Henry Armistead Hoomes   " 22nd Feby 1810 - died 10th Feby 1882.

Armistead Hoomes and Lucy M. Willis (2nd wife) Married Sept 20 1813.

Children

1. Lucy Mary Hoomes born July 1814.

Ann A. Allen & N. Lewis Battaile married 31 Octo 1844.
1. Lizzy Taylor Battaile Born Sept 7 1845.
2. Not named   "   Augt 1846.
3. Lewis Armistead Battaile " Jany 6 1848.
4. Gertrude Battaile   " Octo 8 1849 - died July 13th 1850
   Aged 90 mo & 11 days.

Adaline M. Allen & Robert B. Tunstall Married 5th Octo 1840.
1. Fanny Byrd Tunstall   born 8th Mar 1842 - died 8 Dec 1843.
2. Allen Hoomes Tunstall   " 13 July 1843.
3. Richard Cathbert Tunstall " 20 July 1845.
4. Lelia Sophia Tunstall   " 6 Apr 1847.
5. Robert Byrd Tunstall   " 26 Sep 1848.
6. Fanny Byrd Tunstall   " 31 Aug 1850.
7. Ann Carter Tunstall   " 21 Feby 1852 - died 30 June 1852.
8. Mary Adaline Armistead Tunstall born 8 June 1853.

Alfred Dandridge Allen and Hannah Battaile Pendleton Married November 14 1866.
1. Sophia Hoomes Allen born July 27 1872.

HOOMES FAMILY BIBLE NO. 2

The Hoomes family seat in Caroline County, originally known as "Bowling Green Farm" is now named "Old Mansion". This was the homestead of John Hoomes. "Milford Plantation", now named "Aspen Hill" was the homestead of Armistead Hoomes and "Oak Ridge", just south of Old Mansion and now longer standing was the homestead of Sophia Hoomes. This Bible was published by D. Hitt and T. Ware For the Methodist Connexion in the United States. It was printed in 1815. A copy of the Bible records is in the Virginia Historical Society.

John M. Hoomes and Louisa Dixon his wife were married the twenty fourth of December 1822. Elizabeth Lee Hoomes married Thos C. Robins who was from "Point Lookout" Robin's Neck 1745.

Pricilla Hoomes Married Robert Pollard of King & Queen Co.

Martha married Davis: children Joseph & William Davis.

John Hoomes No. 1 married Bettie Claiborne daughter of Dandridge Claiborne 1752.

B. Claiborne Hoomes & Catherine Pendleton 1776.

Francis G. Bridges and Mary C. his wife were married the fourth November 1845. Son of Robertson Bridges descendant of Joseph Bridges of Macclesfield England. Came to Isle of Wight Co., Va. America. Paymaster English Army - Bacon's Rebellion. Buried St. Lukes Church Yard Smithfield, Va.

Thomas E. Lambeth and Maria Louise (Bridges) his wife were married the 26 of Nov. 1866.

August F. Schultz & Annie Hoomes (Bridges) his wife were married July 13, 1816.

Claiborne Hoomes married Elizabeth Pollard of King & Queen Co. daughter of Robt Pollard.

John Macon Hoomes Married Dec. 24, 1822 Louisa Dixon Taliaferro widow of George Taliaferro.

Benj. Pendleton Hoomes Married Mary Eleanor Dabney daughter of Major George Dabney of King & Queen.

Martha Pendleton Hoomes of Plains [King and Queen Co] & Mordecai Booth Dabney Married Nov. 15, 1821.

Benjamin Clabourn son of John & Louisa Hoomes born seventh of December 1823.

Mary Catharine daughter of John & Louisa Hoomes born the 13th day of May 1827.

Francis G. son of Robertson and Ann Bridges was born the Twenty ninth of March 1822.

Benjamin Pendleton son of Francis & Mary C. Bridges was born seventieth of January 1846.

Maria Louisa daughter of Francis & Mary C. Bridges was born the Sixteenth of February 1850.

Sarah Ann daughter of Francis & Mary C. Bridges was born the Twenty ninth of February 1852.

Annie Hoomes daughter of F.G. & Mary C. Bridges was born the 12th day of February 1857.

Annie Maria Taliaferro daughter of George & Louisa Taliaferro was born the [illeg] March 1821.

Mary Alice daughter of F.G. & M.C. Bridges was born the twenty fourth of October 1858.

Mary Alice the Daughter of Thomas E. and Maria Louisa Lambeth was born the 25 of Oct. 1868. [1868 marked through and 1867 substituted]

Johnnie Francis the infant Son of Thomas E. and Maria Louisa his wife was born the 11 of July 1872.

Mary Maude infant daughter of August F. & Annie H. Schultz was born in Richmond City August 3rd 1877.

Bernard Francis son of A.F. and Anie H. Schultz was born Dec. 5, 1879.

Frederick August, son of August F. & Annie H. Bridges Schultz born Aug 11 - 1881. Died Aug 27 - 1881.

Harleigh Bridges son of A.F. and Annie H.B. Schultz was born Oct. 12 - 1883.

Annie Louise daughter of A.F. and Annie H.B. Schultz was born Oct. 14 - 1888.

August Gwynn, Son of A.F. & Annie H.B. Schultz born Mon. Oct 13 - 1890.

Virginia Ernestine daughter of A.F. & Annie Schultz born May 21st 1897 - Died Oct. 8th 1898.

Walter Schultz Maclelland, Son of Mary Maude Schultz & Walter Shackford Maclelland born May 4 - 1905.

Temple Fairfax Maclelland, Son of Mary Maude S. and Walter S. Maclelland born June 25, 1906.

Annie Louise Maclelland, daughter of Maude S. and Walter S. Maclelland born Mch. 9, 1916.

Evelyn Maude Maclelland, daughter of Maude S. and Walter Maclelland, born November 8, 1917.

John M. Hoomes husband of Louisa Hoomes Died March eleventh 1836.

Louisa Hoomes Wife of John M. Hoomes Died January 20th 1844.

Benjamin C. Hoomes son of John and Louisa Hoomes Died January 7th 1847.

Mary Catherine Hoomes Bridges wife of Sgt. Francis Gwynn Bridges passed Mch. 4, 1904.

Annie Hoomes Bridges Schultz wife of August F. Schultz passed July 18, 1915.

August F. Schultz passed July 18, 1915.

August F. Schultz passed Feb. 12, 1914. [listed twice with different dates]

Temple Fairfax, second son of Mary Maude Schultz and Walter Shackford Maclelland Died Oct. 29, 1972.

Sarah Ann daughter of F.G. and Mary C. Bridges died 21st day of July 1852.

Benjamin Francis son of F.G. and Mary C. Bridges died the 14th day of July 1855 at half past 11 o'clock P.M.

Mary Alice, daughter of F.G. and Mary Catharine Bridges, died 12th of Jan 1860 at half past 11 o'clock, aged 15 mons and three days.

Maria Louisa Bridges wife of Tomas E. Lamberth [sic] died at Marlfield Gloucester Co, Va. Oct 12th 1872.

Annie Louise Schultz - daughter of August Frederick Schultz and Annie Hoomes Bridges Schultz died May 20, 1974 at Baptist Home for Ladies, Richmond, Virginia.

Deacon Francis G. Bridges was killed at the battle of Seven Pines the 31st day of May A.D. 1862. Aged forty years and two months.

Mary Catharine Hoomes Bridges seventy six year of age died last night at the home of her son-in-law A.F. Schultz 2203 W. Main St March 4 - 1904. She was the widow of Sgt. Francis G. Bridges Funeral tomorrow afternoon. Burial in Hollywood.

August Frederick Schultz died night of Feb. 12, 1914 in his home 2203 W. Main St. Richmond Virginia. Funeral services at house Sunday Feb. 15. Burial in his Section Hollywood Va.

Mrs. Annie Hoomes Bridges Schultz wife of August Frederick Schultz died at her home 2203 W. Main St. Richmond on July 18, 1915 services Tabernacle Baptist Church. Burial in family section Hollywood Richmond.

Bernard Francis Schultz died Nov. 30, 1941 in his house 113 N. Crenshaw Ave. Funeral services 3 days after laid to rest in section in Hollywood Oct. 22, 1958.

Harleigh Bridges Schultz. Retired Editor of [illeg] Associate Editor [illeg] Died in Los Angeles California 75 yrs of Age. Burial Oct 25 Valhells Memorial Park North Hollywood Calif.

Mrs. Walter S. Maclelland Mary Maude Schultz wife of Walter S. Maclelland passed away at her home 2205 W. Main St. Richmond Va - Sept 11, 1956.

Walter Shackford Maclelland died April 18, 1958.

Thomas Claiborne Hoomes was born 16th of June 1781.

Betsy Hoomes his wife, daughter of Robt. & Betsy Pollard was born on the 5th day of June 1800.

Martha P. Hoomes Daughter of Benjamin and Mary Hoomes, was Born Jan 21st ....[no year listed]

Mary Eliza Daughter of Mordecai B. and Martha P. Dabney was born February 3rd 1823.

Sarah Catharine Daughter of M. B. and Martha P. Dabney was born January 1 first day of the week and year 1826.

Maria C. Daughter of M. B. and Martha P. Dabney was born March 27th 1829.
Busrod Washington Son of M. B. and Martha P. was born April 21st 1830.
Martha Booth Daughter of M. B. and M. P. Dabney was born Novr 6th 1835.
William Claiborne Son of M. B. and Martha P. Dabney was born Novr 20th [no year listed].
Thomas Claiborne eldest Son of Thomas A. and Maria C. Pierce was born December 18th 1853 A.D.
Anna Pendleton daughter of Thomas A. and Maria C. Pierce was born   December 9th 1855 A.D.
Mary Booth daughter of Thomas A. and Maria C. Pierce was born October 9th 18589 A.D.
Dabney J. Pierce Son of Rev. T.A. Pierce and Maria C. was born Feb. 23rd 1865 A.D.
Edwin McRae Rucker Aug. 13, 1907
Derrell Scott Rucker Mar 17, 1901.
Josephine Pierce Rucker Sept. 14, 1910.
Denpas Pendleton Rucker Nov. 15, 1914.
Thomas Claiborne Hoomes and Betsy Pollard on the 16th day of December 1817 were married.
Mordecai Booth Dabney and Martha P. Hoomes [married] pm the 15th day of November 1821.
Thomas A. Pierce of the Va. Con.[?] and Maria C. Dabney on the 30th day of April 1852 A.D.
Edward T. Rucker, M.D. was married to Annie P. Pierce on the 18th day of November 1879 A.D.
George E. Sangster and Mary Booth Pierce on the 25th day of January 1883 A.D.
Also in the Bible are printed death notices for Martha P. Dabney, consort of Mordecai B. Dabney who died at White Plains, King William County 4 Mary 1851; Mary Eliza the 21 year old daughter of Mordecai B. and Martha P. Dabney who died 11th Sept. 1843 in King William County; Mordecai Booth Dabney who died June 9, 1857 at White Plains, King William County in his 69th year; and Mrs. Mary C. Bridges, widow of Frank G. Bridges of Gloucester County, who died at age of 67 years and was buried in Hollywood, notice dated Mar. 7, 1904.

HUDGIN FAMILY BIBLE

This is a copy of the Bible record left by Mrs. Sallie Graham Hudgin, wife of Robert Hudgin of Bowling Green, Virginia, which was later in the possession of Mrs. Ellen W. Downing of Bowling Green, Virginia. It has been preserved by Mary Robertson Boulware Campbell of Redmond, Washington, who has furnished this copy.

The Hudgin family home named "Auburn" is still standing just north of the intersection of Routes 301, 2, and 307 in Bowling Green, Caroline County and next to the old Glassell house named "Glasselton". It was first occupied by Robert Hudgin and his wife Ellen Downing. Members of this family are buried in Lakewood Cemetery, Bowling Green. Auburn is presently owned and occupied by Dr. and Mrs. Larry Motor and is on the Virginia Landmarks Register and the National Register.

(Beginning of Bible Record)
Walter Graham, fourth son of John and Elizabeth Graham of Dumfries, Virginia, was born March 18, 1759, and the 9th of April 1784, married Sally Richards, the fourth daughter of John and Susannah Richards of Falmouth, Virginia, who was born May 4, 1763. Walter Graham died the 21st of Feb., 1829.

Children of Walter and Sally Graham:
Elizabeth, born Jan. 19, 1785.
Wm. Richards, born Sep. 1, 1786.
Susanna Sydney, born Feb. 11, 1788.
Margaret Sevenia, born May 18, 1789.
Catherine Matilda, born Oct. 30, 1791.
Margaret Mildred, born Nov. 24, 1792.
Jane Catherine, born Nov. 16, 1794.
Elinoe [Elinor] Whitehead, born Feb. 18, 1796.
Catherine Richards, born Apr. 24, 1797.
Walter Allen, born Sep. 9, 1798.
Mary Jane, born Feb. 28, 1800.
Sarah Richards, born May 3, 1801, married R. Hudgin.
Thomas Marshall, born Sep. 3, 1808.

Robert Hudgin and Sarah Richards Graham were married April 30, 1828.
Their children were:
Wescom, born Mar. 27, 1829.
Milly Stone, born in Bowling Green, Va. June 27, 1830, married Gray Boulware.
Elinoe Walker, born in Bowling Green, Va., July 12, 1832.
Walter Graham, born in Bowling Green, Va., Dec. 27, 1833.
Robt. Tunstall, born in Bowling Green, Va., Mar. 5, 1835.
Sallie Graham, born in Bowling Green, Va., Aug. 25, 1837.
John Marye, born in Bowling Green, Va., June 8, 1839.
Notes in the Bible made by Mary Blanche Boulware:
Sarah Richards Graham died Nov. 21, 1837.
Elizabeth Graham married Luckett.
Sarah Richards Hudgin died April, 1865.
Robert Hudgin, born in Fredericksburg, Va. Aug. 10, 1802, died April 20, 1892.
Robert Hudgin and Sarah Richards Graham were married April (30 or 20?).
Wescom Hudgin, physician in Culpeper Cty. Died 1884.
Milly Stone Boulware died June 1906.
Elinor Walker Hudgin died April 1906.
Walter Graham Hudgin, served in Confederacy, died June 19, 1918.
Robt. Tunstall Hudgin, served in Confederacy, died 1881.
Sallie Graham Hudgin, died April 4, 1888.
John Marye Hudgin, served in Confederacy, died Feb. 5, 1899.
Walter Graham Hudgin and Caroline Daggs McClintic of Bath County, Virginia, were married on December 13, 1859.
Caroline Daggs McClintic was born July 2, 1836 on a farm near Covington, Virginia, and died in Hinton, West Virginia, on January 20, 1914, at the home of her daughter Mr. Charles S. Falconer.
Walter Graham Hudgin of Bowling Green, Virginia, died in Covington, Virginia, on June 27, 1918, at the home of his daughter, Mrs. Charles Irving Smith. Their children were:

Mary Daggs, born April 30, 1861 at Bowling Green, Virginia.

Sara Graham, born March 12, 1864 at Bowling Green, Virginia.

Caroline, born March 16, 1866 at Bowling Green, Virginia.

Margaret, born Nov. 17, 1867 at Bowling Green, Virginia.

Katherine, born April 26, 1870 at Bowling Green, Virginia.

Ellen Hardia, born Feb. 21, 1872 at Bowling Green, Virginia.

Robert, born Feb. 2, 1876 at Bowling Green, Virginia.

Doctor Wescom Hudgin, son of Robert Hudgin and Sarah Graham Hudgin, of Bowling Green, Virginia, was married to Anna Yates Billups of Athens, Georgia, on January 26, 1859. Their children were:

Anna Graham, born Jan. 2, 1870, Sunday.

Wescom, born March 20, 1871.

Jane Billups, born Dec. 17, 1872.

Thomas Billups [sic], born Dec. 17 [sic] 1876.

[also added, author, unknown]}

Sallie Graham Hudgin, daughter of Robert Hudgin and Sarah Richards Graham Hudgin, married Corydon Sutton in 1857.

Her son, Garnett was born November 12, 1858. Left a young widow who returned to Bowling Green, and her son grew to manhood in the home of his grandfather, Robert Hudgin. In 1880, Sallie Graham Hudgin Sutton married Mr. Adams of Rockbridge Baths, Virginia. She died in Bowling Green on April 2, 1888 of cancer of the breast..

Garnet Sutton married Sarah Burge Cox on December 15, 1887. He died in Clifton Forge, Virginia, on July 10, 1898. Their children were:

Virginia Graham Sutton, born Dec. 9, 1888.

Ross Claiborne Sutton, born Nov. 15, 1890.

Garnett Wallace Sutton, born Jan. 28, 1893.

Ella Burge Sutton, born Jan. 12, 1896.

Mildred Cooper Sutton, born Nov. 1, 1898.

Notes made by Kate George Hudgin Jennings:

There is a tradition that several Hudgin brothers landed in Jamestown about the middle or latter part of the 17th Century. My grandfather, Robert Hudgin, of Bowling Green, Virginia, said that his Hudgin ancestor came from Wales but he was not sure when. He was an only son and his father was an only son, and as his father died when he was only three years old, he never knew any of his Hudgin relatives. Robert Hudgin was the son of Capt Westcomb Hudgins and his wife Eleanor Hardia Hudgin, both of Fredericksburg, Virginia. Capt. Westcomb Hudgin was a sea captain who made frequent voyages to the West Indies and died at Barbadoes in May, 1805, of yellow fever. Westcomb Hudgin was the son of Robert Hudgins of Mathews County, Virginia, who married Eliza Westcomb.

From the Fredericksburg Herald of Nov. 5, 1799, in the Congressional Library, Washington, D.C. is the following record:

Married on Oct. 31, 1799, Capt. Westcomb Hudgins to Miss Nelly Hardia of this town.

From Fredericksburg Virginia Herald is the following record:

Died at Barbadoes of yellow fever early last month, Captain Westcomb Hudgins of this town. A gentleman much esteemed by all acquaintances.

His wife, Eleanor Hardia Hudgins died Oct. 1819, so my grandfather was only 17 years old when his mother died. Elenor Hardia Hudgins was daughter of John and Clarissa Hardia of Fredericksbuirg, Va. Just when the Hardias came to Fredericksburg I have never been able to ascertain.

From the record of Kingston Parish, Mathews County, Virginia, now deposited in the archives of the Virginia State Library at Richmond, Virginia, it is recorded that on December 22, 1770 Robert Hudgin was married to Eliza Westcomb.

Included in the Bible is the death notice from the Fredericksburg Free Lance of Robert Hudgin in the Ninetieth Year of His Age and the Sixty-fifth of his Official Service. Mr. Robert Hudgin, the venerable clerk of Caroline County Court, died at his home in Bowling Green, last Sunday, the 24th Instant. Mr. Hudgin was born in Fredericksburg, Va. On the 10th of August 1802, and served as apprentice in the chancery court of that city until he was twenty-one years old.

In 1827 he became deputy clerk of Caroline county, Va. And was soon thereafter made clerk of the circuit court of said county by Judge John Tayloe Lomax. He filled this position and acted as deputy clerk of the county court until 1860, when he became purchaser of the Fauquier Springs property. He removed there and settled for a short time, but the Federal force, after using the hotel as a hospital, wantonly burned the property in 1863 and thereby rendered it worthless to him as a watering place. From a ruined home in Fauquier county he returned to Caroline at the close of the war, to find the clerk's office of the county in dire confusion and disorder. The Federal troops had ruthlessly overturned everything and woefully scattered all the papers of the office on the floors in one mingled mess of rubbish and waste and for weeks and months he worked patiently to assort and rearrange the same. He was soon restored to the official discharge of his duties as clerk of both courts, and held them until the separation of the clerkship by the Legislature in 1875. He was retained as clerk of the county court until the time of his death, making an official service, with a very short interregnum, of sixty-five years.

Too old to be in the Confederate army himself, he gave three sons in active service, Walter G., Robert T., and John M. Hudgin, and his oldest son, Dr. Wescom Hudgin, who was resident physician in Culpeper county, waded Hazel river at midnight and gave timely warning to General J. E. B. Stuart that the enemy were about to surprise his camp at Brandy Station. Several times during the war this devoted son of Virginia periled his life between the lives of the contending armies to shelter his friends from destruction. Two of his sons survive him, Judge W.G. Hudgin and Captain J. M. Hudgin. Robert Hudgin was a genuine type of the old Virginia gentleman. He was for a number of years a practicing attorney-at-law and a candidate for the Constitutional Convention in 1849. His life has been spent among memorable events and scenes, among resolutions and convulsions in society and government. None of his contemporaries are left to follow him to the grave, but the hearts of his countymen in Caroline and his friends in distant localities will receive with sorrow and sympathy the news that this worthy citizen, Robert Hudgin, is dead.

Also included is the death notice from the Fredericksburg Free Lance of Captain John M. Hudgin February 6, 1899 [died February 4]:

Captain Jack M. Hudgin, soldier, lawyer, citizen, and Christian gentleman, is dead. The end came peacefully Saturday night at his home "Shepherd's Hill," in Caroline county. For some months past Captain Hudgin had been gradually failing and for the past two weeks his death had been daily expected. The deceased was born in Caroline county in 1838, and was a son of the late Robert Hudgin, who for many years, was Clerk of the County and Circuit Court of Caroline. At the breaking out of the civil war, true to his people and his teachings, his fate and fortune were cast with the Confederacy. He enlisted in the Thirtieth Virginia Regiment, and for distinguished bravery was promoted to captain. At the close of the war he took up the practiced of law and shortly afterwards graduated with distinguished honors at the University of Virginia. He was not only well known in this section, but throughout the entire State, having for several terms served his county ably and faithfully in the lower house of the Virginia Legislature, and on two occasions was a prominent candidate before the Democratic District Convention for Congress. During Mr. Cleveland's second term, he was United States Marshal for the Eastern District of Virginia. He also had held other minor offices of trust and responsibility, which he filled with credit to himself and full satisfaction to his constituents. He leaves one sister--Mrs. Ellen Downing, of Caroline--and a brother--Judge Hudgin of Hinton, W. Va. His funeral took place from his home. Rev. E.H. Rowe conducting the services, at 3:30 o'clock this afternoon, and the remains were interred in Lakewood Cemetery, Bowling Green. His death removes from the stage of life a noble and generous Christian gentleman, an able lawyer, and loyal supporter of the South and her people.

HUDGIN FAMILY RECORD

This family record was included with the Hudgin Bible records as separate pages and not a part of the Bible. They were probably put together by a later family member, not identified. It was entitled as the family of Walter Graham Hudgin and his wife Caroline McClintic Hudgin.

1. Mary Daggs Hudgin was married on February 28, 1889, in Alderson, West Virginia, to Charles Stuart Falcomer of Petersburg, Virginia. They went to live in Hinton, West Virginia. Their only child, Mary Stuart Falcomer, was born in Hinton, August 19, 1894.

Mary Stuart Falconer was married on April 30, 1924, in Alderson, West Virginia, to Lloyd Crescent Halloran of Hinton. Their son, Charles Lloyd Halloran, was born in the Hinton Hospital on February 7, 1925.

2. Sara (Sallie) Graham Hudgin has never married.
3. Caroline Hudgin was married on October 30, 1894, at her home in Hinton, West Virginia, to James Robert Campbell. Their child, Anna Hudgin Campbell, was born in Hinton, West Virginia, on March 14, 1896. Anna Hudgin Campbell was married on October 23, 1919 at 420 Cook Avenue, Trenton, New Jersey, to Walter Beatty. Their daughter, Sara Hudgin Beatty, was born in St. Francis Hospital, Trenton, New Jersey, on November 6, 1926.
4. Margaret Hudgin was married on June 4, 1896 to Hiram Seaborn Douthitt, of Howard, Kansas (born near Richmond, Kentucky). Judge Hiram S. Douthitt died Howard, Kansas, of Pneumonia on February 11, 1904. Their children were Margaret Ayres Douthitt, born November 19, 1897, and Caroline Hudgin Douthitt, born June 19, 1900. After the death of her husband, Margaret Hudgin Douthitt, with her two daughters went to live in Greenville, Indiana. There in June, 1918, Margaret was graduated from DePauw University and Caroline from high school.

The following summer the three moved to Akron, Ohio, where Margaret took a position as chemist with Goodrich Company, and Caroline entered the University of Akron. On October 5, 1920, Margaret [widow] was married to Frederick Hughes Amon, also of Akron (he was born near Greenville, Ohio).

They had two children:

Frank Douthitt Amon, born December 21, 1924 and Richard Frederick Amon, born June 6, 1926.

Caroline Douthitt was married on June 12, 1924, in Frederick, Maryland, to Virgil Eugene Martin of Atlanta, Georgia. They now live in Birmingham, Alabama, and have one child, Eugenia Douthitt Martin, born September 30, 1931, in the Highland Hospital.

5. Katherine (Kate George Hudgin) was married on May 31, 1900, in Hinton, West Virginia, to Stephen P. Jennings of Amherst County, Virginia, a contractor. Their daughter, Margaret Hudgin Jennings, was born on February 27, 1901, in Hinton, West Virginia.

Margaret Hudgin Jennings was married on October 10, 1923 to Leonard Harrison Woods, at her home near Station 29, Richmond and Petersburg Electric Line. There, on November 23, 1924, was born their daughter, Carolyn Jennings Woods.

6. Ellen Hardia Hudgin was married June 2, 1897 in Hinton, West Virginia, to Charles Irving Smith, also of Hinton, but born in Richmond, Virginia. Their children were:

Virginia Montross Smith, born Feb. 2, 1898, at Hinton, W. Va.

Walter Irving Smith, born Jan. 7, 1900, at Hinton, W. Va.

Ellen Hudgin Smith, born May 21, 1906 at Covington, W. Va. Virginia Montross Smith was married on Aug. 11, 1934 to George Martin Farrar, Jr., of Clifton Forge, Virginia, at her home in Covington.

Walter Smith was married to Mary Curlin Jones of Rawlings, Virginia, on June 26, 1936, at the home of the bride.

Ellen Hudgin Smith was married in Lexington, Virginia, to Isaac Rose of Covington, Virginia.

7. Robert Hudgin has never married and now lives in Richmond, Virginia, and is a machinist for the Chesapeake and Ohio Railroad.

HUTCHESON FAMILY BIBLE NO. 1

This Bible belonged to John Hutcheson of "Locust Hill", Caroline County. It is now in the Smith County Historical Society, Tyler, Texas. A copy of it has been printed in *Virginia Bible Records* by Jeannette Holland Austin, Willow Bend Books, Westminster, Maryland, 2000.

John Hutcheson married Elizabeth Chiles of Caroline Co., Va. August 30, 1763.
Jemimah Hutcheson born August 4, 1766.
William Hutcheson born January 12, 1776.
Samuel Hutcheson born January 17, 1774.
Mary Hutcheson born April 18, 1768.
Susannah C. Hutcheson born July 27, 1777.
Chiles Hutcheson born April 30, 1770.
Elizabeth Hutcheson born August 13, 1779.
John Hutcheson born April 7, 1772.
Richard Hutcheson born August 30, 1782.

John Hutcheson married Nancy Stone of Mecklenburg Co., Va. December 24, 1793.
Martha R. Hutcheson born October 9, 1794.
Elizabeth C. Hutcheson born July 12, 1798
William Hutcheson born July 11, 1796.
Frances A. Hutcheson born April 8, 1800.
John Hutcheson married Mary Sugget, widow (nee Jones) September 10, 1801.
Rebecca I. Hutcheson born March 3, 1803.
Mary M. Hutcheson born August 12, 1806.
Ann J. Hutcheson born May 4, 1841.
John Hutcheson married Mary Clay of Mecklenburg Co. February 25, 1840.
Nancy Hutcheson, consort of John Hutcheson died January 16, 1801.
Mary Hutcheson, consort of John Hutcheson died June 25, 1839.
John T. Legrand born May 7, 1862.
James A. Legrand born October 11, 1867.
Eveline O. Legrand born May 19, 1866.
John T. Legrand born January 18, 1863.
Mary Hutcheson, wife of John Hutcheson died February 21, 1868.
Her husband died 14 yrs. before in December 1849
Thomas S. Legrand married Annie Hutcheson May 1, 1863.
John T. Legrand died January 18, 1863.
Thomas S. Legrand died January 5, 1869.
Eveline G. Legrand died October 17, 1868.

HUTCHESON FAMILY BIBLE NO. 2

This Bible was published by N. Bands and J. Emory for The Methodist Episcopal Church, New York, 1828. The Bible originally belonged to the family of Peter Hutcheson of Caroline County, who married Eliza Fisher Carleton, daughter of Gabriel and Elizabeth Edwards Carleton, March 19, 1818. He later moved to Mecklenburg County, Virginia and the Bible became that of son Peter Wesley Hutcheson. The Brame family of Caroline County lived across the highway from old Needwood Tavern.

Peter Hutcheson born December 30th 1743.
Elizabeth Brame who intermarried with said Peter born September 2d 1751.
John Hutcheson son of the above born June 26th 1768.
Peter Wesley do born March 17th 1794.
Elizabeth Whitfield do born November 6th 1795.
Gabriel Carleton born July 27th 1764.
Elizabeth Edwards who intermarried with Gabriel born October 5th 1767.
Jane Swepson daughter of Gabriel & Elizabeth was born November 22d 1788.
Eliza Fisher do born September 4th 1791.
Sarah Edwards do born December 15th 1794.
Peter Hutcheson Departed this life October 16th 1820.

Elizabeth Brame Departed this life February 17th 1821.

John Hutcheson, son of [Peter and Elizabeth] Departed this life April 17th 1825.

Peter Wesley [Hutcheson] Departed this life December 9th 1875 at 6 o'clock P.M.

Elizabeth Whitfield [Hutcheson] Departed this life July 9th 1870.

Gabriel Carleton [Hutcheson] Departed this life Sept. 2d 1803.

Elizabeth Edwards (Hutcheson) Departed this life December 24th 1839 at a quarter past three in the morning.

Jane Swepson [Carleton] Departed this life on the morning of the 7th day of April 1851.

Eliza Fisher [Carleton] Departed this life October 6th 1875 about 12 o'clock noon.

Sarah Edwards [Hutcheson] Departed this life October 20th 1876.

Peter W. Hutcheson and Eliza F. Carleton were married the 19th day of March 1818.

Ellen Maria daughter of the above born December 8th 1818.

Thomas Dance do born September 11th 1820.

Peter Wesley do born July 19th 1822.

Sarah Jane Virginia do born January 28th 1824.

Gabriel Carleton do born December 30th 1825.

Mary Ann Elizabeth do born November 13th 1827.

Two twin children do born July 7th 1829. The first departed this life the 8th day of July, the other the 16th afterwards, 1829.

Ellen Maria [Hutcheson] Departed this life November 29th 1825.

Thomas Dance [Hutcheson] Departed this life June 17th 1891.

Peter Wesley [Hutcheson] Departed this life March 22d 1880.

Sarah Jane Virginia [Hutcheson] Departed this life August 21st, 1914.

Gabriel Carleton [Hutcheson] Departed this life July 17th 1845 at a quarter after 9 in the morning.

Mary Ann Elizabeth [Hutcheson] Departed this life Dec. 14, 1893.

Susannah Rebecca born August 10th 1830.

A female child born dead the 7th day of December 1833.

Edward Hutcheson son of Thomas & Arabella G. Hutcheson born Dec. 4th 1846.

Gabriel Carleton Johnson son of L.[Luke]G.[Garnett] & Mary Ann Elizabeth Johnson born March 11th 1849. [He never married and died in Florida in 1884.]

Elizabeth Hutcheson daughter of Thomas D. and Arabella Hutcheson born 4th September 1850.

Henry Osborn Johnson son of L.G. and Mary Anne [Elizabeth Hutcheson] Johnson born December 13th 1850.

Margaret Eliza daughter of P. W. Hutcheson Jr. and Mary Anne Elizabeth his wife born August 10, 1849.

Thomas Edward son of the above born June 15th 1851.

Swetson O'Neil son of the above born Nov 29th 1853.

Mary Hutcheson daughter of Thomas D. & Arabella Hutcheson his wife born January 23d 1853.

Lucious Fletcher son of L.G. & Mary Anne Elizabeth Johnson his wife born Sept 19th 1852.

Nathan Wesley son of the same born Feby 18th 1854.

George Thomas son of Luke G. & M.A.E. Johnson born March 28th 1855.

Thomas, son of T.[Thomas]D.[Dance] & A.S. Hutcheson born Apr 7th 1855.

Arabella Hutcheson daughter of T.D. & A.S. Hutcheson born July 10th 1856.

James Hutcheson son of the same born Dec 11th 1857.

Mary Hutcheson daughter of Thomas D. and Arabella Hutcheson married Thomas H. Dozier. Died Oct 14, 1927. Buried Oconee Cemetery, Athens, Ga.

Lucious Fletcher son of L.G. & Mary Anne Elizabeth [Hutcheson] Johnson died Nov. 16, 1928. Unmarried. Buried Monticelli, Fla.

Nathan Wesley son of L.G. & Mary Ann Elizabeth Johnson Died [in infancy] the 29th Sept 1854 at a quarter past 12 in the morning.

George Thomas son of Luke G. & M.A.E. Johnson Buried Oconee Cemetery, Athens, Ga.

Thomas son of T.D. & A.S. Hutcheson Died June 26th 1883.

Arabella Hutcheson daughter of T.D. & A.G. Hutcheson Died Sept 23, 1916. Buried Winterville, Ga.

James Hutcheson son of T.D. & A.S. Hutcheson Died Feby 19th 1914. Buried Winterville, Ga.

Also recorded in this Bible are 145 Negro slaves referred to as "servants" with names of births, deaths and in some cases names of husbands and wives, from the dates ranging from 1771 to 1865. Most of these, if not all, are during the time the family was living in Mecklenburg County, Virginia.

JESSE/COLLINS FAMILY BIBLE

This Bible probably originated with the Jesse family of "Hunter's Hill" on U.S. Route 2 north of Bowling Green. It appears to have descended into the family of Robert Emmett Collins and his children, who lived in the southern end of Caroline County. A copy of the family register from the Bible is in the Library of Virginia. For further information concerning this family, see *The History and Genealogy of the Collins Family* by Herbert R. Collins, 1954 and *Todds of Virginia* by Rubey, Stacy and Collins, 1960.

John Jesse [died] January 1 1823. [He was born in 1765].

Mary Elizabeth Jesse [died] May 21st 1837. [She was born circa 1769, the daughter of Captain Charles Tod Sr.]

Charles Collins [died] June 15 1853.

John Jesse January 1 1823.

Mary Elizabeth Jesse May 21st 1837. [these are listed twice].

Charles Jesse son of Charles T.[Tod] and Ann H.[Harriett] Jesse died Sep 15 1839.

Charles Collins died June 15 1853 [He was born January 28, 1793, the son of James & Clarissa Collins and married Catherine Jesse February 12, 1832].

Belle Ham[p]ton Collins was Born the 19th of Dec. 1886.

Sarah Muse Collins The Second daughter Of Bell G. & R.E.[Robert Emmett] Collins was born April 8 1880.

Thomas M. Collins was born December 8th 1883.

Charles Jesse Son of Chas. T.[Tod] and Ann H.[Harriett Thornton] Jesse died Sep 15 1839.

Emett Burk Collins Was born 16 September 1811.

Mary Lou Collins daughter of Emmett & Belle Collins born November 28 1875.

Sarah Muse Collins was born 8th of Apr 1880.

Adelaide B. Jesse daughter of Charles T. Jesse and Ann H. born August 11th 1839.
Charles Jesse Son of Charles T. and Ann H. Jesse born Oct. 25th 1836.
Mildred P. Collins Mother[?] of Catherine Collins born 16 April 1840.
James Collins Son of Charles Collins and Catherine Collins was born 30 November 1841.
George R.[Richard] Collins Son of Charles Collins and Catherine Collins was born 21 November 1844.
Charles Beazley, son of Arthur and Millie Beazley born October 4, 1858.
Richard T.[Thornton] Jesse Son of Robert and Mary D.[Diggs] Jesse born January 26th 1838.
Mary Ellen Jesse daughter of Robert and Mary D. Jesse born May 25th 1840.
Ann Maria Jesse daughter of Robert and Mary D. Jesse born May 6th 1842.
Sarah Louisa Collins was born 10 of March 1847.
Robert E.[Emmett] Collins Son of Charles and Cath. Collins born 18th of June 1850.
Ann E. Beazley daughter of Millie and Arthur Beazley born November 5, 1858.
Belle Hampton Collins was born the 19th Dec 1886.
Mary Jesse born Sept 25 - 1828.
Ann H. [Harriett] Jesse born Decm. 16 - 1830.
Susan T. Jesse daughter of Charles T. Jesse and Ann H Jesse born December 19th 1832.
John J. Collins son of Charles & Catharine born Dec 29th 1832.
George Robert Jesse son of John & Mary Jesse born January 28th 1831.
Mary Gray Jesse daughter of John & Mary Jesse born November 5th 1832.
Jane Margaret Jesse daughter of Joseph & Ann Jesse born September 25th 1831.
Mary Elizabeth Jesse [born] Sept 30th 1833 daughter of Joseph & Ann Jesse.
William Matthew Gray Jesse Son of Joseph and Ann Jesse Sept 29 1836.
Belle Hampton was born Dec 19, 1886.
Wm P. & Sarah Jesse Dec 18 1887.
John Jesse [born] July 31 1799.
Charles Jesse [born] March 23 1800.
George T Jesse [born] Dec 16, 1802.
Joseph Jesse [born] Jany 16, 1804
Robert Jesse [born] March 16, 1807.
Richard Jesse [born] June 3rd 1808.
Catharine Jesse [born] June 3rd 1810.
Mary Tod Collins daughter of Chas & Catherine Collins born October 15th 1836.
Sarah Mildred Jesse daughter of John & Mary Jesse born Dec 18 1834.
Richard T Jesse son of Robt & Mary D. Jesse born Jan 26th 1838.
Charles Collins son of Charles and Catharine Collins born Nov 30th 1838.
James Jesse Son of Charles T Jessie & Harriet born Decr 26th 1838.
Charles T. Jesse and Ann H. Thornton 24 Decr 1827.
Joseph Jesse and Frances Ann Gray 7 Octo 1829.
John Jesse and Mary M. Gray 26 November 1829.
Charles Collins and Catharine Jesse 21st February 1832.
Robert Jesse & Mary Digges Thornton 23 March 1837.
Married on the 23rd of Dec 1874 By Elder J. W. Williams R.E. Collins to Bell B. Burke Both of Caroline Co., Va.

Charles Jesse and Ann H. Thornton [no date listed].
Charles W. Collins and Marie T.[Mary Todd] Collins [his cousin] January 18, 1855.
George Waveley Collins born 11th of February 1882.
Philip A. Beazley son of Arthur and Millie Beazley born April 29th 1864.
Willie A. Beazley son of Arthur and Millie Beazley born March 10th 1867.
George R. Beazley son of Arthur and Millie Beazley born March 23rd 1869.
Marie C Beazley daughter of Millie and Arthur Beazley born March 2, 1861.

JOHNSTON FAMILY BIBLE

This Bible was reproduced in *Johnston of Caroline County, Virginia, Some of the Descendants of William and Chew Johnston (1697-1778)* by Elbert Felton Johnston, The Henington Publishing Company, Wolfe City, Texas, 1964. It is believed to have been written by Larkin Johnston. The Johnstons were well represented in colonial Caroline County. The family operated taverns at both the first and second courthouse sites and also were at Port Royal. Larkin Chew of Caroline County, about 1700, married Hannah Roy, daughter of John and Dorothy Roy of Port Royal. Their third child, Ann Chew, married William Johnston and became the parents of Larkin Johnson. Another child, Judith, married Robert Farish, another Caroline County family. Larkin Johnston's wife, Mary Rogers, was sister to Ann Rogers, mother of George Rogers Clark and William Clark of Caroline County. Another sister, Lucy Rogers, married Capt. Samuel Redd of Caroline County and another sister, Mildred Rogers, married Reuben George of Caroline County. Her brother George Rogers married Frances Hoomes Pollard of Caroline County. In 1748, Larkin Johnston wrote on one page: "God give me Grace therein to look, And when for me the bell doth toll, The Lord of Heaven receive my soul". Larkin Johnston's Bible was given him by his father William Johnston and bears the date on one page as 1747. It next went to Littleton Johnston, son of Larkin Johnston Feb. 19, 1801. Next it went to Thomas Johnston and to his son James Henry in 1849. It was printed in London by Robert Barker, in 1605. It was in the possession of George Porter Wilthies Jr. of Minden, Louisiana in 1957. A copy of the Bible record was published in the December, 1940 issue of the DAR Magazine. All of the Johnstons of Caroline County during the colonial period seem to have left the county by the 19th century or thereabouts.

The Bible begins with the following statement: "Births, deaths, and marriages of the children of Larkin and Mary [Rogers] Johnston who were married May 7, 1745, being then eighteen years old - 1 day. My wife, eighteen years three months old. I was born May 1, 1727 -- my wife, January 2, 1727, and she departed this life 25th of October 1800 on the same day of month and same month our first child was born."

William, the son of Larkin and Mary Johnston was born in Virginia, October 14, 1746 old style --
   now October 30 new style. Deceased November 29, 175;9. Aged 13 years, one month and 15
   days -- Granville Co., N.C.
Ann, daughter of Larkin and Mary Johnston born June 22, 1749, Thursday -- Spotsylvania Co.
Virginia. Married to Samuel Cush, August 26, 1772 -- Caroline Co., Virginia.
Larkin, son of Larkin and Mary, his wife, born 11th of July 1752, old style, Saturday, 2 o'clock
   in the afternoon -- Spotsylvania Co., Virginia. Deceased March 9, 1757, aged 4 years, 8

months and 29 days. Halifax Co., Va.

Lucy, daughter of Larkin and Mary Johnston, born May 1, 1755, Halifax Co., Va. Dan River. Married to John Landers, 30th of November 1783.

Sarah, daughter of Larkin and Mary Johnston born May 18, 1758 -- Granville Co., N.C. Married Francis Howard, January 25, 1778, 1st marriage. Since to Henry Fuller of Person Co., N.C.

Littleton, son of Larkin and Mary Johnston born February 18, 1761, Thursday 9 o'clock in the evening, Granville Co., N.C. Married to Lucy Childs, January 4, 1781.

John, son of Larkin and Mary Johnston born December 22, 1763, Granville Co., N.C. 1st wife Leah Long. 2nd wife Mary Warren.

Theodorick, son of Larkin and Mary Johnston born December 22, 1763, Granville Co., N.C. -- Harrisburg -- married to Elizabeth Stuard.

Sophia, daughter of Larkin and Mary Johnston born December 15, 1769, Granville Co., N.C. Married to Larkin Herndon, August 26, 1802, of Caswell Co.

Richard, son of Larkin and Mary Johnston born March 14, 1778. Married to Elizabeth Hemphill, March 1802.

My wife departed this life October 25, 1800, and was buried by her brother John at his old place on Hico, on the Tuesday after she died, being kept out of the grave 4 days, according to her request. We lived together upward of 55 years in which time she Brought me ten children, eight of whom are now alive — 1802.

JONES FAMILY BIBLE

This Bible was printed and published by Matthew Carey, Philadelphia, 1809. A copy is in the Library of Virginia.

Ann Edmonds Jones born January 3rd. 1797.
Elizabeth Buckner Jones born December 12, 1798.
Lucy Jones born 6th of September 1800.
Lillian Jones born Jany. 9th. 1803.
Emily Jones born April 3 d. 1805.
Harriett Jones born April 19th. 1807.
Sarah Jones born July 15th 1809.
John Richard Jones born Jany. 3rd. 1818.
Madison Taliaferro Jones was born January 29, 1818.
Butler Baker born July 4, 17--.
Mary Frances Jones born January 1813.
Samuel Baker born September 2nd. 1824.
Elizabeth B. Baker born May 23rd. 1827.
Susanna Baker born May 14, 1830.
Samuel B. Baker born January 5th. 1833.
Elizabeth Jones wife of Capt. William Jones departed this life February 22nd. 1818.
Capt. William Jones departed this life April 15th. 1818.
John R. Jones departed this life May 1822.
William Jones Married to Elizabeth Buckner daughter of Major Richard Buckner of Caroline the

first of October 1795.
Ann E. Jones married to John Dishman October 10th. 1816.
Lucy Jones married to Butler Baker December 14 1820.
Elizabeth B. Jones married to Robert Haile November 3 1821.
Harriett Jones Married to Robert Davis November 22 - 1835.
Samuel Baker departed this life September 10th. 1832.
Elizabeth Baker departed this life September 26 - 1832.

KAY FAMILY BIBLE NO. 1

This family lived near Naulakla, Caroline County, on land granted Martha by her father James. He owned a very large estate and his home was near Enon Church, Essex County. "Great grandmother Frances (called Fannie) boarded the carpenters who built Enon Church. Great grandfather John Williams' father had a large farm in the vicinity of and including P.O. of Alps, Va. William had a portion of that farm left him." [Written by Helen Yates]. The old home place near Alps was named "Midway". This Bible record was copied by Helen Kay Yates some years ago and was owned by Harry L. Kay of Woodford, Caroline County. The Bible was published in Troy, N.Y. in 1846. The earlier members of the family were believed to have been born in England.

Richard Kay and Ann his wife had the children named below:

Thomas Kay born Nov. 24th 1781.
James born 20th August 1783.
Betsey born 21st April 1786.
John born 26th Feb 1788.
Robert born 20th September 1789.
Richard born 10th Nov. 1790.
Sarah born 11th Dec. 1793.
Edward born 24th May 1795.
Wilesey born 2nd Feb 1797.
Polly born 25th March 1800.
William born 17th Jan. 1803.
James Kay and Frances G. Spindle were married on the 24th dayu of March 1820. (Their home was near Enon Church, Essex County.
Their children:
　Joseph W. Kay was born Mar. 3, 1821.
　Ann Elizabeth was born Oct. 4th 1823.
　Martha M. Kay was born Aug 17 1838.
　A. Hamilton Kay was born Sept 30 1840.
(Notes by Helen Yates: "Handed down to me verbally Joseph Kay married Julia Baylor. His son Tommie became a doctor. Built up a hospital in Phila, Pa. His daughter Georgia married Stephen Watts. Ann married Dick Gouldman. They lived near Brandywine [Caroline County])
Partial Family Record of William and Martha M. Kay married about 1855.

James H. Kay Born July 19, 1857.
Appolos Kay born (date not known).
Mildred Kay born (date not known).
William B. Kay born (date not known).
Annis Kay born (date not known).

KAY FAMILY BIBLE RECORD NO. 2

This Bible Record of Richard Kay and his wife, Elizabeth Kay was copied by Mrs. Aladdin Campbell Kay (Mary Belle Jordan) from the original and furnished the author by Helen Kay Yates.

Lucy Ann Kay borned May 3rd 1818.
Edward Kay borned 9th (month not listed) 1820.
James Kay borned 11th of Sept. 1821.
Sarah Kay borned 23rd Dec. 1822.
Christopher Kay borned 14th (month not listed) 1824.
Richard H. Kay borned 12 of Mch. 1827.
Elizabeth Jane Kay borned 4th Jan. 1829.
William Kay borned 29th of Feb. 1831.
Polly Kay borned 7th (month not listed) 1833.
Sally Kay borned 16 July 1836.
John Kay borned 12th Oct. 1837.
Richard Kay was borned 11 Nov. 1782.
Richard Kay died 26 Mch 1868.
Elizabeth Kay borned Mch 31st 1794.
Richard H. Kay died 20 Sept. 1863.
Elizabeth Kay died Sept. __ 1852.

KIDD FAMILY BIBLE

This Bible belonged to the family of Captain William Kidd, who lived at "Hedge Hill", adjacent to what later became Kidds Fork Post Office in Caroline County. Captain Kidd's mother, Elizabeth Ann Davenport Kidd, widow of Thomas Kidd, moved here with her two children, William, who later married Harriet M. Wright from the adjoining farm and Lucy A. Kidd, who married Matthew B. Hundley from "Needwood Tavern". The old Kidd homestead was torn down in 1994 and another house built on the site. The cemetery, without stones, was located back of the original house. The Bible passed to the daughter of Ropon Bowers in Richmond, Virginia. It was published by Andrus, Judd & Franklin, Hartford, Connecticut, 1838.

William Kidd born May 7, 1789.
Harriet M. Wright born May 3rd, 1800.
Children born to said Wm Kidd and Harriet M., his wife.
Robert H. [Hawkins] Kidd born 3rd December 1822.

Thomas D. Kidd Sept. 13th 1825.
Maria L. [Louisa] Kidd April 22nd 1827.
Margaret E. [Elizabeth] Kidd Aug. 26th 1830.
Burton W. [Wright] Kidd May 3rd 1832.
Harriet F. Kidd Jany. 14th 1834.
James H. [Henry] Kidd May 16th 1836.
Lucy Anne Kidd born 4th July 1840
William B. [Burton] Kidd 22 Decr 1828
[end of listing of children]
William [Willie] L. [Lee] Kidd Pollard Born March 6, 1862 son of Margaret Kidd and Dr. L. [Leonadas] C. Pollard. Other children born who died in infancy.
Louise Lee Pollard born 1858.
Burton Pollard born September 10, 1863 and died June 1864.
[end of children who died in infancy]
Alice L. Gray born May 26th, 1867.
Children born to said Wm and Alice L. his wife.
Margaret E. Pollard born April 7, 1885.
William K. [Kidd] L. [Lee] Pollard born Dec. the 12 1886.
Annie M. Pollard born October the 27 1888.
E. Cary Pollard born Feb. the 8, 1889.
Robert B. Pollard born June the 13, 1892.
Callie O. Pollard born June the 11, 1893.
[end of listing of children]
Ropon Stuart, son of S.C. and Margarite E. Bowers, born Sept 14, 1907. May God guide, guard and lead him through life.
James Henry Kidd died May 26th 1838.
John W. Kidd died 4th December 1845.
Harriet F. Kidd died 24 September 1847.
Lucy Anne Kidd died 9th November 1852.
William Kidd died Febry 9th 1854.
Maria L. Kidd died Jany 14th 1904.
Margaret Kidd Pollard died September 10, 1863 wife of Dr. L.C. Pollard, died July the 22, 1902.
Robert B. Pollard died Aug the 7, 1892.
Callie O. Pollard died 27 of Sept. 1895.
William L. Kidd Pollard died August 9, 1917.
Alice Lee Gray Pollard wife of William Kidd Pollard died March 7, 1946.
Harriett M. Wright married to William Kidd December 24th A.D. 1821.
Margaret E. Kidd married to L.C. Pollard 28 Oct 1857.
Attie M. Broaddus married to Wm. B. Kidd 18th Nov. A.D. 1858.
Margaret E. Pollard married to S.C. Bowers July 11th 1906.

KNOX FAMILY BIBLE

This Bible dates from 1763 to 1862. It apparently belonged to James and Rebecah Knox. A copy is in the Library of Virginia and is identified as a Caroline County Bible in their records. There are no family members by that name in Caroline County today, however, there was a Susannah Knox listed in the census of 1850 as being 75 years old and living in Caroline. The Knox family intermarried into the Fitzhugh and Gordon families of Caroline County. Another Knox Bible (Thomas Fitzhugh Knox 1807) with records 1793-1876 was at one time owned by George H.S. King and a copy is in the Virginia Historical Society, but not reproduced in this study since most seem to be from another county.

Ages of the Children of James and Rebecah Knox.
Sarah was born July 23 1822.
Nancy Jane born May 3 1824.
Ages of the children of Henry N. Knox and Ester A. Knox.
Child dead born September the 4 1845.
James Knox was married the 23 August 1821.
Joseph Knox was married the 26 September 1822.
Samuel Knox was married June 17 1824.
John Knox was married Sept the [blank] 1824.
Matthew Knox was married April the 5 1831.
Henry N. Knox was married October 30 1844.
Samuel Knox was born May the 16th 1763.
Nancy Knox was born March the 19th 1765.
Nancy Watson was born September 1st in the year of our Lord 1802.
Samuel Knox Died March the 10th 1833.
Mary Knox Died 4 September 1835.
Nancy Knox Died 4 November 1839.
Jane H. Knox Died 22nd September 1840.
Ester Adaline Knox Died September the 20th 1845.
Henry H. Knox Departed this life May 30, 1847 after an illness [illeg].
John Knox died June the 28 1857.
Ages of the children of Saml and Agness Knox.
John was born June 4th 1790.
James born January 22d 1792.
Joseph born September 23d 1794.
Samuel born February 18 1797.
Matthew born December the 25 1799.
Mary born October the 28 1800.
Henry Noel born October 24 1803.
Nancy born September the 30 1805.
Jane Hannah born January the 19 1808.
Nancy Knox Departed this life July the 26 A.D. 1850.
Samuel J.H. Knox Died February the 17 A.D. 1847.
Matthew Knox Died September the 20 1862.

LEAVELL FAMILY BIBLE

Copies of this Bible are in the Alderman Library at the University of Virginia and at the Library of Virginia. This Bible concerns Gayle family members who lived in the Shumansville area of Caroline County before going to Spotsylvania County. Inscribed: "Benjamin L. & Roberta [Gayle] Leavell From Their Affectionate Brother Wm Thos Leavell Sept 1858."

Benjamin F. Leavell youngest son of Burwell & Ann G. Leavell was born at Clover Dale, Spotsylvania County Fa. February 14th 1826.

Roberta E. Gayle Second Daughter of Josiah P. Gayle and Fannie M. Gayle was born 13th Day of May 1830 at the residence of her Father in Caroline County Virginia.

Fannie Goldie Leavell Fifth child of B.L. & R.E. Leavell was born August 1st Tuesday 1854 at Rose Mount the resident of her Grandfather J.P. Gayle in Spotsylvania County Virginia.

Mary Almedia Leavell second child of B.L. & R.E. Leavell was born April 20th 1857 at Oak Grove, the residence of her parents in Spotsylvania County Virginia.

John Thomas Leavell Third child of B.L. & R.E. Leavell was born Thursday March 16th 1860 at Oak Grove the residence of his parents in Spotsylvania County Virginia.

Died suddenly of heart disease at his residence Oak Grove, Spotsylvania Co. Va Benjamin L. Leavell in the 67th year of his age April 10th 1880 at 5 o'clock A.M.

Died after a lingering illness at Oak Grove in her 96th year Roberta E. Leavell, wife of Benj L. Levell Dec.____.

Benjamin L. Leavell and Roberta E. Gayle were married October 11th 1853(or 55) at the residence of her Father Josiah P. Gayle Spotsylvania County Virginia.

William L. Leavell and Fannie G. Leavell were married in Fredg. December 2nd 1875 by Rev. S.S. Dunaway.

Cecil B. Durrett and Mary A. Leavell were married at Massaponnox Church on the 15th January 1878 by Rev. E.G. Baptist.

John G. Leavell and Rosa L. Mills were married Dec 13th 1885 at the residence of her father J. G. Mills Richmond Virginia.

Also included are printed newspaper death notices of Benjamin L. Leavell Apr 10th 1880 at Oakley Grove, Spot Co & the Rev. Mr. Leavell (Baltimore Co Jan 7, 1888).

LIGHTFOOT FAMILY BIBLE NO. 1

The Lightfoot family lived at Port Royal, Caroline County, Virginia and intermarried with several Caroline County families. A copy of this Bible record is in the Library of Virginia. The Lightfoot house is still standing at Port Royal. Another house, "Waverley", named for the ancestral home in Gloucester Co., Va. also stands just outside of Port Royal off Route 17.

Wm Bernard oldest son of John B. and Harriet Ann Lightfoot was born in Port Royal Caroline Co., Va. March 16 1845 - baptized.

Emelina Allmond oldest child of Wm W and Mary S. Crump born in Richmond Va December 26th 1847 and baptized at "Waverley" Gloucester Co. Va. by Revd Chas. Mann.

Wm Crump first child of Wm B. and Emmeline Crump Lightfoot was born at her father's residence in Richmond Va. on the 13th day of January 1873 baptized at the same place 29th March 1873 by Rev. Charles [F.E.] Minnigerode.

Harriet Field - second child of Wm B. and Emmelina Crump Lightfoot was born in Port Royal Caroline Co. Va. on the 12th day of March 1875 baptized in St. Peters Church Port Royal Va September 23rd 1875 by Revd. James Poindexter.

John Bernard third child of Wm. B. and Emmelina Crump Lightfoot was born at "Waverley" near Port Royal Caroline Co., Va. on the 31st of October 1876 - baptized 21st January 1877 (3rd Sunday after Epiphany, in Port Royal Va. by Rev'd. James Poindexter.

Marie Tabb fourth child of Wm B. and Emmeline Crump Lightfoot was born at "Waverley" near Port Royal Caroline County Va on the 10th day of May 1882 - baptized All Saint's day November 1st at her Grandfather's home in Richmond Va. by Revd. Chas. Minnigerode.

Marie Tabb youngest daughter of William Bernard and Emeline Crump Lightfoot was married to Thomas Brown Jr. of Westmoreland Co Va. in St. James' Church By the Rev. G. Freeland Peter Rector on the Second day of October at High Noon, 1918.

Harriet Ann (Field) Lightfoot died at her home in Port Royal Caroline County, Va. June 11th 1871 Aged 49 years.

John Bernard Lightfoot of Port Royal Caroline died at his home in Port Royal Caroline County Va on the 10th day of July 1888 Aged 73 years.

Mary Susan (Tabb) Crump died at her home corner of 12th and Broad Sts. Richmond Va. on the 7th day of April, 1891 Aged 77 years.

"O blest communion fellowship divine
we feebly struggle they in glory shine:
yet all are one in thee -- for all
are Thine" Allelula.

William Crump Lightfoot - oldest Son of Emmiline C. and William B. Lightfoot Died June 3rd 1924 in the 52nd year of his age in N.Y. Buried in Shockoe Cemetery Richmond, Va.

Died at his home in Richmond Virginia January 16th 1929 William B. Lightfoot of Port Royal Va. in the 84th year of his age. Buried in Shockoe Cemetery, Richmond, Va.

John Bernard Lightfoot of Port Royal Caroline County Va. was married to Harriet Ann Field at "Poplar Grove" Matthews County Va 11th August 1841 by Rev. Chas. Mann.

Wm Wood Crump of Richmond Va was married to Mary Susan Tabb at her home "Waverley" Gloucester County, Va January 1st 1846 by Revd. Charles Mann.

Wm Bernard Lightfoot oldest son of John B. and Harriet A. Lightfoot was married to Emmeline Almand oldest daughter of Wm W. and Mary S. Crump at 12th & Broad St. Richmond Va (her home) by Revd Chas. Minnegrode October 17th 1871.

Harriet Field oldest daughter of Wm B. and Emmie C. Lightfoot was married to Doctor Edwin B. Claybrook of Westmoreland County Virginia at St. James' Church, Richmond, Virginia on the 29th day of October 1901 by Rev. Jno J. Gravatt.

This marriage was to have taken place on the 17th day of October 1901 but for the illness of Dr. Claybrook.

John Bernard Second Son of William B. and Emmie C. Lightfoot was married to Nan Maury Lemmon of Charlottesville Va. on the 20th day of April 1912 by the Rev. Harry B. Lee.

Evelyn Lightfoot, daughter of Doctor Edwin B. and Harriet Lightfoot Claybrook, was born in Cumberland Maryland on the twenty second day of June 1907. Baptized in St. James' Church Richmond Va by Rev. W. M. Clarke December 25 1907.

Emmy Lightfoot Brown daughter of Thomas Brown Jr. and Marie Lightfoot Brown was born - Monday July 5th 1920 - 6:25 P.M. Richmond Va.

Edwin Brown Claybrook, son of Edwin Brown and Judith Newton Claybrook, died at his home in Cumberland Md. February 28th 1831, aged 59. buried in Rose Hill Cemetery Cumberland Md.

LIGHTFOOT FAMILY BIBLE NO. 2

This is a second Lightfoot Bible of a family once prominent in the Port Royal area of Caroline County. A copy of this family record is located at both the Virginia Historical Society and the Library of Virginia.

"Presented to our dear Father by his Mother Mrs. Philip Lightfoot of Port Royal Virginia & by him presented to his son John B. Lightfoot Jr. June 7th Tuesday 1881. J. B. Lightfoot to D.B. Lightfoot April 10th 1883."

Born on the 7th Jul 1743 Fanny daughter of J. B. & H.A. Lightfoot.
William B. Lightfoot son of J. B. & H.A. Lightfoot was born the 16th of March 1845.
Born on the 19th of Oct. 1826 Harriet A. second daughter of J. B. & H.A. Lightfoot.
Born on the 24th of Aug 1848 Maria Evelyn third daughter of J. B. & H.A. Lightfoot.
Born the 29th of March 1852 John Bernard second son of J. B. & H.A. Lightfoot.
Born on the 12 September 1853, Philip Howell, third son of J. B. & H.A. Lightfoot.
Born on the 25th May 1856 Sally Virginia fourth daughter of J. B. & H.A. Lightfoot.
Born on the 27th March 1858 George Patterson, fourth son of J. B. & H.A. Lightfoot.
Born on the 13th December 1863 Lewis Herbert, fifth Son of J. B. & H.A. Lightfoot.
Born at Toddsbury, Gloucester Co Va Harriet A. daughter of George Field & Sally Virginia Todd, on the 28th June 1822.
Born in Port Royal on the 24th December 1814 J. B. Lightfoot Son of Philip & Sally S. Lightfoot.
Phillip Lightfoot born 24th September 1784.
Sally S. Lightfoot wife of Philip Lightfoot of Port Royal born 7th March 1790.
Born on the 12th September 1868 Francis Edward, eldest son of Dr. Francis T. & Harriet A. Brooke.
Born on the 1st Day of December 1874 William H. Kennon Esqr. & Maria Ruby his wife.
Born on 13th January 1873 in Richmond William Crump eldest son of William B. & Emmaline A. Lightfoot.
Born on 12 March 1875 Harriet Todd grandchild of Dr. F.V. & L.A. Lightfoot in Port Royal.
Born at Mill Farm Louisa County on the 28th March 76 - John Lightfoot Brooke Son of Dr. F. V. & L.A. Lightfoot.
Born at Waring in the county of [Essex?] 3rd October 1876 John Bernard Son of Dr. F.V. & L.A. Lightfoot.

Born in Petersburg Va on the 3rd October 1878 Herbert Claiborne oldest Son of R. Howell Lightfoot & Nannie A. Lightfoot.

Born at Mill Farm Louisa Co Philip Howell Brooke 3rd son of Dr. F.T. & H.A. Brooke November 16, 1881.

Born at Petersburg Philip Howell Lightfoot April 22nd 1881 Son of Dr. P. Howell & Nannie A. Lightfoot.

Married in St. Peters Church, Port Royal, Caroline Co, Va. Maria Evelyn Lightfoot to Wm H. Kennon Esq. by the Revd. Jas. E. Poindexter on the 9th January 1872.

Births

Born in Petersburg Va on the 22nd of April 1881 Philip Howell, second son of Dr. Philip Howell & Anna Augusta Lightfoot.

Born at Mill Farm Louisa Co Va on the 16th November 1881 Philip Howell Brooke third son of Dr. F. T. & H.A. Brooke.

Born at Waverley, Caroline Co Va on the 15th of May 1887 1/2 past 8 P.M. Maria Tabb Lightfoot second daughter of W.H. & E.C. Lightfoot.

Died on the 17th of June 1844, Fanny, eldest child of J. B. & H.A. Lightfoot.

Died on the 16th June 1876 in Richmond Va William Henry Kennon, in the Forty Fourth year of his life.

Died on the 30th September 1881 in Petersburg John Philip Howell third son of J. B. & H.A. Lightfoot.

Died in Richmond, Virginia on the 31st of March 1892 Dr. Francis T. Howell, husband of H.A. Howell & [H.A. being] daughter of J. B. & H.A. Lightfoot.

Died in Richmond on the 4th April 1882 Maria Evelyn Kennon wife of W.H. Kennon & third daughter of J. B. & H.A. Lightfoot.

Died in Port Royal on the 11th June 1871 Harriet A. beloved wife of J. B. Lightfoot & in the forty ninth year of her life.

Sally S. Lightfoot wife of Philip Lightfoot of Port Royal died 22nd August 1859.

Philip Lightfoot of Port Royal died 22nd July 1865.

Married in St. James Church, Richmond on the 8 February 1882 by Revd Joshua Peterson, Dr. J. B. Lightfoot to Mary Ball Washington Minor daughter of Robert & Landonia Randolph Minor.

LIGHTFOOT FAMILY BIBLE NO. 3

A copy of this Bible Record is in both the Virginia Historical Society and the Library of Virginia. Philip Lightfoot, the first of that name in Virginia came to Gloucester County prior to 1671. The first to come to Caroline County was his grandson Philip, who was the son of William. He lived at Cedar Creek in Caroline County and died in 1786. He married Mary Warner Lewis and had one child, Philip of Port Royal, born 1784, died 1865. A good account of the Lightfoot family appeared in the *William and Mary Quarterly*. There is also a Randolph family Bible record in the Library of Virginia on reel 701 which gives repeated information on this family and which was not copied.

Inscribed in the front of the Bible: "Presented as a bridal gift to Mary Washington Ball Minor by her attached friend and teacher Miss Fannie H. Kearr Wednesday February 8, 1882."

John Bernard Lightfoot of Port Royal Virginia and Mary Washington Ball Minor of Richmond Virginia on Wednesday February 8th 1882 at 4 P.M. at Saint James Church by Rev. Joshua Peterson. Witness Landonia Randolph Minor.

John Bernard, son of Philip & Sallie Bernard Lightfoot Born in Port Royal Caroline Co Va Dec 24th 1814.

Harriet Ann, dau. of George & Sallie Todd Field Born at Toddsburg, Gloucester Co, Va June 28th 1822.

John Bernard Lightfoot Jr. son of J. B. & Harriet Ann Lightfoot Born Port Royal Va March 29th 1851.

Robert Dabney, son of Garret & Elizabeth McWilliams Minor. Born in Fredericksburg Va Sept 13th 1827.

Landonia, dau of Charles Carter & Mary Mortimer Randolph Born at "Cedar Grove" Stafford Co Mar 24th 1830.

Mary Washington Ball, dau of Robert D. & Landonia Randolph Minor Born Sept. 16th 1851 in Leesburg, Loudoun Co Va.

Landonia R. dau. R. D. & S. R. Minor Born Dec 11th 1855 at "The Grove" Fauquier Co Va.

Ann Mortimer dau. R. D. & S. R. Minor Born Sep 25, 1870 at "Lindon" Fauquier Co, Va.

Roberta Dabney, son of R. D. & S. R. Minor Born July 3rd 1872 in Leesburg, Va.

Philip Lightfoot & Sarah [Sally] S. Bernard married August 31st 1804.

John Bernard Lightfoot & Harriet Ann Field married at "Poplar Grove" Matthews Co. Va. Aug 12th 1841.

John Bernard Lightfoot & Mary [Mollie] Washington Ball Minor married at St. James Church Richmond Va by Rev. Joshua Peterson February 8 1882.

Charles Carter Randolph & Mary Ann Mortimer married at "Lisconey" Fredericksburg, Va July 1825.

Robert Dabney Minor U.S. Navy & Landonia Randolph married at "The Grove" Fauquier Co Va. Dec 17th 1850.

Landonia R. [Randolph] Minor & Wm Sparrow Dashield married at St. James Church Richmond, Va Dec 12 1888.

Philip Lightfoot died in Port Royal Va July 22nd 1865.

Sallie S. Bernard died in Port Royal Va August 22nd 1859.

Harriet N. Field died in Port Royal Va June 11th 1871.

John Bernard Lightfoot died in Port Royal Va July 10, 1888.

Charles Carter Randolph died in Fauquier Co, Va Dec 20th 1863.

Mary A [Ann] Mortimer died at "The Grove" Fauquier Co Va Aug 25, 1858.

Capt Robert D. Minor died suddenly in Richmond Va Friday November 25th 1871.

LINDSAY FAMILY BIBLE

Bible of Colonel James Lindsay of Caroline County, the son of Adam, the emigrant. This Bible was in the possession of Mason Gordon Esq of Charlottesville in 1902. It was recorded in *The Magazine of History and Biography*, Volume 10, pp.96-97, 203, 310, Virginia Historical Society, 1902-03; *Genealogies of Virginia Families from the Magazine of History and Biography*, Volume IV, page 235. Genealogical Publishing Co., Baltimore, Maryland, 1981.

The Bible was owned by Mason Gordon Esq of Charlottesville as late as 1979, when it was printed at page 287 in *More than Skin Deep* by Mary Douglas Blaydes, Goins Printing, Lexinton, Kentucky, 1979. [Colonel Lindsay of Caroline, to whom this Bible belonged, married Sarah Daniel. He was the son of Adam, the emigrant, who is believed to have come from Scotland to Virginia in the late 17th or early 18th century. Some of his descendants are now in Albemarle County, Virginia. Caleb Lindsay, the oldest son of Col James Lindsay of Caroline and his first wife, Sarah Daniel, had no children. Reuben Lindsay, son of Colonel James Lindsay, married the adopted daughter of his brother Caleb, Hannah Tidwell, daughter of John Tidwell.] James Lindsay died 1782, age 82. He lived and died in Caroline County about 12 miles from Port Royal where he ran a mill. This mill, on Beverley's Run in Drysdale Parish was later called White's.

Caleb Lindsay, the son of James Lindsay and Sarah, his wife, was born 14th Feb'y 1720.
Elizabeth Lindsay, daughter of James Lindsay and Sarah, his wife, was born the 29th March, 1724.
John, son of James and Sarah, was born 27th August 1728.
William, son of James and Sarah, was born 7th Feb'y 1731.
Jacob, son of James and Sarah, was born 11th March 1733.
Sarah, daughter of James and Sarah, was born 15th June 1735.
Mary, daughter of James and Sarah, was born 3rd April 1738.
James, son of James and Sarah, was born 23rd May 1740.
Daniel, son of James and Sarah, was born 23rd May 1742.
Reuben, son of James and Sarah, was born 15th Jan'y 1747.
Sukie, daughter of James and Lucy Lindsay, was born _____.
Sarah Lindsay, daughter of Thomas Walker & Mildred, his wife, was born the 28th of May, 1758. Married 20th of October, 1774.
Mildred Thornton Lindsay, Daughter of Reuben and Sarah Lindsay, was born ye 5th May, 1776.
James Lindsay, son of Reuben and Sarah Lindsay, was born the 3rd June 1778, died 3rd Sep'r 1778.
Sarah Walker Lindsay, daughter of Reuben and Sarah Lindsay, was born ye 14th May, 1780.
Elizabeth Grimes Lindsay was born 25th January, 1783 and died _____.
William Lindsay, son of Reuben and Hannah Lindsay, was born 6th October, 1790.
Elizabeth was born 22nd April, 1792. Married, the 22 January, 1813.
Mary was born 6th September, 1796 & married, 16th day of May, 1816.

LINDSAY/LOMAX FAMILY DIARY

This family data is taken from *Leaves from an Old Washington Diary 1854-1863* by Elizabeth Lindsay Lomax, E.P. Dutton and Company, Inc., 1943. Both the Lindsay and Lomax families were from the Port Royal area of Caroline. The Lindsay family lived in Port Royal and operated Lindsay's Mills, about 12 miles from Port Royal. The Lomax family lived at "Port Tobago", the Lomax-Waring-White estate near the Caroline-Essex line. After the marriage of Elizabeth Lindsay to Mann Page Lomax, the family moved to Newport, Rhode Island, where he was stationed in the military. After his death, the widow and children moved to Washington, D.C. and later to Warrenton, Virginia.

Sir William L. Lindsay of Port Royal and Miss Taliaferro were married in 1749.

Colonel William Lindsay, son of Sir William L. Lindsay and Miss Taliaferro and father of Elizabeth Lindsay Lomax, died September 1, 1797. He served in the Revolution with George Washington. He came to Port Royal from Scotland in the early 1700's. He is buried in Trinity Churchyard at Newport.

Major Mann Page Lomax died at Watertown Arsenal, Newport, where he was in command, March 27, 1842.

Elizabeth Lindsay, daughter of Colonel William Lindsay was born September 22, 1796 and died of a heart attack while working in her garden May 17, 1867. Aged 70 years 8 months.

Mann Page Lomax, Captain, U.S. Artillery, and Elizabeth Lindsay, youngest daughter of the late Major William Lindsay, were married May 11th 1820 at Norfolk by Rev. Mr. Low. She was 16 years of age.

Jane Taylor Lomax, first child of M.P. & Elizabeth Lindsay, was born February, 1821 and died at the age of 22 in 1846 at the birth of her daughter Alice Anne Corbin Lomax, second child of M.P. & Elizabeth Lomax was born January 5th.____.

Virginia L. Lomax, third child of M.P. & Elizabeth Lomax

Julia Lawrence Lomax, fourth child of M.P. & Elizabeth Lomax, was born December 10th._____.

Mary L. Lomax, firth child of M.P. & Elizabeth Lomax and twin to Julia Lawrence Lomax, was born December 10th.____.

Ellen Victoria "Vic" Lomax, sixth daughter of M.P. & Elizabeth Lomax, was born July 20, ____ and died January 20, 1880. She was buried from St. James Church.

Lindsay Lunsford Lomax, only son of M.P. & Elizabeth L. Lomax, was born November 4, 1835 and died in 1913.

Jane Taylor Lomax, daughter of M.P. & Elizabeth L. Lomax, married Francis Worthington.

Anne Corbin Lomax, daughter of M.P. & Elizabeth L. Lomax, married Thomas Green, her first and his third marriage, January 6, 1862.

Lindsay Lunsford Lomax, only son of M.P. & Elizabeth Lomax, married Elizabeth Winter Payne.

LIPSCOMB/WILSON FAMILY BIBLE

This Bible was published and sold by Kimber and Sharpless, Philadelphia in 1824. There are four pages to the printed family register provided in the Bible and three handwritten pages inserted. A copy of the family record is in the Library of Virginia. The Beazley family mentioned in these records are the same family in the Beazley-Samuel Bible elsewhere in this book. The Jackson family in the two Bible records are buried in the Jackson cemetery off Route 30 on the Caroline-King William line at what was later Camp Discovery. See *Cemeteries of Caroline County, Virginia*, Volume 2, Private Cemeteries by Herbert R. Collins, Family Line Publications, Westminster, Maryland.

Samuel A. [Anderson] Lipscomb Departed this life the 7 day April 1822.
Elizabeth Coleman Lipscomb Departed this life Sept 9th 1825.
Elizabeth Christian Departed this life the 6th of November 1825.

George P. Lipscomb departed this life the 18th June 1826.

Magdalena Lipscomb departed this life the 12th day of August 1827.

Pembleton Lipscomb departed this life the 7th day of May 1832.

J.J. Wilson departed this life 11th Nov 1890.

Thomas Wilson son of J.J. & M.P. Wilson departed This Life the 10 July 1841.

John Wilson son of M.P. and John J. Wilson departed this life the 21st day of November 1845.

Magdalena Wilson daughter of M.P. & Jno. J. Wilson departed this life the 22nd day of December 1846.

Marietta Wilson daughter of M.P. & Jno. J. Wilson departed this life 19th February 1847.

Rose Wilson daughter of M.P. and Jno. J. Wilson departed this life 15th June 1848.

M.P. Wilson the beloved wife of Jno. J. Wilson departed this life the 5th day of November 1848.

Ann C. Lipscomb departed this life the 10th day of December 1849.

Pemberton Lipscomb and Ann Coleman Pemberton was married the 10th of Jany 1818.

John James Wilson and Magdalena P. Lipscomb was married the 2nd of February 1837.

Archs. S. Beazley and Maria E. Wilson was married the 28th December 1856.

John T. Wright and A.T. Wilson was married the 1st day of March 1864.

Philip Samuel and Lillie W. Beazley were married June 2nd 1903.

Marietta Wilson & Magdalena Wilson were twin sisters and daughters of M.P. and Jno. J. Wilson born 10th day of December 1848.

Rose Wilson daughter of M.P. & Jno J. Wilson was born 22 day December 1846.

John James Wilson Son of Magdalena P. & Jno. J. Wilson was born the 21st September 1849.

Boyd Latane Samuel Son of Philip and Lillie Beazley Samuel was born Oct 30th 1906.

Pemberton Lipscomb Son of Anderson Lipscomb & Mary his wife was born the 11th day of Sept 1796.

Ann Coleman Pemberton Daughter of Wilson C. Pemberton & Walthey Ann his wife was born the 27th day of June 1799.

Departed this life on Feb 23rd 1892 Maria E. Beazley daughter of J. J. & M.P. Wilson in the 54th year of her age.

Samuel Anderson Lipscomb Son of Pemberton and Ann C. Lipscomb was born Sept 10th 1819.

Magdalena Pemberton Lipscomb Daughter of P. & a.C. Lipscomb was born the 6th of April 1822.

Elizabeth Coleman Lipscomb Daughter of P. & a.C. Lipscomb was born the 17th day of February 1824.

George Pemberton Lipscomb Son of P. & A.C. Lipscomb was born the 8th of April 1825.

Maryetter Lipscomb Daughter of P. & A.C. Lipscomb was born the 30 day of Sept 1826.

John J. Wilson was Born the 20th of March 1818.

Maria Ellen Wilson Daughter of M.P. and John J. Wilson was born the 19th day of March 1838.

Thomas Wilson son of M.P. and John J. Wilson was born 16th day of February 1840.

Ann Thomas Wilson Daughter of John J. & M.P. Wilson was born the 14th day of March 1842.

John Wilson son of M.P. and John J. Wilson was born 15th day of Jany 1845.

[handwritten pages added]

Fanny Maud [Beazley] was born in Caroline Co Va. Feb 8 1873.

Roland Custer [Beazley] was born in Caroline Co Va. Dec 14 1874.

Oliver B. [Beazley] was born in Caroline Co Va. Feb 9th 1877.

Departed this life on Feb 23rd 1892 Maria Ellen - wife of A.S. Beazley and oldest child of J.J. & M.P. Wilson in the 54th year of her age.

Departed this life on March 21 1891 Ann Thomas - wife of J. T. Wright and second daughter of J. J. Wilson in the 54th year of her age.

Departed this life Dec 24th 1895 A.S. Beazley in the 72nd year of his age.

Departed this life Jan 21st 1896 Anne Jackson wife of Robert L. Jackson & second daughter of A.S. and Maria Beazley in the 35th year of her age.

Departed this life Aug 1907 Magdalena Capitola Stone oldest daughter of A.S. and Maria E. Beazley in the 49th year of her age.

Departed this life June 21st 1908 Gertrude Leslie Jennings 3rd daughter of A.S. and Maria Ellen Beazley in the 39th year of her age.

Dates of births of the children of A.S. & Maria E. Beazley:

Magdelena Capitola was born in Caroline Co Va May 2nd 1859.
Matha [sic] Ann was born in Caroline Co Va. Feb 13th 1861.
Archibald Lewelln was born in Caroline Co Va. Nov 2nd 1862.
John Wilson was born in Caroline Co Va. June 15th 1866.
Gertrude Leslie was born in Caroline Co Va. Nov. 23 1868.
Sallie Almeter was born in Caroline Co Va. April 10th 1870.
William Alpin was born in Caroline Co Va. June 18th 1871.

LUCK FAMILY BIBLE

This Bible originated with John Marshall Luck. It was printed and published by Ziegler & McCurdy, Philadelphia, 1872. It was owned in 1995 by Janet D. Littlejohn, who lives in Dumfries and published in *Magazine of Virginia Genealogy*, Volume 33, No.2, 1995, p.115. Jordan B. Luck's parents were John M. and Milley Luck of St. Margaret's Parish in Caroline County. Jordan Luck married Adaline Gatewood left Caroline County sometime after 1820 and moved to Loudoun County, Virginia. John Marshall Luck lived in Stafford County at a 580 acre farm known as "Mountain View".

Jordan B. Luck was born 1 December 1791.
Adaline Gatewood was born 4 July 1792.
George Rowe was born 21 January 1793.
Lucy Leitch was born 22 February 1798.
John Marshall Luck was born 6 January 1827.
Mary Ann Rowe was born 28 October 1824.
Lucy Agnes Luck was born 20 March 1854.
Drusilla Ann Luck was born 13 June 1855.
Sarah Emily Luck was born 6 December 1858.
Mary Marshall Luck was born 14 January 1865.
Jordan B. Luck died 26 August 1853.
Adaline Luck died 22 February 1864.
Lucy Rowe died 27 March 1863.

George Rowe died 18 January 1866.
Drusilla A. Luck died 18 Oct 1860.
Mary Marshall Luck died 18 August 1867.
Absalom P. Rowe died 1 June 1900.
John M. Luck died ____ 1888.
Mary A. Luck died July 5, 1902.

MADISON FAMILY BIBLE

This Bible was published by Thomas Baskett, London, England, 1759. The Bible record was copied by Major Isaac Hite of Belle Grove, Frederick County, Va. aide to General Muhlenburg at the seize of Yorktown, and was taken from his notebook by Miss S. Jaquelin Davidson for publication in the *William and Mary Quarterly*, but has discrepancies from the original. It was also printed at page 97 in Volume II of *Old Churches, Ministers and Families of Virginia* by Bishop Meade. A copy of this Bible is located both in the Virginia Historical Society and in the Library of Virginia. The record has also been published in *Virginia Bible Records* by Jeannette Holland Austin, Willow Bend Books, Westminster, Maryland 2000.

The Madison family has connections both to early Caroline County and to Orange County, Virginia. Ambrose Madison, grandfather of President Madison was one of the first magistrates of Caroline County in 1728. Nelly Conway, mother of President James Madison was born and raised in Caroline County. The Conway estate is known as "Mount Zion", located off Route 2 near Corbin in Caroline County and is still standing.

Ambrose Madison was Married to Frances Taylor August the 27th 1721.
James Madison was born March 27, 1723 and was Baptized April 23 and had Godfathers
  Thomas Madison & James Taylor & for Godmothers Martha Taylor & Elizabeth Penn.
Elizabeth Madison was born June 14th 1725, and was Baptized July 5 & Godfathers James
  Taylor & Richard Thomas and for Godmothers Martha Taylor & Elinor Madison.
Frances Madison was Born March 6th 1726 and was Baptized April 9th and had Godfather
  James Pendleton & for Godmothers Isbell Pendleton & Elizabeth Pendleton.
Ambrose Madison Departed this life August 29 1732 being Sunday Night.
Frances Madison Departed this life on Wednesday Morning about 2 o'clock 25 of December
  1761 and was intered the Sunday following. Her Funeral Sermon was preached on Wednesday
  the 30th of Decemr. following by Revd. Mr. James Marye Jr. on Revelations Ch. 11 v. 13.
Nelly [Eleanor Rose] Conway was Born January 9th 1731 [mother of President James Madison].
John Wilis was married to Elizabeth Madison the [rest not completed].
James Madison was married to Nelly Conway September 15th 1749 [parents of President James
  Madison].
James Madison Junr. was Born on Tuesday night at 12 o'clock, being last of the 5th and the
  beginning of the 6th Day of March 1751 and was Baptized by the Revd. Mr. Wm Davis Mar. 31
  and had for God Fathers Mr. John M. Jones & Wm Gibson & for Godmothers Mrs. Rebecca
  Moore, Miss Judith Catlett & Miss Elizabeth Catlett. Died the 28 June 1836. Intered 30 June.
  [President James Madison].

Frances Madison was Born on Monday Morning abt. 9 o'clock June 18 1753 & was Baptised by the Revd. Mr. Mungo Marshall July 1st & had Godfathers W. Taverner Beale & Mr. Erasmus Taylor & for Godmothers Miss Milly Taylor & Mrs. Frances Beale.

Ambrose Madison was Born on Monday Night between 9 & 10 o'clock January 27th 1755 & was Baptized by the Revd. Mr. Mungo Marshall & had Godfathers Mr. James Coleman & Col. George Taylor & for Godmothers Mrs. Jane Taylor & Alice Chew.

Catlett Madison was Born on Fryday [sic] Morning at 2 o'clock February 10 1758 & was Baptized by the Revd Mr. James Maury February 22nd & has Godmothers Mrs. Elizabeth Beale & Miss Milley Chew.

Nelly Madison was Born February 14th 1760 and was Baptized March 5th by Rev. Mr. Wm Geterne & had for Godfathers Mr. Larkin Chew & W. M. Moore & for God Mothers Miss Elizabeth Catlett & Miss Catharine Bowie the said Nelly was born on thursday morning just after Daybreak.

William Madison was Born May 1st 1762 & Baptized May 23rd by Rev. James Marie [Marye] Junr. & had for God Fathers Capt. Richard Barbour & Andrew Shepherd & for God Mothers Mrs. Sarah Taylor & Miss Mary Conway. She was born 45 minutes after 5 o'clock P.M. on Fryday.

Elizabeth Madison was Born February 19th 1768 half an hour after 12 o'clock & was Baptized February 22nd by Revd. Mr. Thomas Martin & God Fathers Major Zachariah Burnley & Capt. Ambrose Powell & God Mothers Miss Alice & Miss Milly Chew.

Mrs. Madison Delivered of a Still born Child July 10th 1770. Reuben Madison was born Sep 19, 1771 between 5 & 6 o'clock in the evening & Baptized November 10th by the Revd. Mr. John Barnatt and had God Fathers Mr. Thomas Barbour & Mr. James Chew & for God Mothers Misses Alice & Milly Chew.

Frances Taylor Madison was Born Octr. 4th 1774 & was Baptized Oct ___ by the Revd Mr. John Wingate & had God Fathers Mr. Thomas Bell & Richard Taylor & for God Mothers Miss Frances Taylor & Miss Elizabeth Taylor. She was born on Tuesday morning abt. a quarter after 3 o'clock.

Catlett Madison Departed this life on Saturday 18th of March 1758 at 3 o'clock in morning. Aged 36 Days.

Elizabeth Madison departed this Life May 17th 1775 abt. half after 12 o'clock being Wednesday. Aged 7 years & 3 months lacking 2 Days.

Reuben Madison Departed this Life June 5th 1775 at 10 o'clock in the Morning Monday. Aged 3 years 8 months & 17 days.

Ambrose Madison Departed this Life October 3d 1793 between 2 & 3 o'clock in the morning being Thursday Thirty eight years eight months & ___ days.

Francis Madison departed this Life April 5th 1800 abt. 10 o'clock being Thursday. Aged 46 Years 3 Months & 17 Days.

James Madison departed this Life February 27th 1801 abt. 10 o'clock in the morning being Fryday. Aged 77 years and 10 Months.

Nelly Madison departed this life February 11th 1829 abt. 8 o'clock in the morning being Wednesday. Aged 97 years and one month. [mother of President Madison].

Lucy Hartwell Conway daughter of Thomas & Sally Madison departed this Life Saturday May 13th 10(?) 4 P.M. 1871. Aged abt. ____ years 2 months & 20 days.

There are newspaper death notices pasted the back for Conway C. Mason, died 1864 in Richmond. Aged 68th year. Born in Orange County, Virginia in 1792. Col Edgar Macon died Key West, Fla., 11 Nov. 1929. Elizabeth, daughter of C.C. Macon, died May 21, 1831, age 19. Reuben Macon died May 1, 1893, age 45. Mrs. Lucy Conway died 3 ___ 1856 in Orange in 59 year of age. Reuben Conway died Jan. 3, 1838 of Orange, born 10th of March 1788 & was married to Lucy Haswell Macon daughter of Thomas & Sally Macon July 25, 1811. Mrs. Sarah Conway Macon relict of late Thomas Macon died 17 ___ in 80 yr of age. Penciled note: My father Thomas Macon died Febry 26, 1838 in the 73 year of his age. An obituary appeared in the Richmond Enquirer of which I never got newspaper of. --Signed L.H. Conway.

MAHON FAMILY BIBLE

This Bible was published by B.F. Johnson & Company, Richmond, Virginia, 1886. It was originally the Bible of Joseph "Joe" Carter Mahon who married Lizzie O. Butler, sister of Mattie V. Butler, born November 2, 1853, died at age 6 years, Dr. Edward Everett Butler, born August 28, 1856;; Leonidas C. Butler, born November 8, 1859. They were all children of Colonel J. O. Butler who died April 10, 1857 age 56 years 3 months. He married Anne E. Bagby, daughter of Travis and Mary Ann Bagby January 1850. For more information on the Bagby-Butler connections, see the Bagby Bible elsewhere in this study. Anne E. Bagby and her son Dr. Edward Everett Butler are buried in Lakewood Cemetery, Bowling Green. Other earlier members of the Bagby and Kidd family are buried at Cedar Grove on Fork Bridge Road near Gether, Caroline County.

Joe and Lizzie Butler Mahon purchased the old Harrison place located on Route 627 (Mattaponi Trail) back of Gether Post Office. The place is presently owned by Mr. and Mrs. Jack Upshaw. Joe Mahon died here and was buried on the place in the Harrison-Upshaw Cemetery before being later moved to Upper King and Queen Church Cemetery. The Bible is presently owned by Mrs. Jo (R.E.) Ogden, Petersburg, Virginia.

J. C. Mahon of King Wm and Lizzie O. Butler of Caroline on Dec. 19 1878 at Riverside by Rev. John O. Turpin. Witness: Travis Bagby/E.E. Butler.

Births:
Mary L. Mahon	Sept. 29, 1879
Josephine E. Mahon	July 31st 1881
Lizzie Lee Mahon	Aug. 7th 1883
Annie Vernon Mahon	June 17th 1885
Jennie Carter Mahon	April 10, 1887
Mattie Bagby Mahon	May 17th 1890
Carrie Baylor Mahon	May 10th 1895[1896]

Grandchildren of J. C. Mahon
Frederick W. Moore, Jr.	Feb. 25th 1903
Joseph Mahon Moore	Aug. 9th 1906
Peter Allen Haley, Jr.	Jan. 13th 1907
Ann Elizabeth Moore	May 23, 1909
John Bagby Haley	July 16th 1909

Mary Louise Crittenden	Oct. 24th 1909
Carolyn Vernon Crittenden	July 26th 1915
Florence Bagby Moore	Aug. 9th 1915
Josephine Bagby Donald	Dec. 4, 1922
Holt Crittenden	June 29th 1908
Betty Anne Kay	Nov. 13th 1932
Robert "Bob" Allen Kay	July 21st 1934

Marriages:
Josephine E. Mahon to Frederick Washington Moore Oct. 22, 1901
Mary Louise Mahon to Peter Allen Haley June 25, 1902
Lizzie Lee Mahon to Holt Wilson Crittenden June 26, 1907
Annie Vernon Mahon to Robert Kerr Donald June 17, 1912
Jennie Carter Mahon to Barrett W. Crittenden June 16, 1909
Mattie Bagby Mahon to Carl B. Brown [no date listed]
Carrie Baylor Mahon to Robert Allen Kay May 16, 1931

Deaths:
Lizzie Butler Mahon	October 19th 1904
Holt Crittenden	July 4th 1908
Joseph Carter Mahon	Feb. 1st 1938
Peter Allen Haley	Feb {blank} 1924
William Barrett Crittenden	Nov. 21, 1924
Frederick W. Moore	Oct. [blank] 1931
Holt Wilson Crittenden	Nov. 10, 1931
Josephine Mahon Moore	Aug. [blank] 1945
Robert K. Donald	Nov. 23, 1952
Robert Allen Kay, Sr.	Feb. 8, 1968
Lizzie Lee Mahon Crittenden	Nov. 28, 1969
Mary Louise Mahon Haley	Dec. 18, 1970
Carrie Mahon Kay	June 28, 1975
Carolyn Vernon Crittenden Turpin	April 18, 2000

MARSHALL FAMILY BIBLE

These records were found in the Anderson family Bible record in the Library of Virginia. A copy is also in the Virginia Historical Society.

William Marshall married Ann McLeod, daughter of Torquail McLeod & Ann Clark.
Elizabeth [Marshall] born 18 July 1769, married Hugh Roy of Spotsylvania County, Va.
Ann C. Marshall born 10 February 1772; married William Samuel, Henry Co. Ky.
Fanny Marshall born 1 September 1774; m. Robert Tompkins of Caroline Co. Va.
Mary Marshall born 10 November 1776, married William Webb of Henry Co. Va.
Sarah Marshall born 10 April 1779, married 17 Sept. 1797, Col. Richard Anderson.
George [Rogers] Marshall born 10 April 1782, married Mary Hoskins, Henry County, Ky.
John Marshall born 27 Sept. 1784, married Amelia Fields (2 Nov. 1788-20 April 1876, aged 87

years, 5 months, 18 days)Jefferson County, Kentucky.
John Marshall died 19th April 1830.
Robert Marshall born 25 Feby. 1787.
Lucy Marshall born 6 October 1789.

Notes: Ann McLeod's mother was Nancy Clark, sister of John Clark who married Ann Rogers and were parents of General George Rogers Clark. Ann Clark McLeod was married the day she was 18; had her only child Ann McLeod the day she was 19; and died the day she was 20 years of age. Torquail McLeod started back to Scotland, but believed to have been lost at sea, as he was never again heard from.

McGRUDER FAMILY BIBLE NO. 1

This Bible was printed and sold by Collins & Co., New York, 1816. The McGruder, also spelled Magruder, family lived in the Port Royal area of Caroline County and married into several local families, including the Bankheads, Worthams, Woolfolks, and Scotts. A copy of this Bible family register is in the Library of Virginia.

Sublett McGruder Born 16 of October 1791 *
Mary M. Woolfolk Born 12 of July 1799.
Louisa Frances McGruder Born 7 of April 1819.
Ann Eliza McGruder Born November 29 1820.
Charles McGruder Born November 1st 1822.
Richard Woolfolk McGruder Born November 21, 1824.
Sarah Angelina McGruder Born 18 December 1826.
Mary McGruder Born 20 of May 18__.
Sublett McGruder & Mary M. Woolfolk married the 20 of November 1817.
Samuel G. Scott & Louisa F. McGruder married 26th May 1842.
Frances Woolfolk departed this Life 3rd of January 1825 Aged 65 years.
Mary M. McGruder Departed this Life February 18 1833 in the 34th year of her age.
    They died in Jesus and are blest
    How sweet their numbers are
    From sorrow and from sin released
    They dwell with Jesus there
Ann Elizabeth McGruder married Edwin Wortham [16 April 1845] and died Sept 15 1880.
Sublett McGruder Died July 3d 1852.
Mary Woolfolk departed this life February 18, 1833 in the 34th year of her age.
*Wortham Bible gives date of Sublett McGruder's birth year as 1781.]

McGRUDER FAMILY BIBLE NO. 2

This Bible was published by the American Bible Society, New York, 1850. A copy of this Bible record is in the Library of Virginia.

Richard W. McGruder & Angelina Frances Woolfolk 16th November 1848.
Walter Withers Lucke & Mary Gay McGruder 30th December 1874.
Charles McGruder & Virginia Kinney Whitcomb 29 April 1885.
Wm Purcell McGruder & Ella Virginia Foster 19th October 1886.
Births:
Richard Woolfolk McGruder 23 November 1824.
Angelina Francis Woolfolk 8th April 1824.
Ellen Woolfolk McGruder 23 Nov 1849.
Angelina Winston McGruder 28 March 1851.
Mary Gay McGruder 29 April 1853.
Charles McGruder 1st May 1857.
William Russell McGruder 30th March 1861.
Clarence Linden McGruder 29 Dec 1866.
Deaths:
Ellen Woolfolk McGruder 10 Oct 1851.
Richard W. McGruder 23rd Aug 1886.
Mary Gay Lucke 13 Sept 1887.
Charles McGruder 25 Dec 1888.
William R. McGruder 13 April 1894.
Angelina F. McGruder 2nd Aug 1897.

McGRUDER FAMILY BIBLE NO. 3

This Bible was published by the American Bible Society, New York, 1854. A copy of the Bible is in the Library of Virginia.

R.W. McGruder & Anelina Francis Woolfolk 16th November 1848.
Walter W. Lucke & Mary McGruder 30th December 1874.
Charles McGruder To Virginia Kinney Whitcomb 29 April 1885.
Wm Russell McGruder To Ella Virginia Foster 19th October 1886.
Births:
Richard W. McGruder 28 Nov 1824.
Angelina Frances Woolfolk 8 April 1824.
Charles Woolfolk married Anne Nutting - Their children: Pichegru, Anne, Emily, Mary, Sallie.
Pichegru married Angelina McGruder Winston - Their children: William, Pichegru, Charles, James Edmund Clarence, Gaybrella, Sallie, Angelina.
Wm married Ann Turner.
Pichegru married Louisa Poindexter.
James Edmund Clarence never married.
Gaybrella married Gabriel Williamson.
Sallie married John Dickinson.
Angelina married Richard McGruder, son of Mary Woolfolk & Sublett McGruder.
[children of Charles & Anne Woolfolk]:
Anne married _____ Coleman.

Emily married Archie Dick.
Mary married Sublet McGruder.
Sallie married Robert Staples.
Children of Mary Woolfolk & Sublet McGruder:
Ellen W. McGruder 23 Nov. 1849.
Angelina W. McGruder 28 Mar 1852.
Mary Gay McGruder 29 Apr 1853.
Charles McGruder 1 May 1857.
William Russell McGruder 30 Mar 1861.
Clarence Linden McGruder 29 Dec 1866.
Deaths:
Ellen Woolfolk McGruder 10 Oct 1851.
Richd W. McGruder 23rd Aug. 1886.
Mary Gay Lucke 13th Sept 1887.
Charles McGruder 25th Dec. 1888.
William Russell McGruder 13th April 1894.
Angelina F. McGruder 2nd Aug 1897.
Clarence Lindon McGruder March 17th 1916.
Angelina W. McGruder Dec. 20, 1931.

McGRUDER FAMILY BIBLE NO. 4

A typewritten copy of this family Bible register is in the Library of Virginia. Some of the material in the McGruder Bibles overlap, but since they are all somewhat different, I have included all four. Some of the same material is found in the Woolfolk and Wortham Bibles. Sublett McGruder is listed as a resident of Richmond City in the U.S. Census of 1820. This Bible was in very poor condition when it was auctioned July 29, 1981 at Valentine Auction and Storage Company, Richmond, Virginia. The Bible record here is a transcript made before it was sold. The Bible was published by Harper & Brothers, New York, 1846.

Sublett McGruder and Mary W. Woolfolk Married the 20th of November 1817.
Samuel C. Scott and Louisa F. McGruder married the 26th April 1842.
Edwin Wortham and Ann Eliza McGruder married the 16th April 1845.
Sublett McGruder and Mary L. James married the 15 April 1847.
Charles McGruder and Ann Hite Maury married the 1st of December 1847.
Francis W. Baker and Sally A. McGruder were married on Tuesday, September 12th, 1865 by the Rev. Lewis Walke.
Sublett McGruder born 16 Oct 1781.
Mary W. Woolfolk born 12th July 1799.
Louisa Frances McGruder born 7th April 1819.
Ann Eliza McGruder born 29th Novr. 1820.
Charles McGruder born 1st November 1822.
Richard Woolfolk McGruder born 21st November 1824.
Sarah Angelina McGruder born 18 December 1826.

Mary McGruder born 26th May 1831.
Mary L. James born January 1804.
Frances Woolfolk departed this life 3rd January 1825 aged 65 years.
Mary W. McGruder departed this life 18th Feby 1833.

> They die in Jesus and are blest
> How sweet their slumber are
> From sorrow and from sin released
> They dwell with Jesus there.

Sublett McGruder died July 3d 1853 - born 1781.
Mrs. Louisa F. Henley died April 16th 1863. born 1819.
Mary McGruder (born 1831) died Dec. 8, 1859.
Mrs. Sallie A. Baker (born 1826) died May 15, 1868.

MICOU FAMILY BIBLE

This Bible was in the possession of William H. Micou of Montgomery, Alabama in 1939. He worked in the Tallassee Cotton Mills. He later moved to New York City by 1939. The Bible may also contain Boutwell family records as well, since William H. Micou was a descendant of Richard Micou and Anne Boutwell. The whereabouts of this Bible is unknown today.

MILLER FAMILY BIBLE NO 1

This old Bible belonged to the family of James Miller, who was born in Scotland in 1730 and died in the town of Port Royal, Caroline County in 1808. The Bible was inherited by James Miller's great-great grandson, the late Captain Henry Howell Lewis, U.S.N and C.S.N., of Baltimore in 1933. The whereabouts of this Bible is unknown today.

MILLER FAMILY BIBLE NO 2

This record was from a Bible published in 1811 by Matthew Cary of 122 Market Stree, Philadelphia, and was found in a book store in Kansas City, Missouri. It was copied by Mrs. Milton Welsh of Liberty, Missouri and published in *National Genealogical Society Quarterly*, Volume XI, No. 3, p.3, October 1922. This family lived in Port Royal, Caroline County; Springfield, Westmoreland County; Louisa County; and Orange County, Virginia.

James Miller and Elizabeth Robb, married July 24, 1799.
James Robb Miller married Emily Hayden Jan. 25, 1828.
John Tahlor Thornton, m. Ann Benger Hipkins July 29, 1818.
Peter A. Hansbrough m. Fannie Miller Oct., 1831, at J. T. Thorntons, Orange Co., Va.
James Miller and Peggy Hipkins, widow of Wm. A. Hipkins, m. Dec. 23, 1809.
Franklin Kownslaw, m. Elizabeth M. Miller, Aug. 2nd, 1832, at the home of John G. Thornton, Orange Co., Va.

Joseph P. Babbitt m. Bettie Hansbrough Nov. 7, 1855, in Boonville, Missouri.
Elizabeth Lucy Miller, dau. of James and Elizabeth Miller, b. July 23, 1801.
James Robb Miller, son of James and Elizabeth Miller, born Sept. 28, 1802.
James Miller Hansbrough, son of Peter A. and Fannie, b. July 24, 1832.
Ann Elizabeth, dau. of Peter and Fannie, b. Sept. 29, 1834.
John Hansbrough, b. Oct. 3, 1840.
Charlotte Taylor Thornton, dau of John T. Thornton and Ann Berger Thornton, b. July 13, 1819.
Arthur Wade, son of John T. Thornton and Ann Berger, b. May 11, 1831.
Ann Taylor Thornton, dau. of John T. and Ann Berger, b. 1834.

MINOR FAMILY BIBLE NO 1

This Bible was published by B. & J. Collins, New York, 1819 as the Collins's Sterotype Edition. It was owned by James Minor, Louisa, Va in 1826 and in 1870 by Jas. Minor Rawlings. A copy is in The Albemarle County Historical Society, Charlottesville, Va. Both the Minor and the Magruder are Caroline County families, the latter well established in the Port Royal area, the former at "Topping Castle" in Caroline County. There were four DeJarnette family homeplaces in Caroline, two of which are still standing. The Tyler homestead "Blemheim" is still standing in Caroline County. The Magruder family lived at Port Royal. The Rawlings family lived both in Caroline and Spotsylvania Counties.

James Minor & Mary Watson were married on the 20th July 1813.
John L. Holladay & Julia Ann Minor were married on the 17th May 1836.
Benjamin H. Magruder & Maria L. Minor were married on the 15th Decr. 1836.
James H. Rawlings & Virginia W. Minor were married on the 18th July 1843 at Bracketts by Revd. Joseph Ernest.
Julia V. Magruder & Geo. Tyler were married at Glenmore.
Married at Glenmore 1864 by Rev. Charles Beach Elliott DeJarnette of Spottsylvania Co., Va. to Evelyn May Magruder.
Married in Charlottesville Novr. 7th 1855, by Rev. R. K. Meade, James A. Latane' to Mary Minor Holladay.
Married in Charlottesville Novr. 11th 1858 by Rev. R. K. Meade, Wilson C. N. Randolph to Ann E. Holladay.
Married in Charlottesville, April 19th 1860, by the Rev. R. K. Meade, T. Henry Johnston to Sally W. Holladay.
Married in Charlottesville by Revd. Edgar Woods on July 7th 1868 James Minor Rawlings to Helen Carter Watson.
Married at Ridgeway, Albemarle Co Va. by Revd Hanckle, Henry M. Magruder to Sallie Minor married on the 7th of April 1869.
Married in Clarksville, Tenn. at the home of her Father, Dr James Minor R.[Rawlings], Bettie Watson Rawlings to Dr. Charles West Thomson of Spartanburg, S.C. June 9, 1892.
Married in Charlottesville, Va. at the home of her Mother, Mrs. Thomas Paye Carver, Velora Ames Carver to James Rawlings Thomson by Dr. Henry Alford Porter March 3d 1934.
(inserted pages)

Julia Latane' & Claggett Jones were married April 7th, 1880.
Nannie R. Latane' & Wm. DuBose Stevens were married Nov 7th, 1889.
Mary Minor Latane' & Samuel McLenahan were married June 26, 1889.
John H. Latane' & Elina J. J. Cox (nee Junkin) were married Oct 17th, 1905.
Lettica Latane' & Carroll Mason Sparrow were married Dec 14th, 1912.
James Allen Latane' & Mary Douglas Dabney were married Sept 14th, 1912.
Virginia Minor Randolph & George Scott Shackelford were married July 1st, 1884.
Virginia Randolph Shackelford & Peachy Gassoigne[?] Lynn were married Nov 10th, 1910.
Nannie Holladay Shackelford & Karl Morgan Block were married Oct 1st, 1913.
Thomas Henry Johnston & Anna Alexander Johnston were married Dec 27th, 1894, by R.G. McArthur in New York.
Thomas Henry Johnson & Mary Helen Johnston were married Nov 8th, 1905 by Rev. J. A. Dickinson in Birmingham.
Leonora Johnston & Robt. L. Preston were married in Buchanan, Va., by Rev. J. M. Rawlings.[no date given]
Julia Johnston & John G. Gerrell were married Dec 23rd, 1894, in Birmingham, Ala., by Rev. A.B. Case.
(end of inserted sheet)
Maria Louisa Minor daughter of James & Mary W. Minor was born 7th April 1815.
Julia Ann Minor was born 15 Nov. 1816.
Virginia Watson Minor was born 25 April 1822.
Mary Minor Holladay daughter of John Z. & Julia Ann Holladay was born the 4th May 1837.
Ann Elizabeth Holloday daughter of John Z. and Julia A. Holladay, was born on the 24th of July 1839.
Sally Watson Holladay daughter of John Z. and Julia A. Holladay was born on the 1st of April 1842.
Julia Latane' daughter of James A. & Mary M. Latane, was born on the 17th Novr. 1856 in Charlotte[sville].
Susan Latane' daughter of James A. and Mary M. Latane was born on the 19th day of June 1858, in Staunton.
Henry Waring Latane', son of J. A. & M.M. Latane', was born on the 15th Novr. 1859 in Staunton.
Nannie Randolph Latane', born Feb. 13th 1862 - Married Wm. DuBose Stevens, Nov. 7th 1889.
Mary Minor Latane' daughter of J. A. & M.M. Latane' was born in Staunton Jan. 17th 1864.
Lucy Temple Latane' daughter of J. A. & M.M. Latane' was born in Staunton Feb. 20th 1866.
John Holladay Latane' son of J. A. & M.M. Latane' was born in Staunton April 1st 1869.
Lettice Latane', daughter of Jas. A. and Mary M. Latane, born Jan. 15th 1878.
(inserted page)
Augusta Stuart, born Aug. 22nd 1771. Died April 14th 1872.
Edith Latane' born April 26th 1873.
Samuel Peachy Latane' born Dec. 14, 1874.
Elinor, daughter of John H. Latane' & Elinor his wife born Nov. 15th 1907.
James Allen Latane', son of Jas. A. & Mary M. Latane', was born Jan. 15th 1880.
Virginia Minor Randolph, daughter of Nannie Holladay and Dr. W. C. N. Randolph, born at

"Northwood", Charlottesville Nov. 28th 1859.

Virginius Randolph Shackelford Son of Virginia Minor Randolph, and her Husband, George Scott Shackelford, was born April 15th 1885.

Nannie Holladay Shackelford, born Feb. 25th 1887.

George Scott Shackelford Jr. born Jan 22nd 1897.

Margaret Wilson Shackelford born Oct. 27th 1898.

Walter Nash Johnson, son of T. Henry and Mary Helen Johnston was born Sept. 28th 1911 in Birmingham.

Julia Johnston, daughter of T. Henry and Mary Helen Johnston was born in Birmingham Jan. 11th 1914.

Edward Johnston, Son of Sally Holladay and T. Henry Johnston born Jan 23rd 1861.

Thomas Henry Johnston, Son of Sally Holladay & T. Henry Johnston born March 22nd 1863.

Lenora Johnston, born June 24th 1864.

John William, Son of Thomas Henry & Anne A. Johnston, was born in Birmingham Ala, Feb. 19th 1896.

Julia Johnston, born Feb 11th 1866.

Thomas Henry, son of same, was born in Birmingham April 17th 1898.

Helen Johnston, daughter of T. Henry and Mary Helen Johnston, was born in Birmingham Aug. 18th 1906.

Andrew Barnes Johnston, Son of same, was born in Birmingham August 23rd 1908.

James Rawlings, son of T. Henry and Anna A. Johnston was born in Birmingham Apr 3rd 1901.

Edward Bowyer Johnston, Son of T. Henry and Mary Helen Johnston, born in Birmingham April 3rd 1910.

(inserted sheet)

Catherine Anne, daughter of James Allen Latane' & Mary Douglas Dabney, his wife, born March 28th 1914.

James Allen, son of Jas. Allen Latane' and his wife Mary Douglas Dabney, was born Dec. 4th 1918.

Bettie Watson Rawlings daughter of Jas. M. & Helen C. Rawlings, was born in Charlottesville on the 1st of April 1869 at 8 o'clock A.M.

James Henry Rawlings son of Jas. M. & Helen C. Rawlings was born in Charlottesville, on the 7th day of June 1871.

Mary Norris Rawlings, daughter of Jas. M. & Helen C. Rawlings was born in Charlottesville on the 15th of December 1873.

James Rawlings Thomson Son of Bettie W. & Dr. Charles W. Thomson, was born in Spartanburg, S.C. April 21st 1893.

(end of inserted sheet)

Dr. James Minor died on the 24th March 1828.

Mary W. Minor died on the 20th June 1832.

John Z. Holladay died on the 12th October 1842 at Scottsville.

Virginia W. Rawlings died on the Tenth day of May 1847 at Woodbury in Spottsylvania and was buried at Sunning Hill.

James Henry Rawlings died [no date] & was buried at Sunning Hill.

Maria Louisa Magruder died [no date] & was buried at Glenmore, Albemarle.

Col. John Bowie Magruder Son of B.H. & Maria L. Magruder died at Gettysburg of wounds received in the battle & was buried at Glenmore in Albemarle Co Va.

T. Henry Johnston died on the [no day listed] of November 1866.

Mrs. Julia A. Holladay died in Baltimore Dec. 12 1892 - Aged 76.

Mrs. Bettie Rawlings Thomson daughter of James M. & Helen C. Rawlings & wife of Dr. Charles W. Thomson, died in Spartanburg S.C. June 19th 1893 - Aged 24.

Dr. James Minor Rawlings died in Charlottesvile of Angina Pectoris Feb. 1st 1898. Aged 51.

Dr. Samuel Peachy Latane' died May 1st 1910.

Dr. James Henry Rawlings, Son of James M. & Helen C. Rawlings died in Lynchburg, Va. April 4th 1945.

Helen Carter Watson, widow of Dr. James Minor Rawlings died in Charlottesville Dec 13, 1933.

Mary Norris Rawlings, 86, daughter of Dr. James Minor & Helen C. Watson Rawlings, died in Charlottesville, Va. June 8, 1860 - buried in Maplewood Cemetery, Charlottesville, Va.

[From the J. Rawlings Thomson Family Bible filed with the Minor Bible in the Albemarle County Historical Society, Charlottesville, Virginia.]

Bettie Watson Rawlings Born in Charlottesville, Va. April 1st, 1869 at the home of her Grandfather, Judge Egbert R. Watson Married in Clarksville, Tenn. to Dr. Charles West Thomson of Spartanburg, S.C. June 9th, 1892 at the residence of her Father Rev. James Minor Rawlings. Died in Spartanburg, S.C. June 19th, 1893 at her home on Converse St. leaving an infant, James Rawlings Thomson two months old.

James Rawlings Thomson son of Dr. Charles West Thomson & Bettie Rawlings Thomson was born in Spartanburg, S.C. April 21st, 1893.

James Rawlings Thomson married March 3, 1934 Velora Ames Carver (June 28, 1900-   ) at the home of her mother Mrs. Thomas Payne Carver 100 W. High Street, Charlottes, Virginia.

James Rawlings Thomson son of Dr. Charles West & Bettie Rawlings Thomson, died November 27, 1964, in Charlottesville. Buried in Maplewood Cemetery, Charlottesville, Va.

[newspaper clipping of the obituary of James Rawling Thomas, 71, November 27, 1964 is included]

MINOR FAMILY BIBLE NO. 2

This Bible, of which there is a copy on Reel 701 in the Library of Virginia, has on it's title page "Dorothea B.B. Buckner 1826 Braynefield, Caroline County". The seat of the Minor family in Caroline County was named "Topping Castle". Some members of the Minor family also lived at "Springfield", Caroline County and also at "Jerico". Dorothea Brayne Buckner's family lived and are buried at "Braynefield". The information in brackets which disagrees with the Bible record is taken from *The Minor Family of Virginia* by John B. Minor, 1923. Rather than trying to sort it out and most likely make mistakes, I have offered both versions to the reader, who can do additional research and make the right decision.

Garrit Minor & Eliza McWilliams were married 31st of March 1803.

Dorothea Butler Brayne Benger their first child born 25th of March 1854 married to Dr. William Bankhead Oct. 7th [11th] 1829.

William Garritt [Minor] born 1st of February 1806 married Annie T. [French] Rootes in Fredericksburg 4th of December 1840 (died in Missouri April 1851).

George [Buckner] born May 9th 1808 married Ann Eliza Chew August 1841.

Mary Overton born January 16th 1811 married Capt Theodore Rootes [Jan. 24] 1838.

James Lawrence born 9th of June 1811 married (lst wife Sally [C.] Goode [Mar 25, 1844] & 2nd wife Smith) Louise Smith of Missouri 1843 {Sept 11, 1846].

Andrew Jackson born 8th of September 1815 married 1st Mary A. Massy [Mary A. Massey] of Missouri 1st wife - 2nd wife Mary Baldwin of St. Louis, Mo. October 1846 [Dec 29, 1852].

Dorothea Brayne Bankhead Minor daughter of & first child of Garrit & Elizabeth Minor was Born on the 25 [26] day of March 1804 [1805] and on Oct. 14, 1829 Married Wm Bankhead.

William Garrit Minor Born Feb 1st 1806 and on Dec. 4, 1840 [Dec 11, 1839] married Anne F. Rootes.

George Buckner Minor Born May 12th 1808 and on Aug. 1841 married Ann Eliz Chew.

Mary Overton Minor Born 16 of January 1811 [or 1810] Married Thos. R. [Read] U.S.N. [Jan. 24, 1838].

James Lawrence Minor, Born 9th June [Jan] 1813. First wife Sally [C.] Goode 1848 [Mar 25, 1844]. 2nd wife Louise [Mrs. L.G.] Smith.

Andrew Jackson Minor, Born 4th of Sept. 1815 married Mary A. Massey 1st wife - 2nd wife [Mrs] Mary Baldwin [nee Smith of St. Louis Dec 29, 1852].

Peter Overton Minor Born January 14th 1819.

Robert Dabney Minor born Sept. 13, 1827.

Ann Banger Minor married [Thomas H. Walker 1847.

Robert D. [Dabney] married Landonia Randolph 1850 [Dec 17 of Fauquier Co] Died 20 of Nov '71.

George Buckner died of Apolexy Nov. 18th 1828 at 7 o'clock P.M.

"It has become my duty which I perform with sorrow and regret to inform the General Assembly that a vacancy has occurred in the Electoral body of this State occasioned by the lamented death of George Buckner Esquire of Caroline County". Message of Gov. Giles to Va. Legislature Dec. 11 1828.

Garrit Minor born Dec. 25, 1799 died at Fredericksburg 25 June 1832.

Elizabeth Minor his relick born 19th Aug. 1784 died at Braynefield on the 21st August 1832.

Dorothea Brayne Buckner born March 1, 1765 died at Braynefield on the 26th August 1839.

William Garrit Minor died in Jefferson City Missioui of Pneumonia Feby 20th 1851 in the 45th year of his age.

Ann Benger Walker 3rd daughter & 8th child of G & E Minor died near Jackson Cape, Girandian Co., Mo. Feby _th 1853 in the 31st year of her age leaving two children, Lucy & Louisa Minor.

Dorothea Brayne Buckner Minor 1st child of G. & E. Minor died at Sumerset, Stafford Co., Va. July 1868. Relict of Dr. Wm Bankhead.

Peter Overton born 14th of January 1819 bachelor in California. [in later writing] married Sallie [Susan of Oneida, N.Y] Rhodes in Calif. 186_. [May 16, 1865].

Ann Benger [Minor] born 26th day of October 1822 married to [Thomas] Henry Walker of Missouri 1847 (died December 1853).

Robert Dabney [Minor] born 13th of September 1827 married Landonia Randolph December

[17] 1850. Died 10 Nov. 1871.

Georgie [Georgiana] Cary Bankhead and John [William] E. [Edwin] Moncure were married on the 18 of October 1853.

Charles L. Bankhead and Mary Wagner Lewis Bankhead were married on 26th of Sept 1855.

Rosalie [Rose] Stuart Bankhead in the 21st her age & Richard M. Winston in the 23rd year of his age were married at Edgemont, Orange Co., Va. on the 10th of November 1857. [She married 2nd to the son of Miles Seldon].

Elizabeth [Betty] Bankhead married to [Bickerton] Brokerton L. Winston (no date) [June 1, 1853].

Eleanor [Ellen] Bankhead married [Rev. Jacquelin] Meredith at Edgemont, Orange Co., Va.

John [T] Bankhead married Mrs. [Eliza] Saunders (no date) [Nov. 24, 1831].

Nora Bankhead married at Signal Hill Oct (29) 1871 to Major John Lee of Stafford [brother of Gen/Gov Fitzhugh Lee].

MINOR FAMILY BIBLE NO. 3

This Bible was owned by D. Minor of Albemarle County, who made a transcript copy and placed it in the Virginia Historical Society. The Bible was given to D. Minor by Doctor John Minor of Salving-ton, Stafford County. The Minors and Carrs lived at "Topping Castle", Caroline County. Garritt Minor lived in Fredericksburg, Virginia, but his daughter is buried at "Braynefield" in Caroline County. Matthew Fontaine Maury's grandparents were of the Minor family of Topping Castle, where he visited as a child and played with a boat in the bathtub and tradition holds that he conceived the idea for the submarine at that time.

Mary Dabney was born June 22nd 1680.

John, son of Garritt & Diana Minor, was born June 28th 1707 and departed this life June 23rd 1755 - He was married to Sarah Carr daughter of Thos & Mary Carr, on the 14th Nov: 1732. She, Sarah, was born Novr 14th 1714 & died Sept: 28th 1772.

John, son of John & Sarah, was born Nov: 18th 1755 and died March 21st 1800.

William, son of John & Sarah, was born Aug: 30th 1736 and died Decr 14th 1758.

Thomas, son of John & Sarah, was born Aug: 5th 1740 - Died March 1816.

Mary, daughter of Jno & Sarah, born Mar: 7th 1741 and died [no date listed].

Garritt, son of Jno & Sarah, born Mar: 14th 174_ and died June 25th 1790.

James, son of Jno: & Mary [Sarah?] born Feb: 18th 1745 - died June 9th 1791.

Diana, daughter of Jno: & Sarah, born Feb: 28th 1747 - died March 28th 1748.

Dabney, son of Jno: & Sarah, born June 11th 1749 - Died Nov: 4th 1797.

Vivian, son of Jno: & Sarah, born Nov: 4th 1750 - Died Octo: 15th 1791.

Elizabeth, daughter of Jno: & Sarah, born Aug: 3rd 1852 [1752?] died March 30th 1777.

Peter, son of Jno: & Sarah, born Aug: 16th 1755 - Died Aug: 4th 1789.

[A manuscript note lying in the Bible has the following:]

Major John Minor was born the 25th day of November 1735. Departed this life Friday the Twenty first of March 1800. [This was Jno: the son of Jno: & Sarah.]

MORRIS FAMILY BIBLE

A copy of this Bible record is in the Library of Virginia. They lived in several places in the lower end of Caroline County near the Pamunkey River. They intermarried with the Woolfolk family of "Mulberry Place" and much of the information recorded is also in the Woolfolk family Bible.

Richard Morris son of Dr B. W. Morris & Ann F. Morris born 22nd Apr. 1850.
John Woolfolk son of Jno W. & Lucy T. Woolfolk was born 14 Apr 1852.
Ellen B. Morris daughter of Dr. B. W. Morris & Ann F. Morris was born 11 Apl 1852.
Sallie W. Roper daughter of Dr. W. W. Roper & Bettie C. Roper was born Apr 30th 1852.
Edmond Woolfolk son of J. W. Woolfolk & Lucy T. Woolfolk born 10 Feby 1844.
Jourdan W. Morris son of B. W. Morris & Ann F. Morris born 10 March 1854.
Elizabeth Winston Morris daughter of Dr. B. W. Morris & Ann F. Morris was born Apr 25 1856.
Sallie Winston Woolfolk daughter of Jno W. Woolfolk & Lucy T. Woolfolk was born 25 May 1856.
Louise Roper daughter of W. W. & B.C. Roper born [date not listed, but tombstone has Aug 23, 1851 or 1855].
Barton W. Morris son of B. W. & Ann F. Morris born 3 Apr 1858.
George Roper son of W. W. & E.C. Roper born Feb 18, 1859 [Woolfolk Bible has 19th of February].
Francis W. Woolfolk, son of J. W. & Lucy T. Woolfolk born 27 Sept 1839.
Julia B. Morris daughter of B. W. & A.F. Morris born May 18 1860.
Elizabeth Taylor Woolfolk daughter of J. W. Woolfolk & Lucy T. Woolfolk was born Novr. 4th 1861.
Thomas [E.T. in Woolfolk Bible] son of Dr. B. W. Morris & A.F. Morris was born 18th Jan 1863.
Mary M. Woolfolk born Feby 25th 1867.
Annie Barton Woolfolk was born July [18th] 1870.
Lucy Marshall Woolfolk was born 1st of ___ [Feb. 1839, tombstone].
Charles Woolfolk departed this life 8th Mar. 1886 at 20 minutes past 2 o'clock P.M.
John G. Woolfolk departed his life Friday Morning 16th April 1819 at half past One O'clock aged 68 years 6 1/2 months.
Mary Woolfolk daughter of Jourdan & Elizabeth T. Woolfolk died 14th July 1828.
Elizabeth P. Woolfolk departed this life Wednesday morning July 11 1835 at about Quarter past 7 O'clock Aged 73 years 4 months 8 days.
Ellen Broadnax Woolfolk died June 16th about half past eight O'clock A.M. 1848 aged 14 Years 4 Months & 19 days.
Ann E.[Eliza]Roper daughter of Dr. W. W. Roper & B.C. Roper died 19 Apr. 1850.
Sally W. Woolfolk died Jany 22nd 1851 at 1/2 past 4 P.M. Aged 21 years 8 Months 14 days.

MORSON FAMILY BIBLE NO. 1

This Bible was published by A.J. Holman & Co., 1885. This family has it's connections to the Port Royal area of Caroline County. The Bible was last owned by the late James Patton at "Gay

Mont", Port Royal, Virginia.

My Husband from his most devoted wife December 25th 1885.
  Bless thee & keep thee
  Lord make His face shine upon thee & be gracious unto thee
  Lord lift up His countenance upon
  thee and give thee peace. [title page]

Hugh Morson and Sallie T. Field were united by me in St. Peter's Church, Port Royal, Va. on the fifteenth day of April in the year of our Lord 1879. [printed page filled in]

Hugh A. Morson married to Sarah Phifer Jones at Charlotte, N.C., Oct. 4th 1911.
Margaret Morehead Morson born in Charlotte July 16, 1912. Died April 22, 1954 in Charlotte N.C.
Sarah P. Jones (Mrs. Hugh A. Morson) born April 17, 1888 in Charlotte N.C. died May 5, 1968 in Charlotte N.C.
Harriet Lightfoot, daughter of Hugh and Sallie J. Morson, born in Raleigh N.C. Feby 28th 1880.
Hugh Alexander, son of Hugh & Sallie J. Morson, born in Raleigh N.C. July 19th 1882.
William Field, second son of Hugh and Sallie J. Morson, born in Raleigh, N.C. March 6th 1885.
John Lightfoot, third son of Hugh and Sallie J. Morson, born in Raleigh N.C. July 10th 1888.
Hugh Morson born July 19, 1850.
Sallie Todd Field born Sept. 10, 1852.
My dearly Beloved Husband Hugh Morson died March 29th 1925. His sweet spirit is with me always.
Sallie T. Morson wife of Hugh Morson died Dec. 28th 1932.
Hugh Alexander Morson died April 15, 1956.
William Field Morson died June 13, 1964.
Harriet (Hal) Lightfoot Morson died Nov. 21, 1965.
John Lightfoot Morson died Oct. 22, 1969.

MORSON FAMILY BIBLE NO. 2

This Bible was published by Jesper Harding, Philadelphia, 1851. The family lived in the Port Royal area of Caroline County. The Bible was last owned by James Patton at "Gay Mont", Port Royal, Va. "Little Falls" mentioned in the Bible was in Stafford County, about 6 miles above Fredericksburg.

Married in Port Royal on the 10th of August 1848 by the Rev. William Friend, Hugh Morson to Rosalie Virginia Lightfoot daughter of Philip and Sallie S. Lightfoot.
Born in Port Royal on the 30th of May 1849 Fanny Lightfoot Morson.
Born at Little Falls 6 miles from Fredericksburg on the 19th of July 1850 Hugh Morson.
Born in Port Royal on the 28d of January 1855 Ellen Lightfoot Morson.
Born in Port Royal on the 27th day of August 1858 Philip L. Morson Second son and fifth child of Hugh & Rosalie V. Morson.

Died at Little Falls July 10th 1851. Fanny Lightfoot Morson.
Died at Little Falls March 1st 1857. Ellen Lightfoot Morson.
Died in Raleigh, N.C. March 29th 1925 Hugh Morson.
Died in Newport News, Va. Jan. 3rd 1930 Philip Lewis Morson.
Died in Raleigh, N.C. Feb. 15th 1938. Sallie Bernard Morson.

MOTLEY FAMILY BIBLE

This Bible belonged to the family of Nathaniel Motley, who lived at "Clear Mount", now known as "Mount Clear", 1.4 miles off Route 640 (Pendleton Road) near Sparta. He was the son of Henry and Ann Motley. Henry Motley owned an estate of 920 acres and died in 1817. Nathaniel Motley married Lucy Broaddus and died in 1867, leaving his estate to his son, John Leland Motley, who died in 1891. His daughter, Laura Motley Puller, owned the estate in 1937, when the W.P.A. recorded that the Bible was in the house at that time and copied it in the W.P.A. report, from which this is reproduced. The Bible was printed and published in 1828. The whereabouts of the Bible today is unknown.

Nathaniel Motley was born May 4, 1796 and died Feb 2, 1867 of typhoid pneumonia. He married Lucy G. Motley, who was born Jan 8, 1796 and died July 7, 1849. They were married by Andrew Broaddus August 10, 1820.

Their children:
Elizabeth Garland Motley, born May 11, 1825, married Garland Samuel, Jan 9, 1846.
John Leland Motley, born Feb 15, 1827, married Maria L. Broaddus, Nov 15, 1854.
Sally Ann Motley, born August 10, 1828, married Richard Green, Feb 3, 1857.
Lucy Christina Motley, born July 17, 1830, married Woodson Broaddus, Dec 12, 1848.
Polly Segar Motley, born May 5, 1832, married George W. Marshall, Dec 15, 1853.
Laura Temple Motley, born Feb 5, 1834, married John W. Broaddus, May 20, 1858.
Alice Lunsford Motley, born Dec 20, 1835, married Dr. Cornelius C. Broaddus, Nov 3, 1851.
Virginia Priscilla Motley, born Sep 20, 1837, married Robert G. Green, Dec 30, 1857.
Rubina Victoria Motley, born Feb 8, 1839, married J. Franklin Gouldin, May 20, 1852.

NOEL FAMILY BIBLE

This Bible was printed in 1829 and is in the possession of Mrs. Ruth (Noel) Powell, Fredericksburg, Virginia. It was copied by Mrs. Gloria Gatewood of Maryland. The records in this Bible concern both Essex and Caroline Counties. Berkley Muscoe Noel married Alberta S. Taylor, daughter of John C. and Lucy Myra (Dillard) Taylor in February 1876, in Caroline County, Virginia. Berkley and Alberta (Taylor) Noel are buried in a family cemetery at Elevon, Essex County. A log fence encloses the cemetery, however, there are stones. A receipt was found between the pages of the Bible: "Received May 1st 1878 of Mrs. Cath. E. Noel one cow (valued at about $15.00) which I accept as payment in full for Professional services and medicines to this date. /s/ C. S. Webb, M.D.[of Caroline County]. This Bible record has been published in the *Virginia Genealogical Society Quarterly*, Volume 10, No. 3, July 1972, p.70.

Berkley Muscoe Noel, son of Richd. L. Noel and Cathrine E. Noel was born June 11, 1847 [or 1849?, later written above].
Charles Muscoe Noel, son of James L. Noel and Susannah S. Noel was born 27 day of July 1850.
Edwin Wellford Walker, a son of John M. Walker and Emily F. Walker was born the 28th day of October 185? [page torn].
James L. Noel, son of Maria Noel departed this life 15th April 1862.
James R. Noel, son of Berkley Noel and Alberta Noel was born the 5th of February 1877.
William L. Noel, son of Berkley Noel and Alberta Noel was born October 2nd 1878.
Elmer M. Noel was born October 30, 1880.
Irene Noel was born September 16, 1881, a daughter of Burkley [sic] M. Noel and Alberta Noel.
Mary C.[Catharine] Noel, daughter of Berkly [sic] M. Noel and Alberta Noel was borne [sic] February 26, 1884.
Grace D. Noel was born the 12th day of February 1886.
James R. Noel died June the 12th [year not legible].

OVERTON FAMILY BIBLE

This Bible has no publisher nor date. A copy is in the Library of Virginia. The only reference to Caroline County found in the Bible is that of Emily Wilson Overton who married James Clevie Chewning July 1922 in Bowling Green, Virginia. There are other references to Virginia, although, many refer to Camden, North Carolina. The Library of Virginia lists the Bible as being a Caroline County Bible. The Overton family married into the Harris family.

Benjamin Franklin Overton and Welthy Burgess were married August 1865.
Simeon Burgess Overton and Margaret Dozier Sawyer were married Jan 26th 1847, Camden Co, N.C.
Emily Wilson Overton and James Clevie Chewning were married July 1922 Bowling Green, Va.
Edward Franklin Overton and Frances Andrews Willis were married August 14th 1937 Remington, Va.
Jennie Filmore Overton and George L. Morrisett were married 1891[?].
Benjamin Franklin Overton was born 1828, Camden, N.C.
Welthy Burgess Overton, daughter of Simon and Elizabeth Burgess was born Feb. 17th 1834.
Jennie Filmore Overton daughter of B.F. Overton and Wethy his wife was born June 24th 1866 Camden, N.C.
Simeon Burgess Overton son of B.F. Overton and Welthy his wife was born Oct. 9th 1867.
Margaret Dozier Sawyer daughter of Edmund S. Sawyer and Sarah Anne his wife was born Oct 4th 1865 Camden Co, N.C.
Emily Aileen Overton dau of S.B. and Margaret Sawyer Overton was born Dec 6, 1897 Camden Co, N.C.
Sawyer Overton, son of S.B. and Margaret Sawyer Overton, was born Sept 9th 1900 Norfolk Co, Va.
Alton S. Overton Son of S.B. and Margaret Sawyer Overton was born Sept 9th 1904 Norfolk Co Va.
Edward Franklin Overton son of S.B. and Margaret Sawyer Overton, was born Feb 27th 1961

Indian Neck, King & Queen Co Va.

Margaret Sawyer Overton daughter of Edward F. and Frances Willis Overton was born June 29th 1938 University Hospital Va.

Frances Willis Overton was born Jan 11, 1941 Charlottesville Va.

Eugene Willis Overson, son of Edward F & Frances Willis Overton was born March 5, 1943 Charlottesville, Va.

James Gordon Overton, son of Edward F. & Frances Willis Overton, was born Friday July 13, 1945, Charlottesville Va.

Benjamin Franklin died Friday night Oct 28, 1880 Camden, N.C. age 52 years.

Wethy Burgess Overton, wife of the late B.F. Overton died July 31st 1901, Camden Co, N.C.

Sawyer Overton son of S.B. and Margaret Sawyer Overton died Sept 11th 1902 Norfolk Co, Va.

Alton S. Overton son of S.B. Overton and Margaret Sawyer, his wife, died Oct. 8th 1906, Lloyd's Essex Co Va.

Margaret Sawyer Overton, wife of S.B. Overton died Sept. 24th 1931 Louisa, Va.

Simeon Burgess Overton, son of B.F. and Welthy Burgess Overton, died May 1, 1942 Fredericksburg, Va.

Emily Aileen O. Chewning, daughter of S.B. and Margaret Sawyer O. died March 20, 1958, W. Palm Beach Fla.

PARKER FAMILY BIBLE

This Bible was copied some years ago by Helen Kay Yates. The location of the original is now unknown. They married into the Gouldman family of Caroline County. See Gouldman Bible in this study.

Virgin Alice Parker was born Dec. The 10th 1853.
Emma S. Parker was born April the 17th 1855.
Sarah F. Parker was Born Feb. the 13th 1858.
Richard H. Parker was Born April the 10th 1863.
Robinet Parker was Born April 24th 1865.
John R. Parker was Born ___ 13th 1867.
Charles B. Parker was Born August 12th 1869.

PARSONS FAMILY REGISTER

Lying loose in the Rozell family Bible is a typed register of the Parsons family. Labon D. Parsons and Mary W. Hughes were married by Gilbert Wright, a Justice of the Peace in Decab Co. Witnesses Ira Young and Sarah Brown. The Rozell Bible is owned by Maxie Rozell, Caroline County.

A.J. Little and Ellen Parsons Married Feb. 26th 1880.
James Judge and Martha Mattie Parsons married April 28, 1880.
Ellis Judge and Isabell Parsons Married Oct. 14th 1886.

B.L. Crabtree and Rozelle Parsons Married Jan. 30th 1887.
David Allen Crabtree and Rozelle Parsons Married Jan. 30th 1887.
Henry Crabtree and Caldonia Parsons Married July 19th 1894.
Harrison Lafayette Parsons and Mary Jane Simms Married Jan. 17th 1900.
R.A. Moneyt and L.D. Parsons Married April 12th 1901.
Labon D. Parsons was born Sept. 16th 1840.
Mary E. Hughes, was born Feb. 3rd 1844.
The children births of Labon B. and Mary E. Parsons:
Mary Ellen Parsons was Born March 6th 1863.
Martha M. Parsons was born March 12th 1866.
Sarah M. Isabell Parsons was born Nov. 12th 1868.
Rozelle A.G. Parsons was born June 12th 1871.
Ida A. Parsons was born April 3rd 1875.
Caldonia A. Parsons was born Sept. 2nd 1877.
Harrison Lafayette Parsons was born July 27th 1880.
Green Labon Parsons was born Jan. 3rd 1883.
L.D. Parsons was born Nov. 9th 1885.
Labon D. Parsons died April 10th 1885 Pneumonia.
Mary K. Parsons died Aug. 17, 1929 Stomach trouble.
Green Labon Parsons died Feb. 2nd 1887 Pneumonia.
Mattie Parson Judge died Apgil 12th 1885 Pneumonia.
Mary Ellen Parsons Little died Aug. 22nd 1929 Leaking Heart.
Sarah M. Isabell Parsons Judge died Feb. 2nd 1941 Pneumonia.
Rozelle A .G. Parsons Crabtree died Oct. 30th 1941 Heart and Stroke.
Ida A. Parson Crabtree died Aug. 29th 1943 Blocked Heart.

PARTLOW FAMILY BIBLE

This Bible is known as the Elizah Partlow Bible, although its original owners were probably William and Catherine White, who had 15 children, one of whom, Ann T. White, became the second wife of Elijah J. Partlow. The Bible was owned in 1923 by Mrs. John F. Ellison, Red Bluff, California and the records were published in *The Virginia Magazine of History and Biography*, Volume 31, July, 1923.

John Partlow and Sarah, his wife, were residents of Caroline County as early as 1730. They owned 200 acres on the South River in Upper St. Margaret's Parish. Also living in Caroline County, was Wiliam Partlow, who died there in 1744 leaving wife Sarah, also Samuel Partlow and Mary Oliver, his wife. According to Erminia Jett Darnell in her book *Forks of Elkhorn*, Louiville, Kentucky, 1946, John Partlow came from Wales to Virginia, had 3 sons, John, Samuel and David, the latter who settled in Spotsylvania County, sold his land there in 1786, and went to Elkhorn, Ky. The Bible states that Elijah J. Partlow left Spotsylvania and went to Tennessee in 1840. The Bible apparently was taken with him and later taken by descendants to California.

Elijah J. Partlow, son of John and Sarah Partlow of Caroline County, married first Betsy Cason

February 15, 1805. He married 2ndly to Ann Thomas White, also known as Nancy, February 9, 1813, both marriages recorded in Spotsylvania County. Partlow, just over the border with Caroline County but now in Spotsylvania County, is named for this family.

William White was born March 15, 1751.
Catherine, his wife, was born June 9, 1762.
Richard B. White was born July 17, 1784.
Lewis G. White was born Dec. 22, 1785.
William White, Jr. was born Jan. 24, 1787.
Lipscomb White was born Sept. 5, 1788.
Ann Thomas White was born Jan. 17, 1790.
Milicent White was born Oct. 7, 1791.
Elizabeth White was born March 10, 1793.
Alice L. White was born May 16, 1794.
Chilton O. White was born Jan. 18, 1796.
Warner W. White was born Aug. 3, 1798.
Reuben White was born Nov. 17, 1799.
Silas White was born Jan. 2, 1801.
Edmond White was born Jan. 20, 1802.
James Thomas White was born Dec. 27, 1803.
Eliza White was born Oct. 10th, 1805.
Elijah Partlow, son of John and Sarah Partlow his wife, was born in the year of our Lord 28th of Oct. 1775.
Ann T. Partlow, the daughter of Wm. White & Catherine his wife, was born Jan. 17th, 1790.
Elijah J. Partlow was born 7th of Aug. 1813.
Wm. E.J. Partlow was born Feb. 10, 1815.
Catherine Sarah Ann Partlow was born Dec. 30, 1816.
Richard B. Partlow was born 15th of April 1819.
Martha Ann & Mary E. Partlow were born Sept. 23, 1822.
James M. Partlow was born April 11, 1824.
Eliza M. Partlow was born Jan. 4, 1826.
Maria E. Partlow was born Feb. 11th, 1806.
James B. Partlow was born Aug. 23rd, 1808, departed this life Dec. 23rd, 1832.
Maria E. Cason started out for Missouri Monday 5th of Sept. 1831.
William M. Phillips was born Jan. 4th 1814.
Geo. P. Phillips was born Feb. 2nd 1817.
James M. Lewis was born & Baptized by Rev. H.C. Booggs Sept. & June 1814.
Columbia Ann Elizabeth Phillips was born July 31, 1835.
Maria Ann Phillips, Catherine & Ann Phillips went to the West on Thursday 1st of Oct. 1835.
William L. White born Aug. 16, 1819.
Elijah J. Partlow started to Tennessee on Monday 14th 1840.
Eliza I. White was married to Andrew McDowell 21st of Dec. 1831.
Ann T. Anderson was married to Thomas U. Lipscomb on Thursday 15th of Sept 1831.
Elizabeth Smith was married to Samuel Luck on Thursday 25th of Oct. 1830.

Tindale Carpenter was married to Miss Southlin 1831.
Catherine S. Ann Partlow was married to W.M. Phelps on Thurs. Dec. 6th 1831.
Elijah M. Partlow married to Elliner Farrar on Thurs 22nd 1830.
Mary E. Partlow married William L. White on Thursday 12th Sept 1839.
Benj. C. Cason was married to M.A. Brown on 7th of Dec. 1852.
George B. Cason was born March 2, 1793.
Benj. C. Cason was born Sept. 1821.
M.A. Brown was born 7th Feb. 1834.
George I. Cason was born 9th Sept. 1853.
James B. Cason was born 21st of Dec. 1854.
Minnie B. Cason was born 4th of May 1859.
Daisy Cason was born 7th Dec. 1860.
Mary Adaline Robinson born Howard Co. Mo. Feb. 7th 1834. Died at Red Bluff, Cal. March 29, 1912. Maiden name Mary Adaline Brown.
Eliza M. Partlow departed this life Aug. 29, 1826.
John B.L. Partlow departed this life Dec. 23, 1832.
Ann T. Partlow departed this life on Sat. 20 of Aug. 1840.
Catherine S. Ann Phillips departed this life 2nd of Nov. 1840.
Richard B.L. Partlow was murdered & burned by his fathers 2 negro women Nance & Isabell on Thursday the 20th of Nov. 1840.
Elijah Partlow departed this life on Friday morning seven minutes after two o'clock the 9th day of July in the year of our Lord, 1841 at his son in laws George Cason in the county of Howard Missouri.
William White departed this life 1812.
My father desired for Douglas to preach from the text "Mark the perfect man & behold the upright: For the end of that man is peace."
I, George Cason bought this book at the sale of Elijah Partlow, deceased and gave it to my son Benj. Cason in the year of our Lord 1841.
John B. Cason departed this life the 18th day of Feb. 1858.
Benj. C. Cason died Wed. at 3 A.M. at Jacksonville. Ill. on the 17th of May 1865.
Minnie B. Cason married John F. Ellison at Lake View, on Tues Aug. 31, 1880.

PENDLETON FAMILY BIBLE

Edmund Pendleton lived at "Edmundsbury", Caroline County, which burned in the 1930's. Edmund Pendleton's large estate in Caroline County consisted of six square miles. Three other houses on his adjoining properties, "Edmundston", later named "White Plains", "Mt. Clear", and "Auburn Hills" still stand. A fourth Pendleton house, called the "New Gate Plantation" in his will has not been located by the author. A fifth house, known as a "Quarter House" or overseer's house has been moved to the yard of the author at "Green Falls", some nine miles from its original site, which is now occupied by Lake Holly. Edmund Pendleton, his two wives and infant son were all buried at Edmundsbury, but were re-interred in the aisle of Bruton Parish Church, Williamsburg in 1907. For further information concerning the Pendleton family, see a recent publication; The Descendants of Phillip Pendleton, A Virginia Colonist by David Ellis

Pendleton, 2007, Heritage Books, Inc., 65 East Main Street, Westminster, Md. 21157-5026.

The Pendleton family Bible containing the Old and New Testament is now owned by Colonial Williamsburg. The family records between the Old and New Testament were written by Edmund Pendleton in 1792. Additional entries were added by him during his lifetime. After his death various persons have made other entries, which are reproduced here in italic. This Bible record has been published several times and was last published in *The Letters and Papers of Edmund Pendleton* by David John Mays, University of Virginia Press, 1967. Following is the record as it appears today in the Bible.

About the year 1674, Nathaniel Pendleton a Minister, and Philip Pendleton a school-master sons of Henry Pendleton of the City of Norwich, County of Norfolk in England, came from thence to Virginia in America. Nathaniel died leaving no Issue, Philip went to England about 1680, returned to Virginia and Philip intermarried with Isabella Hurt and died leaving issue three sons and four daughters, in November 1721. His two younger sons John and Philip severally married, died long ago, and a considerable number of descendants from each are now living, but of them I can give no Particular Account. Elizabeth the eldest daughter intermarried with Samuel Clayton. Rachael the second with John Vass, Catharine the third with John Taylor and Isabella with Richard Thomas: are dead and the Posterity of each is numerous--but neither of these can I be particular.

Henry Pendleton the eldest son was born about 1683; in 1701 was married to Mary Taylor (daughter of James Taylor) who was born in 1688...so that he was eighteen, she 13. He died in May 1721. She married a second husband Edward Watkins, whom she survived and died in 1770 aged 82.

James Pendleton oldest son of Henry was born in 1702, and died in 1762, leaving 4 children Henry, James, Philip and Anne, all married, now living and have Issue. James and Anne are since dead. Philip Pendleton the second son died in 1778 leaving issue 5 daughters, all of whom married and have Children, two are dead, three living, one since dead.

Nathaniel Pendleton, thrid son, was born in 1715, and is still living [1792] having several children and grand children. He died in August 1794.

John Pendleton fourth son was born in 1719, and is still living [1792] having children grand children and great great children. He died in 1799.

Edmund Pendleton fifth and youngest son was born in September 1721, (four months after the death of his father) was married in January 1741/2 to Elizabeth Roy, who in November following was delivered of a dead child, and died in childbed. In June 1743 he was married to Sarah Pollard born in 1725 - both are now living, and have never had a child. Her father Joseph Pollard was born in 1701 and died December 26th, 1791, aged 90. Her mother still living aged 88. They lived together upwards of 68 years. She died July 27, 1794, age 92. *The said Edmund [died] in Richmond whilst attending the Court of Appeals of which he was President on the 26th day of October 1803 in the 83rd Year of his age.*

Isabella daughter of Henry was married to William Gaines by whom she had many children and died long ago. I believe there are descendants of her to the 5th generation; they are numerous and he is still living, died about 1790.

Mary the youngest daughter married James Gaines and is still living having descendants to the

4th generation. Her husband died a few years past.

Edmund Pendleton, eldest son of John the son of Henry, was born *January 24th, 1744 and 45*, and in August 1764 married Millie, the youngest daughter of Mr. Pollard, who was born the 11th day of May 1747, *died 4 July 1827-83*. Their children are as followeth:

John Pendleton born June 22, 1765. married September 20, 1789 to Anne Lewis daughter of John Lewis Merchant deceased. She was born the __ day of 17__ .

Frances .... born the 18th day of September 1767, intermarried with Mr. Robert Taylor son of Erasmus Taylor, the 7th day of July 1784, he was born April the 29th 1763.

Edmund .... born and died very young.

Mille .... born the 19th day of June, 1771, intermarried with Mr. Thomas Taylor Page the 15th day of June 1793. He was born ____ 17__ .

Edmund .... born the 18th day of April 1774 Intermarried in 1794 with Jane B. Page, who died October the 7th 1796. In May 1798 he married Lucy, 2nd daughter of Colonel Hugh Nelson born 17th May 1776.

Elizabeth .... born the 24th day of October 1776, intermarried with Mr. Reuben Turner on the 17th day of January, 1793. He was born September 16th, 1766.

Sarah .... born the 24th day of January 1781. Married to Daniel Turner February 1796.

Lucy .... born the 3rd day of October 1787, *intermarried the 7th of February 1805 with Thomas Richards son of William Richards deceased.*

The Children of John Pendleton junior:

John Lewis .... born the 9th day of July, 1790.

Edmund Allen .... born the 19th day of December 1791.

Elizabeth Allen .... born the 11th day of August 1793.

Mary Ann .... born 11th day of May 1795, and died October 5th 1799.

Evilina Mildred .... born 5th day of March, 1797.

Francis Armistead .... born   day of December, 1798 and died July 25th 1799.

William Armistead .... born the 17th day of June 1801.

Charles Lewis .... born the 16th day of November 1803.

Robert Taylor .... born 8th day of July 1805.

Benjamin Franklin .... born 1st day November 1806.

Nathaniel Philip Henry .... born   day of January 1809.

The Children of Frances Taylor:

Robert .... born May 30th 1785.

Milley .... born August 27th 1787. *Intermarried the 7th of February 1805 with Hay Taliaferro son of Robert Taliaferro deceased.*

Edmund Pendleton .... born April 1st 1790, and died in June following.

Edmund Pendleton, 2nd .... born September 17. 1791.

Lucinda .... born April, 1794.

Jacqlin .... born January 20th 1797.

Jane Frances .... born January 9th, 1799.

Alexander Fenelon .... born 4th March 1807.

Howard .... born 22 May, 1810.

Children of Milley Page:

Thomas Taylor .... born March 2nd 1794 and died December 25th, 1794.

Mildred .... a daughter born January 17th 1796.
John Tayloe .... a son born December 19th, 1797.
Jane Byrd .... a daughter born August 30th, 1799.
Eliz Pendleton .... a daughter born June 4th, 1801.
Edmund Pendleton .... a son born August 18, 1803 died 1823.
Thomas Taylor .... born September 16th, 1805.
Robert Carter .... born September 10th and died 19th, 1807.
Judith Frances .... born November 29th, 1808.
Robert Carter .... born June 8th, 1811.
William Henry .... born January 9th, 1814.
  Children of Edmund Pendleton 3rd:
Elizabeth Page .... a daughter born April 8th, 1796.
Hugh Nelson .... a son born April 13th, 1800.
Mildred .... born 21st March 1802.
Judith Page .... born December 8th, 1804.
Edmund .... born the 3rd of February 1805 and departed this life 26th June, 1806.
Thomas Nelson .... born the 16th of February, 1806, departed this life July 6th following.
John and Nathaniel .... Twins born the 29th of December, 1807.
Francis Walker .... born 7th December 1808.
William Nelsen .... born 26th December 1809 and married to Anzolette E. Page 15th July 1831.
  Robert Carter .... born 7th September 1812.
James Lawrence .... born 16th June 1814.
Gurdon A. Bacchus .... born 4th April 1817.
  Children of Elizabeth Turner:
George .... born 29th October 1793.
Edmund Pendleton .... born 3rd March 1796.
James Madison .... born 2nd of July, 1798.
Mildred Edmonia .... born September 29th, 1799.
Anne .... born January 29th, 1802.
Lucy Pendleton .... born April , 1804.
Eliz .... born 2nd June, 1805.
John Maddison .... born the 26th of December, 1807, and died the February following.
Mary Taylor .... born April 6th, 1809.
  Children of Sarah Turner:
George Pendleton .... born December 2nd, 1797.
Edmund .... born September 18th, 1799.
John Pendleton .... born December , 1801.
Robert Taylor .... born March 16th, 1804.
Thomas .... born February 1st, 1806.
Ann Maddison .... born the 18th December, 1807.
Sarah Frances .... November 4th, 1809 married F.W. Pendleton 1834.
  Children of Milley Taliaferro:
Robert Taylor .... born the 23rd of March, 1806.

Elen Bankhead .... *19th November, 1807.*
Edmund Pendleton .... *15th November, 1809.*
Felix H.G. Taliaferro .... *26th April, 1812.*
William Gray son of William Gray, Port Royal, married Eliza A. Pendleton daughter of John Pendleton, son of Edmund and Milley Pendleton the 20th day of September 1811. No children as yet but soon expected.
Isabella their daughter born
Elizabeth Page, daughter of Edmund and J.E. Pendleton was married to John C. Sutton 18th April 1817. Their children are Edmund P., William, Sarah Jane, Norborne, John, Lucy Carter, Patrick H., Ann Lewis, Robert W.
Hugh, 1st son was married 12th March 1829 to Lucy Nelson daughter of Chancellor Ro Nelson. Julia, their daughter, was born 21 January 1830.
Mildred, daughter of E. and Lucy Pendleton was married to Edmd A. Pendleton 17th November 1825. Their children are Edmund, William Thomas (dead), Charles, John and Hugh (Twins), Judy Page.
Judith Page, 2nd daughter, was married to Rob. H. Harrison June 1826. She died 9th July 1834, leaving a son William Lucius born 11th September, 1829 and a daughter, Mary Temple born 31st August, 1833.
Francis Walker, was married to Sarah Frances daughter of Daniel and Sarah Turner, 7th January, 1834. Lost a daughter at birth 12 November 1834.
William Nelson was married to Anzolette E. daughter of Francis and Susan Page on 15th July 1831. their children are Susan, born 28th May 1832, Lucy born 2nd February 1834.
Children of Hugh N. Pendleton, eldest son of Edmund 3rd - entered 1868:
Julia Nelson .... *daughter of his first wife Lucy Nelson (who was the only child of Chancellor Nelson of Williamsburg) - was born 21 January 1830. In 1856 she was married to James W. Allen, Colonel of the 2nd regiment Virginia volunteers, Stonewall birgade, who was killed a the battle Gaines's mill, near Richmond. She died 23rd day of July, 1865.*
Dudley Digges .... *Eldest son of his second wife Elizabeth Frances Mann Digges, who was only daughter of Dudley Digges of Louisa County, and grand-daughter of Dudley Digges of the King's Council, and of Governor John Page. Dudley was born on the 2nd day of March 1840. Was married on the 25th day of April 1866, to Helen M. daughter of Honorable Alexander R. Boteler of Jefferson County.*
Robert Nelson .... *Born 4th day of February 1843.*
Kenneth Murray .... *Born 15th day of March 1845 - died 20th June 1846.*
Kenneth Murray - 2nd .... *Born 16 day of October 1852. An infant born in 1848 lived only 24 hours.*
Hugh N. Pendleton, eldest son of Edmund 3rd, died at Springfield, Wythe County, Virginia, May 27, 1875.
Gurdon H. Pendleton youngest son of Edmund 3rd died near Wytheville January 30th, 1879.
William N. Pendleton son of Edmund 3rd died at Lexington Virginia January 15, 1883.

PENN FAMILY RECORD

The Penn family in Caroline were interconnected with the Pendleton, Taylor and Pollard families of Caroline County. Three of Caroline's most distinguished sons were from this family, Judge Edmund Pendleton, John Taylor of Caroline and John Penn, the signer of the Declaration of Independence. The latter went to North Carolina at the beginning of the American Revolution because his native county of Caroline fined him a penny for being disloyal to the British crown. A copy of this Bible record is in the Library of Virginia and is listed as Amherst Co., Va. Bible. See Taylor Bible elsewhere in this volume.

Moses Penn married Katherine Taylor of Caroline Co. Va. & had seven children via.:
Frances Penn born Jan. 9th 1735.
George Penn born Dec. 12th 1737.
Philip Penn born Jan. 27th 1739.
Gabriel Penn born July 17th 1741 died 1799.
Abram Penn born Dec. 27th 1743 died 1801.
William Penn born April 7th 1745.
Moses Penn born January 13th 1748.
  The children of Abram Penn & Ruth Stovall daughter of James Stoval & Mollie Cooper of Amherst Co. Va.
Lucinda Penn born Sept. 3rd 1771.
Gabriel Penn born Nov. 14th 1773.
Horatio Penn born Nov. 14th, 1775.
Polly Penn born July 1st 1777.
Greensville Penn born May 16th 1779.
Thomas Penn born June 15th 1781.
Abram Penn born March 14th 1783.
James Penn born Jan 31st 1785.
Luvenia Penn born Jan 8th 1787 died in childhood.
Edmund Penn born Jan. 8th 1789.
George Penn born Jan 6th 1790.
Philip Penn born March 5 1792.
Lucinda Penn married Samuel Staples (Clerk of Patrick Co. Va.)
Col. Abram Penn lived for years with John Penn the signer of Declaration. The sword of Col Abram Penn is now in possession of the Family.

PENNEY FAMILY BIBLE

This Bible was published by C. Alexander & Co., Philadelphia in 1839. A copy of the family register is in the Library of Virginia. This family lived, until 1941, in that area of Caroline County, which is now within the bounds of Fort A.P. Hill. The original owners of this Bible appear to have been Edward M.C. Penney and Sophia Jane Cobbs, who were married in Caroline County February 3, 1841.

Cornelieus C. Penney was born the 5 of January 1842 and died Oct 19, 1861.
Julia Elizabeth Penney was born Sept 23, 1844 and died May the 8th 1863.
Edmonia Alice Penney was born the 6th June 1848.

Sally Terrell Penney was born the 5 of Nov 1852.
Mary Mollie Jesse Penney was Born the 1st of February 1857.
Edward M. Penney was Born 30th of March 1860 and died 12th of April 1860.
Irving C. Trainham was born July 19th 1878.
Daisey Trainham was Born May 12 1882 & Died May the 19 1883.
Tillie E. Smith was born 18th Jan 1880.
W.B. Smith was born the 4 November 1853.
Edward M.C. Penney Was Born the 18 of July 1814.
Sophia J. Cobbs was born 12th of April 1819 and died December __.
Elizabeth's children:
Lyla May Smith born November 1876.
Alfred (Allie) Jessee Smith was born the 27th of June 1880.
Edward M.C. Penney Son of William & Elizabeth Penney was married to Sophia Jane Cobbs Daughter of Overton & Rhoda Cobbs the 3 of February 1841.
Married on the 21st June 1874 Sallie F. Penney daughter of Sophia J. and E. M. C. Penney, to Samuel H. Trainham of Caroline County Virginia.
Married on the 2nd of March 1876 E.A. Penney daughter of Sophia J. and E. M. C. Penney to L.A. Smith, son of William & Lucy Smith of Caroline County Va. by C.R. Dickinson.
Married on the 26 of June 1879 M. J. Penney to W.B. Smith by Rev. C.R. Dickinson.

[newspaper obituary:
"Died February 6, 1865, in Caroline County at her own residence after a long and painful disease of cancer, Mrs. Elizabeth A. Penney, age between 75 and 80 years.[*] She had been a member of the Baptist Church for thirty-five or forty years. Her sufferings were great but borne with Christian patience and fortitude. She often expressed herself as being fully resigned to death. She has left five children to mourn their irreparable loss, but they mourn not without hope in the death of this aged Christian. We can exclaim Oh Death where is thy sting, Oh grave where is thy victory. E.M.O.P."]
[* She is listed in the *Caroline Death Register* as dying Feb. 27, 1865 at the age of 80, being the wife of Wm Penney and mother of Ann E. Taylor.]

[newspaper obituary:
Died on Saturday October 19th 1861, at hospital No. 2 in Fredericksburg of Typhoid fever,[*] Cornelius C. Penny, only son of E.M.C. and Sophia Penny of Caroline Co aged 18 years 6 months 14 days. Cornelius was a member of company G, 30th regiment Va. volunteers. At the call of his country, he cheerfully volunteered to assist in driving the northern invaders from our soil, but alas he has fallen a victim to disease" etc. signed R.S.A.
[* *Caroline Death Register* shows pneumonia as cause of death.]

[newspaper obituary:
"Died at her residence in Caroline County January 1, 1874 in the forty five, Mrs. Virginia H. Woolfolk, wife of Deacon Robert Woolfolk of Beaverdam" etc.
Her funeral sermon was preached by her pastor the Sunday following her death, and an unusually large attendance of people on the occasion and in the procession to the grave attested the deep

feeling evoked by her death. She sleeps in the churchyard of Bethel, the church of her choice, the congregation of the saints so dear to her heart, and the place of her active Christian effort in her Saviour's cause. We do not doubt that absent from the body, she is present with the Lord, and now enjoys the rest that remaineth to the people of God"
[This notice appeared in *The Religious Herald* April 23, 1874]

[newspaper obituary:
"At his residence, Tudor Hall, in King and Queen county, on the second Sunday in September 1873 died Mr. LOVELL P. TODD, in the sixty-fourth year of his age. His sainted wife, Mrs. Fanny [Spindle] Todd, had preceded her husband to their heavenly home, in the spring of the year before, exclaiming in her last moments, in a exercise of a faith which had been the unfailing consolation of her beautiful life as she enumerated the ties that bound her to this world. 'None of these things move me, neither count I my life dear to myself, so that I may finish my course with joy.'
Brother Todd was a deacon of Bethesda, Caroline, of which church he had been a valuable member for about twenty years. He was a man of high character and lovely life; and of the many big-hearted Virginian whose lives have been shortened by overstrained hearts, few, if any, have lived more loved or died more regretted. The religion of his life was his comfort in death, and his end was one of triumphant peace".
[This notice appeared in *The Religious Herald* April 23, p.3]

PITTS FAMILY BIBLE NO. 1

This Bible belonged to Robert Woodford Pitts, who lived at the intersection of Kidds Fork Road and Mattaponi Trail. He built the house on a tract of 50 acres which was carved off of nearby "Aberfoyle". The house was destroyed by the owners in the Spring of 2003. This family is buried at Mt. Hermon Church at nearby Shumansville. Sabernie Pitts was killed by lightening while sitting in front of the fireplace in her home at Kidds Fork in 1900. The Bible is now in the possession of Stuart Tyler Pitts, Greenwood, South Carolina.

Robert W. Pitts born August 25, 1845.
Cindarella Pitts born October 18, 1855.
Fernando Pitts born November 4, 1873.
Charles B. Pitts born July 2, 1877.
Sabernie Pitts born January 17, 1880 Died July 22, 1900.
Harry W. Pitts born November 27, 1887.
Carroll F. Pitts born March 11, 1896.
Carrie Pitts wife of Fernando Pitts Died March 11, 1896.

PITTS FAMILY BIBLE NO. 2

This Bible was published by A.J. Holman & Co., Philadelphia, 1890. It originally belonged to Fernando H. Pitts, son of Robert Woodford Pitts. They lived in the house built by Woodford Sirles at the intersection of Reedy Mill Road and Mattaponi Trail in Caroline County and between Kidds Fork and Shumansville. The Bible is presently owned by Joyce Pitts Carter, Milford, Virginia.

Fernando H. Pitts of Shumansville and Mollie K. Barlow of Shumansville on February 20th 1901 at Bowling Green by Dr. Mc Cowen. Witness: Charles Pitts, W. L. K. Pollard.
Howard F. Pitts and Laura C. Christian was united in Marriage June 4, 1927.
Bernice Pitts & William Irving Hudson Married May 1, 1941.
Fernando H. Pitts was born November 4, 1873.
Mollie K. Barlow was born October 21, 1868.
Howard F. Pitts was born March 7, 1902.
Bernice M. Pitts was born April 6, 1905.
Jeanne R. Pitts was born February 29, 1928.
Joyce M. Pitts was born May 23, 1930.
Stuart T. Pitts was born Dec. 23, 1935.
Roger B. Pitts was born Oct. 11, 1937.
Rosa B. Barlow died April 15, 1921.
Edward D. Barlow died Jan. 12, 1926.
Mollie Barlow Pitts died March 4, 1941.
Fernando H. Pitts died July 8, 1856.
William Irving Hudson died Mar. 22, 1983.

POLLARD FAMILY BIBLE

This Bible was in possession of the family when its family register was published in the *William and Mary Quarterly*, Series I, Volume 5 at pp. 64-65 in 1907. The original records were recorded in the handwriting of Judge Edmund Pendleton of Caroline County, whose second wife was Sarah Pollard. The Pollard family also married into the Hoomes family of Caroline County.

Sarah Pollard, born the 4th, May, 1725, was married the 20th June 1743, to Judge Pendleton. She is now in her 90th year.
Anne Pollard, born the 22d February, 1732. She is now in her eighty-third year - married a Mr. Taylor and was mother of Colonel John Taylor, of Caroline, the great statesman.
Elizabeth Pollard (now Meriwether), born October, 1736, is now in her 76th year. These three ladies lived under one roof-- keep no housekeeper--families entire.
Thomas Pollard, born September 30th, 1741, is nearly 73. He rode on horseback from Kentucky, a year or two ago, and means to return shortly.
Milly Pollard, now married to Colonel Edmund Pendleton, was born the 12th of May, 1747, and is now in her 68th year, and lives within two miles of her sisters.
Jane Pollard, now the wife of Thomas Underwood, was born the 25th of May, 1744, and is in her 71st year, living in Hanover.
Joseph Pollard, the father of the above, died 26th December, 1791, nearly 91.
Priscilla Pollard, the mother, died 28th July, 1795, above 91.

PRATT FAMILY RECORD NO. 1

Taken from the Pratt Family Record Book, which is now at "Camden", Caroline County, Virginia. John Pratt crossed the Rappahannock River from King George and settled in Caroline County in 1790, at the time he married the widow of a prominent Port Royal merchant. He built the original house on a large tract just outside of Port Royal, Caroline County and named it for Charles Pratt, the first Earl of Camden. In 1853, the original house was razed and the present Italian Villa house was constructed. The place has always been in the Pratt family. A copy of this family record is also at the Virginia Historical Society.

John Pratt Sr. was born 4th September 1761.
Alice Fitzhugh Pratt born 20th January 1759.
Alice F. Pratt born 11th August 1785.
Caroline M. Pratt born 21 June 1787.
John Pratt Jr. born 22 August 1789.
Thomas Pratt born 11 November 1791.
Maria Pratt born 29 April 1795.[Mrs. Patrick C. Robb]
Harriet Pratt born 25 November 1797.[Mrs. Yerby of "Belvoir"]
Jno Edwd Henry Turner Dixon born 18th February 1780.
Elizabeth T. Dixon born 4 March 1781.
John Pratt was married to Columbia Stanard [youngest dau of late Wm S.] May 6, 1819 [at residence of Samuel Slaughter Esqr. in Culpeper by E.C. McGuire, see Va. Herald for May 15, 1819].
John Pratt, first son, was born March 23d 1820.
William Carter Pratt, second son, born May 1st 1821.
Wm C. Pratt was married to Eliza H. Turner May 8th 1860.
First son, born July 26, 1861; Died Aug. 9th 1861.
Second, a daughter, born Nov. 25, 1862; Died Dec. 6th 1862.
Maggie Stanard Pratt Born April 2nd 1864.[April 3rd on tombstone]
Ida Vivian Pratt Born Nov. 10th 1866.
Wm Turner Pratt born Aug. 2nd 1869. [d. Mar. 1948, m.(1) Mary Marshall d.Jan 1917, m.(2) Mary Custis Lee]
Richard Turner Pratt born Jany 20th 1886.

PRATT FAMILY RECORD NO. 2

This record of the Pratt Family of Stafford County, Va. appears in a volume entitled *THE WHOLE DUTY OF MAN* which seems to be a treatise on the Bible. The record is written near the center of the volume where is a page entitled: *The Second Part of the Works of the Learned and Pious Author of the Whole Duty of Man,* printed at the Theater in Oxford and are to be sold by Edward Paulet Bookseller in London. 1704. On the fly leaf of this book is written "Taken at Fredericksburg, Va., Dec. 14, 1862, the day after the Battle." On the second page is written: "Elizabeth Bernard - Mansfield - August 8th., 1819". This book was taken by a Northern Officer. It was returned in July 1938 by a member of his family, Mrs. C. N. Fitch, 509 Valentine

Road, Kansas City, Missouri, to Mr. Richard Turner, "Camden", Caroline County, Virginia. A copy of this record was made by George H.S. King of Fredericksburg and is now in his papers in the Virginia Historical Society. The original book is at Camden. The Bible record of William Streshley, mentioned at the end of this Record is at the Library of Virginia, no. 20705.

Frankey Pratt Daughter of Thos. Pratt and Margret his wife was born the 14 day of Sept. 1748.
Margret Pratt daughter of Thos Pratt and Margret his wife was born the 30 Day July 1750. [m. 1771 Bernard Hooe of Prince William County]
Ann Pratt was Born the 27th Day March 1752 & was married to William Streshley the 28 day of August 1772.
Elizabeth Pratt was Born the 8 Day of March 1754. [m. John Hipkins]
Susanna Pratt was Born the 8 Day of February 1756.
Molly Pratt was Born the 28 Day January and Departed this Life 23 of March 1758.
Milley Pratt was born the 4 Day of September 1759 and married Henry Washington. [Mar 12, 1779]
John Birkett Pratt Born the 4th day of September 1761 about 1 o'clock in the morning and Baptiz'd the 16th by the Rev. Mr. Stewart. [Aug 6, 1761, St. Paul's Register]
Birkett Pratt Departed this life the 27 of December 1760.
Thomas Pratt was Born the 28 day of June 1765. [m. Jaine Brockenbrough June 23, 1789]
Thomas Pratt Senr. died March the 16th 1766.
William H. Hooe died Mar. 19th 1818.
Frankey Pratt of Boyd's Hole, widow of Wm Hooe, Senr., died on Monday Evening the 16th of August 1830.
[facing the above record on the opposite page is written]:
William Streshley was born the 22 day of December 1749.
William Streshley, Caroline County
Elizabeth Pratt E.

PULLER FAMILY BIBLE

This Bible belonged to the Puller family, who lived at Lauraville, Caroline County. Copies of the original Bible records were furnished by Rachael Puller Harris, Midlothian, Virginia.

Title Page:
J. E. Puller of Caroline and G. (Glenmore) L. (Lora) Chiles of Caroline on Nov. 20th 1902 by Rev. A. Broaddus Witness J. E. Chiles & R. Puller.

Lucye E. Puller Born March 29, 1896.
Battle Everet Puller Born Oct. 3, 1903.
Andrew Floyd Puller Born March 1, 1906.
Roda (Rhoda) Alice Puller Born Sept. 12, 1908.
Eva Christine Puller Born Dec. 24, 1910.
Annie Lora Puller Born Nov. 23, 1913.
James Cave Puller Born Feb. 13th. 1919.

Virginia Ann Puller born April 15 (changed to 14), 1929.
Mildred Lane Puller born June 3, 1932.
Jane Rachel Puller born Sept. 25, 1933
William Floyd Puller born June 13, 1936.
Joanie Kathrinia Puller born March 5, 1957.
Evert B. Puller and Virginia Barlow Married Jan 2nd 1928 Bowling Green, Va.
Floyd A. Puller and Janie B. Southworth married Dec. 12, 1931 Sparta, Va.
Annie L. (Lora) Puller and Julius P. (Preston) Hines married July 31, 1937 - Longdale, Va.
Rhoda Puller and Harry H. Fowler married August 19, 1941 Bennettsville, S.C.
James Cave Puller and Dora Moore married May 22, 1953 Richmond, Va.
Mordecai E. Puller Died Dec. 31st 1906, age 68.
John E. Chiles Died May 30, 1914.
Mr. A.E. Young Died Oct. 29th, 1925, age 57.
Mrs. J.R. Puller Died Jan. 13th 1931, age 45.
Mr. J.R. Puller Dioed April 4, 1931.
Mr. S.L. Chiles Died Sept. 1, 1931, age 24.

REDD/ANDERSON FAMILY BIBLE

This Bible was copied by the late Judge Leon Bazile and a copy is in his papers in the Virginia Historical Society. In the Bible is a siluelette of Dr. Thomas B. Anderson, which reveals him as a handsome man. Also a letter from Dr. Wm. H. Shitsett Jan. 1905 which states the following: "Cedar Vale was the home of the Redds for nearly 200 years. Mr. Samuel Redd was the son of Capt Samuel Redd. His mother was Lucy Rogers sister of Rachel wife of Donald Robertson and of Anne wife of Gen. George Rogers Clark. They were of K & Q. Co. Dr. A. Bagby says that Donald Robertson was a graduate of both Aberdeen and Edinburgh Universities and when he came to K & Q Co. he opened an academy & is known to have taught President Madison who give him great credit for his success in after life. There was reason to believe that he also taught President Monroe and Gen George Rogers Clark one of the noted men of the Revolution." "Topping Castle" in Caroline County was the seat of the Carr-Minor-McLaughlin families, where many are buried and is located near the North Anna River. In a letter addressed to Mrs. S. Redd by Mrs. R.W. Christian, she writes: "I copied this out of Cousin Eliza's Bible for grandmother to show her how Topping Castle came into the family".

Samuel Redd & Elizabeth Taylor were married 2 March 1797.
Thomas Bates Anderson and Harriet McLaughlin Redd were married 18 Sept 1815.
James Temple Redd and Thomasia Anderson were married 10 May 1838.
Alexander England and Elizabeth Barbara Redd were married 30 April 1873.
William T. Dandridge and Harriet S. Redd were married 1 Aug.1895.
Fannie Cornelia Redd and George Preston Smith were married 21 Dec 1875.
John Robinson Redd and Mary J. Eubank were married 31 Jan 1878.
James Thomas Redd & Kate C. Taylor were married 4 Feb 1880.
James Thomas Redd and Addie W. Walter were married 26 Oct 1886.

Lnynette W. Redd and Robert W. Christian Jr. were married 20 June 1888.
Lemuella C. England and George H. Boyd were married 19 Dec 1894.
Samuel Redd born 19 March 1764.
Elizabeth Taylor born 31 March 1776.
Thomas Bates Anderson born 14 Jan. 1792.
Harriet McLaughlin born 20 November 1798.
James Temple Redd born 28 May 1815.
Thomasia Anderson born 18 Nov. 1817.
Llewelyn Wentwoth Redd born 4 Jan. 1840.
Julia Lehmonia Redd born 7 Nov. 1841.
Mary Elizabeth Redd born 10 Feb. 1843.
Harriet Samuella Redd born 3 Nov. 1844.
John Robinson Redd born 5 Nov. 1846.
James Thomas Redd born 25 Feb. 1849.
Thomasia Temple Redd born 29 Jan. 1851.
Elizabeth Barbara Redd born and
Lucy Edmonia Redd born 6 March 1853. [twins]
Fanny Cornelia Redd born 4 June 1855.
Louisa Bates Redd born 6 Aug 1857.
Elishia Pendleton Redd born 14 Oct 1859.
Lynette Wentwoth Redd born 7 Aug 1865.
Llewela Carrington England first grand daughter of James T. & Thomasia Redd born 6 July 1874.
Abner Venon England 1st grandson of James T. & Thomasia Redd was born 22 May 1876.
William T. Dandridge Jr. 2nd grand son was born 7 July 1877.
    baby (no name) was born 7 April 1879 and died 7 June 1879.
Willie Bryant England was born 24 March 1881.
Lwynette Waller Christian 2nd grand daughter was Born 28 Oct 1889.
Samuel Ragland Redd son of J.R. & Mary J. Redd was born 19 Feb 1880.
Andrew Walter Redd was born 23 Nov. 1888.
Samuel Redd died 4 Sept. 1841.
Elizabeth Redd died 5 Nov. 1858.
Thomas B. Anderson died 3 May 1871.
Harriet Anderson died 30 May 1845.
Julia E. Redd died 6 Nov. 1842.
Mary E. Redd died 29 Jan. 1847.
Lucy E. Redd died 30 June 1853.
Thomasia T. Redd died 13 May 1856.
Llewellyn W. Redd died 15 May 1864.
Elethia P. Redd died 18 Nov. 1864.
Kate C. Redd died 10 Oct. 1880.
James Temple Redd died 11 April 1878.
Thomasia Redd died 2 May 1895.
Abner Venon England died 10 July 1848.

Lizzie B. England d. 20 Nov. 1881.
Harriet S. Dandridge d. 8 Jan. 1888.
William J. Dandridge d. 24 March 1888.
George Preston Smith died 21 Nov. 1913.
Lizzie C. Smith died 19 Dec. 1913.
John R. Redd died 20 May 1920.
Willie Bryant England died 27 May 1821 in Washington D.C.
Elizabeth Wentwoth Christian died 9 Nov. 1928.
James Thomas Redd died 27 Aug 1930.
Thomas Anderson father of John and grand father of Thomas B. Anderson was born on the 10th day of February 1733.
Frances Jones (his wife) was born on the 11 day of May 1733.
They were married on the 29th day of March 1754.
Martha d. of the same was born 5 May Died Nov. 1781.
Matthew son of same was born 1 Sept. 1761.
Mary d. of same was born 4 Aug 1763.
Fanny d. of same was born 26 July 1765.
John s. of same was born 3 May 1767.
William s. of same was born 18 Jan. 1769 and died July 1774.
Elizabeth d. of same was born 5 Nov 1770.
Sally d. of same was born 1 Nov 1772.
Nancy d. of same was born 14 May 1775.
Thomas s. of same was born 26 Oct 1778.
Thomas Anderson Sr. Died 20 Sept 1794. Funeral preached by Parson Goodloe. Dust there art and unto dust shalt there return.
Fanny Anderson wife of same died 19 Feb 1799.
Matthew Anderson married Martha Tanner.
Mary married John Hope.
Fanny married Robert Clopton.
John married Mary Trevillian. John Anderson died 4 Dec. 1830.
Elizabeth married Benjamin Bartin Hope.
Sally married George Baber & after his death married Richard Harris.
Nancy married William Harris.
Thomas married Lucy Trevillian.
James Redd married Miss Eastham. Their issue were:
Samuel Redd born 1729 married Miss Lucy Rogers 1755. She was b. 1732. Their issue:
1. Fannie married Col. Samuel Temple of King & Queen Co. Va.
2. Lucy married John Fitzhugh.
3. Anne married Thomas Carr Miner brother of John Minor of Topping Castle Caroline Co. Va.
4. Archilas died young.
5. Jesse m. Miss Woodeck 21 Nov. 1785.
6. Samuel Redd b. 19 March 1764. Married 2 March 1797 to Miss Elizabeth Taylor of Hanover Co. Va. He died 4 Sept. 1841.
Elizabeth Taylor born 30 March 1776. Died 5 Nov. 1858 at Cedar Vale Caroline Co. Va.

Issue of Samuel Redd & Elizabeth Taylor:
1. Lucy Anne b. 15 Dec 1797. Married 28 Feb. 1822 to Dr. Littleton Goodwin Coleman of Caroline Co. Va.
2. Edmund born 19 Nov. 1799. Married 25 Aug. 1825 Sophia R. Burton.
3. Elizabeth Taylor b. 1802 m. William Talley 26 Oct. 1820.
4. Samuel b. 18 March 1804 m. Cornelia McLaughlin 12 Dec. 1827. She was b. 2 Dec 1810 & d. 12 April 1889.
5. Emily Harris born 2 June 1806 m. Simon Gouldin 11 Feb. 1830.
6. Sarah Taulor b. 29 Aug. 1808. Unmarried.
7. John Robinson born 7 Sept. 1810 m. Lucy Redd Fitzhugh 24 April 1838 & then m. Anna Hill.
8. Mary Frances born 21 Dec. 1812 died young.
9. James Temple Redd born 28 May 1815 m. Thomasia Anderson of Topping Castle Caroline Co. She was born 18 Nov. 1817 m. 10 May 1837.
10. Genisa b. 12 Dec. 1817 m. Thomas Warren Goulding 5 Dec. 1839.

Linnae Bates Redd Southworth d. 30 Jan. 1935 8 P.M.

Addie Waltin Redd d. 15 April 1941. Buried at Oakwood Cemetery Louisa Co. Va.

Died in Richmond Va. on the 18th ult Wm T. Dandridge infant son of William T. and Mrs. Harriet S. Dandridge age 6 mos & 11 days. 18 Jan. 1878.

Kate Carter Taylor d. of Edwrd C. and Mary L. Taylor was born 12 March 1855.

James T. Redd & Kate C. Taylor were married 4 Feb. 1880.

Kate C. Redd died at 10 o'clock Sunday Morng 10 Oct 1880.

Llewllyn Carter Redd only child of the above died at 8:30 P.M. 18 Nov. 1880.

Alexander England m. Miss Lizzie Redd 30 April 1873.

Mrs. Harriet Anne Anderson was b. in Caroline Co. Va. 25 Jan. 1819. married M.D. Anderson 20 March 1849. Moved to Tenn. & there resided for 6 years moved from there to Texas. Settled at Gaudaloupe Co. & there remained until 12 Sept 1887. After a life of faithful service in her dear Redeamer's cause of more than 47 years the Lord called her away at the ripe age of 78 years. Sister Anderson was converted and joined the First Baptist Church Richmond moved to Texas joined Staples Baptist Ch. of which she lived a faithful and worth member until death. In the death of this our Mother in Israel our church has lost one of her brighter & stars, for in her heart there was a hale of the sunshine of God's love a kind and loving word for everyone from her kind help was always available when in her power. So pure and perfect was her life that few excel and none surpass. Truly our church, our community, has lost a great and grand woman. Yes, we shall miss Aunt Harriet in the social realms of life. Her seat is vacant in church, thou our loss is her eternal gain. Our hearts go out in sympathy to the bereaved ones of this family. Her pastor C.C. Gaddy.

Mary Dabney the wife of Major Thomas Carr of Topping Caster was born 22 Jan 1688 died 7 Sept. 1748.

Sarah Carr their youngest d. was born 19 March 1714. She m. John Minor 14 Nov. 1732 & died 20 Sept. 1772. They had issue:
1. John born 18 Nov 1735.
2. William born 30 Aug 1738 d. 18 Sept 1758.
3. Thomas born 5 Aug 1740.
4. Mary born 7 March 1742.

5. Garrett born 4 March 1744.
6. James born 18 Feb 1746.
7. Dianne d. young.
8. Dabney born 11 June 1749.
9. Vivian born 3 Nov 1750.
10. Elizabeth born 3 Aug 1752.
11. Peter born 16 Aug 1754.

I copied this out of Cousin Eliza's Bible for grandmother to show you how Topping Castle came into the family. In the Redd-Anderson Bible. Addressed to Mrs. S. Redd by Mrs. R.W. Christian.

Samuel Redd b. 10 March 1804. Died 5 March 1889.

Llewelyn Wentwith Redd died 15 May 1864 from wounds received in the battle of Spotsylvania C.H. on the 10th of same month aged 24 years.

Mrs. Louisiana Redd widow of John R. Redd d. 4 Aug 1872 at the Residence of her son in law J. F. Tompkins near Indianapolis Ind.

Mrs. Elizabeth D. England wife of Alexander England a printer of Richmond formerly employed the Whig d. Sunday afternoon at 3:30 in the 29th year of her age. Interred in Caroline Co.

Died at Hyleka N.C. Mr. Samuel Redd Tuesday 5 March [no year] at 1:15 A.M. Aged 84 years 11 mos & 25 days. A good man, honest upright and sincere. He commanded the respect of all who knew him A Christian his path shine brighter to the last perfect day. Blessed are the dead who died in the Lord.

Died Sunday 8 Jan 1888 at 10 A.M. at Providence Caroline Co. Mrs. Harriet S. Dandridge wife of W. J. Dandridge.

Bythe A. Southworth and Linnia Bates Redd were married 25 Nov 1905.

Willie Bryant England & Charlotte A. Beach were married 21 Dec 1904.

Willie Bryant England d. 27 May 1921.

Dr. Thos Bates Anderson a Lecturer upon the Institutes of Practice of Medicine and upon Clinical Cases by Benj. Rush M.D. 1810, University of Pennsylvania.

This was my mother's Bible the first I ever had in the 19 Psalm the first I ever committed to memory. Thomasia Redd.

My Mother Mrs. Harriet Anderson Bequeathed to Linnie B. Redd By her Mother Thomasia Redd 2 May 1895. This Bible was printed 1808 in Edinburgh.

In Memory of James Temple Redd 28 May 1815 - 11 April 1878 and his wife Thomasia 18 Nov 1817 - 2 May 1898.

In Memory of Samuel Redd 10 March 1804 - 5 March 1889 and his wife Cornelia M. McLaughlin 2 December 1810 - 12 April 1889.

Henry Miner Friend, 163 Lexington Ave. Buffalo, N.Y. 22. [apparently the writer of the above description of the Bible].

RICHARDS FAMILY BIBLE NO. 1

A copy of this Bible record is in the Library of Virginia. The Richards family lived in several locations in Caroline County. Moses Green, listed below, was in the Revolutionary Army from Caroline County. He enlisted in the 2nd VA Regt in Feb 1777 in King and Queen County and fought at Valley Forge, Stony Point and Monmouth. He was 68 years old in 1822. See *Caroline*

County Court Records and Marriages, 1787-1810 by William Lindsay Hopkins, Richmond, Virginia, 1987.

John Richards, son of William Bird Richards was born in Drysdale Parish, Virginia, married Susanna Coleman daughter of Robert Coleman January 1st 1754.
John Richards departed this life February 13, 1785.
Susannah, his wife died April 16, 1778.
Children of John and Susannah
Patsy born November 9, 1755 married John Horner.
James born October 1758.
Elizabeth born May 22, 1760 married Daniel Triplett.
Sarah born May 4, 1763 married Walter Graham.
John born August 11, 1764 lost at sea.
William born December 1765 married Ann Blackwell.
Milley born December 17, 1767 married William S. Stone.
Fanney born March 25, 1770 married Moses Green.
Catherine born September 3, 1772 died single.
[William Richards of Stafford County, Va. married Ann Blackwell of Fauquier County, Va. Feb. 23, 1786. She was the daughter of John Blackwell.]

RICHARDS FAMILY BIBLE NO. 2

This Bible was printed by A.J. Holman, Philadelphia, 1872. It is presently owned by Daniel I. Hansen, Fredericksburg, Virginia, grandson of Alice Purcell Richards DeJarnette, who with husband, Joe Willis DeJarnette, lived in Bowling Green, Virginia.

Nattie Maude Rowe to James Tazwell Richards Oct.
Alice Purcell Richards to Joe Willis DeJarnette Oct. 27, 1920.
  Alice 21 yrs old. Joe Willis 22 yrs old.
James Edgar Richards born Aug [1897].
Alice Purcell Richards born April 21, 1898.
Mary Winslow Richards born Sept 24, [1907].

Additional information, not in Bible, from death records:
Janes Tazewell Richards was born November 2, 1863, died January 2, 1925, age 65.
Nettie Rowe Richards was born August 6, 1874, died March 12, 1926.
James Edgar Richards, 79, died in New York January 5, 1976.
Mary Winslow Richards married Arthur Percy Baldwin.
Mary Winslow Richards died in Mount Pleasant, S.C. September 1, 1990, age 82.
Arthur Percy Baldwin of Alexandria, Virginia died December 8, 1988, age 57.
Alice Richards DeJarnette died October 28, 1985, age 86.
Joe Willis De Jarnette died November 18, 1982, age 84.

RICHERSON FAMILY BIBLE

This Bible was probably first owned by Thomas Richerson, who married Eleanor Broaddus. Thomas Richerson purchased "Auburn Hills", near Sparta in Caroline County, from the Pendleton family. The house is still standing, although the Richerson cemetery has been destroyed. Thomas Richerson died in 1819, leaving a little son, Reuben B., and older son John. He left Auburn Hills to Reuben, who was born circa 1810, and who married Susan F. Saunders November 1, 1830. They had issue: Eugene Saunders, who was killed in the Battle of Gettysburg in September 1863; Thomas H., born ca. 1834, married first Virginia Sale and secondly Nannie Broaddus; Francis B., born ca. 1836, died of consumption in February 1863 at age 29; Anna M., born ca. 1838; James R., born ca. 1839; and William A., born ca. 1841, was killed in the Battle of Gettysburg September 1863 at age 24. Reuben left Auburn Hills to his son, James R. Richerson, who married Kate Butler (1853-1917) and died in 1898. Their son was Francis "Frank" Buckner Richerson (May 17, 1878-October 8, 1947), who married Mattie Sutton and kept a store at Gether, Caroline County.

The Bible passed from Thomas and Nannie Broaddus to their daughter, Martha Ellen Richerson, who married Edward Pearce Souder. They last lived at 1633 Wisconsin Avenue, Washington, D.C. She died in 1957 and the Bible was accidently sold in an estate sale in Georgetown. The whereabouts of the Bible is today unknown. Prior to that time, one page of the Bible was photocopied and is now preserved by Robin S. McAfee of Manassas, Virginia and is copied here.

Children of Thomas H. Richerson and Nannie E. Richerson
Nina Thomas Richerson born Oct 1st 1873.
Frank Richerson born Jan 3rd 1876.
Aubrey Clinton Richerson born June 14th 1877.
Robert Riter Richerson born March 30th 1890.
Ella Richerson July 1883.
Junius Richerson born April 25th 1885.
Martha Ellen Richerson born October 7th 1889.
Wm Buckner Spindle Died November 2d 1860. "Asleep in Jesus, Blessed Sleep" J. R. R.
Frank Richerson infant son of "Thos H. and Nannie E. Richerson his wife" Died June 24th 1876.
Ella Richerson infant daughter of Thos. H. and Nannie E. Richerson Died July 1893 aged 2 days.

ROSE FAMILY BIBLE NO. 1

This Bible originated with the family of Cornelius C. Rose, who resided on Lot 44, Port Royal, Caroline County, Virginia between 1856-1859. Other members of the Rose family lived in that area of Caroline County, which later became Fort A.P. Hill. Cornelius C. Rose, born January 16, 1832 in Caroline County, was the son of John Prince Adams Rose and Anna Roseanna Taylor. He married Sarah Ann James, born July 5, 1837 in Caroline County, the daughter of Albert James and S.A. Mary Nancy Mildred Fontain, 1858 in Caroline County. Corneluis C. Rose died in King George County July 25, 1877 and his wife in February 1893. He served in the Civil War as a Private in Co. E, 47 Reg. Va. Inf. and was a prisoner of War at Point Lookout, Maryland. He had brothers named Lovell M., Mike, John and Philip M. Rose, who also served in the Civil War. Many of this family later settled in King George County. This Bible is presently owned by Willard "Willie" Rose in Minot, North Dakota, who furnished this copy. Additional research was done by Gloria Weeden Sharp, King George County.

Henry Thornton Rose Son of C. C. Rose & Sarah A. James born April 21 - 1868.
John Alfred Rose Son of C. C. Rose & Sarah A. James born Jan 19 - 1871.
James Ryland Rose Son of C. C. Rose & Sarah Ann James born May 6 1872.
R.[Richard] A. Rose Son of C. C. Rose & Sarah A. James born Mar 4 1877.
Frank A. Rose Son of C. C. Rose & Sarah A. James born March 4, 1877.
Mary Susan Rose daughter of C. C. Rose & Sarah A. James born May 31 - 1874 died Feb 7 - 1917.
Albert James & Mildred Fontain.
John Prince Adams Rose & Anna Taylor.
C. C. Rose son of J. P.A. Rose & Anna Taylor born Jan 10 - 1832.
Sarah Ann James daughter of Albert James & Mildred Fontain was born July 5 - 1837.
Sarah Ann Rose died Feb 1893.
P.[Phillip] M.[Montaque] Rose Son of C. C. Rose & Sarah Ann James born Sept 11 - 1860.
Rosa Anna Rose daughter of C. C. Rose & Sarah Ann James born Feb 6 1863.
C.[Cornelius] H.[Hyson] Rose Son of C. C. Rose & Sarah Ann James born Nov 26 - 1865.
Henry T.[Thornton] Rose Son of C.C. Rose & Sarah Ann James - [was born in King George County April 21, 1868].
O. F. Gray Son of Morgan Gray & Patsie Chinault born Jun 2 1847 died Aug 9 - 1921.
Martha Ellen Chinault daughter of William Chinault & Sallie Noeil born April 4 1847 died Jan, 10 - 1892.

ROSE FAMILY BIBLE NO. 2

This Bible originated with Henry T. Rose, who married Mattie Gray. It is presently owned by Willard "Willie" Rose of Minot, North Dakota, who furnished this copy.

Henry T. Rose born April 21 1868.
Wife Mattie [Martha] J. Gray born March 4 1880.
Henry Rose & Mattie Gray was married Mar- 6 1899.
Henry Rose son of C. C. Rose & Sarah Ann James.
Mattie Gray daughter of O. F. Gray and Martha Shinnalt.
Children's Names.
Bennie [Benjamin] L. Rose, born 1 August 1900.
Sarah D. Rose, born 15 Sept. 1902.
John R. Rose, born 15 August 1904.
Forest H. Rose born 11 Augst 1907.
Henry H. Rose born 3 May 1910.
Anna E. Rose born 20 Jun 1914.
Ungin [Eugene] C. Rose born 18 February 1917.

Aguss Willard Rose born Aug. 25, 1919.
Marriages.
S.D. Rose - Gusty Dillon - Aug 2 - 1922.
B.L. Rose - Mattie [B.] Rose - Aug 25 - 1927.
J.R. Rose - Viola [S.] Gray - Nov. 23 - 1927.
F.H. Rose - Stella [F.] Gray - Aug. 1 - 1931.
H.H. Rose - Alberta Shelton - Dec. 8, 1933.
A.E. Rose - Elmer Worrell - July 13 1940.
A.W. Rose - Elizabeth [J.] Carpenter - Jan 9, 1946.
E.C. Rose - Margie Synan Married June 12, 1948.
Deaths.
Henry T. Rose - Nov 24 - 1930.
John R. Rose - Mar. 10 - 1937.
F.[Forrest] Hyson Rose - Mar. 20 - 1937.
Baby - Betty Jean Rose - May - 1 - 1937.
Eugene C. Rose - Apr. 3 - 1959.
Martha James Rose - May 16 May 16 1967 (Mattie).
Agus Willard Rose Jan 25 1980.

ROW/ROWE FAMILY BIBLE

This Bible belonged to the Row/Rowe family of "Row"s Hill", now in the Fort A.P. Hill area of Caroline County. It also contains records of the Cassidy family who also lived in the army area. The 30 graves in the two family cemeteries at these two home sites were moved to Greenlawn Cemetery. The Bible was published by Thomas, Cowperthwait & Co., Philadelphia, Pa., 1836 and is now owned by Louise Childress of Spotsylvania County.

Keeling Rowe and Rebecca Dillard were married 17th of January 1811.
William H. Farrish and Rachel Keeling Row were married 2nd February 1836.
Keeling Row & Fanny Bates were married 10 Feb. 1836.
James W. Rowe and Jane B. Sanford were married 12th day of December 1867.
Mary E. Row and Mitchel J. Smith were married 22nd of January 1884.
Piece of page cut and destroyed
1816   (information missing)   20 August
Duval Dillard Row was born 18th December 1818.
Children of Keeling and Fanny Row
Keeling Row was born 8th day of July 1837.
Carlton Row was born 23 January 1839.
James William Row was born 19th January 1840.
Keeling Row died 4 August 1837.
Mary Elizabeth Row was born February 17th (15) 1842.
Robert B. Row was born 15 Octr. 1844.
Allice D. Row died 20 November 1852.
Keeling Row was born 25th of February 1785.

Rebecca Dillard was born [no date] First wife of Keeling Row.
Thomas Row was born 20th October 1811.
John Row was born 1st July 1813.
Thomas Row died 11th of November 1813.
John Row died 1st of September 1813.
Rebecca Row died 20th October 1820.
Duval Dillard Row died 20th August 1834.
Fanny Row died 12th August 1832 second wife of Keeling Row.
Carrie G. Smith was born July 3rd 1885.
Helen Geraldine Cassidy was born Feb. 2, 1907.
Mary Elizabeth Cassidy was born June 29, 1909.
Charles William Cassidy was born May 27, 1911.
Carlton Row Cassidy was born Dec. 15, 1912.
Keeling Row died July 24, 1869 aged 84.
Carlton Row died 27th of August 1864 [Virginia Bureau of Vital Statistic Death Register shows 1865] in the Seabrook hospital Richmond from wounds received in battle near White Oak Swamp.
Fannie Row third wife of Keeling Row died 20th of Feb. 1883.
Michel J. Smith died 8th of Nov. 1887.
Robt. Beverly Row died 26th of August 1898.
James W. Row died Oct 12th 1901.
Mary E. Smith died June 10, 1913.
William Vernon Bradshaw Born in town of Manchester, Va. February 10th 1859.
Carrie Gifford Smith Cassidy Bradshaw was born in Caroline County, Va. July 3rd 1885.
Wilton Wallace Bradshaw son of W. V. & Carrie Bradshaw was Born in Caroline County, Va. December 20th 1916.
Mitchel Augustus Bradshaw Son of W. V. & Carrie was born in Spotsylvania County September 3rd 1918.
Louise Gifford Bradshaw Daughter of W. V. & Carrie Bradshaw was born in Spotsylvania County May 7th 1920.
Lucy Esta Bradshaw Daughter of W. V. & Carrie was Born in Spotsylvania County April 10th 1922.
John Franklin Bradshaw son of W. V. & Carrie Bradshaw was born in Spotsylvania County April 2nd 1924 still born.
Warren Sanford Bradshaw Son of M. V. & Carrie was born July 3rd Spotsylvania County Virginia.
Kenneth Beverly Bradshaw was born Nov. 4, 1927 in Spotsylvania Co., Va.
Carrie Frances Bradshaw daughter of M.V. & Carrie was born Dec. 28, 1929 in Orange Co., Va.
Charles W. Cassidy died March 29, 1914 age 42 years.
John Franklin Bradshaw son of W.V. & Carrie Bradshaw died April 2nd 1924.
Wm. V. Bradshaw son of Richard C. and Sarah Bradshaw died June 12, 1945. Age 86.
Baby Girl Born to Warren S. & Emma G. Bradshaw Stillborn Feb. 25, 1950.
[The following entries are recorded on onion skin sheets pasted in the family register]
Kenneth Beverly Bradshaw was married to Dorothy Lee Mills on Oct. 27, 1950 by Rev. Stanley

Willis in Fredericksburg at 3:00 P.M.

Panila Ann Bradshaw daughter of Wilton & Marie Bradshaw born May 31st 1953 at Washington, D.C.

Mary Margaret Bradshaw daughter of Warren S. & Emma Bradshaw was born Nov. 4, 1953 in Mary Washington Hospital Fredericksburg, Va.

Stephen Eugene Lamb son of Carrie Frances and Eugene B. Lamb, born May 2, 1957 in Augsburg, Germany. SFC of U.S. Army.

Karen Lee daughter of Kenneth B. and Dorothy Bradshaw was born Oct. 16, 1957 in Hosp. Fredsburg Va.

W. Keven son of W. S. and Emma Bradshaw was born Nov. 19, 1957.

Carol Ann daughter of Carlton K. and Emma Cassidy was born June 3, 1959.

Carrie Frances Bradshaw was married to Eugene B. Lamb on June 6, 1953 by Rev. Charles Moyer at Zoan Church Spot Co Va.

Raymond Leslie Mason, son of Geraldine & Curtis Mason was born Sept. 10, 1929.

Barberry Elizabeth Cassidy daughter of Chas W. & Pearl Cassidy was born Oct. 5, 1942.

Diane Marie Bradshaw daughter of Wilton W. & Marie Bradshaw was born July 13, 1944.

Judith Louise Childress daughter of James W. & Louise Childress was born November 12, 1944.

Dennis Mitchell Bradshaw son of Mitchell A. & Irene C. Banta Bradshaw Born March 12, 1946 Newark, N.J.

Michiel Allen Cameron, son of William Frederick Cameron & Lucy Bradshaw was Born Sept 3, 1948.

Linda Irene Bradshaw daughter of Mitchell A. & Irene Banta Bradshaw was born Feb. 25, 1949 in Newark, N.J.

Wm Vernon Childress was born Mar. 15, 1949 son of James & Louise Childress.

Patricia Michele Cameron - daughter of Frederick W. Cameron & Lucy Bradshaw Cameron born Feb. 16, 1951 in Santa Ana, Calif.

Mitchell A. Bradshaw was married to Irene C. Banta on January 20, 1945.

Carlton R. Cassidy was married to Emma S. Stevens on March 19, 1947.

Warren S. Bradshaw was married to Emma Frances Gallahan on June 28th 1949 by Rev. David R. Hepler.

Keeling H. Row and Family

Keeling H. Row was born 25 of February 1785. Place of birth unknown.

Children of Keeling Row and Frances Bates third wife of Keeling Row.

Keeling Row Jr. was born 23 of Jan 1837.

Carlton D. Row was born 23 Jan 1838.

James W. Row was born 19 Jan. 1840.

Mary E. Row was born 15 Feb. 1842.

Robert B. Row was born 15 Oct 1844.

To James and Jane Row were born two sons Carlton & Sanford born in Caroline. No date of their birth.

Keeling H. Row and Fannie Bates (third wife of him) were married 10 Feb 1835.

James W. Row and Jane B. Sanford ware married 12 Dec. 1867 Orange Co. Va.

Mary E. Row and Mitchell F. Smith were married at Round Oak Church Caroline Co. 22 January 1884.

Robert B. Row never married.
Carlton D. Row never married.
Keeling H. Row died July 24, 1869. Age 84.
Carlton D. Row died 21 of August 1864 [1865] in the Seabrook Hospital Richmond, Va. from wounds received in Battle near white oak swamp. Age 31 years.
Fannie Bates Row, third Wife of Keeling Row died Feb. 20, 1883.
Mitchell J. Smith died 18 Nov. 1887.
Robert Beverly Row died 26 Aug. 1898 age 54 years.
James Row died Oct 12, 1901 age 61 years.
Mary E. Smith died June 6, 1913 age 71 years.
Carrie Gifford Smith only child of Mary E. Smith and Mitchell J. Smith was born July 3, 1883.
Charlie W. Cassidy was born to Patrick and Lizzie Cassidy in Holton, Maine Feb. 25, 1876.
Helen Geraldine Cassidy was born to Carrie and Charles Cassidy Feb. 2, 1901.
Mary Elizabeth Cassidy was born June 29, 1909.
Charles W. Cassidy was born May 27, 1911.
Carlton Row Cassidy was born Dec. 15, 1912.
These 4 children were born to Carrie & Charles Cassidy in Caroline Co., Va.
Grandchildren of Carrie and Charles Cassidy
Raymond L. Mason, Son of Helen G. and Curtis J. Mason was born Sept. 10, 1939 in Washington D.C.
Barbara Elizabeth Cassidy was born to Charles & Pearl Cassidy Oct. 5, 1942 at Mary Washington Hospital Fredericksburg, Va.
Curtis Raymon Mason son of Raymon & Maria Mason on Feb. 23, 1959.
Carrie Ann Msson, daughter of R. L. Mason & Maria was born Feb. 19, 1964.
Carrie L. Smith and Charles W. Cassidy were married Feb. 7, 1906 at Round Oak Church, Caroline, Va.
Helen J. Cassidy and Curtis J. Mason were married March 8, 1928 in Orange Co. Va.
Charles W. Cassidy and Pearl E. Brown were married Oct. 20, 1939 in Orange Co. Va.
Mary E. Cassidy was married to Charles H. Beighey Sept. 5, 1943 in Wash, D.C.
Carlton R. Cassidy and Emma S. Stevens were married March 12, 1947.
Raymon L. Mason was married to Marie Martin Aug. 1958 in Maine.
Charles W. Cassidy died March 29, 1914. Age 42 years.
William Vernon Bradshaw was born to Sarah W. and Richard Bradshaw in Manchester Va. Feb. 10, 1859.
Children of Carrie & W. V. Bradshaw
Wilton Wallace Bradshaw Dec. 20 1916 Caroline Co, Va.
Mitchell Augusta Bradshaw September 3, 1918 Spots Co.
Louise G.[Gifford] Bradshaw May 7, 1920 Spot Co., Va.
Lucy Esther Bradshaw April 10, 1922 Spot Co. Va.
John F. Bradshaw was still born on April 2, 1924 Spot Co, Va.
Warren S. Bradshaw was born July 3, 1925 Spot Co. Va.
Kenneth R. Bradshaw was born Nov. 4, 1927 Spot Co. Va.
Carrie F. Bradshaw was born Dec. 28, 1929 in Orange Co. Va.
Eugene Stephens Son of Sfc. Eugene & Frances Lamb was born May 2, 1957.

Karen Lee Bradshaw daughter of Kenneth & Dorothy was born Oct. 16, 1958.

Carrie F. Smith only child of Mary and Mitchell J. Smith was married to W. Vernon Bradshaw April 23, 1915.

Louise G. Bradshaw and James W. Childress were married June 14, 1971 by Rev. H. Ford in Fredersburg [sic], Va.

Lucy E. Bradshaw and W. Fred Cameron were married Nov. 18, 1943 in Washington, D.C.

John F. Bradshaw was still born on April 2, 1924.

Warren S. Bradshaw was born July 3, 1925 Spot Co. Va.

Kenneth R. Bradshaw was born Nov. 4, 1927 Spot Co. Va.

Carrie F. Bradshaw was born Dec. 28, 1929 in Orange Co. Va.

Carrie F. Smith only child of Mary and Mitchell J. Smith was Married to W. Vernon Bradshaw April 23, 1915.

Louise G. Bradshaw and James W. Childress were Married June 14, 1971 by Rev. H. Ford in Fredsburg, Va.

Lucy E. Bradshaw and W. Fred Cameron were married Nov. 18, 1943 in Washington, D.C.

Mitchell A. Bradshaw and Irene C. Banta were married Jan. 20, 1945 in New York City, N.Y.

Warren S. Bradshaw and Emma F. Gallahan were married June 28, 1947 by Rev. R.D. Helpler Fred Va.

Wilton W. Bradshaw and Marie Mason were Married Oct. 1941 in Silver Springs, Md.

Kenneth B. Bradshaw and Dorothy L. Wills were married Oct. 27, 1950 in Fredsburg, Va.

Carrie F. Bradshaw and Eugene B. Lamb were married June 6, 1953 at Zoan Baptist Church, Spot Co Va.

Carrie G. Mason died at General Hospital Washington, D.C. Nov. 9, 1954.

Judith Louise Childress died July 6, 1969 Mary Washington Hospital Fredericksburg, Va.

Grandchildren of Carrie and W.V. Bradshaw

Diane M. Bradshaw daughter of Marie and Wilton Bradshaw was born July 13, 1944.

Pamila Ann was born May 31, 1903 in Wash D.C. Second daughter of Wilton & Marie Bradshaw.

Judith L. Childress was born daughter of Louise and James Childress Nov. 12, 1944 in Mary Washington Hospital Fredericksburg, Va.

William V. Childress son of Louise and James Childress was born Mar. 15, 1949 in Fredericksburg Hospital, Fred. Va.

Dennis M. Bradshaw son of Irene and Mitchell Bradshaw was born Mar. 12, 1996 in New York, N.Y.

Linda J. Bradshaw daughter of Irene and Mitchell Bradshaw was born Feb. 25, 1949 Newark N.J.

Michiel Allen Cameron son of Lucy and Fred W. Cameron was born Sept. 3, 1948 in Hospital Wash, D.C.

Patricia Mitchell Cameron, daughter of Lucy and Fred W. Cameron was born Feb. 16, 1951 at Hospital in Santa Anna Calif.

Susan G. Lamb, daughter of Frances and Eugene B. Lamb was born June 1960.

Helen Maria was born Jan. 19, 1961 to Raymond & Maria Mason - 3 children.

ROY FAMILY BIBLE NO. 1

This old Bible was formerly in the possession of the Roy family of Essex and Gloucester Counties. It was printed in *The Magazine of History and Biography*, Volume 8, 1900-01, p.331. The Virginia Historical Society. Much of the data in this Bible refers to members of the family that resided in Caroline County, which was formed from three counties, including Essex, in 1727.

Mungo Roy, born March 25, 1742, died September 16, 1815.
Catherine Micou, born 19 Jan. 1746, died at Locust Hill, her residence in Caroline county, May 10, 1827.
Mungo Roy and Catherine Micou were married 29 April 1766.
John Baylor, of Newmarket, Caroline County, and Maria Roy, daughter of Mungo and Catherine Roy, were married by the Rev. Mr. Wilson of Fredericksburg, Thursday May 6, 1819, at the mansion house of Mrs. Catherine Roy.
Mungo, son of Mungo and Catherine Roy, was born 17 February, 1767, died 2d of April, 1771.
William, 2d son was born 7 November, 1768, died April 11, 1815.
John, their 3d son was born Feb. 18, 1770, died 7 June, 1772.
Mungo, the 4th son was born Jan. 11, 1772, and died 27 November, 1802.
Beatrix, the 1st daughter, born 20 of Jan 1773 and died Sept. 12, 1798.
James Henry, their 5th son was born 23d Dec 1775.
Catherine, their 2d daughter, born Feb 2d, 1778, died May, 1850 [married David Bullock, Esq. of Richmond]
Jean, their 3d daughter born Dec. 9, 1779, died 12 Feb., 1825.
John, their 6th son born 25 April, 1782.
Walker, their last son born 25 Feb., 1784.
Judith, their 4th daughter born March 27, 1786, died 11th Nov., 1809.
Maria, their 5th daughter, born 27 Sept, 1790, died March 23d, 1850.
John Roy Baylor son of John and Maria Baylor, born at early candle light on the evening of Tuesday, May 29, 1821, at Locust Hill, residence of his grandmother Roy.

ROY FAMILY BIBLE NO. 2

There are copies of this Bible record in both the Virginia Historical Society and the Library of Virginia. The Roy family lived at Port Royal, Virginia where they operated a tobacco warehouse and tavern.

Mungo Roy born 25 March 1762 and died 25 September 1815.
Catherine Micou born 1st January 1746 and died May 10, 1827.
Mungo Roy was married to Catherine Micou 29th April 1766.
Married on the evening of Thursday May the Sixth 1819 at the Mansion House of Mrs. Catherine Roy by the Revd. Mr. Wilson of Fredericksburg John Baylor of New Market Caroline County to Maria Roy Last Daughter of Mungo & Catherine Roy.

"It is my wish that my daughter Jane Jones shall have this Bible at my death. [signed] Catherine Roy Oct 21st 1821."
"Presented to the Va. Historical Society by Robert Catesby Jones Jr. June 25, 1937."

Mungo, son of Catherine and Mungo was born 17th February 1767 and died 2nd August 1771.
William their second Son was born 7th November 1768 and died April 11, 1815.
John their third Son was born February 18th 1770 and died 10th June 1772.
Mungo their fourth Son was born January 11th 1772 and died 27th November 1802.
Beatrice their first Daughter born 20th January 1773 and died September 13th 1798.
James Henry their Son was born 23rd December 1775.
Catherine their Daughter born February 2d 1778 and died May 1850.
Jean their Daughter born December 9th 1779 and died 19 February 1825.
John their Son born 25th April 1782.
Walker their last Son born 25th February 1784.
Judith their Daughter born March 27th 1786 died 11th Nov 1809.
Maria their Daughter born 27 September 1790 died March the 23rd 1850.
Jno Roy Baylor Son of Jno & Maria Baylor born at early candle light on the evening of Tuesday May 29 1821 at "Jones Hill" residence of his Grandmother Roy.
Catherine Jean Roy daughter of William & Jean was born 14th Novr. 1820.
Mungo Roy, the father of Mungo, William, Jno 1st, Mungo 2nd, Beatrice, James Henry,
Catherine Jean, Jno 2nd, Walker, Judith & Maria nee Baylor, said Mungo (the father was born at Dumphriesburg on the Rappahannock Essex County; he died September the 16th 1875).
Catherine Micou afterwards wife of said Mungo was born on the Rappahannock on 19 Jany 1746 died at Locust Hill her residence Caroline [County] May the 10th Thursday morning 1827.
1850 - My ever dear wife Maria Roy Baylor departed this life on the night of Saturday March the 23d 1850 Thirty minutes after eight o'clock at this place "Locust Hill" in her Sixtyeth [sic] year after a long and painful confinement which she bore with great firmness and resignation Having fought the good fight & & & Sinking her poor desolate Husband here in a Land of woe.

Departed this life during the night of 18th April 1848 my dear brother George Daniel Baylor in his sixtyeth year. A valuable man and a Bright Christian.
James Henry Roy, brother of my late wife Maria Roy Baylor died at Old Point Comfort on the 17th day of March 1825 in the fiftyeth [sic] year Same month Maria died Viz He the 17th & She the 23rd.

ROYSTON FAMILY BIBLE

The Royston family homestead of R. and Thomas Royston, now a part of Fort A.P. Hill in Caroline County joined "Acadia" which joined Cornelius Campbell's "Old Egypt", and the Kay property. We know that Acadia was 7.6 miles s. w. of Port Royal off Route 207, now 301, so the Royston property was next to that. This would have been in the Liberty Church area. Another reference refers to a Mr. Royston as having lived next to Lovel P. Tod within what is now A.P. Hill, however, this puts a second home near "Fox Springs" on Rt. 17 and in the former Bethesda Church area and

Rappahannock Academy area. In later years, the Royston family has lived near Guinea where there are presently two later Royston family cemeteries. In about 2002, some soldiers, while training at Fort A.P. Hill dug into the slave cemetery on the Royston plantation and unearthed bodies which were taken to the Smithsonian Institution for identification and later buried in an Africa-American cemetery in Caroline County. There is no evidence that any white Royston graves were moved when the government took over the area, so they probably still remain there.

The Bible reproduced here was published by Kimber and Sharpless, Philadelphia, 1824. A copy has been placed in the Virginia Historical Society. The Lightfoot family mentioned in the Bible lived in the Port Royal area of Caroline County.

Births:
Richard Cary Royston July 1st 1766.
Polly Read May 2th 1778.
Laurinday R. Royston January 30th 1798.
Dudley C. Royston August 19th 1797.
Richard C. Royston July 13th 1805.
Charlott R. Royston March 22th 1808.
Dammaris Royston December 10th 1809.
Thomas Andrew Royston December 28th.13.[1813]
Caroline Royston Jany 22nd 1817.
Mary Ann Royston May 22th 1822.
Marriages:
Richard Cary Royston & Mary Read Jany 1st 1797.
Simeon Geron to Laurinday Royston 27 April 1820.
Volney Peel & Charlott Royston was Married the 16 August 1827.
R.C. Royston Jun & Mildred was marryed the 13 August 1827.
R.C. Royston & Caroline Lightfoot was Married Septe 20 1842.
Thomas A. Royston & Rebecca S. Brown was Married the 22nd Sept 1842.
M.A. Royston Was Married the 4th Jany 1843 to Jno. Hatley.
Mary Anne Elizabeth Hatley was married to James Madden on the 8th day of March 1855.
Anne Elizabeth Hatley was married to James William on the 6th day of December 1866.
Wiley A. Hatley was married to James C. Watson on the 12th day of April 1868.
Mollie Royston Madden to William Benjamin Waller on the 25th November 1875 by Rev. R. B. Alston.
Deaths:
Richard Cary Royston Departed this life 1837.
Thomas Andrew Royston Departed this life February 17th 1849.
Rebecca his wife departed this life April 25th 1847.
John Hatley departed this life September the 19th about 2 o'clock in the evening on Thursday at Dr. Bethels in Dalis County Arkansas and was buried at the grave yard near Tulip.
Polly Royston died Jan. 11th 1859 about 2 O'Clock in the morning.

ROZELL FAMILY BIBLE

This Bible was published by N.D. Thompson & Co., St. Louis, Missouri, 1879. While the Bible itself does not date early, the family recordings date to the eighteenth century. There are several sheets of research by a family member inserted in the Bible. One states that J.W. Rozell is a son of Enoch & Mary (Sawyer) Rozell and that Enoch was a native of North Carolina, who was brought to Madison County about 1820 by his parents. An envelope in the Bible contains tintype pictures of Mary Rozell Married John Winsett, Beverly Rozell and an 8 x 10-inch tintype of a Rozell ancestor in his Confederate uniform. The Rozell family settled in the Guinea area of Caroline County. Some members of the Rozell family are buried in Sunset Cemetery, Spotsylvania County.

Ashley B. Rozell and Elizabeth Baker was Married January 15th 1846.
Ashley B. Rozell and Eliza Beverly was married August 30, 1868.
John J.W. Rozell and Mary Steel Beverly was married Oct. 6, 1874.
John C. Patterson and Sarah N.M. Rozell was married Nov. 20, 1878.
Robert J. Ivey and Laura May Patterson was married Dec. 24, 1899.
John R. Stuart and Viola Elizabeth Patterson was married Aug. 1, 1903.
A.B. Rozell was Born April 29th 1828.
Elizabeth J. was Born Oct. 30, 1847.
Mary L. L. was born Nov. 5, 1849.
Margaret A.B. was Born June 29, 1851.
John J. W. was Born April 15, 1853.
Sarah N.M. was Born April 7, 1855.
William A.B. was Born Oct. 27, 1856.
Dawson Z.B. was Born Aug. 2nd 1858.
John C. Patterson was borned April 30, 1853.
Laura May was borned May 5, 1881.
Viola Elizabeth was borned June 6, 1883.
Robert Ashley was borned Oct. 4, 1885.
James William Morse was borned Aug. [July added here] 18, 1890.
Lee R. Rozell Borned Nov. 8, 1848, grandson of A.B. Rozell.
Dasson Girlen Son of Lee R. Rozell Borned July 10, 1927.
Elizabeth Rozell died July 8th [?] 1860.
Elizabeth Jane daughter of Ashley and Elizabeth Rozell died May 6th 1848.
Mary S. Rozell, wife of J.W. Rozell died April 22, 1894.
Emily Rozell wife of Dawson Z. Rozell died April 19, 1896.
Eliza Rozell wife of A.B. Rozell died November 3, 1901.
A. B. Rozell died January 19, 1902.
D. G. B. Rozell (1858-1929) & Emily Rozell Husband & Wife. Emily died 1892. Parents of L. R. Rozell Borned 1848.
Ages of the parents of A.B. Rozell borned 1802.
Wm Rozell son of Richard and Elizabeth was born February 24, 1772 and died December 14, 1854.

Mary Rozell daughter of James and Sophiah Bareness (Barnes) was borned September 18, 1779 and died April 15, 1865.
1. Richard Rozell No Date 1779.
2. William Rozell, Sr. Borned February 24, 1772 died 1854.
3. A.B. Rozell Sr. Borned around 1802, son of William Rozell.
4. Ashley B. Rozell Jr. Borned 1826, son of A.B. Rozell died 1903.
5. John J. W. Rozell Borned Apr. 15, 1853.
6. W. A. B. Rozell Borned Oct. 27, 1856.
7. D. G. B. Rozell, Ashley B. Rozell's son Borned Jany. 2, 1858 Died 1928. Brother to W. A. B. Rozell.
8. L. R. Rozell Son of Dauson G.B. Borned Nov. 8, 1888.
William Rozell (wife Mary) & Soloman Rozell were Brothers. Was Father to A.B. Rozell Borned 1802. A.B. Rozell Sr. (wife Henretta) was Father to A.B. Rozell Sr. (wife Elizabeth) Borned 1826.
Lee Rozell (wife Lola) Borned 1888 Son of D.G.B. Rozell
Children of L. R. Rozell (born Nov. 8, 1888) and Lola [Crabtree] his wife:
Hector Rozell Borned 1915.
Anelda Rozell Borned 1917.
Bonnie Rozell Borned 1920.
Margie Rozell Borned 1922.
Ray Rozell Borned 1925.
Dasson Rozell Borned 1927.
Gene Rozell Borned 1930.
Cecil Rozell Borned 1933.
McWayne Rozell born 1936.
Larome Rozell born 1936, twin to above.
1. Richard Rozell No date wife Elizabeth.
2. William Rozell Sr. Borned 1772.
Children of William Rozell Sr.:
Ashley B. Rozell Borned 1802.
Ruford Austin Rozell Borned 18__.
William Rozell Jr. Borned 1822.
Enock Rozell Borned 1813.
End sheet in front of Bible:
Rozell Generations
Richard Rozell
William A.B. Rozell Borned 1772.
William A.B. Rozell father to Ashley B. Rozell Enoch Rozell Milton Rozell William Morse _____ Rozell.
End sheet in back of Bible:
Rozell family as follows:
Richard Rozell No Date
William M. Sr. Borned 1772-4.
A.B. Rozell Sr. Borned 1802.

Ashley B. Rozell Jr. Borned 1826.
Richard Rozell the Father
Rozell family 2 Brothers Solomon & William Born 1772 & 4.
A.B. Rozell 1802.
Ashley B. Rozell 1826.

SALE FAMILY BIBLE

On the fly leaf of this Bible is the dedication: "To Dr. Tho.J. Sale, this family Bible is presented by his uncle Tho. Joyes. 30th Decr. 1850." This Bible was discovered by Dr. M.H. Harris in New Kent County, Virginia and was at that time in the possession of Miss Jennie Sale Jones. It was copied by George H.S. King and published in *The Kentucky Genealogist*, Volume 17, No. 3, p.242, April 1973. It is also referenced in the King Papers at the Virginia Historical Society. The Bible concerns the family of Anthony Sale and his wife, Agnes, of Caroline County, who moved to Jefferson County, Ky. about 1785. Unfortunately, the Bible record has been edited by Mr. King and the wording and arrangement is not as it appeared in the original. In addition, there are lying loose in the Bible invitations to the funeral of Mrs. Elizabeth B. Sale, consort of William Sale Nov. 27th, 1852 and Mrs. Nancy Joyes Jan. 23, 1840. On a separate piece of paper in the Bible are the names of Robert Sale, John Sale, Thomas Sale, Cornelius Sale, Anthony Sale and Richard Sale, where were the grandfather, father and uncles of Capt. Wm Sale who was born in Jefferson Co, Ky. Sept 16th 1792.

Anthony Sale and Agnes, his wife, were both born in Caroline County, Virginia, in 1740.
Anthony Sale departed this life in April 1826 aged about 86 years. His wife, Agnes, departed about 26 years before him.
Lewis Sale, born 14 March 1782, Caroline County, Virginia.
Horace Sale, born 25 April 1784, Caroline County, Virginia.
Edmund Sale, born 13 June 1786 in Jefferson County, Ky; died 31 January 1832.
Richard Sale, born 2 April 1789 in Jefferson County, Ky; died [info not entered].
Captain William Sale, born 16 September 1792, Jefferson County, Ky; died 11 July 1856 aged 63 years, 9 months and 26 days. Married 22 April 1816, Louisville, Ky., Elizabeth B. Joyes.
Elizabeth B. Joyes was born 1 May 1796 in Louisville, Ky; died 26 November 1852 aged 56 years, 6 months and 25 days.
Charles Sale born 6 April 1796, Jefferson County, Ky; died 19 April 1825.
The children of William and Elizabeth B. [Joyes] Sale were all born in Jefferson County, Town of Louisville, Kentucky, viz:
William Sale, Jr., born 20 October 1820; died 28 August 1822.
[Dr.] Thomas Joyes Sale, born 18 August 1822; died 26 October 1867 in Memphis, Tenn. Married 25 November 1846, Margarette LaFayette Hill, daughter of Major James W. Hill of Holly Springs, Mississippi, and his wife Margarette McGuire Beaty. [One recording says she was born 7 April 1828 in Athens, Limestone County, Alabama, while another says she was born 7 April 1830] She died 1 August 1917 in Richmond, Virginia.
Charles Anthony Sale, born 7 February 1827. Married 5 June 1851, Caroline Williams of Mt. Sterling, Ky. Their daughter, Bettie Joyes Sale was born 31 December 1852 in Jefferson

County, Ky.

Elizabeth Agnes Sale, born 15 April 1830. Married 28 July 1856, Charles J. Morton.

Catharine Ann Sale, born 4 September 1831; died 9 June 1832.

Edmund T. Sale, born 20 March 1833.

Laura Frances Sale, born 29 January 1835. Married 19 December 1854, Henry S. Johnson. Their son, William Sale Johnson, born 18 November 1855, Louisville, Ky.

William Holman Sale, born 17 July 1836, Louisville Ky.

Emma Taylor Sale, born 7 March 1839.

The children of Dr. Thomas Joyes and Margarette LaFayette [Hill]

Sale were as follows:

Margarette Elizabeth Sale, born 8 September 1847 in Holly Springs, Mississippi. [After this recording she is called Maggie B. Sale in this Bible record] She died 18 November 1885. Married [1] 24 January 1866, Memphis, Tenn., James Frederick Maclin. Married [2] 17 September 1884, John Warren Walker. Two children entered viz.: Thomas Sale Maclin, born 21 November 1867 & Willie Bullock Sale, born 6 November 1874.

James William Sale, born 6 November 1851; died 18 August 1852.

Lelia Hubbard Sale, born 30 June 1853, Louisville, Ky; died 2 July 1937 in Richmond, Virginia. Married 8 November 1871, Memphis, Tenn., Felix M. Jones.

Four children entered, viz:

Felix M. Jones, Jr., born 6 September 1874, in Memphis, Tenn.

Robert Brinkly Jones, born 17 May 1876, in Memphis, Tenn.

Jean Sale Jones, a son, born 26 November 1878, Memphis, Tenn.

Jennie Sale Jones, born 21 January 1897 [sic].

Jennie Wylie Sale, born 8 February 1858, Louisville, Kentucky; died 17 January 1897, Richmond, Va. Married 16 April 1884, Memphis, Tenn., Robert Wallace Courtney.

SAMUEL(L) FAMILY BIBLE

This Bible was printed by the American Bible Society in 1856. It originally belonged to Thomas L. Samuell of Caroline County, Virginia. On the front cover is written: "Thomas L. Samuel". On the first page is written: "This Bible I give to Willie Samuel at my death. Written the 28 of January 1945 by his aunt Ida Samuel". Ida Samuel (1864-1952) lived in Caroline County, Va. In 1952, the Bible was owned by Mr. W.W. Samuel, Fredericksburg, Virginia and was still owned by him when the Samuel family history was written. See *The Samuell/Samuel Families of Tidewater Virginia* by Dorothy Stanaland Samuel and Colonel Taliaferro Leslie Samuel III, Southern Historical Press, Greenville, S.C., 1997. It appears that much of this family lived in the area of Caroline County, which later became Fort A.P. Hill. William A. Baynham, who was found dead in his buggy on the side of the road between Bowling Green and Fredericksburg, was pastor of Enon Baptist Church on the Caroline-Essex line back of Fort A.P. Hill. He is buried under the church pulpit there. This Bible was copied by George H.S. King in 1952 and a transcript of the Bible is in the Virginia Historical Society.

Thomas L. Samuell was married to Sarah F. Anderson Nov. 10th 1853.
Bettie G. Samuel was married to Willie P. Watts the 10 of Dec. 1882.

Thomas A. Samuel was married to Sarah J. Watts the 7 of Dec.1884.
Nehemiah B. Samuel was married to Virginia Anderson the 24 of December 1885.
Thomas L. Samuell was born January 9th 1831.
Sarah F. Samuell wife of Thomas L. Samuell born May 8th 1832.
William C. Samuell son of Thomas L. Samuell & Sarah F., his wife, was born August 27th 1854.
James H. Samuell was born September 3rd 1855.
Thomas A. Samuell was born October 29th 1856.
John A. Samuell born May 26th 1858.
Muscan [Muscoe] Peyton Samuel was born July the 29th 1859.
Nehemiah B. Samuel was born November the 26th 1860.
Elizabeth Gray Samuel was born February the 19th 1862.
Ida Walker Samuel was born March the 1st 1864.
Mary Fannie Lee Samuel was born August the 13, 1865.
William Esli Samuel was born August the 11th 1867.
Nannie Burke Samuel was born April the 14th 1869.
Fannie L. Samuel was born May 2th 1871.
Susie Fletie Samuel was Born December 17th 1872.
William A. Baynham was 71 years old the 15th of October 1884.
Dr. W.A. Baynham Departed this life the 16th of June 1887.
John Anderson departed this life February 10th 1858.
John A. Samuel Departed this life the 3 of July 1859.
Muscoe Peyton Samuel departed this life the 20 day of August 1860.
William C. Samuel departed this life the 13 day of December 1862.
Eslie W. Anderson departed this life 22 August 1862.
James W. Anderson departed this life the 3 of October 1863.
Mary Fannie Lee Departed this life the 28 of October 1865.
Henry A. Samuel departed this life 28 day of June 1866.
Willie Esli Samuel departed this life the 19 of April 1868.
Here ends the contemporary recordings in the original Bible.
Here begins certain recordings on added pages in the above Bible. Some of these recordings in pen and some in pencil. Some appear to have been taken from possibly an earlier Bible or some other family record. The records are given below as they appear and in the sequence they appear.
John Anderson -------
Frances Terrell Departed this life the 27 day of April 1888.
Willie P. Watts departed this life the 23 of December 1912.
Fannie Samuel were married Jan. the 2, 1913 [no name entered].
Lou Samuel were married Jan. 16, 1913 [no name entered].
Allie Samuel died Oct. 14, 1931.
Ginnie Samuel died Oct. 21, 1932 the wife of Bagby Samuel.
Elmyra Watts died March 28th 1931, the wife of Willie P. Watts.
John Anderson departed this life the 10th day of February 1858.
Sidney B. Anderson departed this life the 17 day of February 1879 age 75 years.
Esli W. Anderson departed this life the 22 day of August 1862.

James W. Anderson departed this life the 3 day of October 1863.
Mary Anderson the wife of E.D. Anderson departed this life the 14 day of December 1874.
Henry B. Samuel departed this life the 14 January 1882 age 80 years 5 months and 14 days.
Elisabeth Samuel wife of Henry B. Samuel departed this life September 18, 1852 [1882?]
Henry B. Samuel was born the 24th day of July 1801.
Elisabeth B. Samuel his wife was born March 11, 1789.
Elisabeth Samuel daughter of Henry B. Samuel born July 4, 1827 and died August 27, 1846.
Eline J. Watts was born the 27 of April 1884.
Annie T. Watts was born the 27 of April 1884.
Willie B. Samuel was born the 4 of October 1885.
Robbert [sic] L. Samuel was born the 11 of November 1886 [sic].
John E. Samuel was born the 13 of November 1886 [sic].
Sarah E. Watts was born the 2 day of February 1888.
Hilda M. Samuel was born the 31 of December 1888.
Thomas H. Samuel was born the 4th of January 1889.
William Lawson Watts was born the 2 day of May 1890.
Bagby Baby Boy was born 5 of Dec. 1891 and died 25 Feb. 1892.
Edward B. Watts was born April 23, 1892.
Elmyre Samuel was born June 3 1892.
Mary F. Samuel was born August the 20, 1893.
Blanch Bruce Departed this life the 19 day of July 1873 age 17 years.
Ada Noel Departed this life the 5 day of January 1874 aged 27 years.
Clem Bruce Departed this life the 2 day of November 1876.
Fannie Bruce departed this life the 14 day of September 1876.
John F. Watts was born June 1, 1894.
Thomas Alfied [sic] Samuel was born the 26 of November 1894.
Mattie Lean Watts was born the 28 of January 1898.
Nora Lee Watts was born December the 31, 1900.
Annie Ruth Collawn (?) was born the 27 of June 1901.
Loulie & Mr. Pitts were married Feb. 8, 1912.
Henry A. Samuel was born November 10, 1832.
William B.B. Samuel was born November the 30, 1834.
Jennette Samuel died 28 December 1904.
Sarah P. Samuel departed her life 27 day of Sept 1909 aged 77 years.
Spergeon Fortune died 24 day of August 1911 aged 13 years.
Willie P. Watts were born July 25, 1860.
Bagby Samuel died June 30, 1945; he was 84 years old was sick 9 months.

SATTERWHITE/REID FAMILY BIBLE

This Bible was published by The Southwestern Co., Nashville, Tennessee. The date of publication is missing. The Bible originated with the Reid family of King William County which intermarried with the Satterwhite family of Caroline County, Virginia. The Bible is presently owned by Wesley E. Satterwhite, Sr., son of Butler E. Satterwhite, of Sunshine Road, Caroline

County. When Oscar Samuel Satterwhite died, his widow Addie M. Reid Satterwhite married Butler E. Satterwhite, a widower.

Oscar Samuel Satterwhite was born Aug. 1, 1895.
Addie M. Reid was born Dec. 7, 1893.
Butler E. Satterwhite was born Nov. 8, 1901.
Wesley E. Satterwhite was born April 18, 1934.
Addie M. Reid and Oscar Samuel Satterwhite was married on December 26 - 1923.
Addie Reid Satterwhite and Butler E. Satterwhite was Married on July 10, 1937.
Alice Ada Reid died in the year of our Lord Dec. 6, 1927.
Bettie E. Satterwhite died in the year of our Lord Dec. 9, 1927.
Edmund Satterwhite died in the year our Lord Oct. 13, 1925.
Lucille Reed died in the year of our Lord June 22, 1931.
James Edward Noel died in the year of Lord June 30, 1935.
Oscar S. Satterwhite died in the year of our Lord at 9:10 A.M. Feb. 21, 1936.
J.W. Satterwhite died in the year of our Lord at 12:10 A.M. Dec.16, 1937.
Geo. E. Reid died 8:45 P.M. Feb. 21, 1938.
Lucy E. Satterwhite died June 2, 1935.

SCHOOLS FAMILY BIBLE

This Bible was copied some years ago by Helen Kay Yates. The whereabouts of the original is unknown.

Thomas Schools was born April the 28th 1778.
John Schools was born December the 29th 1809.
John Atkins was born January the 12th 1817.
Malinay was born March the 30th 1829.
Thomas Schools died Jan. 8th 1850.
Fannie Schools died the wife of Thomas Schools Dec. 30th 1858.

SCOTT FAMILY BIBLE

This Bible originally belonged to Thomas Scott, son of James Scott, who was born in St. Margaret's Parish, Caroline County, June 15, 1718. He married Martha Williams, daughter of Rice and Frances William, Nov. 2, 1742. The Bible was printed in Oxford England in 1715. It was owned by W.R. Scott of Rensens, Virginia in 1949 and the records published in *Tyler's Quarterly*, Volume 30, 1949, p.272.

Thomas Scott, born 1718, was the progenitor of the Scott families of Caroline, Prince Edward, Campbell, Bedford & Amherst counties in Va. In another part of the original Bible was recorded the births of some 60 slaves from 1722 to 1758 on the plantation of Thomas Scott in Caroline County.

Frances, dau. of Rice Williams and Frances his wife, was born Dec. 2n 1721.
Ann, dau of Rice Williams and Frances his wife, was born Dec. 2nd 1723.
Martha, dau of Rice Williams and Frances his wife, was born May 2nd 1727.
[Thomas Scott and Martha Williams were married Nov. 2, 1742]
Rice Scott, son of Thomas Scott and Martha his wife, was born 12th day of August 1743.
Frances Scott, dau. of Thomas Scott and Martha his wife, was born 27th day of June, 1745.
John Scott, 2nd son of Thomas Scott and Martha his wife, was born 19th day of October, 1747.
Thomas Scott, Jr., 3rd son of Thomas Scott and Martha his wife, was born 29th day of February, 1749. He was Captain in the Army.
James Scott, 4th son of Thomas Scott and Martha his wife, was born 17th day of February, 1752.
Samuel Scott, 5th son of Thomas Scott and Martha his wife, was born 14th of March, 1754.
William Scott, 6th son of Thomas Scott and Martha his wife, was born 15th of December, 1756. [married Ann Jones of Culpeper Co., March 1, 1781, was a Captain in the Revolution and died Oct 6, 1818. He and his brother, Samuel left Caroline County and settled in Campbell County, Va. at the close of the War.
Robert Scott, 7th son of Thomas Scott and Martha his wife, was born the 30th of December, 1758 and died August 1st, 1781.
Frances Scott, dau. of Thomas and Martha Scott, was married 30th day of December, 1766 to James Gatewood, son of Dudley Gatewood and Sarah his wife.
Thomas Scott, Jr., and Isabel, his wife were married August 1st, 1767.
Isabel Scott, wife of Thomas Scott, Jr., died May 20 [or 25?], 1770.
Martha Scott, wife of Thomas Scott, Sr., died April 8, 1777.

[In another part of the Bible in a different handwriting are the records of 60 slaves from 1722 to 1758 on the plantation of Thomas Scott of Caroline County. Unfortunately, only two names were copied by W.R. Scott in 1949 as follows:]
Harry was born ye first of Sept. 1722
Leah was born March the 10th 1745.

SEAL FAMILY BIBLE

This Bible originally belonged to John Seal and Margaret G. Edmundson, who were married January 30th 1811. This family lived below present Mt. Hermon Church on Mattaponi Trail in Caroline County in the area later known as Shumansville. The cemetery still exists on the land where they lived. The Bible was published by A. J. Holman & Co. in Philadelphia, however, there is not publication date. It is presently owned by Joseph Alexander Barlow, a descendant, who lived at an adjacent place.

Joanna Seal was born December 20th 1812.
Catherine Seal was born Aug. 15th 1814.
Lewis Seal was born Aug. 11, 1816.
Mary Seal was born May 1st 1818.
Margaret Seal was born May 1st. 1818.

Marcia Seal was born November 7th 1821.
Ira Seal was born September 3rd 1824.
Festus Seal was born December 1st 1826.
Edmonia [C.] Seal was born December 15th 1828.
Juliet [H.] Seal was born January 13th 1832.
Hester Seal was born October 21st 1834.
Children of
John Wharton and Juliet Seal
John C. Wharton born August 13th 1857.
Van Lue Wharton was born March 28th 1859.
Anna Wharton was born December 26th 1860.
Anna Wharton and Charles E. Dillard were married Jan. 8th 1887.
John G. Wharton was married March 14th 1887.
Van Lue Wharton was married September 26th 1889.
Children of Anna Wharton and Charles E. Dillard
Johnnie Dillard was born 29th of October 1877.
Charlie Dillard was born 24th of February 1879.
Bessie Dillard was born 11th of February 1881.
Edie was born February 13th 1883.
Mountival was born July 14th 1885.
Emmet born February 28th 1887.
John Seal died in the year of our Lord 1856 16th day of November.*
Margaret G. Seal departed this life December the 25th 1864.
Juliet Wharton died February 14th 1895.**
Anna Wharton Dillard died July 10th 1889 aged 28 years & 6 months.
Bessie Dillard died July 11th 1889.
Colie Dillard died September 17th 1883.
Margaret Ellen Wharton departed this life August the 9th 1856.
Hermon Wharton departed this life September 23rd 1856.

Additional data from Caroline County Bureau of Vital Statists Record, not in the Bible:

Juliett Seal Wharton, wife of John Wharton, died February 14, 1895, age 65.
Hiram Wharton, 3 month old son of John W. and Juliett Wharton, died September, 1857.
M.A.S. Wharton, 2 year old daughter of John W. and Juliett Wharton, died September, 1857.
Bessie Dillard, daughter of C.E. and A.L. Dillard died July 11, 1889, age 6 years.
Annie L. Dillard, daughter of John & Julia Wharton and wife of C.E. Dillard, died July 10, 1889, age 27 years.
Joanna Barlow, daughter of John & Margaret Seal and wife of John W. Barlow, died February, 1878.
Margaret Seal, daughter of William & Joanna Edmundson and mother in law of Archilles Southworth, died December, 1865, age 60.
John Seal, father of Ira D. Seal, died December 15, 1858, age 67 years.

*Bureau of Vital Statistics of Caroline County gives DOD as December 15, 1857.
** Bureau of Vital Statistics of Caroline County gives DOD as December 1865.

SHEPHERD FAMILY BIBLE

This Bible was published by B.B. Mussey, Boston, 1844. A copy is in the Library of Virginia and is recorded as a Caroline County Bible. An eighteenth century house known as the old Sheppard place stood until the mid-nineteenth century on Penola Road just before one enters Route 207 in Caroline County and was recorded in the 1937 W.P.A. Survey.

Wm M. Shepherd was born 2nd May 1798.
Eliza Ann Lunsford Baskett was born 2nd February 1808.
John Augustine Shepherd was born 30th Novr. 1827.
Frances Mary Shepherd was born May 14, 1829.
Abram Christopher Shepherd was born 25 Septr. 1830.
Lucy Ann Judson Shepherd was born 4th Augst. 1832.
William Martin Baskett Shepherd was born 23rd Apr 1834.
Infant Son was born 17 February 1836.
Sarah M.___ Shepherd was born 1 June 1837.
Eliz Joan Shepherd 29 March 1839.
Susan Turner Shepherd was born 31st Jany 1841.
Thomas Henry Shepherd was born 10th Jany 1840.
Robert D. Shepherd was Born Septr. 24th 1847.
James M. Shepherd was Born 28th June 1849.
Jenny Hurt was born 21st March 1851.
Mary Susan was born 27th August 1852.
Richard Hoge was born the 11th February 1854.
Martha Catherine was born 14th March 1855.
George Washington was born 31st August 1856.
Infant son born 10th Feby 1855.
Wm M. Shepherd amd Eliza A.L. Baskett was Married 13 December 1846.
Wm M. Shepherd and Mary M. Turner was Married 17th December 1866.
David S. Baker and Fanny M. Shepherd was Married the 20 Septr.1849. My daughter.
Robt. J. Adames & Sarah M. Shepherd was Married the 16th May 1858.
Richard F. George & Eliza Joan Shepherd was Married the 19th May 1859.
Thos. H. Shepherd & Mary Lou West was married 6th Sept. 1865.
James M. Shepherd & Mil [illeg] Turner was Married 7th January 1874.
Infant son born the 24th May 1860 Still born.
Infant Son departed this life 20th February 1836.
Susan Turner Shepherd departed this life 15th Novr. 1841.
Eliza A.L. Shepherd departed this life 19th March 1844.
the mother above ones
Martha Catherine departed this life the 11th September 1855.
George Washington departed this life the 27th July 1857.

Infant son departed this life 13th February 1858.
Lucy A.L. Shepherd departed this life the 15th October 1870.
Mary M. Shepherd departed this life the 10th of May 1872.
Jenny H. Shepherd departed this life the 1st of June 1877.
W.H. Shepherd departed this life 4th of April 1878.
Wm. M.B. Shepherd departed this life 25th of February 1892.
Robert D. Shepherd departed this life 18th August 1892.
Richd. Hoge Shepherd departed this life February 14, 1926.
Thomas Henry Shepherd departed this life November 4th 1927.
On Apr 2, 1931 at 7:30 p.m. God called to his Heavenly Home My precious husband Robert Sidney Shepherd.
Abram Baskette m. Frances D. Turner. They were the parents of Eliza Ann Lunsford Baskette. Abram Baskette was a Son of Rev. William Baskette.

[In the back of the Bible are newspaper obituaries of Rev. P.C. Hoge, Mrs. Frances D. Baskette, Mr. T. H. Shepherd, and a handwritten obituary of Abram Basket and Mrs. Frances D. Baskett, but no mention of Caroline County in any of them. There is also a lengthy printed obituary of Mrs. Mary Turner who died at the home of her son-in-law Wm M. Shepherd. It states that she was formerly Miss Hurt and was born in Caroline County where she has many relatives now living. Died 10th July 1860 at age 84. She had moved to Fluvanna Co with her husband when she was quite young. This appears to have been taken from *The Religious Herald*.

SIZER FAMILY BIBLE NO. 1

This Bible concerns families which lived in the Chilesburg area of Caroline County. The Comprehensive Bible containing the Old and New Testaments was published by J.B. Lippincott & Company, 1856. It was owned by the late Miss Kathleen Sizer of Chilesburg.

Greenville A.[Alexander] Sizer, Born July 1830, Died Jan. 14, 1909 and [his] 1st Wife [his cousin] Angelina G. Sizer [daughter of Reuben Sizer & Catherine H. Dickinson, who were married 27 June 1858] and 2nd Wife Cordelia C. Watkins [daughter of H. & Ann E. Watkins] Born Mar. 30, 1867.
Anna E. Sizer, 3 months old 1860, when she died, dau of Greenville & Angelina.
Married 12 of Dec. 1850, Reuben M. Sizer to Martha Winston Dabney by J.R. Bagby.
Col. J. M. Waller married to A.E. Waller Mar 12th 1857 by Dr. J. M. Pendleton.
Mar. Cedar Point, Married Dec. 15, 1881 Harry Baskum White to M. Jennie Waller by E. W. Winfrey.
Reuben Mason Sizer, son of John & Elizabeth Sizer, born Sept. 15th 1816.
Martha Winston Dabney, daughter of William & Jemima B. Dabney, was born Augst. 6th 1824.
Harry B. White, son of Chas & Emily B. White, was born June 18, 1857.
M. Jennie White, daughter of John Mercer & Anne Elizabeth Waller, born 21st Augst 1858.
Emily Elizabeth, daughter of R.B. & M.J. White, was born near Trevilian, Louisa Co, Jan. 10, 1883.
Elias May, son of H.B. & M.J. White, was born at same locality July 26th 1882.

Elias White was born May 13, 1826.
Emily B. Kent was born Jan. 24th 1831.
Mollie Bell White was born June 15th 1861.
Col. John Mercer Waller, born Augst 6th 1814, was the son of Dabney & Elizabeth Minor Waller, Cedar Point.
A. Elizabeth, daughter of Wm & Jenning Burnett Dabney, was born Dec. 18th 1818, married to Wm Carr Waller Jan. 1st 1889.
Willietta Miner Waller, daughter of J. M. & A. E. Waller, was born Feb. 6th, 18__ and departed this life April 6th 1876 age 6ly 8m 4d.
Departed this life July 18, 1893, A. E. Waller aged 74 years & 5 months.
Departed this life Dec. 23rd 1893, Maria Perkins Aged 78 years 8 months & 37 days.
Departed this life Feb. 22, 1901, Mary S. Pendleton Aged 86 years.
Departed this life, Frances J. Goodwin, Aged 73 years, March 4, 1901.
Departed this life R.M. Sizer, November 16th, 1903, Aged 87.
Martha W. Sizer died March 17, 1911.
Jennie Waller White died Jan. 17, 1907.
H.B. White died Sept. 1, 1928.
Emily Elizabeth White [died] Jan 27, 1938.
Willie M. Waller [died] Dec. 28, 1942.
Elias May White, born July 26, 1884, died March 1950.

SIZER FAMILY BIBLE NO. 2

This Sizer family Bible record, a copy of which is in the Library of Virginia dates from 1802 to 1870.

John Sizer and Hannah C. Robinson were married on 23rd of June 1831.
Ann W. Sizer and Jno. M. Fauntleroy were married on the 20th Octr 1852.
Lucy E. Sizer and Thos. A. Dobyns were Married on 3rd of March 1858.
Augustus Sizer and Betsy H. Ryland were Married on 18th November 1838.
John Sizer was born on 17th of October 1802.
Hannah C. Robinson was born on 20th December 1802.
Children of John & Hannah C. Sizer.
Ann Willis Sizer was born on 9th of April 1832 at 3 o'clock P.M.
Augustus Sizer was born on 12th of February 1834 at 5 minutes past 3 o'clock.
Lucy Ellen Sizer was born on 10th of October 1835 at 15 minutes past 7 o' clock P.M.
John Henry Sizer died on 11th October 1843 at 30 minutes past 10 o'clock P.M.
John Sizer Jur died on 27 December 1860 Aged 58 years.
Hannah C. Sizer died on the 11th March 1870 Aged 66 years & 3 months.
Also there newpaper death notices for:
Augustus M. Fauntleroy died March 21, 1893.
John S. Fauntleroy January 14, 1901.
George L. Fauntleroy March 6, 1913.
John M. Fauntleroy Oct 24, 1906 age 75.

Wedding notices of:
George F. Vose & M. Eloise Fauntleroy June 18, 1903.
Elise Watkins & George Latane Fauntleroy June 30, 1905.

SMITH FAMILY BIBLE

This Bible is known as the family Bible of William Rowley Smith of "Alton Farms", Fauquier County. He married Lucy Steptoe Blackwell and had 19 children. Catherine Harrison Smith, listed in this Bible, married Birkenhead Hawkins Boutwell (June 9, 1777-Sept. 19, 1853) of Caroline County, son of William H. Boutwell and Sabrina Hawkins of near Port Royal. Both are buried in the Boutwell-Smith cemetery at the homeplace locally known as "Jack's Hill" just outside of Port Royal on Route 17 (Tidewater Trail), 3.1 miles SE of Port Royal. This Bible was owned by Judge Anderson Doniphan Smith in Fayetteville, West Virginia in 1927. A copy was sent to Miss Ida Birkenhead Smith in Caroline County in 1902. The Bible record has been published in *The Sydney-Smith and Clagett-Price Genealogy* by Lucy Montgomery Price Smith and printed by Shenandoah Publishing House, Strasburg, Virginia, 1927, p.59.

Joseph Smith [no dates listed].
William Smith Sr. born February 5, 1741, died January 22 [1803], between hours of 11 and 12
  o'clock, age 61 years, 10 months, 17 days].
Elizabeth Doniphan, wife of William Smith Sr., was born April 13, 1744, died fifteenth day of
  January 1809, between the hours of 10 and 11 o'clock.
Their children:
  Mary Waugh, born January 1, 1775.
  Ann Anderson, born October 7, 1776.
  Walter Anderson, born February 7, 1779.
  William Rowley, born February 12, 1781.
  Joseph Doniphan, born October 26, 1782.
  Elizabeth Doniphan, born July 30, 1784.
  Catherine Harrison, born June 12, 1787.

SMITH FAMILY RECORD

The family register for this Smith family of Caroline County was kept in a record book rather than a Bible. It is known as the Thomas D. Smith Family Record. The original record is now in the possession of Ray Smith Campbell, Jr. of Caroline County.

Thomas D. Smith was married to Lethe A.G. Cleire the 21st day of November 1826 A.D.
Thomas D. Smith married Agnace M. Quesenberry (his 2nd wife) July 21, 1850.
Minerva Ann Smith married Robert S. Cobbs.
Mary Susan Smith married William F. Luck.
Martha Jane Smith married N.J. Hancock.
Leah E.A.H. Smith married Wm T. Hewlett.
John Thos. Smith married Virginia Curtis.

Ella Lavinia Smith married Jas. Quesenberry October 23, 1860.
C.T. Smith married Sallie Collins [1874].
Adoniram G. Smith married Sallie Owen.
Adoniram G. Smith married Ida May Bondurant (his second wife) April 1, 1880.
Thomas D. Smith married Sarah J. Quarles October 11, 1874 (his 3rd wife).
Thomas D. Smith was born Jan. 28, 1805.
Lethe Ann G. Cleire was born July 12, 1809.
Their children:
Minerva Ann Smith was born Dec. 11, 1827.
Mary S. Smith was born July 16, 1829.
Lethe E.A.H. Smith was born Nov. 16, 1830.
James H. Smith was born June 19, 1832.
Martha J. Smith was born Dec. 6, 1833.
John Thomas Smith was born July 2, 1835.
Robert Judson Smith was born Jan. 16, 1837.
William Powell Smith was born March 19, 1841 and died April 11, 1841.
Cornelius T. Smith was born Jan. 30, 1844.
Lilburne Moren Smith was born Jan. 30, 1844.
Adoniram G. Smith was born Dec. 7, 1845.
Lavinia Ella was born Jan. 26, 1840.
Lathe Ann G. Smith died Nov. 25, 1847 with her 13th infant child.
James H. Smith died Dec. 16, 1855 Sunday night after an illness of 5 weeks of Typhoid fever.
Robert Judson Smith died April 7, 1857.
Minerva A. Cobbs died October 14, 1860 from Typhoid fever.
Agnace M. Smith died Oct. 7, 1873.
Thomas D. Smith died Oct. 16, 1884.
Mary Susan Luck died Nov. 19, 1908.
Lethe E.A. Hasseltine Hewlett died Feb. 12, 1914.
Martha Jane Hancock died May 28, 1928.
John Thomas Smith died 1861.
Lavinia Ella Quisenberry died Oct. 9, 1921.
Cornelius Timothy Smith died Dec. 1937.
Lilburn Mason Smith died Mch. 5, 1925.
Adoniram George Smith died Aug. 19, 1934.
Adoniram George Smith was born Dec. 7, 1845.
Ida May Bondurant was born Dec. 14, 1858.
Their children:
Bessie B. Smith was born March 27, 1881.
Lilburn Mason Smith was born Aug. 28, 1882.
Mary Ella Smith was born June 26, 1884.
Thomas D. Smith was born July 26, 1887
John W. Smith was born August 14, 1889.
Ida George Smith was born Aug. 23, 1891.
Infant son was born July 30, 1893.

Vernon Owen Smith was born Nov. 15, 1894.
Adoniram George Smith Jr. was born Apr. 2, 1897.
Cornelius Smith was born March 2, 1899.
Infant son died August 9, 1893.
Cornelius Smith died October 26, 1906.
Lilburne Smith Marks died Jan. 22, 1911.
Ida May Bondurant Smith, wife of A.G. Smith, died May 19, 1933.
Adoniram George Smith, son of Thomas Dillard and Lethe Ann Smith and husband of Ida May Bondurant, died August 19, 1934.
John W. Smith died 1937.
T. E. Campbell, husband of Bessie B. Smith, died 1937.
Thomas Dillard Smith died Nov. 5, 1964.
Ida Smith Jackson died March 1965.
Mary Ella Smith died December 25, 1968.
Bessie B. Smith Campbell died April 8, 1970.
Carroll Vernon Jackson, husband of Ida Smith Jackson, died [no date listed]
Annie Nottingham Smith, wife of John W. Smith, died 1974.
Family of A.G. Smith Jr.
Parents' Names
Husband, Adoniram George Smith Jr. Born April 2, 1897.
Wife, Esther Reese Born March 15, 1904.
Married September 15, 1925 Atlee, Virginia
Children's Names
Frances Carolyn Smith Born September 11, 1926.
Lilburne Mason Smith Born August 5, 1931.
George Albert Smith Born May 19, 1941.
Marriage and children of Frances Carolyn Smith and Henry W. Obaugh September 19, 1953 First Baptist Church, Staunton, Va.
Michael Dean Obaugh Born April 28, 1958.
Alan Obaugh Born October 4, 1959.
Family of Lilburne Mason Smith
Parents' Names
Husband, Lilburn Mason Smith Born August 5, 1931
Wife, Thelma Grace Nolan Married June 23, 1956 Marion Baptist Church, Marion, S.C.
Their children
Nancy Carol Smith Born February 14, 1958.
Donna Gayle Smith Born February 11, 1960.
Joan Reese Smith Born August 20, 1962.
Family of George Albert Smith
Parents' Names
Husband, George Albert Smith Wife, Jayne Wood Smith Married August 29, 1965 Bowling Green Baptist Church, Bowling Green, Va.
Children's Names
Emily Louise Smith Born July 9, 1968

Joel Adoniram Smith Born August 7, 1975.
Dana Cameron Smith Born December 30, 1971.
Family of T.D. Smith
Parents' Names
Husband, Thomas Dillard Smith Born July 26, 1887.
Wife, Ida Mary Manwaring Born November 28, 1900.
Married June 10, 1921 Princess Ann, Maryland.
Children's Names
Ruth Bondurant Smith Born July 30, 1922.
Thomas Dillard Smith, Jr. Born September 14, 1923.
Marriage and children of Ruth Bondurant Smith and John Rolfe Hargrave June 1952 Central Baptist Church, Miami, Fla.
Children
Jacqueline Smith Hargrave Feb. 10, 1954.
Lucy Carol Hargrave Dec. 25, 1955.
John Rolfe Hargrave, Jr. Nov. 17, 1957.
Marriage and children of Thomas Dillard Smith, Jr. and Shirley Donna Vern Johnson March 18, 1950 First Baptist Church, Homestead, Fla.
Children
Thomas Dillard Smith III July 23, 1951.
Terrill Vern Smith Nov. 16, 1953.
Cynthia Dawn Smith April 10, 1958.
Family of Ida George Smith Jackson
Parents' Names
Husband, Carroll Vernon Jackson Wife, Ida Smith Jackson
Child's Name
Carroll Vernon Jackson Jr. Born July 12, 1929. Married Mildred Hill Jackson Born October 12, 1931.
Children's Names
Susan Ann Jackson Born February 1, 1954.
Janet Carol Jackson Born June 28, 1957.
They died January 11, 1959.
Carroll Vernon Jackson Jr. Born 7/12/29
Mildred Hill Jackson Born 10/12/31
Susan Ann Jackson Born 2/1/54
Janet Carol Jackson Born 6/28/57
All died 1/11/59.

SOUTHWORTH FAMILY BIBLE

This Bible was printed by B.F. Johnson & Co., Richmond, Va., 1886. It originally belonged to William Lewis Southworth and his wife Sarah Ella "Ellie" Robinson. They lived for a while back of the Jeter property at Penola and later moved to the Emmett Hutcheson's place off Signboard Road near Ruther Glen, Caroline County. This was originally the Old Luck Home Place and in more recent years was the home of Onan Taylor, back of Onan's Taylor's store. William Lawrence Southworth and probably one of the children, Wilson who died in 1911, is buried in the Luck-Hutcheson cemetery to the right of the house in an open field. On July 1, 1915, Ellie Southworth purchased "Stanhope" near Kidds Fork from Mrs. Louisa B. Pugh and her husband. Here she raised the family and the Southworth family lived here until after her death, after which it became the home of her son, Wesley. She was buried here and later moved to Salem Baptist Church. The Bible is presently owned by her grandson, William Roy Southworth.

William L. [Lawrence] Southworth, 29, of Jerrell, Va. and Sarah E. Robinson, 18, of Reedy Church on December 20, 1890 at Caroline Co.
Wilson [Southworth, son of above] died March 22, 1911.
Mr. W.L. [William Lawrence] Southworth died July 22, 1912.
J. E. Southworth [died] April 3, 1894.
Ellie R. Southworth died July 24, 1920.
Lawrence Earl Southworth [died September 8, 1951].
Lewis Wesley Southworth Died December 3, 1958.
Bernard [Bernie] Monroe Southworth Died Oct. 28, 1976.
J. [Junius] Roy Southworth Died Feb. 10, 1982.
Janie Barrett Southworth Puller Died Aug. 3, 1985.
J. J. (Uncle Johnnie] Southworth died July 1932.
Aunt Minnie died Oct. 22, 1933.
Births:
J. E. Southworth 3/22/1893.
L. E. Southworth 11/22/1894.
J. R. Southworth 9/15/1896.
L. W. Southworth 8/26/1898.
G. V. Southworth 7/25/1900.
B. M. Southworth 2/24/1902.
J. B. Southworth 6/5/1907.
Wilson Southworth 7/4/1909.

Lying loose in the Bible are the following wedding invitations:

Mrs. Fannie Dew's daughter Lucy DeJarnette to Dudley Dean Davis June 28, 1905 at Emmaus Church, Penola, Va.
Mrs. Ollie Bullock's daughter Bertie S. to J. W. Blanton April 26, 1899 at Summit Union Chapel, Spotsylvania County.
Mr. & Mrs. John Mansfield Holladay's daughter Mary Virginia to Phillip Augustus Dew November 25, 1903 at Trinity Church, Louisa County.
Mr. & Mrs. Wesley Wright's daughter Mayme Butler to Melville Garland Wright November 3, 1904 at St. Margaret's Chapel, Caroline County.
Mrs. Fannie Dew's daughter Gertrude Pirkinson to William Earnest Reynolds July 3, 1900 at Emmaus Christian Church, Caroline County, Virginia.
Mr. & Mrs. J.H. Blackley's daughter Irene Hilda to Earley Meredith Burruss May 9, 1900 at

Emmaus Christian Church, Penola, Va.

Mrs. Fannie Dew's daughter Fannie Scott to James Franklin Swann April 12, 1998 at Emmaus Church, Caroline County, Virginia.

NOTE by author: Emmaus Christian Church burned in February of 1943 and was never rebuilt)

SPILLMAN FAMILY BIBLE

This Bible was published by A. J. Holman & Co., Philadelphia, 1894. It is owned by Myrtle Dabney who also owned the Price Family Bible, which is filed with the Spillman Bible Records. A copy of both is in the King George Historical Society, King George, Va. Since the Price Bible records do not specifically mention Caroline County they have not been included. The Price family included the Owens family. Rev. Andrew Broaddus was pastor of Salem Baptist Church in Caroline County.

THIS CERTIFIES THAT THE RITE OF HOLY MATRIMONY WAS CELEBRATED BETWEEN Lemuel Stillman of King George Co. Va. and Mary E. Chinault of Caroline Co. Va. on the 18th day of Dec 1870 at the home residence by Rev. Andrew Broaddus of Caroline County.

Lemuel Spilman son of Joseph Spillman and Martha Poates his wife was born the 13th day of December 1831.

J. Frank Spillman, son of Lemuel Spillman and Mary E. Spillman his wife, was born the 27th day of February 1870.

Geneva Spillman of the same was born on the 7th of November 1877.

Ernest B. Spillman son of the same was born on the 4th day of September 1879.

Elizabeth Spillman daughter of the same was born on the 4th day of March 1881.

Carrie F. Spillman daughter of the same was born on the 2nd day of December 1883.

Robert E. Spillman son of the same was born on the 8th day of August 1888.

Dan Toy Spillman son the of the same was born on the 17th day of February 1890.

Carrie Fleet Spillman daughter of the same was born on the 18th day of September 1891.

Joseph L. Spillman son of the same was born on the 9th of September 1893.

Richard Lemuel Spillman son of Grace F. & Joseph 2nd Spillman was born Sept 22 1920.

Mary Magdalene Spillman daughter of Grace F. & Joseph L. Spillman born Sept 14 1921.

William Spillman son of Grace F. & Joseph L. Spillman was born May 25 1923.

Joseph Bernard Elmer Spillman, son of [unable to read] was born on 13th day of December 1831.

Geneva Spillman daughter of Lemuel Spillman and Mary E. Spillman, his wife, was married to Thomas H. Powell on the 7th of July 1896 by Rev. William H. Owens.

Ernest B. Spillman son of Lemuel Spillman and Mary E. Spillman his wife died on the 30th day of May 1880 age 8 months.

Mary E. and Carrie F. Spillman daughter of the same died on the 9th day of December 1887. Mary E's age was 6 years and Carrie's was 11 years.

SPINDLE FAMILY BIBLE

This Bible was printed and published by M. Carey, Philadelphia, Pennsylvania in 1817. It was owned by William Taliaferro Spindle, who was 88 years old in 1994, and who lived at Hustle, Essex County, Virginia. Members of the Spindle family lived in both Essex and Caroline County. The homestead in Essex was known as "Bloomsburg" and dated to the late 1700's. It is believed that this Bible originally belonged to Barbee Spindle, Sr. Copies of these records are also located in the Library of Virginia and at the Virginia Historical Society.

The Spindle family was in Caroline County as early as the eighteenth century. Caroline court papers of June 10, 1806 show Lewis Spindle, Barbee Spindle, Philip Spindle and Mordecai Spindle, executors of John Spindle. Mrs. Elizabeth Spindle owned 231 acres in Caroline in 1823 and Benjamin Long, Jr. was her tenant. Lewis Spindle died in Caroline County in 1820 leaving William G. and Elizabeth Spindle coexecutors of his estate. Elizabeth B. Spindle married a Mr. Garnett and had among her issue a son James B. Garnett, and died in Caroline County November 3, 1881. E. J. Spindle, husband of Alice Spindle, died in Caroline County August 21, 1893 at age 72. Mary A. Spindle, daughter of James and Mary Bagby, died in Caroline County August, 1861 at age 57. George Richard Pollard married Maria Spindle, sister of Cornelius Spindle. The Spindle family was also connected with the Todd family of Caroline.

Barbee Spindle [Sr.] was married to Rebeca Jones the 24th of August 1795. [married 2nd to Ann R.___]
Barbee Spindle [Sr.} was married [3rd] to Frances Gatewood the 27th day of June 1821.
Julia Ann Bowie, daughter of Barbee Spindle, was married the 27th October 1814.
Frances J. Rennalds, daughter of Barbee Spindle, was married the 18th day of June 1818.
Martha Spindle, daughter of Barbee Spindle, was married November 29, 1822.
Elizabeth M. Spindle was married the 2nd of December 1835.
Barbee Spindle [Sr.] was born June 22, 1773.
Polly Spindle, daughter of Barbee Spindle by Rebeca, his wife, was born February 1st, 1797.
Julia A. Spindle, daughter of Barbee Spindle by Rebeca, his wife, was born November 22, 1798.
Frances J. Spindle, daughter of Barbee Spinle by Rebeca, his wife, born April 29, 1803.
Martha Spindle, daughter of Barbee Spindle by Rebeca, his wife, was born July 25, 1805.
Elizabeth A. Spindle, daughter of Barbee Spindle by Ann R., his wife, was born 15 September 1810.
Lewis E. Spindle, son of Barbee Spindle by Ann R., his wife, was born January 28, 1813.
Virginia Spindle, daughter of Barbee Spindle by Ann R., his wife, was born September 13, 1815.
Penelope E. F. Spindle, daughter of Barbee Spindle by Frances, his wife, was born August 11, 1822.
Barbee Spindle [Jr.] son of Barbee Spindle by Frances, was born October 1, 1823.
Joseph [C.] Spindle, son of Barbee Spindle by Frances, was born August 5, 1825.
Elizabeth B. Spindle, daughter of Barbee Spindle by Frances, his wife, was born August 1, 1827.
Fannie Gatewood [3rd] wife of Barbee Spindle, Sr.] was born March 1, 1789 [signed] J. C. Spindle.
Rebeca Spindle, [1st] wife of Barbee Spindle, departed this life the 29th of April 1808.
Polly Spindle, daughter of Barbee Spindle by Rebeca, his wife, departed this life in September 1797.
Rebeca Spindle, daughter of Barbee Spindle by Rebeca, his wife, departed this life in November

1808.

Lewis E. Spindle, son of Barbee Spindle by Ann R., his wife, departed this life January 9, 1814.

Ann R. Spindle, [2nd] wife of Barbee Spindle, departed this life April 15, 1818.

Julia Ann Bowie departed this life December 1821.

Martha [Spindle] [illeg] died in June 182[illeg].

Elizabeth [Spindle] [illeg] departed this life September 18__ [illeg],

Barbee Spindle [Sr.] departed this life April 5th, 1838 in his 65th year at his own residence, Bloomsbery, Essex County, Virginia [initialed] J. B. G.

Barbee Spindle, son of Barbee Spindle, departed this life July 15th, 1856 in the 33rd year of his life at his own residence, Bloomsbery, Essex County, Virginia.

Fanny [Gatewood] Spindle, [3rd] wife of Barbee Spindle [Sr.] departed this life September 20th, 1873 in the 84th year, six months and twenty days [signed] J.C. Spindle.

[The following information was found on two tattered pages that were folded and inserted in the preceding Spindle family Bible that belonged to Barbee Spindle, Sr. It is believed these pages came from a family Bible that belonged to Joseph Clarence Spindle, Sr., a son of Barbee Spindle, Sr.]

Sofia Frances Spindle, daughter of J. C. and S. F.[Sofia Frances Burke] Spindle, was born 17th of July 1848 [signed] J. C. Spindle.

Maria L. [Lula] Spindle, daughter of J. C. and Sofia F. Spindle, was born the [illeg] day of July 1849 [signed] J. C. Spindle.

John M.B. [Muse Burke] Spindle, son of J. C. and Sofia F. Spindle, was born [illeg] day of June 1851 [signed] J. C. Spindle.

[next item is completely illegible]

Julia H. [Hoomes] Spindle, daughter of J. C. and Sofia F. Spindle, was born the 19th of May 1853 [signed] J. C. Spindle.

Betty G. [Garnett] Spindle, daughter of J. C. and Sofia Spindle, was born on 17 March 1855 [signed] J. C. Spindle.

Cordelia F. [Fauntleroy] Spindle was born 12 January 1857, daughter of Joseph C. Spindle and Sofia F. Spindle [signed] J. C. Spindle.

[next item is nearly illegible, probably Joseph Clarence Spindle, Jr.]

Francis Woolfolk Spindle, Son of J. C. Spindle and Sofia F. Spindle, was born the 22nd of November 1860.

Resa [Theresa] Burke, daughter of J. C. and Sofia F. Spindle, was born the 9th day of April 1871.

Sofia F. Spindle, daughter of J. C. and Sofia F. Spindle, died 26th day of [illeg, probably Nov. or Dec.] 1850.

Julia [Hoomes] Spindle Carter, daughter of J. C. Spindle and Fanny, his wife, departed this life the 15th day of March, 1884 [signed] J.C. Spindle.

[the items which follow are completely illegible]

STARKE FAMILY BIBLE

This Bible was published by the American Bible Society, N.Y., 1839. It contains handwritten records of the Bailey, Doswell, Hankins, Savage and Starke families, 1828-1871. Kept by Harriet Reynolds (Savage) Starke, in part, while a student at Elson Green Seminary, Caroline County, Virginia. It was given to the Virginia Historical Society by Mrs. John C. Wysor, Harrisonburg, Virginia in 1991. The main importance of this Bible is that it is the only place the author has seen that documents the Elson Green Seminary in Caroline County, heretofore unpublished in other Caroline County histories. "Elson Green" still stands in restored condition on Mt. Gideon Road on top of the hill from the Pamunkey River in Caroline County. Although most of this family seem to have resided in New Kent and Hanover Counties, there were Starke family members in Caroline County during the 18th and 19th centuries. The Starke family intermarried with the Wyatt family of Caroline as well as several other families.

Harriet Reynolds Savage
Elson Green Seminary
Caroline County
Married at Windsor Forest New Kent County on the 23d Day of May 1850 Harriet K. Savage and Marcellus T. Starke.
Sarah C. Doswell was born the 7 of February 1827.
Harriet R. Savage was born the 21st of April 1828.
Willinette Bailey was born 28 of July 1827.
Emily A. Savage was born on the 21st day of July 1829.
Alice Brown Hankins was born the 21st Sept. 1837.
William W. Starke was born the 12th April 1853.
Harriet R. Starke wife of Marcellus T. Starke died June 1871.
Bettie L. Starke daughter of Harriet R. Starke died Oct. 30th 1875.
Also in this Bible is a newspaper clipping "Seven Short Rules for Young Christians".

STERN/STERNE FAMILY BIBLE

There were two separate Stern families in Caroline County early on. One was that of Levi Stern, who lived in the Ruther Glen area and whose member was an officer in the Confederate Army. The other, no kin to the former, lived in the area of Caroline County, which in 1941 became Camp A.P. Hill. This Bible belonged to the latter family. The spelling appears both with and without an "e". They married into the Cash family who were their neighbors. The graves of both the Cash and Stern families were moved from the private cemeteries on their home places to Greenlawn Cemetery, Bowling Green, Virginia, in 1941, when the Camp area was created. All the narrative notations which appear here are original to the Bible record and were added by members of the family.

Francis G. Sterne was born the 16 April 1819.
David Sterne was born the 15th March 1762.
David Stern ran away from home in Caroline Co. Va. at the age of 14 years - and joined Genl. Green's Army as a bugler, was wounded in his shoulder at Cowpens, S.C. later rejoined the army and was wounded 2nd time in the hip permanently lame and unable to do further service in

war. He rec'd a pension as did his widow. He mustered out as a dragoon or cavalryman. Record on file at Wash D.C. Subscribed by his great grand Son. Walter Scott Cash 1931.

Mary Sterne was married the 28 March 1837.

Francis G. Sterne was Married the 14th September 1857.

Mary Sterne married Oscar Cash the father of David Semple Cash, the father of Walter Scott Cash which makes him the great grand Son of David Sterne born, See next page.

The family name is properly Stern and not Sterne because David Stern the first of the family whose signature we find in several books and numerous papers is David Stern. Subscribed by his great grand Son 1932 Walter Scott Cash.

David Sterne departed this life the 23rd of October 1837.

Lucy Sterne wife of David Sterne Departed this life 28th of October 1878.

Lucy Samuel died May 2nd 1908. daughter of David Stern.

S. Elizabeth Tiffey Died Sept. 14th 1858.

Lucy Beazley Daughter of Reuben Beazley and Mary his wife was Born December the-- 2 ---- 1794. Lucy Beazley married David Sterne. See death notice recorded - W. S. Cash.

Lucy Beazley daughter of Rubin Beazley and Mary his wife was born Dec 2nd 1794. [entry written twice in Bible and the name "Reuben" spelled differently the second time]

The marriage of David Stern and Lucy Beazley is recorded in the Court Order book at Bowling Green, Va. For 1812.

STHRESHLEY FAMILY BIBLE

Captain William Sthreshley was quite a prominent citizen of Caroline County from the close of the Revolution to the date of death in 1830, and at one time (1793) offered to donate the necessary land and build a court house at his own expense for a new county proposed to have been carved out of Caroline. This Bible was owned by Marius Streshley, grandson of Capt. William Sthreshley of Caroline County, and in 1934, was owned by Mrs. M.C. Cline of Stafford Co, daughter of Marius Sthreshley. A copy of this Bible is at the Virginia Historical Society and at the Library of Virginia.

The Streshley family intermarried with the Wyatt family of Caroline County and the Skinker and McGruder families of Port Royal, Caroline County. In 1805 Robert B. Sthreshley was a merchant in the town of Port Royal. On 12 January 1808, Robert B. Sthreshley and Amelia Magruder were married in Caroline County by James Elliott. James S. Sthreshley married Sarah Skinker and was a maker of cartwheels in Port Royal in 1810. Fanny B. Sthreshley, daughter of W. Sthreshley, married Henley Woodward 9 July 1804 in Caroline County. Henry B. Sthreshley was executor of Willian Streshley of Caroline County in 1831.

William Sthreshley was born December 22, 1749.
Elizabeth Sthreshley was born 1760.
Richard F. Sthreshley, son of William and Elizabeth Sthreshley was born Sept. 29th 1811.
Marius Sthreshley was born Apr. 16, 18_7.
Mary A. Sthreshley was born October 20th 1870.
Charlie A. Sthreshley was born June 3rd 1872.

James M. Sthreshley was born Oct 26th 1873.
Fannie E. Sthreshley was born May 15th 1875.
Annie E. Sthreshley was born Dec 27th 1876.
Lucy Beale Sthreshley was born Aug 6th 1878.
Lawrence F. Sthreshley was born Feb 9th 1880.
Lillie M. Sthreshley was born Dec 19th 1882.
Attawa L. Sthreshley was born June 14th 1884.
Alice T. Sthreshley was born Feb 10th 1886.
Sadie Virginia Sthreshley born August 20th 1888.
Eva Bowling Sthreshley born June 30th 1890.
Ada Custis Sthreshley born Jan 11, 1892.
Frances Lewis Sthreshley born Nov 13 1905.
Frances R. Maupin born Dec 13 1897.
Fitzhugh Maupin born Nov 27, 1900.
Joseph H. Maupin and Fannie E. Sthreshley were married Dec 28 ____.
_____ Smith & Lucy Beall Sthreshley were married Feb. 4th 1903.
Martin G. Hitt & Lillie Marion Sthreshley were married Aug 18, 1911.
Marius Sthreshley and Fannie M. Clift [only dau. of A.H. Clift of Stafford County were married Dec. 13, 1869.
R. B. McCalley and Mamie A. Sthreshley were married Nov 16, 1892.
Charles A. Sthreshley and Lillie C. Jenkins were married Feb 27, 1892.
Elizabeth Sthreshley died Jany 6th 1830.
William Sthreshley died May 11th, 1850.
Richard F. Sthreshley died Oct 5th 1805.
Ada Custis Sthreshley died July 3rd 1862.
Charlie A. Sthreshley died Decr 5th 1898 Age 26 years and 11 months.
James W. Sthreshley died Sept 30, 1899 Age 25 years.

There is also a letter dated March 30, 1934 to the Virginia Historical Society which states that around 1804-05 two brothers Henley and Richard Woodward of New Kent Co then living at Tappahannock in Essex Co married two sisters Fanny B. and Ann Sthreshley, daughters of Capt William Streshley of Caroline County. The eldest brother of these two ladies was James Madison Sthresley, who married Mary P. B. Fitzhugh in 1828 and they had located his family Bible in the possession of his granddaughter Mrs. Frances Elizabeth Sthreshley Maupin of Chuckey, Tenn.

SUTTON FAMILY BIBLE

The Sutton family was one of the earliest families to settle in what is now Caroline County. John Sutton patented land here as early as 1711. This Bible seems to have originated with Joseph Sutton and his wife Judith Carter, daughter of Captain John Carter and Hannah Chew. She was born March 27, 1769 and died March 2, 1827. Joseph Sutton, born August 22, 1764, died February 6, 1823, was the son of John Sutton and grandson of John and Sarah Sutton of St.

Margaret's Parish in Caroline County. For further information concerning these families see: *Descendants of Captain Thomas Carter of Lancaster County* by J.L. Miller and *The Suttons of Caroline County* by T. Dix Sutton, Richmond Press, 1941. The Bible was in the possession of T. Dix Sutton until his death.

The Sutton family lived at various sites in Caroline County. Stephen Sutton lived at "Chesterfield" which was also a tavern. John Sutton was established at Union Tavern, where he ran an ordinary a few miles below Burk's Bridge on the Old Stage Road near Edmund Pendleton School, and John Carter Sutton established "Pine Forest" near Penola, where a Sutton cemetery with markers exist. None of these places are standing today. This Bible record was copied by Marsha C. Owen from the original and a copy has been placed in the Library of Virginia.

Joseph Sutton and Judith Carter was married March 3, 1785.
John Sutton and Maria C. Sutton was married on July the 11, 1811.
Robert C. Sutton and Catherine Washington was married October the 20th 1811.
Stephen Sutton and Eliza M. Oliver was married May 30, 1816.
John O. Sutton and Martha E. Chapman was married 27th May 1829.
Armistead Oliver Sutton and Sarah D. Lewis was married the 3rd of October 1843.
Joseph Sutton was born August 22, 1764.
Judith Carter was born March 27, 1769.
Stephen Sutton was born on Tuesday March 14, 1786.
Robert C. Sutton was born on Wednesday June 18, 1788.
Maria Chew Sutton was born on Sunday February 14th, 1790.
John Orville Sutton was born on Saturday night eight o'clock May 28, 1803.
George B. Sutton was born on the 25th of October 1813.
Susanna Maria Eliza Sutton was born 4th March, 1816.
Joseph Pike Sutton was born on the 14th of February, 1815.
Children of John O.[Orville] Sutton:
Maria Chew Sutton was born 1st day of April 1831.
Judith C. Sutton was born June 20, 1833.
Charles Manners Sutton was born July 29, 1840.
Robert Joseph Sutton was born April 18, 1842.
Frank Logan Sutton was born the 16th of February 1845.
William Armistead, the son of Armistead O. & Sarah D. Sutton, was born the 23rd of July, 1844.
Cadwallader Lewis Sutton, the son of A. O. & Sarah D. Sutton, was born the 5th of Dec. 1845.
Maria Chew Sutton departed this life on the 27th of February 1815.
George B. Sutton, son of Robert, departed this life on Tuesday the 3rd day of October 1815.
Mrs. Hannah Carter departed this life (at the house of Joseph Sutton) on Monday the 15th day of January at half past one o'clock in the morning in the year of our Lord 1821.
Joseph Sutton departed this life on the 6th day of February at precisely 45 minutes after one o'clock a.m. in the year 1823 in the 54th year of his age.
Judith Sutton departed this life---2nd day of March, 10 minutes after 5 p.m. 1827.
Caty Sutton, consort of Robert C. Sutton, departed this life on 2nd day of Jan 1840.

Stephen Sutton, the oldest of Joseph and Judy Sutton, died at his residence Towinque in the county of King William on Wednesday the second of December 1840 between four and five o'clock a.m.

Eliza M. Sutton, relict of Dr. Stephen Sutton died February 1867 at Towinque, King William county in the sixth sixth year of her age.

William Armistead Sutton the son of A. O. and Sarah D. Sutton died on the 29th of December, 1846.

Samuel Hamlet & Mary E. Sutton (daughter of Stephen and Eliza Oliver Sutton) were married 23rd of Dec 1852.

Laura Sutton, daughter of Stephen & Eliza Sutton departed this life on Friday 12th Nov 1852 at 3 o'clock a.m.

Elvira Maria Sutton departed this life on Thursday 2nd July 1857 at twenty minutes to 8 o'clock p.m.

SWEENEY/HUTCHESON FAMILY BIBLE

This Bible, known as the Martin Sweeney Bible, was owned in 1971 by Mrs. Andrew Robert, Williamsburg, Virginia, who sent a copy to Mrs. Floyd Hutcheson, Richmond, Virginia . It was furnished the author by the late Virginia Lee Hutcheson Davis, editor and publisher of *Tidewater Virginia Families*.

Martin Sweeney [son of Stephen Booker Sweeney and Virginia Elizabeth Martin] was married to Lucy Ann Barnes Nov. 6, 1850 [by Rev. B.F. Woodward].

E. H. Hutcheson was married to L. Jennie Sweeney on May 27th 1873 at 6 o'clock P.M.

R.W. Hutcheson Son of Richard Hutcheson and Mary his wife nee Frances Ann Peatross daughter of John Peatross and Mary his Wife was married Feby 4th 1844.

Lucy Ann Barnes daughter of Richard and Lucy Ann Barnes was born May 27th 1832.

L. Jennie daughter of Martin and Lucy Ann Sweeney was Born December 18th 1856.

Udora Daughter of Martin and Lucy Ann Sweeney was Born April 7th 1854.

Edward Hebious Hutcheson son of Richard W. and Frances A. Hutcheson was born Feby 20th 1845.

Henry Chiles Hutcheson son of R.W. and F.A. Hutcheson was born Sept 16th 1846.

Martin Sweeney son of Stephen and Virginia Sweeney was born Nov 5th 1825.

Mary Permilia Chiles Hutcheson daughter to R.W. and F.A. Hutcheson was born May 22nd 1850.

Sarah Frances Hutcheson daughter to R.W. and F.A. Hutcheson was born Aug. 9th 1852.

Anna Morton Hutcheson daughter to R.W. and F.A. Hutcheson was born Aug. 24th 1854.

Richard W. Hutcheson Jr. Son of R.W. and F.A. Hutcheson was born May 21st 1857.

Martin Sweeney Departed this life 21st day of March at 10 o'clock A.M. 1871.

R.W. Hutcheson died Sept 3rd 1887 in the sixty third year of his age.

F.A. Hutcheson Wife of R.W. Hutcheson died March 23rd 1893 in the seventy fifth year of her age.

Henry C. Hutcheson son of R.W. and F.A. Hutcheson died June 9th 1895 in the 49th year of his age.

Lucy Ann Sweeney Wife of Martin Sweeney Departed this life 12th day of August 1854 15 minutes past 5 o'clock P.M. Age 22 years 2 months and 10 days.

Udora Sweeney Departed this life the 28th day of May 1854.

Died on March 6th 1893 at 8 1/2 o'clock P.M., L. Jennie Sweeney wife of E. H. Hutcheson. Age 41 yrs, 2 months & 16 days.

[The following additions to the Bible records appeared in Mrs. Andrew Lee Roberts' letter to Mrs. Floyd Hutcheson, Richmond, Va., dated October 14, 1971.]

Martin Sweeney the son of Stephen B.(Brocker) Sweeney and Virginia (Elizabeth Martin) his wife was born November 5, 1825.

Martha (Dunnavant) Willis daughter of Vaden and Rebecca (Dunnavant) Willis was born October 7, 1830.

Lucy Virginia daughter of Martin and Lucy Ann Sweeney was born December 18, 1851 1/2 past 8 in the evening.

Alice V.(Vernon) Willis daughter of Martin and Martha D. Sweeney was born the 9th of June Sunday Morning 1867 6 o'clock.

Martin Sweeney was married to Martha D. Willis July 18, 1855 by the Rev. R.(or M) Adams.

Luther Judson Davidson was married to Alice Vernon Willis Sweeney February 21, 1889 by Dr. Hatcher [from marriage certificate].

Udora Sweeney daughter of Martin and L.A. Sweeney departed this life the 23rd day of May 1854. Aged, 1 month and 16 days.

Martha A. Dunnavant Willis Sweeeney, widow of Martin Sweeney, died August 29, 1903.

TALIAFERRO FAMILY BIBLE NO 1

This Bible originally belonged to Charles Taliaferro Sr. and his wife Isabella McCullock. It was printed in Edinburgh in 1756. A copy is in the Library of Virginia. The Bible was rebound in 1870, having been greatly mutilated by the wear and tear. The Bible also contains a handwritten history written by James Govan Taliaferro (Zach-Chas-Rich'd-John-Robt) in 1871. "By tradition, the Taliaferros are descended from immigrants who came from Italy to VA about 1650. There were 3 brothers, one died without descendants, one settled in Fredericksburg & one in Caroline. [the 3 brothers story is a myth told by nearly all early researchers, whether this is true would have to be proved]. According to my uncle Benj Taliaferro, my great-grandfather Richard Taliaferro was the grandson of the immigrant. He was born at 'Taliaferro's Mount' in Caroline [County, Va.] Before he died at Port Royal in Caroline 09.27.1748, Richard bought land in that newly settled country 'tho he never resided there. Son Charles Taliaferro moved to his land at Tobacco Run Mountain about 1761 & lived at the home erected by his father until his death in 1798. Chas' children were born in this house except for son Richard who was born in Westmoreland. For additional reading concerning the Taliaferro family, see *Our Most Skillful Architect - Richard Taliaferro & Associated Colonial Virginia Constructions - Life and Works of Richard Taliaferro 1705-1779* by Claude Lanciano, Lands End Books, Gloucester, Va.

Isabel McCullock, daughter of the Revd. Roderick McCullock was born the 9th of Feb 1739 and departed this life 23rd August 1794.

Charles Taliaferro was born 6th of July 1735 and was married to Isabell McCullock 13th of April

1758 and died on the night of 23rd of August 1794.
Richard Taliaferro Son of Charles and Isabel Taliaferro Born the 23d of May 1759.
Charles Taliaferro was Born the 2d of March 1761.
Peter Taliaferro was Born the 4th of March 1763 and died the 9th of July 1782.
John Taliaferro was Born the 4th of May 1765 and died the 4th November 1807 at 10 o'clock.
Zacheryas Taliaferro was Born September 23d 1767 and died about 4 o'clock P.M. of Friday the 12th day of September 1823 of dropsy produced by the decrease of the liver.
Benjamin Taliaferro was born the 9th of January 1770.
Sarah Taliaferro was born August the 16th 1774.
Roderick Taliaferro was born May the 16th 1777.
James Taliaferro was born April the 12th 1779.
Rose Taliaferro was born January the 2d 1783.
Richard Taliaferro was married to his loving wife whose maiden name was Rose Berryman on the 10th of June 1726 & dyed Sept 27th 1748 Tuesday 12 o'clock.
Sarah Taliaferro was born ye 7th of June 1727 10 o'clock Wednesday Night.
Benja Taliaferro was born ye 21st November 1728 at 1 o'clock thursday and died the 6th Day of March 1751.
Zacha Taliaferro was born the ___ day of Aug 1730 at 8 o'clock Sunday Night.
Richard Taliaferro was born the ___ day of Feby 1731/2 and Died the 26th of the Same month.
John Taliaferro was born the 7th day of April 1733.
Charles Taliaferro was born the 16th day of July 1735.
Beheathland Taliaferro was born the 20th of May 1738.
Peter Taliaferro was born ye 12 day of February 1739.
Elisabeth Taliaferro was born with Rose the 2d Day of November 1741. [Elisabeth and Rose were twins]
Mary Taliaferro was born the 16 Day of October 1743.
Francis Taliaferro was born the 9th Day December 1745.
Richard Taliaferro was born the 2d Day of Sept 1747.

TALIAFERRO FAMILY BIBLE NO. 2

This Bible record was apparently written by James Govan Taliaferro in 1871 when the old original Bible above was rebound. A copy is in the Library of Virginia. Listed below are the children of Charles Taliaferro, son of Richard.

Richard Taliaferro the oldest child, married [Mildred] Powell of Amherst county, removed in 1784 or 5 to Chester District, South Carolina and died in that District in that State on the 4th of April 1806.
Charles Taliaferro the next oldest Son died June 29th 1824.
William Taliaferro the seventh Son died 4th of October 1805.
Roderick Taliaferro died 7th of December 1820.
The three last named died in Amherst County Virginia.
Sarah Taliaferro married John William Loving settled in Kentucky near Russelville.
Rose Taliaferro married Joseph Loving who moved to Brownsville Tenneesse.

James Taliaferro settled in Haywood County. He was twice married- He left two children.

Benjamin Taliaferro the Sixth Son married Mildred Franklin. Had one Son and Seven daughters. He died in Amherst Co.

Zacharias Taliaferro the fifth Son of Charles Taliaferro married Sally Warnick of Amherst County Virginia. He immigrated from Virginia in 1806 and settled in the State of Mississippi (then a Territory) and afterward moved to Louisiana where he died on the 12th of September 1823 - His wife was born on the 26th of ___ 1767 and died on the 25th day of September 1844. Two children were born of this marriage to note: Elvira Taliaferro and James Govan Taliaferro of these brief memoirs.

Elvira Taliaferro was born the 12th of October 1797 and died on the 22nd of October 1807.

James G. Taliaferro was born on the 28th day of September 1798. Was married to Elizabeth M. Williamson of Lexington, Kentucky on the 1st day of May 1819. She was born the 15th of June 18__ and died the 27th of April 1850.

Their children were as follows viz:

James Gowan Taliaferro Jr. was born May 2nd 1821 died in the City of Mexico in February 1848, the day __. He married Mary Lacy. He left one Son William James Taliaferro who was born ___ and died on the 20th of September 1867. He was the only child.

Zacharias Taliaferro was born on the 4th of July ___ and died on the 21st of September 1824.

Samuel Butler Taliaferro was born on the 7th of November 1823 and died on the 7th of April [no year listed]___.

Susannah Bryson Taliaferro was born August 20th 1825.

John Quincy Adams Taliaferro was born the ___ of August 1827 and died on the 9th of July 186_.

William Williamson Taliaferro was born the 9th of July 1829. He died the 12th of September 1831. He was drowned.

Robert Williamson Taliaferro was born May 20th 1831.

David Webster Taliaferro was born 7th June 1833, and died on the 18th of April 1837.

Sarah Elvira Taliaferro was born the 7th of August 1837 and died the 6th of July 1838.

Elizabeth Ann Maria Taliaferro was born the 31st day of May 1839.

Henry Bullard Taliaferro was born October the 16th 1841.

Of the foregoing descendants of James G. Taliaferro and Elizabeth M. B. Williamson, five died young. John Q. A. Taliaferro never married.

Susannah B. Taliaferro was married on the 27th day of December 1842 to Dr. John Steel Alexander who was born on the 25 day of March 1818, and died on the 5th of October 1855, of yellow fever contracted while on the manly performance of his duty as a physician, attending the Sick of that disease, which was then prevailing with great violence at Trinity, La. Four children were the issue of this marriage.

James Robert Alexander born 21st of May 1844.

Taliaferro Alexander born 17th of March 1846.

Sallie Armstrong Alexander, born 13th of February 1849 and died 27th of July 1850.

John Steel Alexander born 15th of January 1851.

Elizabeth Ann Maria Taliaferro was married on the ___ day of October A.D. 1860 to Richard Wooton who departed this life on the 23rd day of February 1870. He was born on the 12th of April 1832. Of this marriage there were four children viz:

Richard Green Wooten was born 8th of September 1861.
Lizzie Beatrice Wooten was born 9th of July 1863.
Lillie Morton was born 28th of October 1865.
Flora Morton was born 12th of April 1867.

TALIAFERRO FAMILY REGISTER

The family register of Nicholas Taliaferro was originally written in a family medical and receipt book which the family termed "Old Buchan" and was transcribed by Thomas Thomas A. Marshall of Vicksburg, Mississippi for his sister, Mrs. Mary A.P. Doniphan of Augusta, Kentucky on the 21st day of June 1849. The book was burned when the Marshall home "Openwoods" in Vicksburg, Mississippi, when that city was burned during it's seize during the Civil War. A copy of it was reproduced in the *William and Mary College Quarterly Historical Magazine,* Second Series, Volume I, No. 3, July, 1921, pp. 145-166. Notes on the errors in this Register appear later as a letter to the Editor to the *William and Mary Quarterly*, dated January 7, 1922.

My Honored Grandfather, John Taliaferro, was married to my honored grandmother, Mary Catlett, the 22d day of December, 1709; my honored grandfather departed this life the 3d of May, 1744. My Uncle, Lawrence Taliaferro was born the 8th of September, 1721; he married Susanna Power, youngest daughter of Major Henry Power, and had issue, Sarah Taliaferro, born 13th October, 1746, o.s., now the wife of Captain William Dangerfield. He died the first of May, 1748.

My Aunt, Martha Taliaferro, was born the 24th of June, 1724 and married Mr. William Hunter, and had issue by him, James Hunter, born 6th November, 1746, William Hunter born 24th August
Anno 1748 o.s., Martha Hunter born 20th October 1749 o.s. Mr. William Hunter died the 25th of January, 1754.

My honored father, William Taliaferro, was born at "Snow Creek", Spotsylvania County, Rappahannock, Va., the 9th of August, 1726, and departed life at "Newington", his seat on Mountain Run, Orange County, Virginia, after a painful illness without a groan the 21st of April 1798, aged seventy two in August, 1798.

My honored father William Taliaferro was married to my honored mother, Mary Battaile, the 4th October 1751 by the Reverend Musgrove Dawson. She was born the 18th September 1731 and died the 9th of November 1757, the daughter of Captain Nicholas Battaile, of "Hays", Caroline County, Rappahannock Virginia. My grandmother's maiden name was Thornton.

John Taliaferro, son of William and Mary Taliaferro, was born Tuesday morning, seven o'clock, the 31st July 1753 and was baptized by the Reverend Musgrove Dawson; his sureties were Colonel John Thornton, Colonel Henry Fitzhugh's lady, Mr. Charles Lewis and his lady, the 24th August, 1753.

Lucy Mary Taliaferro was born the 13th of December Anno 1755, Tuesday nine o'clock at night and was baptized by the Reverend Mungo Marshall, her sureties were Mr. Reuben Thornton, Mr. Henry Willis for Mr. Henry Heath Mrs. Elizabeth Thomas and Miss Mary Waugh.

Nicholas Taliaferro was born the 30th October, A.M., 1757; his sureties were Colonel George

Taylor, Mr. Erasmus Taylor, Mrs. Sarah Slaughter, Miss Betty Slaughter and Mrs. Mildred James.

My Honored father was was married to Miss Elizabeth Taliaferro, a second wife, on Tuesday the 5th of December 1758 by the Reverend Musgrove Dawson. She was the daughter of Francis and Elizabeth Taliaferro of "Epsom", Spotsylvania County, Rappahannock, Virginia, and was born the 4th October 1741.

Ann Hay Taliaferro was born Wednesday the 27th February 1760 at three quarters after eleven o'clock at night and had private baptism by the Reverend James Marye, Jr., and died the 2d March, 1760 at seven o'clock A.M.

Nicholas Taliaferro was married to Ann Taliaferro on Saturday the 3d November 1781, eleven o'clock, by the Reverend James Stevenson. My beloved wife, Ann Taliaferro, was the daughter of Colonel John and Ann Taliaferro, of "Dissington", was born the 7th of April 1756 and departed this life the 3d February 1798.

Lucy Mary Taliaferro, daughter of Nicholas and Ann Taliaferro was born Tuesday morning nine o'clock, 6th August, 1782 and was baptized by the Reverend William Douglas the 18th January 1783; Her sureties were Mr. Winslow Parker, Mrs. Lucy Mary Thurston, Miss Ann Thurston, my wife and self.

John Champe Taliaferro was born Tuesday morning 7 o'clock, the 12th of October 1784 and was baptized by the Reverend James Stevenson the 27th of April 1786. His sureties were Mr. John Grinnan, Mr. Joseph Stewart, Miss Francis Willis Stewart and his mother and departed this life 26th February 1811 after a painful illness.

Matilda Battaile Taliaferro was born Sunday morning eight o'clock the 30th September Anno 1787 and was baptized by the Reverend James Stevenon the 24th August 1788; her sureties were Mr. John and Miss Ann Grinnan, and her mother.

Mary Willis Taliaferro was born One o'clock the 11th August 1789 and was baptized by the Reverend James Stevenson the 15th November 1789. Her sureties were Mr. John Stevens, Mr. Joseph Morton, Miss Elizabeth Taliaferro, Miss Ann Hay Taliaferro and her mother. She departed this life the 25th January 1797 and was buried in Pennsylvania, where General Braddock was defeated, Alleganey County.

George Catlett Taliaferro was born Wednesday evening, four o'clock, the 21st of March Anno 1792 and was baptized by the Reverend Mr. Woodville the 23d December 1794; his sureties were Mr. John Grinnan, and wife, Lucy and myself.

William Thornton Taliaferro was born Friday, January 16th, 1795, at eleven P.M. and was baptized by the Rev. Mr. O'Neal; his sureties were his grandfather who named him, Mr. Hay Taliaferro and Hay Taliaferro Jr, his grandmother, mother and Miss Abby Gibson.

Nicholas Taliaferro was a second time married, to Miss Frances Blasingame, daughter of Mr. James and Mary Blasingame, and had issue:

Carr Blasingame Taliaferro who was born Tuesday 13th August 1799 half after two in the evening.

Lawrence Washington Taliaferro was born Tuesday, nine o'clock, 28 October 1800.

Ann Patterson Taliaferro was born Friday night ten o'clock 29th October 1802, and departed this life Tuesday night about twelve o'clock, 25th November 1803; she was cutting teeth and was taken with the epilepsy fits; her two eye teeth came through the gums before she died.

James Hay Taliaferro was born the second day of September 1804; very warm sunshiny day.

Nicholas Taliaferro was born Thursday half after eight o'clock the 14th August 1806, in the morning.

Marshall Howe Taliaferro was born the ninth of March, 1809, eleven o'clock at night.

Carr Blasingame Taliaferro departed this life Thursday morning half after nine, 1806.

James Hay Taliaferro departed this life Thursday night twelve o'clock, 18th August, 1808.

John Champe Taliaferro died 26th February, ten minutes after two in the morning, 1811.

Frances Ann Taliaferro was born Saturday, eleven o'clock P.M. Nine November, 1811.

William Buckner was born the 19th June, 1780, and was married to Lucy Mary Taliaferro 26th June, 1799, and had issue:

Philip Johnson Buckner, born 8th August, 1800.

Ann Whitaker Taliaferro Buckner born 8th January 1803.

Nicholas Taliaferro Buckner, born 29th June, 1805.

My brother, John Taliaferro, married Ann Stockdell, daughter of Captain John and Mary Stockdell of Orange County Virginia and had issue:

Mary Taliaferro, born 17th June 1773, married Robert Reynolds and died with her first child which is called Thornton.

Elizabeth Hay Taliaferro was born 4th May 1778.

Lucy Mary Battaile Taliaferro was born 14th May 1780.

William Taliaferro was born 23d March, 1782.

Sarah Taliaferro was born 20th February, 1784.

John Taliaferro was born 6th April 1786.

Martha Taliaferro was born 22d January 1789.

Nicholas Hay Battaile Taliaferro was born 15th June, 1793.

Lawrence Wesley Taliaferro was born 5th August 1796.

A Register of the Names and Ages of My Negroes.

1. James, born in March 1756.
2. Rachel was born in November 1773.
3. Clemintina was born in February 1781.
4. Anthony born 12th March 1784, 9 o'clock in the morning.
5. Billy was born 9th December 1785, eleven o'clock at night.
6. Hannah, born 19th August 1786, four o'clock in the morning.
7. Sarah born 10th June 1773.
8. Betty born 15th Sept 1788.
9. Sally born 10th July 1788.
10. Phil, born 5th August 1789.
11. Daniel born the 12th January 1792.
12. Jenny was born the 6th November 1794.
13. Sharlotte was born the 10th February ____.
14. Ben was born the 25th October 1798.
15. Nelly was born the 5th January 1801, in the morning.
16. Mary born 12th March 1803, half after eleven, apparently still born.
17. Lucy, born 11th August 1805, three o'clock in the afternoon.
18. Joe, born 9th November 1806, twelve o'clock, Sunday.
19. Prissy, born Sunday night 11th December, 1808.

20. Caroline, born Tuesday morning 28th September 1809.
21. Simon, born Sunday morning 2d September, 1810.
22. Henry born 22d May, 1811.
23. Charles, born 1810.

I left "Totter-down-hill", my seat on Cedar Run, Culpeper County State of Virginia on the 11th of October 1796 and landed at the lower brooks at Limestone, in the State of Kentucky on the fifth of February 1797 and bought a lease of Lewis Day on John Craig's land where I lived till the 15th March 1798 and then moved to Bracken County, my present seat, the Grampain Hill, [signed] Nicholas Taliaferro, 15 March 1811.

TAYLOR FAMILY BIBLE NO. 1

This is probably the earliest known Bible of the ancestors of the Taylor family who lived in the Port Royal area of Caroline County and from whom John Taylor of Caroline descended. Another Bible kept by John Taylor's family appears here as Taylor Bible No. 3 and some of that same information appears in this earlier Bible. This Bible was printed in Manchester, England by Joseph Harrop in the year 1767. It was owned by John Moore Taylor Hamilton at the time the Bible was copied. That copy is now in the Virginia Historical Society.

The ages of the children of James Taylor the Elder
Jane Taylor was born 27 December 1668.
James Taylor was born 14 March 1675.
Sarah Taylor was born 30 June 1676.
The above children were by his first wife [Frances Walker] who died ss September 1680. He married as his second wife Mary [Bishop] Gregory on 10 August 1682. Their children were:
Anne Taylor born 12 January 1685.
Mary Taylor born 29 June 1688.
Edmund Taylor born 5 July 1690.
John Taylor born 18 November 1696.
James Taylor the Elder died 30 April 1698. The second James Taylor married Martha Thompson on 23 February 1699. Their children were:
Frances Taylor born 30 August 1700.
Martha Taylor born 27 January 1702.
James Taylor born 20 March 1704.
Zachary Taylor born 17 April 1707.
George Taylor born 11 February 1711.
Tabitha Taylor born 2 March 1713.
Erasmus Taylor born 5 September 1715.
Milly Taylor born 11 December 1724.
Hannah Taylor was born 15 March 1718.
Jane Moore married Erasmus Taylor in the year 1750.
Jane Moore Taylor was born 22 December 1728.
Milly Taylor daughter of Erasmus and Jane Taylor was born 15 December 1751.

Frances Taylor daughter of Erasmus and Jane Taylor was born 16 December 1753.
Elizabeth Taylor was born 22 September 1755.
Lucy Taylor was born 13 December 1757.
John Taylor was born 26 October 1760.
Robert Taylor was born 29 April 1763.
Jane Taylor was born 2 March 1766.
Anne Gilbert, who married John Taylor, the son of Erasmus and Jane Moore Taylor, was born 13 June 1769.
Anne daughter of John and Anne Taylor was born 4 August 1787.
John Taylor (John Moore Taylor) was born 28 June 1788.
Gilbert Dade Taylor was born 18 November 1791.
William Taylor was born 21 March 1795.
Felix Taylor was born 19 August 1797.
Felix Haywood Taylor was born 21 October 1800.
Maria Taylor was born 9 October 1803.
Anne Foote, who married John Moore Taylor was born 17 March 1788.
Anne Gilbert Taylor, daughter of John Moore Taylor and Anne Foote Taylor was born 28 Jan. 1812.
William Foote Taylor was born 27 December 1813.
Maria Eliza Taylor was born 1 November 1815.
Felix H.G. Taylor was born 21 February 1818.
Children of John Moore Taylor and his wife Anne Foote Taylor continued:
Third son (name not given) was born on 9 May 1820.
Felix H.G. Taylor was born 28 March 1822.
John William Taylor was born 20 October 1824.
Sigismunda Mary Taylor was born 8 September 1827.
Matilda Foote Taylor was born 19 September 1833.
John Moore Taylor married as his second wife Mrs. Caroline E. Thurman who was born 29 July 1824. They were married 24 December 1850.
John Moore Taylor son of John Moore Taylor and Caroline Taylor was born October 1851.
Feliz H.G. Taylor, son of John Moore Taylor and Anne Foote Taylor married Medora Davis born 22 June 1828. They were married 1846.
Felix H.G. Taylor and Medora Davis Taylor had the following children:
John Anthony Taylor was born 2nd August 1847.
Emma Aldridge Taylor was born 27 July 1849.
Anne Taylor was born 18 December 1851.
Medora Taylor was born 9 April 1853.
Anne Troupe Carter was the second wife of Felix H.G. Taylor. She was born 14 June 1827.
James Taylor's first wife (name unknown) died 23 September 1680.
James Taylor the Elder, died 10 September 1698.
James Taylor the 2nd died 23 January 1730.
Martha (Thompson) his wife died 19 November 1762.
Erasmus Taylor died December 1794.
Anne daughter of John Taylor and Anne (Foote) Taylor died 21 August 1787.

Felix Taylor, son of same died 17 February 1799.

Felix H.G. son of same died 1822.

Maria, daughter of John Taylor and Anne died 1st October 1804.

William Taylor son to same died February 1822.

Jane (Moore) Taylor wife of Erasmus died September 1812.

Third son of John Moore Taylor and Anne died 19 May 1820.

Maria Elizabeth Taylor, daughter of same died 20 September 1820.

Felix H.G. Taylor son of same died 8 May 1821.

William F. Taylor son of same died 1st October 1822.

Anne (Foote) Taylor wife of John Taylor the Elder died December 1823.

John William Taylor son of John Moore Taylor died 9 December 1825.

John Taylor the Elder died 6 August 1826.

Matilda Foote Taylor daughter of John Moore Taylor and Anne died 6 April 1836.

Anne G. Davis died 29 October 1837.

Anne Taylor daughter of William Foote and wife to John Moore Taylor died 5 May 1849.

John Anthony son of Felix H.G. Taylor died 20 June 1850.

Anne daughter to same died 1st January 1852.

Medora E. Taylor wife to Felix H.G. Taylor died 27 April 1853.

John Moore Taylor, Senior died 28 February 1856.

James Taylor, the Elder and Mary Gregory were married on 10 August 1682.

James Taylor, the second and Martha Thompson were married on 23 February 1699.

Erasmus Taylor and Jane Moore were married on 13 October 1749.

John Taylor, son of Erasmus Taylor, was married to Anne Gilbert on 6 September 1786.

John Moore Taylor, son of John Taylor and Anne Gilbert Taylor, was married to Anne Foote on 26 March 1811.

Anne Gilbert, daughter of John Moore Taylor and Anne married F.A.W. Davis on 17 January 18--.

Sigismunda Mary, daughter of John Moore Taylor and Anne was married to Oscar Hamilton [date runs off page].

Isabella Taylor was married on January 25th 1750 to Samuel Hopkins and they had the following children:

Samuel Hopkins, Jr. was born on April 9th 1753 GENERAL SAMUEL HOPKINS.

Catherine Hopkins was born March 23rd 1755.

James Hopkins was born on July 27th 1757 and died August 20th 1759.

Elizabeth Hopkins was born on October 30th 1759.

John Hopkins was born on February 20th 1762.

Mary Hopkins was born March 13th 1764.

Edmund Hopkins was born on February 27th 1767.

JOHN PENN SON OF MOSES AND CATHERINE TAYLOR PENN WAS BORN ON MAY 6TH 1740 and DIED SEPTEMBER 14TH 1788. HE WAS A SIGNER OF THE DECLARATION OF INDEPENDENCE.

Felix H.G., son of John Moore Taylor and Anne was married to Medora E. Davis on 29 Jan. 1846.

John Moore Taylor Hamilton, son of Sigismunda Mary Taylor Hamilton and Dr. Oscar Hamilton was married to Sarah E. Collins on 27 January 1876.

TAYLOR FAMILY BIBLE NO. 2

This Bible once belonged to John Taylor, born November 19, 1696, died March 22, 1780. At the time this copy was made the Bible belonged to Mary Blackwell, daughter of James Taylor, deceased. This Bible duplicates some of the information concerning John Taylor of Caroline's family, but appears to be a different Bible, belonging to another branch of the family. A copy of the record is in the Virginia Historical Society. For family connections, see the Pollard Bible elsewhere in this study.

John Taylor, son of James Taylor and Mary his wife, was born on November 18th, 1696 and died March 22, 1780.
Catherine Pendleton, daughter of Philip Pendleton and Isabella [Hurt] his wife, was born December 8th, 1696 and was married to John Taylor on February 14th 1716 and departed life July 26, 1774.
Mary Taylor born May 13, 1718 died September 13, 1757. She was married to Joseph Penn on February 3rd, 1735.
Anne Taylor was born May 10th 1721 and died August 10th 1761.
Edmund Taylor was born May 12th 1723. He was married to Anne Lewis on 25 January 1750.
Isabella Taylor was born June 26, 1725. She was married to Samuel Hopkins on January 25, 1750.
John Taylor was born July 27, 1727.
James Taylor was born September 9, 1729 and died September 20, 1756.
Philip Taylor was born February 17th 1732 and died September 7th 1765.
Elizabeth Taylor was born July 9th 1737. She was married on December 25th 1752 to James Lewis.
William Taylor was born on December 19th 1737 and died November 5th 1803.
Joseph Taylor was born on February 19th 1742. Joseph Taylor was married on April 7th 1763 to Frances Anderson.
William Taylor married July 28th 1763 to Elizabeth Anderson, daughter of Thomas and Sarah (Hardiman) Anderson.
William Taylor and Elizabeth (Hardiman) Anderson Taylor had the following children:
Sarah Taylor born March 5, 1766 and died August 6, 1823.
Anderson Taylor born December 9, 1770 and died December 26, 1858.
John Taylor born February 22, 1773 and died 1847.
Edmund Taylor and Anne Lewis Taylor had the following children:
Lewis Taylor was born August 17th 1751.
Richard Taylor was born January 7th 1753.
Howell Taylor was born October 10th 1754.
John Taylor was born December 4th 1756.
Mary Taylor was born December 3rd 1760.
Edmund Taylor was born 6 July 1753.
Anne Taylor was born 1765.

Elizabeth Taylor was born in 1768. She was married to Josiah Bucks.
Frances Taylor was born on July 24th 1774. She married the Rev. Nathaniel Moore.
James Taylor was born---(1770?). He was married to Anne Pollard they had two children.
John Taylor was born December 19th 1753. HE WAS THE FAMOUS JOHN TAYLOR OF CAROLINE.
Elizabeth Taylor was born January 5th 1756.
Philip Taylor married Mary Walker and they had the following children:
Walker Taylor born November 3rd 1752.
Catherine Taylor born November 4th 1754.
Mary Taylor born December 14th 1756.
Philip Taylor born March 28th 1759.
Anne Taylor born March 10th 1761.

TAYLOR FAMILY BIBLE NO. 3

This Bible belonged to John Taylor of Caroline, who lived at "Hazelwood" near Port Royal in Caroline County. Fortunately the Bible was copied in its entirety by Mrs. Mary Blackwell, formerly Mary Taylor of Bartlett, Tennessee and sent to Joseph W. Taylor who communicated it to Woodson T. White of Waco, Texas in 1870. After Mrs. Blackwell copied the Bible, her home in Bartlett was destroyed by fire and so was the Bible. The record was published in the *William and Mary Quarterly*, Volume 12, 1903, p.128. It has also been reproduced in *Virginia Bible Records* by Jeannette Holland Austin, Willow Bend Books, Westminster, Maryland 2000.
See Penn Bible elsewhere for related information.

John Taylor, son of James Taylor and Mary, his wife, was born November 18, 1696; died March 22, 1780.
Catherine Pendleton, daughter of Phillip Pendleton and Isabella, his wife, was born December 8, 1699, was married to John Taylor, February 14, 1716, and died July 26, 1774.
Mary, daughter of John and Catherine Taylor, was born May 30, 1718, and died September 13, 1757.
Catherine, daughter of John and Catherine Taylor, was born December 30, 1719; died November 4, 1774.
Ann, daughter of John and Catherine, was born May 10, 1721, and died November 4, 1774.
Edmund, son of John and Catherine, was born May 12, 1723.
Isabella, daughter of John and Catherine Taylor, was born June 26, 1725.
John, son of John and Catherine Taylor, was born July 17, 1727, and died October 26, 1787, between 5 & 6 o'clock A.M.
James, son of John and Catherine Taylor, was born Sep. 7, 1729, and died Sep. 26, 1750. Age, 21 years.
Phillip, son of John and Catherine Taylor, was born Feb. 17, 1732, died Sep. 7, 1765.
Elizabeth, daughter of John and Catherine Taylor, was born July 9, 1735.
William, son of John and Catherine Taylor, was born December 19, 1735; baptized January 18th; died November 5, 1803.
Joseph, son of John and Catherine Taylor, was born Feb. 19, 1742, at 10 o'clock in the morning,

and baptized 20th of same month.

William Taylor married Elizabeth Anderson, July 28, 1763.

Sarah, daughter of William and Elizabeth Taylor, was born March 5, 1766.

Anderson, son of William and Elizabeth Taylor, was born October 18, 1761; died 1808.

William, son of William and Elizabeth Taylor, was born December 9, 1770; died December 26, 1854.

John, son of William and Elizabeth Taylor, was born Feb. 20, 1773. Died 1847.

July 4, 1739, I gave my daughter Catherine [Taylor] in marriage to Moses Penn, who died Nov. 4, 1759.

John, son of Moses and Catherine [Penn], was born May 6, 1740, and died Sep. 14, 1788. He was one of the signers of the Declaration of Independence.

February 3, 1735, I gave my daughter Mary [Taylor] in marriage to Joseph Penn.

_____, son of Joseph and Mary Penn, was born Dec. 13, 1736. [Name is obliterated in the original, perhaps George.]

Joseph, son of Joseph and Mary Penn, was born Sep. 27, 1738, died ____.

Catherine, daughter of Joseph and Mary Penn, was born March ll, 1741.

Phillip, son of Joseph and Mary Penn, was born Feb. 6, 1742-3.

Moses, son of Joseph and Mary Penn, was born Dec. 3, 1744.

Elizabeth, daughter of Joseph and Mary Penn, was born 174__.

James, son of Joseph and Mary Penn, was born Aug 12, 174__.

Thomas, son of Joseph and Mary Penn, was born April 25, 174__.

January 25, 1750, I gave my daughter, Isabella, in marriage to Samuel Hopkins.

Samuel, son of Sanuel and Isabella Hopkins, was born April 9, 1753.

Catherine, daughter of Samuel and Isabella Hopkins, was born March 3, 1755.

James, son of Samuel and Isabella Hopkins, was born July 27, 1755, at 9 o'clock in the morning and departed this life on the 20th of August, 1758.

Elizabeth, daughter of Samuel and Isabella Hopkins, was born Oct. 30, 1759.

John, son of Samuel and Isabella Hopkins, was born Feb. 20, 1762.

Mary, daughter of Samuel and Isabella Hopkins, was born Mar. 13, 1764.

Edmund, son of Samuel and Isabella Hopkins, was born Feb. 27, 1767.

Lewis, son of Edmund and Ann Taylor, was born Aug. 17, 1751.

Richard, son of Edmund and Ann Taylor, was born Aug. 17, 1753.

Howell, son of Edmund and Ann Taylor, was born Oct. 16, 1754.

John, son of Edmund and Ann Taylor, was born Dec. 4, 1756.

Mary, daughter of Edmund and Ann Taylor, was born Dec. 3, 1760.

Edmund, son of Edmund and Ann Taylor, was born July 3, 1763.

Eliza, daughter of Edmund and Ann Taylor, was born 1767.

Frances, daughter of Edmund and Ann Taylor, was born July 24, 1771.

James Taylor, born 1763 [this date of birth could be in error]

John, son of James and Ann Taylor, was born Dec. 19, 1753.
  [this is John Taylor of Caroline]

Elizabeth, daughter of James and Ann Taylor, was born January 5, 1756.

Walker, son of Phillip and Mary Taylor, was born Nov. 3, 1752. Died Oct.[no year]

Catherine, daughter of Phillip and Mary Taylor, was born November 4, 1754.

John Taylor, Jr., answered for Mary, daughter of Phillip and Mary Taylor, was born Dec. 14, 1756, and died.[no date]
Phillip, son of Phillip and Mary Taylor, was born Mar. 28, 1759.
Ann, daughter of Phillip and Mary Taylor, was born Mar. 20, 1761.
John, son of Phillip and Mary Taylor, was born Feb. 10, 1763, and died August, 1792.
James, son of Phillip and Mary Taylor, was born Jan. 8, 1765.
December 25, 1752, I gave my daughter Elizabeth in marriage to James Lewis.
James, son of James and Elizabeth Lewis, was born Aug. 28, 1755.
John, son of James and Elizabeth Lewis, was born Oct. 18, 1757.
Charles, son of James and Elizabeth Lewis, was born Aug. 2, 1760.
Mary, daughter of James and Elizabeth Lewis, was born November 22, 1762.
Capt. James Lewis departed this life May 21, 1764, on Monday at 10 o'clock.
Joseph Taylor was born Feb. 19, 1742, and Frances Anderson, his wife, was born Mar. 30, 1743, and they were married April 7, 1763.
Elizabeth, daughter of Joseph and Frances Taylor, was born Octo. 31, 1764.
Mary Ann, daughter of Joseph and Frances Taylor, was born Sep. 24, 1769.
Thomas, son of Joseph and Frances Taylor, was born July 18, 1771.
Joseph, son of Joseph and Frances Taylor, was born Aug. 14, 1773, about 3 o'clock in the morning.
Lucy Penn, daughter of Joseph and Frances Taylor, was born Dec. 9, 1782; died Aug. 22, 1787.
Frances Anderson, daughter of Joseph and Frances Taylor, was born Oct. 11, 1786, and was married 18 Dec., 1804, to John Sumerville.

TAYLOR/BARLOW FAMILY BIBLE

This Bible originally belonged to Frank L. Taylor and his wife Annie B. Barlow, who lived most of their married life at the home place on Ashville Road near Shumansville, Caroline County. The house is no longer standing. They are buried at nearby Mt. Hermon Baptist Church. The Bible is now owned by Herbert Taylor, Jr., Richmond, Va.

This is to Certify that Frank Leon Taylor of Caroline County and Annie Bell Barlow of Caroline County were united by me in the Bonds of Holy Matrimony at Bowling Green on the 21 day of July in the year of our Lord 1890. In the Presence of Mrs. Boggs & daughters. Signed Rev. Boggs. [title page of family register]

Births [children of Frank & Annie B. Taylor]
Maude Virginia - Dec. 10, 1891.
Frank Manley - Oct. 6, 1892.
Harry Mack - Aug. 24, 1895.
Annie Kate - Aug. 4, 1897.
Rosa Myrtle - Sept. 10, 1899.
John Edward - Mar. 11, 1901.
Myrah Alleyne - Mar. 14, 1902.
Wirt Leon - July 25, 1903.

Henry Herbert - Aug. 12, 1905.
Herminia Alice - Feb. 23, 1907.
Clarence Lynwood - May 18, 1908.
Laura Mabel - May 7, 1910.
Everette Dalgus - Feb. 29, 1912.
Deaths
Harry Mack - Oct. 12, 1918.

TAYLOR/BORKEY FAMILY BIBLE

This Bible was in the possession of Mrs. Grace Taylor Borkey, widow of Clyde Borkey of Bowling Green Virginia. She died May 1, 2003 at the age of 99 years.

William H. Taylor, son of William and Delia Taylor born 13 September 1850.
O.J. Taylor, daughter of J. H. and Emily Allen born 7 January 1858.
Eugene Madison Taylor, son of Wm and O. J. Taylor born 13 January 1877.
Park C. Taylor, daughter of Wm and O. J. Taylor born 30 May 1878.
Henry Wesley Taylor, son of Wm and O. J. Taylor born 12 September 1881.
William Albert Taylor, son of Wm and O. J. Taylor born 3 April 1883.
Emmerson Levi Taylor, son of Wm and O. J. Taylor born 9 June 1886.
Harold Quarles Taylor, son of Wm and O. J. Taylor born 16 August
  1889.
Clarice Estell Taylor, daughter of Wm. and O. J. Taylor born ll April 1894.
Brook Olympia Taylor, daughter of Wm. and O.J. Taylor born 17 August 1899.
Grace Eulalia Taylor, daughter of Wm. and O.J. Taylor born 23 August 1903.

TAYLOR/PITTS FAMILY BIBLE

This Bible was in the possession of Mrs. Ollie Taylor Pitts at Kidds Fork, Caroline County, Virginia, when copied by Mrs. Donald Gatewood and published in the *Virginia Genealogical Society Bulletin*. It has also been reproduced in *Virginia Bible Records* by Jeannette Holland Austin, Willow Bend Books, Westminster, Maryland 2000. Most of this family lived in Caroline County.

John C. Taylor and Lucy M., his wife were married 13 day of July 1846. [Lucy was Lucy Myra
  Dillard]
John C. Taylor son of Thomas B. Taylor and Margaret, his wife, was born December 27, 1816.
Lucy M. Taylor was born October 11, 1828.
Burton Lewis Taylor was born 19th day of October 1847 a son of John C. and Lucy Taylor.
Laura A. Taylor was born 23 day January 1850 a daughter of John C. and Lucy Taylor.
James L. Taylor was born 17 day February 1852 a son of John C .and Lucy Taylor.
Virgin T. Taylor was born 13 day January 1854, a daughter of John C. and Lucy Taylor.
Alberta S. Taylor was born 22 day January 1856, a daughter of John C. and Lucy Taylor.
John Lawrence Taylor born October 16, 1858 a son of John C. and Lucy Taylor.

Letha A. Taylor, a daughter of John and Lucy was born October 30, 1861, and died 24 November 1861.
Mary Elizie Taylor was born February 17, 1863, a daughter of John C. Taylor and Lucy M.
Francis L. Taylor was born May 18, 1866, a son of John C. and Lucy M. Taylor.
Margaret P. Taylor the wife of Thomas B. Taylor died November 23, 1845.
Thomas B. Taylor died January 24, 1854.

TERRELL FAMILY BIBLE NO. 1

This Bible, known as the Chiles Terrell family Bible, was owned by the family in Paducah, Kentucky in 1934, when it was copied into the publication *Richmond, William and Timothy Terrell, Colonial Virginians* by Celeste Jane Terrell Barnhill, The Mitchell Company, Greenfield, Indiana, 1934, p.64. Chiles Terrell was the son of Jonathan and Margaret Hunnicutt Terrell, the grandson of David and Agatha Chiles Terrell, and the great-grandson of William and Susannah Water Terrell. William Terrell, son of Robert and Jane Baldwin Terrell of Berkshire, England. William Terrell came to America circa 1670. This Terrell family settled in Caroline County before moving west into Kentucky. Chiles Terrell, was born in Albemarle Co, where he lived 3 years, before moving back to Caroline County with his parents to the estate of his grandfather David, where he grew up. Soon after his marriage to Mary Upshaw, he moved to Richmond, Virginia, where he lived 15 years before moving west. The Terrell family in Caroline County were Quakers and belonged to either the Golansville Meeting House in Caroline or the Cedar Creek Meeting House in Hanover County, Va.

Children of Jonathan and Margaret Hunnicutt Terrell
Elizabeth Terrell, b. March 28, 1778.
Chiles Terrell, b. Feb. 26, 1770; m. May 14, 1810 to Mary Cordelia Upshaw, at the home of her brother, Col. Edwin Upshaw of King & Queen Co., Va. They moved to Kentucky.
Nancy Terrell, b. June 17, 1782 n. m. [never married]
John Terrell, b. May 24, 1784.
Miriam Terrell, b. Nov. 2, 1786; m. Memon Terrell, son of Charles and Susan Tyler Terrell.
Matilda Terrell, b. March 18, 1789; m. Col. Fleming Terrell.Caleb Terrell, b. May 17, 1891; was disowned from Friends for military service.
Thomas Terrell, b. Feb. 24, 1794; m.; went to Paducah, Ky.
Children of Chiles and Mary Upshaw Terrell
John Terrell
Horace Terrell
Ellen E. Terrell
Thomas F. Terrell
Edwin H. Terrell, moved to Spring Creek, Iowa, Jan. 1854. n.m.
Charles J. Terrell.
Mana Terrell.
Martha Terrell, d.y. [died young].
Cordelia Terrell, d.y.

TERRELL FAMILY BIBLE NO. 2

This Bible is owned by Thomasia Hancock Spencer and was copied by Mrs. John P. Jarvis, Georgetown, Kentucky. She has compiled a short history of this Terrell family. A copy of the Bible record is found in the George H.S. King Papers, Virginia Historical Society and a copy was also published in the *Hanover County Historical Society Bulletin*, June 1981. This family lived in both Caroline and Hanover Counties and one branch lived at Beaverdam, Virginia, at a place known as "Emmetts", which is no longer standing. The Bible originally belonged to Joseph Terrell, who married Elizabeth Mills and who was the son of Joseph Terrell.

Joseph Terrell was born 28th January 1745.
Elizabeth [Mills] Terrell was born 26 January 1747.
Ann Terrell was born 6th May 1770.
Charles Terrell was born 3rd July 1768.
Joseph Terrell was born 6th December 1771.
Sarah Terrell was born 14th October 1773.
John Terrell was born 10th October 1775.
Frances & Elizabeth Terrell were born in Sept. 1777.
Mary Mills Terrell was born 8th April 1780.
David Terrell was born 19th August 1782.
Henrietta Terrell was born 11th of March 1784.
Barbara Terrell was born 31st March 1786.
John W. Terrell, Jr. was born 8th October 1809.
John O. Pendleton, son of J. W. & E. H. Pendleton, was born February 6th 1829.
Anne L. Harris, daughter of John O. & B.W. Harris, was born February 25, 1835.
Sarah Harwood Pendleton, daughter of John O. & A. L. Pendleton, was born Sept. 26, 1852.
John Overton Harris Pendleton was born February 6th 1861.
Elizabeth Barbara, daughter of John O. & A. L. Pendleton, was born Jan. 26th 1864.
Joseph and Elizabeth [Mills, daughter of Nicholas Mills] Terrell were married September 29, 1767.
John O. Pendleton of Louisa Co., Virginia and Nannie [Ann Lewis] L. Harris of Albemarle Co. were married the 2nd of October, 1851.
Joseph Terrell, Sr., departed this life 9th April 1787, aged 41 years.
Joseph Terrell, Jr., departed this life 15th December 1790, aged 19 years & 9 days.
Barbara Terrell departed this life 27th February 1797, aged 11 years, 11 months & 24 days.
Ann Terrell departed this life 20th August 1814, aged 44 years, 8 months and 16 days.
David Terrell departed this life August 1839, aged 72 years.
Charles Terrell departed this life August 1839, aged 72 years.
Ann Terrell, wife of Charles Terrell departed this life November 1842, aged 68 years.

TERRELL FAMILY BIBLE NO. 3

This Bible was copied by Mrs. John P. Jarvis, Georgetown, Kentucky. A copy is in the George H.S. King Papers, Virginia Historical Society. It was also published in the *Hanover County*

Historical Society Bulletin, June 1981. Members of this family lived both in Hanover and Caroline Counties.

Harriett A. Jackson was married to Timothy Terrell Sept. 23, 1830.
Catherine F. Terrell was married to Wm. P. Jackson Nov. 18, 1851.
Fannie H. Terrell was married to Chas. R. Francis Feb. 13, 1866.
Chas. N. Terrell son to Timothy and Harriet A. Terrell, born July 25, 1831.
Catherine F. Terrell daughter to Timothy and Harriet A. Terrell, born June 8, 1836.
Fannie H. Terrell daughter to Timothy and Harriet A. Terrell, born Sept. 12, 1842.
John Samuel Francis son to Fannie H. & Chas. R. Francis born Dec. 16, 1866.
Wm. Price Jackson died Aug. 4, 1907.
Catherine F. Terrell Jackson wife of Wm. Price Jackson died Feb. 9, 1918.[buried on the Harris farm on Little River, Hanover Co]
Harriet Anderson Terrell died Dec. 22, 1888 in her 84th year.
John Samuel Francis died Jan. 21, 1889.
Elisabeth Terrell, born Dec. 17, 1794.
Frances B. Terrell born 2nd March 1796.
Hunnarett was born and Sidney B. was born at the same time 21 July 1798.
Courty Benchete [born] 23 March 1800.
Mary Terrell [born] 28 July 1803.
Timothy Terrell [born] 29 May 1804.
Ralph H. Terrell born 22 Apr. 1806.
Sarah Terrell [born] 10 Dec. 1808.
Alexander M. Terrell born 17 Apr. 1813.
Barbara E. Terrell [born] 29 Jan. 1816.
John Quarles Terrell born 8th May 1817.
Richmond Terrell was born 12 Dec. 1810.
Joseph Terrell was born 22 Jan. 1745/6.
Richard L. Jones was born Feb. 13, 1794 and was married to his wife Frances Terrell the 13th day of August 1816, and his wife was born the 21st March 1796.
Lewis Lawrence born Oct. 8th __.
Sarah Ann Terrell daughter of Joseph Terrell and Mary his wife was born 23 June 1753.

TERRELL FAMILY BIBLE NO. 4

This Bible is known as the Ralph H. Terrell Bible. It was copied by Mrs. John P. Jarvis, Georgetown, Kentucky. A copy is in the George H.S. King Papers, Virginia Historical Society. It was also published in the *Hanover County Historical Society Bulletin*, June 1981.

Ralph Henry Terrell was married to Mary Grace Jackson Nov. 17, 1831.
Julian Fox Terrell their son was born June 3, 1833.
George Littleton Terrell was born June 23, 1835.
Richmond Q. Terrell was born April 23, 1838.
William Nelson Terrell was born Aug. 21, 1840.

Mary Elizabeth Terrell was born Sept. 6, 1842.
Almira Jackson Terrell was born Aug. 24, 1844.
Lucy Marian Terrell was born July 16, 1848.
Arabella C. Terrell was born February 3, 1852.
Ralph Henry Terrell departed this life May 22, 1872.
Mary Grace Terrell departed this life 1896.
Lucy Marian J. Terrell departed this life 1915.
Almira Terrell departed this life 1922.
Arabella Terrell and Chas. Clements married Dec. 18, 1879.

TERRELL FAMILY BIBLE NO. 5

This Bible belonged to Samuel and Elizabeth Harris Terrell of "Prospect Hill", later known as "Shannon Mills" on the North Anna River, and now in the Caroline Pines subdivision in Caroline County. The Bible was published in Philadelphia, 1808-09. It was then owned by R. Arnold Ricks, Bennington, Vermont, who donated it to the Virginia Historical Society in 2001. This family were Quakers and worshiped at the Golansville Meeting House in Caroline County. This Bible is important in that it further establishes the burying ground at the Golansville Meeting House, identifying some buried here and the location of the graves.

The ages of the children of Samuel & Elizabeth Terrell are as
 follows viz
Mary Ann Terrell born 3rd day of the 11th months 1801.
Samuel Terrell born 29th day of 12th month 1802.
Walter Terrell born 15th of 4th month 1805.
James P. Terrell born 2nd of 12th month 1808.
Henry O. Terrell born 2nd of 3rd month 1815.
George Fox Terrell born 16th of 10th month 1817.
Mary Ann Terrell daughter of Walter & Margaret Talitha Terrell was born in Iowa City on the
 10th of 8th month 1851.
Names & births of the children of Pleasant & Caty [Farish]Terrell
Lucy Terrell was born on 17th 9th mo 1763.
Jesse Terrell was born on 5th 10th mo 1765.
Robert Terrell was born on 24th 1st mo 1868.
Saml. Terrell was born on 8th 1st mo 1770.
Rachel Terrell was born on 3rd 1st mo 1772.
Nancy Terrell was born on 17th 2nd mo 1775.
Pleasant Terrell was born 26th 11th mo 1778.
Lemuel Terrell was born 2nd 7th mo 1781.
Mary Terrell was born 3rd 2nd mo 1784.
Samuel Terrell and Elizabeth Harris were married the 7th day of the 5th month 1800 which took
 place in the City of Richmond, and believed to be the first marriage of Friends that took
 place there.

Alfred Ricks of Southampton County & Mary Ann Terrell daughter of Samuel & Elizabeth Terrell, were married at Friends Meeting House, Caroline County the 14th of 4 Month 1822.

Walter Terrell, 2nd son of Samuel & Elizabeth Terrell, was married to Margaret T. Crew, daughter of Walter & Sarah Crew, at the Henry House in Mt. Pleasant, Iowa, on the 3rd of 10th month 1850. Both natives of Virginia.

Robert Terrell was married to Nancy Nelson on 4th 1st mo 1817.

Robert Terrell was married (second time) to Sarah T. Burruss on 14th 9th mo 1826.

Departed this life Samuel Terrell Jr son of Samuel & Elizabeth Terrell aged 23 years & some months on 19th day of 10th month 1826. He suffered great excruciating pain with a bilious cholic about 25 days.

Died here on 13th of 10th month 1842 Samuel Terrell Ricks, aged about 16 years. The 2nd son of Alfred & Mary Ann Ricks, of congestive fever, which continued about twenty days. He was here on a visit with his mother. He was interred the next day a[t] Friends meeting house at Golansvile at the east end of the burying ground.

Died at Prospect Hill on 21st 8th mo 1847 Mary Harris Sister to Elizabeth Terrell wife of Saml Terrell. Said M. Harris had been insane for years.

Nancy Terrell wife of Robert Terrell died on 27th 5 mo 1825.

Departed this life Samuel Terrell Sr Husband to Elizabeth Terrell in his 75th year on 14th 8 mo 1844 about 12 minutes after 12 O'clock A.M. He died of Disease of the Heart, which it is supposed he had labored under for 35 or 40 years but recently had assumed an aggravated form. His sufferings were intense for several months before death, but for several hours before death his pains were much mitigated & he died easily & without a convulsion.

Pleasant Terrell father of the above Saml. died on 1st 11 mo. 1803.

Caty Terrell wife of the above Pleasant died on 24th 4th mo. 1813.

Lucy Hargrave daughter of the above Pleasant & Caty Terrell died on __ day 5th mo. 1811.

Robert Terrell son of the above Pleasant & Caty Terrell died on 9th 2 mo 1845.

The four last items are taken from R. Terrell's book of Records.

  G.F.T. [George Fox Terrell]

Elizabeth Terrell, widow of Saml. Terrell Sr. departed this life on 5th 1st mo 1853 about 11 A.M. about 75 years of age. Her disease was pulmonary consumption, with which she lingered & slowly declined for several years. She was interred at Friends Meeting house in Caroline, on 7th 1st mo 1853 at the east end of the burying ground.

Margaret Talitha Terrell wife of Walter Terrell departed this life at their residence near Iowa City the 13th 10th mo 1853.

Taken from a Plaquemine paper La. ---

Died in Palquemine the 14th day 10th mo (1867) James P. Terrell aged about 54 years. __(59_) James P. Terrell had been for over 20 years a resident of the Parish of Ilesville, La, & has during that time pursued his profession of Civil Engineering and Surveyor. He was born in Virginia & has relations in that state, & in the Northwest. With them we mourn his demise. Unobtrusive in manner - always perfectly honest, correct & sincere in all his dealings with his fellow men, he has made himself respected & highly esteemed by all the needy & suffering. Many have been the recipients of his generous gifts. During his last illness he was not neglected, & his body now rests in the Protestant Cemetery of our town, having been deposited by his friends, later most appropriate funeral ceremonies performed by the Rev. C. S.

Dod, Pastor of the Presbyterian Church of this place. [obituary in the handwriting of Mary Ann Terrell Ricks]

TERRELL FAMILY BIBLE NO. 6

This Bible was published by the American Bible Society, N.Y., 1869. A copy is recorded in The Library of Virginia. This appears to be a branch of the Caroline County Terrell family who went to Tennessee in the late 19th Century.

Births

J.C. Terrell Summer Co, Tenn October 29th 1831.

Mary V. Terrell Marshall Co, Tenn Feb 28th 1832.

Sue Anna, daughter of J.C. & Mary V. Terrell 15 minutes before 3 o'clock P.M. May 13th 1872 Fort Worth Texas.

John Lawrence Terrell Son of J.C. & Mary V. Terrell two (2) o'clock P.M. August 1st 1873 Fort Worth, Texas.

Mrs. Susan Penn March 27 1805 Mother of J.C. Terrell.

Joe [probably abbreviation for Josephine] daughter of J. C. and M. V. Terrell died May 1st 1875 at 7 o'clock P.M. Fort Worth.

Mary V. Terrell Daughter of J. C. and Mary V. Terrell January 12th at 4 o'clock A.M. 1877.

Alexander Watkins (A.W.) Terrell Born December 26 1878 Four o'clock A.M. Son of J.C. & M. V. Terrell.

Mrs. Susan Penn [died] Jan. 29, 1901 near Lynchburg, Va.

Joseph C. Terrell & Mary V. Lawson June 1st A.D. 1871 at 9 A.M. by Rev. Davis,[&] P.C. Fox. [probably Percy C. Fox of Caroline County]

Christopher Johnson Terrell baptized August 26 1883 by Rev. Horace Bishop pastor Fort Worth Station N. W. Texas Conference.

Joseph C. Terrell & Mary Peters Young Married at Marshall, Texas March 30 1889 by Rev. John T. McBridge.

Sue A. Terrell baptized by Rev. Wm Price Sept 13th A.D. 1872. P.E. Fox at Ft. Worth Texas N. W. T. Conference.

John Lawrence Terrell baptized Aug. 30th A.D. 1874 by Rev. T. W. Hine & P.E. Fox Fort Worth Texas N. W. Texas Conf.

Jos. C. & Mary V. Terrell baptized August 30, 1877 By M.D. Fly Pastor Ft. Worth Stat. at N. W. Texas Conference.

Alexander Watkins Terrell Baptized July 18 1876 by Rev. M. H. Well Pastor Ft. Worth Station N. W. Texas Conference.

Mrs. Mary V. Terrell [died] November 23 1885 at 1:14 o'clock A.M. Fort Worth Texas.

Joseph C. Terrell [died] Oct 15 1909 at Ft Worth, Texas/ Age 97 yrs ll Mo 15 days.

Little Christopher [died] January 1st 1884, 6:30 A.M. Ft Worth, Texas.

Christopher Johnson Terrell Son of J. C. & Mary V. Terrell Born January 22, 1883 at 1 1/2 P.M. Monday.

Catherine P. Terrell baptized Apr 12 1903 by Rev. Whitehunt.

James Y. Smith Jr. baptized by Dr. Day May 1912.

Samuel Christopher Smith Jr. baptized by Dr. ___ 191___.[illeg]
Mary V. Terrell married James Young Smith April 24 1906 by ___ ___.[illeg}
Births
Catherine ___ [illeg] Terrell, daughter of John ___ Terrell & Anna B. Terrell, Dec. 12, 1902, 5:25 p.m.
John Peter Smith Son of Y. & Mary Terrell Smith Mch. 18, 1909.
Josephine Terrell Smith daughter of Y. & Mary Terrell Smith March ___ [illeg] 1909.
J. Y. Smith Jr. Son of J. Y. & Mary Terrell Smith born Jan 30th 1912, 12 p.m. Tuesday.
Samuel Christopher Smith Son of J. Y. & Mary Terrell [Smith] born ___ ___ [illeg] Apr 20 1916.

TERRELL FAMILY BIBLE NO. 7

This Bible was owned by Mrs. Roberta Terrell Jarvis of Georgetown, Kentucky in 1979 when she made it available to be included in the publication *More Than Skin Deep* by Mary Douglas Meriwether Blaydes, Goins Printing Company, Lexington, Kentucky. Some earlier ancestors were buried in the Quaker Meeting House Cemetery in Caroline County, Virginia. This family is the same as Terrell Bible No. 2.

John Terrell was the son of Joseph & Elizabeth Mills Terrell. She was daughter of Nicholas Mills. Register of the ages of the children:
Chiles Terrell b. 3rd day of July 1766.
Ann Terrell, b. 6th of May 1770.
Joseph Terrell b. 6th day of December 1771.
Sarah Terrell b. 14th of October 1773.
John Terrell b. 10th of October 1775.
Mary Mills Terrell b. 8th of April 1780.
David Terrell b. 19th of August 1782.
Henrietta Terrell b. 11th of March 1784.
Barbara Terrell b. 21st of March 1786.
John Terrell was b. 10th of October 1775 and Elizabeth Terrell, his wife, b. 2nd March 1783. Register of their children:
Joseph C. Terrell was born 7th of December 1807.
John W. Terrell was born 8th of October 1809.
Sarah Ann Dabney Terrell born 5th of December 1811.
Elizabeth Agnes Terrell b. 25th of September 1813.
Mary Maria Terrell b. 7th June 1814.
Thomas Jackson Terrell, born 31st of July 1818.
Dorothy Barbara Terrell b. 16th of June 1821.
Thomas J. Terrell departed this life 21st day of April 1839. At the time of his departure he was 22 years, 5 months and 21 days.
John Terrell Sr died on March 4, 1852. At the time of his death he was 46 years, 4 months and 23 days.

Dorothy B. Terrell died July 30th 1852. She was 31 years, 1 month and 13 days old.

Joseph Carr Terrell married Ann E. Terrell on August 31, 1845. Their son, Charles Thomas Terrell, b. in May 1852 and married Fannie Pierce McGehee (b. Nov. 27, 1852) on Oct. 12, 1876.

Joseph Stuart Terrell, b. Oct 18, 1886; m. Roberta Yancey Winfred (b. Oct 11, 1882) on June 24, 1914.

TERRELL/COBB FAMILY BIBLE

This Bible was published by Ziegler & McCurdy in 1872. It was originally owned by John Thomas Terrell and Ella Anderson Cobb, both of Caroline County. It is presently owned by Vivian Jackson, Brewton, Alabama, who is a descendant of the original owner. It was given her by her grandmother, Louise Terrell Campbell of Caroline County, Virginia., whose daughter, Ertelle Campbell was Vivian Jackson's mother.

John Thomas Terrell the son of Linsey L. Terrell & Mary A. Terrell was born August 90th 1880.
Ella Anderson Cobb the daughter of James E. & Maria L. Cobb, was born March 30th 1855.
Linsey Lewis Terrell Jr. the son of John T. & Ella A. Terrell was born September 25th 1872.
James Edward Terrell the son of John T. Terrell & Ella A. Terrell was born August 27th 1874.
Eva Adelaid Terrell the daughter of John T. & Ella A. Terrell was born December 10th 1876.
Aubin Cobb Terrell the son of John T. & Ella A. Terrell was born October 6th 1880.
Maria Louise Terrell the daughter of John T. & Ella Terrell was born Dec. 10th 1883.
John Thomas Terrell Jr. the Son of John T. & Ella A. Terrell was born Dec. 31st 1885.
Conway Ella Terrell the Daughter of John T. & Ella A. Terrell was born March 14th 1887.
William Lewis Terrell the son of John T. & Ella A. Terrell was born Jan. 29th 1892.
Eva Ade;aode Terrell, the daughter of John T. & Ella A. Terrell was married to Edward Franklin Cobb son of M.T. & Maggie A. Cobb, Oct. 18, 1899.
Linsey L. Terrell Jr. departed his life August 19th 1873.
James E. Terrell departed his life November 1874.

TERRELL/RICKS FAMILY BIBLE

This Bible belonged to Mary Ann Terrell and Alfred Ricks, who lived at "Prospect Hill", now known as "Shannon Mills", located in the Caroline Pines subdivision in Caroline County. The Bible probably was originally owned by Dr. George Fox Terrell of Caroline County. It was published in Philadelphia in 1850 and was last owned by a descendant, R. Arnold Ricks of Bennington, Vermont, great-grandson of Alfred & Mary Terrell Ricks. He donated it to the Virginia Historical Society in 2001. Alfred & Mary T. Ricks are both buried near the house at "Shannon Mills". George Fox Terrell is buried in the cemetery at the Golansville Quaker Meeting House, Caroline County. Some of this material duplicates the material in the preceding Bible since it is the same family.

The ages of the children of Samuel & Elizabeth Terrell are as follows - viz -
Mary Ann Terrell was born 3rd day of 11th mo. 1801.

Saml Terrell Jr. was born 29th day 12 month 1802.

Walter Terrell was born 14th 4th Month 1805.

James P. Terrell was born 2d 12 mo 1808.

Henry O. Terrell was born 2d 2rd mo 1808.

Geo. F. Terrell was born 16th 10th mo 1817.

Saml Terrell and Elizabeth Harris were married the 7th day of 5th month 1800, which took place in the City of Richmond and believed to be the first marriage of Friends that took place there.

Alfred Ricks, of Southampton County, & Mary Ann Terrell daughter of Samuel & Elizabeth Terrell, were married the 14th 4 mo 1822 at Friends Meeting House Caroline County Va.

Robert Terrell was married to Nancy Nelson on 4th 1st month 1817. Robert Terrell was married the Second Time to Sarah T. Burruss on 14th 9 month 1826 & left no children by either wife. Later Sarah Burruss Terrell married Elis Wortham.

Departed this life, Saml. Terrell Jr. Son of Saml & Elizabeth Terrell aged 23 years & some months on 19th day 10 month 1826. He suffered great excruciating pain with a bilious cholic for 25 days.

Died here (at Prospect Hill Caroline) on 13th 10 mo 1842 Saml Terrell Ricks aged about 16 years, the 2d Son of Alfred & Mary A. Ricks, of congestive fever which continued about 20 days. He was here on a visit with his mother. He was interred the next day at Friends Meeting House at Golansville at the east end of the burying ground. Died at Prospect Hill on 21st 8 mo 1847 Mary Harris Sister of Elizabeth Terrell wife of Saml Terrell. Mary Harris had been insane for years.

Nancy Terrell fist wife of Robt. Terrell died on 27th 5 mo 1825.

Departed this life Saml. Terrell Sr husband of Elizabeth Terrell in his 75th year on 14th 8 mo 1844 about 12 minutes after 12 o'clock A.M. He died of a disease of the heart which it is supposed he had laboured under for 35 or 40 years. His sufferings were intense for several months before death but for several hours before death his pains were much mitigated & he died easily & without a convulsion.

Pleasant Terrell father of the above Saml died 1st 11 mo 1803.

Caty Terrell wife of the above Pleasant died on 24th 4th mo 1813.

Lucy Hargrave daughter of the above Pleasant died on __ day 4 mo 1811.

Robert Terrell Son of the above Pleasant & brother of Saml Terrell Sr died on 9th 2nd mo 1845.

Note The four last items are taken from Robt. Terrell's book of records [this reference was written in the Bible]

Elizabeth Terrell widow of Saml Terrell Sr. departed this life on 5th 1st mo 1853 about 11 A.M. about 75 years of age. Her disease was pulmonary consumption, with which she lingered & slowly declined for several years. She was interred at Friends Meeting House in Caroline on 7th 9th mo 1853 at the east end of the burying ground.

Departed this life on the 28th of the 5th March 1855 Dr. George F. Terrell aged about 37 the youngest son of Samuel & Elizabeth Terrell. An eminent physician of high intellectual & scientific attainments which were made subservient to his practices; his ardious duties & devotion to which it is believed, wore on a naturally feeble constitution & shortened his days - He was taken off suddenly supposed of Congestion of the brain while engaged in an extensive sphere of usefulness. He was interred at Friends Meeting House in Caroline County on the 30th of 5th mo 1855 at S. east end of the burying ground near his mother. His memory is embalmed in the hearts of the poor and afflicted.

E.A.R.[Ricks]

Died in Plaquemine the 14th day 10 mo 1869 - James P. Terrell, aged about 54 years. Mr. Terrell has been for over twenty years a resident of the Parish of Iberville, Louisiana, and has during that time pursued his profession of civil Engineering and Surveyor. He was born in Virginia and his relations in that state, and in the North-West. With them, we mourn his demise. Unobtrusive in manner - always perfectly honest, correct and sincere in all his dealings with his fellow men, he has made himself respected and highly esteemed by all who came in contact with him. Silently and even secretly, he helped from his purse the needy and suffering. Many have been the recipients of his generous gifts. During his last illness he was not neglected and his body now rests in the Protestant Cemetery of our town, having there been deposited by his friends after most appropriate funeral ceremonies performed by the Rev. C.S. Dod, Pastor of the Presbyterian Church of this place.

THOMAS FAMILY BIBLE NO. 1

The family record of this family was recorded in a John Wesley Prayer Book published in Bristol, September 9, 1784. It was first owned by Susannah Boulware who married William Thomas Jr. It passed from them to a grandson James Thomas Jr. and his wife, Elizabeth Andrews, who moved from Thomas' Neck, Essex County to "Vernon" plantation, Caroline County. By the 1890's, the little book had traveled with a family member to Detroit, Michigan. Somehow the prayer book found its way to a Washington, D.C. antique shop, where it was purchased by someone and taken to an Arlington County, Virginia book dealer, from which the author of this study purchased it. It is now deposited in the Virginia Historical Society. Much of the data is recorded on added pages which have been sewn into the original book. Mention of the existence of this prayer book was made when *The Thomas Book* was published in 1896 in a footnote on page 103. Information concerning the slaves owned by this family is also recorded in the prayer book. Some of the material in the prayer book is recorded in duplication, and is included here in its entirety. The records in this prayer book have been published in *Tidewater Virginia Families*, Volume 6, Number 6, November 1997, pp.160-170.

Slaves of James and Elizabeth Thomas, Caroline Va.
Rachel the daughter of Judy was Born the 18th Day of December 1792.
Billy the Son of Judy was Born the 17 Day of November 1793.
Cook the Son of Judy was Born the 12 Day of February 1796.
Affiah The daughter of the above was Born the 17 of April 1790.
Sam The Son of The Above was Born The 15 Day of February 1799.
Leeannah The Daughter of The Above was Born The 10 Day of Augst 1802. [end of entry of slaves]
Isabella M. Thomas [name on first inside page]
Susannah Thomas [name on back of first page]
Names of Children of James & Elizabeth Thomas
Nancy Thomas, The daughter of James Thomas and Elizabeth Thomas Was Born The 3 Day of November 1793 and Departed This Life July 30th 1795.

Archer Thomas Born March 28th Day 1796.
Susannah Thomas was Born August 12, 1798.
James Thomas Born January The 1 Day - 1801 and departed This life March 13 - 1804.
Ira Thomas and Emmiline Born May 13 = 1803.
Elizabeth Andrews 1791 [name written at top of page A5].
August 18 - 1892 [written on a sliver of paper used as a bookmark at page 17].
By Rachel Thomas/Caroline County [written on page 166]
Feb 16th 1905 [written in pencil on page 193].
James and William Thomas were born 8th of February 180[6]. [page torn] The latter departed this life May 14th 1810.
Elizabeth Thomas Born November The 22 = 1812.
Elizabeth Thomas [no further info listed].
Silas, slave was born the 1st Day of October 1811.
James Thomas The Son of Thomas was born the 2 Day of March 1765.
Elizabeth Thomas was born November 28, 1768.
James Thomas was married to Elizabeth Andrews the 9 Day of January 1793.
Nancy Thomas the daughter of the above was Born 3 day of November 1795.
Archer Thomas Born March The 28 Day 1796.
Susannah Thomas The Daughter of James Thomas and Elizabeth Andrews, was born the 12th of August 1798.
James Thomas and Elizabeth Andrews were married 9 day of January 1793.
James Thomas the Son of James Thomas was born February 8, 1806.
Hannah, Slave of James Thomas came from Essex, Va.
James Thomas & Elizabeth [no further info listed]
Fanny, the slave of William Thomas of Thomas Neck, Essex Co., Va. inherited by James Thomas, also her son John & daughter Winnie.
James Thomas was born March 2, 1765.
Elizabeth his wife Novr 28, 1762.
Nancy Thomas Do.[ditto] Nov 3, 1793.
Archer Thomas do. March 28, 1796.
Susannah Thomas Aug 12, 1798.
James Thomas do. Jany 1, 1800.
Ira & Emeline Thomas May 13, 1803.
James & Wm Thomas do. Feby 8, 1806.
Elizabeth G. Thomas do. Nov 11, 1811.
James Thomas was born the 8 Febry 1806.
James Thomas and Elizabeth Andrews were married The 9 day of January 1793.
[2 lines illegible]
Cynthia, slave died [no date]
Ira Thomas the Son of James [blank] 13, 1803.
Slaves of James & Elizabeth Thomas
Sam & Nancy came [illegible].
Dinah, the daughter of Sally Was Born the 30 May 1813.
Robert the Son of Hannah was Born The 4 Day of August 1813.

Issac was Born the 17 Day of May at Dommi__ 1811 The Son of Sally.
Phillip The son of Hannah was Born Nover 30 Day 1805.
Mahulda was born the 27 of Aug 1815.
Nelson was born the 14 of December 1815.
Maria was born August 15th 1803.
Henry was born August 28th 1806.
Nutty was born July 29th 1809.
Issac was Born 17th of May 1811.
Matilda daughter of Sally was born [no date].
Delilah daughter of Sally was born [no date].
Sidney wife of Billy [no further info]
Cupid the son of Sally was born the 18th Octr 1821.
William Roane was born [no date].
Amelia the daughter of Leah was born March 23rd 1822.
Leannoh was born 1822.
Nancy wife of Cook [no further info].
Mary was Born April 25, 1824.
Barbary was Born September the 15 - 1824.
[The following slaves are listed "was born" without dates given]
Eliza, Henry, Samuel, Ned, Frank, Elizabeth, Isaac, Waller, Jessie, William, Albert, Kemp, Hannah, Leah, Henry & Milly, Frank, Jenny & Frank.
Iran Thomas bought Margaret and Henry of Semple Broaddus.
Judy & Rachel & Sam and Henry were slaves of Elizabeth Andrews of Caroline County, Va. who was born 1768 in Essex Co. and was married to James Thomas, son of William Thomas of Thomas' Neck, Essex Co. Va. Said James Thomas born 2 March 1765 and married Elizabeth Garnett Andrews 9th Jan. 1793. Joicie Garnett married Joshua Andrews.

Slaves

Fannie and her children John & Winnie, James Thomas inherited from his Father Wm Thomas of Thomas' Neck, Essex Co Va. He also brought with him out of Essex, his slave Hannah and when he married brought home his slave man Will & slave Sally.
Susannah Thomas Seventeen hundred and [rest not finished].
William Thomas of Thomas' Neck, Essex Co Va. was son of William Thomas of England, his sons were Lewis, Edmund and James. Capt. William Billy Thomas, inherited Thomas' Neck in Essex Co., Va. from his grandfather Wm and father Lewis_____. William Thomas sold Thomas' Neck to Payne Warring. He had one male descendant who went West & left no descendants. Archer, Ira Lomax Thomas, and James Thomas Jr. son of James Thomas, were the representatives of William Thomas of Thomas' Neck Essex Co Va. Said Thomas' Neck was sold in the year of (seventeen) [scratched out and 18 written in] hundred. His Father Wm Thomas having come from England. Archer Thomas left a son Wilson Cary Thomas of Richmond Va.. Ira Thomas had a son James Thomas in the Army of the South killed at Gettysburg 1862, Pickett's Div. James Thomas Jr. left one son Dr. Wm D. Thomas in Richd, Va. when he died Oct 8th 1882. James Thomas Jr. left one son Dr. Wm D[andridge] Thomas in Richd, Va. when he died Oct 8th 1882.
William Thomas, of Thomas' Neck, had besides his sons Lewis, Edmund and James in

seventeen hundred & sixty [sixty marked out] daughter Catharine who married Capt Billy White of Hanover Co. Va., Susannah Thomas, who married J[oseph] Cropp of Stafford and Elizabeth Thomas who married Joe [Joseph] Brame of Caroline Co., Va. Catharine Thomas White & Capt. Billy White of Hanover Co., Va had sons Dick, Warner, James, etc. others. Warner White's son Malvern lives at old place Chilesburg, near Western boundary of Hanover Co., Va. Achillian White married a wealthy widow of Bedford. His son Sam and daughter Anna live near Salem, Roanoke Va. The daughters of Catharine Thomas White & Capt. Billy W. were Eliza (married a Methodist Minister McDowell. Elizabeth White married Partloe and Alice (married Phillips). Susannah Thomas of Stafford Co. Va born Thomas' Neck, Essex Co. Va had sons Warner & Dick. Elizabeth Thomas of Thomas' Neck, Essex, married Brame of Caroline County, Va. {had a daughter Betsy Brame who moved West with half brothers and sisters [sisters marked out] and never heard from [never heard from marked out]James Rowzee Thomas of Essex Co. Va. born at Thomas' Neck, Essex Co. Va. 1765 had daughters Nancy, Susan, Emmeline & Elizabeth. Susan Thomas married Thomas Patterson and {had 2 sons} and ["and" marked out] left a son Dr. R. Archibald Patterson of Richd., who has five sons Fuller & Purnet & James, Archie & Melvian & 2[?] daughters Lizzie and Josephine [above the name Josephine and in between the lines is written "married Cottrell"] & Emmeline Patterson. Lottie [sic] married John Hutcheson and {they have} left sons in Richd. Va. James & John & daughters Florrie & Susan. Florrie Hutcheson married W.H.A. Smith of Washington [Washington marked out] Russell Co. Va. and has four sons Douglas, James Thomas, John Henry of Richd, Va., and Garnett. James Thomas, Jr. had daughters Ella who married Dr. W.D. Quisenberry of Caroline Co. Va., Mary married Dr. J. L. M. Creasy from Ala (then of Rich'd), Alice married Col.J[ohn] K[err]Conally of N.C., Louisa married Thomas Rutherford of Rich'd, Va., Bettie married Wallers Allison of Rich'd, Va., Kate {Kornick, Carmick} married Colderon Carlisle of Washington, D.C. and Gabrielle married Richmond Pearson of Asheville, N.C. Ira L. Thomas, son of James Thomas of Caroline Virginia married Mary Jones Morgan of Richd. Va. The had sons James, Daniel H., Ira and Archibald and daughters Emiline, Mary Hannah, Isabell, Alice & Ann Eliza. Ann Eliza married J[ames] T[homas] Hurt of Caroline Va. had a daughter Lizzie Rowland Hurt & moved to Detroit, Michigan. His son Ira Hurt died at five [marked through, four added in pencil] years old Mary Hannah Elizabeth Thomas married Rowland Green Tyler of Detroit, Michigan and moved there. Emilie Thomas James R. McTyre of Chesterfield Co. Va. Isabelle Thomas moved to King Wm Co Va. Archer Thomas had daughters Julia who married Dr. A. E. Wortham of Richd Va. & A. E. Wortham of Richd. & Caroline V. Thomas who married Josiah Ryland, Richd., Va. Julia Wortham had daughters Bertie who married John Williams, Richd., Va., Kate married Col A.S. Bufort, Richd. and Deanie married Josiah Ryland [Josiah apparently married sisters]. Callie Thomas Ryland left a daughter Callie Ryland. Ira L. Thomas, born 1803, son of James Thomas & Elizabeth Garnett Andrews Thomas of Caroline Co., Va. was educated in classics and sciences by Thos Nelson of Humanity Hall Academy, Hanover Va. as well as James White his cousin and other White cousins, son of Capt. Billy & Catharine Thomas White of Hanover Co., Va. Also his cousin Henry Garnett, a lawyer, of King & Queen Co., Va., son of Thomas & Frances Garnett, was educated at same school, and practiced at bar in Essex & K & Queen Co. His sister Emily Garnett was educated by Miss Hill in Hanover Co, Va. They were cousins of Muscoe Garnett & their brothers were John etc. of King & Queen Co. Va. The Favors [Favor] of Essex were related to Wm Thomas of Thomas' Neck in Essex Co in seventeen hundred and one of these moved to Caroline & married [John] DeJarnette.Isaac was born the 17 Day May A. Donn__ 1811.

Susanna Thomas was born 12th Day of August 1790.

William Thomas' Slaves Sam to Henry came by Elizabeth Andrews who married James Thomas 1793.

Nelson was born December 14th 1815.

[Joseph Brame and Elizabeth Thomas were married in Caroline County January 9, 1794.]

THOMAS FAMILY BIBLE NO. 2

This Bible originally belonged to William Thomas, son of Lewis & Margery Thomas, who was born in 1788. According to a deposition made concerning George Thomas, son of Sally Thomas and made in 1844, the family record was cut from this Bible, before the Bible was sold by the sheriff. (See Deposition and other documents taken in Caroline County related to the contested election to the House of Delegates between Archibald Samuel and Andrew S. Broaddus, April, 1844, Virginia General Assembly Contested Elections 1842-1844, Caroline County folder, Box 12, Library of Virginia). A copy of this Bible record is also in the Bible Record Collection, Library of Virginia. No date is given as to when the record was cut by the sheriff. George Thomas owned land both in Caroline and Essex Counties in 1844. The deposition states that this George Thomas was born 9 Feb. 1823 and also states that one of Sally Thomas' children went to Louisville, Kentucky and had not been heard of since. In 1844, the family register was owned by Edward Kay, uncle of George Thomas.

William Thomas, son of Lewis Thomas & Margery his wife, was born July 28 1788.
Robert Thomas, son of above, was born 13 January 1790.
Polley H. Thomas, daughter of above, was born 15 Sept 1791.
Patsy Thomas, daughter of above, was born 30 August 1793
Lewis Henshaw Thomas, son of above, was born 19 September 1795.
Salley Newman Noel, daughter of Ellison Noel and Margery his wife, was born 6 April 1799.
James Thomas, son of William Thomas and Salley his wife, was born 10 March 1812.
John Miles Thomas, son of above, was born 14 May 1814.
William Richard Thomas, son of the above, was born 19 Feb. 1816.
Mary Thomas, Daughter of above, was born 19 Oct. 1817.
Robert Lewis Thomas, Son of above, was born 8 Nov. 1819.
Edmond Thomas, son of above, was born 27 May 1821.
George Franklin Thomas, son of above, was born 9 Feb. 1823.
William Thomas and Sally his wife was Married 14th May in the year of Our Lord 1811.
Edward Clarke was admitted into this world by my kind master in the year of our Lord eighteen hundred and sixteen. This was written March the 10th 1835. E. L.C. was born the year 1815. March 10th 1835 I was 18 years 2 months ten days old.

THOMAS FAMILY BIBLE NO. 3

This Bible record was submitted to the Federal Government for a pension for services in the Revolutionary War for Catlett Thomas Sr., who was born November 14, 1763 and died October 27, 1847 in Caroline County, Virginia. He signed up for duty in both Essex and King & Queen Counties, but resided in Caroline County. He married Mary Dobson December 27, 1788 in Essex County, Virginia. She submitted the cut Bible pages when she applied for a widow's pension. The Bible apparently originated with this couple and contains data on their 13 children. The handwriting appears to have all been done at the same time by the same person.

This Thomas family married into the LeFoe families of Caroline and King George Counties, the Green family of King George County, and the Rose family of Caroline County. Of the descendants in Caroline County, Pittman Thomas married Sarah Ragan December 22, 1824 in Caroline County. Their son, Pittman A. Thomas, was deputy treasurer for Caroline County, married twice, first to Emma Haynes, daughter of George L. Haynes, and secondly to her sister Lucy Haynes, and died December of 1940, at the age of 82. His son Pitman A. Thomas died in 1992, at the age of 99; and a daughter Ruth Virginia Thomas, married James Clarence Collins in 1922. Some of this family are buried at "Berry Grove" and others at Lakewood Cemetery, both in Caroline County. Alma J. Giddis, who lives at Partlow, Virginia, is a direct descendant of Catlett Thomas, Sr. and still lives in the area of Caroline County.

Catlett Thomas was born the 14th day of November 1763.
Mary Dobson, the wife of Catlett Thomas was born the 5th day of February 1768.
The age of their Children
William Thomas was born the 13th day of September 1789.
Elizabeth Thomas was born the 9th day of October 1799 & Lewey with her and is not but Dead.
Catlett Thomas was born the 11th day of September 1794.
[Note: The next three entries are for Mary, Rebekah, and Nancy Thomas, were marked out and re-entered later in the Bible]
Pitman Thomas & Phebe Thomas was born the 14th day of September 1797.
Mary Thomas was born the 2th day of October 1799.
Rebekah Thomas was born the 29 day of October 1801.
Nancy Thomas was born the 29th day of January 1804.
Susanna Thomas was born the 2th day of October 1805.
Thomas [sic] Thomas was born the 12th day of September 1807.
James Thomas was born the 29th day of August 1810.
Silas Thomas was born the 12th day of September 1812.
William Jones the son of Thomas Jones & Elizabeth his wife was born the 9th of March 1816.
Catlett Thomas was married to Mary Dobson the 27th day of december [sic] 1788.
Thomas Jones was married to Elizabeth Thomas the 15th of October 1813.
Catlett Thomas Jr the son of Catlett Thomas Sr was married the 13th of Apr 1819 his wife was Ann Toombs.
Pittman Thomas was married to Sarah Ragan the 23 of December 1825.
Ann Thomas was married to Allen Rose the 3rd day of April 1832.

Thomas Thomas was married the 19th day of January 1848.

THOMSON FAMILY BIBLE

This Bible is known as the J. Rawling Thomson Family Bible and is filed with the Minor Bible in the Albemarle County Historical Society, Charlottesville, Virginia.

Bettie Watson Rawlings Born in Charlottesville, Va. April 1st, 1869 at the home of her Grandfather, Judge Egbert R. Watson. Married in Clarksville, Tenn. to Dr. Charles West Thomson of Spartanburg, S.C. June 9th, 1892 at the residence of her Father Rev. James Minor Rawlings. Died in Spartanburg, S.C. June 19th, 1893 at her home on Converse St. leaving an infant, James Rawlings Thomson two months old.

James Rawlings Thomson son of Dr. Charles West Thomson & Bettie Rawlings Thomson was born in Spartanburg, S.C. April 21st ,1893.

James Rawlings Thomson married March 3, 1934 Velora Ames Carver (June 28, 1900-   ) at the home of her mother Mrs. Thomas Payne Carver 100 W. High Street, Charlottesville, Virginia.

James Rawlings Thomson, son of Dr. Charles West & Bettie Rawlings Thomson, died November 27, 1964, in Charlottesville, Va. Buried in Maplewood Cemetery, Charlottesville, Va.

[newspaper clipping of the obituary of James Rawlings Thomas, 71, November 27, 1964 in included in record.]

THORNLEY FAMILY BIBLE NO. 1

This family record is taken from an old Prayer Book, which copy was given a Mrs. Grayson by her cousin, Mary Amelia Smith, daughter of William Smith ("Extra Bill"), twice Governor of Virginia. It was reproduced in the *National Genealogical Society Quarterly*, Vol XXII, No. 4, p. 96, December 1934. John Thornley came from Bristol, England and married Ann Berry and died before 1790. Their son, Aaron Thornley lived at "White Plains" and "Poplar Grove", both in King George County and he was twice married. He died in King George County at the age of seventy years. Most of their children settled in Caroline County.

Aaron Thornley and Catherine, his wife, married April 9, 1772.
(Their Children):
Enoch Berry Thornley, born February 6, 1773; died April, 1778.
William Thornley, born January 2, 1775; died February 27, 1837.
Judith Berry Thornley, born May 31, 1777; died February 28, 1788.
Francis Ann Thornley, born Sept. 8, 1779.
Elizabeth Thornley, born November 18, 1781.(married William Murdock and had issue).
Jean Thornley, born Sept. 26, 1783.
Mary Matilda Thornley, born January 27, 1786.
Thomas Berry Thornley, born February 17, 1788.*

Judith Ann Thornley, born February 17, 1788.
Catherine Thornley, born July 22, 1790.
Lucy Thornley, born January 25, 1793.

*[Thomas Berry Thornley married Mary ____ and had a daughter Mary S. Thornley, born in King George County, who married Henry Thornton in Caroline County. Mary S. Thornton died in Caroline County June 1876 at the age of 54.]

THORNLEY FAMILY BIBLE NO. 2

This Bible was printed and published by Matthew Carey, Philadelphia, 1811 and sold by William F. Gray, Bookseller and Stationer, Fredericksburg, Va. It originally belonged to Jane (Riding) Thornley, wife of William Thornley. It passed to Mrs. John Cooke Grayson, Charlottesville, Virginia, only daughter of Dr. John Thornley. Mrs. Grtayson was given these records from an old Prayer Book, which copy was given her by her cousin, Mary Amelia Smith, dau. Of William Smith ("Extra Billy") twice Governor of Virginia. A copy is now in the King George Historical Society, King George, Va. A copy was printed in the *National Genealogical Society Quarterly*, Vol. XXXII, No. 4, p. 98, December, 1944. The two copies vary slightly and have been meshed together here. More than half of this family married and lived in Caroline County. The old Dangerfield estate in Caroline County was "Belvidere", still standing south of New Post on Route 17. The Stevens Farish estate as "North Point" on the Mattaponi River near Woodford and burned some years ago. A later Farish place stood on Route 17 just west of Port Royal and was named Hazelwood after Hazelwood Farish. It was later the home of John Taylor of Caroline. The Thornley place was in the Fort A.P. Hill Reservation.

MARRIAGES:
Aaron Thornley and Catherine, his wife, m. 4/9/1792.
William Thornley and Jane, his wife, were married December 22nd, 1796. [lived entire life in
  Caroline County]
Emily Thornley, Daughter of William Thornley and Jane, his wife and Hazelwood Farish, son of
  Stephen [Stevens] Farish and Catherine [Tod], his [second] wife, were married March the
  15th, 1821 [in Caroline County].
Ann Eliza Thornley, daughter of William & Jane Thornley, and Bland Dangerfield, son of
William Henry Dangerfield, were married Sept 2nd, 1824 [in Caroline County].
[Martha] Jane Thornley, daughter of William & Jane Thornley, and Thomas West, son of Ellis
  West and Charity, his wife, were married May 11th, 1830 [in Caroline County].
Aaron Thornley, son of Wm Thornley and Jane, his wife, and Mary M., daughter of Thomas
  Buckner and Lucy, his wife, were married May 14, 1833 [in Caroline County].*
William Thornley, son of William Thornley and Jane, his wife, and Sarah P., daughter of Mark
  Boulware and Lucy, his wife, were married [in Caroline County] December 20th, 1838.**
James Thornley, son of William Thornley and Jane Thornley, and Catherine C., daughter of Jesse
  & Helen White, were married on the 16th day of April 1850, in the town of Charlottesville, Va.
John, 3rd son of William & Jane Thornley, was married to Mary Downes, 1st daughter of
  Nathaniel & Rose Pearce in Baltimore, April 2nd, 1856.

Caroline Virginia Thornley, daughter of William and Jane Thornley, was married to George C. Omohundro, son of John Omohundro and Nancy Crank, his wife, October 5, 1858.

BIRTHS:

Children of Aaron Thornley and Catherine, his wife:

Enock Thornley 2/6/1773-4/1778.

William Thornley, son of Aaron Thornley and Catherine, his wife, was born Jan. 2, 1775.

Judith Berry Thornley 5/31/1777-2/28/1788.

Frances Ann Thornley 9/8/1779.

Jane Riding, Daughter of George T. Riding and Winney, his wife, was born June 18, 1780.

Elizabeth Thornley 11/18/1781.

Jean Thornley 9/26/1783.

Mary Matilda Thornley 1/27/1786.

Thomas Berry Thornton 2/17/1788.

Judith Ann Thornley 2/17/1788.

Catherine Thornley 7/22/1790.

Lucy Thornley 1/25/1793.

Children of William and Jane Riding Thornley:

Emily Thornley, daughter of William Thornley and Jane, his wife, was born Nov. 10, 1797.

Ann Eliza Thornley, daughter of William and Jane Thornley, was born October the 25th, 1800.

Aaron Thornley, son of William and Jane Thornley, was born April 23, 1803.

Maria Thornley, daughter of William and Jane Thornley, was born December 9, 1805. (she never married)

Jane Thornley, daughter of William and Jane Thornley, was born January 6th, 1808.

Catherine Thornley, daughter of William and Jane Thornley, was born September 6th, 1810.

William Thornley, son of William and Jane Thornley, his wife, was born March 15, 1813.

John Thornley, the son of William Thornley and Jane, his wife, was born August 27, 1816.

James Thornley, son of William and Jane Thornley, was born October 20th, 1818.

(all of the above born at "White Plains", King George County)

Caroline Virginia Thornley, daughter of William and Jane Thornley, was born Sept 11th, 1822 [in Caroline County, Va.]

James P., son of James and C.C. Thornley, was born in Fredericksburg, Va., Feb. 28, 1851.

Catherine Jane, [only] daughter of Hazlewood and Emily Farish, was born [in Caroline County] 23rd of March, 1822 [She married Edwin F. Ware May 12, 1841].

Note: Ann Eliza Dangerfield 8/6/1825 (listed in the other Bible)

Sarah Jane, Daughter of Bland and Ann Eliza Dangerfield, was born August 6th, 1825 [in Caroline County].

Lucy Jane, Daughter of William Thornley and Sarah, his wife, was born November 11th, 1839. [probably in Caroline County]

(Note: William Thornley and Sarah P. Boulware, his wife, had three other children not mentioned in the Bible: Sally Thornley, Andrew Glassell Thornley and John Thornley.)

William, Son of William Thornley and Sarah, his wife, was born Sept. 23rd 1841.

George Omohundro, son of George C. Omohundro and Caroline Virginia, his wife, was born May 6th, 1860.

Carrie Omohundro, daughter of George C. Omohundro and Caroline Virginia, his wife, was born February 6, 1865.

Clarence, son of Joh & Mary Downes Thornley, was born in New York, Feb. 1, 1857.

John, son of John & Mary Downes Thornley, was born in Balt., Md. Feb. 8, 1858.

DEATHS:

Catherine Thornley, daughter of William & Jane Thornley, died March 8th, 1814.

Hazlewood Farish, husband of Emily Farish, formerly Emily Thornley, died Sept. 12, 1821.

Aaron Thornley, father of William Thornley etc, died July 29, 1821.

William Thornley, Senior, died on the Island of St. Croix, February 27, 1837. [For the division of his estate, see Hopkins' *Abstracts of Caroline County*, pp. 190-191.]

Winifred, wife of Aaron Thornley, Senior, Died July 28, 1842.

Maria, daughter of William Thornley, Senior, & Jane, his wife, died in Charlottesville, Va., Sept. 10, 1856--Buried in Maplewood Cemetery.

Bland Dangerfield died December, 1843.

Mary Downes Pearce died in Morristown, N.J., April 22nd, 1861.

Jane Thornley, wife of Thos. J. West, died Sept. 6th, 1854, in the City of Richmond, Va.

Jane, relict of William Thornley, Senior, died in Charlottesville, Va. June 12, 1865. Buried in Maplewood Cemetery.

John, infant son of John Thornley and Mary Downes Pearce, his wife, died in Balto., Md., February 10, 1859.

John T., son of Jane & T. J. West, died in Richmond, Va., Sept. 3rd 1863.

Mary Downes Thornley 7/21/1873 in Charlottesville, Va.

Clarence, son of John & Mary Downes Thornley, died July 21, 1873, in Charlottesville, Va.

Aaron, son of Wm & Jane Thornley, died April 8, 1880.

Emily Farish, daughter of Wm & Jane Thornley, died April 16, 1881.

Ann Eliza Dangerfield, daughter of Wm & Jane Thornley, died in Balto., Md., Mar. 3rd 1882.

Julian Thornley, son of John & Julian H. Payne Thornley, died in N.Y.City, Dec. 21, 1912.

*[Aaron Thornley, 47, was living in that part of Caroline County, which later became Fort A.P. Hill, in 1850 with his wife, Mary, 46, and children Thomas W., 13, Frances A., 11, Mary J., 8, Ella F., 6, and Allen, 2 years of age.]

** [Had a son, H.G. Thornley, who reported his mother's death at the age of 65 in Caroline County in June 1877. William Thornley, 37, his wife Sarah P., 37, and children William, 8, Lucy J., 3 and Sarah P., 1, were all living in the area of Caroline County, which later became Fort A.P. Hill in 1850.]

THORNLEY FAMILY BIBLE NO. 3

This Bible was published at the University Press, Oxford and sold by E. Gardner and Son, Oxford Bible Warehouse, Paternoster Row, London and by J.& C. Mozley, Derby, MDCCCLIII. It belonged to Dr. John Thornley, U.S.N. It was printed in the *National Genealogical Society Quarterly*, Vol. XXII, No. 4, p. 100, December, 1934. This family originated from King George and Caroline Counties.

John Thornley, son of William and Jane Thornley, was born in King George Co, Va., August 27,

1816.

Mary Downes Pearce, Daughter of Nathaniel & Rosetta Pearce, was born in the City of Baltimore, Oct. 3, 1831.

Clarence, son of John & Mary Downes Thornley, was born in New York, Feb. 1, 1857.

John, son of John & Mary D. Thornley, was born in Balto., Md., Feb. 8, 1858.

Julia Henrietta, Daughter of Josiah Smith Payne & Isabella J. Rolando Payne, was born in Charleston, S.C., Sept. 19th, 1835.

Josiah Payne, son of John & Julia H. Thornley, was born July 17, 1867.

Julian, son of John & Julia H. Thornley, was born Oct. 28th, 1876.

Jane Riding, daughter of John & Julia H. Thornley, was born Sept. 2, 1870, in Charlottesville, Va.

John, son of John & Julia H. Thornley, was born Oct. 28th, 1876.

Maria Julia Grayson, daughter of Jane Riding Thornley & her husband, John Cooke Grayson of Culpeper, Va., was born in Culpeper, May 17, 1894.

Sarah Mason Cooke Grayson, daughter of Jane Riding Thornley & John Cooke Grayson, born Oct. 30, 1895, Culpeper.

John Thornley Grayson, son of Jane Riding Thornley & John Cooke Grayson, born Oct. 27, 1897, in Pulaski City, Va.

John Thornley and Mary Downes Pearce were married in Balto., Md., April 2, 1856.

John Thornley and Julia H. Payne were married in Emmanuel Church, Balto., Md., Oct. 4, 1866.

Jane Riding Thornley, daughter of Dr. John Thornley, U.S.N., & his wife, Julia Henrietta Payne of Charleston, S.C., and John Cooke Grayson, son of Dr. John Cooke Grayson of "Salubria", Stevensburg, Culpeper Co., Va., & his wife, Lena Pettus (widow Walton), were married in St. Michael's Church, Charleston, South Carolina, June 14, 1893, by Dr. Trappier, Rector. Witnesses, Josiah Payne Thornley, Brother of the Bride, and John Strode Barbour, Best Man.

Sarah Mason Cooke Grayson, daughter of John Cooke & Jane Riding Thornley Grayson, his wife, was married to Lewis Benjamin Johnson of Albemarle Co., Virginia, 1920.

Julia H. Payne, 2nd wife of John Thornley, Sr., died Jan. 23rd 1885 in Charlottesville, Va., buried in Greenwood Cemetery, N.Y.

Isabella Rolando Payne, widow of Josiah Smith Payne of Charleston, S.C., died in Charlottesville, Va., Dec. 4, 1884, and was buried in Greenwood Cemetery, N.Y.

John Thornley, Sr., son of William and Jane Riding Thornley, died in Charlottesville, Va., November, 1887; buried in Greenwood Cemetery, N.Y.

Julian Thornley, son of John & Julia H. Thornley, died in New York City, Dec. 21, 1912. Buried in Greenwood Cemetery.

THORNLEY FAMILY BIBLE NO. 4

This Bible is known as the Jane Riding Thornley Bible of Charlottesville and the owner is Mrs. John Cooke Grayson, Charlottesville, Va. Mrs. Grayson was given these records from an old Prayer Book, which copy was given her by her cousin, Mary Smith, daughter of William Smith ("Extra Billy"), twice Governor of Va. A copy is in the King George County Historical Society. This is a repeat in part of Thornley Bible No. 1.

Aaron Thornley and Catherine, his wife, m. 4/9/1772.
BIRTHS OF THEIR CHILDREN:
Enoch Thornley 2/6/1773-4/1778.
William Thornley 1/2/1775-2/27/1837.
Judith Berry Thornley 5/31/1777-2/28/1785.
Frances Ann Thornley 9/8//1779.
Elizabeth Thornley 11/18/1781.
Jean Thornley 0/26/1783.
Mary Matilda Thornley 1/17/1786.
Thomas Berry Thornley 2/17/1788.
Judith Ann Thornley 2/17/1788.
Catherine Thornley 7/22/1790.
Lucy Tghornley 1/25/1793.
MARRIAGES:
William Thornley to Jane 12/22/1796.
Emily Thornley, dau. of William and Jane, to Hazelwood Farish, son of Stephen and Catherine, 2/15/1821.
Ann Eliza Thornley, dau. of William and Jane, to Bland Dangerfield, son of William Henry, 0/2/1824.
Jane Thornley, dau. Of William and Jane, to Thomas J. West, son of Ellis West and Charity, his wife, 5/11/1830.
Aaron Thornley, son of Wm and Jane, to Mary M. Buckner, dau. of Thomas and Lucy, 5/14/1833.
William Thornley, son of William and Jane, to Sarah P. Boulware, dau. of Mark and Lucy, 12/20/1838.
James Thornley, son of William and Jane, to Catherine C. White, dau. Of Jesse and Helen, 4/16/1850 in town of Charlottesville. John Thornley, third son of William and Jane, to Mary Downes, 1st dau. of Nathaniel and Bose Pearce Downes in Baltimore 4/2/1856.
Caroline Virginia Thornley, dau. of William and Jane to George C. Omohundro, son of John Omohundro and Nancy Crank 10/5/1858.
BIRTHS of Children of William and Jane Riding Thornley.
Emily Thornley 1/10/1797.
Ann Eliza Thornley 10/25/1800.
Aaron Thornley 4/23/1803.
Maria Thornley 12/9/1805.
Jane Thornley 1/6/1808.
Catherine Thornley 8/6/1810.
William Thornley 3/15/1813.
John Thornley 8/27/1816.
James Thornley 10/20/1818.
Caroline Virginia Thornley 9/11/1822.
James P. Thornley, son of James and C.C. 2/28/1851, Fredericksburg, Va.
Catherine Jane Farish, dau. of Hazelwood and Emily, 3/23/1822.
Sarah Jane, dau. of Bland and Ann Eliza Dangerfield, 8/6/1825.

Lucy Jane, dau. of William and Sarah Thornley, 11/11/1839.
George, son of George C. and Caroline Virginia Omohundro, 5/6/1860.
Carrie, dau. of George C. and Caroline Virginia Omohundro, 2/6/1865.
Clarence, son of John and Mary Downes Thornley, 2/1/1857.
John, son of John and Mary Downes Thornley, 2/8/1858, Baltimore, Maryland.

DEATHS:
Catherine Thornley, dau. Of William and Jane, 3/8/1814.
Hazelwood Farish, husband of Emily Farish, formerly Emily Thornley, 9/12/1821.
Aaron Thornley, father of William, 7/29/1821.
William Thornley, Sr. 2/27/1837 on Island of St. Croix.
Winifred, wife of Aaron Thornley, Sr. 7/28/1842.
Maria, dau. of Wm Thornley, Sr./ and Jane, 9/10/1856, Charlottessville, Va., bur. Maplewood Cem.
Bland Dangerfield 12/1843.
Mary Downes Pearce 4/22/1861 Morristown, New Jersey.
Jane Thornley, wife of Thomas J. West, 0/5/1864, in City of Richmond, Virginia.
Jane, relict of William Thornley, Sr. 6/12/1865 in Charlottesville, Va., bur. In Maplewood Cemetery.
John, infant son of John Thornley and Mary Downes Pearce, his wife, 2/10/1859, Baltimore, Md.
John T., son of Jane and T.J. West, 0/3/1863 in Richmond, Va.
Clarence, son of John and Mary Downes Thornley 7/21/1873 in Charlottesville, Va.
Aaron, son of William and Jane Thornley, 4/8/1860.
Emily Farish, dau. of William and Jane Thornley, 4/16/1881.
Anna Eliza Dangerfield, dau. of William and Jane Thornley, 3/3/1882 in Baltimore, Maryland.
Julian Thornley, son of John and Julian H. Payne Thornley, 12/21/1912 in N.Y. City.

Note: The following was omitted from this version but printed in the copy in the King George County Historical Society version.

Josiah Smith Payne Isabella J. Rolando Payne, 9/19/1835, Charleston, South Carolina.

THORNTON FAMILY BIBLE NO. 1

This small Bible was printed in London in 1672 and brought to the colonies by the Thorntons of Virginia, who settled first in Gloucester County. They later settled in Spotsylvania, Stafford, King George, Orange and Caroline Counties. Rowland Thornton and his wife Elizabeth Catlett, mentioned in these records lived at "Crowes", King George County. Anthony Thornton lived at "Ormesby", Caroline County and Philip Thornton lived both at "Ormesby", Caroline County and "South Garden", also in Caroline. Ormesby burned in the last half of the 20th century; however, North Garden is still standing. Later members of the Thornton lived at "Mt. Zephyr", Caroline County. Inscribed in the front of the Bible is the following: "This Bible you have was the one that belonged to mother's father and she gave it to dear Uncle Lewis". Copies of this Bible record are in both the Virginia Historical Society and the Library of Virginia.

Rowland Thornton was born 5 August About sun rise 1685 [later Bible records and other references give the date as 1 August].

Ann Thornton born 22nd of March 1689.

Anthony Thornton born 27 day of June in the year of our Lord 1695.

Anthony Thornton born 27 day of September in 1691.

Catlett Conway was born ye 11th January in the year of our Lord 1719.

Edwin Conway of London St. was married to Elizth Thornberg on tuesday the 21st day of May 1695.

Francis Conway the Son of the Said Edwin Conway & Eliza Conway was born on Thursday at 10 o'clock at night being the 15th day of Apr 1690.

Rowland Thornton was married to Rebecca Catlett the 25th day of October in the year of our Lord 1717 it being a Monday.

Ann Thornberg Elder born Novr 5, 1641.

Eliz. Their Daughter born the 3 of Jan 1694.

Margaret born the 2nd of April 1678.

Wm & Sarah born the 14 of Decemr 1681.

Francis born the 4 of Jany. 1682.

Rowland born the 1st of Aug. 1685.

Anthony born 27 of Septr 1691.

Philip Thornton was born at Ormesby Caroline County Va on 28th day of April 1777.

Sarah T [Taliaferro] Conway [wife of Philip Thornton] was born at "Belleair" Stafford County, Va. October 7th 1781.

P.T. [Philip Thornton] died 27th of November 1829 at Clearville, Spotsylvania Co Va. Intered at South Garden, Caroline County, Va.

S. T. T. [Sarah Taliaferro Thornton] died at the Grove, Chesterfield Co, Va - 30th July 1839. Buried at Gum Swamp Same County.

Philip Thornton and Sarah T. Conway were married at Mount Zion, Caroline Co., the 26th of May 1800.

Their first child

Elizabeth Fitzhugh Thornton was born the 8th of August 1801

Their second child

Sarah Taliaferro Thornton was born 6th August 1804.

Rowland Conway was born the 6th of April 1808.

Frances Fitzhugh Conway their 2nd son was born 6 of Sept 1810.

THORNTON FAMILY BIBLE NO. 2

This Bible belonged to the Thornton who lived at "Ormesby" near Guinea in Caroline County, Virginia. The old house, built in the 18th century, burned a few years ago when a tramp set if afire one cold night. The Bible is dated 1769 and its present whereabouts are unknown. The records were published in the *Virginia Magazine of History and Biography*, Volume 21, 1903, p.204.

Henry Fitzhugh Thornton, son of Anthony and Susannah Thornton, born July 14, 1765, married

Ann R. Fitzhugh, Sept. 22, 1785.

Wm. Thornton, born Sept. 20th. 1767; died Oct. 14, 1783.

John Thornton, born March 4, 1771; married Sarah Fitzhugh, Sept. 17, 1765, she born July 22, 1779; died Feb. 25, 1810.

John Thornton married "[2nd]" Jane Laughlin, Oct. 22, 1812; died Dec. 22, 1821; ["3rd wife Miss Dade - First wife only one who had children"].

Thomas Griffin Thornton, born June 11, 1775, married Ann H. [Harrison] Fitzhugh, Oct. 29, 1795.

Anthony Thornton son of Henry and Ann Thornton, born 29th July 1786, baptised [sic] by Rev. Robert Buchan, had for sureties Mr. John Henry, George and Daniel Fitzhugh. Mrs. Susannah Thornton, Mrs Alice Fitzhugh, Miss Fanny Richards, Mrs. George Fitzhugh.

Susannah Fitzhugh Thornton, daughter of John and Sarah Thornton, born Oct. 13th 1797, baptised by Rev. Tredale, had as sureties Mr. William, George, Thomas and Henry Fitzhugh, Mrs. Mary, Miss Ann D. Baylor, Miss Mary Fitzhugh.

George Fitzhugh Thornton, born May 22nd 1799, baptised by Rev. John Wiley. Sureties Mr. Griffin Thornton, Mr. John Baylor, Mr. George Fitzhugh, Jr., Mrs. Lucy Burrell, Mrs. Ann H. Thornton, Mrs. Ann D. Baylor, Miss Mary Fitzhugh.

John Griffin Thornton, born Nov. 13, 1800, baptised by Rev. Thompson. Sureties Mr. George Fitzhugh, Edward Diggs, Thomas Knox, Mordica, Edward and Henry Fitzhugh, Mrs. Elizabeth Powell, Mrs. Sarah Fitzhugh, Mrs. Elizabeth Diggs, Miss Sarah Fitzhugh, Miss Porcia Diggs. [Mrs. Tompkins the mistress at that time of Ormesly added the comments in quotation marks].

THORNTON FAMILY BIBLE NO. 3

A copy of this Bible is at both the Virginia Historical Society and the Virginia State Library. It apparently was originally owned by Philip and Sarah Thornton. Philip Thornton was born at "Ormesby", Caroline County 28 April 1777 and died 27 November 1829 at "Clearville", Spotsylvania County and was buried at "South Garden", Caroline County. He married Sarah Taliaferro Conway, daughter of Francis Conway at "Mount Zion", Caroline County. She was born at "Belleair", Stafford County, October 7, 1781 and died at "The Grove", Chesterfield County 30 July 1839 and was buried at Gun Swamp in that county.

Philip Thornton was married to Sarah Taliaferro Conway on the 28th of May 1800.

Sarah T.[Taliaferro] Thornton was married to John C. Glanard Esq on 15th of September 1829.

Philip Thornton was born 28th of April in the year 1777.

Sarah Taliaferro Conway was born the 7th of October 1781.

The first Child Elizabeth Fitzhugh was born the 8th day of August 1801.

Their 2nd Child Sarah Taliaferro was born the 6th of August 1804.

Their third Child died in a few minutes after his birth September 1806.

Their 4th Child Rowland Conway was born the 6th day of April 1808.

Their 5th Child Francis Fitzhugh Conway was born the 6th of September 1810.

Betsey Fitzhugh the 6th Child was born the 9th day of April 1813.

Lewis Bedford the 7th Child was born the 29th day of May 1815.

Philippus Antonius the 8th Child was born the 2nd day of Septr. in the year 1817.

Charles Walker their 9th Child was born on the 4th day of December 1819.
Thomas Jefferson, their 7th Son & 10th Child was born the 24th day of January 1822 at 3 o'clock.
Elizabeth Fitzhugh Thornton died on the 5th of March 1806.
Betsey Fitzhugh died the 24th day of July 1814.
Charles Walker died on the 25th day of November 1822.
Phillip Thornton died on the 29th day of November 1829.
Sarah T. Thornton died on the 30th July 1837.

THORNTON FAMILY BIBLE NO 4

This Bible belonged to Anthony Thornton and Sarah Taliaferro, his wife, of Caroline County, Virginia. The seat of the Thornton family was "Ormesby" near Guinea. It burned the last quarter of the 19th Century. The Bible was copied by George H.S. King and a copy of the records is in the Virginia Historical Society.

Anthony Thornton & Sarah Taliaferro married Dec. 31, 1746.
Anthony Thornton & Susannah Fitzhugh, married June 28, 1764.
Aylette Buckner & Judith Presley Thornton, married Apr. 1768.
Anthony Thornton Jr. & Mary Rootes, married May 8, 1772.
George Thornton & Margaret Stanley, married Jan. 1, 1774.
Charles Thornton & Mary Jones married [no date listed].
Reuben Thornton & Mildred Grymes, married [no date listed].
Charles Thornton & Sarah Fitzhugh, married [blurred] 1782.
Freeley Thornton & Alice Thornton, married [no date listed].
Henry Thornton & Ann Rosa Fitzhugh, married Sept. 22, 1784.
John Thornton & Sarah Fitzhugh, married Sept. 16, 1795.
Thomas Griffin Thornton & Ann Harrison Fitzhugh, married Oct. 29, 1795.
John Thornton & Jane Laughlin, married Oct. 22, 1812.
Anthony Thornton born Nov. 15, 1727.
Sarah Taliaferro, born [blurred] 1728.
Anthony Thornton Jr., born Feb. 1, 1748. [Col. Anthony Thornton of Harrison Co., Ky., died 2 Jan. 1829, formerly of Caroline Co, Va. but for last 20 years a resident of Ky. Officer in American Revolution.]
Judith Presley Thornton born June 6, 1750.
George Thornton, born Nov. 18, 1752.
Charles Thornton, born Oct.--- 1754.
Peter Thornton, born Dec. 3, 1756.
Reuben Thornton, born Sept. 15, 1758.
Presley Thornton, born Dec. 31, 1760.
Henry Thornton, born July 14, 1765.
William Thornton, born Sept. 20, 1767.

John Thornton, born March 11, 1771.
Thomas Griffin Thornton, born June 11, 1775.
Sarah Thornton, wife of Anthony Thornton, died Feb. 6, 1762 age 33.
Anthony Thornton Sr., died [blurred] 1782, aged 55.
William Thornton, died Oct. 14, 1783, aged 16.
Mary Jones Thornton, wife of Charles Thornton, died [no date listed].
Sarah Fitzhugh Thornton, wife of John Thornton, died [no date listed].
Charles Thornton, died April --- 1824.
Susannah Fitzhugh Thornton, wife of Anthony Thornton Sr. died [no date listed].

THORNTON FAMILY BIBLE NO. 5

This Bible is known as the George Washington Thornton Bible and at one time was owned by John Thornton of Tulsa, Oklahoma. It was copied by George H.S. King and a copy of the record is in the Virginia Historical Society. The Thornton families of Caroline County, Fredericksburg and Stafford were all interrelated and are buried in all three locations.

Married at St. Paul's Parish, Stafford Co. by Rev. William Stewart on October 9, 1773 George Washington Thornton & Mary Alexander.
George Washington Thornton born on 6th of Dec. 1737.
Mary Alexander born on the 26th. of Nov. 1756.
George Washington Thornton Jr. born on 6 of Sept. 1774.
Reuben Thornton born 1st of Dec. 1776.
Benjamin Thornton born on 3rd of April 1779.
Lucy Francis Thornton born on 5th of Jan. 1781.
George Washington Thornton died on 30th of April 1781 in the 54th year of his age.
George Washington Thornton died on the --th of Dec. 1816 aged 42 years.
Mary A. Thornton Posey, died on the 18th of May 1837 in her 81st year. [Mary Alexander married 2ndly to Thomas Posey]

TOD(D) FAMILY BIBLE

This Bible was published by Sage and Clough for William Durell, New York, 1803. This Bible originally belonged to Colonel Charles Tod Jr. (1777-1832) [son of Capt Charles and Mary Tod and grandson of Dr. George Tod] and his wife Elizabeth Muse Pierce Tod (1791-1826). The Tod or Todd family of Caroline lived at four large plantations at differing times in Caroline County. Recent information reveals that Dr. George Tod was the son of Charles Tod, res. Westshore, Orkney Islands (See p. 157, Scots on the Chesapeake 1607-1830 by David Dobson). They were "Sycamores", "Villeboro", "Spring Hill" and "Hickory Grove". For further information concerning this family see *Todds of Virginia* by Rubey, Stacy and Collins, Artcraft Press, Columbia, Missouri, 1960.

Charles Tod and Elizabeth his Wife was Married the 15th day of December 1807.
Lovel Pierce Tod their first Son was born the 2nd day of February 1809.
Charles Tod Jr. their second Son was born the 20th day of January 1811.
George Tod Jr. their third Son was born the 28th day of October 1812.
John Burke Tod their fourth Son was born the 15th day of December 1814.
Joseph Tod their fifth Son was born the 4th day of February 1817.
Mary Elizabeth Tod their first Daughter was born the 19th day of Feby 1819.
Martha Muse Tod was born the 11th day of June 1823.
Chas. Tod was born the 10th day of May 1777.
Elizabeth M. Tod his wife was born the 14th day of April 1792.
Martha Muse Tod died the 27 day of Septr. 1823.
Mira-Ann Cordelia Muse Tod was born the 7th of Augst. 1824.
Caroline Virginia Tod was born the 15 of August 1820.
Mrs. Elizabeth M. Tod Departed this life on the night of the 6th of December 1826 aged 34 years, seven Months & 22 days.
Joseph Tod Jr. and Frances Ann his wife was married the 23d day of November at 1/2 past 9 o'clock in the morning 1837.

JOHN B. TOD FAMILY

John B.[Burke] Tod and Clemenza [L. Miller] his wife were married on the 12th day of Feby 1835.
Susan E. Tod their first daughter was born the 2d day of December 1835.
Euphemia M. Tod their second daughter was born the 12th of November 1837.
John B.[Burke} Tod and Martha A. Taliaferro his [2nd] wife was Married on the 26th day of August 1841 By Elder Robert Ryland.
Sarah Alice Tod Their first daughter was born on the 20th day of July 1842.
John B.[Burke] Tod was born the 25th of December 1814.
Clemenza L. [Miller] his wife was born the 19th day of Jany 1814.
Mrs. Clemenza L. Tod departed this life on Saturday the 4th of Jany 1840 aged twenty four years eleven months and fifteen days.
Mrs. Martha Alice Tod departed this life on Monday morning 5 o'clock the 29th day of November 1827.

TOMPKINS FAMILY BIBLE

This Bible record was published in *The Virginia Magazine of History and Biography*, Volume 19, p.196. The Virginia Historical Society, 1911.

Christopher Tompkins, born on North River Gloucester County, Oct 17th 1705 - Departed this life in Caroline County where he lived upwards of forty years, Mar. 16, 1779.
Joyce, His wife [who was a Read], born in Gloucester Co on Gwyn's Island was born Mar. 6th 1701 - and Departed this life in Caroline County Aug. 8th 1771 leaving six sons and a daughter all she ever had. Robert, Eldest son, died the 7 of June 1795, in the sixty fifth year of his age.
Wm Tompkins, 4th son, was born in Gloucester County on North River 1736 and Departed this life in Caroline County February 24th 1772 leaving four children 2 sons and 2 daughters.

TRIBBLE FAMILY BIBLE

This Bible originally belonged to Reverend Andrew Tribble, who was born in Caroline County March, 1741, the son of George Tribble and Betty Clark. He married Sally Burruss, daughter of Thomas Burruss and Frances Tandy. He died in Clark County, Kentucky December 22, 1822. The Bible was owned in 1936 by Mrs. B.F. Buckley, Lexington, Kentucky, when it was published in *Tyler's Quarterly*, Volume 18, pp.59-61.

Frances T. Tribble born Sept. 3, 1769; married Michael Stoner; he was born Sept. 30, 1753; died Sept. 3, 1814.
Samuel Tribble born Dec. 30, 1771.
Peter Tribble born Oct 8, 1773; married Oct. 8, 1893 to Polly Boone. She died Sept. 14, 1831.
Thomas Tribble born June 13, 1776.
Nancy Tribble born Nov. 6, 1778 married April 1794 David Chenault.
Sally B. Tribble born Feb. 9, 1781; married Mar. 7, 1789 David Crews. She died Feb. 2, 1810. Crews married again.
Silas Tribble born June 3, 1783. Married Oct. 30, 1809 Jerusha White. He died Nov. 18, 1842.
Andrew Tribble born Dec. 2, 1785. Married June 24, 1810 Lucy Boone.
Mary Tribble born March 29, 1788. Married Dec. 23, 1806, Joseph Stephenson; their son James M. Stephenson died Sept. 1809.
John Tribble (Gen.) born August 15, 1790. Married 1st Martha A. White. Had several children. Martha died June 10, 1850. Gen. Tribble then married Sally Coffee. She died Jan. 3, 1865.
Patsey Tribble born March 7, 1794. Married Oct. 5, 1812 Jacob White.
Dudley Tribble born May 1, 1797; married Jan. 21, 1819 Matilda H. Tevis (b. Jan. 10, 1805)
Parents of James P. Tribble, Dudley Tribble now a citizen of Richmond, Ky., Robt G. Tribble and others.
Children of Sally Burruss born Sept. 30, 1753; died Dec. 15, 1830.
Roger Burruss b. April 18, 1769. Cynthia his wife [formerly Cynthia Mills] b. Sept. 19, 1772. They were married Jan. 14, 1790. Issue:
Nathaniel Burruss b. Nov. 20, 1790.
Henry Tandy Burruss b. Sept. 23, 1793.
Peggy Burruss b. Jan. 25, 1794.
Roger Burruss b. Dec. 11 [or 17?] 1795.
Frances Burruss b. Sept. 8, 1797.
Mary Ann Burruss b. May 30, 1800.
Sally Ellen Burruss b. Nov. 14, 1802.
Cynthia Mills Burruss b. Feb. 15, 1805 m. Mar. 25, 1824 Robt. Kay [brother of Gabriel Kay who m. Anna Tandy Mason, grandau of Henry Tandy]
Charles Mills Burruss b. Feb. 19, 1807.
Celia Ann Burruss b. June 20, 1809.
Virginia Banks Burruss b. May 26, 1811.
Rebecca Massie Burruss b. June 19, 1814.
Mildred Thompson Burruss b. Feb. 13, 1818.
Roger Burruss Sr. d. Sept. 30, 1926 aged 57 yrs. 5 mo. 12 days.

Cynthia Burruss died Jan. 26, 1853, aged 80 yrs. 4 mo. 6 days.

TUNSTALL FAMILY BIBLE NO.1

The Tunstall Bible record is in the Alderman Library, University of Virginia, Charlottesville. A copy of the record is also in the Library of Virginia. The Tunstall family lived both in King and Queen as well as Caroline County. Prior to the Civil War, L.H. Tunstall, who served in Picketts Divion during that war, lived at "Elson Green" on top of the hill from the Pamunkey River in Caroline County. His son, C. S. Tunstall owned it next until 1937. Robert S. Tunstall was in Caroline County in 1853 and lived at "Bloomfield", now in the Fort A.P. Hill area. A reference to this family may be found in *Genealogies of Virginia Families From The Virginia Magazine of History and Biography,* Volume I, Genealogical Publishing Co., Baltimore, Md., 1981. Also see *The First Tunstalls in Virginia and Some of Their Descendants*, The Clegg Company, San Antonio, Texas, 1950.

Ann Tunstall the Daughter of Richard & Ann Tunstall was born the 19th day of October 1728.
Elizabeth Tunstall was born the 10th day of Augst. 1730 & departed this Life the 23rd day of June 1743.
John Tunstall was born the 8th day of July 1733.
Katherine Tunstall was born 19th day of August 1734 & dyed [sic] the 23d of June 1743.
Frankey Tunstall was born the 29th day of December 1736 & dyed the [blank] day of [blank].
Richard Tunstall was born the 22d day of July 1738.
Thomas Tunstall was born the 16th day of November 1739 & dy'd the [blank] day of December 1769.
Leonard Tunstall was born the 4th day of March 1741.
William Tunstall was born the 25th day of May 1843.
William Tunstall the Son of Richd & Esther Tunstall was born the 2d day of June 1768.
Richard Tunstall was born the 17th day of August 1769.
Cuthbert Tunstall was born the 3d day of July 1774.
Edward Tunstall was born the 7th day of May 1707 and departed this life the 23 day of October 1791.
Sarah Hill Tunstall was born the 29 October 1774.
Richard Cowin Tunstall was born the 7th day Jany 1777 and departed this life the 23rd day of August 1790.
John Grayson Tunstall was born the 28 Febry 1779.

TUNSTALL FAMILY BIBLE NO. 2

This Bible was kept by Lewis Hill Tunstall, son of Richard Tunstall and Jane Graham Hill of Caroline County. It was reproduced in *The First Tunstalls in Virginia and Some of Their Descendants* by Whit Morris, Press of The Clegg Company, San Antonio, Texas, 1950 at page page 22. The Tunstall family lived at "Elson Green" and the Hill family lived at "Mt. Gideon", both in lower Caroline County, near the Pamunkey River.

Richard Tunstall was b. 27 Oct. 1803, d. 8 Mar. 1875 and lived in Richmond up to the War Between the States and thereafter at his country place "Elson Green" in Caroline County. Richard Tunstall married 21 Nov. 1833 his first cousin once removed, Jane Graham Hill, daughter of Henry Hill of Caroline Co., granddaughter of Robert Hill and wife Hannah Garlick and great-granddaughter of Col. Humphrey Hill.

Children:

Maria Emily Tunstall, b. 21 Feb. 1835, d. unm. 5 June 1873.

Lewis Hill Tunstall, b. 7 May 1837, d. 2 Dec. 1826, m. 2 May 1867 Mary Ellen Hill.

Sarah Ann (Nannie) Tunstall, b. 14 Sept. 1839, d. unm. 10 Apr. 1910.

Mary Camm Tunstall, b. 1 Apr. 1842, d. 30 Dec. 1907, m. 24 Dec.1872, Archibald Samuel.

Agnes Tunstall [no further information].

Lucy Tunstall [no further information].

TURNER/THORNTON FAMILY BIBLE

Bible printed and published by Matthew Carey, Philadelphia, 1812. This book was given Robert T. Turner by his Mother Sarah Turner the Year 183[?]6. A copy is in the Library of Virginia. The Turner family was well established in Caroline County. One branch came from King George County and settled in the Port Royal area, one family on lands which later became "Moss Neck". The other branch seems to have come out of New Kent County, later King William County, one settling in Caroline County on Route 30 near the King William-Caroline line. Another settled near Ruther Glen at a place known as "Fairfield" and another settled at "Turner's Store", near the old Kidds Fork Post office in central Caroline. The Turner family married into the Magruder family at "Aberfoyle" nearby. For information concerning the Fairfield, consult *Descendants of Daniel Turner 1750-1806* by Alfred Wilmer Turner, 1977. The seat of the Thornton family in Caroline was "Ormesby" near Guinea in Caroline County. The house burned in the late 20th century.

Robert T. Turner was married to Elizabeth D. Thornton on the 13 November 1828.

Robert G. Turner Married on 25th of December 1856 to Sarah E. Purks.

Ann H. Turner Married to John W. Woolfolk the 24th of November 1858.

James M. Turner Married to Genevive Turner Daughter of W.D. & Maria Louisa Turner 22nd Dec. 1869.

Daniel Turner and Georgie Gardiner Married Mch. 1st. 1876.

Henry E. Turner and Grace Christain married March 28, 1908.

Jas. Ro. Turner son of J.M.T. & Viver Turner born 12th Jany 1871.

William D. Turner born 1st June 1873.

Henry Edmund son of Daniel and Georgie Turner was born Feb. 24 1877.

Edmund Christian Turner son of Henry E. and Grace Christian was born June 18 1806.

Anne Harrison daughter of Henry E. and Grace C. was born Nov. 21 1907.

Louise Waddill, daughter of Henry E. and Grace C. was born March 29 1915.

Katherine Stiles daughter of Henry E. and Grace C. was born April 3, 1916.

Thomas G. Thornton born on 11th day of June 1775.

Ann Harrison Fitzhugh was born 13 day September 1780.

Susan Elizabeth Thornton daughter of the above Thos. G. and Ann Harrison was born the 29 day Oct. 1797.

William Fitzhugh Thornton was born 9 day Sept. 1800.

Sarah D. Thornton was born the 13 Augt 1802.

Ann H. Thornton was born 29th May 1804.

Adeline Thornton was born 19 day of March 1806.

Elizabeth D. Thornton was born 22 Feby 1808.

Elizabeth D. Thornton was born 20th April 1811. [apparently named for her sister who must have died in 1808]

Samuel G. Thornton was born 18 June 1813.

Thomas G. Thornton was born the 19th Sept. 1815.

Mary D. Thornton was born the 24 May 1817.

Henry F. Thornton was born the 16th Sept. 1819.

Ellen R. Thornton was born the 29 June 1821.

Robert T. Turner was born on the 16th March 1804.

Elizabeth D. Turner born on the 20th of April 1811.

Edward Turner was born on the 13th of February 1830.

Robert Griffin Turner was born on 30th December 1831.

Sarah P. Turner was born the 7 of January 1834.

Ann Harrison Turner was born on the 19 of October 1835.

James M. Turner was born on the 20 of May 1837. Died the 15 March 1839.

Edmund Turner born 25th March 1840.

Mary Willis Turner was born 5th Feby. 1842.

Daniel Turner born on the 25 of January 1844.

Henry Turner born on the 6 of Jany. 1846.

John Thomas Turner born the 6th June 1848.

Daniel Turner died 1st September 1846.

Edmund P. Turner son of Daniel & Sarah Turner died Augt. 1834.

Thomas Turner died the 27 of Sept. 1847.

Sarah Turner died the 22 March 1849.

Edmund Turner died the 13 of Feby. 1865.

Robert Taylor Turner died 12th July 1870 at Stevensville King & Queen.

Nannie Winston Turner [Turner marked through] Woolfolk died 18th July 1870.

Geo. P. Turner died Aug. 1871.

Elizabeth D. Turner died 1st Dec. 1865.

Robert G. Turner died Son of Eliz & D.T. Nov. 20th 1884.

Thomas G. Thornton died on the 12th June 1830.

Ann H. Thornton died on the 9 of March 1841.

Adaline Thornton died the 24 September 1807.

Elizabeth Dedmen Thronton died the 16 Augt. 1810.

Edward Digges Thornton died the 2nd September 1826.

Sally Digges Battaile died the 9 of Augt. 1842.

Samuel G. Thornton died 3 of September 1847.

Mary D. Jesse died 2 Feby 1857.

Ann H. Jesse died 21st May 1864.
Ellen Catlett died 21 Sept. 1864.
Edward Turner died on the 6 of October 1830.
Sarah P. Turner died on the 12 of October 1836.
Mary W. Turner died on 12 of October 1846.
John Thomas Turner died 16th June 1848.
Born dead 31st July 1849.[no name listed]
Daniel Turner died May 16, 1894 in the 51st year of his age.
James M. Turner died May 6, 1905 in the 68th year of his age.
Wm W. Woolfolk died 17th January 1897 in his 67th yr.
Nannie E. Woolfolk daughter of R. T. Turner & Elizabeth Turner died Mch. 19, 1915 in the 80th year of her age.
Henry P. Turner died in Richmond Va.[no date listed]
Henry Edward Turner son of Daniel & Georgia Turner died Dec. 19, 1933.
Anne Harrison daughter of Henry E. & Grace C. died July 1908.
Edmund Christian Turner son of Henry Edmund & Grace Christian died Nov. 13, 1930.
[note in back of Bible]:
Hollywood - William Daniel T. wife Maria Louisa Turner. daughter Genievive T. married James M.T. son of Robt. T. & Eliz. D.Thornton.
Also the following two newspaper obituaries:
Died at the residence of his son-in-law, Mr. W. W. Woolfolk, in King & Queen county, July 12th [1870], ROB'T T. TURNER, Esq. in the 67th year of his age. A native of Caroline county, Mr T. removed years ago to this county. A gentleman by birth and education, polished and refined in manners, sociable and kindly in disposition. When grey hairs had gathered upon his brow, he added yet this, above all, he became a sincere lover of our Lord Jesus Christ. For several months before death came, he was the subject of disease which baffled the skill of eminent physicians, but which yet proved a blessing in disguise, affording time for serious reflection. He eagerly embraced the opportunity and died an humble Christian. He leaves an affectionate daughter and four sons to lament the death. May his death be a blessing to each of them.

Sudden Death of This Prominent Citizen and Member of the Masonic Fraternity.
Mr. George P. Stacy, the well-known furniture dealer, died very suddenly last night about 9 o'clock at his residence, No. 406 east Cary street. He was born in Lincolnshire, England, forty-seven years ago, and with his father and brothers came to this city in 1848, and long had been prominent in business and social circles. His wife was a Miss Turner, of Caroline, who with two sons and two daughters survive him. For a week of more, at times, Mr. Stacy had complained of pain about the region of his stomach, and his son Charlie had earnestly besought him to obtain medical advice but he sad no; that he was suffering from something he had eaten and that he felt sure he knew what was the matter with him and would soon be all right again. He was at his store, on Main street near Twelth, Friday and was tolerably well until he went home to dinner. At home about 4 o'clock he was seized with paroxylsms of pain about the bowels, and none of the remedies tried affording relief. Doctors Stone and Taber were called in and gave him their best attention, but he continued to suffer greatly until within a short time before death, which was probably caused by abdominal neuralgia. The blow fell with crushing

effect upon the aged father, who had just come down from Amelia on a visit, and the wife and children. They were altogether unprepared for the sudden end of their beloved one. Mr. Stacy was a man of quiet and agreeable manners, and was widely known and beloved. He was a deacon of the Seventh-Street Christian church, and was an active and earnest church worker. He belonged to a Masonic lodge and was the second officer of the Commandery of St. Andrew. He was also a member of Acca Temple of the Mystic Shrine.

The hour of the funeral has not yet been set.

TURNER/WRIGHT FAMILY BIBLE

This Bible was originally the property of Benjamin H. Turner of Hanover County, who married Jane C. Sale. After her death, he married Louisa Tod Wright, daughter of Burton B. Wright of "Elmwood", Caroline County, Virginia. It was passed down in that family to Dr. Charles Wright's family at "Aberfoyle", Caroline County and is today owned by Herbert R. Collins at nearby "Green Falls", another Wright home place. The Bible was published by G & C Merriam, Springfield, Mass., 1846. A typewritten copy of the Bible has been placed in The Library of Virginia.

Benjm. H.[Harrison] Turner and Jane C.[Columbia] Sale were married on the 20th January 1842.
B.H. Turner married the second time to Louisa T. Wright Dec. 16th 1852.
Benjm. H. Turner was born on the 15th Nov. 1823.
Jane C. Sale was born on the 11th May 1820.
Louisa T.[Tod] Wright was born 5th May 1827.
Burton [Birkenhead] B. [Boutwell] Wright the Father of L.T. Turner was born August 1st 1802.
Ann [Tod] Wright his wife [was born] the 24th of February 1806.
Ann Maria Wright [was born] the 21st of May 1829.
Charles Wright [was born] the 11th of December 1831.
Eliza Wright [was born] the 19th of February 1834.
Burton B. Wright [was born] the 30th of June 1837.
George Tod Wright [was born] the 8th of February 1840.
Mary Margaret [Maggie] Wright [was born] the 14 of December 1842.
Catharine & Julia Wright [twins were born] the 31st of July 1846.
Lucy Daniel Turner was born on the 28th Novr. 1842.
Louisa Columbia Turner was born on the 15th July 1847.
Ann Burton Turner was born January 1st 1854.
Benjamin Harrison Turner [Jr] was born on the 25th June 1855.
Maxwell S. [Summerville] Hudgins [was born] August 25th 1855.
Alice E. [Eugenia] Hudgins [was born] April 7th 1857.
Burton B.W. [Boutwell Wright] Hudgins [was born] July 3rd 1858.
Clarence Hudgins [was born] September 20th 1860.
Ann Tod Hudgins [was born] November 5th 1864.

Joseph Burton Wright [was born] December 23rd 1860.
George Tod Wright son of Charles & Lizzie Wright [was born] December 11th 1864.
Robert Ridgway Wright [was born] October 5th 1866.
Ida Louisa Wright [was born] November 7th 1868.
Eva V. [Virginia] Wright [was born] January 19th 1871.
Maggie [Margaret] L. [Lewis] Wright [was born] June 3rd 1875.
George R. [Ridgeway] Wright [was born] November 11th 1877.
Lina M. [Moore] Wright [was born] June 7th 1880.
Burta L. [Lee] Wright [was born] July 21st 1882.
Etta J. [Josephine] Wright [was born] October 31st 1884.
Julia A. [Anne Alexandria] Wright [was born] December 13th 1889.
Lizzie J. [Jesse] Wright Wife of Chas. Wright born April 13th 1846.
Jane Columbia Turner the beloved wife of Benjamin H. Turner departed this life Monday evening July 1st 1850 Aged 30 years 1 month and 20 days "Blessed are the dead that die in the Lord".
Benjamin H. Turner died the 19th of February 1855.
Burton B. Wright father of Louisa T. Turner died the 17th of March 1856.
Ann Wright his wife [died] the ll of April 1864.
George Tod Wright [died] the 25th of May 1847.
Robert Ridgway Wright [died] December 3rd 1868.
George Tod Wright [died] December 10th 1868.
Charles Wright [died] Jan [17, 1893].
Louisa T.[Wright] Turner [died] July 4 [1898].
Burton B. Wright [Jr. died August 25, 1903]
Mary Margaret Wright [George, Bibb died August 30, 1916]
Julia [Wright] Brown [died February 25, 1913].
Eliza [Tod] Wright [died July 27, 1917].

TYLER FAMILY BIBLE

This Bible was published by the American Bible Society, N.Y. 1857. A copy is in the Library of Virginia. The family lived at "Braynefield" in Caroline County and George Hoge Tyler of this family became Governor of Virginia. Members of this family are buried at "Braynefield" and at "Spring Grove" in Caroline County. The Magruders are another Caroline family.

Married on the 5th of February 1862 at Glenmore in Albemarle County by the Rev. Chas. Beach, George Tyler of Caroline County & Julia Virginia, oldest daughter of B. H. Magruder.
George Tyler, son of Henry & Lucinda Coleman Tyler Born at his Grandfather's Capt. George Tyler of Spotsylvania Co on December the 17th 1817.
Married by the Rev. L. W. Burton, at 2308 E. Grace St. Richmond Va. on Wednesday July 21, 1886 - Henry M. Tyler (son of Geo. & Julia V. Tyler) & Mary A. (Daughter of Geo. K. & Annie H. Taylor of Richmond, Va.)

UPSHAW FAMILY BIBLE NO. 1

This Bible was published by S. Andrus and Son, Hartford, Connecticut, 1848. It is presently owned by June Upshaw Guiles, Richmond, Virginia. The Upshaw family in Caroline County had its roots in Essex and King & Queen Counties before settling in Caroline County in the Bagby and Gether area. This Bible originally belonged to Robert Harrison Upshaw and his wife Margaret Elizabeth Green.

Robert Harrison Upshaw was the son of Colonel Edwin Upshaw and Martha "Patsy" Harrison. Edwin Upshaw was the son of John and Mary Lafoon Upshaw. Margaret Elizabeth Green, wife of Robert Harrison Upshaw, was the daughter of Eldred Green and Suburnah Hawkins Wright, who was the daughter of Robert Wright and Margaret Boutwell of "Green Falls", Caroline County. Eldred Green was the son of George Green of Caroline County. The old Upshaw cemetery, enclosed by a brick wall, is on the place now owned by Jack Upshaw at Gether.

Robert H. Upshaw. son of Edwin Upshaw & Martha his wife, & Margaret E. Green, daughter of Eldred Green & Suburnah his wife, were married in the holy bonds of Matrimony on Tuesday the 18 of March 1851.
Doctor Thomas G. Ritchie & Margaret Eva Upshaw, daughter of Robert H. Upshaw & Margaret his wife, were married 4th of June 1877.
Willie E. Upshaw son of Robert H. Upshaw & Margaret his wife, and Gay Garnett daughter of James Garnett & Bettie his wife, were married on Thursday the 29th Aug. 1879.
Tommie E. Upshaw & Callie D. Atkinson were married on the 9th of December 1885.
Lulie K. Upshaw and Willie L. Campbell were married on the 24th of November 1891.
Lillie D. Upshaw and John G. Broaddus were married on the 24th of December 1891.
Robert E. Lee Upshaw and Emma Kidd were married the 19th of December 1896.
Tommie E. Upshaw and Annie Broaddus were married on 16th of December 1896.
William Edwin son of Robert H. and Margaret E. Upshaw was born on the 19th of January 1852.
Mary Virginia Upshaw [was born] on March 30th 1853.
Margaret Eva Upshaw [was born] August 26th 1854.
Robert Green Upshaw [was born] 18th of December 1855.
Oliver Crump Upshaw [was born] 30th August 1857.[named for the Crump brothers who married the two sisters of Suburnah Wright Green.]
Suburna Hawkins Upshaw [was born] 23rd April 1859.
Robert G. Upshaw son of Robt H. Upshaw & Margaret E. his wife died on the 18th day of Augst 1858.
Oliver Crump Upshaw died on the 30th of July 1865.
Robert H. Upshaw died on the 25th of November 1881.
Mamie [Margaret Elizabeth] V. Upshaw died on the 14th of August 1883.
Wayland Smith Broaddus son of Jack Broaddus & Lillie his wife was born on tuesday the 8th of November 1892.
John Massie Broaddus was born on 22nd of March 1894.
Robert Ross Broaddus was born on the 7th of July 1895.
Eva Lois Campbell was born on Sunday the 1st of December 1889.

Leonard Lee Campbell was born on March 31st 1891.
Charlie Edward Campbell was born on February 28th 1893.
L. K. Campbell's twins Louise & Kate Aubrey were born on the 22nd of June 1900.
Robert Ross Broaddus died July 18, 1967.

UPSHAW FAMILY BIBLE NO. 2

This Bible was published by Charles Foster Publishing Company, Philadelphia, Pennsylvania [no date]. It is presently owned by June Upshaw Guiles, Richmond, Virginia, who was raised in the Gether area of Caroline County.

Robert Lee Upshaw Son of Robert and Margaret Upshaw was born March 20th 1863.
Emma E. Kidd daughter of Henry and Ella Kidd was born December 20th 1875.
Oliver Dewey Upshaw Son of Emma & Lee Upshaw was born April 5th 1898.
Mary Evline [Lynn] Upshaw daughter of Emma and Lee Upshaw was born December 1st 1900.
Margaret Ella Upshaw daughter of Emma and Lee Upshaw was born May 27th 1904.
Russell Lee Upshaw Son of Emma and Lee Upshaw was born Nov 25th 1905.
Robert Henry Upshaw born Feb. 9, 1910.
Ludolph Kidd Upshaw born Dec. 16, 1912.
Alice June Upshaw born June 21 1915.
Willard Bates Upshaw born Nov. 26, 1917.
[above are] Sons and daughters of Emma & Lee Upshaw.
Robert Lee Upshaw and Emma E. Kidd was Married December 9th 1896 by Rev. A. Broaddus.
Oliver Dewey Upshaw and Evelyn Eubank Vaughan were married Dec. 12, 1936.
Phillip H. Minor and Mary Evline Upshaw were married Jan. 1, 1924.
Bryan Boswell and Margaret Ella Upshaw were married June, 19__.
Russell Lee Upshaw and Ruby Mae Richerson were married July 16 , 1932.
Ludolph Kidd Upshaw and Nellie Margiarite Whalen were married November 28, 1935.
George Earl Guiles and Alice June Upshaw were married July 6th 1942.
Willard Bates Upshaw and Evlyn Broaddus Penny were married March 18, 1939.
Mrs. Ella Kidd daughter of Lencie and John Tennant Died May 5th 1905.
Mary Campbell died October 8 1903.
Robert Lee Upshaw died March 26, 1944 .
Mrs. Lula Kate Campbell sister of Robert Lee Upshaw died December 27 1944.
Mrs. Bernie Ancarrow sister of R.L. Upshaw died March 2, 1936.
Mrs Maggie Ritchie sister of R.L. Upshaw died [Sept. 12, 1936].
Robert Edwin Lee Upshaw Born 3-20-1863 Died 3-26-1944.
Emma Ella Kidd Upshaw Born 12-20-1875 Died 12-29-1951.
Evelyn Eubank Vaughan Upshaw B. 5-1-1912 D. 8-7-1955.
Russell Lee Upshaw B. 11-25-1905 D. 9-5-1973.
Ann Wayne Minor Middleton B. 12-7-1926 D. 11-13-1974.
Nicholas Lee Upshaw B. 11-21-1938 D. 12-4-1980.
Philip Henry Minor B. 8-5-1900 D. 3-10-1984.
Oliver Dewey Upshaw B. 4-5-1898 D. 9-22-1987.

Marylyn Upshaw Minor B. 12-1-1900 D. 8-23-1992.
Willard Bates Upshaw B. 11-26-1917 D. 3-23-1994.
Robert Henry Upshaw B. 2-9-1910 D. 9-23-1994.
Ludolph Kidd Upshaw b. 12-16-1912 d. 8-3-1996.
Margaret E. Upshaw Boswell b. 6-27-1903 d. 11-1998.
E. Bryan Boswell b. 1908 d. 12-2-1998.

UPSHAW FAMILY BIBLE NO. 3

This Bible was published by The Southwestern Co., Nashville, Tennessee. It was originally the Bible of Ernest Linwood Upshaw, Sr. and Bertha Gouldin, his wife, who lived at Bagby, Caroline County, Virginia. It is now owned by Barbara S. Upshaw, the widow of Ernest Lynwood Upshaw, Jr. of Milford, Virginia.

Ernest Linwood [Lynwood] Upshaw of Bagby Va. and Bertha Anna Gouldin of Bagby Va. were united in marriage June 4, 1927 at Bowling Green by L.A. Ritter, Baptist Minister. Witness Irvin Broaddus and Thomas Broaddus. Bertha, the daughter of Roderick Butler Gouldin Sr. and Bettie Pitts. Ernest, the son of Tommie Eldred Upshaw and Callie Atkinson.
Elizabeth Anne Upshaw married Marvin Wright Jr. Wed. The 3rd of August at Shiloh Methodist Church.
Ernest Lynwood Upshaw married Barbara Jean Schools on Saturday Feb. 23rd 1937 at St. Stephen Baptist Church.
Roderick Eldred Upshaw married Amelia Elizabeth Safrett on Sat. The 8th of Oct. 1960 Fairmont Methodist Church, Richmond Va.
Tommy Waller Upshaw married Jean Elizabeth Gravatt Saturday June 18, 1966 at Bowling Green Baptist Church, Bowling Green, Va.
Ernest Linwood {Lynwood] Upshaw born March 8, 1928 at Bagby, Caroline Co.
Roderick Eldred Upshaw born December 23, 1929 at Bagby Caroline Co.
Thomas Waller Upshaw born February 2, 1945 at Bagby Caroline County.
Grandchildren
Kathleen Anne Wright May 20th 1956 in New Mexico.
Barbara Lynwood Upshaw Dec 23 1957.
Vin Wright (Otho Marvin) 29 March 1958 in New Mexico.
Emily Marcie Wright June 20, 1960.
Ernest Lynwood Upshaw III "Woody" Sept 8, 1960.
Anita Michelle Upshaw May 26, 1971.
Thomas Michael Upshaw July 17, 1976.
At the age of 66 Died at his home 1:30 P.M. Ernest Linwood [Linwood] Upshaw Sr. October 24, 1960.
Roderick Eldred Upshaw second son of Bertha & Ernest Upshaw passed to his Eternal Home Mar. 8, 1966, M. C. V. Hospital 7:15 P.M. He was 36 yrs. 10 mo. And 8 days old.

VAUGHAN FAMILY BIBLE NO. 1

This Bible was published by L.W. Jewell & Co., Washington, D.C., 1876. It was originally the Bible of William Henry Vaughan and was owned Roderick Dew "Jiggs" Vaughan, son of J.A. and Sadie Virginia Young Vaughan, who died August 12, 2002 at Port Royal. The Vaughan family lived at "Fleetwood" .2 mile north of Mica on route 603, now in the A.P. Hill Military Reservation. William H. Vaughan purchased this estate from his father-in-law, E.M. Richardson about 1860.

This Certifies that William H. Vaughan & Lucy E. Richardson [Richerson] were solemnly united by me in the Holy Bonds of Matrimony on the 26th day of November in the year of our Lord One Thousand Eight Hundred and Sixty Three.
Elliott T. Vaughan Son of Wm H. Vaughan was married to Miss Minnie J. Daughter of Andrew Gravatt on the 21 st day of June 1892.
William Henry Vaughan Jr. was married to Miss Theresa, Daughter of Rev. Jas. H. Marshall on the 12th of February A.D. 1896.
Elliott Toler Vaughan born March 8th 1865.
William Henry Vaughan born February 27th 1869.
John Albin Vaughan born April 6th 1874.
Joseph Coleman Vaughan born July 15th 1878.
Lucie Mary Vaughan born July 18th 1894.
William Adrew Vaughan born Dec 17th 1895.
Mary Lucille Vaughan born February 19th 1897.
Minnie Patsy Gravatt Vaughan Born July 30th 1897.
Bessie Dew Vaughan Born Jany 19th 1899.
Annie Lee Vaughan Born Jany 19th 1899.
Eller Cora Kay Richerson Marshall Vaughan [Born] Febry 12th 1900.
Edna Broaddus Vaughan Born Febry 12th 1900.
William Henry Vaughan born August 22nd 1831.
Lucie Elliott Vaughan born January 1st 1846.
Mrs. Martha A. Rollow Born Nov 13th 1828.
Mrs. Mary Richerson Born Oct 9th 1822.
Lucelle Vaughan born Feb. 19, 1897.
Cora Richerson Vaughan born Aug 21, 1899.
Elliott Eugene Vaughan born April 29, 1901.
Theresa Marshall Vaughan born Dec. 25, 1903.
Anna Johnston Vaughan born Dec. 6, 1905.
William Henry Vaughan born Sept. 10, 1907.
Mary Kay Vaughan born July 23, 1909.
Frank Marshall Vaughan born June 28, 1911.
Bessie Tulloch Vaughan born Feb. 24, 1916.
Martha Richerson Vaughan born Jan. 15, 1939.
Mrs. Mary Richerson Died May 7th 1889.
Mr. Elliott M. Richerson Died Nov 21st 1891.

Mrs. Martha A. Rollow Died July 12th 1898.
Bessie Dew Vaughan Died Jany. 20th 1899.
Mrs. Lucy E. Vaughan died June 9th 1906.
Mrs. Lucille Hutt died Sept. 15, 1923.

VAUGHAN FAMILY BIBLE NO. 2

This Bible belonged to John Albin Vaughan. Members of this family are buried at Bethany Baptist Church on the Caroline-Spotsylvania line.

This Certifies that John Albin Vaughan and Sadie Virginia Young Were Solemnly United by me in the Holy Bonds of Matrimony at Bethany Church on the Twenty seventh day of June in the year of our Lord, One Thousand Nine Hundred One in the presence of Rev. J.S. Ryland.
John Albin Vaughan born Caroline Co. Va. April 2, 1874.
Sadie Virginia Young born North Garden Spotsylvania Co. Va. Aug. 9th 1879.
John Albin Vaughan Jr. born Caroline Co. Va. Nov. 16th 1902.
Emma V. Vaughan born Caroline Co. Va. April 26th 1904.
Clarice R. Vaughan born Caroline Co. Va. April 14th 1906.
Sadie Esther Vaughan born Caroline Co. Va. June 27th 1908.
Elwood Young Vaughan born Caroline Co. Va. June 7th 1910.
Bryan Wilson Vaughan born Caroline Co. Va. May 26th 1912.
Christine Vaughan born Caroline Co. Va. June 7th 1914.
Edith Louise Vaughan born Caroline Co. Va. Sept. 7th 1916.
Douglas Karl Vaughan born Caroline Co. Va. Dec. 28th 1919.
Katheryn Elizabeth Vaughan born Caroline Co. Va. June 5th 1923.
Roderick Dew Vaughan born Caroline Co. Va. Sept. 13th 1926.
Lucy E. Vaughan born Caroline Co. Va. died June 9th 1906.
M.L. Young Sr. born Spotsylvania died Feb. 10th 1912.
Carrie O. Young born Spotsylvania died Oct. 10th 1916.
W.A. Young born Spotsylvania died June 18th 1929.
Ethel M. Young born Spotsylvania 1904 died Oct. 18th 1927.
John Alvin Vaughan born Caroline Co. Va. died Nov. 10th 1945.

VAULX FAMILY BIBLE

The Catherine Vaulx Bible was bought in 1827. It was published by Kimber and Sharpless, Philadelphia, Pa. and printed by Matthew Carey & Son, Philadelphia, Pa., 1818. There are several variations in the spelling of this name, the second most common being " Vaux". Although there have not been members of this family in Caroline County for sometime, they were here as early as the 18th century. They married into the Raines family who lived at "Robin's Roost", Bowling Green, Va. and also into the Clements family. Catharine Clements, wife of Daniel Vaulx was born in Caroline County 20 July 1755. Hannah Bolling, the maternal grand mother of Joseph Vaulx was born about 1717 in Caroline County. For further information concerning this family, see *Vaulx Family for 1900 Years* by James G. Horsfall, a copy of which is in the Library of Virginia.

Joseph Vaulx and Susan Ellis Hobson were married on Thursday the 21st day of December 1826.

Joseph Vaulx and Eleanor Ryburn Nichol Armstrong were married on Wednesday the 27th day of August 1840.

My Grand Mother

Mary Elizabeth Cowan daughter of Joseph Vaulx and Harriet Rains Cowan born at Rains home Sept 29, 1914.

Joseph Vaulx Cowan Jr. son of Joseph Vaulx & Harriet Rains Cowan born in Harching Court 30th & West End in Nashville Tenn Dec 26 1915.

James Robert Cowan still born infant son of Joseph Vaulx & Harriet Rains Cowan born home on Central Ave nr. Nash ville Tenn 1917.

Daniel Vaulx & Catherine Clements, parents of Joseph Vaulx, were married on the 15th day July 1772 in Halifax County, N. Carolina.

Note - My maternal GrandMother's maiden name was Bolling and of that branch of the Bollings which descended from Pocahontas July 1852.

Margaret N. Vaulx and George Bill Crockett were married on Tuesday 29th August 1871.

Martha Vaulx and Robert S. Cowan were married on Thursday June 14, 1883 and started for California Friday morning at 1:45 A.M. on a Bridal tour.

Joseph Vaulx Cowan Born at Nicholson House Tralane Hotel at Nashville Tenn May 4 - 1884.

Joseph Vaulx Cowan & Harriett Rains were married at Rains home on Nolensville Pike in Davidson County Tenn Nov 15 - 1910.

Joseph Vaulx was born on the 5 day of January 1799.

Susan Ellis Hobson was born on the 3d day of November 1807.

William Hobson Vaulx, son of Joseph & Susan E. Vaulx was born on Wednesday the 4th day of March 1829 at half past 12 oclk P.M in Nashville.

Ellen Clements Vaulx daughter of Joseph & Susan E. Vaulx was born on the 14th of July 1830 at 2 o'clk A.M. (Wednesday) in Nashville.

Susan Josephine Vaulx daughter of Joseph and Susan E. Vaulx was born in Nashville on the 7th day of July 1832 at 2 oclk A.M. Saturday.

Joseph Vaulx Jr. Son of Joseph Vaulx and Susan E. Vaulx his wife, was born on Sunday the 13th day of September 1835 at 3 oclk P.M. born in Nashville and in the same room where the balance of our children were born.

Robert Armstrong Vaulx, son of Joseph & Eleanor R.N. Vaulx, was born on Sunday morning about 5 o'clock the 10th day of April 1842 in Nashville.

Daniel Vaulx Son of Joseph Vaulx & Eleanor R.N. Vaulx was born on Thursday July 6th 1843 about 3 o'clk P.M. in Nashville.

Margaret Nichol Vaulx daughter of Jos. & Eleanor R.N. Vaulx was born on Tuesday 17th December 1845 at about 10 Oclk P.M. Nashville.

Catharine Clements Vaulx daughter of Jos & Eleanor R.N. Vaulx was born on Sunday 7th November 1847 at 1/2 past 7 oclk A.M. born at Mount Alban.

Mary Ann Vaulx daughter of Jos. & Eleanor R.N. Vaulx, was born on Friday 5th July 1850 born at Mt. Alban Brown Cr.

Martha & Mary Vaulx, daughters of Jos. & Eleanor R.N. Vaulx was born on Friday September 3rd 1852 at 11 1/2 Oclk P.M. (Twins) Born at Mount Alban our residence on Brown's Creek.

Births of Daniel and Catharine Vaulx's children taken from the original records this 11th day of December A.D. 1819.

Mary Vaulx born 19th day of December 1775.

Hannah Vaulx born 23rd day of August 1780.

James Vaulx born 20th day of March 1783.

Martha Vaulx born 27th day January 1786.

Susan Vaulx born 6th March 1789.

William Vaulx born 31st day of October 1792.

Margaret Vaulx born 10th June 1795.

Joseph Vaulx born the 3rd January 1799.

Catharine Vaulx, daughter of William & Hanna Clements born the 20th July 1755.

Catharine Vaulx's age was omitted to be registered in its proper place. [sic]

Eleanor Ryburn Nichol Armstrong was born in Nashville 27th January 1816.

Bolling Vaulx, Son of Jos & Eleanor R.N. Vaulx was born at "Mount Alban" on Wednesday 23rd August 1854 at 10 oclock P.M. (on Brown's Creek).

Catharine Clements, wife of Daniel Vaulx and Mother of Joseph Vaulx was born in Caroline County Virginia on the 20th day of July 1755.

Hannah Bolling, the maternal Grandmother of Joseph Vaulx was from what I can understand born about the year 1717 & I Think she was born in Caroline County Virginia her only child, my mother was born 1856. Joseph Vaulx.

Susan E. Vaulx, the beloved wife of Joseph Vaulx, departed this life on Tuesday the 13th day of October 1835 at 48 minutes Past 9 Oclk P.M. - universally regretted by all who knew her.

Robert Armstrong Vaulx son of Joseph & Eleanor R.N. Vaulx died on Monday morning the 16th day of December 1850 at 40 Minutes past 5 oclk. Aged 8 yrs 8 mos & 6 days.

William Hobson Vaulx, son of Jos & Susan E. Vaulx died on Tuesday 25th February 1851 at 45 Minutes past 2 oclk P.M. at the residence of Gen Armstrong, Nashville.

Mary Ann Vaulx daughter of Jos & E.R.N. Vaulx died on Sunday the 13th July 1851 at 45 Minutes past 2 oclk P.M. Aged 1 yr 1 week & 1 day.

Ellen C. Vaulx daughter of Jos & Susan E. Vaulx, died on Friday the 9th April 1852 at 25 Minutes past 9 oclk A.M.

Mary Vaulx daughter of Jos & E.R.N. Vaulx died Friday 21st June 1853, 10 min. past 8 A.M.

Daniel Vaulx Father of Joseph Vaulx, departed this life on the 18th day of August 1815, aged about 65 years. He was born in Maryland.

Daniel Vaulx son of Jos & E.R.N. Voulx died 13th day July 1844 Aged 1 year 1 week.

Catharine Vaulx Mother of Joseph Vaulx, died on Wednesday 12th November 1851 Aged 96 years, 3 Mos & 23 days.

Susan Josephine Vaulx died on Monday Morning 18th July 1853 about 2 oclk.

Bolling Vaulx son of Jos & E.R.N. Vaulx died on the 6th day Novemr. 1856 at 11 1/4 O'clk P.M.

Joseph Vaulx (Gr F.) died on the 22nd October 1878 at 2 oclk P.M at his residence No. 23 North High Street Nashville Tennessee in the 80th yr of his age.

Eleanor Ryburn Nichol Armstrong wife of Joseph Vaulx died in Nashville Dec 21st 1895 at 2

A.M. in the 80th year of her age.
Daniel Vaulz died the 18th August 1815.
Catharine Vaulx died the 12th November 1851 Aged 96 years, 3 mo. & 23 days.
Margaret Williams their youngest daughter died while on a visit to West Tennessee the 8th of January 1859 aged 63 yrs 6 mo. & 23 days. [corrected] Aged 64 years 6 mos 24 days, was the age of Margaret Williams, when she died - [signed] Joseph Vaulx February 17th 1873.
Times of births of Danl & Catharine Vaulx's children
Mary Vaulx born 11 December 1775.
Hannah Vaulx born 23 Augt. 1780.
James Vaulx born March 1783 died 10 _____ 1862.
Martha Vaulx born 27 Jany 1786 died young.
Susan Vaulx born 6 March 1789 .
William Vaulx born 31 October 1792.
Margaret Vaulx born 15 June 1795.
Joseph Vaulx age recorded in his bible (this book).
Taken from Mrs. Catharine Vaulx's Bible in the possession of Mrs. Margaret Williams May 1858 Joseph Vaulx.

WALDEN FAMILY BIBLE

Lord Walden [John Walden] came to this country from England in 1715, landing at Port Royal, Caroline County. He settled on lands adjoining the site of the first courthouse in Caroline County just below the old Kidds Fork Post Office and across from "Stanhope". He named the place "Walden Towers" after the estate in England. This house burned in the late 19th century. The Bible survived and was kept in the family of the descendants, owned by the late Mrs. Eula Andrews Southworth, who lived nearby. After her death it passed to Ethel Broaddus Andrews Barlow of Caroline County. No publication date is given in the Bible, however, there is a page with the inscription "This Bible is the Property of George G. and Elizabeth Walden. Bot [Bought] in the year 1802 price 7 s [shillings]". There are loose pages which appear to have been from another Bible and which contain data on the Oliver and Newman families. The records from this Bible have been published in *Tidewater Virginia Families*, Volume 4, Number 4, February 1996, pp.150-152.

Geo Walden was born 13th March 1758 Dec'd April 19th 1835.
Elizabeth Walden [was born] Nov 1790 Dec'd 3rd Sep 1822.
Nancy Walden 1st daughter of Geo & Elizabeth Walden [was born] December 18th 1781 Deceased 26 May 1783.
Charles Walden [was born] May 24 1784 Dec'd 16 December 1784.
Ambrose Walden [was born] Nov 23 1785 Dec'd 27 Aug 1786.
W.L. Walden [was born] Oct 3 [date appears to be 1787].
J.P. Walden [was born] Sep 13 1788.
Mary L Walden [was born] July 7 1792 Dec'd 6 Aug 1793.
Elizabeth Walden [was born] Apr 25 1794.
Patsy Walden [was born] Oct 4 1796.

Milly Walden [was born] December 20 1798 Dec'd 2 Sept 1799.
George Walden [was born] 13th July 1806 Dec'd 2 July 1821.
R [Rachel] A.P. Walden [was born] 30 Oct 1802 Dec'd 5 Nov 1852.
William L. Walden intermarried with Ann Berry daughter [not legible] on 13th December 1810.
Elizabeth D. Walden intermarried with William E. Gayle on 16th Nov 1815.
John P. Walden intermarried with Mary Robertson on 21st Dec 1816.
Rachel A.P. Walden intermarried with Philip T. Munday on Dec 17th 1818.
William L. Walden son of Geo [&] Elizabeth Walden died May [blank]
Geo Walden son of Geo Walden [&] Elizabeth died July 25th [blank].
William L. Walden married Sarah Vaughter 13th Dec 1810.
His children's names
Charles Franklin born 17th Sept 1811.
Elizabeth Berry Walden Born 3rd Oct 1813.
Elizabeth D. Walden married W E G 16th Nov 1815.
Patsy E. Walden married Theo. F. Green 24 [blank] 1816.
R.[Rachel] A.P. Walden married Phillip [sic] Munday 4th Dec 1799.
R .A. P. Walden was born 30th Oct 1802 Phillip Munday.
William L. Munday son of Phillip Munday and R.A.P. Munday was born 29th of Sept 1820.
John S [?] Munday 2nd son of P.T. Munday & Rachel A. his wife born April 6 [blank].
Thomas, Mary and Lucy Oliver's children's names and ages recorded below the 5th of July 1806.
John Harris Oliver son of Thomas and Mary Oliver born the 11th of February 1797.
George Lee Oliver Ditto son of Thomas and Lucy Oliver born 24th of March 1799.
Harriet Oliver daughter of Ditto Thomas and Lucy Oliver born the 11th of April 1800.
Julia Oliver 2nd daughter Ditto-Ditto-born 3rd of October 1805.
[end of listing of Oliver children]
James Madison Newman son of James and Nancy Newman was born March 31 1808.
John Mozell Newman was born the 12th of August 1809.
January 14th 1831 the great snow commenced falling and continued until the 17th of the month [noted in family record entry].
Francis Oscar Newman 1st son of James and Elizabeth Newman was born May the 23rd 1836.
John O. Newman born May the 29th 1838.
Alpheus Newman born December 28th 1840.
Daughter Octava born February the 23rd 1842.
Leonora Newman born December the 23 1844 [?].
James V. Newman October 26 1854.
Thos Berry was born October 2nd 1789.
Theo F. Green died April 14th 1862.

WALLER FAMILY BIBLE

This Bible was published by G.E. Eyre, London, England [no date listed]. A copy of the family register is in the Library of Virginia. This family lived at a place known as "Walnut Hill", then in Caroline County, but now in the edge of Spotsylvania County. Walnut Hill was built in 1837 by a Mr. Wright. It was purchased by Dabney Washington Waller, who lived here and operated

Walnut Hill Academy for many years. He died August August 16, 1880 and his son Dabney Jordan Waller lived here. He married Sophia Pleasants and Garland Thompson Waddy of "Oak Hill", Louisa County, June 26, 1867. Both he and his wife Catherine are buried here. They had 8 children: Caroline Waddy, Kate Clarke, Edward Pinckney, Rose Garland, Sophia Woodson, Georgia Tyler, Dabney Jordan Jr., and Hampden Pleasants Waller. After his first wife's death, Dabney Jordan Waller married Alice C. Lee of England October 29, 1889 and had three more children: Roberta Lee, Raymond Minor and Dorothy Vivian Waller. This family were members of Bethany Baptist Church and some are buried there. For more information concerning this family see *The Virginia Magazine of History and Biography*, Volume 36, 1928, pp.381-384. The Bible record of Judge Benjamin Waller of Spotsylvania County, Virginia is published in *Virginia Bible Records* by Jeannette Holland Austin, Willow Bend Books, Westminster, Maryland 2000.

Sophie W. [Woodson] Waller daughter of D.J.[Jordan] & A.C.[Annie Catherine] Waller was born July 17th 1875 [at Walnut Hill].
Georgie T.[Tyler] Waller daughter of D.J. & A.C. Waller was born Oct. 16th 1877 [at Walnut Hill].
D.J. Waller Jr. son of D.J. & A.C. Waller was born March 22 1879 [at Walnut Hill].
Hampden P.[Pleasants] Son of D.J. & A.C. Waller was born March 1st 1882 [at Walnut Hill].
Roberta L.[Lee] Waller daughter of D.J. & Alice Waller was born Aug. 16th 1890 [at Walnut Hill].
Alice [Caroline] Waller was born Aug 16 th 1890 [at Walnut Hill].
Garland Waddy Wilde was born Nov 23rd 1856.
Abner Pleasants Wilde was born Dec. 25th 1859.
D.J. Waller Son of D.W. and Caroline Waller was born June 29th 1841.
Annie C. Waller daughter of G.L. and L.A. Waddy was born Dec.25th 1847.
Callie [Caroline] W.[Waddy] Waller daughter of D.J. and A.C. Waller was born May 8th 1868 [at "Oak Hill", Louisa County].
Kate C. Waller daughter of D.J. and A.C. Waller was born Sept.21st 1869 [at Oak Hill, Louisa County].
Edward P.[Pinckney] Waller son of D.J. and A.C. Waller was born March 21st 1871 [at Walnut Hill].
Rosiebelle [Rose] G.[Garland] Waller daughter of D.J. and A.C. Waller was born Nov. 30th 1872 [at Walnut Hill].
Raymond M.[Minor] Waller son of D.J. and Alice Waller was born June 21, 1892.
Dorothy V.[Vivian] Waller daughter of D.J. and Alice Waller born July 13, 1895 [at Walnut Hill].

[Following newspaper clippings:]
Chewning-Waller 1891. Bethany Baptist church, Caroline county, Va., was the scene of a beautiful marriage on the evening of the 25th. The church was tastefully decorated with mottoes of evergreens and other floral designs, and nearly filled with a very appreciative audience, at 5 o'clock, when Mr. L.P. [Lynn Purcell] Chewning of Spotsylvania, and Miss Kate C. Waller, of Caroline, preceded by twelve couples of waiters, marched gracefully down the aisle and were united in holy wedlock by the Rev. O.T. Taylor of Richmond College. After the ceremony the

bridal party with quite a number of relatives of the bride and groom, drove to the residence of the bride's father, Mr. A.J. Waller, where they enjoyed a very hospitable reception, a magnificent supper, and several hours of pleasant conversation.

D. Jordan Waller. Prominent Caroline County Citizen Passes Away Sunday Night April 12th 1925. D. Jordan Waller, a highly esteemed and prominent citizen at Caroline county died Sunday night at his home, "Walnut Hill", in the upper part of the county, after an illness of several years. Mr. Waller was slightly more than 80 years of age and his death was not unexpected.

The deceased was born in Caroline county and had made his home there all his life, practically all of which was spent in farming, he having never aspired to public office, though he was for some time a justice of the peace, a capacity in which he served more for the convenience of the neighborhood than for the pleasure he derived from his duties. Mr. Waller was an ex-Confederate soldier, having served nearly three years with the Southern forces, coming out of the conflict with a creditable and honorable record.

Mr. Waller is survived by his second wife, who was a Miss Lee prior to her marriage and by the following children: Mrs. S.W. Hancock and Mrs. Georgia Dalton, of this city; Mrs. L.P. Chewning, of Partlow; Mrs. Frederick Frazer, of Massaponax; Mrs. Roberta Anderson, of Midlothian; Hampden Waller, of Washington; Raymond Waller, of Caroline; Miss Callie Waller, of Caroline; Jordan Waller, of Caroline and Miss Dorothy Waller, who lived with her father at the home place. He also is survived by a large number of grandchildren.

On the 8th of September, 1880, after a long and painful illness, being at the time in the thirty-ninth year of her age, Mrs. ANNIE WALLER *nee* Waddy, beloved wife of Jordan Waller, Esq., gently passed from "the land of the dying" into that of endless life.

In girlhood she professed faith to the Lord Jesus and united with Elk Creek church, but for the last eighteen years she had been a member at Bethany, where she will be greatly and sadly missed. One who knew her well testifies that hers was a life of gentleness, meekness and patient continuance in well-doing. To the writer she was a friend faithful and true - a sister who knew how to sympathize and help. There are many who will not soon cease to mourn that she is with us no more. But our loving father knows and does just what is best for each and all of his Children.

May the stricken husband, eight motherless children, aged mother, and all who grieve that she is gone, realize that in this afflictive dispensation of His providence the Lord designs and is accomplishing for them enlargement of character and eternal honor. K.W.W.

Death of a Good Woman. Mars. Annie Waddy Waller, wife of Dr. Jordan Waller, of Caroline county, died yesterday at her home, Walnut Hill, near Goodloe's postoffice, after a brief illness. She was a daughter of the late Garland Thompson Waddy of Louisa county, and had many friends in Richmond, who will deeply regret the passing away of this most amiable and lovely lady. Deceased was an aunt of Mr. G. Waddy Wilde, secretary of the Democratic City Committee. She leaves many to lament her death, including a loving husband and children. She was always a good woman in the interpretation of that term, and therefore her translation had no terrors for her. Her memory, with those who survive her, will always "bloom and blossom in the dust."

Mrs. D. Jordan Waller died at her home, Walnut Hill, Caroline Co., Va. on Monday morning Sept. 6th, 1886. She leaves a husband, an aged mother and eight children to mourn their loss.

WARE FAMILY BIBLE NO. 1

A copy of this Bible record is in the Library of Virginia. Robert Ware was in Caroline County records as early as 1769. He served on the Committee of Safety in 1775. Ware Creek which flows into the Rappahannock River in Caroline County is named for this family. Nicholas Ware died in Caroline County in 1744 leaving Nicholas Ware Jr. as executor. Nicholas Ware operated a grist mill in St. Mary's Parish in 1771. For further information see *Colonial Caroline, A History of Caroline County, Virginia* by T. E. Campbell, The Dietz Press, Richmond, Virginia, 1954.

Robert Ware and Peggy his wife were married 29 December 1767.
Susannah Ware the daughter of Robert & Peggy Ware, was married to Daniel Banksdale Jany 1780.
Joseph Ware was married January 11, 1780.
Nicholas Ware was married December 1800 to his first wife and the 12 of June 1816 to his second.
Sarah Ware was married to Lewis Harris 18 June 1795.
Lucy G. Ware was married to Wm Brown 7 March 1803.
Robert Ware was married 23 Dec 1805.
Thompson Ware was married 5 February 1807.
Aspry Ware was married to Miss Comelia Jones on the 19 Jany 1817. George G. Ware was married to Miss Jane E. Middleton on the 24 of February 1835.
Samuel R. Tucker was married to Eliza Ware on the 7th October 1834.
Robert Ware Son of Nicholas Ware and Sarah his wife was born 3rd April 1750.
Peggy Ware the wife of Robert Ware was born 5 November 1750.
Susannah Ware, the daughter of Robert Ware and Peggy his wife was born 11th November 1758.
Joseph Ware Son of Robert and Peggy Ware was born 6th December 1772.
Nicholas Ware Son of Robert and Peggy Ware was born the 16th February 1776.
Sarah Ware the daughter of Robert and Peggy Ware, was born the 3rd August 1778.
Lucy Green Ware, daughter of Robert and Peggy Ware, was born the 2 August 1781.
Robert Tankersley Ware, Son of Robert & Peggy Ware was born the 18 December 1783.
Thompson Ware, Son of Robert and Peggy Ware was born the 12th May 1786.
Henry Ware Son of Robert and Peggy Ware, was born the 1st February 1789.
Nicholas Ware Senior died 4th November 1817 in the 68th year of his age.
Lucy G. Bacon daughter of Robert & Peggy Ware died at Mt. Pleasant 15th Sepr 1821.
Nicholas Ware Son of Robert & Peggy Ware died in the City of New York on the 7th Septr. 1824. Aged 28 years & Seven Months.
Peggy Ware Wife of Robert Ware Senior died on the 22nd of December 1829 in the 80th year of her age.
George Green Tankersley Ware, Son of Robert and Peggy Ware was born the 18 February 1794.
Nicholas Ware the father of Robert Ware was born 29th December 1709.
Margaret Lucy Ware Daughter of George & Jane Ware was born on the 4 of December 1825.

Nicholas Ware Senr. died the 10th November 1799 aged 90 years.
Joseph Ware, Son of Robert and Peggy Ware died the 24th March 1808.
William Bacon died at Mt. Pleasant 18 June 1811.
Susannah Barksdale Daughter of Robert Ware and Peggy his wife died 26th September 1812.
Henry Ware Son of Robert & Peggy Ware died the 10 September 1817.
Robert Ware Son of Robert & Peggy Ware died the 27th October 1820.

WARE FAMILY BIBLE NO. 2

Albert G. Ware and his wife, Judith, lived at a farm named "Solitude" in the north western part of Caroline County. The house is now gone. They are buried on this place. There are two pages of family records in this Bible. For information concerning the military service, see *History of 47th Virginia Infantry* by Homer D. Musselman. The Bible records have recently been donated to the Virginia Historical Society by Ray S. Campbell, Jr. who furnished the copy for publication here.

Albert G. Ware and Judith T. Ware were married on the 9th day of January, 1834.
A.G. Ware was born 21st [?] day of October, 1810.
Indiana Pleasants Ware was born the 9th of January, 1835.
Martha Lindsay Ware was born on the 13th day of February, 1837.
Jordan Pleasants Ware was born on the 14th of February 1839.
William Wallace Ware was born on the 11th day of August, 1841.
Francis Calvin Ware was born on the 15th of August 1843.
Francis Calvin Ware died on Tuesday morning 4 1/4 o'clock 10th of Decmr. 1861 at R.M. [Randolph Macon} College.
Judith T. Ware died on Monday evening the 24th day of February, 1862.
Margaret F. Ware died the 25th day of August, 1872.
Jordan P. Ware was [killed] by a ball passing through the crown of his hat just grasing the top of his head on the first day of Octo, about sunrise in the morning, 1864, near Petersburg.
William Wallace Ware died the 16th of May, 1865, at home (disease chronic diorea); came from the army sick several months before he died.
Jordan P. Ware & Wallace W. Ware joined the seckond [sic] Regiment of Virginia Artillery and started to Camp the 23rd of June, 1861.
Servants births:
Betty was born in January 1831.
Jack was born in 1830.
Dick was born in 1832.
Elizabeth was born in 1834.
Milly was born in 1838.
William was born 3rd or 8th of Jany, 1841.
Eliza was born 3rd of Jany, 1841.
Wilton was born 19 August, 1842.
Susan was born ____.
Patsey was born the 27th of August 1842.
John Minor was born 29th of March, 1861.

Eady was born 2nd of April 1861.
_____ was born December 6th, 1861.
Clara died 26th April, 1841.
Winney died ____.
Mary died ____.
Mary Jane ____.
Elizabeth died l4th November, 1861.

WASHINGTON FAMILY BIBLE

This Bible was printed and published by M. Carry & Son, Philadelphia. In the front is written: Wm S. Courts. The records of this Bible were copied by W. H. Washington, Laurens, S.C. in 1911 and published in part in the *William and Mary Quarterly*, Volume 20, p.32 and in the *Virginia Magazine of History and Biography*, Volume 22, 1914, p.114. This family lived at "Woodpecker" plantation in the northern part of Caroline County. A typewritten copy is also in the Burke folder of the George H.S. King Papers, Virginia Historical Society, from which the following is reproduced. The original Bible was last owned by the late Mrs. Florence Lucy, Caroline County.

John Washington was married to Elizabeth Buckner in 1770.
John Washington, son of John Washington and Elizabeth Washington was born September 24, 1772.
George Washington son of John and Elizabeth Washington was born July 8, 1775.
Catharine Washington was born June 22. 1796.
George Washington was born August the 6th 1798.
John Washington [born] September 13 - 1800.
Susan Elizabeth Knox Washington was born Oct. 7, 1802.
Ann Washington was born September 11, 1804.
Selina R.C. Washington was born Oct. 15th 1806.
Dorothea B. Washington was born November 11th 1808.
George Washington son of John & Elizabeth Washington was married to Elizabeth Courts the Daughter of Doct. John Courts January 1, 1794.
Catharine Washington intermarried with Robt. Sutton Oct. 10, 1811.
John Washington and Ann Haws [Hawes] was married the March the 7, 1820.
Susan Washington and Thos. H. Burke was married the 5 day Decr 1821.
Ann Washington and E.D. Withers was married the 24th day of February in the year of our Lord 18[torn] A.L.5825.
Dorothea B. Washington was married to Norborne E. Sutton Augst 21st 1829.
Eliza F. Washington was [married] to Wm. Taliaferro 1st day April 1830.
William Washington and [short name obliterated, probably Ann] E. Vass were married in January 1831.
William Washington was born March 22nd 1810.
Eliza Washington was born February 8th 1812.
Caroline Washington was born the 15th of May 1814.

Geo. B. Sutton the son of Robt. and Catherine was born the 25 Oct. 1813.
Susan M.E. Sutton was born March the 4, 1816.
Judith Ann Sutton was born March the 1, 1818.
William Robert Sutton was born Oct. 29, 1819.
Adaline W. Sutton was born Augst. 19 - 1822.
Henry C. Sutton was born February 25 - 1823.
George W. Burke the son of Thos. H. and Susan Burke was born the April 4, 1823.
George Washington son of John & Ann Washington was born Jany. 23rd 1821.
Dorothea Washington daughter of John & Ann Washington was born April 22nd 1822.
Walker Washington son of Jno. & Ann Washington was born Oct. 26, 1824.
William Henry Burke son of Thos. H. and Susan Burke was born the 1 day of December 1824.
Rolls Montgomery Withers son of Ezekiel D. and Ann Withers was born the 1st day of January 1826. A.L. 5826.
Edward Gray son of Thomas H. and Susan Burke was born the 29th of August 1826.
William Washington was born in 1810.
Eliza Washington was born the 8th of February 1812.
Ann Eliza Withers daughter of Ezekiel D. Withers and Ann Withers was born 22nd Sept. 1827.
Selina W. Burke Daughter of Tho. H. and Susan Burke was born the 11th day of August 1828.
George W. Sutton son of N.E.S. D.B.S. was born the 1st day of July 1830.
Selina H. Taliaferro daughter of Wm F. & Eliza Taliaferro was born 28 of January 1831.
John Washington son of John and Elizabeth Washington departed this life Oct. the 2nd 1802.
John Washington, father of John and George Washington, departed this life August the 22nd 1804.
Elizabeth the wife of John Washington departed this life Oct. the 15th 1812.
George Washington departed this life January 15th 1815.
George Washington son of Geo. and Elizabeth Washington departed this life Feb. 1815.
Caroline Washington daughter of Geo. and Elizabeth Washington departed this life Augst. 15, 1815.
George B. Sutton departed this life Oct. 3, 1815.
John Washington son of John and Ann Washington was born April 17th 1827.
Elizabeth Selina Payne was born 9th of November 1827.
Bettie S. Payne [written with no further info]
Elizabeth Washington the wife of Geo. Washington died Feby. 8th 1834.
Edward G. Burke son of Thos. H. & Susan Burke died the 22nd of Feby. 1844.
Wm Washington son of Geo. & Elizabeth died 4th Aug. 1844 [this has been altered to 1843. Will published 11 Sept. 1843 in Caroline County.]
Edward G. Burke son of Thomas H. & Susan Burke died on 22nd of February 1844.
Dorothea Sutton the wife of Norborne E. Sutton died on 17th of November 1844.
Betty Washington the daughter of John & Ann Washington died Oct. 28th 1827.
Mary daughter of John & Ann Washington died January 26, 1831.
Dorothea Burke daughter of John & Ann Washington died Jany. 11th 1849.
Col. John Washington son of George & Elizabeth Washington died at Woodpecker the 27 of September 1850 in the 50 year of his age.
Mrs. Ann Washington wife of Col. John Washington died on the 24th day of August 1863.

WASHINGTON/BURKE FAMILY BIBLE

This Bible was printed by C. Ewer & T. Bedlington, J. H. A. Frost, printer, Boston, 1827. It is now owned by John W. Burke, Jr. of "Braynefield', Caroline County, Virginia. A typewritten copy is in the Burke folder of the George H.S. King Papers, Virginia Historical Society, from which this is copied.

Thomas H. Burke and Susan E. K. Washington was Married on the 5th day of December 1821.
Geo. M. Burke and Dorothea B. Washington were married on 2 July 1844.
John Washington and Ann Hawes were married the 7th March 1820.
George W. Burke and Eliza F. Taliaferro were married 28th of Nov. 1850.
G.W. Burke & Bettie C. DeJarnette were married on the 1st day of November 1882.
Bessie W. Burke and T.J. Higgins were married on the 10th day of September 1907.
J.D. Burke & Beatrice L. Knapp were married Oct. 8, 1914.
Lucy H. Burke & William P. Goodwin were married May 5, 1915 by S.B. Overton, Bowling Green, Va.
John W. Burke & Hazel S. Bellerby were married on December 24 - 1924.
Thomas Henry Burke was born 3rd of October 1800.
Susan E.K. Washington was born the 7th of October 1802.
George Washington Burke, son of Susan & Thos. H. Burke, was born the 4th day of April 1823.
William H. Burke, son of Tho. H. & Susan Burke was born the 1st day of December 1824.
Edward G. Burke, son of Tho. H. & Susan Burke was born the 29th of August 1826.
Selina W. Burke, Daughter of Tho. H. & Susan Burke was born the 11th day of August 1828.
Thomas H. Burke, son of Dorothea & G. W. Burke was born the 18th day of April 1845.
Eliza F., Daughter of William & Eliza F. Taliaferro was born the 21st day of March 1833.
James DeJarnette Burke, son of G. W. Burke and Bettie D. Burke was born the 11th of November 1883.
Lucy Herndon Burke, daughter of G. W. Burke and Bettie D. Burke, was born the 18th of March 1886.
Bettie Washington Burke, second daughter of G. W. Burke and Bettie Burke was born April 16th 1889.
4 O'Clock, Sunday, August 23, 1891, John W. Burke, second son of Bettie Burke and G. W. Burke [was born].
T. J. Higgins, Jr., son of Bessie Burke and T. J. Higgins was born the 4th of July 1908.
John W. Burke, Jr., son of John W. and Hazel Burke, born Sept. 30, 1925 at 9:25 A.M., being Wednesday.
Rosalie T.--- Burke, daughter of Eliza & G. W. Burke was born 30 day of November 1851.
William Taliaferro Burke, son of Eliza F. and George W. Burke, was born February 6, 1854.
John Washington Burke, son of Eliza F. and George W. Burke, was born 6 of February 1855.
George W. Burke, third son of Geo. & Eliza Burke, was born the 30th day of April 1859. Twin brother Edward was born & died 1 May 1859.
George Washington, the son of John & Ann Washington was born Jany. 23rd 1821.
Dorothea Washington, the daughter of John & Ann Washington was born April 22nd 1822.
Walker Washington, the son of Jno. & Ann Washington was born Octr. 26th 1824.

Jno. son of Jno. and Ann Washington was born April 16th 1827.

Betty, daughter of Jno. & Ann Washington was born Feby. 2nd 1826.

Mary, Daughter of John & Ann Washington was born Augst. 27th 1828.

Robert Lee Burke, 5th son of Eliza & Geo. W. Burke, was born 28th of July 1862.

Eliza F. Burke, second daughter of Eliza & Geo. W. Burke born 16th of September 1863.

Susan S. Burke, 3rd daughter of Geo. W. & Eliza F. Burke born 3rd December 1864.

Betty, Daughter of Jno. & Ann Washington, died Octr. 28th 1827.

Mary, Daughter of John & Ann Washington, died 26 January 1831.

Dorothea B. Burke, the wife of G.W. Burke and daughter of Col. John and Ann Washington, died 11 of January 1849.

Col. John Washington, son of Major George and Elizabeth Washington, died at Woodpecker the 27 of September 1850.

Edward G. Burke, son of Thos. H. & Susan Burke died on 22nd Feby 1844.

William Washington, son of Geo. & Elizabeth Washington, died 11 August 1844 [this has been altered to read 1843].

Dorothea Sutton the wife of N. E. Sutton died 17 Novr. 1844.

Susan S. Burke, 3rd daughter of Geo. W. & Eliza F. Burke, died 9th June 1865.

Rosalie F. Burke, daughter of George Burke and Eliza Burke, died the 8th of July 1852.

John Washington Burke, second son of Eliza & Geo. Burke, died 10 of November 1855.

Wm. Taliaferro Burke, 1st son of Eliza & Geo. W. Burke died the 23d of August 1863.

Eliza F., second daughter of Eliza & Geo. Burke died the 26th of September 1863.

Robert Lee Burke, son of Eliza & Geo. Burke died the 24th Oct.1863.

Eliza F. Burke, wife of G.W. Burke and daughter of William and Eliza Taliaferro, died the 5th of March 1878. For more than two long years she scarcely saw a well day. It was a long trail of faith, but she endured it all with Christian resignation.

George Washington Burke born the 4th of April 1823 died at Braynefield July 28th 1896 after an illness of ten days.

Bettie D. Burke was born November the 8th 1851, died July 23, 1930, at 5:25 at Braynefield. She was true devoted wife. A fond and loving Mother. She was in failing health for years, but bore it all with Christian fortitude. An Angel in her Earthly home, An Angel in Heaven.

James C. DeJarnette, son of Elliotte & Elizabeth DeJarnette, was Born September 21st 1817. Died March 9th 1894. Mr. DeJarnette was a great sufferer for two years or more with a combination of diseases he bore them all with a Christian resignation. I have never seen equaled. Surely he was a GODly man. Just, upright in a all of his dealings with his fellow man, honest to a fault, Cannot it be well ------.

Lucy Mary DeJarnette born Sept. 15th 1824, Died May 13th 1896.

Beatrice Knapp Burke, wife of J.D. Burke, died Feb. 26, 1935, buried at Braynefield Feb. 28, 1935. A true Christian, a faithful wife, a devoted Mother. Loved by all who knew her.

Jennie L. DeJarnette died in Ashland, July 25, 1937. Buried July 27, 1937 at Poplar Grove her old home. She was daughter of the late James Coleman and Lucy Mary DeJarnette.

Dorothy Knapp Burke, oldest daughter of James D. Burke and Beatrice Burke, married July 4, 1937, to Scott Hall.

Florence Amelia Peane Bellerly, mother of Hazel B. Burke, died April 11, 1934 at her home in Chesterfield County. She was born in Kent, England, April 12, 1878. Came to San Antonio,

Texas, when about twelve years of age. She was a devoted Mother, true and faithful wife. She was a graduate of St. Mary's Hall Episcopal School in San Antonio. She died very suddenly, was sick only two hours.

Edward Ballery, Father of Hazel B. Burke, was born in Durham, England, Sept. 18, 1872, came to Texas in 1885, lived on a ranch in Bexer County near Pasadena, Texas, until 1907 when he brought his family to Chesterfield County, where he lived the remainder of his life. He was a good father, true and faithful husband. He died after a few months sickness (heart trouble) on Sept. 24, 1939, leaving two daughters, Mrs. Thelma Clarke & Hazel B. Burke.

WHITE FAMILY BIBLE NO. 1

This Bible originally belonged to the family of James J. White Sr., who lived in the Guinea area of Caroline County. Their neighbors were the families of Catlett, Thornton, Dillard, the Jesses, and Matthew Campbell. A copy of this family register is in the Library of Virginia.

James J. White Sr. was born 6th Nov. 1776.
Elizabeth White, his wife was born 18th October 1781. Married 26 December 1798.
Ann J. White was born 3rd November 1799. Died in Tennessee.
George Green White was born September 20th 1801.
Elizabeth S. White was born February 5th 1803. Died in Albemarle Co.
Martha G. (Green) White was born February 6th 1805. Died in Goochland.
Ambrose L. White was born November 24th 1807. Died in Tennessee.
James J. Whites Jr. was born March 15th 1815. Lived 69 years Died in Caroline Co.
Mary A.G. (Ann Green) White was born August 29th 1816. Died in Caroline Co.
William S. White was born March 29th 1819. Lived 75 years. Died in Tenn.
Henry Buckner White was born Oct. 28th 1820. Died in Ga.
Julia A. Banks White was born February 22nd 1823. Lived 75 years & Died in Tennessee.
Virginia Nelson White was born April 12th 1825. Died in Caroline Co.
James J. White Sr. and Elizabeth his wife were baptized by Elder Addison M. Lewis September 8th. 1827.
James J. White and Elizabeth Green were married 26 December 1798.
Bennet Wright and Ann J. White were married the 9th. Dec. 1819.
Rice G. Barksdale and Elizabeth White were married 22nd Nov. 1821.
Roland H. Goodman and Martha G. White were married 14th Nov.1822.
Wesley Wright and Mary A.G. White were married May 20th 1834.
James J. White Jr. and Margaret A. T. Campbell were married 18th Dec. 1834.
H. B. White and Ann E. Wigglesworth were married 25th Oct. 1842.
Virginia N. White and George R. Samuel were married Sept. 21st 1843.
Julia A.B. White and Matthew T. Campbell were married 14th December 1844.
William S. White and Lavinia C. Gouldin were married 23 November 1845.

WHITE FAMILY BIBLE NO. 2

This Bible was published by Jesper Harding & Son, Philadelphia, 1857. The Bible belonged to Lawrence Battaile White (1838-1901) son of Dr. Edmond Pendleton White and Ann Champe Battaile of "Port Tobago", Caroline County, Virginia. Dr. White, his wife and members of his family are buried in the cemetery at Port Tobago, the Lomax family estate outside of Port Royal. The house burned many years ago, but the site remains undisturbed. A copy of this Bible record is in the Library of Virginia.

Married in Washington, D.C., by the Rev. J.S. Kinnard, on the 6th of July 1860 Laurence B. White to Eliza L. Taliaferro, both of Fredericksburg, Virginia.

John White Junior of Louisa Co Va., son of William & Caty - married Matha Key, daughter of Martin Key of Albemarle Co Va 1st day January 1796. John White was the grand father of Laurence B. White.

Edmond P. [Pendleton] White, son of John & Matha White of Spotsylvania Co, Va., married Ann Champe Battaile, daug of Laurence Battaile of Caroline Co Va 1st day of October 1826.

William F. White, son of John White & Matha, married Catherine L. White, daughter of Gen William White of Davidson Co, Tennessee, 25 Aug 1831.

Jesie Martin Key White of Spotsylvania Co, Va., married Helen Thomly of King [King George?] Co, Va.

Nancy Bibb White, only daughter of John & Matha White of Spotsylvania Co Va., married Hawes Graves of Fayette Co, Kentucky 8 April 1819 & moved to Tennessee. They had 3 children, viz:

Matha who married Wm B. Ewing of Tennessee.

Louisa Catherine, who married 1st a Hatcher, a Methodist minister of distinction; 2nd, Dr. McClain. She resides near Nashville, Tennessee.

Edmond P. Graves, who married Miss Helen Clarissa Strich of Louisiana, resides near Nashville, Tennessee, has six children.

Children of Wm F. White are as follows & their marriages:

Louisa, only daughter, married Robert Graves, resides near Pine Grove, Clarke Co., Kentucky, has five daughters.

George Arthur White married Annie Elizabeth Taliaferro of Fredericksburg, Va., and had no children. He died in Hospital for Sick Soldiers during the Confederate War of 1861. He was maimed Feb 1862 at Fredericksburg, Virginia.

John Wesley White, son of William White, the son of John & Matha White, married and had 6 children, his children reside in Tenn.

Charles White, son of William White, son of John & Matha White of Va, married 1st, a Miss Cork; 2nd time, a widow, has no children, resides at Nashville, Tennessee.

These are the children of Jessie Martin Key White, the son of John & Matha White, viz:

John White who married and died and left one child at Mt. Sterling, Montgomery Co, Kentucky.

Edmond Pendleton, single, resides with his mother, Mt. Sterling, Kentucky.

Catherine, married Dr. James Thomley of King George Co, Va., is dead and leaves 1 child, a son, now 25 years of age - yr 1878.

Jessie, daughter of Jessie White, died 16 or 17 years of age, single, having never married.

These are the children of Doctor Edmond P. White & their marriages, who was the son of John & Matha White, who married Ann C. Battaile, viz:

John Laurence, died 12 or 13 yrs of age.

William Wirt, died 8 or 10 yrs of age.

Edmond Pendleton, died 7 or 8 yrs of age.

Anna Robinson, died 10 or 12 yrs of age.

John B. White married Fannie B. Taliaferro of Fredericksburg, Va., Oct 10, 1860.

LAURENCE B. WHITE (author) married Eliza L. Taliaferro, sister of Fannie B. Taliaferro, daughters of John W. Taliaferro of Fredericksburg, Va., July 6, 1860.

These are the children of Laurence & Eliza White of Porto Bago, Caroline County, Va.:

John Pendleton, died at Fredericksburg & buried in cemetery there Jan 1st, 1862.

Laurence Gustavus, born Nov 10, 1862, at Fredericksburg, Va (died 1954).

George Arthur, born Nov 13, 1864, at Port Tobago, Caroline Co, Va.

Edmond Pendleton, born Nov 20, 1866, at Port Tobago, Caroline Co, Va. (died 1952).

Mary Wilhelmina, born Sept 15, 1868, at Port Tobago, Caroline Co, Va.

Sallie Francais Brooke, born Feb 22, 187_(date inked out), Port Tobago.

John Addison, born July 17, 187_(date inked out), Port Tobago.

Edmond Champ Gaines White, son of Dr. E.P. White, single and afflicted, born April 26, 1847.

William R.W. White, son of Dr. E.P. White, born Sept 19th, 1849, died March 20th, 1876, being 27 years of age, he was buried in Cemetery of Lunatic Asylum at Williamsburg, Va.

(same handwriting but different ink):

Robinson Spurgeon White, second son of Laurence B. White & Mary B. White, born Feb 19, 1886, at Planna Terra, Caroline Co, Va.

Benjamin Battaile White, 3rd son of L. B. & Mary B. White, born Aug 11, 1889 (died 1919).

Eugene Fitzhugh, 4th son of L. B. & Mary B. White, born Jan 30, 1892, at Planna Terra, Caroline Co, Va.

Edmonia Brown White, 2nd daughter of L. B. & M. B. White, born Planna Terra, Caroline Co, Va., on July 24, 1894.

(Pinned in Bible, mostly in same handwriting):

Born at Planna Terra, Caroline Co, Va., September 30th, 1895, William Temple White, 4th son of L. B. & Mary B. White.

Annie Elizabeth White, 3rd daughter of Laurence B. & Mary B. White, born May 24, 1898, at "Planna Terr[a]", a part of "Port Tobago", Caroline Co, Va.

Born at Planna Terra, Caroline County, Va, July 4, 1901, Lauryce Battaile White, 4th daughter of Laurence B. & Mary B. White.

Edmond Pendleton White, son of Laurence B. & Eliza L. White, married Annie L. Battaile of Westmoreland, at Benning D.C., Jan 11, 1892.

Mary Wilhelmina, oldest daughter of Laurence B. White & Eliza L. White, married R.E. Hudson of West Virginia, formerly of Richmond, Va.

John Addison White, youngest son of Laurence B. & Eliza L. White, married Washington, D.C. April 25, 1900, Annie Reamy of Westmoreland Co, Virginia.

(continuing with the original Bible)

Born in King George County 17th of July 1840, Eliza L. Taliaferro, 5th daughter of John W.

Taliaferro and Sarah Brooke.

Born at Port Tobago in Caroline County 27th of January 1843, LAURENCE B. WHITE, son of Edmond P. White and Ann Champ Battaile.

Born at Fredericksburg April 19, 1861, John Pendleton, first son of Laurence B. & Eliza L. White.

Born at Fredericksburg Nov 10th, 1862, Laurence Gustavus, second son of Laurence B. & Eliza L. White.

Born at Port Tobago, Caroline Co, Va., Nov 13th 1864, George Arthur White, 3rd son of L. B. & E. L. White.

(Also, pinned in original Bible)

EDMUND PENDLETON WHITE, son of Dr. E. P. & A.C. White, died at "Runnymede", the home of his uncle, Dr. Benjamin R. Battaile, July 1911. He was a member of Enon Baptist Church and a earnest Christian and died believing in Christ. His sudden death was mourned by his many friends and relatives.

(continued from original Bible):

Born at Port Tobago, Caroline County, Va., Edmond Pendleton, 4th son of Laurence B. & Eliza L White, Nov 20, 1866.

Born at Port Tobago, Caroline County, Va., Mary Wilhelmina, 1st daughter of Laurence B. & Eliza L White, September 15, 1868.

Born at Planna Terra (a part of Port Tobago Farm), Caroline County, Virginia, Sarah Francais Brooke, 2nd daughter of Laurence B. & Eliza L White, February 22nd, 1873.

Born at Planna Terra (a part of Port Tobago Farm), Caroline County, Va., John Addison White, fifth son of Laurence Battaile & Eliza Laurence Taliaferro White, July 17th, 1870.

(inserted but same handwriting):

Born at Planna Terra Edith Hawthorne White, 1st daughter of Laurence B & Mary B. White Dec 17th, 1884.

Nancy Bibb White, daughter of John and Matha White, was born 1st day March 1797.

Jessie Martin Key White, son of John & Matha White, born 12 day August 1798.

William F. White, son of John & Matha White, born 12 day Sept 1800.

Dr. Edmond P. White, son of John & Matha White, born 12th Sept 1803. Died at Port Tobago August 15, 1856.

[following newspaper clippings]

Married on the 6th Nov 1882 in Richmond City, Va., at the residence of the bride's sister, Mrs. Virginia H. Clayton, by the Rev Z. Tyler of Christian Church of said City, Rev. Laurence B. White, son of Dr. E. P. White of Caroline Co, Va., to Miss Mary Bettie Battaile of Westmoreland Co, Va., daughter of Dr. Benjamin R. Battaile. May God crown this institution of marital union with high blessings of His merciful Hand.

Died January 1st 1862 John Pendleton, 1st son of Laurence B. & Eliza L White, aged nine months. "Suffer little children to come unto men and forbid them not, for of such is the Kingdom of God".

Died at Williamsburg, Va., March - 1876, William R.W. White, brother of Laurence B. White.

He never married. His brother heired his estate. "Many are the afflictions of the Righteous but the Lord deliverth them out of them all".

Dr. Edmond P. White died at Port Tobago, Caroline Co, Va. Aug 14, 1856. He was a member of Enon Baptist Church, a kind father, an affectionate husband, a useful citizen, a charitable Christian. In his death, his children lost a noble parent, a wise protectorate; his country and neighbors, a true patriot and friend; the Church of Christ, a charitable member. Their loss has been his eternal gain. His funeral was attended by a concourse of Masonic and Christian and friendly mourners, with the services of Christian religion appropriate for such occasions and Masonic burial ceremonies. His earthly remains were committed to the dust till Jesus shall bid them rise. "May they rise in resplendent glory of the Redeemed of God".

Ann C. White, consort of Dr. E. P. White, in her widowhood, died at Port Tobago May 18, 1863 of dropsey. Owing to a Civil War then in progress, she was deprived of the association of her children but she was not alone. She confided in Jesus Christ, our Lord, her Redeemer, and the arms of the everlasting covenant of the Mercy of God upheld her spirit in the trying hour of her dissolution. She sung the sweet songs of Zion on her bed of affliction. She was a affectionate mother tho composed with infirmities of health. She left 4 children to mourn her loss while she departed to be with Christ. She was a member of the Protestant Episcopal, St. Peter's, Port Royal, Caroline Co, Va. Her earthly remains interred by the side of her husband's and children in the "White" family cemetery on Port Tobago Farm on the Rappahannock River, Caroline County, Virginia.

John W. Taliaferro, father of Eliza L. White, the wife of Laurence B. White, died at Fredericksburg, Va., Sept 12, 1877. In the 90th year of his life. He left children and grandchildren to mourn his death. "Like Jacob of old, he gathered himself up and gave up willingly the Ghost". Religion was a frequent theme with him. He avowed faith in Christ. He was buried in Cemetery, Fredericksburg, Va.

Gustavus S. Taliaferro, son of John W. Taliaferro and brother of Eliza L. White, died at Fredericksburg, Va. March 9th 1877 of typhoid pneumonia in the 55th yr of his age. After an illness of 14 days, all of which he was said to have borne with Christian patience. He served in various capacities of public usefulness, as clerk of The Treasury Department of the Federal Government. At the breaking out of the War of Secession, he cast his destinies with his native state and the South. He was appointed to clerkship of like department of the Confederate Government. In all of which capacities, he served with honor to his family and country. He died a member of the Episcopal Church. He never married. He was buried in Cemetery at Fredericksburg Va.

Eliza L. White, beloved wife of Laurence B. White, died at Planna Terra April 14, 1882, in the 41st year of her age. She died in the triumphants of the Christian faith, was made perfect through suffering. Many wives and mothers have done certainly but she seemingly excelled them all. Her loss to her husband and children has been her eternal gain. "Blessed are the dead that died in the Lord for they rest from their labors and their works do follow them". Eliza L. White was buried at Port Tobago, Caroline Co, Va. A good attendance of her neighbors and friend took part in the burial services of her funeral.

George Arthus White, son of Laurence B. & Eliza L White, died at Planna Terra, July 9th 1891, died single.

John Addison White, last son of Laurence B. & Eliza L. White, died Sept 11, 1900, leaving a widow with no offspring.

REV. L.B. WHITE, son of Edmond P. White, and Ann Champe Battaile White of Caroline Co, Va., died his home, Planna Terra, Jan 28th 1901 suddenly. He was a faithful member of Enon Baptist Church, Essex Co., Va., and an earnest Christian, devoted to greater part of his life in the work for Christ. He was an affectionate father and husband, a thoroughly conscientious man. His death was mourned by his family and his many friends. "May his spirit rest with God". He was buried in the "White" cemetery at Port Tobago, Virginia.

WHITE FAMILY BIBLE NO. 3

While this family register, a copy of which is in the Library of Virginia, has no title page information, the family is the same as the White Bible (No.1), which lived in the Guinea area of Caroline County. It covers the period 1776-1884.

Geo. Green White departed this life Sept. 26th 1813.
Ambrose L. White departed this life at Chickasaw Bluff Tennessee in his twenty first year on Friday Oct. 13th 1828.
James J. White Sen departed this life on the 5th of June at his residence Edge Hill 1850.
Virginia N. Samuel departed this life on the 5th day of May 1851.
Elizabeth White wife of James J. White Sen departed this life Apl. 5th 1853.
Mary Ann G. Wright wife of Dr. Wesley Wright departed this life July 9th 1855.
Note: There is no record of the death of Elizabeth P. White Barksdale & Martha G. White Goodman. Wm. L. White and Julia A.D. White Campbell died Near Ripley Tenn in recent years of whom there is no record.

Jas. J. White Sen was born on the 6th Nov. 1776 and Elizabeth Green White his wife was born on the 18th Oct. 1781.
Ann J. White was born on the 3rd Nov. 1799.
Geo. G. White Born 20th Sept. 1801.[named for his grandfather George Green]
Elizabeth S. White Born 5th Feby 1803.
Martha G. White Born 6th Feby 1805.[named for her grandmother Martha Green]
Ambrose L. White Born 24th Novr. 1807.
James J. White Jr. Born 15th Mar. 1815.
Mary Ann G. White (2nd wife of Dr. Wesley Wright & Mother of his children) Born 29th Aug 1816.
Wm. S. White Born 29th March 1819.

Nancy B. White Born 28th Octo. 1820.

Julia A.B. White Born 22d Feby 1823.

Virginia N. White Born 12th Apl 1825.

James J. White Sen and Elizabeth his wife were baptized by Elder Adison M. Lewis on the 8th day of Sept. 1827.

Bennet Wright and Ann J. White were married on the 9th day Dec 1819.

Rice G. Barksdale was married to Elizabeth J. White on the 22d Nov. 1821.

Roland H. Goodman and Martha G. White were married 14th Nov. 1822.

Wesley Wright and Mary A.G. White were married on the 20th day of May 1834.

James J. White Jr. and Margarite A. Campbell were married 18th Dec 1834.

A.B. White and Ann E. Wigglesworth were married on the 25th Octo.1842.

Virginia N. White and Geo. R. Samuel were married on the 21st Sept. 1843.

Matthew T. Campbell and Julia A.B. White were married on the 14th of Dec. 1844.

Wm. P. White and Lavinia C. Gouldin were married 23d Nov. 1845.

WILLIS FAMILY BIBLE NO.1

The title page to this Bible is missing. The Bible is now owned by Daniel I. Hansen, Fredericksburg, Virginia.

This is to certify that J. G. Willis and Pattie DeJarnette Willis were united by me J. R. Wilmoth Texas near Richmond Ky. on the 30 day of Sept. in the year of our Lord One Thousand Eight Hundred and Sixty Nine 1869. Signed Amelia Turner & J.P. Simmons.

Joe B. Willis b. Crab Orchard died 6 Oct 1919 teething and pneumonia, lacked one day being 11 months. Has headstone marker.

Nancy Richards Born July 2, 1929 Bowling Green, Va. daughter of Joe Willis DeJarnette & Alice Richards.

Daniel C. De Jarnette died at "Spring Grove" Feb 21st 1926. Buried Wednesday Feb. 24th 1924.

Alice Purcell Richards daughter of Nettie & James Richards was born April 21st 1899 in Bowling Green, Va.

Grandchildren of J. B. & Pattie Willis

1. Nancy Everlin Willis Daughter of T. C. & Etta Finnell.
2. Willis Born Feb 16, 1898 at Richmond, Va.
3. Joe Willis DeJarnette Son of D.C. & Nancy Willis DeJarnette born Aug 29, 1898 at Bowling Green Va.(Spring Grove).
4. Joe Bronaugh Willis son of J.D. & Katherine Bronaugh Willis Born Nov. 13, 1918 at Lexington, Ky.
5. Nancy Everlin Willis married Sept 30, 1918 to Cyril B. Alsoine of Greenburg Pa.
6. Joe Willis DeJarnette son of D.C. & Nancy DeJarnette was married to Alice Richards Oct 27, 1920 at Bowling Green Va.

Nancy Richards DeJarnette born July 2nd 1923 at Bowling Green Va daughter of Alice & Joe Willis DeJarnette.

George W. Hansen born Sept 7th 1921 Winside Nebr.

Balance are his parents - Mother & Father & names of their family (my husband J .B. Willis).

1. John Willis Born 29 Oct 1796 Madison Ky died 1871 married 10 Jan 1822 Drury Willis. Parents Drury Willis-Nancy Philps-Michael.
2. Susan Baker Born 21 Nov 1804 Madison Ky died 1871 dau of Michael Baker.
3. Mary Willis Born abt. 1824 Madison Ky marr _____ Crutcher.
4. Amos B. Willis Born abt. 1826 Madison Ky, Bachelor.
5. William Willis Born abt 1828 Madison Ky married Dora Oldham.
6. Ann Willis Born abt. 1830 married Alex Cornelison.
7. Nancy J. Willis Born abt. 1832 married John Arnold.
8. David B. Willis Born abt. 1834 married Sallie Simmons.
9. Susan E. Willis Born abt. 1836 married John March.
10. Dr. Samuel Willis Born abt. 1838 marr Anna Coleman, dau of Samuel Coleman.
11. Thomas Willis Born abt. 1842, Bachelor, died young.

Lying loose in the Bible are the following:

Huldah Hawes Coleman DeJarnette second wife of Daniel DeJarnette and mother of Daniel Coleman DeJarnette. She was born in Spotsylvania Co. in 1795 died 1861. Portrait painted 1837 at age 44.

On a family genealogy sheet lying in the Bible is the following:

Dr. Robert T. Willis Born 2 July 1844 in Madison Ky.

Joseph B. Willis Born 1848 in Madison Ky.

Richard Willis Born 1850 in Madison Ky.

Dr. Robert T. Willis married to Lula Gateskill.

Joseph B. Willis married to Miss Pattie DeJarnette Sept 30, 1869.

Drury Willis born Culpepper Va.

Nancy Philps born Madison Ky + John Willis born 29 Oct 1796 Madison Ky married Susan Baker.

Above are my husband's grandparents.

Loose in Bible

Black bordered 5"x 7" printed funeral notice for Louis Heath Willis Nov. 17 1909 at First Christian Church thence his burial in Richmond Ky.

Black bordered 5"x 7" printed funeral notice for Mr. J. B. Willis at the Christian Church, Crab Orchard burial at Richmond Apr 11, 1917.

WILLIS FAMILY BIBLE NO. 2

This Bible was copyrighted by J. R. Jones, 1871. The title page is missing. On the outside cover board to the Bible is the following inscription: " Presented to Pattie Willis by Her Parents Geo. & Sarah DeJarnette." The family register pages are missing from the Bible. The Bible is presently owned by Daniel I. Hansen, Fredericksburg, Virginia. There are three printed funeral notices prepared by the funeral home in Richmond, Kentucky, where Mrs. Nancy (Daniel Coleman) DeJarnette was from before she moved to Caroline County.

Printed black bordered 5"x 7" funeral notice for Mrs. Kate Brown at residence of her husband Nat. C. Brown, thence her burial in the cemetery Richmond May 20 '82 [1882].

Printed black bordered 5"x 7" funeral notice for Blanche, infant daughter of D.B. and Annie F. Armer thence burial in the Cemetery Richmond June 12th '82 [1882].

Printed black bordered 4"x 6" funeral notice for James S. Jones at Presbyterian Church in Richmond thence burial in Richmond Oct 2d, 1873.

WILTSHIRE/DUGGINS FAMILY BIBLE

This Bible was printed by the American Bible Society, New York, 1857. A copy of the family register is in the Library of Virginia. The title page contains the following: From Miss Mary L. Hill To Wm B. Wiltshire. Take care of this good book dear children and study it daily; making it the man of your counsel as your dear father always did; & may God bless the reading of it to your everlasting good is the prayer of your affectionately W. B. W. Sept. 23rd 1867.

Married on the 3rd day of September 1845 Virginia Ellen Wash and Wm B. Wiltshire.
Married on the 23rd of May 1858 William B. Wiltshire and Henrietta B. Hill.
Married on the 24th day of November 1867 Josiah H. Duggins and Virginia Ellen Wiltshire.
Married on the 19th of Dec. 1893 Tyree Wingfield and Willie Virginia Duggins.
Married on [blank] Francis Winston Dabney and Mary Lewis Duggins.
Married on the 8th day of November 1871 Richard L. Wiltshire and Martha V. Brooke.
William B. Wiltshire son of Richard L. and Martha V. Wiltshire was born the 19th of December 1872.
Richard E. Wiltshire son of Richard L. and Martha V. Wiltshire was born the 17th day of December 1874.
Russell Stewart Wingfield Son of Willie V. and J.P. Wingfield was born September 16th 1894.
Mary Lewis Duggins Daughter of J. H. & V. E. Duggins was born 29th day of August 1868.
Willie Virginia Duggins Daughter of J. H. & V. E. Duggins was born February 27th 1870.
Charles Franklin Duggins Son of J. H. & V. E. Duggins was born 2nd day of August 1872.
Lucy Colly Duggins Daughter of J. H. & V. E. Duggins was born the 17th day of October 1876.
Wm. B. Wiltshire was born the 6th day of October 1819.
Virginia E. Wiltshire wife of Wm B. Wiltshire was born the 13th day of April 1827.
Henrietta B. Wiltshire wife of Wm B. Wiltshire and daughter of Richard & Nancy Hill was born the 2nd day of July 1816.
Edmund Wash was born September 20th 1790.
Nancy Wash was born March 22nd 1788.
Richard Lewis Wiltshire Son of Wm B. & V. E. Wiltshire was born the 17th day of June 1847.
Virginia Ellen Wiltshire Daughter of Wm B. & V. E. Wiltshire was born the 29th day of August 1848 married Josiah H. Duggins).
Edmund Wash departed this life on the 8th of April A.D. 1858.
Nancy Wash departed this life on the 4th of October A.D. 1858.
William B. Wiltshire departed this life on the 4th of October A.D. 1858.
Josiah H. Duggins departed this life on the 15th of Sept. 1806.
Virginia E. Duggins departed this life on the 14th of Sep. 1916.
Willie Virginia Duggins Wingfield departed this life on [blank].

Mary Lewis Duggins Dabney departed this life on [blank] 1960.
Charles Franklin Duggins departed this life on the twenty second of October 1961 (87 yrs).
Lucy Colly Duggins departed this life on the [blank] of December 1974.

WOODFORD FAMILY BIBLE

From the Bible of General William Woodford, we find on the frontispiece - "Presented by his grandmother, Elizabeth Holloway." According to *The Life of Brigadier General William Woodford of the American Revolution* by Mrs. Catesby Willis Stewart, Whittet & Shepperson, Richmond, Va. 1973, this Bible is now in the Library of Virginia. However, when searching there, it was not found. Mrs. Stewart records that the frontispiece is missing, but a brief account of births and deaths of his immediate family are recorded. At the end of each entry is the abreviations for old style calendar and new style calendar.

William Woodford, born the 6th day of Oct. 1734, o.s.
Mary Thornton Woodford, born the 4th day of May 1743, o.s.
The above persons married the 26th day of June 1762, o.s.
John Thornton Woodford, born July 29, 1763, n.s.
Anne Cocke Woodford, born the 21st day of Oct. 1765.
Departed this life the 27th of said month in the same year, n.s.
William Catesby Woodford, born Dec. 2, 1766, n.s.
Brigadier General William Woodford died in New York 13th November, 1780, being in
  captivity.

June 11th, 1773, n.s. A smart Frost that bit the vines, some snow fell mixed with hail and rain.
May 4th, 1774, a violent frost that bit the corn, wheat, and destroyed the fruit entirely.

WOODFORD FAMILY RECORD

The family register was recorded in *The Gentleman's Annual Remembrance for the year 1812*, published by W.Y. Bersh, No. 275 2nd St. Philadelphia. The book originally belonged to William Woodford, who lived at "Jamappe", Caroline County, Virginia in 1816. He was a descendant of General William Woodford, who lived at "Windsor", Caroline County, Virginia. In 1945, the book was in the possession of Elizabeth Buckner Steele, Paris, Ky. A copy of these record is in the Library of Virginia. William Catesby Woodford is buried at "White Hall", Caroline County, Va.

Wm Woodford and Ann Cocke were married Sept. 2, 1732.
Wm Woodford was born Oct. 6, 1734.
Thos. Woodford was born Aug. 14, 1736.
Catesby Woodford was born June 19, 1741.
John Woodford was born Mar. 23, 1742.
Henry Woodford was born Jan. 7, 1744.
General Wm. Woodford died Nov. 13, 1780.

Mary Woodford, wife of the above died 1792 on Feb. 8th.
John Thornton Woodford was born July 29th 1763.
Mary T. Taliaferro was born March 13, 1772.
The above persons were married May 4th Thursday 1786.
Wm. Woodford son of the above was born March 25th 1787.
John Woodford son of the above was born March 22, 1789.
Thoms. Woodford son of the above was born Feb. 21, 1791.
Lucy Woodford daughter of the above was born July 11, 1793.
Mary Woodford daughter of the above was born June 14, 1796.
Sally Taliaferro Woodford daughter of the above was born Sept. 9,   1798.
Catesby Woodford son of the above was born Nov. 13th, 1801.
Ann Cocke Woodford daughter of the above was born Dec. 19, 1801. [must be in error, probably 1802]
Betty Thornton Woodford daughter of the above was born July 2nd 1805.
Mildred Gregory Woodford daughter of the above was born July 19th, 1807.
Mark Henry Woodford son of the above was born March 30th 1810.
Wm. Taliaferro of Bath died February 11th 1817 aged 48.
Mary Taliaferro Woodford Died March 1, 1828.
Wm. Woodford son of John Thornton Woodford & Mary T. Woodford was born 25 March 1787.
Anna Maria Archer wife of the said Wm. & daughter of Samuel and Mary Archer was born Feb. 14, 1788.
Mary T. Woodford was born at Bath [Caroline County] Oct. 15th 1810.
John Thornton Woodford was born August 26, 1812 at Jamappe C..C. V. [Caroline County Virginia]
Samuel Bedford Archer Woodford [born] Feb. 14th 1815 at Fredericksburg, Va.
Wm. Taliaferro Woodford was born January 26, 1819 Springfield.
Lucy Woodford was born March 30, 1821 at Bath C. C. Va.
Thomas Woodford was born Oct. 3, 1823 at Bath C. C. Va.
Sally Taliaferro Woodford was born June 25, 1826 and 16 hours later my wife has a [child] which was born dead at Clark Co. Ky.
Thomas Madison Taylor Woodford was born Jan. 24th 1829 at Woodstock Fayette Co. Ky.
Dr. John Taylor and Lucy Woodford were married------.
John Taylor was born Sept. 24, 1810.
Lucy P. Taylor was born May 20, 1812.
Edmund P. Taylor was born------.
Dr. Simeon Ambrose Dudly and Sally Taliaferro Woodford were married 5th December 1820.
Dr. Simeon A. Dudley died at his residence-------.
Mrs. Sally Taliaferro Dudley died Sept. 5th 1830 Windsor C. C. Va.
Dr. Thomas Madison Taylor and Ann Cocke Woodford were married Feb. 1, 1822.
John Thornton Taylor son of the above was born 1st Dec. 1824.
James Hubbard Taylor son of the above was born 28 Oct. 1826.
Clarisa Minor Taylor son of the above was born 3 Nov 1828.
Edmund Hockida Didlake and Mildred Gregory Woodford were married 27 April 1824.
Robert Baker Didlake was born 22 May 1825.

Mary Taliaferro Woodford Didlake was born 5 Mar. 1828.
Lucy Woodford Didlake was born 23 May 1830.
John Robertson Montgomery and Betty T. Woodford were married 31st Oct. 1822.
Mary Woodford Montgomery was born 13 July 1823.
Alexander Montgomery was born 25 March 1825.
Mildred Gregory Montgomery was born 10 July 1827.
John T. Woodford and Elizabeth Hawes Buckner were married 1840.
Sally Archer Woodford daughter of the above was born March 24, 1841.
Mary Woodford daughter of the above was born May 3, 1843.
Wm. Thomas Buckner Woodford son of the above was born Feb. 5, 1845.
John Thornton Woodford son of the above was born Aug. 12, 1847.
Thomas Catesby Woodford son of the above was born Aug. 12, 1849.
Elizabeth Hawes Buckner son of the above was born May 9th 1852.
Henry Madison Woodford son of the above was born Sept. 2, 1854.
Benj. Walker Buckner Woodford son of the above was born Oct 1856.
Maria Archer Woodford daughter of the above was born Nov 1858.
Thomas Buckner was born August 31st 1755 and died Apr 5, 1805.
Elizabeth Hawes was born Nov 20, 1859.
Walker Buckner, son of Thomas Buckner was born March 7, 1781, d. March 14, 1855.
The above Walker Buckner married Elizabeth Buckner.
Wm Buckner Son of Walker & Eliabeth W. Buckner was born Aug 10th 1810 in Henderson Co. Ky.

[Also included in this accession in the Library of Virginia is a Genealogy of the Woodford Family written by Lucy Woodford, wife of William Thomas Buckner II, and sent to Martha W. Hiden by her great grandaughter Mrs. Harry M. (Jane Clay) Blanton in 1945.]

William Woodford the first of the family in America was a native of England, and a merchant. He settled in Caroline County, Virginia, and called his estate Windsor. He married lst Mrs. Whittaker, the widow of an East Indian merchant, she died leaving no heir, next the widow Battaile, she also died without heirs. Lastly in 1732 he married Ann the daughter of John Cocke, Secretary of State, under the Colonial Government. Her mother was a Miss Catesby, sister of Mark Catesby, a writer on Natural History. He visited Virginia and passed sometime at Windsor. After his return to London, he published his work. Frequent references are found in works, on that subject, subsequently he was admitted a fellow of the Royal society. There was a copy in the Library at Windsor.

William, the oldest son of William and Ann Woodford, was born October the 6th, 1734. He early entered the army, and was an officer under the Colonial Government. He was also a Brigadier General in the United States service. He married Mary the daughter of John and Mildred Thornton. Mildred was a Miss Gregory, her mother was Mildred Washington, sister of Augustine Washington, consequently General Washington's aunt, she was also his God Mother, for farther information see "Sparks" life Washington. General Woodford was taken prisoner at the surrender, of Charleston, with his Brigade taken round to New York, died and buried there. They landed, & buried him with military honors.

John Thornton Woodford, oldest son of William and Mary, was born on the 23rd of July, 1763, was pupil of Dr. Witherspoon at Princeton College, married Mary Turner Taliaferro in 1786.

William Woodford oldest son of John and Mary, married Anna Maria Archer 25th December, 1819. He died 1831.

Mary Elizabeth Woodford born October 1810, died May 1836.

John Thornton Woodford born August 1812, married Elizabeth Hawes Buckner.

Samuel Bedford Archer Woodford born 1815 married Martha Holliday.

William Taliaferro Woodford born Feb. 1817 married Mary Halleck.

Thomas Woodford born October 1823.

Sallie Taliaferro Woodford born October 1826 married William Buckner.

Madison Woodford born March 1829 married Mrs. Eliza LaRue.

William Catesby Woodford second son of William and Mary, was born in 1769 married Elizabeth Battaile, and resided at "White Hall" until his death which took place in 1820. He was educated in Liverpool England. [he is buried at "White Hall", near Woodford in Caroline County]

Mary Thornton Woodford daughter of W.C. married W.W. Taliaferro and died age 22.

William Woodford was born in April 1795 married Elizabeth Goodwin, both died young leaving no heirs.

John B. Woodford was born the 13 of June 1797 married Sarah Goodwin.

Elenor Woodford born Jan. 24th 1800 married William Taliaferro.

Mary Catesby Woodford daughter of John and Sarah was born June 1822, married in Spotsylvania Vir whether or living or not, do not know.

John Battaile Woodford born April 1824.

Bettie Battaile Woodford born October 1826.

Children of John T. Wooford's & Mary T.

John second son was born March the 22 1789 died 1814.

Thomas 3rd Woodford was born the 20th of Feb. 1791. He married 1st Sally Thornton she died leaving no heir 2nd Elizabeth B M Taylor and 3rd Mrs. Lucy Thomas Catesby Buckner (whose maiden name was Woodford).

Lucy Taylor Woodford daughter of Thomas & Elizabeth married Edmond Taylor, they died leaving two daughters.

Thomas died 24th of March 1852.

Lucy Woodford born July 11th 1793 married Dr. John Taylor, and died 1832.

Mary Woodford generally called Maria, was born June 14th 1726, and died in 1836.

Sally Taliaferro Woodford born Sep 9th 1783 married Dr. Simeon Dudly, and died September 8th 1830.

Catesby Woodford [born] Nov 13th 1800 died March 1816.

Ann Cocke Woodford born Dec. 19th 1802, married Dr. Madison Taylor.

Bettie Thornton Woodford born July 2nd 1805 married John R. Montgomery.

Mildred Gregory Woodford born July 19 1807 married Edmond H. Didlake, whose father was Robert Didlake, and his mothers maiden name was Mary Baker, they were both natives of King William Virginia.

Mark Henry Woodford born Mar 31st 1810 married Sarah Ann Haden.

Children of William and Ann Woodford

Thomas the 2nd son born August 14th 1734. He was educated at Cambridge England for the church, but loved to roam on the dark blue sea, and lived & died a Sea Captain. He never married and soon after the close of Revolutionary War he was preparing for a voyage was taken ill of fever and died at Cherry Point in the lower part of Virginia 1791.

C Woodford died at the Warms Springs Augusta Co. Mar. 28th 1742.

Catesby Woodford 3rd son of William & Ann was born June the 19th 1738, married Mary Buckner in October 1771.

John Woodford 4th son of W W was born March the 23rd 1742 and died in London of the Small Pox age 21.

Henry Woodford 5th son of William and Ann, was born Jan 7th 1744. He was also a Sea Captain engaged in the Merchants Service, but died in Caroline County Virginia and was the only one of his Bro interred at Windsor their Birthplace.

Children of Catesby & Mary Woodford

Judith Thornton Woodford was born Dec 5th Married Thodtius Hansford on the 19th of May 1795 and died Jan 8th 1803.

Mark Catesby Woodford born Nov. 5th 1774 died Feb 27th 1817.

Elizabeth Buckner Woodford born June 22 1780 married Roger Laughlin October 1799 and died 1853.

William Thomas Woodford born June 23rd 1784 married Mary Aylett Buckner in October 1807 and died Jan 11th 1852.

Lucy Thomas Catesby Woodford born July the 16th 1759 and married Spencer Monroe Buckner 1801.

Lucy Taylor daughter of Thomas and Elizabeth B M Woodford was born May 15 1826 married Edmond Taylor. They died early leaving 2 daughters.

Mary Elizabeth daughter of Henry and Sarah Woodford married Henry White.

John Thornton son of H. and S. W. was born Nov 2nd 1839.

William Haden son of H and Sarah born 1845.

WOOLFOLK FAMILY BIBLE

Printed and published by M. Carey 1816, Philadelphia. Stamped at
top of title page "Jourdan Woolfolk Bowling Green Va." This Bible belonged to the Woolfolk family of "Mulberry Place", Caroline County. It is now in the possession of the Skinker family, who are descendants. A copy of the records is in the Library of Virginia.

John G. [George] Woolfolk and Elizabeth [Powers Broadnax] his wife were married 5th January 1790.

William G.[Grymes] Maury and Ann H.[Hoomes] his wife were married 14th July 1808.

Hawes Coleman & Maria [Woolfolk] his wife were married 5th Jany. 1809.

John M. Burke & Sophia Frances [Woolfolk] his wife were Married 21st May 1817.

Jourdan Woolfolk and Elizabeth Taylor Winston were married the 9th day of November 1820.

Jno Woolfolk & Louisa F. Scott were married 10 Jany 1850.

Andrew M. Woolfolk & Frances Hanes were married Feb. 9th 1929.
Edmund Winston Woolfolk & Virginia Gertrude Saunders November 24th 1926.
Elizabeth Woolfolk Jordan & William John Furr Aug 29th 1930.
Jourdan Woolfolk and Elizabeth Taylor Winston were married the 9th day of November 1820.
Dr. William W.[Winston] Roper & Elizabeth [Betty] Carr Woolfolk were married 1st day of June 1843.
Dr. Barton W. Morris and Ann F.[Ferrell] Woolfolk were married the 18th Novr 1847.
Jno W.[William] Woolfolk & Lucy T.[Trevillian] Winston were married 12th June 1851.
Jourdan W.[Woolfolk] Roper and Rebecca [Gowan] were married the 19th September 1876.
John Woolfolk & Lucy M. Marshall were married the 23d Jan. 1878.
E.W. Woolfolk and Emma L. Blackerly were married Dec. 15, 1887.
Pearl Buckner Woolfolk and Wm Stanford Webb were married July 15, 1937.
Sally W. Woolfolk and J.L. Jordan were married Jan 13th 1892.
George Woolfolk & Harriett G.[Grace] Cunningham April 14, 1906.
Lucy Winston Jordan and B.M. Skinker married April 22, 1922.
Roper Blackerly Woolfolk & Louise Young married April 1, 1918.
Barton Gregory Woolfolk and Jane Merle Hill married May ___.
John G.[George] Woolfolk was born 1st October 1750.
Elizabeth P.[Powers] Broadnax was born 3rd March 1765.
1st Maria Woolfolk daughter of John & Elizabeth was born 28 Octr 1790.
2nd Ann Hoomes Woolfolk was born 17th March 1793.
3. Jourdan Woolfolk was born 23rd July 1796.
4. Sophia Frances Woolfolk was born 12th Jany 1799.
5. Still born & a Boy.
6. Charles Woolfolk was born 26th Sept 1802.
7. John Woolfolk was born 7th July 1805.
Lucy T. Winston daughter of Edmund and Sally A. Winston Born March 25, 1832.
Jourdan Woolfolk was born the 23rd day of July 1796.
Elizabeth T. Woolfolk wife of Jourdan Woolfolk was born the 26th day of March 1796.
Betsy Carr Woolfolk was born Octr 23rd 1821.
John William Woolfolk was born June the 27th 1823 & L. T. W. his wife 25 Mar 1832.
Ann Ferrell Woolfolk was born August 2nd 1825.
Mary Woolfolk was born 11th June 1827.
Sarah Winston Woolfolk was born the 8th May 1829.
Ellen Broadnax Woolfolk was born Jany. 27th 1834.
Jourdan Woolfolk Roper Son of Dr. W. W. Roper & E.C. Roper was born June 10th 1846.
Charles Dabney Morris, Son of Dr. B. W. Morris & Ann Ferrell Morris, Sept. 15, 1846, was born
Richard Morris, son of Dr. B. W. Morris & Ann F. Morris born 22nd Apr 1850.
John Woolfolk son of Jno W. & Lucy T. Woolfolk was born 14 Apr 1852.
Ellen B. Morris daughter of Dr. B. W. Morris & Ann F. Morris, was born 11 Apr 1852.
Sallie W. Roper Daughter of Dr. W. W. Roper & Bettie C. Roper was born Apr 30th 1852.
Edmund Woolfolk son of J. W. Woolfolk & Lucy T. Woolfolk born 16th Feby 1854.[date given 1844 in Morris Bible]

Jourdan W. Morris, son of B. W. Morris & A.F. Morris born 10 March 1854.

Elizabeth Winston Morris daughter of Dr. B. W. Morris & Ann F. Morris was born Apr 25 1856.

Sallie [Sarah] Winston Woolfolk, daughter of Jno W. Woolfolk & Lucy T. Woolfolk, was born 25 May 1856.

Louise Roper daughter of W. W. & E.C. Roper born [no further infor given. Aug 23, 1851 or 1853 according to tombstone]

Barton W. Morris son of B. W. & A.F. Morris born 3rd Apr 1858

George Roper son of W. W. & E.C. Roper born Feby 19 1859.

Jourdan Woolfolk, son of J. W. & Lucy T. Woolfolk born 27 Sept 1859.

Julia B. Morris daughter of B.W. & A.F. Morris born May 17th 1860.[May 18 listed in Morris Bible].

Elizabeth Taylor Woolfolk daughter of J. W. Woolfolk & Lucy T. Woolfolk was born Novr. 4th 1861.

E.T. Morris son of Dr. B. W. Morris & A.F. Morris was born 13 Jan. 1863.

William Roper, son of Dr. W. W. Roper & E.C. Roper born Aug 4th 1864.

Mary M.[Morris] Woolfolk born Feb. 25th 1867.

Annie Barton Woolfolk was born July 18th 1870.

Charles Woolfolk departed this life 8th Nov. 1806 at 25 minutes past 2 o'clock P.M.

John G.[George] Woolfolk departed this life Friday morning 16th April 1819 at half past one o'clock aged 68 years 6 1/2 months.

Mary Woolfolk, daughter of Jourdan & Elizabeth T. Woolfolk died 14th July 1828.

Elizabeth P. Woolfolk departed this life Wednesday evening July 11, 1838 at about Quarter past 7 o'clock Aged 73 years 4 months 9 days [9 days marked through]

Ellen Brodnax [Broadnax] Woolfolk died June 16th about half past eight o'clock A.M. 1848 aged 14 years 4 months & 19 days.

Ann [Anne Eliza] E. Roper daughter of W.W. Roper & B.C. Roper died 19 Apr 1850.

Sally W. Woolfolk died Jany 22nd 1857 at 1/2 past 4 P.M. Aged 21 years 8 Months 14 days.

Lucy Marshall Woolfolk born 1st of [page torn, Feb 1839 on tombstone].

Richard Morris second child of B. W. & A.F. Morris died May 29 1851 aged thirteen months & seven days.

John Woolfolk, son of J. G. & E. P. Woolfolk, died 11th July 1851 Aged 47 years.

Ann H. Maury, wife of W.G. Maury, died July 10th 1856.

W.G. Maury husband of A.H. Maury, died Jany 1860.

Dr. Barton W. Morris died 11th Dec. 1862 aged 44 years 10 Months & 15 days.

Dr. W. W. Roper died July 1866.[died August 15, 1866 according to the Caroline County Death Register].

Jourdan Woolfolk died June 6th 1868, in the 72 year of his age.

Elizabeth T. Woolfolk died December 16th 1876 in the 81st year of her age.

John Wm Woolfolk died July 8th 1891 in the 68 year of his age.

Anne F. Morris died Mar 20, 1897 in the 72 year of her age at Glamorgan [estate in Caroline County next to Meadow Farm]

John Wm Woolfolk Second son of John & Lucy M. Woolfolk died June 19th 1885.

Virginia Alice second daughter of John & Lucy M. Woolfolk died 12th of September 1890.

Bettie C. Roper wife of Dr. W.W. Roper died July 29, 1902 in her 81 year.
Lucy T. Woolfolk wife of John W. Woolfolk died January 27, 1914 at 9:15 at night.
John Woolfolk son of John Wm Woolfolk & Lucy T. Woolfolk, died June 1st 1909 at Ha___[illeg].
E. W. Woolfolk, son of John Wm & Lucy T. Woolfolk died Aug 2nd 1933 in his 80th year.
Jourdan Woolfolk, son of John Wm & Lucy T. Woolfolk died February 17th 1934 in his 75th year.
Mary Morris Woolfolk daughter of John Wm Woolfolk & Lucy T. Woolfolk died May 16, 1958.
William Roper Woolfolk son of John Wm & Lucy T. Woolfolk, died Dec. 24, 1948.
George Woolfolk son of John & Lucy M. Woolfolk born Nov 4th 1878.
Sallie C. Woolfolk daughter of John & Lucy M. Woolfolk born Sept 6th 1881.
John Wm Woolfolk son of John & Lucy M. Woolfolk born Oct 16th 1883.
Lucy M.[Marshall] Woolfolk born July 6, 1886.
Edmund W. Woolfolk, son of John & Lucy M. Woolfolk born May 26th 1889.
Virginia Alice, daughter of John & Lucy M. Woolfolk born Aug. 12th 1890.
Jourdan Woolfolk son of John & Lucy M. Woolfolk born July 1st 1891.
John M. Woolfolk son of L. M. Woolfolk & John Woolfolk born Jan 1893.
Died John M. Woolfolk son of John & L. M. Woolfolk 1894.
Barton Gregory son of John Woolfolk & Lucy M. Woolfolk born July 18, 1897.
John Woolfolk son of John & L. M. Woolfolk born Oct 11th 1902.
Virginia Marshall, daughter of George Woolfolk and Grace C. Woolfolk born Dec 18, 1908.
Harriett Cullen, daughter of George Woolfolk and Grace C. [Cunningham] Woolfolk born Nov 21, 1911.
Jno George Woolfolk son of Geo & Grace Woolfolk born Nov 2, 1918.
Roper B. Woolfolk son of Edmund & Emma Woolfolk born Jul 6th 1890.
Born a Son April 6th 1892 of J. L. & Sallie W. Jordan Died April 6, 1893.
Born Lucy Winston, daughter of J .L. & Sally W. Jordan June 2, 1895.
Pearl Buckner daughter of E. W. and Emma Woolfolk born June 11, 1896.
Edmund Winston son of E. W. & E. B. Woolfolk born Sept 15, 1890.
Elizabeth Woolfolk daughter of Sallie W. and J. L. Jordan born February 23 ___[page torn].
Louise Garrison Woolfolk, daughter of Roper B. & Louise Woolfolk born Sept 12, 1919.
Viola Hubbard Woolfolk, dau of Edmund W. & Alice Woolfolk born Aug [smeared] 1922.
Margaret B. Woolfolk daughter of Roper B. & Louise Woolfolk born 29 Sept 1923.
Ben M. Skinker, son of Lucy W. & B.M. Skinker born [page torn] May 1925.
Sarah Jane Skinker, daughter of Lucy W. & B.M. Skinker born May 1, 1925.
Edmonia Winston, daughter of Edmund Winston & Alice Woolfolk [page torn].
[also lying in the Bible is a three page handwritten eulogy to John G. Woolfolk of Shepherd's Hill entitled "A picture of modest but solid merit" unsigned and undated.
Also included are newspaper death notices for Mrs. Emma Blackerby Woolfolk, March 27, 1945; John Woolfolk, June 1; Jourdan Woolfolk, February 17th 1934; Ellen B. Woolfolk, June 16, 1848; Sally Winston Woolfook, Jan. 22, 1857; and Mrs. Betty Carr Roper, July 29, 1902.

WORMELEY FAMILY BIBLE

This Bible was printed by Joseph Bentham and sold by Benj Dod Bookseller in London, 1762. This family lived in Port Royal, Caroline County. A copy of the family register from the Bible is in the Library of Virginia. On the title page is "To my Darling precious boy Baynham" with a five line memoriam.

Carter Warner Wormeley son of Warner Lewis & Maria C. Wormeley was born on the 22d of Feb 1815 at Wormeley Cove King William County.

Ellen Bankhead Lightfoot was born in Port Royal Caroline county on the 29th of May 1818 - daughter of Philip & Sally S. Lightfoot.

Carter W. Wormeley was married to Ellen B. Lightfoot on the 5th of Octr. 1836 in Port Royal by the Rev. Wm Friend.

Sally Lightfoot Wormeley daughter of Carter W. & Ellen B. Wormeley was born in Port Royal, Va. on the 23d of Oct 1837.

Warner Lewis Wormeley son of Carter W. & Ellen B. Wormeley was born in Port Royal Va. on the 27th (twenty seventh) of August 1839.

Ralph Wormeley son of Carter W. & Ellen B. Wormeley was born in Port Royal Va. on the 22d (twenty second) July 1841.

Ralph Wormeley son of Carter W. & Ellen B. Wormeley died at Manskin Lodge King William county on Monday morning the 20th of Dec 1841 at 23 minutes past 1 o'clock a.m. Aged 4 months & 28 days.

William Baynham Wormeley was born at Manakin Lodge in King William county on Saturday night the 18th of February 1843 at 9 o'clock & he was named after my most intimate & dearest friend the Rev. Wm A. Baynham, M.D. of Essex, whose virtues truly he will imitate. [Rev. Baynham, pastor of Enon Baptist Church, buried under the pulpit of the church].

Maria Carter Wormeley was born in Port Royal Va. on the 13th of November 1845 at 10 o'clock a.m.

Sophie Wormeley was born in Port Royal Caroline county on the 17th of June 1848 - she is called after her aunt Sophie Caldwell.

Philip Lightfoot Wormeley was born at Manskin Lodge, King William County on the 17th of January 1851 - he is called after his grandfather Philip Lightfoot of Port Royal.

Wm Baynham Wormeley died at Fork Church Hanover Co (the summer residence of his parents on the 16th of July 1853 of dysentery after an illness of 14 days - aged 10 years, 5 months & 28 days.

"But though beneath the dull cold sod
Sweet Baynham form doth lie
His spirit liveth with its God
Above the agure (sic, agru?)sky
For in a purer realm above
More meet he now do thy dwell
An angels form of heaven & love
Brighter than words can tell
Ten bid adieu to gentle Baynham

For his bright home is now
Where sorrow never more shall survive him
And sadness mark his brow."

Carter Landon Wormeley was born at Manskin Lodge King Wm County on the 16th of Dec. 1853 at 9 o'clock A.M.

William Braxton Wormeley son of Carter W. and Ellen B. Wormeley was born at Manskin Lodge May 23rd (at 8 1/2 o'clock A.M.) 1856 he is named after our friend Dr. Wm P. Braxton of Oak Spring King Wm Co.

Ellen Byrd Wormeley, daughter of Carter W. & Ellen B. Wormeley, was born at Manskin Lodge Feb. 18th 1858 at 1 1/2 o'clock A.M.

(fifteen years ago our beloved and now sainted Baynham was born)

Maria Carter Wormeley was married Dec 22nd 1865 to Benj. E. Perkins of Camden So. Carolina.

Lawrence Jumelle Perkins Perkins, son of B.E. & Maria C. Perkins, was born at Manskin Lodge, King William Co Va. Jan 10th 1867.

Sophy Wormeley was married to Thomas F. Nelson Dec. 24th 1872.

Maria C. Perkins died at Manskin Lodge July 3d 1873.

Lawrence Jumelle Perkins died in Charlottesville July 23d 1873.

P. Lightfoot Wormeley was married Oct 8th 1873 to Lucy W. Duval of Richmond.

Carter W. Nelson was born March 1874 and lived three months.

Carter L. Wormeley was married in Philadelphia Jan. 25th 1875 to Miss Jeanie Bucknor.

Robert Burwell Nelson was born March 14th 1875.

Sophy Nelson, wife of Thos. F. Nelson, died in Lynchburg Va. Oct. 1st 1878.

Warmer L. Wormeley was married to Lydia [runs off bottom of page]

[a five paragraph verse appears handwritten at the back of the family register concerning the death of "my darling boy Baynham].

WORTHAM FAMILY BIBLE NO. 1

This Bible was published by B.B. Mussey in 1841. A copy of the family record is in the Library of Virginia. The Wortham family purchased "The Grove" in the lower end of Caroline, on the top of the hill from the Pamunkey River, in 1855 and lived there well into the 20th century.

Annie Guy Wortham daughter of R. C. Wortham & Sallie L. W., was born 20 Jany 1868 about 3 1/2 P.M.

Sallie McGruder Wortham daughter of R. C. Wortham & Sallie L. W., was born 26 November 1869.

Richard C. Wortham Son of R. C. Wortham & Sallie L. W., was born 16 Decm. 187_.

Ellen Gordon Wortham daughter of Richard C. Wortham and Sallie L. Wortham was born 14th March 1880.

Robert [Olin?] Wortham son of R. C. Wortham & Sallie L. Wortham was born 7 March 1882.

Fannie Burbage Wortham daughter of Richard C. Wortham & Sallie L. Wortham born 13 October 1884.

Ages of Edwin and Frances Wortham's children Richard C. Wortham son of Edwin and Frances

Wortham born 2nd August 1841.

Fanny Guy Wortham was born Wednesday Morning about 2 o'clock 16th August 1843.

Ages of the children of Edwin & Ann E. Wortham

Alice Wortham born 17th March 1846 about 7 o'clock A.M.

Edwin Wortham born 12th July 1847 at 12 1/2 o'clock A.M.

Allen Williamson Talley, son of Dr. W. Warren Talley & Annie Guy Wortham Talley was born Jany 16th 1895.

William Warren Talley Jr., son of Dr. W. W. & Annie W. Talley, born Feb 24, 1897 in New York City.

James Sidney Swan, son of Fannie Burbage Wortham & James A. Swan was born Dec 6 [illeg].

Charles Wortham and Mary Jane Chandler were married 24th Decm. 1780.

Thomas Coleman and Mary Woolfolk were married 26 of March 1776.

Richard C. Wortham and Mary Coleman were married 6th April 1809.

Albert G. Wortham & Julia Ann Thomas were married 21st April 1836.

Edwin Wortham & Frances Hopkins were married 15th November 1838.

Ro H. Maury and Sarah Ann Wortham were married 17 December 1840.

C.J. Wortham and Mary Jane Hutcheson were married 1st Febry 1842.

James Thomas Jr. and Mary Woolfolk were married 5th October 1841.

Edwin Wortham and Ann Eliza McGruder were married 16th April 1845.

Coleman Wortham and Eunice D. Shepherd were married 14 July 1849.

Saml Wortham & Mary Conway Spelman were married 20 Nov 1851.

Luther R. Spelman and Lucy T. Wortham were married 25 Novr 1851.

Richard C. Wortham (son of Edwin Wortham) & Sally L. Staples were married 30th April 1867.

Sam Wortham & Edmonia Taylor were married 12 July 1865.

Charles T. Wortham & Annie C. Peatross were married 17 October 1865.

Rev. F.M. Baker and Sallie C. McGruder were married 12th Sept.1865.

W. Warren Talley and Annie Guy Wortham were married Dec 8th 1892.

James Sidney Swann Jr. and Fannie Burbage Wortham were married Oct 7th 1903.

Richard Wortham Talley and Jane Lee Blackburn Hutcheson of Gloucester, Va. married June 20th 1935.

Frances Wortham Swan Daughter of Fannie B. Wortham Swan & James Sidney Swan Jr was married to Walter Howard Ackund-Kelley of New Zealand & N.Y. on Aug 2nd 1941 at Manuet N.Y.

Frances Wortham Swan daughter of Fannie Burbage Wortham & James Sidney Swan Born March 13th 1908 in Richd Va.

Richard Wortham Talley 3rd Son of Annie Guy Wortham & Dr. W. Warren Talley Born March 31st 1908 in N Y City.

Jan Howard Ackroyd-Kelly, Son of Frances Wortham Swan & Ackroyd- Kelly born Aug 24, 1944 Manuet NY.

Michael Hopkins Ackroyd-Kelly 2nd Son of Frances Wortham Swan A. K. and W. Howard Ackund-Kelly, born Aug 2nd 1946 Manuet NY.

Robin, daughter of Frances Swan and W. Howard Ackroyd-Kelly born Sept 24, 1948 Manuet NY.

Charly Wortham father of R. C. W. died 4 June 1818.

Richard Woolfolk Wortham died 22nd Sept 1815 and buried at Mr. Thos Coleman's Caroline [county].

Mary Jane Wortham died 8 June 1807 and buried at Mr. Thos Coleman's Caroline [county].

My dear wife Frances Wortham died in Richmond on tuesday 26 March 1844 about 10 minutes before 8 A.M. [eulogy follows written by her husband Edwin Wortham, who states that she was buried in the grave yard near the poor house.

Fanny Guy Wortham died at her grandfather Dr. Hopkins Thursday Morning 4 July 1845. She is buried near her mother.

Alice Wortham died 11th July 1847. The Lord gave and the Lord Taketh away, blessed be the name of the Lord.

Sarah Ann Maury, wife of R.H. Maury died in Washington City whither she went in pursuit of health.

Sublett McGruder died on the 30th July 1853 Saturday from disease of the heart. He had been suffering with it for some months.

Our father Robert C. Wortham --[illeg]--died on the 25th of May 1856 about 1 1/2 o'clock P.M. He was --[illeg, perhaps "loving"]--Husband, Father & Christian. He has now gone to rest.

Our Mother Mary Wortham died the 16th December 1861 at 5 1/2 o'clock A.M. in the full assurance of a blessed immortality.

Father & Mother are intered side by side in Hollywood Cemetery.

Charles Wortham Sr born July 13, 1759.

Jane Chandler born 31 Augt 1759.

Ages of the children of Charles and Jane Wortham

Sally T. Wortham born Thursday 28th November 1782.

Richard C. Wortham born Thursday 2 June 1785.

Mary Wortham born Tuesday 9 January 1787.

Samuel Wortham born Monday 15 September 1789.

Charles Wortham born Monday 29 March 1790.

Jane Wortham born Friday 10 August 1792.

Elliott Wortham born tuesday 13 January 1795.

Timothy Wortham born Wednesday 18 April 1798.

Andrew Broaddus Wortham born Friday 21 November 1800.

Ages of the children of Thomas and Mary Coleman

Samuel Coleman born 31 December 1778.

Robert Coleman born 15 June 1780.

Ann Coleman born 9 December 1783.

Mary Coleman born 11 Jany. 1786.

Jno W. Coleman born 26 May 1788.

Thomas Coleman father of the above children born 17 June 1745.

Mary Woolfolk, mother of the above children born sometime in the year 1754.

Ages of R. C. and Mary Wortham's Children

Albert G. Wortham born Wednesday night about 11 o'clock 17 January 1810.

Edwin Wortham born Tuesday about 12 o'clock 23 July 1811.

Charles T. Wortham born Monday Morning about 2 o'clock 4 January 1813.

Richard Woolfolk Wortham born Thursday Morning about 4 o'clock 17 April 1814.

Mary Jane Wortham born Friday 8 o'clock P.M. 16 February 1816.
Sarah Ann Wortham born Thursday 9 o'clock A.M. 30 October 1817.
Gabriel Wortham born Monday 4 o'clock A.M. 8 March 1819.
Coleman Wortham born Friday 6 o'clock P.M. 22 Decem 1820.
Mary Woolfolk Wortham born Saturday P.M. 15 March 1823.
Samuel Wortham born Friday P.M. April 1, 1825.
Lucy T. Wortham born 1st April 1828.
Ages of the children of Dr. Geo V. and Frances Hopkins nee Guy Augustus Hopkins born 30th June 1818 7 o'clock P.M.
Frances Hopkins born 14th March 1820 4 o'clock A.M.
Delia Hopkins born 8 January 1822 5 1/2 o'clock P.M.
Erasmus Hopkins born 24 Nov 1824 4 o'clock P.M.
Josephine Hopkins born 15 July 1827 3 3/4 o'clock P.M.
George Hopkins born 2 Nov 1829 5 1/2 o'clock
Died on Thursday afternoon September 10th 1885 at a quarter to four o'clock our Father Edwin Wortham in the seventy fifth of his age.
Sublett McGruder Born 16 Oct 1781.
Mary M. Woolfolk Born 12 July 1799.
Louisa F. McGruder Born 7 April 1819.
Ann Eliza McGruder Born 29 Nov 1820.
Charles McGruder Born 1 Nov 1822.
Richard Woolfolk McGruder Born 21 Nov 1824.
Sarah Angelina McGruder Born 18 Decr 1826.
Mary McGruder Born 20 May 1831.
Sublett McGruder and Mary M. Woolfolk were married on the 20th Nov 1817.
Ann Eliza McGruder was Baptized by James Henshall in 1840.
Lucy T. Spelman died June 20, 1865 [newspaper death notice pasted below].
I now 16th day May 1868 have to record the death of Sallie A. Baker wife of Rev. F.M. Baker who died last night 10 1/4 o'clock 15 May 1868 [newspaper death notice pasted below].
Mrs. Sarah W. Staples died 11 May 1867 [with newspaper death notice written by Rev. J. B. Taylor pasted below].

WORTHAM FAMILY BIBLE NO. 2

This Bible consist only of the New Testament published by Harper & Brothers, N.Y., 1846. The Bible covers the period 1749-1963 in 11 leaves, a copy of which is in the Library of Virginia. The Wortham family lived in the lower end of Caroline County near the Pamunkey River. Parts of this Bible duplicate the above Wortham Bible.

Charles T. Wortham and Mary Jane Hutchison were married on the 1st day Feby 1842.
John A. Sloan and Mary Morton Wortham were married on the 30 Apl 1865.
Charles T. Wortham and Anne C. Peatross were married on 17th Octo. 1865.
Jennie H. Wortham & G. Percy Hawes married 8th Apr 1874.

Coleman Wortham and Mary Marshall Gilliam were married Novr. 21, 1901.
Garret B. Wall Jr. and Mary Hoge Wortham were married April 13, 1929.
Coleman Wortham and Mary Virginia Wood were married February 10th 1945.
Samuel Spenser Jackson and Nancy Scott Wortham were married April 14th 1951.
Charles T. Wortham born 4th Jany 1813.
Mary Jane Hutchison born 28th Jany 1821.
Children of Charles T. Wortham & Mary Jane Hutchison
Mary Morton Wortham born Saturday Jany 20th 1843.
Albert Carr Wortham born Sept. 9th 1844.
Noah Montgomery Wortham born July 4th 1846.
Charles Montgomery Wortham born April 27th 1848.
Charles T. Wortham Jr. born Sept. 9 1850.
Jennie Hutchison Wortham born April 3 1852.
Robert Coleman Wortham bnorn March 4th 1854.
John Alexander Sloan born July 29th 1839.
Thomas Monahon Wortham born 19 Sept 1866.
Charles Wortham Sloan born 18 Sept 1866.
Sallie Paisley Sloan born July 1, 1869.
Annie Coleman Peatross born 6th Nov 1829.
Bessie Montgomery Wortham born 10 Nov 1899.
Coleman Wortham born 18th June 1872 about 4 o'clock P.M.
Geo. Percy Hawes Jr. born Feby 17th 1876 at 5:10 P.M.
Geo. Percy Hawes born June 29th 1846.
Charles Morris Hawes born May 21, 1878.
Morton Hutchinson Hawes born July 1882.
Coleman Wortham Jr. born Sep. 16 1904.
Mary Hoge Wortham born Jany 3 1908.
Anne (Nancy) Scott Wortham born Feby 25 1911.
Garrett B. Wall Jr. born Sept 17th 1903.
Mary Virginia Wood born April 5th 1920.
Samuel Spencer Jackson born January 23rd 1902.
Children of Charles T. & Mary Jane Wortham
Noah M. Wortham died Augt 4th 1846 Aged one month.
Albert Carr Wortham died on his birthday Sept 9th 1848. Aged four years.
Charles M. Wortham died March 5th 1850. Aged one year 10 mos & 12 days.
Charles T. Wortham Jr. died Feby 19th 1851. Aged Five Mos & 9 days.
Robert Coleman Wortham died June 29 1854 Aged Three Months & 25 days.
My dear wife Mary Jane died Apl 1st 1859 about 25 min after 9 o'clock P.M. after a painful
  illness of ten days. She had been a great Sufferer from heart disease for over nine years and
  allways [sic] even whilst in great pain cheerful. She died as does the Christian, commending her
  children and friends to Christ saying to them that Christ would now be to them a Mother. Aged
  38 years 2 months and 3 days.
Bessie Montgomery Wortham died Monday 12 o'clock A.M. March 6th 1876 after a short illness
  of six days of Dyptheria. Aged 6 years & 24 days.

Jennie Hutchison Hawes died June 6th 1884 at Ashland Va.
Morton Hutchinson Hawes died June 1883.
Charles T. Wortham died March 10th 1881.
John A. Sloan Nov. 9th 1885.
Annie C. Wortham died August 7 - 1918 at 6:35 P.M.
Thomas Monahan Wortham died June 13th 1922.
Coleman Wortham died April 12th 1936
Morton Wortham Sloan died Jan 25th 1931.
Mrs. Coleman Wortham (Mary Gilliam Wortham) died Oct 11 1954.
Coleman Wortham Jr. died May 22nd, 1963.
Charles Wortham and Mary Jane Chaldler were married on the 24th Decr. 1781.
Thomas Coleman and Mary Woolfolk were married on the 26 March 1776.
Richard Chandler Wortham and Mary Coleman were married on the 6th April 1809.
Albert G. Wortham and Julia Ann Thomas were married on 21st April 1836.
Edwin Wortham and Fanny Hopkins were married on 15th November 1838.
Robert H. Maury and Sarah Ann Wortham were married on the 17th Decr. 1840.
James Thomas Jr. and Mary Woolfolk Wortham were married on [no date listed].
Edwin Wortham and Ann Eliza McGruder were married on the 16th April 1845.
John K. Connally and Alice C. Thomas were married on 30 Apl 1865.
Richd C. Wortham & Sally L. Staples were married on the 30th Apl 1867.
Charles Wortham born July 13th 1759.
Jane Chandler born Augst 31st 1759.
Children of Charles Wortham & Jane Chandler
Sally T. Wortham born Thursday Nov 28th 1782.
Richard C. Wortham born Thursday June 2nd 1785.
Mary Wortham born Tuesday Jany 9th 1787.
Sam'l Wortham born Monday Sept 15 1789.
Charles Wortham born Monday March 29 1790.
Jane Wortham born Friday Augt 10th 1792.
Elliott Wortham born Tuesday Jany 13 1795.
Timothy Wortham born Wednesday April 18 1798.
Andrew Broaddus Wortham born Friday Nov 21st 1800.
Children of Thomas & Mary Coleman
Saml Coleman born 31 Decr 1778.
Robt Coleman born 15 June 1780.
Ann Coleman born 9 Decr 1783.
Mary Coleman born 11 Feby 1786.
John W. Coleman born 26 May 1788.
Thomas Coleman father of the above children born 17 June 1745.
Mary Woolfolk Mother of the above children born sometime in the year 1754.
The above Thos Coleman is son of Danl Coleman an emigrant settler in Caroline Co from heir
  Lewis Minor Coleman & Dr. Robert Coleman. Danl Coleman above was a grandson of Sir John
  Coleman of Essex [Eng?]
Danl C. Hutchison born Decr. 18th 1785.

Jane Morton born 1780.
Children of Danl C. Hutchison & Jane Morton
Elizabeth Morton Hutchison born Decr. 8th 1818.
Mary Jane Hutchison born 28 Jany 1821.
Children of Richard C. Wortham & Mary Coleman.
Albert G. Wortham born Wednesday Night about 11 o'clock 17 Jany 1810.
Edwin Wortham born Tuesday about 12 o'clock 23 July 1811.
Charles T. Wortham born Monday Morning about 2 o'clock 4th Jany 1813.
Richard Woolfolk Wortham born Thursday Morning about 4 o'clock 17 Apl 1814.
Mary Jane Wortham born Friday 8 o'clock P.M. 16th Feby 1816.
Sarah Ann Wortham born Thursday 9 o'clock A.M. 30 Octo 1817.
Gabriel Wortham born Monday 4 o'clock A.M. 8 March 1819.
Coleman Wortham born Friday 6 o'clock P.M. 22 Decr. 1820.
Mary Woolfolk Wortham born Saturday 2 P.M. 15 March 1823.
Saml Wortham born Friday Apl 1st 1825.
Lucy T. Wortham April 1st 1828.
Children of Coleman Wortham and Mary Marshall Gilliam
Coleman Wortham born September 16, 1904.
Mary Hoge Wortham born January 3 1908.
Anne (Nancy) Scott Wortham born February 25 1911.
Children of Garrett B. Wall Jr. and Mary Hoge Wortham
Garrett B. Wall III born November 25th 1932.
Mary Marshall Wall born June 3rd 1937.
Children of Coleman Wortham Jr. and Virginia Wood
Coleman Wortham III born February 10th 1946
Virginia Ann Wortham born April 13 th 1948
Child of Samuel S. Jackson and Nancy Scott Wortham
Samuel Spencer Jackson Jr. born June 22nd 1952.
Family of Danl C. & Jane Hutchison
Elizabeth Morton (daughter of D.C. & J. Hutchison) died July 24th 1820. Age 19 mos & 16 days.
Ann Morton (Mother of Jane Hutchison) died Apl 1st 1829. Age 73 years.
Danl C. Hutchison died Jany 16th 1832. Aged 47 years.
Jane Hutchison died November 12th 1850. Aged 70 years.
Danl C. Hutchison and Jane Martin were married on the 29th Octo. 1817.
Bickerton W. Mallory and Ann Curtis Hutchison were married on 7th Nov 1832.

WRIGHT (EUGENE) FAMILY BIBLE

This Bible was published by Charles Foster Publishing Co., Philadelphia, Pennsylvania. [no date given]. This Bible was originally owned by Eugene H. Wright, son of James and Mary Eliza Broaddus Wright, who married Nola E. Pitts. They lived at "Locust Grove", Caroline County. The Bible was next owned by Harry Lee Kay, Jr., son of Mary E. Wright and Harry L. Kay, Sr. He gave the Bible to Mrs. Woodford Broaddus, the present owner, who lives at Gether, Caroline County, Virginia.

Married by A. Broaddus Eugene H. Wright & Nola E. Pitts Jan. 16, 1894.
Mary E. Wright & Harry L. Kay was married Sep. 4, 1920 in Washington.
Eugene M. Wright & Ruth Broaddus was Married on September 10, 1932.
John Butler Wright and Mary Marshall Pitts were Married November 8, 1943.
Leslie B. Wright and Alma M. Arey were Married June 2, 1951.
Born at Locust Grove December 23 1896 John Butler Wright.
Born at Locust Grove March 2, 1899 Mary E. Wright.
Born at Locust Grove June 27, 1903 Roy Wright.
Born at Locust Grove July 31, 1905 Eugene Maxwell Wright.
Born at Locust Grove June 11, 1908 Leslie Brown Wright.
Eugene H. Wright born March 18, 1863.
Nola E. Pitts was born at Locust Grove October 15, 1868.
Roy Wright Died Set--21 1909 in his seventh year.
John Butler Wright Died - June 3, 1963.
Leslie Brown Wright Died March 1969.
Eugene Maxwell Wright Died Sept. 20, 1969.

WRIGHT (LOUIS) FAMILY BIBLE

This Bible was printed by Zondervan Bible Publishers, Grand Rapids, Michigan and belonged to the family of William Louis Wright, son of Robert Moseley Wright and Dorothea Buckner Wright, who lived most of his married life at "Deep Springs" in the Mica area of Caroline County. He married Emma Gray Shackelford.

William L. Wright born Aug. 28, 1896.
Robert Jesse Wright born Jan. 28, 1899.
Belfield Moseley Wright born May 18, 1902.
Mary Dorothy Wright born Dec. 16, 1904.
John Lewis Wright born Jan. 25, 1908.
Robert William Wright born March 23, 1927.
Edward Louis Wright born May 12, 1928.
Dorothy Gray Wright born October 15, 1930.
Charles Jesse Wright born October 31, 1932.
James Paige Wright born February 15, 1937.
William Louis Wright and Emma Gray Shackelford married Nov. 14, 1895.
Robert Jesse Wright and Ethel L. Campbell married Oct. 21, 1925.
John Louis Wright and Elizabeth Bullock married August 22, 1964.
William Louis Wright died June 21, 1919.
Emma Gray Shackelford Wright died Oct. 26, 1933.
Willie L. Wright died March 13, 1905.
Belfield M. Wright died July 27, 1974.

WRIGHT (ROBERT) FAMILY BIBLE

This Bible belonged to Robert Wright of "Green Falls", Caroline County, Virginia. The title page is now missing. It is still at Green Falls and is owned by Herbert R. Collins, a descendant. A copy of the records is on deposit in the Library of Virginia.

Robert Wright to Margaret Boutwell 21 December 1797.
Fanny B.[Bell] Wright to Edmund Crump August 31st 1820.
Harriett M. Wright to Wm Kidd December 24th 1821.
Burton [Birkenhead] B.[Boutwell] Wright to Ann Tod daughter of George T. Tod 30 May 1826.
Margaret B.[Bell] Wright to Hiram Crump 19th Jany 1826.
Subburnah H.[Hawkins] Wright to Eldred Green 18th August 1827.
Robert M.[Moseley] Wright to Mary D.[Dorothea] Buckner daughter of Richd. Buckner Augst 17, 1841.
William H.[Hawkins] Wright to Sarah J.[Jane] Sutton daughter of John C. Sutton Octr. 24th 1841.
Fanny B.[Bell] Wright [born] November 13th 1798.
Harriett M. Wright [born] May 3rd 1800.
Birkenhead B.[Boutwell] Wright [born] August 1st 1802.
Margaret Bell Wright [born] 21st Jany 1805.
Subburnah Hawkins Wright [born] November 28th 1807.
Robert Moseley Wright [born] 2nd May 1810
Mary Elizabeth Wright [born] 14 March 1812.
William Hawking Wright [born] 20 April 1813 [or 1815]
Mary Ann Elizabeth Crump, the daughter of Edmund Crump & Frances his wife was born 7th June 1821.
Robert Hawkins Kidd the son of Wm Kidd and Harriett his wife was born 3rd Dec 1822.
Margret Boutwell Crump [born] the 16 December 1822.
Edward Crump [born] the 25 of February 1825.
Thos D. Kidd [born] 13th Sept. 1825.
Louisa Tod Wright Daughter of Burton B. Wright & Ann his wife [born] 5th May 1827.
Maria Louisa Kidd [born] 22nd April 1827.
Margaret Elizabeth Green [born] 24th July 1828.
William Boutwell Kidd [born] 22nd Dec. 1828.
Humphrey Sale son of Jos. Sale [born] June 1790.
B. Boutwell Son of W. Boutwell [born] 9 June 1777.
Margaret Elizabeth Kidd [born] 26th Augt. 1830.
John C. Crump [born] 17th August 1828.
Moseley M. Wright [born] Nov. 25 1857.
Robert Wright (the Father of Robert Wright II) April 1st 1809 Aged 72 years.
William Boutwell father of Mrs. Wright May 14th 1806. Aged 72 years.
William H. Boutwell brother of Mrs. Wright [died] July 7th 1806. Aged ____.
Thomas Burke [died] January 24th 1807.
Henry Wright [died] Dec. 9th 1822 aged 52.
Robert Wright Sr. [died] Jany 20th 1838 Aged 71.
Margaret H. Wright [died] Octr 29th 1855. Aged ____.

Richard B.[Buckner] Wright departed this life on June the 1st, 1854.
Burton B. Wright MD [died] March 17th 1856.
Mildred A.E. Crump [died] May 8th 1856.
Richard B. Wright [died] June 1st 1854 [repeated entry].
Robert M. Wright [died] November 9th 1857. [marked out and rewritten on next column same way]
Mildred C.[Crump] Wright [died] October 20th 1865 Aged 9 years.
 Suffer little children to come unto me and forbid them not for such is the kingdom of heaven.

WRIGHT (WESLEY) FAMILY BIBLE

This Bible was copied and a copy placed in the Library of Virginia in 1962 with the following affidavit: Richmond Virginia October 12, 1962. "I, Wesley Wright III (b.1893) certify that his photostat is a copy of a page from the family Bible of Dr. Wesley Wright (1799-1879) now owned by Virginia Wesley Broaddus Richardson of Caroline County, Virginia, near Milford; that this Bible was published in Hartford, S. Andrus & Son 1845 and Sterotyped by James Conner New York. Some of the entries are in my father's (Wesley Wright II 1844-1911) handwriting. [signed] Wesley Wright." Wesley Wright lived next to St. Paul's Methodist Church in Caroline County on Signboard Road.

Wesley Wright & Mary Ann his wife were married May 20th 1834.
James J. White father of Mary Ann Green Wright (Wife of Wesley Wright) was born 6th Novr. 1776 and died 5th June 1850.
Elizabeth White wife of James J. White & Mother of Mary Ann Green Wright was born 18th Octr 1781 & died 5th Aprl 1853.
Virginia N. Samuel sister of Mary Ann Green Wright died about the 15th May 1855.
Wesley Wright & Ann Jane Swann were married January 10, 1861.
Ann Jane Swann wife of Wesley Wright was born 9th March 1823.
Wesley Wright was born Apl 8th 1799.
Mary Ann Green wife of Wesley Wright was born 29th August 1816.
William Wright (father of Wesley Wright) was born October 13th 1765.
Frances Wright (Mother of Wesley Wright) was born November 14th 1772.
Mary Ann Green Wright died 9th July 1855. She was the daughter of James J. White & Elizabeth White.
[blank] died 14th January 1829.
[blank] died 7th August 1853.
James Calvin Wright was born April 10th 1838 and was baptized by Henry B. Cowles, was married 5th July 1855 to Ottawa Coleman. Died Feb. 1891.
Luther Wright was born 18th of June 1840 & was baptized by Rev. Mr. Hall. Died 1921.
Victoria Ann Wright was born August 22nd 1842 and was baptized by Reverend Mr. Kennelly. Was married to Doctor Joseph M. Moore October 10th 1861. Died Nov 191[illeg].
Wesley Wright was born 1st Apl 1844 & was baptized by same minister. Died 26 August 1911.
William Buckner Wright was born May 11th 1846 and was baptized by Saml Moorman.

Betty Frances Wright was born Apl 1st 1851.
Mary Virginia Wright was born May 25th 1852.
Alfred Wright was born July 6th 1853.
Betty Frances Wright died 15th May 1851.
Wesley Wright died 13 Sept. 1871. His funeral was preached at Wright's Chapel on following Sunday by Rev. Jno G. Rowe.
Ann Jane Wright wife of Dr. Wesley Wright died Nov 19th 1909. Age 86 years.
Edgar Lynch Wright was born 22nd September 1861 and died 13th of March 1862.
Argyle Wright was born 28 December 1862 and he died May 1st 1863.
Francis Swann Wright was born 19th Sept. 1864 and died February 15th 1865.
Julia W. Swann died at Palestine June 14, 1910 Age 82.
Mary Virginia [Wright] Broaddus died Jany 27th 1926.
Alfred Wright died Dec. 7, 1928.
Wm Buckner Wright Dec. 16, 1928.
Wesley Wright & Martha Hatcher [1st wife] were married 14th December 1826. William their son was born 3 Dec 1827. Martha (wife of Wesley Wright) died 14th May 1828 & William (their Son) died 15th May 1828.

WYATT FAMILY BIBLE

This Bible consists only of the New Testament and was published by J. Emory and B. Waugh. It was printed by J. Collord, N.Y., 1829. The Wyatt family lived in the lower part of Caroline County near the North Anna River. The two estates were "Edgewood" and "Plain Dealing". On the banks of the Pamunkey and North Anna Rivers lie the remains of the early Wyatt families in unmarked graves. For more information concerning this family see *The Virginia Magazine of History and Biography*, Volume 3, 1895-96, pp. 177-180. A copy is also in the Virginia Historical Society.

Capt John Wyatt who marr'd Jenny Pamplin was born 1684.
Wm his son was born 1713.
Richd Wyatt son of John Wyatt was born 20th May 1720 & died Nov 1803.
Richd Wyatt son of Richd. Wyatt was born 1st Jan. 1763.
Elizth Wyatt, daughter of Richd & Nancy Wyatt was born 29th Nov 1798.
Ann H. Wyatt was born 27th July 1802.
Sarah C. Wyatt was born 12th Nov. 1804.
Richd Ware Wyatt was born 22 Dec. 1806.
Nancy Ware daughter of Capt John Ware was born 30th June 1771.
Mary Ann Wilkerson was born 27th Aug 1828.
Mildred H. Wilkerson born 13th Aug. 1830.
John Henry Guy was born 4th Aug. 1831.
Richd Wilkinson was born 1832.
Eliza Frances Guy was born 8th Feby 1824.
_____[blank] Son of Richd & Harriet H. Wyatt was born 25th Sept & died 2nd day of Octr 1824 aged 8 days.

Sarah E. Wilkinson, born 1st day of May 1835.

Martha Ann Wyatt, daughter of Richd W. & H. K. Wyatt, born 12 Oct 1835 & Baptized 1836 by Revd Jos. A. Brown.

Richard Overton Wyatt son of R.W. & H. K. Wyatt born 18th day of April 1837 & Baptized 28th Aug 1838 by Rev. H. B. Cowles.

Mary Eliza Wyatt, daughter of R.W. & H. K. Wyatt born 6th June 1838 & Baptized the 28th Augst 1838 by Rev. H. B. Cowles.

William Henning Wyatt son of R.W. & H. K. Wyatt born the 26th Feby 1840 & Baptized the 7th day of Octr 1840 by Revd. H. B. Cowles.

James Walter Wyatt, Son of R.W. & H. K. Wyatt born 9th June 1841 & baptized 8th June 1845 by Revd. Jos A. Brown.

Evelina Harris Wyatt daughter of R.W. & H. K. Wyatt born 28th Jany 1843 & baptized 8th June 1845 by Revd. Jos A. Brown.

Alice Elizabeth Wyatt daughter of R.W. & H. K. Wyatt born 13th June 1844 & baptized 8th June 1845 by Revd. Jos A. Brown.

Ida May Wyatt daughter of R.W. & H. K. Wyatt born 1st day of May 1846.

_____[blank] Daughter of R.W. & H. K. Wyatt born 20th Aug & died 26th 1847. Aged 8 days.

Overton Harris born 29th Nov. 1767.

Barbara his 1st wife born 16th March 1773.

Patsey Harris (2nd wife of O. Harris) born 20 Sept. 1778.

Amelia A. Harris daughter of O & P. Harris born 6th May 1800.

John W. Harris, son of O. & B. Harris born 9 Sept. 1802.

Evelina O. Harris, daughter of O. & P. Harris born 4th Nov. 1806.

Martha A. & Barbara W. Harris (twins) daughters of O. & P. Harris born 16th July 1808.

Harriet K. Harris daughter of O. & P. Harris born 16th Nov. 1811.

Mary Nelson Wyatt daughter of R.W. & H. K. Wyatt born 1st Jan. 1851.

Kate Harrison Wyatt daughter of R.W. & H. K. Wyatt born 5th Feb 1852.

Harriet Overton Woodard daughter of Martha A. Woodard (ne Wyatt) born 5th Jan 1868.

Annie Pritchard Woodard daughter of Martha A. Woodard (ne Wyatt) born 12th May 1869.

Harriet James Wyatt daughter of Ada May Wyatt (ne Wyatt) born 3rd June - 71.

Amey Wyatt died 16 Dec 1794 in 61st year of her age.

Richd Wyatt her husband died Nov 1803 in the 83rd yr of his age.

Sarah Wyatt (alias) McGhee died 1830.

Elizh Wyatt (alias) Starke died 12 Sept 1830. She raised 13 children in the years of maturity & died at her residence in Hanover age 86.

Nancy Wyatt (alias) New died 11th Jan 1833 at the residence of her husband Colo. Anthony New in Todd Co Ky - Said A. New died 1833.

Colo. Richd B. New son of Colo. Anthony & Nancy New died 1834.

Ann H. Guy daughr. of Richd & Nancy Wyatt died 14th Decr 1836 at the residence of her Husband in Louisa - She died in full hope of Heaven.

Wm G. Wyatt son of Richd Wyatt who married Eliza Streshly died suddenly of apoplexy at his residence in Caroline the 24th day of Jany 1839. Aged 63y 4m 26d.

Nancy Wyatt, wife of Richd Wyatt and daughter of Capt. John Ware of Goochd. died the 17th day of April 1838. Aged 66y 9m & 17d.

Mary E. Wyatt daughter of R.w. & H.K. Wyatt died the 19th March 1841.
Wm Henning Wyatt son of R.W. & H.K. Wyatt died the 25th Aug 1841.
Richd Wyatt (born 1st day of Jany 1763) died 12th day of June 1845. Aged 82y 5m 12 days.
John Wyatt (born ____[blank]day of ____[blank] died 11th Sept 1846, aged ____[blank].
Barbara Harris who was B. Wyatt died 6 Oct. 1904.
Overton Harris died 7th Oct. 1813.
Patsey Wyatt who was P. King died 14 Aug 1847.
Evelina O. Doswell died 22nd Dec. 1840.
Wm R.B. Wyatt son of Wm S. Wyatt died 29 May 1828.
Harriet Overton Woodard b. Jan 5 1868.
Anne Pritchard Woodard b. May 12 - 1869.
John Wyatt Woodard b. Dec 25 - 1873.
Births
Overton Harris born Novr. 1767.
Barbara Wyatt born March 16 - 1773 (wife of Overton Harris).
Amelia Anne Harris May 6 - 1800.
John W. Harris Sept. 9, 1804.
Patsy Harris Sept. 20 - 1778.
Evelina Overton Harris Novr 4 - 1806.
Martha Anne & Barbara Overton (twins) b. July 16 - 1808.
H.K. Harris (Harriet King Harris) b. Novr. 16 - 1811. (Married Richd Ware Wyatt).
Deaths
Barbara Wyatt, wife of Overton Harris d. Octr 6, 1804. He died Octr 7 - 1813.
Evelina Overton Harris Doswell d. Decr. 22 - 1840.
Mag. J. Wyatt d. Septr. 11 - 1846.
Patsey Wyatt d. Aug 14 - 1847.
Overton Harris & first wife Barbara Wyatt married Dec 20 - 1798.
Overton Harris & 2nd wife Patsey King, married Novr 28 - 1805.
John Wyatt & Patsey Harris mar. Decr. 18 - 1817
S.B. White mar. A.A. Harris July 2 - 1818.
Henry Cole Doswell & Evelina Overton Harris mar. Octr. 25 - 1827.
Richard Ware Wyatt & Harriet King Harris mar. Sept. 19 - 1933.
Henry W. King & Barbara Wyatt Harris mar. Novr. 29 - 1838.
Barbara Wyatt Harris King mar. 2nd M. Kelley July 24 1845.
John Wyatt Harris & Judith Cox mar. ____[blank].

Slave Negroes Ages.
Thomas, son of Lucinda, born March 1861.
Stella daug of Mary Jane, born March 1861.
Texana daug of Maria born Aug 1861.
Frank, son of Amanda born Aug 1862.
Jack, son of Emily born Nov. 1862.
Washington, son of Maria born 1864.
Courtney's Children:

Courtney died 1859.
Lewis born 1816 Died 1854.
Edmond born 1818.
Mary Jane born 1820.
Frances born 1822.
Lucinda born 1825.
Oliver born 1827.
Emily born June 1830.
Ellen born April 1833.
Julia born Decr. 1838.
[end of Courtney's children]
John, son of Mary Jane born Decr 1836. Drowned 1854.
Catharine, Daughter of Mary Jane March 1839.
Maria, Daughter of Frances born June 1839.
Sylvester, Son of M. Jane born Mar 1841 Died 1860.
Henry, Son of Lavinia, born June 1841.
_____daughter of Francis Decr. died 1843.
Robert son of M. Jane born July 1844.
Amanda, daug of Lucinda born 1845.
Fanny Daugr of Ed & Lavinia born March 1846.
Wm Son of Mary Jane born Jan 1848.
Ellick Son Lucinda born 28th Jan 1848 Died 52.
Lucy Daugr of Lavinia Oct 49.
Biggerton Son of Lucinda Feb. 50.
Mary, daugh of M. Jane Sept. 50.
Isabella Daugh of Lucinda 1st Jan 54.
Hillary Son of Tempy born about 1824 or 5.
Orange Son of Tempy Senr. born about 1802 or 3. died 61.
Washington Son of Fanny born about 1802 or 3.
Ned son of Jennie born about 1825 or 6.
Jim son of M. Jane born about Feb. 55 died 57.
Oliver Son of Ellen born about Decr 54.
Harry Son of Emily Oct. 55. Died 56.
Josephine, daugr of Lucinda 5th May 56.
Lavinia born (Say) 1819.
Lyon Son of Ellen Decr. 56.
Fleming Son of Emily, born Aug. 57.
Elora Ann, daug of Mary Jane June 58.
Rhoda, daug of Ned & Maria Feb 59.
Vina daug of Lucinda Oct. 58.
Fletcher Son of Emily born May 60.
[end of listing of slaves]
Capt John Wyatt married Jenny Pamplin in the year 1711 by whom he had 9 children:
Wm who married Elizabeth Eggleston.

John who died in the 17 year of his age.

Anne who married John Starke.

Richd - married Elizabeth Streshly who died in child bed with 1st child. This sd. Richd afterwards married Amey Chiles daughter of Capt. Walter Chiles 7th Nov. 1752.

Mary married Capt Henry Gilbert.

Thos & Henry never married.

Lucy married Capt Mills.

John married Elizh. Smith & afterwards Anne Starke.

Mary Wyatt daughr of Richd & Amey Wyatt mard. Wm Peatross & had ten children.

Sarah Wyatt mard. Mathew Thompson & had 5 chidren. She after married Austin McGhee.

Lacy died young.

Lucy marrd. James Hawkins.

Nancy mard. Antho. New 3rd Aug 1782.

Joseph Wyatt died in 17th year of his age.

Richd. Wyatt mard. Nancy Ware daughter of Capt. John Ware (Goochland) 8th Dec 1796.

Walter Wyatt mard. Eliza Brame afterwards Mrs. Bliss of Kentucky.

John Wyatt mard. Lucy Richardson & afterwards Mrs. Patsy Harris Decr 1817.

Barbara Wyatt marrd. Overton Harris 20th Dec 1798.

Wm S. Wyatt mard. Polly New (daughter of Colo. Antho. New by his first Wife) he afterwards mard. Susan Minor 11th Novr. 1813.

Elizth Wyatt daugh of Richd & Nancy Wyatt mard. Revd. Robt Wilkinson 30th Oct 1827.

Ann K. Wyatt daugh of Richd & Nancy Wyatt mard. Saml A. Guy 16th Sept 1830.

Richd W. Wyatt son of Richd & Nancy Wyatt married Harriet K. Harris daughter of Overton & Patsy Harris, the 19th Septr. 1833 - H. K. H. born 16th Nov. 1811.

Wm R.B. Wyatt son of Wm S. & Polly Wyatt married Martha Scott 5th Sept. 1832.

Overton Harris married Barbara Wyatt (his 1st wife) 20th Decr.1798 & afterwards married Patsy King (his 2nd wife) 28th Nov 1805.

Majr. John Wyatt married Lucy Richardson & afterwards Mrs. Patsey Harris 18th Dec 1817.

Amelia A. Harris daughter of Overton & Barbara Harris, married Sam'l B. White 2nd July 1818.

John W. Harris Son of Overton & Barbara Harris married Judith Cox.[no date]

Evelina O. Harris daughter of Overton & Patsy Harris married Henly C. Doswell 25th Oct 1827.

Barbara W. Harris married Revd. Henning W. Kelley 29th Nov 1838 and afterwards Mard. Milton King of Ky. 24th July 1845.

Harriet K. Harris married Richd W. Wyatt 19th Sept 1833.

Martha Anne Wyatt (eldest dau to live to be grown) of Col Richard Ware Wyatt & Harriet King Harris, mar. Theodore Hoyt Woodard of La. Dec 24 - 1866.

Ida May Wyatt sister of above, mar. her cousin Joseph Marion Wyatt of Caroline Co Va Mch 9 - 1870. She was b. May 1 - 1846.

Kate Harrison Wyatt sister of above, mar. Saml E. Wilson of Texas, Sept 22 - 1880. He d. Dec 3 - 1880. No issue. She mar May 5 - 1884 Rev. John Willis Lea - d. May 15 - 1884.

Harriet Overton Woodard, dau of Martha Anne Wyatt Woodard, mar Samuel Downer Hicks. She was b. 1869 & he about 1860.

Anna Pritchard Woodard, 2nd dau of Martha Anne Wyatt Woodard, marr. Edw. Lansing Fox

Septr. 23 - 1890.
Harriet James Wyatt, dau of Joseph Marion Wyatt & Ida May Wyatt mar. Henry S. Washington June 10 - 1895. She was b. June 3 - 1871.
Martha Isabel Wyatt, dau of Ida May Wyatt b. Feb 18 1873.
Ida Marion Wyatt, dau of Ida May Wyatt (single) b. Feb 24, 1875.
William Richard Baynham Wyatt, son of Ida May Wyatt, b. Apr 28 - 1877.
Harriet Wyatt Washington, dau of Harriet James Wyatt b. Thanksgiving day - Novr 29 - 1900.
John Wyatt Woodard son of Martha Anne Wyatt Woodard born Dec 25 -1873.
Doctor Richard Overton Wyatt son of Richard Wyatt & Harriet King Harris d. Dec 16 - 1861.
Capt James Walter Wyatt killed at Cold Harbor in Civil War 3rd June 1864 - He was a brother of Dr. Overton Wyatt above.
Evelina Harris Wyatt, sister of above man, d. of typhoid fever July 22 - 1865.
Col Richard Ware Wyatt father of above children, d. May 25 [no date].
Alice E. Wyatt dau of Col. Richard Ware Wyatt died of pneumonia Feb 11 - 1898.
Harriett King Harris wife of Col Richard Ware Wyatt, d. of pneumonia Octr. 8, 1888.
John Wyatt Woodard, son of Martha Ann Wyatt died Aug 6 - 1886, of typhoid fever - age 13 yrs.
Joseph Marion Wyatt, son of Wm Richard Baynham Wyatt & Martha Scott & husband of Ida May Wyatt who was a sister of Martha Anne & Alice, above, died of paralysis Aug 20 - 1891.

YATES FAMILY BIBLE

The Yates family in Caroline County descends from George Yates, whose son Captain George Yates, born circa 1727 in Caroline County and who died there in 1777 is believed to have married Frances Fielding Lewis. Captain George Yates' son, James Yates, was born in Caroline County May 2, 1752. He married Lucy Partlow, daughter of John Partlow of Spotsylvania County, who was born August 25, 1759. From Caroline County, the Yates family scattered into Spotsylvania, Culpeper, Albemarle, and Loudoun Counties. Others went to Harrisonburg, Virginia; Charlestown, West Virginia; and Adair County, Kentucky. Still others remained in Caroline County, and one particular branch Reuben Yates lived there in the mid-19th century and he and his family lie buried there in marked graves off Long Branch Road in the northern end of Caroline County. Besides James Partlow, the other children of Captain George Yates, not listed in the Bible are: Frances Yates, b. 1750; Richard Yates, b. 1751; John Yates, d. July 1820; Charles Lewis Yates, d. 1807; William Yates, b. 1763; Molly Martha Yates, b. 1767; George Yates; and Warner Yates; all born in Caroline County.

Little is known of the Bible records reproduced here, except that they appeared in 1923 in *The Virginia Magazine of History and Biography*, Volume 31 at pages 255-56. Since it begins with the records of James Yates and his wife Lucy (Partlow) Yates, both of Caroline County, it is assumed the Bible began with them. Also listed are their eight children.

James Yates was born May 3rd, 1763.
Lucy Yates [wife of James Yates] was born Augt. 25th, 1759.
Betsey Yates was born 28th Oct., 1782.
Sarah Yates was born 11th Sept. 1784.

B.[Boswell] P. Yates was born 2nd Oct. 1786.
Lucy P. Yates was born Novr. 4th, 1789.
Gerrard Yates was born 29th April, 1792.
Benjamin Yates was born 4th Augt. 1794.
Frances Yates was born Nov. 1st, 1797.
Aylett R. Yates was born ____ 1800.
Clarissa Ann Yates was born June 13th, 1791.
James Harrison Yates the eldest son of B.P. Yates & Clarissa Ann,
  his wife, was born Feby. 11th, 1814.
Wm. Mortimer Yates was born 31st May, 1815.
Susan Ann Elizabeth Yates was born 20th Feby., 1817.
Mary Frances Yates was born April 24th, 1819.
Lucy Ann Yates was born 4th Feby. 1827.
Thomas Aylett Yates was born 12th Jany. 1831.
James Yates [husband of Lucy P. Yates] departed this life in 1828.
Boswell P. Yates departed this life 12 Day Jany. 1857 in North
  Garden, Albemarle.
Aylett R. Yates departed this life in April, 1815.
Wm. Mortimer Yates departed this life 27th of October, 1840.
Mary Frances Yates departed this life November 18th, 1840.
Lucy Ann (Partlow) Yates [wife of James Yates] departed this life
  22d of Augt., 1829.
Susan A.E. Yates was married to R.G. Anderson October 27th, 1836.
Ann Elizabeth Anderson, eldest daughter R.G. Anderson & Susan his wife was born November
  12th, 1837 (at Stony Pt, Albemarle).
Mary F. Anderson was born 27th Feby. 1845 at North Garden,
  Albemarle, Second daughter of R.G. & S.A.E. Anderson.
Boswell Anderson, Son of R.G. Anderson & Susan A.E. Anderson was
  born 13th Augt. 1847, 7 o'clock in morning.
R.T.W. Anderson was born Sept. 9th 1853.
Clarissa Gaines Anderson daughter of R.G. & S.A.E. Anderson was
  born 19 Nov. 1860.
Charles W. Chamblin (of Loudoun co.) was married to Mary F. Anderson daughter of R.G. & S.A.
  Anderson Jany 4th 1865 by Rev. Wm F. Broadus of Charlottesville, Va.
Clara Anderson infant daughter of R.G. & Susan Anderson departed this life on 26th May 1862, 15
  minutes after 7 A.M.
James H. Yates was married to Juliett E. Hunter February 28th,
  1839.
Juliett E. Yates was born 25th March 1817.
Saml. Boswell Yates was born 15th June 1840--First son of James H. Yates & Juliett E. Yates his
  wife.
Sarah Frances Yates was born 11th January 1843.
Mary Cathrin Yates was born 28th Augt. 1846.
James Mortimer Yates was born 4th Decmr, 1852.

YOUNG FAMILY BIBLE

The following data was copied from the fly-leaf of a Bible in the possession of Miss Kate Garnett of Richmond, Virginia about 1924. A typewritten copy is in the Library of Virginia. This family lived at "White Chimney's", an early tavern, earlier known as "Kerner's Tavern" in Caroline County on the old stage road, now U.S. Route 2. The old chimneys to this tavern were standing as late as the 1930's and were pushed down for safety reasons when the Civilian Conservation Corps [CCC] was established near this site on the high banks along present-day Route 2/301.

Children of John and Sarah Young:
Humphrey son of John and Sarah Young, born 5-10-1733/4 baptized Apr. 1st 1734 by Rev. Adam Decker; departed this life Aug. 22, 1735.
Elizabeth Young born Dec. 1, 1736, baptized Jan. 1. 1736/7 by Rev. Brunskill.
John Young born Jan. 11, 1738/9 at 8 o'clock at night; baptized - June 29 [marked through] Feb. 25.
William Young born May 2, 1740 at 9 o'clock in the morning; baptized June 29 1740 by Rev. John Brunskill.
Mickleborough Young, 1st son of William and Jane Young, was born Feb. 22, 1774.
Ann Young, 2nd daughter of Rich and Maria Young was born 26 October 1798.
Mickleborough Young and Ann Broadus married August 1, 1816.
Sarah Jane Young, 1st daughter of Mickleborough and Ann Young, was born Sept 26, 1818.
William Richard Young, 1st son of Mickleborough and Ann Young, was born Dec. 3, 1820.
Virginia Ann Young, 2nd daughter of Mickleborough and Ann Young, was born May 29, 1822.
Maria Elizabeth Young, 3rd daughter of Mickleborough and Ann Young was born May 17, 1825.
A second son, not named, was born and died on May - 1829.
Caroline Sims Young born Sept 25, 1830.
Henry Mickleborough Young born March 13, 1833.
Mickleborough Young died May 24, 1854, age 80.
William R. Young died Mar. 20, 1865, age 41.
Ann Young died Jan 1, 1876, age 78.
Maria Elizabeth Cheatham died Dec. 28, 1884, age 60.
Sarah Bridges died July 31, 1896, age 78.
[This note was typed at the bottom of the Bible records, apparently by Miss Kate Garnett]
Note: William Young married Jane Mickleborough April 8, 1773. See Christ Church Parish Register, page 200.
Virginia Ann Young married John Mosby Sheppard August 1846. From Bible records as given by Mrs. E. P. Crump (Lizzie Sheppard, their daughter).
William Young and Jane Mickleborough had a daughter, Sarah Garland Young, who married Benjamin Sheppard who died 1855 (See Sheppard Family)
Mickleborough Young and Ann (Broadus) Young's daughter, Sarah Jane Young, married Richard Morgan Bridges. Sarah J. Bridges died in 1896. (Notes from Miss Nannie Haw whose mother was a Bridges).
Jane Mickleborough Young, wife of William Young, died November 9, 1835 at the home of her son in Caroline County. (See *Richmond Whig* for Nov. 24, 1835).

ABOUT THE AUTHOR

The author, HERBERT RIDGEWAY COLLINS, noted genealogist and historian, graduated from the 10th National Genealogical Institute at The National Archives, Washington, D.C., in 1960. He published his first genealogical book at the age of twenty-two and was the youngest Virginia author of such a work at that time. Mr. Collins was a founding member of the Virginia Genealogical Society and became its third president, at which time he started the society's publication which evolved into its present publication, *Magazine of Virginia Genealogy*. He was also a member of the National Genealogical Society. Mr. Collins spent thirty-two years with the Smithsonian Institute as curator and historian. During that time, and since his retirement, he has authored more than twenty books and been contributing author of many more. Among his publications have been topics including U.S. politics, political campaigning, presidential history, state and local history. Some of his publications have been exhibited at the Book Fair in Germany, made the Book-of-the-Month Club, and one appeared in *The New York Times* longer than any other Smithsonian author. Several of his books are now considered rare books and have appeared on the Internet and second-hand bookstores and command prices as high as $800. During his lifetime, he has amassed one of the largest privately owned Virginiana Collections, which he has recently donated to the Caroline County Main Library at Bowling Green, Virginia; the room having been named in his honor. He was also recently honored by having his portrait placed in the Circuit Court Room of the Caroline County Courthouse. His biography is included in state, national, and international *Who's Who* publications. Mr. Collins is now considered the unofficial historian of Caroline County and is always willing to assist researchers from the West Coast to the East Coast and in between, who have roots in Caroline County. He was born in the oldest frame house in Caroline County, which is now placed on the Virginia Landmarks Register and the National Register, and will be maintained after his death by the Association for the Preservation of Virginia Antiquities. Mr. Collins holds memberships in many Virginia county historical societies as well as the Virginia Historical Society and has held offices in some, including president. Several years ago he was commissioned by the Commission for Presidential Debates to write and prepare the brochure distributed at the T.V. Debates and National Conventions.

www.ingramcontent.com/pod-product-compliance
Lightning Source LLC
Chambersburg PA
CBHW080724300426

44114CB00019B/2484